VOLUME TWO

The American Nation

A History of the United States Since 1865

SEVENTH
EDITION

JOHN A. GARRATY

Gouverneur Morris Professor of History
Columbia University

with

ROBERT A. McCAUGHEY

Professor and Dean of the Faculty
Barnard College, Columbia University

HarperCollins*Publishers*

For Kathy, Jack, and Sarah

Sponsoring Editors: Lauren Silverman/Bruce Borland
Development Editor: Kathleen Dolan
Project Editor: Karen Trost
Design Supervisor: Dorothy Bungert
Text and Cover Design: Delgado Design, Inc.
Cover Illustration: *The White Way* (1926), by John Sloan. Philadelphia Museum of Art. Given by Mrs. Cyrus McCormick.
Photo Research: Cheryl Mannes and Suzanne Volkman Skloot
Production: Willie Lane
Compositor: Arcata Graphics Company/Kingsport Division
Printer and Binder: R.R. Donnelley & Sons Company
Cover Printer: New England Book Components

The American Nation: A History of the United States Since 1865, Volume Two, Seventh Edition

The author makes grateful acknowledgment to:
New Directions Publishing Corporation for permission to quote from "Hugh Selwyn Mauberley" by Ezra Pound. From Ezra Pound, *Personae*. Copyright 1926 by Ezra Pound. Reprinted by permission of New Directions Publishing Corporation.

Liveright Publishing Corporation for permission to quote from "the first president to be loved by his . . ." by e. e. cummings. Reprinted from *ViVa* by e. e. cummings, by permission of Liveright Publishing Corporation. Copyright 1931, 1959 by e. e. cummings. Copyright © 1979, 1973 by the Trustees for the E. E. Cummings Trust. Copyright © 1979, 1973 by George James Firmage.

Library of Congress Cataloging-in-Publication Data

Garraty, John Arthur, 1920–
    The American nation: a history of the United States/John A.
  Garraty with Robert A. McCaughey.
      p. cm.
    Includes bibliographical references and index.
    ISBN 0-06-042243-2 (v. 1) (student edition). ISBN 0-06-500036-6 (v. 1) (teacher edition) —ISBN
0-06-042244-0 (v. 2) (student edition). ISBN 0-06-500037-4 (v. 2) (teacher edition)
    1. United States—History. I. McCaughey, Robert A. II. Title.
E178.1.G24 1991
973—dc20
                                        90–48476
                                            CIP

93 9 8 7 6 5

Contents

Maps and Graphs

Maps

Graphs

This is the seventh edition of *The American Nation*, the sixth time I have revised it, and the process remains for me both challenging and endlessly fascinating. Historians try to explain what happened in the past and of course "what happened" does not change. But what is important to point out about the past is that it changes constantly as more information about past events comes to light and as current events raise new questions about the events and people of earlier times. Year by year hundreds of new books and articles are published about various aspects of American history; when those dealing with any particular subject have been digested and synthesized and combined with already existing knowledge, a new, "up-to-date" description of that topic results. This process keeps authors like me who write American history textbooks very busy.

Goals of This Revision

The work of revising a survey of all American history takes many forms. First there are the small alterations involved in incorporating new details and examples, and in clarifying obscurities that have previously escaped notice. Then there is the matter of bringing the narrative as close to the present as possible, something that is relatively easy to do, but difficult to do well. Nearly always revision also involves changes in emphasis—some subjects need to be condensed or eliminated; others require more space either because more has been discovered about them or because recent developments make them seem more significant. Finally, and most important, are the larger changes made necessary because historians, responding to contemporary interests, to noteworthy work being done by colleagues and other specialists, and to the questions and interests of their students, have produced persuasive new interpretations and even opened up entirely new subjects. Dealing with this work, in turn, requires more of the simpler kinds of revisions just mentioned.

This revision of *The American Nation* contains many examples of all these types of change; in sum, I believe it is the most thorough and broad-ranging restructuring and re-thinking of the six such revisions that I have made.

Organizational Changes

To improve the flow of topics, I have shifted many sections to different chapters, for example, moving the discussion of the Great Awakening and the colonial Enlightenment to the chapter on the events leading to the Revolution, where these inter-colonial, "national" topics seem more properly to belong. I have also consolidated the material on the Federalist era and on the Jefferson administrations into separate chapters, and I have divided the previously combined account of the political and economic events of the Monroe and John Quincy Adams period.

Similarly, several chapters covering the period 1877–1896 have been completely reorganized, and the chapter on World War I has been expanded to include an account of the Red Scare and other events of the immediate postwar period. The three chapters dealing with the 1920s and 1930s in the sixth edition have been drastically restructured; that period now is covered in four chapters. I have also made changes only slightly less extensive in the chapters on the post–World War II period.

New Coverage and Features

As to new topics and significantly expanded coverage of old ones, readers will notice that there is much more information about society in the colonial south and about southern political and religious institutions; on the activities of women during the American Revolution and other social changes of the period; on the Whiskey Rebellion and the opening of the Ohio country after the Revolution; on changes in early 19th-century family life; on the westward movement, the Second Great Awakening, the Know-Nothing movement; and on plantation life, particularly the lives of southern women, slave and free.

In Chapter XX, "American Society in the Industrial Age," there is much new information about middle-class life, about the daily activities of farmers, about the family lives and social attitudes of wage earners of both sexes, about social and economic mobility in the 1870s and 1880s, and about the development of spectator sports and other leisure activities. Chapter XXVI treats these and other aspects of social history before and after World War I in much greater detail than in earlier editions. There is also expanded and more up-to-date coverage of radicalism, the effects of the Great Depression on the unemployed, the treatment of minorities during World War II and the contributions of women in that conflict, the "Baby Boom" generation that followed the war, the counterculture of the 1960s, the modern women's movement, and many other subjects.

I have paid a good deal of attention also to the "Suggestions for Further Reading" that follow each chapter. I have eliminated many older titles that, although valuable, are out of print, and I have substituted more recent and in most instances equally worthwhile volumes that are readily available, often in paperback. This edition also contains a new feature, American Lives, designed to give students a better understanding of how ordinary people lived and thought in various times and places. It consists of accounts of the life-styles of "ordinary" people whom we know a great deal about only because they had children who became famous, and of the childhoods and youths of men and women who were later to become important figures. Most of the material comes from biographies, autobiographies, and other personal writings. There are seven of these features, some treating more than one person in a comparative manner.

Approach

In making all these changes and others less important, I have not, I trust, altered my basic approach to American history, which is to deal with the subject in narrative fashion and to use the political history of the nation as the frame or skeleton on which social, economic, and cultural developments depend. The American nation (the United States) is, after all, a political institution.

The people of the United States, in their infinite variety, also remain central to my account. The theory that a few great individuals, cut from larger cloth than the general run of human beings, have shaped the course of past events oversimplifies history. But the past becomes more comprehensible when attention is paid to how the major figures on the historical stage have reacted to events and to one another. Since generalizations require concrete illustration if they are to be grasped fully, readers will find many anecdotes and quotations on the following pages, along with the facts and dates and statistics every good history must contain. This illustrative material is interesting, and most of it is entertaining, but I believe it is instructive as well.

I also believe that one need not be an uncritical admirer of the American nation and its people to recognize that the history of the United States deserves to be treated with dignity and respect. Individually and as a society, we have rarely lived up perfectly to the principles enunciated in the Declaration of Independence and the Constitution, but recent events in Eastern Europe demonstrate how cherished these "American" values are by people who have been deprived of them. American values are not well served by patriotic hoopla or by slighting or excusing dark and discreditable aspects of the American past. The English radical Oliver Cromwell is said to have told an artist who was painting his picture to portray him "warts and all." Cromwell wanted to be remembered as he was, confident that, on balance, history would judge him fairly. This is another principle on which *The American Nation* continues to be based.

Acknowledgments

I wish to thank the many friends, colleagues, and students who, over the years, have given me the benefit of their advice and encouragement in keeping this book up to date. In particular I am grateful to the following reviewers for their comments and suggestions regarding the revision: Robert M. Barrow, Georgia Southern University; Sidney R. Bland, James Madison University; Paul C. Bowers, The Ohio State University; Dean R. Esslinger, Towson State University; George E. Frakes, Santa Barbara City College; David A. Johnson, Portland State University; George M. Lubick, Northern Arizona University; Thomas C. Mackey, Kansas State University; Michael S. Mayer, University of Montana; Howard N. Rabinowitz, University of New Mexico; G. S. Rowe, University of Northern Colorado; Herbert Shapiro, University of Cincinnati; Harry F. Snapp, University of North Texas; Ken L. Weath-

erbie, Del Mar College; and Herbert H. Wubben, Oregon State University.

John A. Garraty
Gouverneur Morris Professor of History
Columbia University

SUPPLEMENTS

An extensive package of supplements has been developed to accompany the seventh edition of *The American Nation*. To order supplements, contact your HarperCollins representative.

■ The *Instructor's Resource Manual*, written by Michael Mayer of the University of Montana, has been designed to aid both the novice and the experienced instructor in teaching the American History course. Each chapter of the *Instructor's Resource Manual* includes a concise chapter overview, a list of points for student mastery, lecture supplements, and questions for class discussion. A special feature of each chapter is a set of excerpted documents with accompanying questions for student analysis. The *Instructor's Resource Manual* also includes essays on teaching American History through films and maps, and a full-length class activity on teaching essay writing using the rhetoric of the Declaration of Independence.

■ The *Test Bank*, prepared by Larry Peterson of North Dakota State University, contains over 2000 test items, including multiple-choice, true/false, and essay questions, and map exercises. The questions are referenced by topic, cognitive type (factual, applied, or interpretive), difficulty level, and relevant text page.

  In addition to the printed format, the *Test Bank* is available on *TestMaster*, HarperCollins's computerized testing system. Available for IBM, Apple, and Macintosh computers, this powerful software allows the instructor to scramble and edit questions from the *Test Bank* and add original questions.

■ The two-volume *Student Study Guide*, co-authored by Kenneth Weatherbie of Del Mar College and Billy Hathorn of Laredo State University, is designed to provide students

with a comprehensive review of text material, and to encourage application and critical analysis of the material. Each chapter contains a chapter overview, learning objectives, important glossary terms, identification, map, and critical thinking exercises, and multiple-choice and essay questions. In addition, an essay on writing about history is provided.

■ *SuperShell*, HarperCollins's computerized tutorial, is an interactive program that provides sophisticated diagnostic feedback including an end-of-session reading assignment based on the student's performance, and tracking of the student's performance from session to session. In addition to review questions in a variety of formats, *SuperShell* contains comprehensive chapter outlines keyed to the headings and subheadings in the text. A "Flash Card" program helps students learn important terms and concepts. *SuperShell* is available for IBM computers only.

■ *Mapping American History*, created by Gerald Danzer of the University of Illinois at Chicago, features numerous varied map exercises and activities for students. In addition to increasing basic locational literacy, these exercises provide students with opportunities for map interpretation and analysis, as well as an appreciation of cartographic materials as historical documents. Each copy of *The American Nation* purchased from HarperCollins entitles the instructor to a free copy of this student map workbook.

■ *Discovering American History Through Maps and Views*, also prepared by Gerald Danzer, provides 140 four-color transparencies of images selected from key primary sources. Assembled in a three-ring binder, the collection begins with an essay on teaching history using maps, and contains detailed commentary on each transparency. The program consists of cartographic materials, various photos and views including urban plans, building diagrams, and works of art, and is free to adopters of the text.

■ *American Historical Geography: A Computerized Atlas,* prepared by William Hambin of Brigham Young University, offers map exercises pertaining to the rise of the Americas, the Revolutionary War, the Civil War, transportation systems, and elections. Free upon adoption of the textbook, the program is available for Macintosh computers only.

■ *Historical Viewpoints: Notable Articles from* American Heritage, *Sixth Edition,* edited by John Garraty, is a collection of interesting and substantive articles that have appeared in *American Heritage.* Available in a two-volume format, the sixth edition contains many new selections.

■ *Visual Archives of American History,* a new laser disk, provides over 500 photos and 29 minutes of film coverage of major events in American history. Each photo or film clip may be instantly accessed, making this collection ideal for classroom use.

■ *The Winner's Circle* is a collection of recent prize-winning films and videos relating to American History. Available for loan at no charge to adopters of the text.

■ *Grades,* HarperCollins's easy-to-use classroom management software, records quiz and exam scores for up to 200 students.

To help instructors make effective use of this comprehensive supplement package, HarperCollins offers *The Integrator,* a cross-reference and index to all print, software, and media supplements available with *The American Nation. The Integrator* also includes teaching techniques for multimedia presentations.

American Lives:
Three Families in the Post–Civil War South

The Village Post Office

William La Fayette Black, a Confederate veteran, was a citizen of Harlan, a small community in a remote section of northern Alabama. He farmed a considerable acreage, but his main business was running the Harlan general store. His wife Martha was the village postmistress.

In his store Black sold farm tools, seed, coffee, tobacco, cloth, and all sorts of other goods. Most of his customers were white farmers; slightly more than 10 percent were black. Some owned their own land, and some were tenants or sharecroppers. (Unlike many southern merchants, Black made a point of treating black customers fairly.)

Local farmers had to buy things on credit because they had many expenses and little money during the planting and growing seasons. They gave Black a lien on their fall crops as security for what they needed during the spring and summer.

Black was therefore an important person in the community. People gathered in his store to talk about politics and crop prospects, to gossip, and perhaps to play a game of checkers. Farmers could scarcely exist without the credit he advanced them, and in hard times he readily carried them as long as possible. It was in his interest to do so, because it was always possible that low prices or a crop failure would hurt him almost as much as the debtors. Still, he also had to borrow to run his business; over the years he accumulated a great deal of land when people who owed him money went bankrupt.

However, the Blacks' life-style was far from easy. Their home was originally a one-room log cabin. As the family grew Black added to it until by 1889 there were four bedrooms and a kitchen as well as the original building. But the house had no cellar. It stood a foot or so above the ground resting on stone pillars. Hogs, chickens, dogs, and cats took shelter beneath it. The house was drafty, heated only by a single stone fireplace. There was no running water.

Black sometimes worked in the fields along with his sons and his tenants. They grew corn, wheat, oats, and of course cotton, which was their cash crop. They worked hard. During the winter they cleared woodland, uprooted stumps, and mended fences and equipment. After plowing and planting, there were the usual tasks of hoeing out weeds and ultimately harvesting the grain. Then in the fall they picked and ginned the cotton. Besides doing the cooking and other household tasks, Martha Black and her daughters milked the family cows, spun cotton, and wove cotton and wool into cloth for the family's use.

In 1889 the Blacks moved to Ashland, a larger town. Black purchased a more substantial house and a part interest in another general store. His partner was a power in the local Democratic party. Black himself was what he called "a Grover Cleveland Democrat." He would have nothing to do with the Populists, who were strong in many sections of Alabama.

When he died in 1900, Black left an estate valued at $25,000. One of his sons, Hugo, became a justice of the United States Supreme Court.

Samuel and Patsy McLeod owned a small cotton farm near Mayesville, South Carolina. The McLeods had been born slaves. Some of their 17 children had been sold away from them. After the war Patsy McLeod continued to work as a cook for her former master. Her wages, carefully saved, had helped make it possible for the family to buy five acres of cotton land.

McLeod and his sons had then built a log house on the property, which the McLeods proudly christened "The Homestead." It was very small (especially for such a large family) and lacking in conveniences. The floor was of dirt and the two windows had shutters, but no glass panes. The children slept in bunk beds built against the walls. A solid brick fireplace supplied heat. A kitchen with its own chimney was later attached to the cabin.

Gradually the McLeods improved the property, building a barn and other outbuildings. Each fall they took their cotton to the farm of a white neighbor, where it was ginned and baled. Patsy McLeod spun some of this cotton and wove the thread to make shirts and underwear for the family. Shoes and most of their other clothes had to be purchased in the town of Sumter, which was 12 miles from the farm. Shopping in Sumter was an all-day trip by horse and wagon, but exciting for the children whose turn it was to accompany Samuel McLeod on such an expedition.

The McLeods were industrious and thrifty. Everyone worked on the farm. The youngest children gathered fruits and vegetables and fed and tended the animals. Others fished and hunted in the steams and woods of the area. The oldest boys worked for wages on nearby farms and what they earned helped pay for more land. Some of this land was too swampy for growing cotton, so the McLeods began to grow rice also.

Most of the McLeod children had little formal education, but Mary, the fifteenth child, born in 1875, was sent to a school for blacks operated by the Presbyterian Church near Mayesville, where the pupils learned to read by studying the Bible. Mary went into teaching and eventually founded a school of her own in Florida. She gradually elevated what began as an elementary school first to high school, then to junior college status. It finally became Bethune-Cookman College, a four-year liberal arts institution.

Simon Baruch emigrated to the United States from East Prussia in 1855, when he was 15. He came to Camden, South Carolina, because two friends from his hometown had started a business there. With their help he was able to go to medical school and become a doctor. He served in the Confederate army during the Civil War, then

The McLeod's "Homestead"

married Isabelle Wolfe. Isabelle's parents had been wealthy, but their home and property (along with nearly everything in the Camden area) had been destroyed by General Sherman's army during the late stages of the war.

Dr. Baruch was a tall, dignified man, very formal. His son Bernard claimed that despite the heat of South Carolina summers, he had never seen his father in shirtsleeves. But Baruch was a typical country doctor. He made his rounds in the countryside, treating both white and black patients. Times were hard in South Carolina during Reconstruction. Since money was scarce, Baruch often had to accept payment in goods—a cord of wood, perhaps, or some cotton or corn. Isabelle Baruch helped out by giving piano lessons for 25 cents an hour.

Gradually things improved. There was never a great deal of money but the Baruchs lived well. They had a large house, servants, and three acres of land on which Baruch ran a genuine farm in miniature. He raised cotton, corn, vegetables, and even sugarcane, which his servants refined into brown sugar for the family's use.

Although he was less prejudiced than most white southerners, Baruch detested the "Black Republican" government that controlled South Carolina in the 1870s. He joined the Ku Klux Klan. His children went to a small private school, but in their free time they mingled freely with black children. Many years later Bernard Baruch wrote: "What a cruel thing it was when I grew old enough to appreciate the gulf that separated the white and black races!" He did not add that it must have seemed much more cruel to the black children than to him.

In 1880 Dr. Baruch gave up his practice in South Carolina and moved the family to New York City.

Reconstruction and the South

No great social revolution ever took place without causing great temporary loss and inconvenience.

THE NATION, *1867*

The experiment has totally failed.

THE NATION, *1871*

This is socialism.

THE NATION, *1874*

n April 5, 1865, Abraham Lincoln visited Richmond. The fallen capital lay in ruins, sections blackened by fire, but the president was able to walk the streets unmolested and almost unattended. Everywhere black people crowded around him worshipfully; some fell to their knees as he passed, crying "Glory, Hallelujah," hailing him as a messiah. But even white townspeople seemed to have accepted defeat without resentment.

A few days later, in Washington, Lincoln delivered an important speech on Reconstruction, urging compassion and open-mindedness. On April 14 he held a Cabinet meeting at which postwar readjustment was considered at length. That evening, while Lincoln was watching a performance of the play *Our American Cousin* at Ford's Theater, a half-mad actor, John Wilkes Booth, slipped into his box and shot him in the back of the head with a small pistol. Early the next morning, without having regained consciousness, Lincoln died.

The murder was part of a complicated plot organized by die-hard prosoutherners. Seldom have fanatics displayed so little understanding of their own interests, for with Lincoln perished the South's best hope for a mild peace. After his body had been taken home to Illinois, the national mood hardened; apparently the awesome drama was still unfolding; retribution and a final humbling of the South were inevitable.

Presidential Reconstruction

Despite its bloodiness, the Civil War had caused less intersectional hatred than might have been expected. Although civilian property was often seized or destroyed, the invading armies treated the southern population with remarkable forbearance, both during the war and after Appomattox. While he was ensconced in Richmond behind Lee's army, northerners boasted that they would "hang Jeff Davis to a sour apple tree," and when he was captured in Georgia in May 1865, he was at once clapped into irons preparatory to being tried for treason and murder. But feeling against Davis subsided quickly. In 1867 the military turned him over to the civil courts, which released him on bail. He was never brought to trial. A few other Confederate officials spent short periods behind bars, but the only southerner executed for war crimes was Major Henry Wirz, the commandant of Andersonville military prison.

The legal questions related to bringing the defeated states back into the Union were extremely complex. Since southerners believed that secession was legal, logic should have compelled them to argue that they were out of the Union and would thus have to be formally readmitted. Northerners should have taken the contrary position, for they had fought to prove that secession was illegal. Yet the people of both sections did just the opposite. Senator Charles Sumner and Congressman Thaddeus Stevens, in 1861 uncompromising expounders of the theory that the Union was indissoluble, now insisted that the Confederate states had "committed suicide" and should be treated like "conquered provinces." Lincoln believed the issue a "pernicious abstraction" and tried to ignore it.

The process of readmission began in 1862, when Lincoln reappointed provisional governors for those parts of the South that had been occupied by federal troops. On December 8, 1863, he issued a proclamation setting forth a general policy. With the exception of high Confederate officials and a few other special groups, all southerners could reinstate themselves as United States citizens by taking a simple loyalty oath. When, in any state, a number equal to ten percent of those voting in the 1860 election had taken this oath, they could set up a state government. Such governments had to be republican in form, must recognize the "permanent freedom" of the slaves, and must provide for black education. The plan, however, did not require that blacks be given the right to vote.

The "ten percent plan" reflected Lincoln's lack of vindictiveness and his political wisdom. He realized that any government based on such a small minority of the population would be, as he put it, merely "a tangible nucleus which the remainder . . . may rally around as fast as it can," a sort of puppet regime, like the paper government established in those sections of Virginia under federal control.* The regimes established under this plan in Tennessee, Louisiana, and Arkansas bore, in the president's mind, the same relation to finally reconstructed states that an egg bears to a chicken. "We shall sooner have the fowl by hatching it than by smashing it," he remarked. He knew that eventually representatives of the Southern states would again be sitting in Congress, and he wished to lay the groundwork for a strong Republican party in the section. Yet he realized that Congress had no intention of seating representatives from the "ten percent" states at once.

The Radicals in Congress disliked the ten percent plan, partly because of its moderation and partly because it enabled Lincoln to determine Union policy toward the recaptured regions. In July 1864 they passed the Wade-Davis bill, which provided for constitutional conventions only after a *majority* of the voters in a Southern state had taken a loyalty oath. Confederate officials and anyone who had "voluntarily borne arms against the United States" were barred from voting in the election or serving at the convention. Besides prohibiting slavery, the new state constitutions would have to repudiate Confederate debts. Lincoln disposed of the Wade-Davis bill with a pocket veto, and there matters stood when Andrew Johnson became president following the assassination.

---

* By approving the separation of the western counties that had refused to secede, this government provided a legal pretext for the creation of West Virginia.

Andrew Johnson, as recorded by Matthew Brady's camera in 1865. Johnson, Charles Dickens reported, radiated purposefulness but no "genial sunlight."

Lincoln had picked Johnson for a running mate in 1864 because he was a border-state Unionist Democrat and something of a hero as a result of his courageous service as military governor of Tennessee. From origins even more lowly than Lincoln's, Johnson had risen to be congressman, governor of Tennessee, and United States senator. He was able and ambitious but fundamentally unsure of himself, as could be seen in his boastfulness and stubbornness. His political strength came from the poor whites and yeomen farmers of eastern Tennessee, and he was fond of extolling the common man and attacking "stuck-up aristocrats."

Thaddeus Stevens called Johnson a "rank demagogue" and a "damned scoundrel," and it is true that he was a masterful rabble-rouser. But few politicians of his generation labored so consistently in behalf of small farmers. Free homesteads, public education, absolute social equality—such were his objectives. The father of communism, Karl Marx, a close observer of American affairs at this time, wrote approvingly of Johnson's "deadly hatred of the oligarchy."

Johnson was a Democrat, but because of his record and his reassuring penchant for excoriating southern aristocrats, the Republicans in Congress were ready to cooperate with him. "Johnson, we have faith in you," said Senator Ben Wade, author of the Wade-Davis bill, the day after Lincoln's death. "By the gods, there will be no trouble now in running the government!"

Johnson's reply, "Treason must be made infamous," delighted the Radicals, but the president proved temperamentally unable to work with them. As Eric L. McKitrick has shown in *Andrew Johnson and Reconstruction,* Johnson was an "outsider," a "lone wolf" in every way. Like Randolph of Roanoke, his antithesis intellectually and socially, opposition was his specialty; he soon alienated every powerful Republican in Washington.

Radical Republicans listened to Johnson's diatribes against secessionists and the great planters and assumed that he was antisouthern. Nothing could have been further from the truth. He had great respect for states' rights and he shared most of his poor white Tennessee constituents' contempt of blacks. "Damn the negroes, I am fighting these traitorous aristocrats, their masters," he told a friend during the war. "I wish to God," he said on another occasion, "every head of a family in the United States had one slave to take the drudgery and menial service off his family."

The new president did not want to injure or humiliate all southerners. He issued an amnesty proclamation only slightly more rigorous than Lincoln's. It assumed, correctly enough, that with the war over most southern voters would freely take the loyalty oath; thus it contained no ten percent clause. More classes of Confederates, including those who owned taxable property in excess of $20,000, were excluded from the general pardon. By the time Congress convened in December 1865, all of the southern states had organized governments, ratified the Thirteenth Amendment abolishing slavery, and elected senators and representatives. Johnson promptly recommended these new governments to the attention of Congress.

Republican Radicals

Peace found the Republicans in Congress no more united than they had been during the war. A small

Matthew Brady's photograph of the stalwart radical Republican, Thaddeus Stevens. Stevens served in the House from 1859 until his death in 1868.

group of "ultra" Radicals were demanding immediate and absolute civil and political equality for blacks; they should be given, for example, the vote, a plot of land, and access to a decent education. Senator Sumner led this faction. A second group of Radicals, headed by Thaddeus Stevens in the House and Ben Wade in the Senate, agreed with the ultras' objectives but were prepared to accept half a loaf if necessary to win the support of less radical colleagues.

Nearly all Radicals distinguished between the "natural" God-given rights described in the Declaration of Independence, and social equality. "Equality," said Stevens, "does not mean that a negro shall sit in the same seat or eat at the same table with a white man. That is a matter of taste which every man must decide for himself." This did not reflect personal prejudice in Stevens's case. When he died, he was buried in a black cemetery. Here is his epitaph, written by himself: "I repose in this quiet and secluded spot, not from any natural preference for solitude, but finding other cemeteries limited as to race, by charter rules, I have chosen this that I might illustrate in my death the principles which I advocated through a long life, equality of man before his Creator."

The moderate Republicans wanted to protect ex-slaves from exploitation and guarantee their basic rights but were unprepared to push for full political equality. A handful of Republicans sided with the Democrats in support of Johnson's approach, but all the rest insisted at least on the minimum demands of the moderates. Thus Johnsonian Reconstruction was doomed.

Johnson's proposal had no chance in Congress for reasons having little to do with black rights. The Thirteenth Amendment had the effect of increasing the representation of the southern states in Congress because it made the Three-fifths Compromise meaningless. Henceforth those who had been slaves would be counted as whole persons in apportioning seats in the House of Representatives. If Congress seated the southerners, the balance of power might swing to the Democrats. To expect the Republicans to surrender power in such a fashion was unrealistic. Former Copperheads gushing with extravagant praise for Johnson put them instantly on guard.

In addition, the ex-Confederates were not overflowing with goodwill toward their conquerors. A minority would have nothing to do with amnesties and pardons:

Oh, I'm a good old rebel,
Now that's just what I am;
For the "fair land of freedom,"
I do not care a dam.
I'm glad I fit against it—
I only wish we'd won
And I don't want no pardon
For anything I done.

Southern voters had further provoked northern resentment by their choice of congressmen. Georgia elected Alexander H. Stephens, vice-president of the Confederacy, to the Senate, although he was still in a federal prison awaiting trial for treason! Several dozen men who had served in the Confederate Congress had been elected to either the House or the Senate, together with four generals and many other high officials. It was understandable that southern people would select locally respected and experienced leaders, but it was equally reasonable that these choices would sit poorly with northerners.

Finally, the so-called Black Codes enacted by southern governments to control former slaves alarmed the North. These varied in severity from state to state. When seen in historical perspective, even the strictest codes represented a considerable improvement over slavery. Most permitted blacks to sue and to testify in court, at least in cases involving members of their own race. Blacks were allowed to own certain kinds of property; marriages were made legal; other rights were guaranteed. However, blacks could not bear arms, be employed in occupations other than farming and domestic service, or leave their jobs without forfeiting back pay. The Louisiana code required them to sign labor contracts for the year during the first ten days of January. A similar rule was put into effect in Mississippi, where, in addition, drunkards, vagrants, beggars, "common night-walkers," and even persons who "misspend what they earn" and who could not pay the stiff fines assessed for such misbehavior were to be "hired out . . . at public outcry" to the white persons who would take them for the shortest period in return for paying the fines. Such laws, apparently designed to get around the Thirteenth Amendment, outraged northerners.

For all these reasons the Republicans in Congress rejected Johnsonian Reconstruction. Quickly they created a joint committee on Reconstruction, headed by Senator William P. Fessenden of Maine, a moderate, to study the question of readmitting the southern states.

The committee held public hearings that produced much evidence of the mistreatment of blacks. Colonel George A. Custer, stationed in Texas, testified: "It is of weekly, if not of daily occurrence that Freedmen are murdered." The nurse Clara Barton told a gruesome tale about a pregnant woman who had been brutally whipped. Others described the intimidation of blacks by poor whites. The hearings strengthened the hands of the Radicals, who had been claiming all along that the South was perpetuating slavery under another name.

President Johnson's attitude speeded the swing toward the Radical position. While the hearings were in progress, Congress passed a bill expanding and extending the Freedmen's Bureau, which had

Agents of the Freedmen's Bureau helped defend former slaves against white attacks and provided them with food, clothing, and medical care. They also set up schools. However, hostility toward the activities of the Freedmen's Bureau was widespread. In 1866, during a race riot in Memphis, mobs killed 46 blacks and burned this Freedmen's schoolhouse.

been established in March 1865 to care for refugees. The bureau, a branch of the War Department, was already exercising considerable coercive and supervisory power in the South. Now Congress sought to add to its authority in order to protect the black population. Although the bill had wide support, Johnson vetoed it, arguing that it was an unconstitutional extension of military authority in peacetime. Congress then passed a Civil Rights Act that, besides declaring specifically that blacks were citizens of the United States, denied the states the power to restrict their rights to testify in court, to make contracts for their labor, and to hold property. In other words, it put teeth in the Thirteenth Amendment.

Once again the president refused to go along, although his veto was sure to drive more moderates into the arms of the Radicals. On April 9, 1866, Congress repassed the Civil Rights Act by a two-thirds majority, the first time in American history that a major piece of legislation became law over the veto of a president. This event marked a revolution in the history of Reconstruction, indeed, in federal-state relations, north as well as south. Thereafter Congress, not President Johnson, had the upper hand.

In the clash between the president and Congress, Johnson was his own worst enemy. His language was often intemperate, his handling of opponents inept, his analysis of southern conditions incorrect. He had assumed that the small southern farmers who made up the majority in the Confederacy shared his prejudices against the planter class. They did not, as their choices in the postwar elections demonstrated. In fact, Johnson's hatred of the southern aristocracy may have been based more on jealousy than on principle. Under the Reconstruction plan, persons excluded from the blanket amnesty could apply individually for the restoration of their rights. When wealthy and socially prominent southerners flocked to Washington, hat in hand, he found their flattery and humility exhilarating. He issued pardons wholesale. "I did not expect to keep out all who were excluded from the amnesty," he explained. "I intended they should sue for pardon, and so realize the enormity of their crime."

The president misread northern opinion. He believed that Congress had no right to pass laws affecting the South before southern representatives had been readmitted to Congress. However, in the light of the refusal of most southern whites to grant any real power or responsibility to the freedmen (an attitude that Johnson did not condemn), the public would not accept this point of view. Johnson placed his own judgment over that of the overwhelming majority of northern voters, and this was a great error, morally and tactically. By encouraging southerners to resist efforts to improve the lot of blacks, Johnson played into the hands of northern extremists.

The Radicals encountered grave problems in fighting for their program. Northerners might object to the Black Codes and to seating "rebels" in Congress, but few believed in racial equality. Between 1865 and 1868 Wisconsin, Minnesota, Connecticut, Nebraska, New Jersey, Ohio, Michigan, and Pennsylvania all rejected bills granting blacks the vote.

The Radicals were in effect demanding not merely equal rights for freedmen but extra rights; not merely the vote but special protection of that right against the pressure that southern whites would surely apply to undermine it. This idea flew in the face of conventional American beliefs in equality before the law and individual self-reliance. Such protection would involve interference by the federal government in local affairs, a concept at variance with American practice. Events were to show that the Radicals were correct—that what amounted to a political revolution in state-federal relations was essential if blacks were to achieve real equality. But in the climate of that day their proposals encountered bitter resistance, and not only from southerners.

Thus, while the Radicals sought partisan advantage in their battle with Johnson and sometimes played on war-bred passions in achieving their ends, they were taking large political risks in defense of genuinely held principles. One historian has aptly called them the "moral trustees" of the Civil War.

The Fourteenth Amendment

In June 1866 Congress submitted to the states a new amendment to the Constitution. The Fourteenth Amendment was, in the context of the times, a truly radical measure. Never before had newly freed slaves been granted significant political rights. For example, in the British Caribbean sugar islands, where slavery had been abolished in the 1830s, stiff property qualifications and poll taxes kept freedmen from voting. The Fourteenth Amendment was also a milestone along the road to the centralization of political power in the United States because it

reduced the power of all the states. In this sense it confirmed the great change wrought by the Civil War: the growth of a more complex, more closely integrated social and economic structure requiring closer national supervision. Few people understood this aspect of the amendment at the time.

First the amendment supplied a broad definition of American citizenship: "All persons born or naturalized in the United States, and subject to the jurisdiction thereof, are citizens of the United States and of the State wherein they reside." Obviously this included blacks. Then it struck at discriminatory legislation like the Black Codes: "No State shall make or enforce any law which shall abridge the privileges or immunities of citizens of the United States; nor shall any State deprive any person of life, liberty, or property, without due process of law." The next section attempted to force the southern states to permit blacks to vote. If a state denied the vote to any class of its adult male citizens, its representation was to be reduced proportionately. Under another clause, former federal officials who had served the Confederacy were barred from holding either state or federal office unless specifically pardoned by a two-thirds vote of Congress. Finally, the Confederate debt was repudiated.

While the amendment did not specifically outlaw segregation or prevent a state from disfranchising blacks, the southern states would have none of it. Without them the necessary three-fourths majority of the states could not be obtained.

President Johnson vowed to make the choice between the Fourteenth Amendment and his own policy the main issue of the 1866 congressional elections. He embarked on "a swing around the circle" to rally the public to his cause. He failed dismally. Northern women objected to the implication in the amendment that black men were more fitted to vote than white women, but a large majority of northern voters was determined that blacks must have at least formal legal equality. The Republicans won better than two-thirds of the seats in both houses, together with control of all of the northern state governments. Johnson emerged from the campaign discredited, the Radicals stronger and determined to have their way. The southern states, Congressman James A. Garfield of Ohio said in February 1867, have "flung back into our teeth the magnanimous offer of a generous nation. It is now our turn to act."

The Reconstruction Acts

Had the southern states been willing to accept the Fourteenth Amendment, coercive measures might have been avoided. Their recalcitrance and continuing indications that local authorities were persecuting blacks finally led to the passage, on March 2, 1867, of the First Reconstruction Act. This law divided the former Confederacy—exclusive of Tennessee, which had ratified the Fourteenth Amendment—into five military districts, each controlled by

Johnson tried to turn public opinion against the Radicals' plan for Reconstruction. He toured the country, stumping for the Constitution with the same speech at every stop. His efforts failed as mobs greeted him with the cry. "Shut up, Johnson." This Harper's Weekly *cartoon reflects public criticism of Johnson as a parrot repeating a single word.*

a major general. It gave these officers almost dictatorial power to protect the civil rights of "all persons," maintain order, and supervise the administration of justice. To rid themselves of military rule, the former states were required to adopt constitutions guaranteeing blacks the right to vote and disfranchising broad classes of ex-Confederates. If the new constitutions proved satisfactory to Congress, and if the new governments ratified the Fourteenth Amendment, their representatives would be admitted to Congress and military rule ended. Johnson's veto of the act was easily overridden.

Although drastic, the Reconstruction Act was so vague that it proved unworkable. Military control was easily established. But in deference to moderate Republican views, the law had not spelled out the process by which the new constitutions were to be drawn up. Southern whites preferred the status quo, even under army control, to enfranchising blacks and retiring their own respected leaders. They made no effort to follow the steps laid down in the law. Congress therefore passed a second act requiring the military authorities to register voters and supervise the election of delegates to constitutional conventions. A third act further clarified procedures.

Still white southerners resisted. The laws required that the constitutions be approved by a majority of the registered voters. Simply by staying away from the polls, whites prevented ratification in state after state. At last, in March 1868, a full year after the First Reconstruction Act, Congress changed the rules again. The constitutions were to be ratified by a majority of the voters. In June 1868, Arkansas, having fulfilled the requirements, was readmitted to the Union, and by July a sufficient number of states had ratified the Fourteenth Amendment to make it part of the Constitution. But it was not until July 1870 that the last southern state, Georgia, qualified to the satisfaction of Congress.

Congress Takes Charge

To carry out this program in the face of determined southern resistance required singlemindedness over a long period to an extent seldom demonstrated by an American legislature. The persistence resulted in part from the suffering and frustrations of the war years. The refusal of the South to accept the spirit of even the mild reconstruction designed by Johnson goaded the North to ever more overbearing efforts to bring the ex-Confederates to heel. President Johnson's stubbornness also influenced the Republicans. They became obsessed with the need to defeat him. The unsettled times and the large Republican majorities, always threatened by the possibility of a Democratic resurgence if "unreconstructed" southern congressmen were readmitted, sustained their determination.

These considerations led Republicans to attempt a kind of grand revision of the federal government, one that almost destroyed the balance between judicial, executive, and legislative power established in 1789. A series of measures passed between 1866 and 1868 increased the authority of Congress over the army, over the process of amending the Constitution, and over Cabinet members and lesser appointive officers. Even the Supreme Court was affected. Its size was reduced and its jurisdiction over civil rights cases limited. Finally, in a showdown caused by emotion more than by practical considerations, the Republicans attempted to remove President Johnson from office.

Johnson was a poor president and out of touch with public opinion, but he had done nothing to merit ejection from office. While he had a low opinion of blacks, his opinion was so widely shared by whites that it is unhistorical to condemn him as a reactionary on this ground. Johnson believed that he was fighting to preserve constitutional government. He was honest and devoted to duty, and his record easily withstood the most searching examination. When Congress passed laws taking away powers granted him by the Constitution, he refused to submit.

The chief issue was the Tenure of Office Act of 1867, which prohibited the president from removing officials who had been appointed with the consent of the Senate without first obtaining Senate approval. In February 1868 Johnson "violated" this act by dismissing Secretary of War Edwin M. Stanton, who had been openly in sympathy with the Radicals for some time. The House, acting under the procedure set up in the Constitution for removing the president, promptly impeached him before the bar of the Senate, Chief Justice Salmon P. Chase presiding.

The trial was conducted in a partisan and vindictive manner. Johnson's lawyers easily established that he had removed Stanton only in an effort to prove the Tenure of Office Act unconstitutional. They demonstrated that the act did not protect Stanton to begin with, since it gave Cabinet members tenure "during the term of the President by whom they may have been appointed," and Stanton had been appointed in 1862, during Lincoln's first term!

Nevertheless the Radicals pressed the charges (11 separate articles) relentlessly. To the argument that Johnson had committed no crime, the learned Senator Sumner retorted that the proceedings were "political in character" rather than judicial. Thaddeus Stevens, directing the attack on behalf of the House, warned the senators that although "no corrupt or wicked motive" could be attributed to Johnson, they would "be tortured on the gibbet of everlasting obloquy" if they did not convict him. Tremendous pressure was applied to the handful of Republican senators who were unwilling to disregard the evidence.

Seven of them resisted to the end, and the Senate failed by a single vote to convict Johnson. This was probably fortunate. Had he been forced from office on such flimsy grounds, the independence of the executive might have been permanently weakened. Then the legislative branch would have become supreme.

The Fifteenth Amendment

The failure of the impeachment did not affect the course of Reconstruction. The president was acquitted on May 16, 1868. A few days later, the Republican National Convention nominated General Ulysses S. Grant for the presidency. At the Democratic convention Johnson had considerable support, but the delegates nominated Horatio Seymour, a former governor of New York. In November Grant won an easy victory in the electoral college, 214 to 80, but the popular vote was close: 3 million to 2.7 million. Although he would probably have carried the electoral college in any case, Grant's margin in the popular vote was supplied by southern blacks enfranchised under the Reconstruction Acts, about 450,000 of whom supported him. A majority of white voters probably preferred Sey-

The black vote helped Grant win five former Confederate states in the election of 1868. Although Republicans had avoided supporting suffrage for blacks during the campaign, they changed course after their victory and proposed the Fifteenth Amendment. In this cartoon, Grant, standing on shore, advises white Southerners to accept black suffrage.

mour. Since many citizens undoubtedly voted Republican because of personal admiration for General Grant, the election statistics suggest that a substantial white majority opposed the policies of the Radicals.

The Reconstruction Acts and the ratification of the Fourteenth Amendment achieved the purpose of enabling black southerners to vote. The Radicals, however, were not satisfied; despite the unpopularity of the idea in the North, they wished to guarantee the right of blacks to vote in every state. Another amendment seemed the only way to accomplish this objective, but passage of such an amendment appeared impossible. The Republican platform in the 1868 election had smugly distinguished between blacks voting in the South ("demanded by every consideration of public safety, of gratitude, and of justice") and in the North (where the question "properly belongs to the people").

However, after the election had demonstrated how important the black vote could be, Republican strategy shifted. Grant had carried Indiana by less than 10,000 votes and lost New York by a similar number. If blacks in these and other closely divided states had voted, Republican strength would have been greatly enhanced.

Suddenly Congress blossomed with suffrage amendments. After considerable bickering over details, the Fifteenth Amendment was sent to the states for ratification in February 1869. It forbade all the

states to deny the vote to anyone "on account of race, color, or previous condition of servitude." Once again nothing was said about denial of the vote on the basis of sex, which caused feminists such as Elizabeth Cady Stanton to be even more outraged than they had been by the Fourteenth Amendment.

Most southern states, still under federal pressure, ratified the amendment swiftly. The same was true in most of New England and in some western states. Bitter battles were waged in Connecticut, New York, Pennsylvania, and the states immediately north of the Ohio River, but by March 1870 most of them had ratified the amendment and it became part of the Constitution.

The debates occasioned by these contests show that partisan advantage was not the only reason why voters approved black suffrage at last. The unfairness of a double standard of voting, North and South, the contribution of black soldiers during the war, and the hope that by passing the amendment the strife of Reconstruction could finally be ended all played a part.

When the Fifteenth Amendment went into effect, President Grant called it "the greatest civil change and . . . the most important event that has occurred since the nation came to life." The American Anti-Slavery Society formally dissolved itself, its work apparently completed. "The Fifteenth Amendment confers upon the African race the care of its own destiny," Radical Congressman James A.

Garfield wrote proudly after the amendment was ratified. "It places their fortunes in their own hands."

Many of the celebrants lived to see the amendment subverted in the South. That it could be evaded by literacy tests and other restrictions was apparent at the time and may even have influenced some persons who voted for it. But a stronger amendment—one, for instance, that positively granted the right to vote to all men and put the supervision of elections under national control—could not have been ratified.

"Black Republican" Reconstruction: Scalawags and Carpetbaggers

The Radicals had at last succeeded in imposing their will upon the South. Throughout the region former slaves had real political influence; they voted, held office, and exercised the "privileges" and enjoyed the "immunities" guaranteed them by the Fourteenth Amendment. Almost to a man they voted Republican.

The spectacle of blacks not five years removed from slavery in positions of power and responsibility attracted much attention at the time and has since been examined exhaustively by historians. The subject is controversial, but certain facts are beyond argument. Black officeholders were neither numerous nor inordinately influential. None was ever elected governor of a state; fewer than a dozen and a half during the entire period served in Congress. Blacks held many minor offices and were influential in southern legislatures, although (except in South Carolina) they never made up the majority. Certainly they did not share the spoils of office in proportion to their numbers.

The real rulers of the "black Republican" governments were white, the "scalawags"—southerners willing to cooperate with the Republicans because they accepted the results of the war and to advance their own interests—and the "carpetbaggers"—northerners who went to the South as idealists to help the freed slaves, as employees of the federal government, or more commonly as settlers hoping to improve themselves.

The scalawags were by far the more numerous. A few were prewar politicians or well-to-do planters, men such as the Mississippi planter John L. Alcorn and Joseph E. Brown, the Confederate governor of Georgia. General James Longstreet, one of Lee's most important lieutenants, was another prominent southerner who cooperated with the Republicans. But most were people who had supported the Whig party before the secession crisis and who saw the

During Reconstruction, fourteen blacks won election to the House of Representatives and two, Hiram Revels and Blanche K. Bruce, served in the Senate. Revels, at far left, won the Mississippi Senate seat that Jefferson Davis had once held. He later became president of Alcorn University. Congressman R. Brown Elliot, at far right, had been educated at Eton in England.

Republicans as the logical successors of the Whigs.

The carpetbaggers were a particularly varied lot. Most had mixed motives for coming south and personal gain was certainly among them. But so were opposition to slavery and the belief that blacks deserved to be treated decently and given a chance to get ahead in the world. Among the most admirable of the carpetbaggers was Adelbert Ames of Maine, who was governor of Mississippi in 1874–1875. Ames was, in the words of historian Richard N. Current, "about as pure and incorruptible a governor as Mississippi or any other state is likely ever to have."

Many northern blacks became carpetbaggers: former Union soldiers, missionaries from northern black churches, and also teachers, lawyers, and other members of the small northern black professional class. Many of these became officeholders, but like southern black politicans their influence was limited.

That blacks should fail to dominate southern governments is certainly understandable. They lacked experience in politics and were mostly poor and uneducated. They were nearly everywhere a minority. Those blacks who held office during Reconstruction tended to be better educated and more prosperous than most southern blacks. In his interesting analysis of black South Carolina politicians, Thomas Holt shows that a disproportionate number of them had been free before the war. Of those freed by the Thirteenth Amendment, a large percentage had been house servants or artisans, not field hands. Mulatto politicians were also disproportionately numerous and (as a group) more conservative and economically better off than other black leaders.

In South Carolina and elsewhere, blacks proved in the main able and conscientious public servants, able because the best tended to rise to the top in such a fluid situation, and conscientious because most of those who achieved importance sought eagerly to demonstrate the capacity of their race for self-government. Even at the local level, where the quality of officials was usually poor, there was little difference in the degree of competence displayed by white and black officeholders. In power, the blacks were not vindictive; by and large they did not seek to restrict the rights of ex-Confederates.

Not all black legislators and administrators were paragons of virtue. In South Carolina, despite their control of the legislature, they broke up into factions repeatedly and failed to press for laws that would improve the lot of poor black farm workers. In *The Prostrate South* (1874), James S. Pike, a northern newspaperman, wrote: "The rule of South Carolina should not be dignified with the name of government. It is the installation of a huge system of brigandage." Like many northern commentators, Pike exaggerated the immorality and incompetence of the blacks, but waste and corruption were common in Reconstruction governments. Half the budget of Louisiana in some years went for salaries and "mileage" for representatives and their staffs. One Arkansas black took $9,000 from the state for repairing a bridge that had cost only $500 to build. A South Carolina legislator was voted an additional $1,000 in salary after he lost that sum betting on a horse race.

However, the corruption must be seen in perspective. The big thieves were nearly always white; blacks got mostly crumbs. Furthermore, graft and callous disregard of the public interest characterized government in every section and at every level during the decade after Appomattox. Big-city bosses in the North embezzled sums that dwarfed the most brazen southern frauds. The New York City Tweed Ring probably made off with more money than all the southern thieves, black and white, combined. While the evidence does not justify the southern corruption, it suggests that the unique features of Reconstruction politics—black suffrage, military supervision, carpetbagger and scalawag influence—do not explain it.

The "black Republican" governments displayed qualities that grew directly from the ignorance and political inexperience of the former slaves. There was a tragicomic aspect to the South Carolina legislature during these years, its many black members—some dressed in old frock coats, others in rude farm clothes—rising to points of order and personal privilege without reason, discoursing ponderously on subjects they did not understand. But those who complained about the ignorance and irresponsibility of blacks conveniently forgot that the tendency of 19th-century American democracy was away from educational, financial, or any other restrictions on the franchise. Thousands of white southerners were as illiterate and uncultured as the freedmen, yet no one suggested depriving them of the ballot.

In fact, the Radical southern governments ac-

The Freedmen's Bureau established 4,329 schools, attended by some 250,000 ex-slaves, in the postwar South. Harper's Weekly *artist Alfred Waud sketched a Freedmen's Bureau school in Vicksburg, Mississippi, in 1866. Many of the teachers were white women from the North.*

complished a great deal. They spent money freely but not entirely wastefully. Tax rates zoomed, but the money financed the repair and expansion of the South's dilapidated railroad network, rebuilt crumbling levees, and expanded social services. Before the Civil War, as Eric Foner points out in *Reconstruction: America's Unfinished Revolution,* "slavery had sharply curtailed the scope of public authority" because the slaves were governed by private individuals (their owners) far more than by the state. The planters possessed a disproportionate share of political as well as economic power, and they spent relatively little public money on education and public services of all kinds. During Reconstruction an enormous gap had to be filled, and it took money to fill it. The Freedmen's Bureau made a start, and northern religious and philanthropic organizations did important work. Eventually, however, the state governments established and supported hospitals, asylums, and systems of free public education that, while segregated, greatly benefited everyone, whites as well as blacks. Much state money was also spent on economic development: land reclamation, repairing and expanding the war-ravaged railroads, maintaining levees.

The former slaves grasped eagerly at the opportunities to learn. Nearly all appreciated the immense importance of knowing how to read and write; the sight of elderly men and women poring laboriously over elementary texts beside their grandchildren was common everywhere. Schools and other institutions were supported chiefly by property taxes, and these, of course, hit well-to-do white farmers hard. Hence much of the complaining about the "extravagance" of Reconstruction governments concealed selfish objections to paying for public projects. Eventually the benefits of expanded government services to the entire population became clear, and when white supremacy was reestablished, most of the new services remained in force, and the corruption and inefficiency inherited from the carpetbagger governments continued.

The Ravaged Land

The South's grave economic problems complicated the rebuilding of its political system. The section had never been as prosperous as the North, and wartime destruction left it desperately poor by any standard. In the long run the abolition of slavery released immeasurable quantities of human energy previously stifled, but the immediate effect was to create confusion. Freedom to move without a pass, to "see the world," was one of the ex-slaves' most cherished benefits of emancipation. Understandably, many at first equated legal freedom with freedom from having to earn a living, a tendency reinforced for a time by the willingness of the Freedmen's Bureau to provide rations and other forms of relief in war-devastated areas. Most, however, soon accepted the fact that they must earn a living; a small plot of land of their own ("40 acres and a mule") would complete their independence.

This objective was forcefully supported by the relentless Congressman Thaddeus Stevens, whose hatred of the planter class was pathological. "The property of the chief rebels should be seized," he stated. If the lands of the richest "70,000 proud, bloated and defiant rebels" were confiscated, the federal government would obtain 394 million acres. Every adult male ex-slave could easily be supplied with 40 acres. The beauty of his scheme, Stevens insisted, was that "nine-tenths of the (southern) people would remain untouched." Dispossessing the great planters would make the South "a safe republic," its lands cultivated by "the free labor of intelligent citizens." If the plan drove the planters into exile, "all the better."

Although Stevens's figures were faulty, many Radicals agreed with him. "We must see that the freedmen are established on the soil," Senator Sumner declared. "The great plantations, which have been so many nurseries of the rebellion, must be broken up, and the freedmen must have the pieces." Stevens, Sumner, and others who wanted to give land to the freedmen weakened their case by associating it with the idea of punishing the former rebels; the average American had too much respect for property rights to support a policy of confiscation.

Aside from its vindictiveness, the extremists' view was simplistic. Land without tools, seed, and other necessities would have done the freedmen little good. Congress did throw open 46 million acres of poor-quality federal land in the South to blacks under the Homestead Act, but few settled upon it. Establishing former slaves on small farms with adequate financial aid would have been of incalculable benefit to them and to the nation. This would have been practicable, but it was not done.

The former slaves therefore had to work out their destiny within the established framework of southern agriculture. White planters, influenced by the precipitous decline of sugar production in Jamaica and other Caribbean islands that had followed the abolition of slavery there, expected them to be incapable of self-directed effort. If allowed to become independent farmers, they would either starve to death or descend into barbarism. Of course the blacks did neither. True, the output of cotton and other southern staples declined precipitously after slavery was abolished. Observers soon came to the conclusion that a free black produced much less than a slave had produced. "You can't get only about two-thirds as much out of 'em now as you could when they were slaves," an Arkansas planter complained.

However, the decline in productivity was not caused by the *inability* of free blacks to work independently. What happened was that since they now held, in the pithy phrase of the economist Robert Higgs, "property rights over their own bodies," they chose no longer to work like slaves. They let their children play instead of forcing them into the fields. Mothers devoted more time to child care and housework, less to farm labor. Elderly blacks worked less.

Noting these changes, white critics spoke scornfully of black laziness and shiftlessness. "You cannot make the negro work without physical compulsion," was the common view. As the economic historians Roger Ransom and Richard Sutch have said, the perfectly reasonable desire of ex-slaves to devote more time to leisure was "taken as 'evidence' to support racist characterizations of blacks as lazy, incompetent, and unwilling to work." A leading southern magazine complained in 1866 that black women now expected their husbands "to support them in idleness." It would never have made such a comment about white housewives. Ransom and Sutch also point out that, while working less, emancipated blacks were far better off materially than under slavery. Their earnings brought them almost 30 percent more than the value of the subsistence provided by their former masters.

The family life of ex–slaves was changed in other ways. Male authority increased when husbands became true heads of families. (Under slavery the ultimate responsibility for providing for women and children was the master's.) When blacks became citizens, the men acquired rights and powers denied to all women, such as the right to hold public office and serve on juries. Similarly, black women became more like white women, devoting themselves to separate "spheres" where their lives revolved around housekeeping and child rearing.

Sharecropping and the Crop Lien System

Before the passage of the Reconstruction Acts, plantation owners tried to farm their land with gang labor, the same system as before, only now paying wages to the ex-slaves. This method did not work well for two entirely different reasons. Money was scarce, and capital, never adequate even before the collapse of the Confederacy, accumulated slowly. Interest rates were extremely high. This situation made it difficult for landowners to pay their laborers in cash. More important, blacks did not like working for wages because it kept them under the direction of whites and thus reminded them of slavery. They wanted to be independent, to manage not merely their free time but their entire lives for themselves. Since the voluntary withdrawal of so much black labor from the work force had produced a shortage, the blacks had their way. "I had to yield," one planter admitted, "or lose my labor."

Quite swiftly, a new agricultural system known as sharecropping emerged. Instead of cultivating the land by gang labor as in antebellum times, plant-ers broke up their estates into small units and established on each a black family. The planter provided housing, agricultural implements, draft animals, seed, and other supplies, and the family provided labor. The crop was divided between them, usually on a fifty-fifty basis. If the landlord supplied only land and housing, the laborer got a larger share. This was called share tenancy.

Sharecropping gave blacks the day-to-day control of their lives that they craved and the hope of earning enough to buy a small farm. But few achieved this ambition because whites resisted their efforts adamantly. As late as 1880 blacks owned less than 10 percent of the agricultural land in the South, although they made up more than half of the region's farm population. Mississippi actually prohibited the purchase of farmland by blacks.

Many white farmers in the South were also trapped by the sharecropping system and by white efforts to keep blacks in a subordinate position. New fencing laws kept them from grazing livestock on undeveloped land, a practice common before the Civil War. But the main cause of southern rural poverty for whites as well as blacks was the lack of enough capital to finance the sharecropping system. Like their colonial ancestors, the landowners had to borrow against October's harvest to pay for April's seed. Thus the crop-lien system developed,

After the Civil War, most blacks worked as sharecroppers on land owned by whites. In this photograph, black sharecroppers pick cotton, a major cash crop of the South. Because the price for cotton remained low, sharecroppers often fell into debt and were tied to the land almost as tightly as under slavery.

and to protect their investments, lenders insisted that the grower concentrate on readily marketable cash crops: tobacco, sugar, and especially cotton.

The system injured everyone. Diversified farming would have reduced the farmers' need for cash, preserved the fertility of the soil, and, by placing a premium on imagination and shrewdness, aided the best of them to rise in the world. Under the crop-lien system, both landowner and sharecropper depended on credit supplied by local bankers, merchants, and storekeepers for everything from seed, tools, and fertilizer to overalls, coffee, and salt. Crossroads stores proliferated, and a new class of small merchants appeared. The prices of goods sold on credit were high, adding to the burden borne by the rural population. The small southern merchants were almost equally victimized by the system, for they also lacked capital, bought goods on credit, and had to pay high interest rates.

Seen in broad perspective, the situation is not difficult to understand. The South, drained of every resource by the war, was competing for funds with the North and West, both vigorous and expanding and therefore voracious consumers of capital. Reconstruction, in the literal sense of the word, was accomplished chiefly at the expense of the standard of living of the producing classes. The crop-lien system and the small storekeeper were only agents of an economic process dictated by national, perhaps even worldwide, conditions.

This does not mean that the South's economy was paralyzed by the shortage of capital or that recovery and growth did not take place. But compared with the rest of the country, progress was slow. Just before the Civil War cotton harvests averaged about 4 million bales. During the conflict, output fell to about half a million, and the former Confederate states did not enjoy a 4-million-bale year again until 1870. Only after 1874 did the crop begin to top that figure consistently. In contrast, national wheat production in 1859 was 175 million bushels and in 1878, 449 million. About 7,000 miles of railroad were built in the South between 1865 and 1879; in the rest of the nation nearly 45,000 miles of track were laid.

In manufacturing the South made important gains after the war. The tobacco industry, stimulated by the sudden popularity of the cigarette, expanded rapidly. Virginia and North Carolina tobacco towns like Richmond, Lynchburg, and

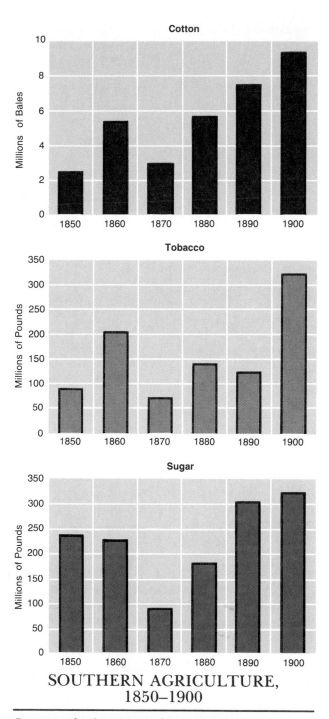

SOUTHERN AGRICULTURE, 1850–1900

Cotton production recovered to its prewar level by 1880, but tobacco and sugar production lagged. Not until 1900 did tobacco growers have a better year than they had in 1860. The years following 1870 saw a general downward trend in wholesale prices for farm commodities. (Statistics are for the 11 states of the Confederacy.)

Durham flourished. The exploitation of the coal and iron deposits of northeastern Alabama in the early 1870s made a boom town of Birmingham. The manufacture of cotton cloth increased, productive capacity nearly doubling between 1865 and 1880. Yet the mills of Massachusetts alone had eight times the capacity of the entire South in 1880. Despite the increases, the South's share of the national output of manufactured goods declined sharply during the Reconstruction era.

The White Counterrevolution

Radical southern governments could sustain themselves only so long as they had the support of a significant proportion of the white population, for except in South Carolina and Louisiana, the blacks were not numerous enough to win elections alone. The key to survival lay in the hands of the wealthy merchants and planters, mostly former Whigs. People of this sort had nothing to fear from black economic competition. Taking a broad view, they could see that improving the lot of the former slaves would benefit all classes.

Southern white Republicans used the Union League of America, a patriotic club founded during the war, to control the black vote. Employing secret rituals, exotic symbols, and other paraphernalia calculated to impress unsophisticated people, they enrolled the freedmen in droves and marched them to the polls en masse.

Powerless to check the League by open methods, dissident southerners established a number of secret terrorist societies, bearing such names as the Ku Klux Klan, the Knights of the White Camelia, and the Pale Faces. The most notorious of these organizations was the Klan, which was organized in Tennessee in 1866. At first it was purely a social club, but by 1868 it had been taken over by vigilante types dedicated to driving blacks out of politics, and it was spreading rapidly across the South. Sheet-clad night riders roamed the countryside, frightening the impressionable and chastising the defiant. Klansmen, using a weird mumbo jumbo and claiming to be the ghosts of Confederate soldiers, spread horrendous rumors and published broadsides designed to persuade the freedmen that it was unhealthy for them to participate in politics:

Niggers and Leaguers, get out of the way,
We're born of the night and we vanish by day.
No rations have we, but the flesh of man—
And love niggers best—the Ku Klux Klan;
We catch 'em alive and roast 'em whole,
Then hand 'em around with a sharpened pole.
Whole Leagues have been eaten, not leaving a man,
And went away hungry—the Ku Klux Klan. . . .

When intimidation failed, the Klansmen resorted to force. After being whipped by one group in Tennessee, a recently elected justice of the peace reported: "They said they had nothing particular against me . . . but they did not intend any nigger to hold office." In hundreds of cases the KKK murdered their opponents, often in the most gruesome manner.

Congress struck at the Klan with three Force Acts (1870–1871), which placed elections under federal jurisdiction and imposed fines and prison sentences on persons convicted of interfering with any citizen's exercise of the franchise. Troops were dispatched to areas where the Klan was strong, and by 1872 the federal authorities had arrested enough Klansmen to break up the organization.

Nevertheless the Klan contributed substantially to the destruction of Radical regimes in the South. Its depredations weakened the will of white Republicans (few of whom really believed in racial equality), and it intimidated many blacks, who gave up trying to exercise their rights. The fact that the army had to be called in to suppress it was a glaring illustration of the weakness of the Reconstruction governments.

Gradually it became respectable to intimidate black voters. Beginning in Mississippi in 1874, terrorism spread through the South. Instead of hiding behind masks and operating in the dark, these terrorists donned red shirts, organized into military companies, and paraded openly. Mississippi redshirts seized militant blacks and whipped them publicly. Killings were frequent. When blacks dared to fight back, heavily armed whites easily put them to rout. In other states similar results followed.

Terrorism fed on fear, fear on terrorism. White violence led to fear of black retaliation and thus to even more brutal attacks. The slightest sign of resistance came to be seen as the beginning of race war, and when the blacks suffered indignities and

A graphic warning by the Alabama Klan "of the fate in store for" scalawags and carpetbaggers, "those great pests of Southern society," from the Tuscaloosa Independent Monitor, *September 1, 1868.*

persecutions in silence, the awareness of how much they must resent the mistreatment made them appear more dangerous still. Thus self-hatred was displaced, guilt suppressed, aggression justified as self-defense, individual conscience submerged in the animality of the mob.

Before long the blacks learned to stay home on election day. One by one, "Conservative" parties—Democratic in national affairs—took over southern state governments. Intimidation was only a partial explanation of this development. The increasing solidarity of whites, northern and southern, was equally significant.

The North had subjected the South to control from Washington while preserving state sovereignty in the North itself. In the long run this discrimination proved unworkable. Many northerners had supported the Radical policy only out of irritation with President Johnson. After his retirement their enthusiasm waned. The war was fading into the past and with it the worst of the anger it had generated.

Northern voters could still be stirred by references to the sacrifices Republicans had made to save the Union and by reminders that the Democratic party was the organization of rebels, Copperheads, and the Ku Klux Klan. "If the Devil himself were at the helm of the ship of state," wrote the novelist

Lydia Maria Child in 1872, "my conscience would not allow me to aid in removing him to make room for the Democratic party." Yet emotional appeals could not convince northerners that it was still necessary to maintain a large army in the South. In 1869 the occupying forces were down to 11,000 men. After Klan disruption and intimidation had made a farce of the 1874 elections in Mississippi, Governor Ames appealed to Washington for help. President Grant's attorney general, Edwards Pierrepont, refused to act. "The whole public are tired out with these autumnal outbreaks in the South," he told Ames. "Preserve the peace by the forces of your own state."

Nationalism was reasserting itself. Had not Washington and Jefferson been Virginians? Was not Andrew Jackson Carolina-born? Since most northerners had little real love or respect for blacks, their interest in racial equality flagged once they felt reasonably certain that blacks would not be reenslaved if left to their own devices in the South.

Another, much subtler force was also at work. The prewar Republican party had stressed the common interest of workers, manufacturers, and farmers in a free and mobile society, a land of equal opportunity where all could work in harmony. Southern whites had insisted that laborers must be disciplined if large enterprises were to be run efficiently. By the 1870s, as large industrial enterprises developed in the northern states, the thinking of business leaders changed—the southern argument began to make sense to them, and they became more sympathetic to the southern demand for more control over "their" labor force.

Grant as President

Other matters occupied the attention of northern voters. The expansion of industry and the rapid development of the West, stimulated by a new wave of railroad building, loomed more important to many than the fortunes of ex-slaves. Beginning in 1873, when a stock market panic struck at public confidence, economic difficulties plagued the country for nearly a decade. Heated controversies arose over tariff policy, with western agricultural interests seeking to force reductions from the high levels established during the war, and over the handling of the wartime greenback paper money, with debtor groups and many manufacturers favoring further expansion of the supply of dollars and conservative merchants and bankers arguing for retiring the greenbacks in order to return to a "sound" currency.

More damaging to the Republicans was the failure of Ulysses S. Grant to live up to expectations as president. Qualities that had made Grant a fine military leader for a democracy—his dislike of political maneuvering and his simple belief that the popular will could best be observed in the actions of Congress—made him a poor chief executive. When Congress failed to act on his suggestion that the quality of the civil service needed improvement, he announced meekly that if Congress did nothing, he would assume the country did not want anything done. Grant was honest, but his honesty was of the naive type that made him the dupe of unscrupulous friends and schemers.

His most serious weakness as president was his failure to deal effectively with economic and social problems, but the one that injured him and the Republicans most was his inability to cope with government corruption. Grant did not cause the corruption, nor did he participate in the remotest way in the rush to "fatten at the public trough," as the reformers of the day might have put it. But he did nothing to prevent the scandals that disgraced his administration. Out of a misplaced belief in the

sanctity of friendship, he protected some of the worst culprits and allowed calculating tricksters to use his good name and the prestige of his office to advance their own interests at the country's expense.

The worst of the scandals—such as the Whiskey Ring affair, which implicated Grant's private secretary, Orville E. Babcock, and cost the government millions in tax revenue, and the defalcations of Secretary of War William W. Belknap in the management of Indian affairs—did not become public knowledge during Grant's first term. However, in 1872 Republican reformers, alarmed by rumors of corruption and disappointed by Grant's failure to press for civil service reform, organized the Liberal Republican party and nominated Horace Greeley, the able but eccentric editor of the *New York Tribune,* for president.

The Liberal Republicans were mostly well educated, socially prominent types—editors, college presidents, and economists, along with a sprinkling of businessmen and politicians. Their liberalism was of the *laissez faire* variety; they were for low tariffs and sound money, and against what they called "class legislation," meaning measures benefiting particular groups, whether labor unions or railroad companies or farm organizations. Nearly all had supported Reconstruction at the start, but by the early 1870s most were including southern blacks among the special interests that ought to be left to their own devices. Their observation of urban corruption and of unrestricted immigration led them to disparage universal suffrage, which, one of them said, "can only mean in plain English the government of ignorance and vice."

The Democrats also nominated Greeley in 1872, although he had devoted his political life to flailing the Democratic party in the *Tribune.* That surrender to expediency, together with Greeley's temperamental unsuitability for the presidency, made the campaign a fiasco for the reformers. Grant triumphed easily, with a popular majority of nearly 800,000.

Nevertheless, the defection of the Liberal Republicans hurt the Republican party in Congress. In the 1874 elections, no longer hampered as in the presidential contest by Greeley's notoriety and Grant's fame, the Democrats carried the House of Representatives. It was clear that the days of military rule in the South were ending. By the end of 1875 only three southern states—South Carolina, Flor-

In 1872, Republicans who opposed Grant's renomination bolted the party and nominated Horace Greeley. These Liberal Republicans—some of them former Radicals—sought to conciliate the South. In this cartoon, Thomas Nast, a Grant supporter, condemns the actions of Greeley and Charles Sumner as they push a black man to shake hands with a Klan member and a Copperhead.

ida, and Louisiana—were still under Republican control.

The Republican party in the South was "dead as a doornail," a reporter noted. He reflected the opinion of thousands when he added: "We ought to have a sound sensible republican . . . for the next President as a measure of safety; but only on the condition of absolute noninterference in Southern local affairs, for which there is no further need or excuse."

The Disputed Election of 1876

Against this background the presidential election of 1876 took place. Since corruption in government was the most widely discussed issue, the Republicans passed over their most attractive political personality, the dynamic James G. Blaine, Speaker of the House of Representatives, who had been connected with some chicanery involving railroad securities. Instead they nominated Governor Rutherford B. Hayes of Ohio, a former general with an unsmirched reputation. The Democrats picked Governor Samuel J. Tilden of New York, a wealthy lawyer who had attracted national attention for his part in breaking up the Tweed Ring in New York City.

In November early returns indicated that Tilden had carried New York, New Jersey, Connecticut, Indiana, and all the southern states, including Louisiana, South Carolina, and Florida, where Republican regimes were still in control. This seemed to give him 203 electoral votes to Hayes's 165, and a popular plurality in the neighborhood of 250,000 out of more than 8 million votes cast. However, Republican leaders had anticipated the possible loss of Florida, South Carolina, and Louisiana and were prepared to use their control of the election machinery in those states to throw out sufficient Democratic ballots to alter the results if doing so would change the national outcome. Realizing that the electoral votes of those states were exactly enough to elect their man, they telegraphed their henchmen on the scene, ordering them to go into action. The local Republicans then invalidated Democratic ballots in wholesale lots and filed returns showing Hayes the winner. Naturally the local Democrats protested vigorously and filed their own returns.

The Constitution provides (Article II, section 1) that presidential electors must meet in their respective states to vote and forward the results to "the Seat of the Government." There, it adds, "the President of the Senate shall, in the Presence of the Senate and House of Representatives, open all the Certificates, and the Votes shall then be counted." But who was to do the counting? The House was Democratic, the Senate Republican; neither would agree to allow the other to do the job. On January 29, 1877, scarcely a month before inauguration day, Congress created an electoral commission to decide the disputed cases. The commission consisted of five senators (three Republicans and two Democrats), five representatives (three Democrats and two Republicans), and five justices of the Supreme Court (two Democrats, two Republicans, and one "independent" judge, David Davis). Since it was a foregone conclusion that the others would vote for their party no matter what the evidence, Davis would presumably swing the balance in the interest of fairness.

But before the commission met, the Illinois legislature elected Davis senator! He had to resign from the Court and the commission. Since independents were rare even on the Supreme Court, no neutral was available to replace him. The vacancy went to Associate Justice Joseph P. Bradley of New Jersey, a Republican.

Evidence presented before the commission revealed a disgraceful picture of election shenanigans. On the one hand, in all three disputed states Dem-

ocrats had clearly cast a majority of the votes; on the other, it was unquestionable that many blacks had been forcibly prevented from voting.

In truth, both sides were shamefully corrupt. Lew Wallace, a northern politician later famous as the author of the novel *Ben Hur,* visited Louisiana and Florida shortly after the election. "It is terrible to see the extent to which all classes go in their determination to win," he wrote his wife from Florida. "Money and intimidation can obtain the oath of white men as well as black to any required statement. . . . If we win, our methods are subject to impeachment for possible fraud. If the enemy win, it is the same thing." The governor of Louisiana was reportedly willing to sell his state's electoral votes for $200,000. The Florida election board was supposed to have offered itself to Tilden for the same price. "That seems to be the standard figure," Tilden remarked ruefully.

Most modern authorities take the view that in a fair election the Republicans would have carried South Carolina and Louisiana but that Florida would have gone to Tilden, giving him the election, 188 electoral votes to 181. In the last analysis, this opinion has been arrived at simply by counting white and black noses: blacks were in the majority in South Carolina and Louisiana. Amid the tension and confusion of early 1877, however, even a Solomon would have been hard pressed to judge rightly amid the rumors, lies, and contradictory statements, and the electoral commission was not composed of Solomons. The Democrats had some hopes that Justice Bradley would be sympathetic to their case, for he was known to be opposed to harsh Reconstruction policies. On the eve of the commission's decision in the Florida controversy, he was apparently ready to vote in favor of Tilden. But the Republicans subjected him to tremendous political pressure. When he read his opinion on February 8, it was for Hayes. Thus, by a vote of 8 to 7, the commission awarded Florida's electoral votes to the Republicans.

The rest of the proceedings were routine. The commission assigned all the disputed electoral votes (including one in Oregon where the Democratic governor had seized on a technicality to replace a single Republican elector with a Democrat) to Hayes.

With the spitefulness common to rejected suitors, the Democrats assailed Bradley until, as *The New York Times* put it, he seemed like "a middle-aged St. Sebastian, stuck full of Democratic darts." Unlike Sebastian, however, Bradley was protected from the arrows by the armor of his Republican faith.

To such a level had the republic of Jefferson and John Adams descended. Democratic institutions, shaken by the South's refusal to go along with the majority in 1860 and by the suppression of civil rights during the rebellion, and further weakened by military intervention and the intimidation of blacks in the South during Reconstruction, now seemed a farce. According to Tilden's campaign manager, angry Democrats in 15 states, chiefly war veterans, were readying themselves to march on Washington to force the inauguration of Tilden. Tempers flared in Congress, where some spoke om-inously of a filibuster that would prevent the re-cording of the electoral vote and leave the country, on March 4, with no president at all.

The Compromise of 1877

Fortunately, forces for compromise had been at work behind the scenes in Washington for some time. Although northern Democrats threatened to fight to the last ditch, many southern Democrats were willing to accept Hayes if he would promise to remove the troops and allow the southern states to manage their internal affairs by themselves. Ex-Whig planters and merchants who had reluctantly abandoned the carpetbag governments and who sympathized with Republican economic policies hoped that by supporting Hayes they might con-

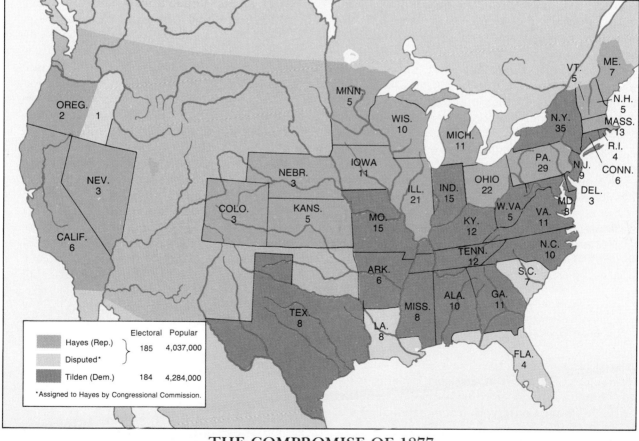

THE COMPROMISE OF 1877

tribute to the restoration of the two-party system that had been destroyed in the South during the 1850s. Ohio Congressman James A. Garfield urged Hayes to find "some discreet way" of showing these southerners that he favored "internal improvements." Hayes replied: "Your views are so nearly the same as mine that I need not say a word."

Tradition has it that a great compromise between the sections was worked out during a dramatic meeting at the Wormley Hotel* in Washington on February 26. Actually, as C. Vann Woodward has demonstrated in his important book *Reunion and Reaction*, the negotiations were long-drawn-out and informal, and the Wormley conference was but one of many. With the tacit support of many Democrats, the electoral vote was counted by the president of the Senate on March 2, and Hayes was declared elected, 185 votes to 184.

Like all compromises, this agreement was not entirely satisfactory; like most, it was not honored in every detail. Hayes recalled the last troops from South Carolina and Louisiana in April. He appointed a former Confederate general, David M. Key of Tennessee, postmaster general and delegated to him the congenial task of finding southerners willing to serve their country as officials of a Republican administration. But the alliance of ex-Whigs and northern Republicans did not flourish; the South remained solidly Democratic. The major significance of the compromise, one of the great intersectional political accommodations of American history, has been well summarized by Professor Woodward:

The Compromise of 1877 marked the abandonment of principles and force and a return to the traditional ways of expediency and concession. It wrote an end to Reconstruction and recognized a new regime in the South. More profoundly than Constitutional amendments and wordy statutes it shaped the future of four million freedmen and their progeny for generations to come.

For most of the former slaves, this future was to be bleak. Forgotten in the North, manipulated and then callously rejected by the South, rebuffed by the Supreme Court, voiceless in national affairs,

they and their descendants were condemned in the interests of sectional harmony to lives of poverty, indignity, and little hope. Meanwhile, the rest of the United States continued its golden march toward wealth and power.

Milestones

1863	Lincoln announces "Ten Percent Plan" for Reconstruction
Mar. 1865	Establishment of the Freedmen's Bureau
Apr. 1865	General Lee surrenders at Appomattox Court House
Apr. 1865	Assassination of Abraham Lincoln, Andrew Johnson becomes President
May 1865	Johnson's Amnesty plan
Dec. 1865	Thirteenth Amendment ratified
1865–1866	Enactment of Black Codes by southern states
Apr. 1866	Civil Rights Act passed over Johnson's veto
Sept. 1866	Johnson campaigns for his Reconstruction policy
Mar. 1867	First Reconstruction Act
Feb. 1868	House of Representatives impeaches Johnson
Mar. 1868	Fourth Reconstruction Act
May 1868	Senate acquits Johnson
July 1868	Fourteenth Amendment ratified
Nov. 1868	Ulysses S. Grant elected President
1868–1872	Ku Klux Klan in action
Mar. 1870	Fifteenth Amendment ratified
1870–1871	Force (Ku Klux Klan) Acts destroys Klan
1872	Liberal Republican party nominates Horace Greeley for President
Nov. 1872	Grant reelected President
1876	Disputed presidential election
Feb. 1877	Electoral Commission awards disputed votes to Rutherford B. Hayes
	Hayes agrees to Compromise of 1877

---

* Ironically, the hotel was owned by James Wormley, reputedly the wealthiest black in Washington.

SUPPLEMENTARY READING

Titles marked with an asterisk have been published in paperback.

The finest of many excellent overviews of the Reconstruction Era is Eric Foner's **Reconstruction: America's Unfinished Revolution*** (1988). The older approach to the period, stressing the excesses of black-influenced governments and criticizing the Radicals, derives from the seminal work of W. A. Dunning, **Reconstruction, Political and Economic*** (1907). W. E. B. Du Bois, **Black Reconstruction in America*** (1935) was the pioneering counterattack against the Dunning view. See also Eric Foner, **Politics and Ideology in the Age of the Civil War** (1980), and Foner's **Nothing But Freedom*** (1984).

Lincoln's ideas about Reconstruction are analyzed in W. B. Hesseltine, **Lincoln's plan of Reconstruction*** (1960), and in many of the Lincoln volumes mentioned in earlier chapters. Albert Castel, **The Presidency of Andrew Johnson** (1979), is a balanced recent account. On Johnson's battle with the congressional Radicals, see H. L. Trefousse, **The Radical Republicans: Lincoln's Vanguard for Racial Justice*** (1969), E. L. McKitrick, **Andrew Johnson and Reconstruction*** (1960), and M. L. Benedict, **The Impeachment and Trial of Andrew Johnson** (1973). A number of biographies provide information helpful in understanding the Radicals. These include David Donald, **Charles Sumner and the Rights of Man** (1970), B. P. Thomas and H. M. Hyman, **Stanton** (1962), R. N. Current, **Old Thad Stevens** (1942), and H. L. Trefousse, **Benjamin Franklin Wade** (1963). J. M. McPherson, **The Struggle for Equality: Abolitionists and the Negro in the Civil War and Reconstruction*** (1964), is also valuable. On the Fourteenth Amendment, see Joseph James, **The Framing of the Fourteenth Amendment*** (1956); on the Fifteenth Amendment, see William Gillette, **The Right to Vote: Politics and the Passage of the Fifteenth Amendment*** (1965).

Conditions in the South during Reconstruction are discussed in R. H. Abbott, **The Republican Party and the South** (1986), Michael Perman, **Reunion Without Compromise** (1973), H. N. Rabinowitz, **Race Relations in the Urban South** (1978), J. L. Roark, **Masters Without Slaves** (1977), and Leon Litwack, **Been in the Storm Too Long** (1979).

For state studies, see W. L. Rose, **Rehearsal for Reconstruction: The Port Royal Experiment*** (1964), Thomas Holt, **Black over White: Negro Political Leadership in South Carolina** (1977), W. C. Harris, **The Day of the Carpetbagger: Republican Reconstruction in Mississippi** (1979) and Joel Williamson, **After Slavery: The Negro in South Carolina During Reconstruction*** (1965). See also Joel Williamson, **The Crucible of Race: Black-White Relations in the American South Since Emancipation** (1984), a psychoanalytical interpretation of racism. G. R. Bentley, **A History of the Freedmen's Bureau** (1955), discusses the work of that important organization, but see also W. S. McFeely, **Yankee Stepfather: General O. O. Howard and the Freedmen*** (1968). On the Ku Klux Klan, see G. C. Rable, **But There Was No Peace*** (1984), and A. W. Trelease, **White Terror: The Ku Klux Klan Conspiracy and Southern Reconstruction** (1971).

On the economic and social effects of Reconstruction, see G. D. Jaynes, **Branches Without Roots: Genesis of the Black Working Class** (1986), R. L. Ransom and Richard Sutch, **One Kind of Freedom: The Economic Consequences of Emancipation*** (1977), Robert Higgs, **Competition and Coercion: Blacks in the American Economy, 1865–1914** (1977), and C. F. Oubre, **Forty Acres and a Mule** (1978). F. A. Shannon, **The Farmer's Last Frontier*** (1945), is also a useful text on southern agriculture. For the growth of industry, see J. F. Stover, **The Railroads of the South** (1955).

On Grant's presidency, see W. S. McFeely, **Grant** (1981); Allan Nevins, **Hamilton Fish: The Inner History of the Grant Administration** (1936), and Matthew Josephson, **The Politicos*** (1938), contain much additional information. On the Republican reform movement, see J. G. Sproat, **"The Best Men": Liberal Reformers in the Gilded Age*** (1968), and M. B. Duberman, **Charles Francis Adams*** (1961). For the disputed election of 1876 and the compromise following it, consult C. V. Woodward, **Reunion and Reaction*** (1951), and K. I. Polakoff, **The Politics of Inertia: The Election of 1876 and the End of Reconstruction** (1973). William Gillette, **Retreat from Reconstruction** (1980), is also an important study.

Blacks in Slavery and Freedom

It is much easier to generalize about what life was like for American blacks under slavery than for free people of that time. Indeed, the fact that the restrictions imposed upon slaves reduced drastically their possibilities for individual development and self-expression was the basic injustice of the slave system. Nevertheless, as these illustrations show, the institution affected its victims in many different ways. Seen from this perspective, the ending of slavery expanded the ability of individual blacks to "be themselves." Even after more than a century, however, the possibilities open to the average black are still more limited than those available to the average white. Finally ending this discrimination is one of the major tasks our society faces today.

The three views of slave life on this page throw different lights on "the peculiar institution." Edwin White, an academic painter, titled his carefully humble yet dignified portrayal of a quite moment Thoughts of Liberia. Actually, few blacks ever returned to Africa in spite of colonization efforts by well-meaning groups.

In 1862, T. H. O'Sullivan made this extraordinary photograph of five generations of a slave family. All were born on the plantation of J. J. Smith in Beaufort, South Carolina.

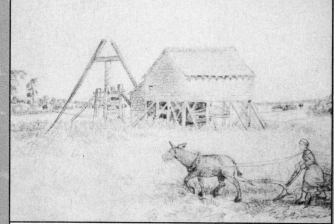

A Northern visitor, George Fuller, traveled through Alabama in 1858 to observe the conditions under which slaves lived. He sketched this woman, her skirts hitched up and the reins of a plantation mule looped around her neck, plowing a field. In the background are a cotton gin (the building on stilts) and a cotton press, which was used to compress the ginned cotton into bales for shipping.

Before 1860, many of the free blacks of the northern states lived in cities and towns. For most, the church was the center of community life. This 1853 scene from Frank Leslie's Illustrated Newspaper *shows a prayer meeting in the African Church of Cincinnati, Ohio.*

Thomas "Daddy" Rice was a popular vaudeville star in the pre–Civil War years. He introduced the character "Jim Crow" in a song-and-dance blackface act ("Wheel a-bout and turn a-bout/And jump . . . Jim Crow") based on the antics of a black stable boy he claimed to have seen. His "Jump Jim Crow" act helped launch the popular minstrel shows of the 19th century. Unfortunately, they also promoted the stereotype of the shiftless black man. The term Jim Crow *later came to be applied to the system of Southern segregation laws and customs in the late 19th century.*

Slaves, of course, could be bought and sold at their owners' discretion, like any piece of property. Edwin Taylor's 1852 painting **American Slave Market** *catches a sense of the mundane way that most owners viewed the trade in human beings. With the slave went a bill of sale. Below is a receipt covering the sale of "a Negro man by the name of Ned about 38 or 40 years of age which negro I warrant to be a slave for life" for $800. The note in the upper right corner, added by the buyer's great-grandson, comments that Ned was reputed to be a good cabinet maker.*

My Great Grand Father Jas. Benson Zachry
Old Henry County Present Newton County
This slave was reputed to be a good cabinet
maker.

Columbus 25th May 1842

Received of James B Zachry by the hands of John Morton Eight Hundred dollars in full consideration for a Negro Man by the name of Ned about 38 or 40 years of age which negro I warrant to be a slave for life to be sound & well both in body & mind & I also warrant him against the Claim of Myself my heirs or against the Claim of any other person or persons whomsoever Given under my hand and seal this day and year above written

Henry Morton
Jois Boswell

Stephen Wall

Reconstruction meant a new set of accommodations to freedom within an older social order. Winslow Homer's tense painting, A Visit from the Old Mistress, *conveys a feeling of the complex relationships that developed between newly freed blacks and their former owners.*

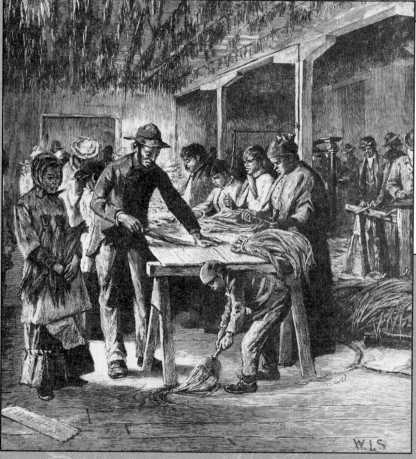

For most former slaves, day-to-day activity in the rural South remained a round of planting, cultivating, and harvesting. For example, the way that hogs were slaughtered and the meat cured or made into sausage did not change. Some blacks, however, did not stay on the land, but instead worked in individual settings, such as this tobacco-processing plant in Danville, Virginia, where men, women, and children were employed stripping tobacco.

In the Wake of War

It may be metaphorically said that natural selection is daily and hourly scrutinizing, throughout the world, the slightest variations; rejecting those that are bad, preserving and adding up all that are good; silently and insensibly working, whenever and wherever opportunity offers.

CHARLES DARWIN, The Origin of Species, *1859*

The way for people to gain their reasonable rights is not by voluntarily throwing them away.

W. E. B. DU BOIS, Of Mr. Booker T. Washington and Others, *1903*

W hen Americans turned from fighting and making weapons to more constructive occupations, they transformed their agriculture, trade, manufacturing, mining, and means of communication. Immigration increased rapidly. Cities grew in size and number, exerting on every aspect of life an influence at least as pervasive as that exercised on earlier generations by the frontier. More and more Americans were flocking to the towns and cities, supporting themselves by laboring at machines or by scratching accounts in ledgers. At the same time farm production rose to new heights, invigorated by new marketing methods and the increased use of machinery. Railroad construction stimulated and unified the economy, helping to make possible still larger and more efficient enterprises. The flow of gold and silver from western mines excited people's imaginations and their avarice, while petroleum, the "black gold" discovered in Pennsylvania shortly before the war, gave rise to a new industry soon to become one of the most important in the nation. These developments amounted to more than a mere change of scale; they altered the structure of the economy and the society.

The American Commonwealth

Most students of the subject have concluded that the political history of the United States in the last quarter of the 19th century was singularly divorced from the meaningful issues of that day. On the rare occasions that important, supposedly controversial measures were debated, they excited far less argument than they merited. A graduated income tax, the greatest instrument for orderly economic and social change that a democratic society has devised, was enacted during the Civil War, repealed after that conflict, reenacted in 1894 as part of the maneuvering over tariff reform, and then declared unconstitutional in 1895 without causing much more than a ripple in the world of partisan politics. This was typical; as the English observer James Bryce noted in the late 1880s, the politicians were "clinging too long to outworn issues" and "neglecting to discover and work out new principles capable of solving the problems which now perplex the country." Congress, another critic wrote, "does not solve the problems, the solution of which is demanded by the life of the nation."

"Root, Hog, or Die"

After Appomattox, the immense resources of the United States, combined with the high value most Americans assigned to work and achievement, made the people strongly materialistic.

After the failures of Reconstruction, Americans seemed even more enamored with material values. They were tired of sacrifice, eager to act for themselves. They professed to believe strongly in a government policy of noninterference, or laissez faire. "'Things regulate themselves' . . . means, of course, that God regulates them by his general laws," Professor Francis Bowen of Harvard wrote in his *American Political Economy* (1870).

Impressed by such logic, people now tolerated the grossest kind of waste and seemed to care little about corruption in high places, so long as no one interfered with their personal pursuit of profit. Mark Twain, raised in an earlier era, called this the

Gilded Age, dazzling on the surface, base metal below.

Certain intellectual currents encouraged the exploitative drives of the people. Charles Darwin's *Origin of Species* was published in 1859, and by the 1870s his theory of evolution was beginning to influence opinion in the United States. That nature had ordained a kind of inevitable progress, governed by the natural selection of the individual organisms best adapted to survive in a particular environment, seemed eminently reasonable to most Americans, for it fitted well with their own experiences. "Let the buyer beware; that covers the whole business," the sugar magnate Henry O. Havemeyer explained to an investigating committee. "You cannot wet-nurse people from the time they are born until the time they die. They have to wade and get stuck, and that is the way men are educated."

Yale professor William Graham Sumner sometimes used the survival-of-the-fittest analogy in teaching undergraduates. "Professor," one student asked Sumner, "don't you believe in any government aid to industries?" "No!" Sumner replied, "It's root, hog, or die." The student persisted: "Suppose some professor of political science came along and took your job away from you. Wouldn't you be sore?" "Any other professor is welcome to try," Sumner answered promptly. "If he gets my job, it is my fault. My business is to teach the subject so well that no one can take the job away from me." Sumner's argument described what came to be known as social Darwinism, the belief that human business and social relationships were governed by the Darwinian principle that the "fittest" will always "survive" if allowed to exercise their capacities without restriction.

Few businessmen were directly influenced by Darwin's ideas. Most eagerly accepted any aid they could get from the government; many were active in philanthropy; some felt a deep sense of social responsibility. Nevertheless, most were sincere individualists. They believed in competition, being convinced that the nation would prosper most if all people were free to seek their personal fortunes by their own methods.

The Shape of Politics

A succession of weak presidents presided over the White House. Although the impeachment proceedings against Andrew Johnson had failed, Congress dominated the government. Within Congress, the Senate generally overshadowed the House of Representatives. In his novel *Democracy* (1880), the cynical Henry Adams wrote that the United States had a "government of the people, by the people, for the benefit of Senators." Critics called the Senate a "rich man's club," and it did contain many millionaires. However, the true sources of the Senate's influence lay in the long tenure of many of its members (which enabled them to master the craft of politics), in the fact that it was small enough to encourage real debate and in its long-established reputation for wisdom, intelligence, and statesmanship.

The House of Representatives, by contrast, was one of the most disorderly and inefficient legislative bodies in the world. As I make my notes, one reporter wrote in 1882 while sitting in the House gallery,

> I see a dozen men reading newspapers with their feet on their desks. . . . The vile odor of . . . tobacco . . . rises from the two-for-five-cents cigars in the mouths of the so-called gentlemen below. . . . They chew, too! Every desk has a spittoon of pink and gold china beside it to catch the filth from the statesman's mouth.

An infernal din rose from the crowded chamber. Desks slammed; members held private conversations, hailed pages, shuffled from place to place, clamored for the attention of the Speaker—all while some poor orator tried to discuss the question of the moment. Speaking in the House, one writer said, was like trying to address the crowd on a passing Broadway bus from the curb in front of the Astor House in New York.

The great political parties professed undying enmity to each other, but they seldom took clearly opposing positions on the questions of the day. Democrats were separated from Republicans more by accidents of geography, religious affiliation, ethnic background, and emotion than by economic issues.

The fundamental division between Democrats and Republicans was sectional, a result of the Civil War. The South, after the political rights of blacks had been drastically circumscribed, became heavily Democratic. Most of New England was solidly Republican. Elsewhere the two parties stood in fair balance, although the Republicans tended to have the advantage.

The personalities of political leaders often dic-

Joseph Keppler's 1890 Puck cartoon "None but Millionaires Need Apply—The Coming Style of Presidential Election," comments acidly on the low status of the presidency. The tag Eight Pieces With This Set on the chief executive's chair refers to the Cabinet. As the examples in this chapter show, the late 19th century was a heyday for political cartoonists.

tated the voting patterns of individuals and groups. In the 1884 presidential election, the banker J. P. Morgan voted Democratic because he admired Grover Cleveland, while Irish-Americans, traditionally Democrats, cast thousands of ballots for Republican James G. Blaine. In the 1892 contest in which Cleveland defeated Benjamin Harrison, a prominent steel manufacturer wrote to his even more prominent competitor, Andrew Carnegie: "I am very sorry for President Harrison, but I cannot see that our interests are going to be affected one way or the other." And Carnegie replied: "We have nothing to fear. . . . Cleveland is [a] pretty good fellow. Off for Venice tomorrow."

The balance of political power after 1876 was almost perfect—"the most spectacular degree of equilibrium in American history." Between 1856 and 1912 the Democrats elected a president only twice (1884 and 1892), but most contests were extremely close. Majorities in both the Senate and the House fluctuated continually. Between 1876 and 1896 the "dominant" Republican party controlled both houses of Congress and the presidency at the same time for only one two-year period.

Issues of the Gilded Age

Four questions obsessed politicians in these years. One was the "bloody shirt." The term, which became part of the language after a Massachusetts con-

gressman dramatically displayed to his colleagues in the House the bloodstained shirt of an Ohio carpetbagger who had been flogged by terrorists in Mississippi, referred to the tactic of reminding the electorate of the northern states that the men who had taken the South out of the Union and precipitated the Civil War had been Democrats and that they and their descendants were still Democrats. "Every man that endeavored to tear down the old flag," a Republican orator proclaimed in 1876, "was a Democrat. Every man that tried to destroy this nation was a Democrat. . . . The man that assassinated Abraham Lincoln was a Democrat. . . . Soldiers, every scar you have on your heroic bodies was given you by a Democrat."

Every scoundrel or incompetent who sought office under the Republican banner waved the bloody shirt in order to divert the attention of northern voters from his own shortcomings.

Waving the bloody shirt was related intimately to the issue of the rights of blacks. Throughout this period Republicans vacillated between trying to build up their organization in the South by appealing to black voters—which required them to make sure that blacks in the South could vote—and trying to win conservative white support by stressing economic issues such as the tariff. When the former strategy seemed wise, they waved the bloody shirt with vigor; in the latter case, they piously announced that the blacks' future was "as safe in the hands of one party as it is in the other."

The question of veterans' pensions also bore a close relationship to the bloody shirt. Following the Civil War, Union soldiers founded the Grand Army of the Republic. By 1890 the organization had a membership of more than 400,000. The GAR put immense pressure on Congress, first for aid to veterans with service-connected disabilities, then for those with any disability, and eventually for all former Union soldiers.

The tariff was another perennial issue in post–Civil War politics. Manufacturers desired protective tariffs to keep out competing products, and a majority of their workers were convinced that wage levels would fall if goods produced by cheap foreign labor entered the United States untaxed. Many farmers supported protection, though almost no competing agricultural products were being imported. Congressman William McKinley of Ohio, who reputedly could make reciting a tariff schedule sound like poetry, stated the majority opinion in the clearest terms: High tariffs foster the growth of

Uncle Sam walks the floor with a fretful "Infant Industries," saying "I guess he won't stop howling till I give him enough Protection Soothing Syrup to burst him!" An 1896 Puck *cartoon by Louis Dalrymple.*

industry and thus create jobs. "Reduce the tariff and labor is the first to suffer," he said.

The Democrats professed to believe in moderation, yet whenever party leaders tried to revise the tariff downward, Democratic congressmen from industrial states like Pennsylvania and New York sided with the Republicans. Every new tariff bill became an occasion for logrolling, lobbying, and outrageous politicking rather than for sane discussion and careful evaluation of the public interest.

A third political question in this period was currency reform. During the Civil War, it will be recalled, the government, faced with obligations it could not meet by taxing or borrowing, suspended specie payments and issued about $450 million in paper money. The greenbacks did not command the full confidence of a people accustomed to money readily convertible into gold or silver. Greenbacks seemed to threaten inflation, for how could one trust the government not to issue them in wholesale lots to avoid passing unpopular tax laws? Thus when the war ended, strong sentiment developed for withdrawing the greenbacks from circulation and returning to a bullion standard.

Beginning during Reconstruction, prices declined sharply. The deflation increased the real income of bondholders and other creditors but injured debtors. Farmers were particularly hard hit, for many of them had borrowed heavily during the wartime boom to finance expansion.

Here was a question of real significance. However, the major parties refused to confront each other over the currency question. While Republicans professed to be the party of sound money, most western Republicans favored expansion of the currency. And while one wing of the Democrats flirted with the Greenbackers, the conservative, or "Bourbon," Democrats favored deflation as much as Republicans did.

In 1874 a bill to increase the supply of greenbacks was defeated in a Republican-dominated Congress only by the veto of President Grant. The next year Congress voted to resume specie payments, but in order to avoid a party split on the question, the Republicans agreed to allow $300 million in greenbacks to remain in circulation and to postpone actual resumption of specie payments until 1879.

Under various administrations, steps were taken to increase or decrease the amount of money in circulation, but the net effect on the economy was not significant. Few politicians before 1890 considered monetary policy as a device for influencing economic development.

The final major political issue of these years was civil service reform. That the federal bureaucracy needed overhauling nearly everyone agreed. As American society grew larger and more complex, the government necessarily took on more functions. The need for professional administration increased. The number of federal employees rose from 53,000 in 1871 to 256,000 at the end of the century. Corruption flourished; waste and inefficiency were the normal state of affairs. "The federal system . . . was generally undistinguished," the historian Leonard D. White concluded after an exhaustive study of the period. "Nobody, whether in Congress or in the executive departments, seemed able to rise much above the handicraft office methods that were cumbersome even in the simpler days of the Jacksonians."

Every honest observer could see the need for reform, but the politicians argued that patronage was the lifeblood of politics, that parties could not function without armies of loyal political workers, and that the workers expected and deserved the rewards of office when their efforts were crowned with victory at the polls. Typical was the attitude of the New York assemblyman who, according to Theodore Roosevelt, had "the same idea about Public Life and the Civil Service that a vulture has of a dead sheep."

Blacks After Reconstruction

Minorities were treated with callousness and contempt in the postwar decades. That the South would deal harshly with the former slaves once federal control was relaxed probably should have been expected. Men like Governor Wade Hampton of South Carolina had promised to respect black civil rights. "We . . . will secure to every citizen, the lowest as well as the highest, black as well as white, full and equal protection in the enjoyment of all his rights under the Constitution," Hampton said in 1877. This pledge was not kept.

President Hayes had urged blacks to trust southern whites. A new Era of Good Feelings had dawned, he announced after making a goodwill tour of the South shortly after his inauguration. By December 1877 he had been sadly disillusioned. "By state legislation, by frauds, by intimidation, and by violence of the most atrocious character, colored citizens have been deprived of the right of suffrage," he wrote in his diary. However, he did nothing to remedy the situation. Frederick Douglass called Hayes's policy "sickly conciliation."

Hayes's successors in the 1880s did no better. "Time is the only cure," President Garfield said, thereby confessing that he had no policy at all. President Arthur gave federal patronage to antiblack groups in an effort to split the Democratic South. In President Cleveland's day, blacks had scarcely a friend in high places, North or South. In 1887 Cleveland explained to a correspondent why he opposed "mixed schools." Expert opinion, the president said, believed "that separate schools were of much more benefit for the colored people." Hayes, Garfield, and Arthur were Republicans, Cleveland a Democrat; party made little difference. Both parties subscribed to hypocritical statements about equality and constitutional rights, and neither did anything to implement them.

For a time blacks were not totally disfranchised in the South. Rival white factions tried to manipulate them, and corruption flourished as widely as in the machine-dominated wards of the northern cities. In the 1890s, however, the southern states, led by Mississippi, began to deprive blacks of the vote despite the Fifteenth Amendment. Poll taxes raised a formidable economic barrier, one that also disfranchised many poor whites. Literacy tests completed the work; a number of states provided a loophole for illiterate whites by including an "understanding" clause whereby an illiterate person could qualify by demonstrating an ability to explain the meaning of a section of the state constitution when an election official read it to him. Blacks who attempted to take the test were uniformly declared to have failed it.

In Louisiana, 130,000 blacks voted in the election of 1896. Then the law was changed. In 1900 only 5,000 votes were cast by blacks. With unctuous hypocrisy, white southerners insisted that they loved "their" blacks dearly and wished only to protect them from "the machinations of those who would use them only to further their own base ends." "We take away the Negroes' votes," a Louisiana politician explained, "to protect them just as we would protect a little child and prevent it from injuring itself with sharp-edged tools."

Practically every Supreme Court decision after 1877 that affected blacks somehow "nullified or curtailed" their rights, Professor Rayford W. Logan writes. In *Hall* v. *De Cuir* (1878) the Court even threw out a state law forbidding segregation on riverboats, arguing that it was an unjustifiable interference with interstate commerce. The *Civil Rights Cases* (1883) declared the Civil Rights Act of 1875 unconstitutional. Blacks who were refused equal accommodations or privileges by hotels, theaters, and other privately owned facilities had no recourse in law, the Court announced. The Fourteenth Amendment guaranteed their civil rights against invasion by the states, not by individuals.

Finally, in *Plessy* v. *Ferguson* (1896), the Court ruled that even in places of public accommodation, such as railroads and, by implication, schools, segregation was legal so long as facilities of equal quality were provided. "If one race be inferior to the other socially, the Constitution of the United States cannot put them upon the same plane." In a noble dissent in the Plessy case, Justice John Marshall Harlan protested this line of argument. "Our Constitution is color-blind," he said. "The arbitrary separation of citizens, on the basis of race . . . is a badge of servitude wholly inconsistent with civil freedom and the equality before the law established by the Constitution." Alas, more than half a century was to pass before the Court came around to Harlan's reasoning and reversed the Plessy decision. Meanwhile, total segregation was imposed throughout the South. Separate schools, prisons, hospitals, recreational facilities, and even cemeteries were provided for blacks, and these were almost never equal to those available to whites.

Most northerners supported the government and the Court. Social Darwinist ideas seemed to demonstrate that since there were physiological differences between whites and blacks and since the whites were in control of the country, they were the "fittest" by nature. Newspapers presented a stereotyped, derogatory picture of blacks, no matter what the circumstances. Northern magazines repeatedly made blacks the butt of crude jokes. "The Negro's day is over," the tough-minded William Graham Sumner explained. "He is out of fashion."

The restoration of white rule abruptly halted the progress in public education for blacks that the Reconstruction governments had made. Church groups and private foundations such as the Peabody Fund and the Slater Fund, financed chiefly by northern philanthropists, supported black schools after

Frances Benjamin Johnston, the first black woman photographer of note, documented Tuskegee Institute's activities in the early years of the century. Here students help with building construction about 1900.

1877, among them two important experiments in vocational training, Hampton Institute and Tuskegee Institute.

These schools had to overcome considerable resistance and suspicion in the white community; they survived only because they taught a docile, essentially subservient philosophy, preparing students to accept second-class citizenship and become farmers and craftsmen. Since proficiency in academic subjects might have given the lie to the southern belief that blacks were intellectually inferior to whites, such subjects were avoided.

The southern insistence on segregating the public schools, buttressed by the "separate but equal" decision of the Supreme Court in *Plessy* v. *Ferguson,* imposed a crushing financial burden on poor, sparsely settled communities, and the dominant opinion that blacks were not really educable did not encourage these communities to make special efforts in their behalf.

Booker T. Washington and the Atlanta Compromise

Since nearly all contemporary biologists, physicians, and other supposed experts on race were convinced that blacks were inferior beings, educated northerners generally accepted black inferiority as fact. James Bryce, whose study of the United States at this time, *The American Commonwealth* (1888), has become a classic, saw many Americans of this type and absorbed their social Darwinist point of view. Negroes, Bryce wrote, were inherently docile, pliable, submissive, lustful, childish, impressionable, emotional, heedless, and "unthrifty." They had "no capacity for abstract thinking, for scientific inquiry, or for any kind of invention." Being "unspeakably inferior," they were "unfit to cope with a superior race."

Like Bryce, most Americans did not especially wish blacks ill; they simply refused to consider them quite human and consigned them complacently to oblivion, along with the Indians, who were also dismissed as racially inferior by Darwinians. A vicious circle was established. By denying blacks decent educational opportunities and good jobs, the dominant race could use the blacks' resultant ignorance and poverty to justify the inferior facilities offered them.

Southern blacks reacted to this deplorable situation in a variety of ways. Some sought redress in racial pride and what would later be called black nationalism. Some became so disaffected that they tried to revive the African colonization movement. "Africa is our home," insisted Bishop Henry M. Turner, a huge, plainspoken man who had served as an army chaplain during the war and as a member of the Georgia legislature during Reconstruction. "Every man that has the sense of an animal must see there is no future in this country for the Negro." Another militant, T. Thomas Fortune, editor of the New York *Age* and founder of the Afro-American League (1887), called on blacks to demand full civil rights, better schools, and fair wages and to fight against discrimination of every sort. "Let us stand up like men in our own organization," he urged. "If others use . . . violence to combat our peaceful arguments, it is not for us to run away from violence."

Militancy and black separatism won few adherents among southern blacks. For one thing, life was better than it had been under slavery. According to the most conservative estimates, the living standard of the average southern black more than doubled between 1865 and 1900. But the forces of repression were extremely powerful. The late 19th century saw more lynchings in the South than any other period of American history. This helps explain the tactics of Booker T. Washington, one of the most extraordinary Americans of that generation.

Washington had been born a slave in Virginia in 1856. Laboriously he obtained an education, supporting himself while a student by working as a janitor. In 1881, with the financial help of northern philanthropists, he founded Tuskegee Institute in Alabama. His experiences convinced Washington that blacks must lift themselves by their own bootstraps but that they must also accommodate themselves to white prejudices. A persuasive speaker and a brilliant fund-raiser, he soon developed a national reputation as a "reasonable" champion of his race. (In 1891 Harvard awarded him an honorary degree.)

In 1895 Washington made a now-famous speech to a mixed audience in Atlanta. To the blacks he said: "Cast down your bucket where you are," by which he meant stop fighting segregation and second-class citizenship and concentrate on learning useful skills. "Dignify and glorify common labor," he urged. "Agitation of questions of racial equality is the extremest folly." Progress up the social and economic ladder would come not from "artificial forcing" but from self-improvement. "There is as much dignity in tilling a field as in writing a poem."

Washington asked the whites of what he called "our beloved South" to lend the blacks a hand in their efforts to advance themselves. If you will do so, he promised, you will be "surrounded by the most patient, faithful, law-abiding, and unresentful people that the world has seen."

This so-called Atlanta Compromise delighted white southerners and won Washington financial support in every section of the country. He became one of the most powerful men in the United States, consulted by presidents, in close touch with business and philanthropic leaders, and capable of influencing in countless unobtrusive ways the fate of millions of blacks.

Blacks responded to the compromise with mixed feelings. Accepting Washington's approach might relieve them of many burdens and dangers and bring them considerable material assistance. Obsequiousness might, like discretion, be the better part of valor. But the cost was high in surrendered personal dignity and lost hopes of obtaining real justice.

Washington's career illustrates the terrible dilemma that American blacks have always faced: the choice between confrontation and accommodation. This choice was particularly difficult in the late 19th century.

Washington chose accommodation. It is easy to condemn him as a toady but difficult to see how, at that time, a more aggressive policy could have succeeded. One can even interpret the Atlanta Compromise as a subtle form of black nationalism; in a way, Washington was not urging blacks to accept inferiority and racial slurs but to ignore them. His own behavior lends force to this view, for his method of operating was indeed subtle, even devious. In public he minimized the importance of civil and political rights and accepted separate but equal facilities—if they were truly equal. Behind the scenes he lobbied against restrictive measures, marshaled large sums of money to fight test cases in the courts, and worked hard in northern states to organize the black vote and make sure that black political leaders got a share of the spoils of office. As one black militant put it, Washington knew the virtue of "sa-

gacious silence." He may not, in retrospect, seem an admirable man, but he was a useful one. His defects point up more the unlovely aspects of the age than those of his own character.

The West After the Civil War

The West displayed these aspects of the age, and a number of others, in heightened form. Many parts of the region had as large a percentage of foreign-born residents as the populous eastern states—nearly a third of all Californians were foreign-born, as were more than 40 percent of Nevadans and over half the residents of Idaho and Arizona. There were, of course, large populations of Spanish-speaking Americans of Mexican origin all over the Southwest. Chinese and Irish laborers were pouring into California by the thousands, and there were substantial numbers of Germans in Texas. Germans, Scandinavians, and other Europeans were also important on the high plains east of the Rockies.

Although the image of the West as a land of great open spaces is accurate enough, the region contained several bustling cities. San Francisco, with a population approaching 250,000 in the late 1870s, had long outgrown its role as a rickety boomtown where the forty-niners bought supplies and squandered whatever wealth they had sifted from the streams of the Sierra. It was still an important warehouse and supply center, but it was also the commercial and financial heart of the Pacific Coast and a center of light manufacturing, food processing, and machine shops. Denver, San Antonio, and Salt Lake City were far smaller but growing rapidly and equally "urban."

There was, in short, no one West, no typical westerner. If the economy was predominantly agricultural and extractive, it was also commercial and entering the early stages of industrial development. The seeds of such large enterprises as Wells Fargo, Levi Strauss, and half a dozen important department store empires were sown in the immediate postwar decades.

Above all, however, the West epitomized the social Darwinist, "every man for himself" psychology of post-Reconstruction American society. In 1879 several thousand southern blacks suddenly migrated to western Kansas. When asked why, one of their leaders replied: "The white people [in the

South] treat our people so bad . . . that it is impossible for them to stand it." But their treatment in Kansas was not much better, certainly not better than the way blacks were treated in the northern states. California had been a free state from the moment of its entry into the Union as part of the Compromise of 1850, but it treated its black citizens poorly, even refusing to ratify the Fifteenth Amendment.

Beginning in the mid-1850s, a steady flow of Chinese migrated to the United States, most of them to the West Coast region. About four or five thousand a year came until the negotiation of the Burlingame Treaty of 1868, the purpose of which was to provide cheap labor for railroad construction crews. Thereafter the annual influx more than doubled, though before 1882 it exceeded 20,000 only twice. When the railroads were completed the Chinese, who were hardworking and willing to work for low wages, began to compete with native workers. A great cry of resentment went up on the West Coast. Riots broke out in San Francisco in 1877. Bigots called Chinese workers "groveling worms" and described them as "more slavish and brutish than the beasts that roam the fields." When the

Construction crew laying tracks along the west slope of the Cascades in 1885. By then, such physically demanding and socially isolated work had largely devolved upon the most recently arrived immigrants, as seems the case here.

migration suddenly increased in 1882 to nearly 40,000, the protests reached such a peak that Congress passed a law prohibiting all Chinese immigration for ten years. Later legislation extended the ban indefinitely.

Chinese immigrants created genuine social problems. Most did not intend to remain in the United States and therefore made little effort to accommodate themselves to American ways. Their supposed attachment to gambling, opium, and prostitutes—over 90 percent of the Chinese in America in the 1880s were men—alarmed respectable citizens. But the westerners' attitude toward the Chinese differed only in degree from their attitude toward the Mexicans who flocked into the Southwest to work as farm laborers and to help build railroads.

The Plains Indians

"Whites," the historian Rodman Paul wrote, "did not shed their old attitudes when they crossed into a new country." His generalization applies with special force to the way the westerners dealt with Indians. For 250 years the Indians had been driven back steadily, yet on the eve of the Civil War they still inhabited roughly half the United States. By the time of Hayes's inauguration, however, the Indians had been shattered as independent peoples, and in another decade the survivors were penned up on reservations, the government committed to a policy of extinguishing their way of life.

In 1860 the survivors of most of the eastern tribes were living peacefully in what is now Oklahoma. In California the forty-niners had made short work of the local tribes. Elsewhere in the West—in the deserts of the Great Basin between the Sierra and the Rockies, in the mountains themselves, and on the semiarid, grass-covered plains between the Rockies and the edge of white civilization in eastern Kansas and Nebraska—nearly a quarter of a million Indians dominated the land.

By far the most important lived on the High Plains. From the Blackfeet of southwestern Canada and the Sioux of Minnesota and the Dakotas to the Cheyenne of Colorado and Wyoming and the Comanche of northern Texas, the plains tribes possessed a generally uniform culture. All lived by hunting the hulking American bison, or buffalo, which ranged over the plains by the millions. The buffalo provided the Indians with food, clothing, even shelter, for the famous Indian tepee was covered with hides. On the treeless plains, dried buffalo dung was used for fuel. The buffalo was also an important symbol in Indian religion.

Although they seemed the epitome of freedom, pride, and self-reliance, the plains Indians had begun to fall under the sway of white power. They eagerly adopted the products of the more technically advanced culture—cloth, metal tools, weapons, cheap decorations. However, the most important thing the whites gave them had nothing to do with technology: It was the horse.

The geological record shows that the genus *Equus* was native to America, but it had become extinct in the Western Hemisphere long before Cortés brought the first modern horses to America in the 16th century. Multiplying rapidly thereafter, the animals soon roamed wild from Texas to the Argentine. By the 18th century the Indians of the plains had made them a vital part of their culture.

Horses thrived on the plains, and so did their masters. Mounted Indians could run down buffalo instead of stalking them on foot. They could move more easily over the country and fight more effectively too. They could acquire and transport more possessions and increase the size of their tepees, for horses could drag heavy loads heaped on A-shaped frames (called *travois* by the French), whereas earlier Indians had only dogs to depend on as pack animals. The frames of the travois, when disassembled, served as poles for tepees. The Indians also adopted modern weapons: the cavalry sword, which they particularly admired, and the rifle. Both added to their effectiveness as hunters and fighters. However, like the whites' liquor and diseases, horses and guns caused problems. The buffalo herds began to diminish, and warfare became bloodier and more frequent.

In a familiar and tragic pattern, the majority of the western tribes greeted the first whites to enter their domains in a friendly fashion. Lewis and Clark and their handful of companions crossed and recrossed the entire region without a single clash with the Indians they encountered. As late as the 1830s, white hunters and trappers ranged freely over most of the West, trading with the Indians and often marrying Indian women. Settlers pushing cross-country toward Oregon in the 1840s met with relatively little trouble.

An Oglala Sioux named Kills Two painted this portrayal of "An Indian Horse Dance." Horses were vital to survival for the Sioux, as their inclusion in such ceremonies demonstrates.

After the start of the gold rush, the need to link the East with California meant that the tribes were pushed aside. Deliberately, the government in Washington prepared the way. In 1851 Thomas Fitzpatrick, an experienced mountain man, scout for the first large group of settlers to Oregon in 1841 and for American soldiers in California during the Mexican War, summoned a great "council" of the tribes. About 10,000 Indians gathered that September at Horse Creek, 37 miles east of Fort Laramie, in what is now Wyoming.

The Indians respected Fitzpatrick, who had recently married a woman who was half Indian. At Horse Creek he persuaded each tribe to accept definite limits to its hunting grounds. In return the Indians were promised gifts and annual payments. This policy, known as "concentration," was designed to cut down on intertribal warfare and—far more important—to enable the government to negotiate separately with each tribe. It was the classic strategy of divide and conquer.

Although it made a mockery of diplomacy to treat with Indian tribes as though they were European powers, the United States maintained that each tribe was a sovereign nation, to be dealt with as an equal in solemn treaties. Both sides knew that this was not the case. Tribal chiefs had only limited power; young braves frequently refused to respect agreements made by their elders.

Indian Wars

The government showed little interest in honoring agreements with Indians. No sooner had the Kansas-Nebraska bill become law than the Kansas, Omaha, Pawnee, and Yankton Sioux tribes began to feel pressure for further concessions of territory. Other trouble developed in the Sioux country. Thus it happened that in 1862, after federal troops had been pulled out of the West for service against the Confederacy, most of the plains Indians rose up against the whites. For five years intermittent but bloody clashes kept the entire area in a state of alarm.

This was guerrilla warfare, with all its horror and treachery. In 1864 a party of Colorado militia fell upon an unsuspecting Cheyenne community at Sand Creek and killed an estimated 450. "Kill and scalp all, big and little," Colonel J. M. Chivington, a minister in private life, told his men. "Nits make lice." A white observer described the scene: "They were scalped, their brains knocked out; the men used their knives, ripped open women, clubbed little children, knocked them in the head with their guns, beat their brains out, mutilated their bodies in every sense of the word." General Nelson A. Miles called this Chivington Massacre the "foulest and most unjustifiable crime in the annals of America," but it was no worse than many incidents in earlier conflicts with Indians and not very different from what was later to occur in guerrilla wars involving American troops in the Philippines and, more recently, in Vietnam.

In turn the Indians slaughtered dozens of isolated white families, ambushed small parties, and fought many successful skirmishes against troops and militia. They achieved their most notable triumph in December 1866, when the Oglala Sioux,

under their great chief Red Cloud, wiped out a party of 82 soldiers under Captain W. J. Fetterman. Red Cloud fought ruthlessly, but only when goaded by the construction of the Bozeman Trail, a road through the heart of the Sioux hunting grounds in southern Montana.*

In 1867 the government tried a new strategy. The concentration policy had evidently not gone far enough. All the plains Indians would be confined to two small reservations, one in the Black Hills of Dakota Territory, the other in Oklahoma, and forced to become farmers. At two great conclaves held in 1867 and 1868 at Medicine Lodge Creek and Fort Laramie, the principal chiefs yielded to the government's demands.

Many Indians refused to abide by these agreements. With their whole way of life at stake, they raged across the plains like a prairie fire—and were almost as destructive.

That a relative handful of "savages," without central leadership or plan, could hold off the cream of the army, battle-hardened in the Civil War, can be explained by the character of the vast, trackless country and the ineptness of many American military commanders. Indian leadership was also poor in that few chiefs were capable of organizing a campaign or following up an advantage. But the Indians made superb guerrillas. Every observer called them the best cavalry soldiers in the world. Armed with stubby, powerful bows capable of driving an arrow clear through a bull buffalo, they were a fair match for troops equipped with carbines and Colt revolvers. Expertly they led pursuers into ambushes, swept down on unsuspecting supply details, and stole up on small parties the way a mountain lion stalks a grazing lamb. Trouble flared here one week, another week somewhere else, perhaps 500 miles away. No less an authority than General William Tecumseh Sherman testified that a mere 50 Indians could often "checkmate" 3,000 soldiers.

If one concedes that no one could reverse the direction of history or stop the invasion of Indian lands, some version of the small-reservation policy would probably have been best for the Indians. Had they been guaranteed a reasonable amount of land and adequate subsidies and allowed to maintain

---

* Fetterman had boasted that with 80 cavalrymen he could ride the entire length of the Bozeman Trail. When he tried, however, he blundered into an ambush.

their way of life, they might have accepted the situation and ceased to harry the whites.

Whatever chance that policy had was weakened by the government's maladministration of Indian affairs. In dealing with Indians, 19th-century Americans displayed a grave lack of talent for administration. After 1849 the Department of the Interior supposedly had charge of tribal affairs. Most of its agents systematically cheated the Indians. One, heavily involved in mining operations on the side, diverted goods intended for his charges to his private ventures. When an inspector looked into his records, he sold him shares in a mine. That worthy in turn protected himself by sharing some of the loot with the son of the commissioner of Indian affairs. "No branch of the national government is so spotted with fraud, so tainted with corruption . . . as this Indian Bureau," Congressman Garfield charged in 1869.

At about this time a Yale paleontologist, Othniel C. Marsh, who wished to dig for fossils on the Sioux reservation, asked Red Cloud for permission to enter his domain. The chief agreed on condition that Marsh, whom the Indians called Big Bone Chief, take back with him samples of the moldy flour and beef that government agents were supplying to his people. Appalled by what he saw on the reservation, Professor Marsh took the rotten supplies directly to President Grant and prepared a list of charges against the agents. General Philip Sheridan was no lover of Indians. "The only good Indians I ever saw," he said in an oft-quoted remark, "were dead." But he understood why they behaved as they did. "We took away their country and their means of support, broke up their mode of living, their habits of life, introduced disease and decay among them, and it was for this and against this that they made war. Could anyone expect less?"

In 1869 Congress created a nonpolitical Board of Indian Commissioners to oversee Indian affairs, but the bureaucrats in Washington stymied the commissioners at every turn. "Their recommendations were ignored, . . . gross breaking of the law was winked at, and . . . many matters were not submitted to them at all," the biographer of one commissioner has written. "They decided that their task was as useless as it was irritating."

But in 1874 gold was discovered in the Black Hills Indian reservation. By the next winter thousands of miners had invaded the reserved area.

Comanche, the only survivor on the army's side at the Battle of Little Bighorn. His rider was among the 264 cavalrymen who perished with General Custer that June afternoon in 1876.

Already alarmed by the approach of crews building the Northern Pacific Railroad, the Sioux once again went on the warpath. Joining with nontreaty tribes to the west, they concentrated in the region of the Bighorn River, in southern Montana Territory.

The summer of 1876 saw three columns of troops in the field against them. The commander of one column, General Alfred H. Terry, sent ahead a small detachment of the Seventh Cavalry under Colonel George A. Custer with orders to locate the Indians' camp and then block their escape route into the inaccessible Bighorn Mountains. Custer was vain and rash, and vanity and rashness were grave handicaps when fighting Indians. Grossly underestimating the number of the Indians, he decided to attack directly with his tiny force of 264 men. At the Little Bighorn late in June he found himself surrounded by 2,500 Sioux under Rain-in-the-Face, Crazy Horse, and Sitting Bull. He and all his men died on the field.

Because it was so one-sided, "Custer's Last Stand" was not a typical battle, though it may be taken as symbolic of the Indian warfare of the period in the sense that it was characterized by bravery, foolhardiness, and a tragic waste of life. The battle greatly heartened the Indians, but it did not gain them their cause. That autumn, short of rations and hard-pressed by overwhelming numbers of soldiers, they surrendered and returned to the reservation.

The Destruction of Tribal Life

Thereafter, the fighting slackened. For this the building of transcontinental railroads and the destruction of the buffalo were chiefly responsible. An estimated 13 to 15 million head had roamed the plains in the mid-1860s. Then the slaughter began. Thousands were butchered to feed the gangs of laborers engaged in building the Union Pacific Railroad. Thousands more fell before the guns of sportsmen. Buffalo hunting became a fad, and a brisk demand developed for buffalo rugs and mounted buffalo heads. The railroads contributed to the decimation of the buffalo by running excursion trains for hunters; even the shameful practice of gunning down the beasts directly from the cars was allowed. In 1871 and 1872 the Grand Duke Alexis of Russia headed a gigantic hunt, supported by "Buffalo Bill" Cody, most famous of the pro-

fessional buffalo killers, the Seventh United States Cavalry under General Sheridan, and hundreds of Indians.

The discovery in 1871 of a way to make commercial use of buffalo hides completed the tragedy. In the next three years about 9 million head were killed; after another decade the animals were almost extinct. No more efficient way could have been found for destroying the plains Indians. The disappearance of the bison left them starving, homeless, purposeless.

By 1887 the tribes of the mountains and deserts beyond the plains had also given up the fight. Typical of the heartlessness of the government's treatment of these peoples was that afforded the Nez Percé of Oregon and Idaho, who were led by the remarkable Chief Joseph. After outwitting federal troops in a campaign across more than 1,000 miles of rough country, Joseph finally surrendered in October 1877. The Nez Percé were then settled on "the malarial bottoms of the Indian Territory" in far-off Oklahoma. The last Indians to abandon the unequal battle were the relentless Apaches of the Southwest, who finally yielded upon the capture of their leader, Geronimo, in 1886.

By the 1880s the advance of whites into the plains had become, in the words of one congressman, as irresistible "as that of Sherman's to the sea." Greed for land lay behind the pressure, but large numbers of disinterested people, including most of those who deplored the way the Indians had been treated in the past, believed that the only practical way to solve the "Indian problem" was to persuade the Indians to abandon their tribal culture and live on family farms. The "wild" Indian must be changed into a "civilized" member of "American" society.

To accomplish this goal Congress passed the Dawes Severalty Act of 1887. Tribal lands were to be split up into individual allotments. To keep speculators from wresting the allotments from the Indians while they were adjusting to their new way of life, the land could not be disposed of for 25 years. Funds were to be appropriated for educating and training the Indians, and those who accepted allotments, took up residence "separate from any tribe," and "adopted the habits of civilized life" were to be granted United States citizenship.

The sponsors of the Severalty Act thought they were effecting a fine humanitarian reform. "We must throw some protection over [the Indian]," Sen-

Preparing to surrender to General Crook, Geronimo (mounted, left) and Natiche stand with their respective sons and Geronimo's grandson; the sons wear ceremonial paint. This photograph was taken in the Sierra Madre mountains of Mexico in 1886, just before the surrender.

ator Henry L. Dawes declared. "We must hold up his hand." But the law had disastrous results in the long run. It assumed that Indians could be transformed into small agricultural capitalists by an act of Congress. It weakened what was left of the Indians' culture without enabling them to adapt to white ways. Moreover, unscrupulous whites systematically tricked many Indians into leasing their allotments for a pittance, and local authorities often taxed Indian lands at excessive rates. In 1934, after about 86 million of the 138 million acres assigned under the Dawes Act had passed into white hands, the government returned to a policy of encouraging tribal ownership of Indian lands.

Exploiting Mineral Wealth in the West

Americans had long regarded the West as a limitless treasure to be grasped as rapidly as possible, and after 1865 they engrossed its riches still faster and in a wider variety of ways. From the mid-1850s to the mid-1870s thousands of gold-crazed prospectors fanned out through the Rockies, panning every stream and hacking furiously at every likely out-

cropping from the Fraser River country of British Columbia to Tucson in southern Arizona, from the eastern slopes of the Sierra to the Great Plains.

Gold and silver were scattered throughout the area, though usually too thinly to make mining profitable. Whenever anyone made a "strike," prospectors, the vast majority utterly without previous experience but driven by what a mining journal of the period called an "unhealthy desire" for sudden wealth, flocked to the site, drawn by rumors of streambeds gleaming with gold-rich gravel and of nuggets the size of men's fists. For a few months the area teemed with activity. Towns of 5,000 or more sprang up overnight; improvised roads were crowded with people and supply wagons. Claims were staked out along every stream and gully. Then, usually, expectations faded in the light of reality: high prices, low yields, hardship, violence, and deception. The boom collapsed, and the towns died as quickly as they had risen. A few would have found wealth, the rest only backbreaking labor and disappointment—until tales of another strike sent them dashing feverishly across the land on another golden chase.

In the spring of 1858 it was on the Fraser River in Canada that the horde descended, 30,000 Californians in the vanguard. The following spring, Pikes Peak in Colorado attracted the pack, experienced California prospectors ("yonder siders") mixing with "greenhorns" from every corner of the globe. In June 1859 came the finds in Nevada, where the famous Comstock Lode yielded ores worth nearly $4,000 a ton. In 1861, while men in the settled areas were laying down their tools to take up arms, the miners were racing to the Idaho panhandle, hoping to become millionaires overnight. The next year the rush was to the Snake River valley, in 1863 and 1864 to Montana. From 1874 to 1876 the Black Hills in the heart of the Sioux lands were inundated with prospectors.

In a sense the Denvers, Aurarias, Virginia Cities, Orofinos, and Gold Creeks of the West during the war years were harbingers of the attitudes that flourished in the East in the age of President Grant and his immediate successors. The miners enthusiastically adopted the get-rich-quick philosophy, willingly enduring privations and laboring hard, always with the object of striking it rich. The idea of reserving any part of the West for future generations never entered their heads.

The sudden prosperity of the mining towns attracted every kind of shady character—according to one forty-niner, "rascals from Oregon, pickpockets from New York, accomplished gentlemen from Europe, interlopers from Lima and Chile, Mexican thieves, gamblers from no particular spot, and assassins manufactured in Hell." Gambling dens, dance halls, saloons, and brothels mushroomed wherever precious metal was found.

Law enforcement was a constant problem. Gold and silver dominated people's thoughts and dreams, and few paid much attention to the means employed in accumulating this wealth. Storekeepers charged outrageous prices; claim holders "salted" worthless properties with nuggets in order to swindle gullible investors. Ostentation characterized the successful, braggadocio those who failed. During the administration of President Grant, Virginia City, Nevada, was at the peak of its vulgar prosperity. It had 25 saloons before it had 4,000 people. By the 1870s its mountainside site was disfigured by ugly, ornate mansions where successful mine operators ate from fine china and swilled champagne as though it were water.

In 1873, after the discovery of the Big Bonanza, a seam of rich ore more than 50 feet thick, the future

of Virginia City seemed boundless. Other discoveries shortly thereafter indicated to optimists that the mining boom in the West would continue indefinitely. The finds in the Black Hills district in 1875 and 1876, heralding deposits yielding eventually $100 million, led to the mushroom growth of Deadwood, home of Wild Bill Hickok, Deadwood Dick, Calamity Jane, and such lesser-known characters as California Jack and Poker Alice. In Deadwood, according to the historian Ray Allen Billington, "the faro games were wilder, the hurdy-gurdy dance halls noisier, the street brawls more common, than in any other western town." New strikes in Colorado in 1876 and 1877 caused the town of Leadville to boom; in 1880 there were 30,000 people in

Nat Love, a cowboy who earned the name of "Deadwood Dick" throughout the Dakotas in the 1880s for his prowess with a lariat. His autobiography, published in 1907, attests to the role blacks played in the settling of the Wild West.

the area. However, this was the last important flurry to ruffle the mining frontier. The West continued to yield much gold and silver, especially silver, but big corporations produced nearly all of it. The mines around Deadwood were soon controlled by one large company, Homestake Mining.

This is the culminating irony of the history of the mining frontier: Shoestring prospectors, independent and enterprising, made the key discoveries. They established local institutions and supplied the West with much of its color and folklore. But the stockholders of large corporations, many of whom had never seen a mine, made off with the lion's share of the wealth. Those whose worship of gold was direct and incessant, the prospectors who peopled the mining towns and gave the frontier its character, mostly died poor, still seeking a prize as elusive if not as illusory as the pot of gold at the end of the rainbow.

The mining of gold and silver was not essentially different from the mining of coal and iron. To operate profitably, large capital investments, heavy machinery, railroads, and hundreds of skilled workers (mostly "deep" miners from Cornwall, in England) were required. Henry Comstock, the prospector who gave his name to the Comstock Lode,

was luckier than most, but he sold his claims to the lode for a pittance, disposing of what became one valuable mine for $40 and receiving only $10,000 for his share of the fabulous Ophir, the richest concentration of gold and silver ever found. More typical of the successful mine owner was George Hearst, senator from California and father of the newspaper tycoon William Randolph Hearst, who, by shrewd speculations, obtained large blocks of stock in mining properties scattered from Montana to Mexico.

Though marked by violence, fraud, greed, and shattered hopes, the gold rushes had valuable results. The most obvious was the new metal itself, which bolstered the financial position of the United States during and after the Civil War. Quantities of European goods needed for the war effort and for postwar economic development were paid for with the yield of the new mines. Gold and silver also caused a great increase of interest in the West. A valuable literature appeared, part imaginative, part reportorial, describing the mining camps and the life of the prospectors. These works fascinated contemporaries (as they have continued to fascinate succeeding generations when adapted to the motion picture and to television). Mark Twain's *Roughing*

An idealized engraving of the interior of a gold mine in Nevada in the 1870s. Neither prospectors like Henry Comstock nor those who dug these mines figured prominently among those enriched by them.

It (1872), based in part on his experiences in the Nevada mining country, is the most famous example of this literature.

Each new strike and rush, no matter how ephemeral, brought permanent settlers along with the prospectors: farmers, cattlemen, storekeepers, teamsters, lawyers, and ministers. The boomtowns had to import everything from bread, meat, and liquor to building materials and tools of every sort. Without the well-worn trails blazed by earlier hunters and migrants headed for Oregon and California and of freighting companies equipped to haul heavy loads over long distances, the towns could not have existed. Some of the gold seekers saw from the start that a better living could be made supplying the needs of prospectors than looking for the elusive metal. Others, failing to find mineral wealth, took up whatever occupation they could rather than starve or return home empty-handed. In every mining town—along with the saloons and brothels— schools, churches, and newspaper offices sprang up.

The philosopher Josiah Royce (1855–1916), the son of forty-niners, grew up in a California mining town and in San Francisco. Many years later, while teaching at Harvard, he wrote a book about life in the camps. "The romantic degradation of the early mining life, with its . . . inevitable brutality and its resulting loathsome corruption, gave place to the commonplace industries of the later mining days," he recalled.

The mines also speeded the political organization of the West. Colorado and Nevada became territories in 1861, Arizona and Idaho in 1863, Montana in 1864. Although Nevada was admitted before it had 60,000 residents (in 1864, to ratify the Thirteenth Amendment and help reelect Lincoln), most of these territories did not become states for decades. But thanks to the miners, the framework for future development was established early.

The Land Bonanza

While the miners were engrossing the mineral wealth of the West, other interests were snapping up the region's choice farmland. The Homestead Act of 1862 had presumably ended the reign of the speculator and the large landholder. An early amendment to the act even prevented husbands and wives from filing separate claims. The West, land

reformers had assumed, would soon be dotted with 160-acre family farms.

They were doomed to disappointment. Most landless Americans were too poor to become farmers even when they could obtain land without cost. The expense of moving a family to the ever-receding frontier exceeded the means of many, and the costs of hoes and scythes, harvesting machines, fencing, and housing presented a formidable barrier. As for the industrial workers for whom the free land was supposed to provide a "safety valve," they had neither the skills nor the inclination to become farmers. Homesteaders usually came from districts not far removed from frontier conditions, and despite the intent of the law, speculators often managed to obtain large tracts. They hired men to stake out claims, falsely swear that they had fulfilled the conditions laid down in the law for obtaining legal title, and then deed the land over to their employers.

Furthermore, 160 acres was not enough for raising livestock or for the kind of commercial agriculture that was developing west of the Mississippi. Congress made a feeble attempt to make larger holdings available to homesteaders by passing the Timber Culture Act of 1873, which permitted individuals to claim an additional 160 acres if they would agree to plant a quarter of it with trees within ten years. This law proved helpful to some farmers in Kansas, Nebraska, and the Dakotas. Nevertheless, fewer than 25 percent of the 245,000 who took up land under it obtained final title to the property. Raising large numbers of seedlings on the plains was a difficult task.

While futilely attempting to make a forest of parts of the treeless plains, the government permitted private interests to gobble up and destroy many of the great forests that clothed the slopes of the Rockies and the Sierra. The Timber and Stone Act of 1878 allowed anyone to acquire a quarter section of forest land for $2.50 an acre if it was "unfit for civilization." This laxly drawn measure enabled lumber companies to obtain thousands of acres by hiring dummy entrymen, whom they marched in gangs to the land offices, paying them a few dollars for their time after they had signed over their claims.

Had the land laws been more precisely drafted, it is still unlikely that the policy of granting free land to small homesteaders would have succeeded. Aside from the built-in difficulties faced by small-scale ag-

The crews of five combines stopped during the wheat harvest on a bonanza farm in northern California to have their picture taken. Combines such as these reaped, threshed, cleaned, and bagged grain in a single operation.

riculturalists, frontier farmers of the 1870s and 1880s had to grapple with novel problems. The soil was rich, but the climate, especially in the semiarid regions beyond the 98th meridian of longitude, made agriculture frequently difficult and often impossible. Blizzards, floods, grasshopper plagues, and prairie fires caused repeated heartaches, but periodic drought and searing summer heat were the worst hazards.

At the same time, the flat immensity of the land, combined with newly available farm machinery and the development of rail connections with the East, encouraged the growth of enormous corporation-controlled "bonanza" farms. One such organization was the railroad-owned empire managed by Oliver Dalrymple in Dakota Territory, which cultivated 25,000 acres of wheat in 1880. Dalrymple employed 200 pairs of harrows to prepare his soil, 125 seeders to sow his seed, and 155 binders to harvest his crop.

Bonanza farmers could buy supplies wholesale and obtain concessions from railroads and processors; even the biggest organizations could not cope with prolonged drought, however, and most of the bonanza outfits failed in the dry years of the late 1880s. Wise farmers who diversified their crops and cultivated their land intensively fared better in the

long run, though even they could not hope to earn a profit in really dry years.

Despite the hazards of plains agriculture, the region became the breadbasket of America in the decades following the Civil War. By 1889 Minnesota topped the nation in wheat production, and ten years later four of the five leading wheat states lay west of the Mississippi. The plains also accounted for large percentages of the nation's other cereal crops, together with immense quantities of beef, pork, and mutton.

Like other exploiters of the nation's resources, farmers took whatever they could from the soil with little heed for preserving its fertility and preventing erosion. The consequent national loss was less apparent because it was diffuse and slow to assume drastic proportions, but it was nonetheless real.

Western Railroad Building

Further exploitation of land resources by private interests resulted from the government's policy of subsidizing western railroads. Here was a clear illustration of the conflict between the idea of the

West as a national heritage to be disposed of to deserving citizens and the concept of the region as a cornucopia pouring forth riches to be gathered up and carted off by anyone powerful and determined enough to take them. When it came to a choice between giving a particular tract to railroads or to homesteaders, the homesteaders nearly always lost out.

Unless the government had been willing to build the transcontinental lines itself—and this was unthinkable in an age dominated by belief in individual exploitation—some system of subsidy was essential. Private investors would not hazard the huge sums needed to lay tracks across hundreds of miles of rugged, empty country when traffic over the road could not possibly produce profits for many years. It might appear that subsidizing construction by direct outlays of public funds would have been adopted, but that idea had few supporters. Most voters were wary of entrusting the dispensing of large sums to politicians. Grants of land seemed a sensible way of financing construction. The method avoided direct outlays of public funds, for the companies could pledge the land as security for bond issues or sell it directly for cash. Moreover, land and railroad values were intimately linked in contemporary thinking. "The occupation of new land and the building of new mileage go hand in hand," the *Commercial and Financial Chronicle* explained in 1886.

There could be no great or continuous opening up of new territory without the necessary facilities in the way of railroads. On the other hand, most new mileage on the borders of our Western territory is prosecuted with the idea and expectation that it is to pave the way for an accession of new settlers and an extension of the area of land devoted to their uses.

In many cases the value of the land granted might be recovered by the government when it sold other lands in the vicinity, for such properties would certainly be worth more after transportation facilities to eastern markets had been constructed. "Why," the governor of one eastern state asked in 1867, "should private individuals be called upon to make a useless sacrifice of their means, when railroads can be constructed by the unity of public and private interests, and made profitable to all?"

About 49 million acres were given to various lines indirectly in the form of grants to the states, but the most lavish gifts of the public domain were those made directly to builders of intersectional trunk lines. These roads received more than 155 million acres, although about 25 million acres reverted to the government because some companies failed to lay the required miles of track. About 75 percent of this land went to aid the construction of four transcontinental railroads: the Union Pacific–Central Pacific line, running from Nebraska to San Francisco, completed in 1869; the Atchison, Topeka and Santa Fe, running from Kansas City to Los

Railroads expanded using bridges and trestles to cross inhospitable terrain that had presented problems for horse and wagon. This bridge east of Santa Fe, New Mexico, was completed in 1880.

Angeles by way of Santa Fe and Albuquerque, completed in 1883; the Southern Pacific, running from San Francisco to New Orleans by way of Yuma and El Paso, completed in 1883; and the Northern Pacific, running from Duluth, Minnesota, to Portland, Oregon, completed in 1883.

The Pacific Railway Act of 1862 established the pattern for these grants. It gave the builders of the Union Pacific and Central Pacific railroads 5 square miles of public land on each side of their right of way for each mile of track laid. The land was allotted in alternate sections, forming a pattern like a checkerboard, the squares of one color representing railroad property, the other government property. Presumably this arrangement benefited the entire nation since half the land close to the railroad remained in public hands.

However, whenever grants were made to railroads, the adjacent government lands were not opened to homesteaders, on the theory that free land in the immediate vicinity of a line would prevent the road from disposing of its properties at good prices. Since, in addition to the land granted the railroads, a wide zone of "indemnity" lands was reserved to allow the roads to choose alternative sites to make up for land that settlers had already taken up within the checkerboard, homesteading was in fact prohibited near land-grant railroads. Grants per mile of track ranged from five alternate sections on each side of the track to the Union and Central Pacific to 40 sections to the Northern Pacific. In the latter case, when the indemnity zone was included, homesteaders were barred from an area 100 miles wide, all the way from Lake Superior to the Pacific. More than 20 years after receiving its immense grant, the Northern Pacific was still attempting to keep homesteaders from filing in the indemnity zone. President Cleveland finally put a stop to this in 1887, saying that he could find "no evidence" that "this vast tract is necessary for the fulfillment of the grant."

Historians have argued at length about the fairness of the land-grant system. No railroad corporation waxed fat directly from the sale of its lands, which were sold at prices averaging between $2 and $5 an acre. Collectively the roads have taken in between $400 million and $500 million from this source, but only over the course of a century. Land-grant lines did a great deal to encourage the growth of the West by advertising their property and by providing cheap transportation for prospective set-

tlers and efficient shipping services for farmers. They were required by law to carry troops and handle government business free or at reduced rates, which saved the government millions over the years. At the same time the system imposed no effective restraints on how the railroads used the funds raised with federal aid. Being able to lay track with money obtained from land grants, the operators tended to be extravagant and often downright corrupt.

The Union Pacific was built by a construction company, the Crédit Mobilier, which was owned by the promoters. These men awarded themselves contracts at prices that assured the Crédit Mobilier of fat profits. When Congress threatened to investigate the Union Pacific in 1868, Oakes Ames, a stockholder in both companies who was also a member of Congress, sold key congressmen and government officials over 300 shares of Crédit Mobilier stock at a price far below its real value. "I have found," Ames said, "there is no difficulty in inducing men to look after their own property."

When these transactions were exposed, the House of Representatives censured Ames, but such was the temper of the times that neither he nor most of his associates believed that he had done anything wrong. According to the president of one western railroad, congressmen frequently tried to use their influence to get railroad land at bargain prices. "Isn't there a discount?" they would ask. "Surely you can give the land cheaper to a friend. . . ." The railroads seldom resisted this type of pressure.

The construction of the Central Pacific in the 1860s illustrates how the system encouraged extravagance. The line was controlled by four businessmen, Collis P. Huntington ("scrupulously dishonest" but an excellent manager); Leland Stanford, a Sacramento grocer and politican; Mark Hopkins, a hardware merchant; and Charles Crocker, a hulking, relentless driver of men who had come to California during the gold rush and made a small fortune as a merchant. The Central Pacific and the Union Pacific were given, in addition to their land grants, loans in the form of government bonds—from $16,000 to $48,000 for each mile of track laid, depending on the difficulty of the terrain. The two competed for the subsidies, the Central Pacific building eastward from Sacramento, the Union Pacific westward from Nebraska. Each put crews to work grading and laying track, bringing up supplies over the already completed road. The

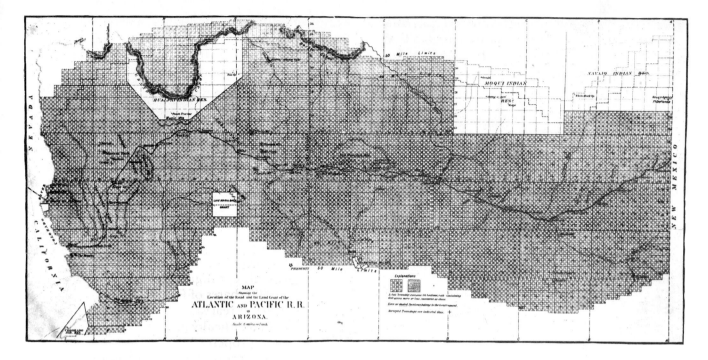

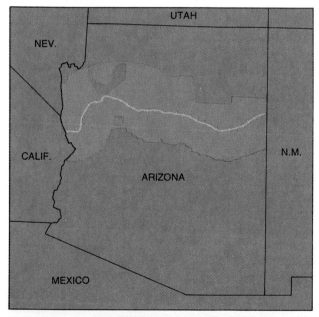

On the contemporary map (upper), the Atlantic and Pacific Railroad land grant in Arizona appears as shaded squares on a checkerboard. The grant cut a 100-mile-wide swath across the entire territory (lower).

Union Pacific employed Civil War veterans and Irish immigrants; the Central, Chinese immigrants.

This plan favored the Union Pacific. While the Central Pacific was inching upward through the gorges and granite of the mighty Sierra, the Union Pacific was racing across the level plains, laying 540 miles of track between 1865 and 1867. Once beyond the Sierra, the Central Pacific would have easy going across the Nevada-Utah plateau country, but by then it might be too late to prevent the Union Pacific from making off with most of the government aid.

Crocker managed the Central Pacific construction crews. He wasted huge sums by working through the winter in the High Sierra. Often the men labored in tunnels dug through 40-foot snowdrifts to get at the frozen ground. To speed construction of the Summit Tunnel, Crocker had a shaft cut down from above so that crews could work out from the middle as well as in from each end. In 1866, over the most difficult terrain, he laid 28 miles of track—at a cost of more than $280,000 a mile. Experts later estimated that 70 percent of this sum could have been saved had speed not been a factor. Such prodigality made economic sense to Huntington, Stanford, Hopkins, and Crocker because of the profits they were making through the construction company and because of the gains they could count on once they reached the flat country beyond the Sierra, where construction costs would amount to only half the federal aid.

Crocker's herculean efforts paid off. The mountains were conquered, and then the crews raced across the Great Basin to Salt Lake City and beyond.

The meeting of the rails—the occasion of a national celebration—took place at Promontory, north of Ogden, Utah, on May 10, 1869. Leland Stanford drove the final ceremonial golden spike with a silver hammer.* The Union Pacific had built 1,086 miles of track, the Central 689 miles.

In the long run the wasteful way in which the Central Pacific was built hurt the road severely. It was ill-constructed, over grades too steep and around curves too sharp, and burdened with debts that were too heavy. Such was the fate of nearly all the railroads constructed with the help of government subsidies.

The only transcontinental built without land grants was the Great Northern, running from St. Paul, Minnesota, to the Pacific. Spending private capital, its guiding genius, James J. Hill, was compelled to build economically and to plan carefully. As a result, his was the only transcontinental line to weather the depression of the 1890s without going into bankruptcy.

The Cattle Kingdom

While miners were digging out the mineral wealth of the West and railroaders were taking possession of much of its land, another group was exploiting endless acres of its grass. For 20 years after the Civil War, cattlemen and sheep raisers dominated huge areas of the High Plains, making millions of dollars by grazing their herds on lands they did not own.

Columbus brought the first cattle to the New World in 1493, on his second voyage, and later *conquistadores* took them to every corner of Spain's American empire. Mexico proved to be so well suited to raising cattle that many were allowed to roam free. They multiplied rapidly, and by the late 18th century what is now southern Texas harbored enormous herds. The beasts interbred with nondescript "English" cattle, brought into the area by settlers from the United States, to produce the Texas longhorn. Hardy, wiry, ill-tempered, and fleet, with horns often attaining a spread of 6 feet, these animals were far from ideal as beef cattle and almost as hard to capture as wild horses. But they existed in southern Texas by the million, most of them unowned.

The lack of markets and transportation explains why Texas cattle were lightly regarded. But conditions were changing. Industrial growth in the East was causing an increase in the urban population and a consequent rise in the demand for food. At the same time, the expansion of the railroad network made it possible to move cattle cheaply over long distances. As the iron rails inched across the plains, astute cattlemen began to do some elementary figuring. Longhorns could be had locally for $3 to $4 a head. In the northern cities they would bring ten times that much, perhaps even more. Why not round them up and herd them northward to the railroads, allowing them to feed along the way on the abundant grasses of the plains?

In 1866 a number of Texans drove large herds northward toward Sedalia, Missouri, railhead of the Missouri Pacific. This route took the herds through wooded and settled country and across Indian reservations, which provoked many difficulties. At the same time Charles Goodnight and Oliver Loving successfully drove 2,000 head in a great arc west to New Mexico Territory and then north to Colorado.

The next year the drovers, inspired by a clever young Illinois cattle dealer named Joseph G. McCoy and other entrepreneurs, led their herds north by a more westerly route, across unsettled grasslands, to the Kansas Pacific line at Abilene, Kansas, which McCoy described as "a very small, dead place, consisting of about one dozen log huts." They earned excellent profits, and during the next five years about 1.5 million head made the "long drive" over the Chisholm Trail to Abilene, where they were sold to ranchers, feedlot operators, and the agents of eastern meat packers. Other shipping points sprang up as the railroads pushed westward. According to the best estimates, 10 million head were driven north before the practice ended in the mid-1880s.

The technique of the long drive, which involved guiding herds of two or three thousand cattle slowly across as much as a thousand miles of country, produced the American cowboy, renowned in song, story, and on film. Half a dozen of these men could control several thousand steers. Mounted on wiry ponies, they would range alongside the herd, keeping the animals on the move but preventing stampedes, allowing them time to rest yet steadily pressing them toward the yards of Abilene.

---

* A mysterious "San Francisco jeweler" passed among the onlookers, taking orders for souvenir watch chains that he proposed to make from the spike at $5 each.

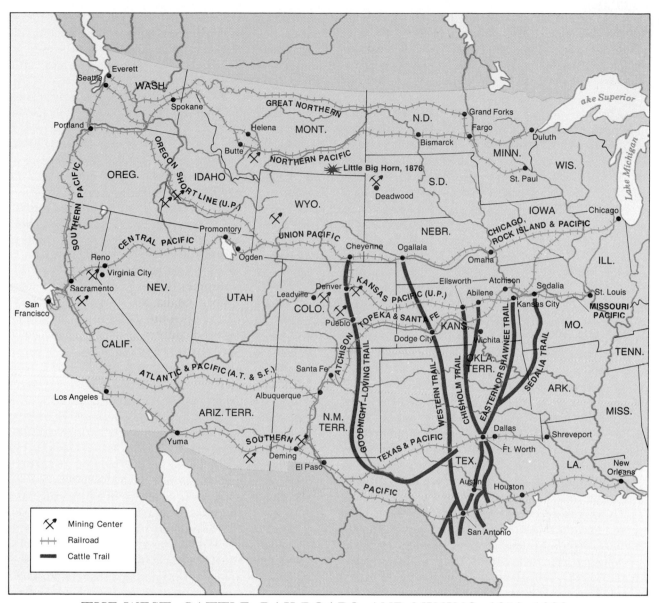

THE WEST: CATTLE, RAILROADS, AND MINING, 1850–1893

The cowboy's life was far more prosaic than it appears in modern legend, consisting mainly of endless hours on the trail surrounded by thousands of bellowing beasts. Cowboys were a mixed lot: Mexican *vaqueros* and blacks made up about a third of them, but there were many local Texans, Civil War veterans, former miners, and, in the words of Theodore Roosevelt, "wild spirits from every land." They virtually lived on horseback, for their work kept them far from human habitation for months on end.

Most, accustomed to solitude, were indeed "strong, silent men." They were courageous—and expert marksmen, too, for they lived amid many dangers and had to know how to protect themselves. Few grew rich, yet like the miners they were true representatives of their time—determinedly individualistic, contemptuous of authority, crude, devoted to coarse pleasures.

The major "cattle towns," Abilene, Wichita, Ellsworth, Dodge City, and Caldwell, had their full share of saloons, gambling dens, and "dance houses" patronized by cowboys and by other transients bent on having a good time. Most were young, male, and single. Violence punctuated their activities, but tales of individual desperadoes and gangs of outlaws "shooting up" cattle towns and terrorizing honest citizens are fictitious. Police forces were well organized. Indeed, the "respectable" town residents tended to urge leniency for lawbreakers because of the money they and their fellows brought to the towns. A careful check of the records by the historian Robert Dykstra revealed that between 1870 and 1885 there were only 45 homicides in these five towns, and some of them had nothing to do with the cattle trade.

Open-Range Ranching

Soon cattlemen discovered that the hardy Texas stock could survive the winters of the northern plains. Attracted by the apparently limitless forage, they began to bring up herds to stock the vast regions where the buffalo had so recently roamed. Introducing pedigreed Hereford bulls, they improved the stock without weakening its resistance to harsh conditions. By 1880 some 4.5 million head had spread across the sea of grass that ran from Kansas to Montana and west to the Rockies.

The prairie grasses offered cattlemen a bonanza almost as valuable as the gold mines. Open-range ranching required actual ownership of no more than a few acres along some watercourse. In this semiarid region, control of water enabled a rancher to dominate all the surrounding area back to the divide separating his range from the next stream without investing a cent in the purchase of land. His cattle, wandering freely on the public domain, fattened on grass owned by all the people, to be turned into beefsteak and leather for the profit of the rancher.

Theoretically, anyone could pasture stock on the open range, but without access to water it was impossible to do so. "I have 2 miles of running water," a cattleman said in testifying before the Public Land Commission. "That accounts for my ranch being where it is. The next water from me in one direction is 23 miles; now no man can have a ranch between these two places. I have control of the grass, the

same as though I owned it." By having his cowhands take out homestead claims along watercourses in his region, a rancher could greatly expand the area he dominated. In the late 1870s one Colorado cattle baron controlled an area roughly the size of Connecticut and Rhode Island even though he owned only 105 small parcels that totaled about 15,500 acres.

Generally a group of ranchers acted together, obtaining legal title to the lands along the bank of a stream and grazing their cattle over the area drained by it. The herds became thoroughly intermixed, each owner's being identified by an individual brand mark. Every spring and fall the ranchers staged a great roundup, driving in all the cattle to a central place, separating them by the brands, culling steers for shipment to market, and branding new calves.

With the demand for meat rising and transportation cheap, princely fortunes could be made in a few years. Capitalists from the East and from Europe began to pour funds into the business. Eastern "dudes" like Theodore Roosevelt, a young New York assemblyman who sank over $50,000 into his Elkhorn Ranch in Dakota Territory in 1883, bought up cattle as a sort of profitable hobby. (Roosevelt, clad in buckskin and bearing a small armory of rifles and six-shooters, made quite a splash in Dakota, but not as a rancher.)

Unlike other exploiters of the West's resources, the ranchers did not at first injure or reduce any public resource. Grass eaten by their stock renewed itself annually, the soil enriched by the droppings of the animals. Furthermore, ranchers poached on the public domain because there was no reasonable way for them to obtain legal possession of the large areas necessary to raise cattle on the plains. Federal land laws made no allowance for the special conditions of the semiarid West. "Title to the public lands [of the West] cannot be honestly acquired under the homestead laws," S. E. Burdett, commissioner of the General Land Office, reported in 1875. "A system of sale should be authorized in accordance with the necessities of the situation."

Such a system was soon devised by Major John Wesley Powell, later the director of the United States Geological Survey. His *Report on the Lands of the Arid Region of the United States* (1879) suggested that western lands be divided into three classes: irrigable lands, timber lands, and "pasturage" lands. On the pasturage lands the "farm unit" ought to be at least 2,560 acres (four sections), Powell urged. Groups of these units should be organized into "pasturage districts" in which the ranchers "should have the right to make their own regulations for the division of lands, the use of the water . . . and for the pasturage of lands in common or in severalty."

Barbed-Wire Warfare

Congress refused to change the land laws in any basic way, and this had two harmful effects. First, it encouraged fraud: Those who could not get title to enough land honestly turned to subterfuge. The Desert Land Act (1877) allowed anyone to obtain 640 acres in the arid states for $1.25 an acre provided the owner irrigated part of it within three years. More than 2.6 million acres were taken up under the act, and according to the best estimate, about 95 percent of the claims were fraudulent—no sincere effort was made to irrigate the land.

Second, overcrowding became a problem that led to serious conflicts, even killings, because no one had uncontestable title to the land. The leading ranchers banded together in cattlemen's associations to deal with overcrowding and with such problems as quarantine regulations, water rights, and thievery. In most cases these associations devised effective and sensible rules, but their functions would better have been performed by the government, as such matters usually are.

To keep other ranchers' cattle from the sections of the public domain they considered their own, the associations and many individuals began to fence huge areas. This was possible only because of the invention in 1874 of barbed wire by Joseph F. Glidden, an Illinois farmer. By the 1880s thousands of miles of the new fencing had been strung across the plains, often across roads and in a few cases around entire communities. "Barbed-wire wars" resulted, fought by rancher against rancher, cattleman against sheepman, herder against farmer. The associations tried to police their fences and to punish anyone who cut their wire. Signs posted along lonely stretches gave dire warnings to trespassers. "The Son of a Bitch who opens this fence had better look

In 1885 masked Nebraskans seeking access to water posed for photographer S. D. Butcher, who captioned the picture "Settlers taking the law in their own hands: cutting 15 miles of the Brighton Ranch fence."

out for his scalp," one such sign announced, another fine statement of the philosophy of the age.

By stringing so much wire the cattlemen were unwittingly destroying their own way of doing business. On a truly open range, cattle could fend for themselves, instinctively finding water during droughts, drifting safely downwind before blizzards. Barbed wire prevented their free movement. During winter storms these slender strands became as lethal as high-tension wires; the drifting cattle piled up against them and died by the thousands. "The advent of barbed wire," Walter Prescott Webb wrote in his classic study *The Great Plains* (1931), "brought about the disappearance of the open, free range and converted the range country into the big-pasture country."

The boom times were ending. Overproduction was driving down the price of beef; expenses were on the rise; many sections of the range were badly overgrazed. The dry summer of 1886 left the stock in such poor condition as winter approached that the *Rocky Mountain Husbandman* urged its readers to sell their cattle despite the prevailing low prices rather than "endanger the whole herd by having the range overstocked."

Some ranchers took this advice; those who did not made a fatal error. Winter that year arrived early and with unparalleled fury. Blizzards raged and temperatures plummeted far below zero. Cattle crowded into low places only to be engulfed in giant snowdrifts; barbed wire took a fearful toll. When spring finally came, the streams were choked with rotting carcasses. Between 80 and 90 percent of all cattle on the range were dead.

That cruel winter finished open-range cattle raising. The large companies were bankrupt; many independent operators, Roosevelt among them, became discouraged and sold out. When the industry revived, it was on a smaller, more efficiently organized scale. Cattle raising, like mining before it, ceased to be an adventure in rollicking individualism and became a business.

By the late 1880s the bonanza days of the West were over. No previous frontier had caught the imagination of Americans so completely as the Great West, with its heroic size, its awesome emptiness, its massive, sculptured beauty. Now the frontier was no more. Most of what Professor Webb called the "primary windfalls" of the region—the

furs, the precious metals, the forests, the cattle, and the grass—had been snatched up by firstcomers and by individuals already wealthy. Big companies were taking over all the West's resources. The nation was becoming more powerful, richer, larger, and its economic structure more complex and diversified as the West yielded its treasures. But the East, especially eastern industrialists and financiers, increasingly dominated the economy of the nation.

Milestones

1859	Charles Darwin's *Origin of Species*
	Comstock Lode discovered
1864	Chivington Massacre
1869	Union Pacific Railroad completed
	Board of Indian Commissioners established
1873	Timber Culture Act
1875	Civil Rights Act
1876	Battle of the Little Bighorn
1877	Desert Land Act
1878	Timber and Stone Act
1879	Major Powell's *Report on the Lands of the Arid Region*
	Specie payments resumed
1881	Tuskegee Institute founded
1883	*Civil Rights Cases*
1886–1887	Blizzards put an end to open-range ranching
1887	Dawes Severalty Act
1888	James Bryce's *American Commonwealth*
1890–1900	Blacks deprived of the vote in the South
1895	Booker T. Washington's Atlanta Compromise speech
1896	*Plessy* v. *Ferguson* sanctions segregation

SUPPLEMENTARY READING

Titles marked with an asterisk have been published in paperback.

Three superb analyses of the political system of the period were written by men who studied it firsthand: James Bryce, **The American Commonwealth*** (1888), Woodrow Wilson, **Congressional Government*** (1886), and Moisei Ostrogorski, **Democracy and the Organization of Political Parties*** (1902). Morton Keller, **Affairs of State** (1977), is an interesting analysis of public life in the period.

The issues of post-Reconstruction politics are discussed in S. P. Hirshson, **Farewell to the Bloody Shirt*** (1962), Allen Weinstein, **Prelude to Populism: Origins of the Silver Issue** (1970), Irwin Unger, **The Greenback Era*** (1964), Milton Friedman and A. J. Schwartz, **A Monetary History of the United States*** (1963), and W. T. K. Nugent, **Money and American Society** (1968).

The economic, political, and legal ideas current in this period are covered in Sidney Fine, **Laissez Faire and the General Welfare State*** (1956), and J. W. Hurst, **Law and the Conditions of Freedom in the Nineteenth-Century United States*** (1956). C. D. Warner and Mark Twain, **The Gilded Age*** (1873), is a useful and entertaining contemporary impression. On social Darwinism, see R. C. Bannister, **Social Darwinism** (1979).

Western development is covered in R. A. Billington and Martin Ridge, **Westward Expansion** (1982), and in R. W. Paul, **The Far West and the Great Plains** (1988), which puts more emphasis on social aspects of the subject. Gunther Barth, **Instant Cities** (1975), deals with the development of San Francisco and Denver. On the Indians, general works include W. E. Washburn, **The Indian in America*** (1975), and W. T. Hagan, **American Indians*** (1961). Of more specialized books, the following are useful: F. G. Roe, **The Indian and the Horse** (1955), R. W. Mardock, **The Reformers and the American Indian** (1971), R. M. Utley, **Frontier Regulars: The United States Army and the Indian*** (1973); and F. P. Prucha, **The Great Father: The U.S. Government and the American Indians** (1984).

On the fate of other minority groups, see R. W. Logan, **The Negro in American Life and Thought: The Nadir*** (1954), Joel Williamson, **The Crucible of Race** (1984), L. R. Harlan, **Booker T. Washington*** (1972), C. V. Woodward, **The Strange Career of Jim Crow*** (1966), Gunther Barth, **Bitter Strength: A History of the Chinese in the United States** (1964), and John Higham, **Strangers in the Land*** (1955). On the mining frontier consult R. W. Paul, **Mining Frontiers of the Far West*** (1963), W. T. Jackson, **Treasure Hill: Portrait of a Silver Mining Camp*** (1963), Paula Petric, **No Step Backward: Women and Family on the Rocky Mountain Frontier** (1987) and D. A. Smith, **Rocky Mountain Mining Camps*** (1967). Mark Twain, **Roughing It*** (1872), is a classic contemporary account, and W. H. Goetzmann, **Exploration and Empire** (1966), throws much light on all aspects of western development. F. A. Shannon, **The Farmer's Last Frontier*** (1945), is excellent on all questions relating to post–Civil War agriculture. Bonanza farming is described in H. M. Drache, **The Day of the Bonanza** (1964).

The development of transcontinental railroads is discussed in R. E. Riegel, **The Story of the Western Railroads*** (1926), O. O. Winther, **The Transportation Frontier*** (1964), and G. R. Taylor and I. D. Neu, **The American Railroad Network** (1956). See also David Lavender, **The Great Persuader** (1970), Albro Martin, **James J. Hill and the Opening of the Northwest** (1976), R. G. Athearn, **Union Pacific Country*** (1971), and L. L. Waters, **Steel Rails to Santa Fe** (1950).

On cattle ranching on the plains, a good account is Lewis Atherton, **The Cattle Kings*** (1961), but see also Don Worcester, **The Chisholm Trail** (1980). On the cowboy and his life, see J. B. Frantz and J. E. Choate, **The American Cowboy** (1955), and R. R. Dykstra, **The Cattle Towns*** (1968). W. P. Webb, **The Great Plains*** (1931), is a fascinating analysis of the development of a unique civilization on the plains.

American Lives:

Clement Vann Rogers and George William Norris

Clem Rogers

Clem Rogers was part Cherokee Indian on both sides. He was born in Indian Territory in 1839, shortly after President Andrew Jackson had forced the Cherokee to migrate there from their ancestral lands in Georgia. Although he was proud of his Indian blood, Rogers lived more like the whites than the Indians. He never learned to speak Cherokee, though he was able to understand the language. His grandfather had actually settled in the region well before the tribe was forced there by Jackson.

The Rogers family had prospered in the Territory and Clem had been given a "white" education. But his father died when he was very young and after his mother remarried, Clem did not get along with his stepfather. When he was 16, his mother gave him enough cattle and horses to get started as a rancher, as well as two slaves (the Cherokee had adopted slavery along with other customs of their white Georgia neighbors).

Under Cherokee law, anyone could occupy and use any tribal land not already being used by another person; Clem settled in Cooweescoowee County, 30 miles south of the Kansas border. There he married Mary America Schrimsher, who was also part Cherokee.

When the Civil War broke out, Clem Rogers joined the Cherokee Mounted Rifles, a Confederate regiment commanded by Chief Stand Watie, one of the signers of the treaty in which the Cherokee had agreed to leave Georgia. He took part in a series of raids and engagements along the Kansas border and emerged from the war a captain.

When he returned from the war, Rogers found his ranch run down, his cattle missing. Of course his slaves were now free. He began anew, first as a laborer, then transporting freight by wagon from Missouri to Texas. With profits from this business he bought cattle and began ranching again. Gradually he extended his holdings of cattle. Reportedly he was the first rancher in the district to fence his land with barbed wire. By 1875 he had a substantial seven-room house with great stone chimneys surrounded by a white picket fence that enclosed Mary America's impressive flower gardens. He was also said to own the only piano in the county. The cowboys Rogers hired to work his cattle lived in a bunkhouse behind his home.

Clem Rogers was tough, shrewd, and ambitious. He was also something of a character. While his son Will was still learning to talk he taught him a number of "cuss words" and trained the baby to let loose with them when Clem snatched his bottle out of his mouth. He continued to prosper, buying cattle in Texas, fattening them on his ranch, and then sending them off, several thousand head each year, to the slaughterhouses of St. Louis. He also raised fine horses and grew substantial amounts of corn and wheat.

By the late 1880s, however, the same forces that were putting an end to open range ranching on the northern plains were also affecting Indian

Beaver City, ca. 1890

Territory. In 1889 the Missouri Pacific Railroad laid track directly across land Rogers had been using for grazing and fenced its right of way with wire. This cut Rogers off from half the natural feed he needed to maintain his operation. At the same time the federal government opened a large section of the Territory to white homesteaders, who poured in by the thousands. Almost two million acres were claimed by these "Boomers" in a single day.

Rogers responded by shifting more of his land from cattle to wheat. He also improved his herds by replacing Texas longhorns with shorthorn steers. These required more care, but they produced greater amounts of higher quality beef. In 1895 he sold out, moved to Claremore, Oklahoma, and became vice president of a bank. He was also involved in politics, being a power in Cherokee affairs. In 1907 he was a delegate to the convention that drafted the state's constitution when Oklahoma was admitted to the Union.

The same forces that influenced the career of Clem Rogers affected in a somewhat different way the career of a young lawyer named George W. Norris. Norris, born in 1861, grew up on a farm in Ohio, taught school for a year, and then earned a law degree at what later became Valparaiso University in Indiana. In 1885 he moved to Beaver City, a farm town in southwestern Nebraska, to open an office.

That part of the country was booming. There was plenty of rain in western Nebraska and Kansas and the corn crop was enormous. Beaver City had only about a thousand residents but it was growing fast and prospering because of the business of the farmers of the region. It had two newspapers and two banks. A high school and a court house had been built recently. There was a flour mill and even a hotel.

Norris rented two rooms in a building near the court house, one to serve as his office, the other as his living quarters. At first he did not have much legal business and took on all sorts of jobs to earn money. He became an agent for the banks and for individuals interested in lending money to farmers and local businessmen. He also sold life insurance, and even applied for a job selling typewriters, but the manufacturer of this recently perfected invention turned him down for the understandable reason that he did not know how to type.

Norris's law practice gradually developed, a high point coming when the Burlington and Missouri Railroad made him its local attorney. He began to acquire farm properties, and he put up a two-story building in town, renting space to the Furnas County Bank and other businesses. He took another big step up the economic and social ladder when he married Pluma Lashley, daughter of Beaver City's leading businessman. When the elder Lashley died shortly thereafter, he left the Norrises the town flour mill.

However, western Nebraska was ravaged by drought in the early 1890s and the dry cycle had a crushing effect on farmers and most local enterprises. Norris's moneylending business shrank to almost nothing. The Furnas County Bank and other tenants of his office building failed. He avoided losing the flour mill only by borrowing money from friends.

In this situation he turned to politics merely to earn a living. In 1892 he was elected prosecuting attorney of the county on the Republican ticket; in 1895 district judge; in 1902 member of Congress.

After five terms in the House of Representatives, Norris was elected to the Senate, a place he was to hold for the next 30 years.

An Industrial Giant

You know how often I had not an unbroken night's sleep, worrying about how it was ail coming out. All the fortune I have made has not served to compensate for the anxiety of that period. . . . If I had foreseen the future I doubt whether I would have had the courage to go on.

JOHN D. ROCKEFELLER

Our organization does not consist of idealists. . . . I look first to cigars.

ADOLPH STRASSER, *president of the Cigar Makers Union, 1883*

hen the Civil War began, the country's industrial output, though important and increasing, did not approach that of the major European powers. By the end of the century the United States had become far and away the colossus among world manufacturers, dwarfing the production of Great Britain and Germany. The world had never seen such rapid economic growth. Modern economists estimate that the output of goods and services in the country (the gross national product, or GNP) increased by 44 percent between 1874 and 1883 and continued to expand in succeeding years. This growth was not confined to the Northeast. Wisconsin, for example, underwent a major transformation between 1873 and 1893; an economy based on grain and lumber became a mainly urban-centered industrial economy.

Industrial Growth: An Overview

American manufacturing flourished for many reasons. New natural resources were discovered and exploited steadily, thereby increasing opportunities. These opportunities in turn attracted the brightest and most energetic of a vigorous and expanding population. The growth of the country added constantly to the size of the national market, and protective tariffs shielded that market from foreign competition. Yet foreign capital entered the market freely, in part because tariffs kept out so many foreign goods. The dominant spirit of the time encouraged businessmen to maximum effort by emphasizing progress, glorifying material wealth, and justifying aggressiveness. European immigrants provided the additional labor needed by expanding industry; 2.5 million arrived in the 1870s, twice that number in the 1880s.

It was a period of rapid advances in basic science, and technicians created a bountiful harvest of new machines, processes, and power sources that increased productivity in many industries and created new industries as well. In agriculture there were what one contemporary expert called "an endless variety of cultivators," better harvesters and binding machines, and combines capable of threshing and bagging 450 pounds of grain a minute. An 1886 report of the Illinois Bureau of Labor Statistics claimed that "new machinery has displaced fully 50 percent of the muscular labor formerly required to do a given amount of work in the manufacture of agricultural implements."

As a result of improvements in the milling of grain, packaged cereals appeared on the American breakfast table. The commercial canning of food, spurred by the "automatic line" canning factory, expanded so rapidly that by 1887 a writer in *Good Housekeeping* magazine could say: "Housekeeping is getting to be ready made, as well as clothing." The Bonsack cigarette-rolling machine created a new industry that changed the habits of millions. George B. Eastman created another with his development of mass-produced roll photographic film and the simple but efficient Kodak camera. The perfection of the typewriter by the Remington company in the

1880s revolutionized the way office work was performed.

Railroads: The First Big Business

In 1866, returning from his honeymoon in Europe, 30-year-old Charles Francis Adams, Jr., grandson and great-grandson of presidents, full of ambition and ready, as he put it, to confront the world "face to face," looked about in search of a career. "Surveying the whole field," he later explained, "I fixed on the railroad system as the most developing force and the largest field of the day, and determined to attach myself to it." Adams's judgment was acute: For the next 25 years the railroads were probably the most significant element in American economic development, railroad executives the most powerful people in the country.

Railroads were important first as an industry in themselves. Less than 35,000 miles of track existed when Lee laid down his sword at Appomattox. In 1875 railroad mileage exceeded 74,000 and the skeleton of the network was complete. Over the next two decades the skeleton was fleshed out. In 1890 the mature but still growing system took in over $1 billion in passenger and freight revenues. (The federal government's income in 1890 was only $403 million.) The value of railroad properties and equipment was more than $8.7 billion. The national railroad debt of $5.1 billion was almost five times the national debt of $1.1 billion! By 1900 the nation had 193,000 miles of track.

The emphasis in railroad construction after 1865 was on organizing integrated systems. The lines had high fixed costs: taxes, interest on their bonds, maintenance of track and rolling stock, salaries of office personnel. A short train with half-empty cars required nearly as many workers and as much fuel to operate as a long one jammed with freight or passengers. To earn profits, the railroads had to carry as much traffic as possible. They therefore spread out feeder lines to draw business to their main lines the way the root network of a tree draws water into its trunk.

Before the Civil War, as we have seen, passengers and freight could travel by rail from beyond Chicago and St. Louis to the Atlantic Coast, but only after the war did true interregional trunk lines appear. In 1861, for example, the New York Central ran from Albany to Buffalo. One could proceed from Buffalo to Chicago, but on a different company's trains. In 1867 the Central passed into the hands of "Commodore" Cornelius Vanderbilt, who had made a large fortune in the shipping business. Vanderbilt already controlled lines running from Albany to New York City; now he merged these properties with the Central. In 1873 he integrated the Lake Shore and Michigan Southern into his empire, and two years later the Michigan Central. At his death in 1877 the Central operated a network of over 4,500 miles of track between New York City and most of the principal cities of the Middle West.

While Vanderbilt was putting together the New York Central complex, Thomas A. Scott was fusing roads to Cincinnati, Indianapolis, St. Louis, and Chicago to his Pennsylvania Railroad, which linked Pittsburgh and Philadelphia. In 1871 the Pennsylvania obtained access to New York; soon it reached Baltimore and Washington. By 1869 another important system, the Erie, extended from New York to Cleveland, Cincinnati, and St. Louis. Soon thereafter it too tapped the markets of Chicago and other cities. In 1874 the Baltimore and Ohio also obtained access to Chicago.

The transcontinentals were trunk lines from the start; the emptiness of the western country would have made short lines unprofitable, and builders quickly grasped the need for direct connections to eastern markets and thorough integration of feeder lines.

The dominant system builder of the Southwest was Jay Gould, a soft-spoken, unostentatious-looking man who was in fact ruthless, cynical, and aggressive. Another railroad president once called Gould a "perfect eel." Gould took over the Kansas Pacific, running from Denver to Kansas City, and consolidated it with the Union Pacific and the Missouri Pacific, a line from Kansas City to St. Louis. Often he put together such properties merely to unload them on other railroads at a profit, but his grasp of the importance of integration was sound.

In the Northwest, Henry Villard, a German-born ex-newspaperman, constructed another great complex based on his control of the Northern Pacific. James J. Hill controlled the Great Northern system, still another western network.

The Civil War had highlighted the need for through railroad connections in the South. Shortly

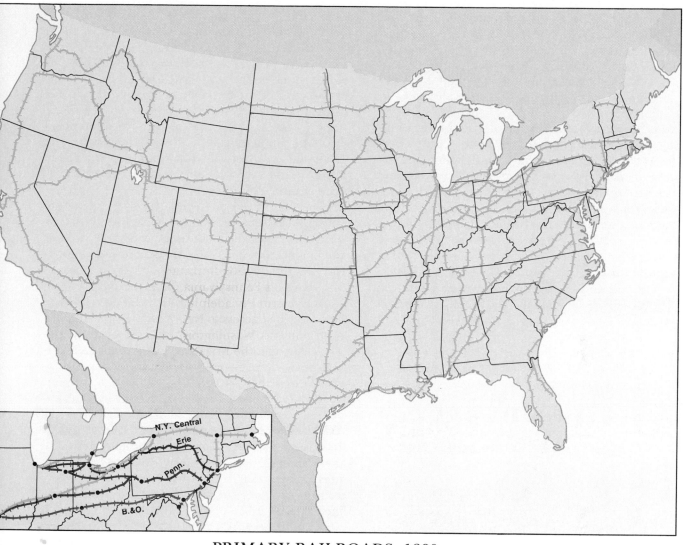

PRIMARY RAILROADS, 1890

By 1890 trunk lines spanned the country, supplemented by networks of smaller feeder lines. The inset shows the trunk lines of four major companies that dominated rail service in the Northeast and linked up with western lines at Chicago and St. Louis.

after the conflict the Chesapeake and Ohio opened a direct line from Norfolk, Virginia, to Cincinnati. By the late 1880s, the Richmond and West Point Terminal Company controlled an 8,558-mile network. Like other southern trunk lines such as the Louisville and Nashville and the Atlantic Coast Line, this system was controlled by northern capitalists.

The trunk lines interconnected and thus had to standardize many of their activities. This in turn led to the standardization of other aspects of life. The present system of time zones was developed in 1883 by the roads. The standard track gauge (4 feet 8½ inches) was established in 1886. Standardized car-coupling and braking mechanisms, standard signal systems, even standard methods of accounting were essential to the effective functioning of the network.

The lines sought to work out fixed rates for carrying different types of freight, charging more for valuable manufactured goods than for bulky products like coal or wheat, and they agreed to permit rate concessions to shippers when necessary to avoid hauling empty cars. In other words, they charged what the traffic would bear. However, by the 1880s the men who ran the railroads had come to recognize the advantages of cooperating with one another in order to avoid "senseless" competition. Railroad management was becoming a kind of profession, with certain standard ways of doing things, even with its own professional journals and with regional organizations such as the Eastern Trunk Line Association and the Western Traffic Association.

The railroads stimulated the economy indirectly. Like foreign commerce and the textile industry in

Widely distributed circular encouraging easterners to migrate to Iowa and Nebraska in 1873. Such advertisements were not noted for their accuracy.

earlier times, they served as a "multiplier," speeding development. In 1869 they bought $41.6 million worth of cars and locomotives; in 1889, $90.8 million. Their purchases created thousands of jobs and led to countless technological advances.

Because of their voracious appetite for traffic, railroads in sparsely settled regions and in areas with undeveloped resources devoted much money and effort to stimulating local economic growth. The Louisville and Nashville, for instance, was a prime mover in the expansion of the iron industry in Alabama in the 1880s.

To speed the settlement of new regions, the land-grant railroads sold land cheaply and on easy terms, for sales meant future business as well as current income. They offered reduced rates to travelers interested in buying farms and set up "bureaus of immigration" that distributed elaborate brochures describing the wonders of the new country. Their agents greeted immigrants at the eastern ports and tried to steer them to railroad property. They sent agents who were usually themselves immigrants—often ministers—all over Europe to recruit prospective settlers.

Technological advances in railroading accelerated economic development in complex ways. In 1869 George Westinghouse invented the air brake. By enabling an engineer to apply the brakes to all cars simultaneously (formerly each car had to be braked separately by its own conductor or brakeman), this invention made possible revolutionary increases in the size of trains and the speed at which they could operate safely. The sleeping car, invented in 1864 by George Pullman, now came into its own.

To pull the heavier trains, more powerful locomotives were needed. They in turn produced a call for stronger and more durable rails to bear the additional weight. Steel, itself reduced in cost because of technological developments, supplied the answer, for steel rails outlasted iron many times despite the use of much heavier equipment.

A close tie developed between the railroads and the nation's telegraph network, dominated by the Western Union Company. Commonly the roads allowed Western Union to string wires along their rights of way, and they transported telegraphers and their equipment without charge. In return they received free telegraphic service, important for efficiency and safety.

Iron, Oil, and Electricity

The transformation of iron manufacturing affected the nation almost as much as railroad development. Output rose from 920,000 tons in 1860 to 10.3 million tons in 1900, but the big change came in the development of ways to mass-produce steel. In its pure form (wrought iron) the metal is tough but relatively soft. Ordinary cast iron, which contains large amounts of carbon and other impurities, is hard but brittle. Steel, which contains 1 or 2 percent carbon, combines the hardness of cast iron with the toughness of wrought iron. For nearly every purpose—structural girders for bridges and buildings,

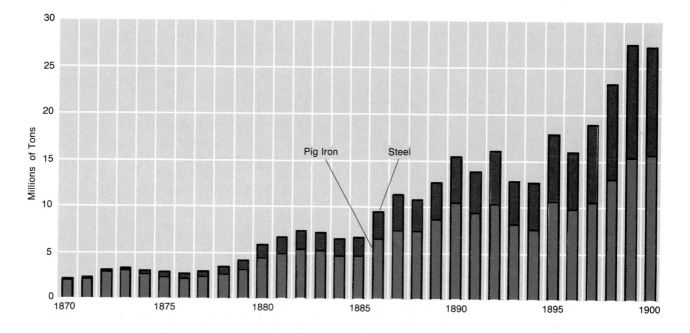

Minnesota's Mesabi Range (shown in 1899) was developed largely with Rockefeller money. It shipped 4,000 tons of iron ore in 1892 and within a decade tripled that amount—an increase reflected in the graph.

railroad track, machine tools, boiler plate, barbed wire—steel is immensely superior to other kinds of iron.

But steel was so expensive to manufacture that it could not be used for bulky products until the invention in the 1850s of the Bessemer process, perfected independently by Henry Bessemer, an Englishman, and William Kelly of Kentucky. Bessemer and Kelly discovered that a stream of air directed into a mass of molten iron caused the carbon and other impurities to combine with oxygen and burn off. When measured amounts of carbon, silicon, and manganese were then added, the brew became steel. What had been a rare metal could now be produced by the hundreds and thousands of tons. The Bessemer process and the open-hearth method, a slower but more precise technique that enabled producers to sample the molten mass and thus control quality closely, were introduced commercially in the 1860s. In 1870 77,000 tons of steel were manufactured. Such growth would have been impossible but for the huge supplies of iron ore in the United States and the coal necessary to fire the furnaces that refined it. In the 1870s the great iron fields rimming Lake Superior began to yield their treasures. The enormous iron concentrations of the Mesabi region made a compass needle spin like a top. Mesabi ores could be mined with steam shovels, almost like gravel.

Pittsburgh, surrounded by vast coal deposits, became the iron and steel capital of the country, the Minnesota ores reaching it by way of steamers on the Great Lakes and rail lines from Cleveland. Other cities in Pennsylvania and Ohio were important producers, and a separate complex, centering on Birmingham, Alabama, developed to exploit local iron and coal fields.

The petroleum industry expanded even more spectacularly than iron and steel. Edwin L. Drake drilled the first successful well in Pennsylvania in 1859. During the Civil War production ranged between 2 million and 3 million barrels a year. By 1890 the figure had leaped to about 50 million barrels.

Before the invention of the gasoline engine and the automobile, the most important petroleum product was kerosene, which was burned in lamps. Refiners heated crude oil in large kettles and, after the volatile elements had escaped, condensed the kerosene in coils cooled by water. The heavier petroleum tars were discarded.

Technological advances came rapidly. By the early 1870s, refiners had learned how to "crack" petroleum by applying high temperatures to the crude in order to rearrange its molecular structure, thereby increasing the percentage of kerosene yielded. By-products such as naphtha, gasoline (used in vaporized form as an illuminating gas), rhigolene (a local anesthetic), cymogene (a coolant for refrigerating machines), and many lubricants and waxes began to appear on the market. At the same time a great increase in the supply of crude oil drove prices down, especially after the German-born chemist Herman Frasch perfected a method for removing sulfur from low-quality petroleum.

These circumstances put a premium on refining efficiency. Larger plants that used expensive machinery and employed skilled technicians became more important. In the mid-1860s only three refineries in the country could process 2,000 barrels of crude a week; a decade later plants capable of handling 1,000 barrels a day were common.

Two other important new industries were the telephone and electric light businesses. Both were typical of the period, being products of technical advances and intimately related to the growth of a high-speed, urban civilization that put great stress on communication. The telephone was invented in 1876 by Alexander Graham Bell, who had been led to the study of acoustics through his interest in the education of the deaf. The invention soon proved its practical value. By 1900 there were almost 800,000 phones in the country, twice the total for all Europe. The American Telephone and Telegraph Company, a consolidation of over 100 local systems, dominated the business.

When Western Union realized the importance of the telephone, it tried for a time to compete with Bell by developing a machine of its own. The man it commissioned to devise this machine was Thomas A. Edison, but Bell's patents proved unassailable. Edison had already made a number of contributions toward solving what he called the "mysteries of electrical force," including a multiplex telegraph capable of sending four messages over a single wire at the same time. At Menlo Park, New Jersey, he built the prototype of the modern research laboratory, where specific problems could be attacked

Edison patented the phonograph in 1878, budgeting $18 for its invention. He was photographed in his laboratory on June 16, 1888, at 5:30 A.M., working on a wax cylinder model.

on a mass scale by a team of trained specialists. During his lifetime he took out more than 1,000 patents, covering machines as varied as the phonograph, the motion picture projector, the storage battery, and the mimeograph.

Edison's most significant achievement was the incandescent lamp, or electric light bulb. Others before Edison had experimented with the idea of producing light by passing electricity through a filament in a vacuum. Always, however, the filaments quickly burned out. Edison tried hundreds of fibers before producing, in 1879, a carbonized filament that would glow brightly in a vacuum tube for as long as 170 hours without crumbling. At Christmastime he decorated the grounds about his laboratory with a few dozen of the new lights. People flocked by the thousands to see this miracle of the "Wizard of Menlo Park." The inventor boasted that soon he would be able to illuminate entire towns, even great cities like New York.

He was true to his promise. In 1882 his Edison Illuminating Company opened a power station in New York and began to supply current for lighting to 85 consumers, including *The New York Times* and the banking house of J. P. Morgan and Company. Soon central stations were springing up everywhere until, by 1898, there were about 3,000 in the country.

The substitution of electric for steam power in factories was as liberating as steam for waterpower before the Civil War. Small, safe electric motors replaced dangerous and cumbersome mazes of belts and wheels. The electric power industry expanded rapidly. By the early years of the 20th century almost 6 billion kilowatt-hours of electricity were being produced annually. Yet this was only the beginning.

Competition and Monopoly: The Railroads

During the post–Civil War era, expansion in industry went hand in hand with concentration. The principal cause of this trend, aside from the obvious economics resulting from large-scale production and the growing importance of expensive machinery, was the downward trend of prices after 1873. The deflation, which resulted mainly from the failure of the money supply to keep pace with the rapid increase in the volume of goods produced, affected agricultural goods as well as manufactures, and it lasted until 1896 or 1897.

Contemporaries believed they were living through a "great depression." That label is misleading, for output expanded almost continuously, and at a rapid rate, until 1893, when production slumped and a true depression struck the country. Falling prices, however, kept a steady pressure on profit margins, and this led to increased production and thus to intense competition for markets. According to economists, competition advanced the public interest by keeping prices low and assuring the most efficient producer the largest profit. Up to a point, it accomplished these purposes in the years after 1865, but it also caused side effects that injured both the economy and society as a whole. Railroad managers, for instance, found it impossible to enforce "official" rate schedules and maintain their regional associations once competitive pressures mounted. In 1865 it had cost from 96 cents to $2.15 per 100 pounds, depending on the class of freight, to ship goods from New York to Chicago. In 1888 rates ranged from 35 cents to 75 cents.

Competition cut deeply into railroad profits, causing the lines to seek desperately to increase volume. They did so chiefly by reducing rates still more, on a selective basis. They gave rebates (secret reductions below the published rates) to large shippers in order to capture their business. The granting of discounts to those who shipped in volume made economic sense: It was easier to handle freight in carload lots than in smaller units. So intense was the battle for business, however, that the roads often made concessions to big customers far beyond what the economics of bulk shipment justified. In the 1870s the New York Central regularly reduced the rates charged important shippers by 50 to 80 percent. One large Utica dry goods merchant received a rate of 9 cents while others paid 33 cents. Two big New York City grain merchants paid so little that they soon controlled the grain business of the entire city.

Railroad officials disliked rebating but found no way to avoid the practice. "Notwithstanding my horror of rebates," the president of a New England trunk line told one of his executives in discussing the case of a brick manufacturer, "bill at the usual rate, and rebate Mr. Cole 25 cents a thousand." In extreme cases the railroads even gave large shippers drawbacks, which were rebates on the business of the shippers' competitors! Besides rebating, railroads issued passes to favored shippers, built sidings at the plants of important companies without charge, and gave freely of their landholdings to attract businesses to their territory. "The force of competition," a railroad man explained, "is one that no carrying corporation can withstand and before which the managing officers of a corporation are

helpless." James F. Joy of the Chicago, Burlington, and Quincy made the same point more bluntly: "Unless you prepare to defend yourselves," he advised the president of the Michigan Central, "you will be boarded by pirates in all quarters." A person trying to run a railroad honestly, wrote Charles Francis Adams, Jr., in *Railroads: Their Origin and Problems* (1879), would be like Don Quixote tilting at a windmill.

To make up for losses forced on them by competitive pressures, railroads charged higher rates at way points along their tracks where no competition existed. Frequently it cost more to ship a product a short distance than a longer one. Rochester, New York, was served only by the New York Central. In the 1870s it cost 30 cents to transport a barrel of flour from Rochester to New York City, a distance of 350 miles. At the same time flour could be shipped from Minneapolis to New York, a distance of well over 1,000 miles, for only 20 cents a barrel. One Rochester businessman told a state investigating committee that he could save 18 cents a hundredweight by sending goods to St. Louis by way of New York, where several carriers competed for the traffic, even though, in fact, the goods might come back through Rochester over the same tracks on the way to St. Louis!

Although cheap transportation stimulated the economy, few people benefited from cutthroat competition. Small shippers—and all businessmen in cities and towns with limited rail outlets—suffered; railroad discrimination speeded the concentration of industry in large corporations located in major centers. The instability of rates even troubled interests like the middle western flour millers who benefited from the competitive situation, for it hampered planning. Nor could manufacturers who received rebates be entirely happy, since few could be sure that some other producer was not getting a larger reduction.

Probably the worst sufferers were the roads themselves. The loss of revenue resulting from rate cutting, combined with inflated debts, put most of them in grave difficulty when faced with a downturn in the business cycle. In 1876 two-fifths of all railroad bonds were in default; three years later 65 lines were bankrupt. Wits called Samuel J. Tilden, the 1876 Democratic presidential candidate, the "Great Forecloser" because of his work reorganizing bankrupt railroads at this time.

Edward Steichen's memorable photograph of J. Pierpont Morgan, taken in 1906. Looking the formidable Morgan in the eye, Steichen said, was like facing the headlights of an onrushing express train.

bankers as Kuhn, Loeb of New York and Lee, Higginson of Boston. The economic historian A. D. Noyes described in 1904 what the bankers did:

> Bondholders were requested to scale down interest charges, receiving new stock in compensation, while the shareholders were invited to pay a cash assessment, thus providing a working fund. [The bankers] combined to guarantee that the requisite money should be raised. They too were paid in new stock. . . . Though the total capital issues were increased, fixed charges were diminished and a sufficient fund for road improvement and new equipment was provided.

Critics called the reorganizations "Morganizations." Representatives of the bankers sat on the board of every line they saved, and their influence was predominant. They consistently opposed rate wars, rebating, and other competitive practices. In effect, control of the railroad network became centralized, even though the companies maintained their separate existences and operated in a seemingly independent manner. When Morgan died in 1913, "Morgan men" dominated the boards of the New York Central; the Erie; the New York, New Haven and Hartford; the Southern; the Père Marquette; the Atchison, Topeka and Santa Fe; and many other lines.

Competition and Monopoly: Steel

The iron and steel industry was also intensely competitive. Despite the trend toward higher production, demand varied erratically from year to year, even from month to month. In good times producers built new facilities, only to suffer heavy losses when demand declined. The forward rush of technology put a tremendous emphasis on efficiency; expensive plants quickly became obsolete. Improved transportation facilities allowed manufacturers in widely separated places to compete with one another.

The kingpin of the industry was Andrew Carnegie. Carnegie was born in Scotland, and came to the United States in 1848 at the age of 12. His first job, as a bobbin boy in a cotton mill, brought him $1.20 a week, but his talents fitted the times perfectly, and he rose rapidly: to Western Union mes-

Since the public would not countenance bankrupt railroads going out of business, these companies were placed in the hands of court-appointed receivers. The receivers, however, seldom provided efficient management and had no funds at their disposal for new equipment.

During the 1880s the major roads responded to these pressures by building or buying lines in order to create interregional systems. These were the first giant corporations, capitalized in the hundreds of millions of dollars. Their enormous cost led to another wave of bankruptcies when a true depression struck in the 1890s.

The consequent reorganizations brought most of the big systems under the control of financiers, notably J. Pierpont Morgan, and such other private

senger boy, to telegrapher, to private secretary, to railroad manager. He saved his money, made some shrewd investments, and by 1868 had an income of $50,000 a year.

At about this time he decided to specialize in the iron business. Carnegie possessed great talent as a salesman, boundless faith in the future of the country, an uncanny knack for choosing topflight subordinates, and enough ruthlessness to survive in the iron and steel jungle. Where other steelmen built new plants in good times, he preferred to expand in bad times, when it cost far less to do so. During the 1870s, he later recalled, "many of my friends needed money. . . . [I] bought out five or six of them. That is what gave me my leading interest in this steel business."

Carnegie grasped the importance of technological improvements. Slightly skeptical of the Bessemer process at first, once he became convinced of its practicality, he adopted it enthusiastically. In 1875 he built the J. Edgar Thomson Steel Works, named after a president of the Pennsylvania Railroad, his biggest customer. He employed chemists and other specialists and was soon making steel from iron oxides that other manufacturers had discarded as waste. He was a merciless competitor. When a plant manager announced, "We broke all records for making steel last week," Carnegie replied, "Congratulations! Why not do it every week?" Carnegie sold rails by paying "commissions" to railroad purchasing agents, and he was not above reneging on a contract if he thought it profitable and safe to do so.

By 1890 the Carnegie Steel Company dominated the industry, and its output increased nearly tenfold during the next decade. Profits soared. Alarmed by his increasing control of the industry, the makers of finished steel products such as barbed wire and tubing began to combine and to consider entering the primary field. Carnegie, his competitive temper aroused, threatened to turn to finished products himself. A colossal steel war seemed imminent.

However, Carnegie longed to retire in order to devote himself to philanthropic work. He believed that great wealth entailed social responsibilities and that it was a disgrace to die rich. When J. P. Morgan approached him through an intermediary with an offer to buy him out, he assented readily. In 1901 Morgan put together United States Steel, the

Andrew Carnegie in later life. His phenomenal rags-to-riches career was one of the real-life models for Horatio Alger's dime novels on the theme "poor boy makes good."

"world's first billion-dollar corporation." This combination included all the Carnegie properties, the Federal Steel Company (Carnegie's largest competitor), and such important fabricators of finished products as the American Steel and Wire Company, the American Tin Plate Company, and the National Tube Company. Vast reserves of Minnesota iron ore and a fleet of Great Lakes ore steamers were also included. U.S. Steel was capitalized at $1.4 billion, about twice the value of its component properties but not necessarily an overestimation of its profit-earning capacity. The owners of Carnegie Steel received $492 million, of which $250 million went to Carnegie himself.

Competition and Monopoly: Oil

The pattern of fierce competition leading to combination and monopoly is well illustrated by the history of the petroleum industry. Irresistible pressures pushed the refiners into a brutal struggle to dominate the business. Production of crude oil, subject to the uncertainties of prospecting and drilling, fluctuated constantly and without regard for need. In general, output surged far ahead of demand.

By the 1870s the chief oil-refining centers were Cleveland, Pittsburgh, Baltimore, and the New York City area. Of these, Cleveland was the fastest-growing, chiefly because the New York Central and Erie railroads competed fiercely for its oil trade and the Erie Canal offered an alternative route.

The Standard Oil Company of Cleveland, founded in 1870 by a 31-year-old merchant named John D. Rockefeller, emerged as the giant among the refiners. Rockefeller exploited every possible technical advance and employed fair means and foul to persuade competitors either to sell out or to join forces. By 1879 he controlled 90 percent of the nation's oil-refining capacity along with a network of oil pipelines and large reserves of petroleum in the ground.

Standard Oil emerged victorious from the competitive wars because Rockefeller and his associates were the toughest and most imaginative fighters as well as the most efficient refiners in the business. In addition to obtaining from the railroads a 10 percent rebate and drawbacks on its competitors' shipments, Standard Oil cut prices locally to force small independents to sell out or face ruin. Since kerosene was sold in grocery stores, Standard supplied its own outlets with meat, sugar, and other products at artificially low prices to help crush the stores that handled other brands of kerosene. The company employed spies to track down the customers of independents and offer them oil at bargain prices. Bribery was also a Standard practice; the reformer Henry Demarest Lloyd quipped that the company had done everything to the Pennsylvania legislature except refine it. Although a bold planner and a daring taker of necessary risks, Rockefeller was far too orderly and astute to enjoy the free-swinging battles that plagued his industry. Born in an upstate New York village in 1839, he settled in Cleveland in 1855 and became a produce merchant. During the Civil War he invested in a local refinery and by 1865 was engaged full time in the oil business.

Like Carnegie, Rockefeller was an organizer; he knew little about the technology of petroleum. His

A regally attired John D. Rockefeller, astride a barrel from his Standard Oil refinery, his crown encircled by the railroads he controlled. His actual attire was considerably less conspicuous.

forte was meticulous attention to detail: Stories are told of his ordering the number of drops of solder used to seal oil cans reduced from 40 to 39 and of his insisting that the manager of one of his refineries account for 750 missing barrel bungs. Not miserliness but a profound grasp of the economies of large-scale production explains this behavior.

Rockefeller competed ruthlessly not primarily to crush other refiners but to persuade them to join with him, to share the business peaceably and rationally so that all could profit. Competition was obsolescent, he argued, though no more effective competitor than he ever lived.

Having achieved his monopoly, Rockefeller stabilized and structured it by creating a new type of business organization, the trust. Standard Oil was an Ohio corporation, prohibited by state law from owning plants in other states or holding stock in out-of-state corporations. As Rockefeller and his associates took over dozens of companies with facilities scattered across the country, serious legal and managerial difficulties arose. How could these many organizations be integrated with Standard Oil of Ohio?

A rotund, genial little Pennsylvania lawyer named Samuel C. T. Dodd came up with an answer to this question in 1879.* The stock of Standard of Ohio and of all the other companies that the Rockefeller interests had swallowed up was turned over to nine trustees, who were empowered to "exercise general supervision" over all the properties. Stockholders received in exchange trust certificates, on which dividends were paid. This seemingly simple device brought order to the petroleum business. Competition almost disappeared; prices steadied; profits skyrocketed. By 1892 John D. Rockefeller was worth over $800 million.

The Standard Oil Trust was not a corporation. It had no charter, indeed no legal existence at all. For many years few people outside the organization knew that it existed. The form they chose persuaded Rockefeller and other Standard Oil officials that without violating their consciences, they could deny under oath that Standard Oil of Ohio owned or controlled other corporations "directly or indirectly through its officers or agents." The trustees controlled these organizations—and Standard of Ohio too!

After Standard Oil's duplicity was revealed during a New York investigation in 1888, the word *trust,* formerly signifying a fiduciary arrangement for the protection of the interests of individuals incompetent or unwilling to guard them themselves, became a synonym for *monopoly.* However, from the company's point of view, monopoly was not the purpose of the trust—that had been achieved before the device was invented. Centralization of the management of diverse and far-flung operations in the interest of efficiency was its chief function. Standard Oil headquarters in New York became the brain of a complex network where information from salaried managers in the field was collected and digested, where top managerial decisions were made, and

whence orders went out to armies of drillers, refiners, scientists, and salesmen.

Competition and Monopoly: Utilities and Retailing

That utilities such as the telephone and electric lighting industries tended to form monopolies is not difficult to explain, for in such fields competition involved costly duplication of equipment and, particularly in the case of the telephone, loss of service efficiency. However, competitive pressures were strong in the early stages of their development. Since these industries depended on patents, Bell and Edison had to fight mighty battles in the courts with rivals seeking to infringe on their rights. When Edison first announced his electric light, capitalists, engineers, and inventors flocked to Menlo Park. He proudly revealed to them the secrets of his marvelous lamp. Many hurried away to turn this information to their own advantage, thinking the "Wizard" a naive fool. When they invaded the field, the law provided Edison with far less protection than he had expected. "My electric light inventions have brought me no profits, only forty years of litigation," Edison later complained. A patent, he said bitterly, was "simply an invitation to a lawsuit."

The attitude of businessmen toward the rights of inventors and industrial pioneers is illustrated by an early advertisement of the Westinghouse Company:

> We regard it as fortunate that we have deferred entering the electrical field until the present moment. Having thus profited by the public experience of others, we enter ourselves for competition, hampered by a minimum of expense for experimental outlay. . . . In short, our organization is free, in large measure, of the load with which [other] electrical enterprises seem to be encumbered. The fruit of this . . . we propose to share with the customer.

Competition in the electric lighting business raged for some years among Edison, Westinghouse, and another corporation, the Thomson-Houston Electric Company, which was operating 870 central lighting stations by 1890. In 1892 the Edison and Thomson-Houston companies merged, forming General Electric, a $35 million corporation. There-

* The trust formula was not "perfected" until 1882.

The glove counter in Rike's Department Store, Dayton, Ohio, 1893. Ferns on the stairs, ornate wall decorations, and an abundance of help distinguished this store from its bargain-basement competition.

after, General Electric and Westinghouse maintained their dominance in the manufacture of bulbs and electrical equipment as well as in the distribution of electrical power.

The pattern of competition leading to dominance by a few great companies was repeated in many businesses. In life insurance an immense expansion took place after the Civil War, stimulated by the development of a new type of group policy, the "tontine," by Henry B. Hyde of the Equitable Life Company.* High-pressure salesmanship prevailed; agents gave rebates to customers by shaving their own commissions; companies stole "crack" agents from their rivals and raided new territories. They sometimes invested as much as 96 percent of the first year's premiums into obtaining new business. By 1900, after three decades of fierce competition, three giants dominated the industry—Equitable, New York Life, and Mutual Life, each with approximately $1 billion of insurance in force.

In retailing, the period saw the growth of urban department stores. In 1862 Alexander T. Stewart

had built an eight-story emporium in New York City that covered an entire block and employed 2,000 persons. John Wanamaker in Philadelphia and Marshall Field in Chicago headed similar establishments by the 1880s, and there were others. These department stores were run like factories. They advertised heavily, stressing low prices, efficient service, and money-back guarantees. High volume made for large profits. Here is how one of Field's biographers described his methods:

His was a one-price store, with the price plainly marked on the merchandise. Goods were not misrepresented, and a reputation for quality merchandise and for fair and honest dealing was built up. . . . Courtesy toward customers was an unfailing rule. Stocks of goods were bought at wholesale for cash in anticipation of consumer demand and then a demand for them was created.

Americans' Reactions to Big Business

The expansion of industry and its concentration in fewer and fewer hands changed the way many people felt about the role of government in economic and social affairs. The fact that Americans

---

* A tontine policy paid no dividends for a stated period of years. The heirs of a policyholder who died received the face value but no dividends. At the end of the tontine period, survivors collected not only their own dividends but also those of the unfortunates who had died or permitted their policies to lapse. This was psychologically appealing, since it stressed living rather than dying and added an element of gambling to insurance.

disliked powerful governments in general and strict regulation of the economy in particular had never meant that they objected to all government activity in the economic sphere. Banking laws, tariffs, internal-improvement legislation, and the granting of public land to railroads are only the most obvious of the economic regulations enforced in the 19th century by both the federal government and the states. Americans saw no contradiction between government activities of this type and the free enterprise philosophy, for such laws were intended to release human energy and thus increase the area in which freedom could operate. Tariffs stimulated industry and created new jobs, railroad grants opened up new regions for development, and so on. As J. W. Hurst has written in a thought-provoking study, *Law and the Conditions of Freedom in the Nineteenth-Century United States* (1956), the people "resort to law to enlarge the options open to private individual and group energy."

The growth of huge industrial and financial organizations and the increasing complexity of economic relations frightened people yet made them at the same time greedy for more of the goods and services the new society was turning out. To many, the great new corporations and trusts resembled Frankenstein's monster—marvelous and powerful but a grave threat to society. The astute James Bryce described the changes in *The American Commonwealth* (1888):

> Modern civilization . . . has become more exacting. It discerns more benefits which the organized power of government can secure, and grows more anxious to attain them. Men live fast, and are impatient of the slow working of natural laws. . . . There are benefits which the law of supply and demand do not procure. Unlimited competition seems to press too hard on the weak. The power of groups of men organized by incorporation as joint-stock companies, or of small knots of rich men acting in combination, has developed with unexpected strength in unexpected ways, overshadowing individuals and even communities, and showing that the very freedom of association which men sought to secure by law . . . may, under the shelter of the law, ripen into a new form of tyranny.

To some extent public fear of the industrial giants reflected concern about monopoly. If Standard Oil dominated oil refining, it might raise prices inordinately at vast cost to consumers. Charles Francis

Adams, Jr., expressed this feeling in the 1870s: "In the minds of the great majority, and not without reason, the idea of any industrial combination is closely connected with that of monopoly, and monopoly with extortion."

Although in isolated cases monopolists did raise prices unreasonably, generally they did not. On the contrary, prices tended to fall until by the 1890s a veritable "consumer's millennium" had arrived. Far more important in causing resentment was the fear that the monopolists were destroying economic opportunity and threatening democratic institutions. It was not the wealth of tycoons like Carnegie and Rockefeller and Morgan so much as their influence that worried people. In the face of the growing disparity between rich and poor, could republican institutions survive? "The belief is common," wrote Charles Francis Adams's brother Henry as early as 1870, "that the day is at hand when corporations . . . swaying power such as has never in the world's history been trusted in the hands of mere private citizens . . . will ultimately succeed in directing government itself."

Some observers believed either autocracy or a form of revolutionary socialism to be almost inevitable. In 1890 former president Hayes pondered "the wrong and evils of the money-piling tendency of our country, which is changing laws, government, and morals and giving all power to the rich" and decided that he was going to become a "nihilist." Campaigning for the governorship of Texas in 1890, James S. Hogg, a staunch conservative, said: "Within a few years, unless something is done, most of the wealth and talent of our country will be on one side, while arrayed on the other will be the great mass of the people, composing the bone and sinew of this government." John Boyle O'Reilly, a liberal Catholic journalist, wrote in 1886: "There is something worse than Anarchy, bad as that is; and it is irresponsible power in the hands of mere wealth." William Cook, a New York lawyer, warned in *The Corporation Problem* (1891) that "colossal aggregations of capital" were "dangerous to the republic."

These were typical reactions of responsible citizens to the rise of industrial combinations. Less thoughtful Americans sometimes went much further in their hatred of entrenched wealth. In 1900 Eddie Cudahy, son of a prominent member of the Beef Trust, was kidnapped. His captor, Pat Crowe, received $25,000 ransom but was apprehended. Crowe's guilt was clear: "I want to start right by confessing in plain English that I was guilty of the kidnapping," he wrote. Yet a jury acquitted him, presumably on the theory that it was all right to rob a member of the Beef Trust.

As criticism mounted, business leaders rose to their own defense. Rockefeller described in graphic terms the chaotic conditions that plagued the oil industry before the rise of Standard Oil:

> It seemed absolutely necessary to extend the market for oil . . . and also greatly improve the process of refining so that oil could be made and sold cheaply, yet with a profit. We proceeded to buy the largest and best refining concerns and centralized the administration of them with a view to securing greater economy and efficiency.

Carnegie, in an essay published in 1889, insisted that the concentration of wealth was necessary if humanity was to progress, softening this "Gospel of Wealth" by insisting that the rich must use their money "in the manner which . . . is best calculated to produce the most beneficial results for the community." The rich man was merely a trustee for his "poorer brethren," Carnegie said, "bringing to their service his superior wisdom, experience, and ability to administer." Lesser tycoons echoed these arguments.

The voices of the critics were louder if not necessarily more influential. Many clergymen denounced unrestrained competition, which they considered un-Christian. The new class of professional economists (the American Economic Association was founded in 1885) tended to repudiate laissez faire. State aid, Richard T. Ely of Johns Hopkins University wrote, "is an indispensable condition of human progress."

Reformers: George, Bellamy, Lloyd

The popularity of a number of radical theorists reflects public feeling in the period. In 1879 Henry George, a California newspaperman, published *Progress and Poverty*, a forthright attack on the maldistribution of wealth in the United States. George argued that labor was the true and only source of

capital. Observing the speculative fever of the West, which enabled landowners to reap profits merely by holding property while population increased, George proposed a property tax that would confiscate this "unearned increment." The value of land depended on society and should belong to society; allowing individuals to keep this wealth was the major cause of the growing disparity between rich and poor, George believed.

George's "single tax," as others called it, would bring in so much money that no other taxes would be necessary, and the government would have plenty of funds to establish new schools, museums, theaters, and other badly needed social and cultural services. Though the single tax was never adopted, George's ideas attracted enthusiastic attention. Single tax clubs sprang up throughout the nation, and *Progress and Poverty* became a best-seller.

Even more spectacular was the reception afforded *Looking Backward, 2000–1887,* a utopian novel written in 1888 by Edward Bellamy. This book, which sold over a million copies in its first few years, described a future America that was completely socialized, all economic activity carefully planned. Bellamy compared 19th-century society to a lumbering stagecoach on which the favored few rode in comfort while the mass of the people hauled them along life's route. Occasionally one of the toilers managed to fight his way onto the coach; whenever a rider fell from it, he had to join the multitude dragging it along.

Such, Bellamy wrote, was the working of the vaunted American competitive system. He suggested that the ideal socialist state, in which all citizens shared equally, would arrive without revolution or violence. The trend toward consolidation would continue, he predicted, until one monster trust controlled all economic activity. At this point everyone would realize that nationalization was essential.

A third influential attack on monopoly was that of Henry Demarest Lloyd, whose *Wealth Against Commonwealth* appeared in 1894. Lloyd, a journalist of independent means, devoted years to preparing a denunciation of the Standard Oil Company. Marshaling masses of facts and vivid examples of Standard's evildoing, he assaulted the trust at every point. Although in his zeal Lloyd sometimes distorted and exaggerated the evidence to make his indictment more effective—"Every important man

THE AGE OF GIANT ENTERPRISE, 1861–1920

This is the second of three price graphs; the first appeared in Chapter 14, pages 372–373. The price scale on the left axis applies to the blue line. It shows changes in wholesale commodity prices as they vary around the base line/trend line of 100. In the 45 years after 1870, wholesale prices were consistently below par, regardless of the periods of relative prosperity and depression shown by the solid peaks and valleys. The green line, scaled to the right axis, shows as a contrast what the retail price of a dozen eggs was between 1870 and 1920. This line reflects the wholesale price line.

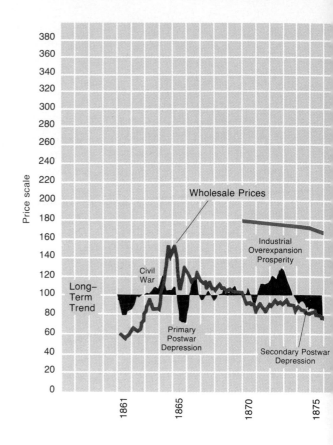

in the oil, coal and many other trusts ought today to be in some one of our penitentiaries," he wrote in a typical overstatement—as a polemic his book was peerless. His forceful but uncomplicated arguments and his copious references to official documents made *Wealth Against Commonwealth* utterly convincing to thousands. The book was more than an attack on Standard Oil. Lloyd denounced the application of Darwin's concept of survival of the fittest to economic and social affairs, and he condemned laissez faire policies as leading directly to monopoly.

The popularity of these books indicates that the trend toward monopoly in the United States worried many people. But despite the drastic changes suggested in their pages, none of these writers questioned the underlying values of the middle-class majority. They insisted that reform could be accomplished without serious inconvenience to any individual or class. In *Looking Backward* Bellamy pictured the socialists of the future gathered around a radiolike gadget in a well-furnished parlor listening to a minister delivering an inspiring sermon.

Nor did most of their millions of readers seriously consider trying to apply the reformers' ideas. Henry George ran for mayor of New York City in 1886 and lost narrowly to Abram S. Hewitt, a wealthy iron manufacturer, but even if he had won, he would have been powerless to apply the single tax to metropolitan property. The national discontent was apparently not as profound as the popularity of these works might suggest. If John D. Rockefeller became the bogeyman of American in-

dustry because of Lloyd's attack, no one prevented him from also becoming the richest man in the United States.

Reformers: The Marxists

By the 1870s the ideas of Marxian socialists were beginning to penetrate the United States, and in 1877 a Marxist Socialist Labor party was founded. Laurence Gronlund in *The Cooperative Commonwealth* (1884) made the first serious attempt to explain to Americans the ideas Marx expressed in *Das Kapital* (*Capital*), not yet translated into English.

Capitalism, Gronlund claimed, contained the seeds of its own destruction. The state ought to own all the means of production. Competition was "Established Anarchy," middlemen were "parasites," and speculators were "vampires." "Capital and Labor," he wrote in one of the rare humorous lines in his book, "are just as harmonious as roast beef and a hungry stomach." Yet like other harsh critics of that day, Gronlund expected the millennium to arrive in a peaceful, orderly manner. The red flag

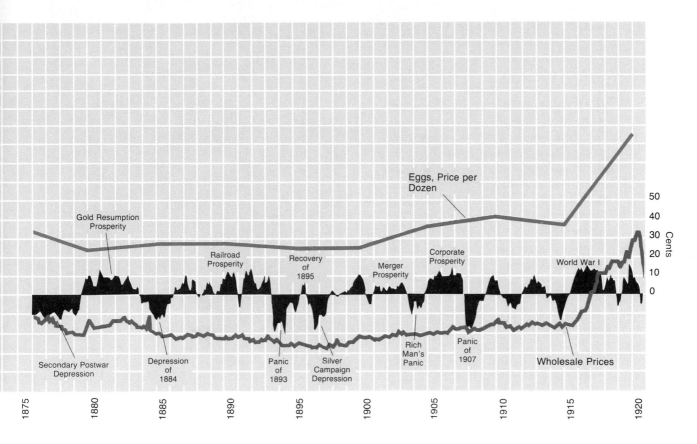

Gold Resumption Prosperity

Eggs, Price per Dozen

Railroad Prosperity

Recovery of 1895

Merger Prosperity

Corporate Prosperity

World War I

Secondary Postwar Depression

Depression of 1884

Panic of 1893

Silver Campaign Depression

Rich Man's Panic

Panic of 1907

Wholesale Prices

Cents
50
40
30
20
10
0

1875 1880 1885 1890 1895 1900 1905 1910 1915 1920

of socialism, he said, "has no relation to blood." The movement could accommodate "representatives of all classes," even "thoughtful" middlemen parasites.

The leading voice of the Socialist Labor party, Daniel De Leon, editor of the party's weekly, *The People,* was a different type. He was born in the West Indies, son of a Dutch army doctor stationed in Curaçao, and educated in Europe. He emigrated to the United States in the 1870s, where he was progressively attracted by the ideas of Henry George, then Edward Bellamy and the Knights of Labor, and finally Marx. Personally mild-mannered and kindly, when he put pen to paper, he became a doctrinaire revolutionary. He excoriated the AFL and the Knights of Labor in *The People*, insisting that industrial workers could improve their lot only by adopting socialism and joining the Socialist Labor party. He paid scant attention, however, to the practical needs or even to the opinions of rank-and-file working people. The labor historian Philip Taft aptly characterized him as a "verbal revolutionary." In 1891 he was the Socialist Labor party's candidate for governor of New York.

Government Reactions to Big Business: Railroad Regulation

Political action related to the growth of big business came first on the state level and dealt chiefly with the regulation of railroads. Even before the Civil War, a number of New England states established railroad commissions to supervise lines within their borders; by the end of the century 28 states had such boards.

Strict regulation was largely the result of agitation by the National Grange of the Patrons of Husbandry. The Grange, founded in 1867 by Oliver H. Kelley, was created to provide social and cultural benefits for isolated rural communities. As it spread and grew in influence—14 states had Granges by 1872, and membership reached 800,000 in 1874—the movement became political too. "Granger" candidates, often not themselves farmers (many local businessmen resented such railroad practices as rebating), won control of a number of state legislatures in the West and the South. Railroad regulation invariably followed, for farmers' eagerness for internal improvements tended to turn to disillusionment after the lines were built. Intense competition might reduce rates between major centers like Chicago and New York and Philadelphia, but most western farm districts were served by only one railroad. In 1877, for example, the freight charges of the Burlington road were almost four times as high west of the Missouri as they were east of the river. It cost less to ship wheat from Chicago to Liverpool, England, than from some parts of the Dakotas to Minneapolis.

Granger-controlled legislatures tried to eliminate this kind of discrimination. The Illinois Granger laws were typical. They established "reasonable" maximum rates and outlawed "unjust" discrimination. The legislature also set up a commission to enforce the laws and punish violators.

The railroads protested, insisting that they were being deprived of property without due process of law. In *Munn* v. *Illinois* (1877), a case that involved a grain elevator whose owner had refused to comply with a state warehouse act, the Supreme Court upheld the constitutionality of this kind of act. Any business that served a public interest, such as a railroad or a grain warehouse, was subject to state control, the justices ruled. Legislatures might fix maximum charges; if the charges seemed unreasonable to the parties concerned, they should direct their complaints to the legislatures or to the voters, not to the courts.

Regulation of the railroad network by the individual states was inefficient, and in some cases the commissions were incompetent and even corrupt. When the Supreme Court, in the Wabash case (1886), declared unconstitutional an Illinois regulation outlawing the long-and-short-haul evil, federal action became necessary. The Wabash, St. Louis and Pacific Railroad had charged 25 cents per 100 pounds for shipping goods from Gilman, Illinois, to New York City and only 15 cents from Peoria, which was 86 miles farther from New York. Illinois judges had held this to be illegal, but the Supreme Court decided that Illinois could not regulate interstate shipments.

Congress filled the gap created by the Wabash decision in 1887 by passing the Interstate Commerce Act. All charges made by railroads "shall be reasonable and just," the act stated. Rebates, drawbacks, the long-and-short-haul evil, and other competitive practices were declared unlawful, and so were their monopolistic counterparts, pools and

A Thomas Nast cartoon ridiculing the willingness of the United States Senate—the "Senatorial Round-House"—to do the bidding of the railroad lobbyists during the debates that led to the Interstate Commerce Act of 1888.

traffic-sharing agreements. Railroads were required to publish schedules of rates and forbidden to change them without due public notice. Most important, the law established the Interstate Commerce Commission (ICC), the first federal regulatory board, to supervise the affairs of railroads, investigate complaints, and issue cease and desist orders when the roads acted illegally.

The Interstate Commerce Act broke new ground, yet it was neither radical nor particularly effective. Its terms were contradictory, some having been designed to stimulate, others to penalize competition. The chairman of the commission soon characterized the law as an "anomaly." It sought, he said, to "enforce competition" at the same time that it outlawed "the acts and inducements by which competition is ordinarily effected."

The new commission had less power than the law seemed to give it. It could not fix rates, only bring the roads to court when it considered rates unreasonably high. Such cases could be extremely complicated; applying the law was "like cutting a path through a jungle." With the truth so hard to determine and the burden of proof on the commission, the courts in nearly every instance decided in favor of the railroads.

State regulatory commissions also fared poorly in the Supreme Court in the last years of the century. Overruling part of their 1877 decision in *Munn* v. *Illinois*, the justices declared in *Chicago, Milwaukee and St. Paul Railroad Company* v. *Minnesota* (1890) that the reasonableness of rates was "eminently a question for judicial investigation." In a Texas case, *Reagan* v. *Farmers' Loan and Trust Company* (1894), the Court held that it had the "power and duty" to decide if rates were "unjust and unreasonable" even when the state legislature itself had established them. Nevertheless, by describing so clearly the right of Congress to regulate private corporations engaged in interstate commerce, the Interstate Commerce Act challenged the philosophy of laissez faire. Later legislation made the commission more effective. The commission also served as the model for a host of similar federal administrative authorities, such as the Federal Communications Commission (1934).

Government Reactions to Big Business: The Sherman Antitrust Act

As with railroad legislation, the first antitrust laws originated in the states, but they were southern and western states with relatively little industry, and most of the statutes were vaguely worded and ill-enforced. Federal action came in 1890 with the passage of the Sherman Antitrust Act. Any combination "in the form of trust or otherwise" that was "in restraint of trade or commerce among the several states, or with foreign nations" was declared illegal. Persons forming such combinations were subject to fines of $5,000 and a year in jail. Individuals and businesses suffering losses because of actions that violated the law were authorized to sue in the federal courts for triple damages.

Where the Interstate Commerce Act sought to outlaw the excesses of competition, the Sherman Act was supposed to restore competition. If businessmen joined together to "restrain" (monopolize) trade in a particular field, they should be punished

and their deeds undone. "The great thing this bill does," Senator George Frisbie Hoar of Massachusetts explained, "is to extend the common-law principle . . . to international and interstate commerce." This was important because the states ran into legal difficulties when they tried to use the common law to restrict corporations engaged in interstate activities.

But the Sherman Act was rather loosely worded—Thurman Arnold, a modern authority, once said that it made it "a crime to violate a vaguely stated economic policy." Critics have argued that the congressmen were more interested in quieting the public clamor for action against the trusts than in actually breaking up any of the new combinations. Quieting the clamor was certainly one of their objectives. However, they were trying to solve a new problem and were not sure how to proceed. A law with teeth too sharp might do more harm than good. Most Americans assumed that the courts would deal with the details, as they always had in common-law matters.

In fact the Supreme Court quickly emasculated the Sherman Act. In *United States* v. *E. C. Knight Company* (1895) it held that the American Sugar Refining Company had not violated the law by taking over a number of important competitors. Although the Sugar Trust now controlled about 98 percent of all sugar refining in the United States, it was not restraining trade. "Doubtless the power to control the manufacture of a given thing involves in a certain sense the control of its disposition," the Court said in one of the greatest feats of judicial understatement of all time. "Although the exercise of that power may result in bringing the operation of commerce into play, it does not control it, and affects it only incidentally and indirectly."

If the creation of the Sugar Trust did not violate the Sherman Act, it seemed unlikely that any other combination of manufacturers could be convicted under the law. In *The History of the Last Quarter Century in the United States* (1896), E. Benjamin Andrews, president of Brown University, delivered a strong indictment of trusts. "The crimes to which some of them resorted to crush out competition were unworthy of civilization," he wrote. Yet he referred only obliquely to the Sherman Act, dismissing it as "obviously ineffectual" and "of little avail."

However, in several cases in 1898 and 1899 the Supreme Court ruled that agreements to fix prices or divide markets did violate the Sherman Act. These decisions precipitated a wave of outright mergers in which a handful of large companies swallowed up hundreds of smaller ones. Presumably mergers were not illegal. When, some years after his retirement, Andrew Carnegie was asked by a committee of the House of Representatives to explain how he had dared to participate in the formation of the U.S. Steel Corporation, he replied: "Nobody ever mentioned the Sherman Act to me, that I remember."

The Union Movement

At the time of the Civil War, only a small percentage of the American work force was organized, and most union members were cigarmakers, printers, carpenters, and other skilled artisans, not factory hands. Aside from ironworkers, railroad workers, and miners, few industrial laborers belonged to unions. Nevertheless, the union was the workers' response to the big corporation: a combination designed to eliminate competition for jobs and to provide efficient organization for labor.

After 1865 the growth of national craft unions, which had been stimulated by labor dissatisfaction during the Civil War, quickened perceptibly. In 1866 a federation of these organizations, the National Labor Union, was founded and by the early 1870s many new trades, notably in railroading, had been unionized.

Most of the leaders of these unions were visionaries who were out of touch with the practical needs and aspirations of workers. They opposed the wage system, strikes, and anything that increased the laborers' sense of being members of the working class. A major objective was the formation of worker-owned cooperatives.

Far more remarkable was the Knights of Labor, a curious organization founded in 1869 by a group of Philadelphia garment workers headed by Uriah S. Stephens. Like so many labor organizers of the period, Stephens was a reformer of wide interests rather than a man dedicated to the specific problems of industrial workers. He, his successor Terence V. Powderly, and many other leaders of the Knights would have been thoroughly at home in the labor organizations of the Jacksonian era. Like the Jacksonians, they supported political objectives that had

A black delegate introduces Terrence V. Powderly at a Knights of Labor convention held in Richmond. At one point the union had some 60,000 black members.

no direct connection with working conditions, such as currency reform and the curbing of land speculation. They rejected the idea that workers must resign themselves to remaining wage earners. By pooling their resources, workingmen could advance up the economic ladder and enter the capitalist class. "There is no good reason," Powderly wrote in his autobiography, *The Path I Trod*, "why labor cannot, through cooperation, own and operate mines, factories, and railroads." The leading Knights saw no contradiction between their denunciation of "soulless" monopolies and "drones" like bankers and lawyers and their talk of "combining all branches of trade in one common brotherhood." Such muddled thinking led the Knights to attack the wage system and to frown on strikes as "acts of private warfare."

If the Knights had one foot in the past, they also had one foot in the future. They supported some startlingly advanced ideas. Rejecting the traditional grouping of workers by crafts, they developed a concept closely resembling modern industrial unionism. They welcomed blacks (though mostly in segregated locals), women, and immigrants, and they accepted unskilled workers as well as artisans. The eight-hour day was one of their basic demands, their argument being that increased leisure would give workers time to develop more cultivated tastes and higher aspirations. Higher pay would inevitably follow.

The growth of the union, however, had little to do with ideology. Stephens had made the Knights a secret organization with an elaborate ritual. Under his leadership, as late as 1879 it had fewer than 10,000 members. Under Powderly, secrecy was discarded. Between 1882 and 1886 successful strikes by local "assemblies" against western railroads, including one against the hated Jay Gould's Missouri Pacific, brought recruits by the thousands. Mem-

An anarchist group printed 20,000 of these bilingual handbills on the day of the Haymarket bombing in Chicago in 1886.

bership passed 42,000 in 1882, hit 110,000 in 1885, and the next year soared beyond 700,000. Alas, sudden prosperity was too much for the Knights. The union's national leadership was unable to control local groups. A number of poorly planned strikes failed dismally, and the public was alienated by sporadic acts of violence and intimidation. Disillusioned recruits began to drift away.

Circumstances largely fortuitous caused the collapse of the organization. By 1886 the movement for the eight-hour day had gained wide support among workers, including many who did not belong to unions. Several hundred thousand (estimates vary) were on strike in various parts of the country by May of that year. In Chicago, a center of the eight-hour movement, about 80,000 workers were involved, and a small group of anarchists was trying to take advantage of the excitement to win support.

When a striker was killed in a fracas at the McCormick Harvesting Machine Company, the anarchists called a protest meeting on May 4, at Haymarket Square. Police intervened to break up the meeting, and someone—whose identity has never been established—hurled a bomb into their ranks. Seven policemen were killed and many others injured.

The American Federation of Labor

Though the anarchists were the immediate victims of the resulting public indignation and hysteria— seven were condemned to death and four eventually executed—organized labor, especially the Knights, suffered heavily. No tie between the Knights and the bombing could be established, but the union had been closely connected with the eight-hour agitation, and the public tended to associate it with violence and radicalism. Its membership declined as suddenly as it had risen, and soon it ceased to exist as a force in the labor movement.

The Knights' place was taken by the American Federation of Labor, a combination of national craft unions established in 1886. In a sense the AFL was a reactionary organization. Its principal leaders, Adolph Strasser and Samuel Gompers of the Cigarmakers Union, were, like the founders of the Knights of Labor, originally interested in utopian social reforms. They even toyed with the idea of forming a workingmen's political party. Experience, however, soon led them to concentrate on organizing skilled workers and fighting for "bread and butter" issues such as higher wages and shorter hours. "Our organization does not consist of idealists," Strasser explained to a congressional committee. "We do not control the production of the world. That is controlled by the employers. . . . I look first to cigars."

The AFL accepted the fact that most workers would remain wage earners all their lives and tried to develop in them a sense of common purpose and pride in their skills and station. Strasser and Gompers paid great attention to building a strong organization of dues-paying members committed to unionism as a way of improving their lot. Rank-and-file AFL members were naturally eager to win wage increases and other benefits, but most also valued their unions for the companionship they provided, the sense of belonging to a group. In other words, despite statements such as Strasser's, unions, in and out of the AFL, were a kind of club as well as a means of defending and advancing their members' material interests.

The chief weapon of the federation was the strike, which it used to win concessions from employers and to attract recruits. Gompers, president of the AFL almost continuously from 1886 until his death in 1924, encouraged workers to make "intelligent use of the ballot" to advance their interests. The federation worked for such things as eight-hour, employers' liability, and mine safety laws, but it avoided direct involvement in politics. "I have my own philosophy and my own dreams," Gompers once told a left-wing French politician, "but first and foremost I want to increase the workingman's welfare year by year. . . . The French workers waste their economic force by their political divisions."

Gompers's approach to labor problems produced solid, if unspectacular, growth for the AFL. Unions with a total of about 150,000 members formed the federation in 1886. By 1892 membership had reached 250,000, and in 1901 it passed the million mark.

Labor Militancy Rebuffed

The stress of the AFL on the strike weapon reflected rather than caused the increasing militancy of labor.

Workers felt themselves threatened from all sides: the growing size and power of their corporate employers, the substitution of machines for human skills, the invasion of foreign workers willing to accept substandard wages. At the same time they had tasted some of the material benefits of industrialization and had learned the advantages of concerted action.

The average employer behaved like a tyrant when dealing with his workers. He discharged them arbitrarily when they tried to organize unions; he hired scabs to break strikes; he frequently failed to provide the most rudimentary protections against injury on the job. Some employers, Carnegie, for example, professed to approve of unions, but almost none would bargain with labor collectively. To do so, they argued, would be to deprive workers of their freedom to contract for their own labor in any way they saw fit.

The industrialists of the period were not all ogres; they were as alarmed by the rapid changes of the times as their workers, and since they had more at stake materially, they were probably more frightened by the uncertainties. Deflation, technological change, and intense competition kept even the most successful under constant pressure.

The thinking of most employers was remarkably confused. They considered workers who joined unions "disloyal," and at the same time they treated labor as a commodity to be purchased as cheaply as possible. "If I wanted boiler iron," Henry B. Stone, a railroad official, explained, "I would go out on the market and buy it where I could get it cheapest, and if I wanted to employ men, I would do the same." Yet Stone was furious when the men he had "bought" joined a union. When labor was scarce, employers resisted demands for higher wages by arguing that the price of labor was controlled by its productivity; when it was plentiful, they justified reducing wages by referring to the law of supply and demand.

Thus capital and labor were often spoiling for a fight, frequently without fully understanding why. When labor troubles developed, they tended to be bitter, even violent. In 1877 a great railroad strike convulsed much of the nation. It began on the Baltimore and Ohio system in response to a wage cut and spread to other eastern lines and then throughout the West until about two-thirds of the railroad mileage of the country had been shut down. Vio-

After the collapse of his American Railway Union in 1897, Eugene V. Debs (shown here addressing a Socialist party gathering) devoted himself to politics.

lence broke out, rail yards were put to the torch, and dismayed and frightened businessmen formed militia companies to patrol the streets of Chicago and other cities. Eventually President Hayes sent federal troops to the trouble spots to restore order, and the strike collapsed. There had been no real danger of revolution, but the violence and destruction of the strike had been without precedent in America.

The disturbances of 1877 were a response to a business slump, those of the next decade a response to good times. Twice as many strikes occurred in 1886 as in any previous year. Even before the Haymarket bombing centered the country's attention on labor problems, the situation had become so disturbing that President Grover Cleveland, in the first presidential message devoted to labor problems, had urged Congress to create a voluntary arbitration board to aid in settling labor disputes—a remarkable suggestion for a man of Cleveland's conservative, laissez faire approach to economic issues.

In 1892 a violent strike broke out among silver miners at Coeur d'Alene, Idaho, and a far more important clash shook Andrew Carnegie's Home-

stead steel plant near Pittsburgh when strikers attacked 300 private guards brought in to protect strikebreakers. Seven guards were killed at Homestead, and the rest were forced to "surrender" and march off ignominiously. The Homestead affair was part of a struggle between capital and labor in the steel industry. The steelmen insisted that the workers were holding back progress by resisting technological advances, while the workers believed that the company was refusing to share the fruits of more efficient operation fairly. The strike was precipitated by the decision of company officials to crush the union at all costs. The final defeat, after a five-month walkout, of the 24,000-member Amalgamated Association of Iron and Steel Workers, one of the most important elements in the AFL, destroyed unionism as an effective force in the steel industry and set back the progress of organized labor all over the country.

As in the case of the Haymarket bombing, the activities of radicals on the fringe of the dispute turned the public against the steelworkers. The boss of Homestead was Henry Clay Frick, a tough-minded foe of unions who was determined to "teach our employees a lesson." Frick made the decision to bring in strikebreakers and to employ Pinkerton detectives to protect them. During the course of the strike, Alexander Berkman, an anarchist, burst into Frick's office and attempted to assassinate him. Frick was only slightly wounded, but the attack brought him much sympathy and unjustly discredited the strikers.

The most important strike of the period took place in 1894. It began when the workers at George Pullman's Palace Car factory outside Chicago walked out in protest against wage cuts. (While reducing wages, Pullman insisted on holding the line on rents in the company town of Pullman; when a delegation called on him to remonstrate, he refused to give in and had three of the leaders fired.) Some Pullman workers belonged to the American Railway Union, headed by Eugene V. Debs. After the strike had dragged along for weeks, the union voted to refuse to handle trains with Pullman cars. The union was perfectly willing to handle mail trains, but the owners refused to run trains unless they were made up of a full complement of cars.

When Pullman cars were added to mail trains, the workers refused to move them. The resulting railroad strike tied up trunk lines running in and out of Chicago. The railroad owners appealed to President Cleveland to send troops to preserve order. On the pretext that the soldiers were needed to ensure the movement of the mails, Cleveland agreed. When Debs defied a federal injunction to end the walkout, he was jailed for contempt, and the strike was broken.

Whither America, Whither Democracy?

Each year more of the nation's wealth and power seemed to fall into fewer hands. As with the railroads, other industries were coming to be influenced, if not completely dominated, by bankers. The firm of J. P. Morgan and Company controlled many railroads; the largest steel, electrical, agricultural machinery, rubber, and shipping companies; two life insurance companies; and a number of banks. By 1913 Morgan and the Rockefeller National City Bank group between them could name 341 directors to 112 corporations worth over $22.2 billion. The "Money Trust," a loose but potent fraternity of financiers, seemed fated to become the ultimate monopoly.

Centralization unquestionably increased efficiency, at least in industries that used a great deal of expensive machinery to turn out goods for the mass market and in those where close coordination of output, distribution, and sales was important. The public benefited immensely from the productive efficiency of the new empires. Living standards rose. But the trend toward giantism raised doubts. With ownership falling into fewer hands, what would be the ultimate effect of big business on American democracy? What did it mean for ordinary people when a few tycoons possessed huge fortunes and commanded such influence even on the Congress and the courts?

The crushing of the Pullman strike demonstrated the power of the courts to break strikes by issuing injunctions. And the courts seemed concerned only with protecting the interests of the rich and powerful. Particularly ominous for organized labor was the fact that the federal government based its request for the injunction that broke the strike on the Sherman Antitrust Act, arguing that the American Railway Union was a combination in restraint of trade. An indirect result of the Pullman strike was that while serving his sentence for con-

tempt, Eugene Debs was visited by a number of prominent socialists who sought to convert him to their cause. One gave him a copy of Karl Marx's *Capital*, which he found too dull to finish, but he did read *Looking Backward* and *Wealth Against Commonwealth*. In 1897 he became a socialist.

Milestones

1859	First oil well drilled in Pennsylvania
1868	Carnegie Steel Company formed
1869	George Westinghouse invents the air brake
	Knights of Labor founded
1870	Standard Oil Company formed
1870–1890	Railroad trunk lines completed
1876	Alexander Graham Bell invents the telephone
1877	Great Railroad Strike
	Munn v. *Illinois* upholds state regulatory laws
1879	Thomas Edison invents the electric light
	Henry George's *Progress and Poverty*
1884	*The Cooperative Commonwealth* by Laurence Gronlund
1886	Haymarket bombing
	American Federation of Labor founded
1887	Interstate Commerce Act
1888	Edward Bellamy's *Looking Backward*
1889	Andrew Carnegie's "Gospel of Wealth"
1890	Sherman Antitrust Act
1892	Homestead strike
	General Electric Company formed
1894	Pullman strike
	Henry Demarest Lloyd's *Wealth Against Commonwealth*
1895	*United States* v. *E. C. Knight Company* weakens Sherman Act
1901	U.S. Steel Corporation formed

SUPPLEMENTARY READING

Titles marked with an asterisk have been published in paperback.

Of works dealing with industrial growth, E. C. Kirkland, **IndustryComes of Age*** (1961), is the best general introduction, but see also Stuart Bruchey, **Growth of the American Economy** (1975). Matthew Josephson, **The Robber Barons*** (1934), is highly critical but provocative. A. D. Chandler, Jr., **The Visible Hand** (1977), covers the way businesses were organized and managed. On technological developments, see H. J. Habakkuk, **American and British Technology in the Nineteenth Century*** (1962), and W. P. Strassmann, **Risk and Technological Innovation** (1959).

On the railroad industry, consult A. D. Chandler, Jr., **Railroads: The Nation's First Big Business** (1965), J. F. Stover, **American Railroads*** (1961), T. C. Cochran, **Railroad Leaders** (1953), and Julius Grodinsky, **Transcontinental Railway Strategy** (1962).

The iron and steel business is discussed in detail in J. F. Wall, **Andrew Carnegie** (1970), and Peter Temin, **Iron and Steel in Nineteenth-Century America** (1964), an economic analysis. On the oil industry, see Carl Solberg, **Oil Power*** (1976), a good survey, and for more detail, H. F. Williamson and A. R. Daum, **The American Petroleum Industry: Age of Illumination** (1959), and Allan Nevins, **Study in Power: John D. Rockefeller** (1953).

The electrical industry is discussed in an excellent study, H. C. Passer, **The Electrical Manufacturers** (1953), and in an equally good biography, Matthew Josephson, **Edison*** (1959). About the telephone, see John Brooks, **Telephone** (1976), and R. V. Bruce, **Alexander Graham Bell** (1973).

Many of these volumes deal with the problems of competition and monopoly. See also, however, Gabriel Kolko, **Railroads and Regulation*** (1965), which is critical of both railroad leaders and government policy. J. D. Rockefeller, **Random Reminiscences of Men and Events** (1909), makes the case for Standard Oil, while H. D. Lloyd, **Wealth Against Commonwealth** (1894), attacks the trust mercilessly.

For discussion of the radical critics, see J. L. Thomas, **Alternative Americas: Henry George, Edward Bellamy, Henry Demarest Lloyd** (1983), H. H. Quint, **The Forging of American Socialism** (1964), L. G. Seretan, **Daniel De Leon: The Odyssey of an American Marxist** (1979), and also the radicals' own writings.

On the growth of unions, see David Montgomery, **Beyond Equality** (1967), G. N. Grob, **Workers and Utopia** (1961), Harold Livesay, **Samuel Gompers and Organized Labor in America** (1978), and Nick Salvatore, **Eugene V. Debs** (1982). The important strikes and labor violence of the period are covered in R. V. Bruce, **1877: Year of Violence** (1959), Paul Arvich, **The Haymarket Tragedy** (1984), Leon Wolff, **Lockout** (1965), and Almont Lindsey, **The Pullman Strike** (1942).

The background of government regulation of industry is treated in Sidney Fine, **Laissez Faire and the General-Welfare State*** (1956), and J. A. Garraty, **The New Commonwealth*** (1968). Other useful volumes include Ari and Olive Hoogenboom, **A History of the ICC*** (1976), H. B. Thorelli, **The Federal Antitrust Policy** (1954), and G. W. Miller, **Railroads and the Granger Laws** (1971).

American Lives:
The Steltzles and the Smiths

New York's Lower East Side

Dora Uhlendorf was the daughter of a baker who had emigrated to New York City from Germany before the Civil War. The family settled on the Lower East Side and developed a prosperous business. When she grew up Dora married John Steltzle, a brewer, but misfortune struck, first when the Steltzle brewery failed, and then when John Steltzle died.

Dora's parents had objected to her marrying Steltzle, so she was determined not to ask them for help. Instead she moved with her five children to cheap quarters on the Lower East Side. There, as her son Charles later recalled, she spent "many years in a hand-to-hand battle with all the horrors of poverty, asking favors of no one."

The family lived in a series of tenements, usually on the top floor where the rent was lowest. Frequently the bedrooms had no outside windows; the only ventilation was a window on a dark hallway, the only running water from a faucet in the hall. Such places were unbearably hot in summer; the Steltzles spent many such nights on the roof. The tenements were also extremely noisy, the din created by crying children, squabbling neighbors, drunks, and children at play.

Dora Steltzle worked day and night in these dingy apartments sewing bathrobes for a local manufacturer for about $2 a dozen, a task that took, on average, three days. "We children soon learned to do a great many things for ourselves, because she was always sewing, sewing, sewing," Charles explained. When the bathrobe business was slow, Dora took in washing. At such times the family subsisted chiefly on stale rolls.

Charles went to school until he was 11, but by the time he was eight he was working too. He earned 50 cents a week stripping tobacco leaves from their stems in a tenement sweatshop, sold newspapers, and peddled oranges and candles door to door. A high point was the summer of 1879, when he got a job in a restaurant. His chief memory of this (perhaps distorted by the passage of many years) involved consuming unfinished portions of cake and ice cream left by departing diners.

Despite its hardships, in later life Charles Steltzle insisted that his boyhood had been a happy one. In summer he and his friends swam in the East River, blissfully ignoring passing ferries. He belonged to a club, "the Orchard Street gang," whose members sat around on old boxes dreaming of "going out West to shoot Indians and eat bear meat." He learned by experience to respect the "human qualities" of the local Tammany Hall politicos, who made it their business to know the social and economic needs of everyone in their district. "The reformers live uptown and . . . seem to be in business for the purpose of taking privileges away from the people, rather than furnishing them with jobs, and coal, and food," he explained. "It is by helping in such matters as these that Tammany Hall gains influence."

Charles Steltzle became a Presbyterian minister, preaching the social gospel and working with slum children and labor groups.

The Steltzles came "down" to the Lower East Side from a better neighborhood. At the same time Alfred E. and Catherine Mulvehill Smith and their three children were also living in the district, but in a part that was far from a slum. Alfred was of German and Italian descent, while Catherine's parents were Irish. Alfred Smith, a Civil War veteran, owned a modest trucking business. The family lived in a comfortable flat near the southern tip of Manhattan Island. Since they were Catholics, the children went to the local

Swimming in the East River

parochial school, which was run by the Christian Brothers order.

In 1886 Alfred Smith died and the family's fortunes turned sharply downward. His widow went to work in an umbrella factory. Two years later, 14-year-old Alfred Jr. had to drop out of school. He went to work as a "chaser," or errand boy, first of a series of such jobs. By the early 1890s he was working in the bustling Fulton Fish Market, supplying restaurants and stores and earning $12 a week.

The Smiths were firm supporters of the Democratic party and of Tammany Hall, the local Democratic machine. In their ward the "boss" was Tom Foley, a big, friendly man with a large black moustache. Young Alfred got to know Foley because he often stopped in at a saloon owned by Foley for a glass of beer. For a time he served as a kind of assistant to the boss, and became one of his most enthusiastic supporters. Later in life he had fond memories of watching the boss walking through the crowded streets of the Lower East Side handing out pennies and nickels to passing children. "When they got a nickel they thought it was Sunday," he recalled.

In 1894 Smith supported Foley in a factional dispute within Tammany and was rewarded with a job serving subpoenas at an annual salary of $800, substantial pay for that time. In 1903 he was elected to the state Assembly, the start of a career that included four terms as governor of New York and the 1928 Democratic presidential nomination.

Fulton's Fish Market in the 1880s

American Society in the Industrial Age

There is in all the past nothing to compare with the rapid changes now going on in the civilized world. . . . Industrial changes imply social changes and necessitate political changes. Progressive societies outgrow institutions as children outgrow clothes.

HENRY GEORGE, Social Problems (*1883*)

T he industrialization that followed the Civil War profoundly affected every aspect of American life. New machines, improvements in transportation and communication, the appearance of the great corporation with its uncertain implications for the future—all made deep impressions on the shape and indeed the very character of American society. The growth of cities and the influx of tens of thousands of immigrants who knew little about urban life and who neither spoke nor understood English had large effects on the lives they led and the world they inhabited.

Middle-Class Life

In so large and diverse a country as the United States, it is hard to generalize about how people lived and worked and how they fared while doing so. Some, as we have just seen, became fabulously wealthy in the new industrial society, in no small part because neither the federal government nor the states taxed their incomes.

Members of the professions and the large and diffuse groups of shopkeepers, small manufacturers, skilled craftsmen, and established farmers that made up the middle class lived in varying degrees of comfort. A family with an annual income of $1,000 in the 1880s would have no need to skimp on food, clothing, or shelter. According to the best modern estimates, about a quarter of the families in the cities employed at least one full-time servant.

In such families, husbands and wives continued to maintain their separate spheres, the men going off to their shops and offices, the women devoting their main energies to caring for (or at least supervising the care of) children and household. Middle-class women maintained the trend toward having fewer children. The children in a family of this type, though treasured, were carefully supervised. Much stress was placed on their being "little ladies and gentlemen," meaning having good manners and doing what their elders told them to do. This was the era of Victorian prudery, so in most families "young people" (today we would call them teenagers) were closely chaperoned when in the company of "members of the opposite sex." Upward-striving parents were much concerned about the status and prospects of their children's marriage partners, but it was no longer considered proper to interfere with the "course of true love" for any materialistic or purely social reason.

Wage Earners

Wage earners felt the full force of the industrial tide in countless ways—some beneficial, others not. As manufacturing and mining became more important, the number of workers in these fields multiplied rapidly: from 885,000 in 1860 to more than 3.2 million in 1890. Though workers lacked much sense of solidarity, they exerted a far greater influence on society at the turn of the century than they had in the years before the Civil War.

More efficient methods of production enabled them to increase their output, making possible a rise in their standard of living. The working day still tended to approximate the hours of daylight, but it was shortening perceptibly by the 1880s in many occupations. In 1860 the average had been

537

11 hours, but by 1880 only one worker in four labored more than ten hours, and radicals were beginning to talk about eight hours as a fair day's work.

This generalization, however, conceals some important differences. Skilled industrial workers—such types as railroad engineers and conductors, machinists, and iron molders—were quite well off in most cases. But unskilled laborers still could not earn enough to maintain a family decently by their own efforts alone.

James H. Ducker's *Men of the Steel Rails*, a study of the work force of the Atchison, Topeka and Santa Fe Railroad, throws much light on working conditions and workers' attitudes at this time. Ordinary track laborers were paid from $1.00 to $1.25 a day, whereas engineers received three times that amount or more. In addition, many of the better-paid workers picked up additional sums, some by legitimate means, such as renting spare rooms to other workers, some by practices ranging from shady to flagrantly criminal.

Railroad management tried to discipline the labor force by establishing rules for each job category, but it had difficulty enforcing them. "There were many schemes to avoid work and evade regulations," Ducker reports. Drunkenness on the job was a constant problem. Many conductors were said to be "color blind," the expression referring not to any physical defect or to their lack of racial prejudice but to their inability to tell the difference between the road's money and their own. Baggage and freight handlers frequently made off with goods ranging from a few cigars or a bottle of whiskey to entire shipments of merchandise. According to Ducker, transient workers, called "boomers," had "a deserved reputation as rowdies who cared more for drink than decorum, cards than church, lust than love." Other workers, of course, were law-abiding, hardworking family men.

Industrialization created problems for workers beyond the obvious one of earning enough money to support themselves. By and large, skilled workers, always better off than the unskilled, improved their positions relatively, despite the increased use of machinery. Furthermore, when machines took the place of human skills, jobs became monotonous. Mechanization undermined both the artisans' pride and their bargaining power vis-à-vis their employers. As expensive machinery became more important, the worker seemed of necessity less important.

Machines more than workers controlled the pace of work and its duration. The time clock regulated the labor force more rigidly than the most exacting foreman. The length of the workday may have declined, but the pace of work and the danger involved in working around heavy, high-speed machinery increased accordingly.

As businesses grew larger, personal contact between employer and hired hand tended to disappear. Relations between them became less human, more businesslike and ruthless. However, large enterprises usually employed a higher percentage of managerial and clerical workers than smaller companies, thus providing opportunities for more blue-collar workers to rise in the industrial hierarchy. But the trend toward bigness made it more difficult for workers to rise from the ranks of labor to become themselves manufacturers, as Andrew Carnegie, for example, had done during the Civil War era.

Another problem for workers was that industrialization tended to accentuate swings of the business cycle. On the upswing, something approaching full employment existed, but in periods of depression, unemployment became a problem that affected workers without regard for their individual abilities. It is significant that the word *unemployment* (though not, of course, the condition itself) was a late-19th-century invention.

Working Women

Women continued to be a significant part of the industrial working force. But now many more of them were working outside their homes; the factory had almost completely replaced the household as the seat of manufacturing. At least half of all working women were domestic servants; textile mills and the "sewing trades" accounted for a large percentage of the rest. But in all fields women were paid substantially lower wages than men.

Women found many new types of work in these years, a fact commented on by *The New York Times* as early as 1869. They made up the overwhelming majority of salespersons and cashiers in the big new department stores. Partly because of the persistence of the "cult of true womanhood" into the postwar era, managers considered women more polite, easier to control, and more honest than male workers, all qualities especially valuable in the huge empo-

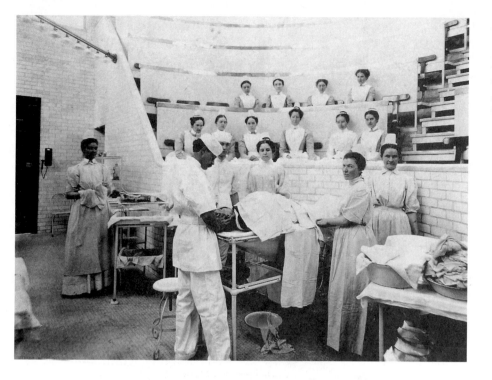

In a society that still believed that the sexes should maintain "separate spheres," the new profession of nursing was viewed as particularly suited to women. Doctoring was reserved for men.

riums. Over half of the more than 1,700 employees in A. T. Stewart's New York store were women.

Educated, middle-class women also dominated the new profession of nursing, which developed alongside the expanding medical profession and the establishment of large urban hospitals. To nearly all doctors, to most men, and indeed to many women of that day, nursing seemed the perfect female profession, since it required the same characteristics that women were thought to have by nature: selflessness, cleanliness, kindliness, tact, sensitivity, and submissiveness to male control. "It seemed obvious," the historian Charles Rosenberg writes in *The Care of Strangers*, "that women were better suited than men to nursing." Typical was this remark of a contemporary authority: "Since God could not care for all the sick, he made women to nurse." Why it had not occurred to the Lord to make more women physicians, or for that matter members of other prestigious professions like law and the clergy, this man did not explain, probably because it had not occurred to him either.

Middle-class women did replace men as teachers in most of the nation's grade schools, and they also replaced men as clerks, secretaries, and operators of the new typewriters in goverment departments and in business offices. Most men with the knowledge of spelling and grammar that these positions required had better opportunities and were uninterested in office work, so women high school graduates, of whom there was an increasing number, filled the gap.

Both department store clerks and "typewriters" (as they were called) earned more money than unskilled factory workers, and working conditions were more pleasant. According to one advertisement of the period, a "Type-Writer" was an ideal Christmas present for "deserving" young women. "No invention has opened for women so broad and easy an avenue to profitable and suitable employment." Opportunities for promotion for women, however, were rare; managerial posts in these fields remained almost exclusively in the hands of men.

Farmers

Long the backbone of American society, independent farmers and the agricultural way of life were rapidly being left behind in the race for wealth and status. The number of farmers and the volume of agricultural production continued to rise, but agriculture's relative place in the national economy was declining. Between 1860 and 1890 the number of farms rose from 2 million to 4.5 million; wheat output leaped from 173 million bushels to 449 million, cotton from 5.3 million bales to 8.5 million. The rural population increased from 25 million to 40.8 million. Yet industry was expanding far faster, and the urban population, quadrupling in the period, would soon overtake and pass that of the countryside.

Along with this relative decline, farmers suffered a decline in status. Compared to middle-class city dwellers, they seemed provincial and behind the times. People in the cities began to refer to farmers as "rubes," "hicks," and "hayseeds" and to view them with bemused tolerance or even contempt.

This combination of circumstances angered and frustrated farmers. Waves of radicalism swept the agricultural regions, giving rise to demands for social and economic experiments that played a major role in breaking down rural laissez faire prejudices. As we have seen, in the 1870s pressure from the Patrons of Husbandry produced legislation regulating railroads and warehouses. This Granger movement also led to many cooperative experiments in the marketing of farm products and in the purchase of machinery, fertilizers, and other goods.

Not all farmers were affected by economic developments in the same way. Because of the steady decline of the price level, those in newly settled regions were usually worse off than those in older areas, since they had to borrow money to get started and were therefore burdened with fixed interest charges that became harder to meet each year. In the 1870s farmers in Illinois and Iowa suffered most, which accounts for the strength of the Granger movement in that region. Except as a purely social organization, the Grange had little importance in the eastern states, where rapidly expanding urban markets made farmers relatively prosperous. A typical eastern farm family raising wheat and other grains and perhaps some livestock worked hard but made a good living. Such a family might employ a neighbor's daughter to help with housework, milking, and similar chores and a hired hand whose work was mainly in the fields.

By the late 1880s farmers in the old Middle West had also become better established. Even when prices dipped and a general depression gripped the country, they were able to weather the bad times nicely by taking advantage of lower transportation costs, better farm machinery, and new fertilizers and insecticides to increase output and by shifting from wheat to the production of corn, oats, hogs, and cattle, which had not declined so drastically in price.

On the agricultural frontier from Texas to the Dakotas, and through the states of the old Confederacy, farmers were less fortunate. The burdens of the crop-lien system kept thousands of southern farmers in penury, while on the plains life was a succession of hardships. The first settlers in western Kansas, Nebraska, and the Dakotas took up land along the rivers and creeks where they found enough timber for home building, fuel, and fencing. Later arrivals had to build houses of the tough prairie sod and depend on hay, sunflower stalks, and buffalo dung for fuel.

Frontier farm families had always had to work hard and endure the hazards of storm, drought, and insect plagues, along with isolation and loneliness. But all these burdens were magnified on the prairies and the high plains. Hamlin Garland, a writer who grew up on a farm in Iowa, described conditions in graphic and moving terms in his autobiography, *A Son of the Middle Border* (1890), and in *Main-Travelled Roads* (1891). Life was particularly hard for farm women, who in addition to child care and housework performed endless farm chores—milking cows, feeding livestock, raising vegetables, and so on. "I . . . am set and running every morning at half-past four o'clock, and run all day, often until half-past eleven P. M.," one farm woman explained. "Is it any wonder I have become slightly demoralized?"

On the plains, women also had to endure drab, cheerless surroundings without the companionship of neighbors or the respites and stimulations of social life. After Hamlin Garland's mother read the grim discussions of women's lot in *Main-Travelled Roads*, she wrote him: "You might have said more, but I'm glad you didn't. Farmers' wives have enough to bear as it is."

Working-Class Family Life

Early social workers who visited the homes of industrial laborers in this period reported enormous

A Minnesota farming family photographed in front of their house in 1895. Winters must have been lonely times on the Northern Plains.

differences in the standards of living of people engaged in the same line of work, differences related to such variables as health, intelligence, the wife's ability as a homemaker, the degree of the family's commitment to middle-class values, and pure luck. Some families spent most of their income on food; others saved substantial sums even when earning no more than $400 or $500 a year. Family incomes varied greatly among workers who received similar hourly wages, depending on the steadiness of employment and on the number of family members holding jobs.

Consider the cases of two Illinois coal miners, each decent, hardworking union men with large families, each earning $1.50 a day in 1883. One was out of work nearly half the year; his income in 1883 was only $250. He, his wife, and their five children, aged 3 to 19, lived in a two-room tenement. They existed almost exclusively on a diet of bread and salt meat. Nevertheless, as an investigator reported, their home was neat and clean, and three of the children were attending school.

The other miner, father of four children, worked full time and brought home $420 in 1883. He owned a six-room house and an acre of land, where the family raised vegetables. Their food bill for the year was more than ten times that of the family just de-

scribed. Two admirable families, probably similar in social attitudes and perhaps in political loyalties, but possessed of very different standards of living.

The cases of two families headed by railroad brakemen provide a different kind of variation. One man brought home only $360 to house and feed a wife and eight children. Here is the report of a state official who interviewed the family: "Clothes ragged, children half-dressed and dirty. They all sleep in one room regardless of sex. . . . The entire concern is as wretched as could be imagined. Father is shiftless. . . . Wife is without ambition or industry."

The other brakeman and his wife had only two children, and he earned $484 in 1883. They owned a well-furnished house, kept a cow, and raised vegetables for home consumption. Although they were far from rich, they managed to put aside enough for insurance, reading matter, and a few small luxuries.

Working-Class Attitudes

Social workers and government officials made many efforts in the 1880s and 1890s to find out how working people felt about all sorts of matters connected with their jobs. Their reports reveal a wide spectrum of opinion. To the question, asked of two Wisconsin carpenters, "What new laws, in your opinion, ought to be enacted?" one replied: "Keep down strikes and rioters. Let every man attend to his own business." But the other answered: "Complete nationalization of land and all ways of transportation. Burn all government bonds. A graduated income tax. . . . Abolish child labor and [pass] any other act that capitalists say is wrong."

Every variation of opinion between these extremes was expressed by working people in many sections and in many kinds of work. In 1881 a female textile worker in Lawrence, Massachusetts, said to an interviewer: "If you will stand by the mill, and see the people coming out, you will be surprised to see the happy, contented look they all have."

Despite such remarks and the general improvement in living standards, it is clear if only from the large number of bitter strikes of the period that dissatisfaction was widespread among industrial workers. Writing in 1885, the labor leader Terence V. Powderly reported that "a deep-rooted feeling of discontent pervades the masses." A few years later a Connecticut official conducted an informal survey of labor opinion in the state and found a "feeling of bitterness" and "distrust of employers" to be endemic.

The discontent had many causes. For some workers, poverty was still the chief problem, but for others, rising aspirations triggered discontent. Workers were confused about their destiny; the tradition that no one of ability need remain a hired hand died hard. They wanted to believe their bosses and the politicians when those worthies voiced the old slogans about a classless society and the community of interest of capital and labor. "Our men," William Vanderbilt of the New York Central said in 1877, "feel that, although I . . . may have my millions and they the rewards of their daily toil, still we are about equal in the end. If they suffer, I suffer, and if I suffer, they cannot escape." "The poor," another conservative spokesman said a decade later, "are not poor because the rich are rich." Instead "the service of capital" softened their lot and gave them many benefits.

Statements such as these, though self-serving, were essentially correct. The rich were growing richer and more people were growing rich, but or-

dinary workers were better off too. However, the gap between the very rich and the ordinary citizen was widening. "The tendency . . . is toward centralization and aggregation," the Illinois Bureau of Labor Statistics reported in 1886. "This involves a separation of the people into classes, and the permanently subordinate status of large numbers of them."

Mobility: Social, Economic, and Educational

To study mobility in a large industrial country is extraordinarily difficult. Americans in the late 19th century believed their society offered great opportunities for individual advancement, and to prove it they pointed to men like Andrew Carnegie and to other poor boys who accumulated large fortunes. How general the rise from rags to riches (or even to modest comfort) was is another question.

Americans had been on the move, mostly westward, since the colonial period, but studies of census records, such as those of Stephan Thernstrom, show that there was considerable geographic mobility in urban areas throughout the last half of the 19th century and into the 20th. Most investigations reveal that only about half the people recorded in one census were still in the same place ten years later; as Thernstrom puts it, "transiency was part of the American way of life. . . . The country had an enormous reservoir of footloose men, who could be lured to new destinations when opportunity beckoned."

In most of the cities studied, mobility was accompanied by some economic and social improvement. On the average, about a quarter of the manual laborers traced rose to middle-class status during their lifetimes, and the sons of manual laborers were still more likely to improve their place in society. In New York City about a third of the Italian and Jewish immigrants of the 1890s had risen from unskilled to skilled jobs a decade later. Even in Newburyport, Massachusetts, a town that was something of an economic backwater, most laborers made some progress, though far fewer rose to skilled or white-collar positions than in more prosperous cities.

Such progress was primarily the result of the

economic growth the nation was experiencing and of the energy and ambition of the people, native-born and immigrant alike, who were pouring into the cities in such numbers. But the public education system gave an additional boost to the upwardly mobile.

The history of American education after about 1870 reflects the impact of social and economic change. Although Horace Mann, Henry Barnard, and others had laid the foundations for state-supported school systems earlier in the century, most of these systems became compulsory only after the Civil War, when the growth of cities provided the concentration of population and financial resources necessary for economical mass education. In the 1860s about half the children in the country were getting some formal education, but this did not mean that half the children were attending school at any one time. Sessions were short, especially in rural areas, and many teachers were poorly trained. President Calvin Coolidge noted in his autobiography that the one-room school he attended in rural Vermont in the 1880s was open only in slack seasons when the 20-odd students were not needed in the fields. "Few, if any, of my teachers reached the standard now required," he wrote, adding that his own younger sister had obtained a teaching certificate and actually taught a class when she was only 12.

Attendance in the public schools increased from 6.8 million in 1870 to 15.5 million in 1900, a remarkable expansion even when allowance is made for the growth of the population. More remarkable still, during a time when prices were declining steadily, public expenditures for education nearly quadrupled. A typical elementary school graduate, at least in the cities, could count on having studied, besides the traditional "three Rs," history, geography, a bit of science, drawing, and physical training.

Industrialization created many demands for vocational and technical training; both employers and unskilled workers quickly grasped the possibilities. Science courses were taught in some of the new high schools, but secondary education was still assumed to be only for those with special abilities and youths whose families did not require that they immediately become breadwinners. As late as 1890 fewer than 300,000 of the 14.3 million children attending public and private schools had progressed beyond the eighth grade, and nearly a third of these were attending private institutions.

In 1880 Calvin M. Woodward opened the Manual Training School in St. Louis, and soon a number

An 1890s classroom with 40-plus kids, all about the same age, from the same economic and social circumstances, and set to the same assignment by a woman teacher. The urban public school had arrived.

of similar schools were offering courses in carpentry, metalwork, sewing, and other crafts. Woodward thought of vocational training as part of a broad general education rather than as preparation for a specific occupation, but by 1890, 36 cities had established purely vocational public high schools.

Because manual training attracted the backing of industrialists, organized labor was at first suspicious of the new trend. One union leader called trade schools "breeding schools for scabs and rats." Fortunately, the usefulness of such training soon became evident to the unions; by 1910 the AFL was lobbying side by side with the National Association of Manufacturers for more trade schools.

Education certainly helped young people to rise in the world, but progress from rags to real riches was far from common. Carnegies were rare. A study of the family backgrounds of 200 late-19th-century business leaders revealed that nearly all of them grew up in well-to-do middle-class families. They were far better educated than the general run, and most were members of one or another Protestant church.

More than the absence of real opportunity, the unrealistic expectations inspired by the rags-to-riches myth explains why so many workers, even when expressing dissatisfaction with life as it was, continued to subscribe to such middle-class values as hard work and thrift—that is, they continued to hope. Professor Thernstrom notes that hundreds of poor people in Newburyport, by practicing what he calls "ruthless underconsumption," gradually accumulated enough money to buy their own homes and provide for themselves in their old age.

The "New" Immigration

Industrial expansion increased the need for labor, and this in turn powerfully stimulated immigration. Between 1866 and 1915 about 25 million foreigners entered the United States. Industrial growth alone does not explain the influx. The launching in 1858 of the English liner *Great Eastern*, which measured nearly 700 feet from stem to stern and weighed about 19,000 tons, opened a new era in transatlantic travel. Although most immigrants traveled in steerage, which was cramped and almost totally lacking in amenities, the Atlantic crossing, once so hazardous, became safe and speedy with the perfection of the steamship. Competition between the great packet lines such as Cunard, North German Lloyd, and Holland-America drove down the cost of the passage, and advertising by the lines further stimulated traffic.

"Push" pressures as well as these "pull" factors had much to do with this "new" immigration. Improvements in transportation produced unexpected and disruptive changes in the economies of many European countries. Cheap wheat from the United States, Russia, and other parts of the world poured into Europe, bringing disaster to farmers from England and the Scandinavian countries to Italy, Greece, and Russia. The spreading industrial revolution and the increased use of farm machinery led to the collapse of the peasant economy of central and southern Europe. For rural inhabitants this meant the loss of self-sufficiency, the fragmentation of landholdings, unemployment, and, for many, the decision to make a new start in the New World.

Political and religious persecutions pushed still others into the migrating stream, but the main reason for immigration remained the desire for economic betterment. "In America," a British immigrant reported, "you get pies and puddings."

While immigrants continued to people the farms of America, industry absorbed an ever-increasing number of the newcomers. In 1870 one industrial worker in three was foreign-born. When congressional investigators examined 21 major industries early in the new century, they discovered that well over half of the labor force had not been born in the United States.

Most of the new millions entered the country by way of New York City. A Serbian immigrant, Michael Pupin, later a distinguished physicist at Columbia University, has left a moving description of what it was like. He arrived in 1874 on the Hamburg-American liner *Westphalia* amid a horde of other newcomers. Disembarking at Hoboken, he was taken by tug to the immigration reception center at Castle Garden on the southern tip of Manhattan Island. He confessed to the authorities that he had only 5 cents to his name and knew no Americans except—by reputation—Franklin, Lincoln, and Harriet Beecher Stowe. But he explained in eloquent phrases why he wanted to live in the land of liberty rather than in the Austro-Hungarian Empire.

The officials conferred briefly, then admitted

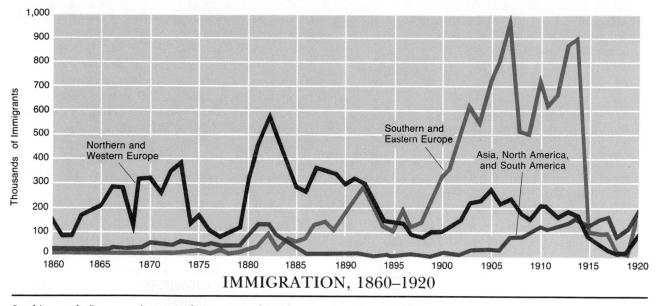

IMMIGRATION, 1860–1920

In this graph Germany is counted as a part of northern and western Europe. Note the tide of "new" immigration from southern and eastern Europe in the early 1900s, and how it plummeted during World War I.

him. After a good breakfast, supplied by the immigration authorities, someone from the Castle Garden Labor Bureau offered him a job as a farmhand in Delaware. Within 24 hours of his arrival he had reached his destination, ready to go to work.

Before 1882, when—in addition to the Chinese—criminals, idiots, lunatics, and persons liable to become public charges were excluded, entry into the United States was almost unrestricted. Indeed, until 1891 the Atlantic Coast states, not the federal government, exercised whatever controls were imposed on newcomers. Even when federally imposed, medical inspection was perfunctory. Public Health officials boasted that with "one glance" at each arrival, the inspectors could "take in six details, namely the scalp, face, neck, hands, gait and general condition, both mental and physical." Only those who failed this "test" were examined more closely. On average, only one immigrant in 50 was ultimately rejected.

Private agencies, philanthropic and commercial, served as a link between the new arrivals and employers looking for labor. Until the Foran Act of 1885 outlawed the practice, a few companies brought in skilled workers under contract, advancing them passage money and collecting it in in-

stallments from their paychecks, a system somewhat like the indentured servitude of colonial times. Numerous nationality groups assisted (and sometimes exploited) their compatriots by organizing "immigrant banks" that recruited labor in the old country, arranged transportation, and then housed the newcomers in boardinghouses in the United States while finding them jobs. The *padrone* system of the Italians and Greeks was typical. The *padrone*, a sort of contractor who agreed to supply gangs of unskilled workers to companies for a lump sum, usually signed on immigrants unfamiliar with American wage levels at rates that assured him a healthy profit.

Beginning in the 1880s, the spreading effects of industrialization in Europe caused a shift in the sources of American immigration from northern and western to southern and eastern sections of the Continent. In 1882 when a total of 789,000 immigrants entered the United States, more than 350,000 came from Great Britain and Germany, only 32,000 from Italy, and fewer than 17,000 from Russia. In 1907—the all-time peak year, with 1,285,000 immigrants—Great Britain and Germany supplied fewer than half as many as they had 25 years earlier, while Russia and Italy were supplying 11 times as many as before. Up to 1880, only about

200,000 southern and eastern Europeans had migrated to America. Between 1880 and 1910, approximately 8.4 million arrived.

The Old Immigrants and the New

Of course, Michael Pupin was not an ordinary immigrant. Though he came from eastern Europe, he preceded the flood of people from there, and he was more sophisticated and better educated than most. The new immigrants, like the "old" Irish of the 1840s and 1850s, were mostly peasants. They also seemed more than ordinarily clannish; southern Italians typically called all people outside their families *forestieri*, "foreigners." Old-stock Americans thought them harder to assimilate, and in fact many were. Some Italian immigrants, for example, were unmarried men who had come to the United States to earn enough money to buy a farm back home. Such people made hard and willing workers but were not much concerned with being part of an American community.

The "birds of passage" formed a substantial minority, but the immigrant who saved in order to bring his wife and children or his younger brothers and sisters to America was more typical. In addition, thousands of immigrants came as family groups and intended to remain. Some, like the eastern European Jewish migrants, were refugees who were almost desperately eager to become Americans, though of course they retained and nurtured much of their traditional culture.

Cultural differences among immigrants were often large and had important effects on their relations with native-born Americans and with other immigrant groups. Italians who settled in the city of Buffalo, the historian Virginia Yans-McLaughlin has shown, adjusted relatively smoothly to urban industrial life because of their close family and kinship ties. Poverty, unemployment, female jobholding outside the home, and other traumas that might have been expected to disrupt family relationships apparently had little effect. Polish immigrants in Buffalo, having different traditions, found adjustment more difficult.

German-American and Irish-American Catho-lics had different attitudes that caused them to clash over such matters as the policies of the Catholic University in Washington. Although (or perhaps because) the Haymarket anarchists were German-born, in 1887 one prominent German-American denounced the Knights of Labor as a hotbed of radicalism—and was said to have claimed that it was dominated by "Irish ignoramuses." Controversies erupted between Catholic and Protestant German-Americans, between Greek-American groups supporting various political factions in their homeland, and so on.

Confused by such differences and conflicts, many Americans of longer standing concluded, wrongly but understandably, that the new immigrants were incapable of becoming good citizens and should be kept out. During the 1880s large numbers of social workers, economists, and church leaders, worried by the problems that arose when so many poor immigrants flocked into cities already bursting at the seams, began to believe that some restriction should be placed on the incoming human tide. The directors of charitable organizations, which bore the burden of aiding the most unfortunate immigrants, complained that their resources were being exhausted by the needs of the flood.

Social Darwinists and people obsessed with pseudoscientific ideas about "racial purity" also found the new immigration alarming. Misunderstanding the findings of the new science of genetics, they attributed the social problems associated with mass immigration to supposed physiological characteristics of the newcomers. Forgetting that earlier Americans had accused pre–Civil War Irish and German immigrants of similar deficiencies, they decided that the peoples of southern and eastern Europe were racially (and therefore permanently) inferior to "Nordic" and "Anglo-Saxon" types and ought to be kept out.

Workers, fearing the competition of people with low living standards and no bargaining power, spoke out against the "enticing of penniless and unapprised immigrants . . . to undermine our wages and social welfare." In 1883 the president of the Amalgamated Iron and Steel Workers told a Senate committee that Hungarian, Polish, Italian, and other immigrants "can live where I think a decent man would die; they can live on . . . food that other men would not touch." A Wisconsin iron-

Contemporary cartoonists reflected the "new nativist" attitude toward unrestricted immigration. Frank Beard's 1885 drawing shows anarchists, socialists, and members of the Mafia arriving from the sewers of Europe and being resisted by Columbia and her watchdogs "Law" and "Order."

worker put it this way: "Immigrants work for almost nothing and seem to be able to live on wind—something I can not do."

Employers were not disturbed by the influx of people with strong backs willing to work hard for low wages. Nevertheless, by the late 1880s many of them were alarmed about the supposed radicalism of the immigrants. The Haymarket bombing focused attention on the handful of foreign-born extremists in the country and loosed a flood of unjustified charges that "anarchists and communists" were dominating the labor movement. Nativism, which had waxed in the 1850s under the Know-Nothing banner and waned during the Civil War, now flared up again, and for similar reasons. Denunciations of "longhaired, wild-eyed, bad-smelling, atheistic, reckless foreign wretches," of "Europe's human and inhuman rubbish," of the

"cutthroats of Beelzebub from the Rhine, the Danube, the Vistula and the Elbe" crowded the pages of the nation's press. The Grand Army of the Republic, an organization of Civil War veterans, grumbled about foreign-born radicals.

These nativists, again like the pre–Civil War variety, disliked Catholics and other minority groups more than immigrants as such. The largest nativist organization of the period, the American Protective Association, founded in 1887, existed primarily to resist what its members called the "Catholic menace." The Protestant majority treated new immigrants as underlings, tried to keep them out of the best jobs, and discouraged their efforts to climb the social ladder. This prejudice functioned only at the social and economic levels. But nowhere in America did prejudice lead to interference with religious freedom in the narrow sense. And neither labor leaders nor important industrialists, despite their misgivings about immigration, took a broadly antiforeign position.

After the Exclusion Act of 1882 and the almost meaningless 1885 ban on importing contract labor, no further restrictions were imposed on immigration until the 20th century. Strong support for a literacy test for admission developed in the 1890s, pushed by a new organization, the Immigration Restriction League. Since there was much more illiteracy in the southeastern quarter of Europe than in the northwestern, such a test would discriminate without seeming to do so on national or racial grounds. A literacy test bill passed both houses of Congress in 1897, but President Cleveland vetoed it. Such a "radical departure" from the "generous and free-handed policy" of the past, Cleveland said, was unjustified. He added, perhaps with tongue in cheek, that a literacy requirement would not keep out "unruly agitators," who were only too adept at reading and writing.

out the national transportation network. But by the final decades of the century, the expansion of industry had become the chief cause of city growth. Thus the urban concentration continued; in 1890 one person in three lived in a city, by 1910 nearly one in two.

A steadily increasing proportion of the urban population was made up of immigrants. In 1890 the foreign-born population of Chicago almost equaled the total population of Chicago in 1880; a third of all Bostonians and a quarter of all Philadelphians had been born abroad, and four out of five residents of New York City were either immigrants themselves or the children of immigrants.

After 1890 the immigrant concentration became even more dense. The migrants from eastern and southern Europe lacked the resources to travel to the agriculturally developing regions (to say nothing of the sums necessary to acquire land and farm equipment). As the concentration progressed, it fed

The Expanding City and Its Problems

Americans who favored restricting immigration made much of the fact that so many of the newcomers crowded into the cities, aggravating problems of housing, public health, crime, and immorality. Immigrants concentrated in the cities because the jobs created by expanding industry were located there. So, of course, did native-born Americans; the proportion of urban dwellers had been steadily increasing since about 1820.

It is important to keep in mind that population density is not necessarily related to the existence of large cities. In the late 19th century there were areas in Asia as large as the United States that were as densely populated as Belgium and England yet overwhelmingly rural. The United States by any standard was sparsely populated, but well before the Civil War it had become one of the most urban nations in the world.

Industrialization does not entirely explain the growth of 19th-century cities. All the large American cities began as commercial centers, and the development of huge metropolises such as New York and Chicago would have been impossible with-

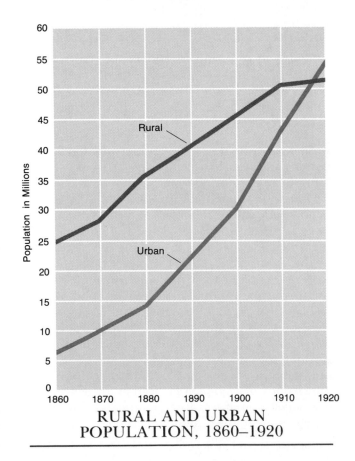

RURAL AND URBAN
POPULATION, 1860–1920

on itself, for all the eastern cities developed many ethnic neighborhoods, in each of which immigrants of one nationality congregated. Lonely, confused, often unable to speak English, the Italians, the Greeks, the Polish and Russian Jews, and other immigrants tended to settle where their predecessors had settled. Eager to maintain their traditional culture, they supported "national" churches and schools. Newspapers in their native languages flourished, as did social organizations of all sorts. Each great American city became a Europe in microcosm where it sometimes seemed that every language in the world but English could be heard. New York, the great entrepôt, had Italian, Polish, Greek, Jewish, and Bohemian quarters, even a Chinatown.

Although ethnic neighborhoods were crowded, unhealthy, and crime-ridden and many of the residents were desperately poor, they were not ghettos in the European sense, for those who lived there were not compelled by law to remain. Thousands "escaped" yearly to better districts. American ghettos were places where hopes and ambitions were fulfilled, where people worked hard and endured hardships in order to improve their own lot and that of their children.

Observing the immigrants' attachment to "foreign" values and institutions, numbers of native-born citizens accused the newcomers of resisting Americanization and blamed them for urban problems. The immigrants were involved in these problems, but the rapidity of urban expansion explains the troubles associated with city life far more fully than the high percentage of foreigners.

The Urban Infrastructure

The cities were suffering from growing pains. Sewer and water facilities frequently could not keep pace with skyrocketing needs. By the 1890s the tremendous growth of Chicago had put such a strain on its sanitation system that the Chicago River had become virtually an open sewer, and the city's drinking water contained such a high concentration of germ-killing chemicals that it tasted like creosote. In the 1880s all the sewers of Baltimore emptied into the sluggish Back Basin, and according to the journalist H. L. Mencken, every summer the city smelled "like a billion polecats." Fire protection became less and less adequate, garbage piled up in the streets faster

than it could be carted away, and the streets themselves crumbled beneath the pounding of heavy traffic. Urban growth proceeded with such speed that new streets were laid out more rapidly than they could be paved. Chicago had more than 1,400 miles of dirt streets in 1890.

People poured into the great cities faster than housing could be built to accommodate them. The influx into areas already densely packed in the 1840s became unbearable as rising property values and the absence of zoning laws conspired to make builders utilize every possible foot of space, squeezing out light and air ruthlessly in order to wedge in a few additional family units.

Substandard living quarters aggravated other evils such as disease and the disintegration of family life with its attendant mental anguish, crime, and juvenile delinquency. The bloody New York riots of 1863, though sparked by dislike of the Civil War draft and of blacks, reflected the bitterness and frustration of thousands jammed together amid filth and threatened by disease. A citizens' committee seeking to discover the causes of the riots expressed its amazement after visiting the slums "that so much misery, disease, and wretchedness can be huddled together and hidden . . . unvisited and unthought of, so near our own abodes." New York City created the Metropolitan Health Board in 1866, and a state tenement house law the following year made a feeble beginning at regulating city housing. Another law in 1879 placed a limit on the percentage of lot space that could be covered by new construction and established minimum standards of plumbing and ventilation. The magazine *Plumber and Sanitary Engineer* sponsored a contest to pick the best design for a tenement that met these specifications. The winner of the competition was James E. Ware, whose plan for a "dumbbell" apartment house managed to crowd 24 to 32 four-room apartments onto a plot of ground measuring only 25 by 100 feet. Oscar Handlin elaborates in *The Uprooted:*

The feat was accomplished by narrowing the building at its middle so that it took on the shape of a dumbbell. The indentation was only two-and-a-half feet wide and varied in length from five to fifty feet; but, added to the similar indentations on the adjoining houses, it created on each side an air-shaft five feet wide. . . . The stairs, halls, and common water closets were cramped into the narrow center of the building so that almost the whole of its surface was available for living quarters.

Despite efforts at reform, in 1890 more than 1.4 million persons were living on Manhattan Island, and in some sections the population density exceeded 900 persons per acre. Jacob Riis, a reporter, captured the horror of the crowded warrens in his classic study of life in the slums, *How the Other Half Lives* (1890):

> Be a little careful, please! The hall is dark and you might stumble. . . . Here where the hall turns and dives into utter darkness is . . . a flight of stairs. You can feel your way, if you cannot see it. Close? Yes! What would you have? All the fresh air that enters these stairs comes from the hall-door that is forever slamming. . . . The sinks are in the hallway, that all the tenants may have access—and all be poisoned alike

An alley known as "Bandit's Roost," on New York's Lower East Side, photographed for the New York Sun *in 1887 by police reporter Jacob Riis, himself an immigrant. "What sort of an answer, think you, would come from these tenements to the question 'Is life worth living?' " Riis asked in his book* How the Other Half Lives.

by their summer stenches. . . . Here is a door. Listen! That short, hacking cough, that tiny, helpless wail—what do they mean? . . . The child is dying of measles. With half a chance it might have lived; but it had none. That dark bedroom killed it.

The unhealthiness of the tenements was notorious; one noxious corner of New York became known as the "lung block" because of the prevalence of tuberculosis among its inhabitants. In 1900 three out of five babies born in one poor district of Chicago died before their first birthday. Equally frightening was the impact of overcrowding on the morals of the tenement dweller. The number of prison inmates in the United States increased by 50 percent in the 1880s, and the homicide rate nearly tripled, most of the rise occurring in cities. Driven into the streets by the squalor of their homes, slum youths formed gangs bearing names like Alley Gang, Rock Gang, and Hell's Kitchen Gang. From petty thievery and shoplifting they graduated to housebreaking, bank robbery, and murder. According to Jacob Riis, when the leader of the infamous Whyo Gang, convicted of murder, confessed his sins to a prison chaplain, "his father confessor turned pale . . . though many years of labor as chaplain of the Tombs had hardened him to such rehearsals."

Slums bred criminals—the wonder was that they bred so few. They also drove well-to-do residents into exclusive sections and to the suburbs. From Boston's Beacon Hill and Back Bay to San Francisco's Nob Hill, the rich retired into their cluttered mansions and ignored conditions in the poorer parts of town.

Modernizing the Cities

As American cities grew larger and more crowded, thereby aggravating a host of social problems, practical forces operated to bring about improvements. Once the relationship between polluted water and disease was fully understood, everyone saw the need for decent water and sewage systems. It is true that some businessmen profited from corrupt dealings with the city machines, but more of them wanted efficient and honest government in order to reduce their tax bills. City dwellers of all classes resented dirt, noise, and ugliness, and in many communities public-spirited groups formed societies to plant trees, clean up littered areas, and develop recreational facilities. When one city undertook improvements, others tended to follow suit, spurred on by local pride and the booster spirit.

Gradually, the basic facilities of urban living were improved. Streets were paved, first with cobblestones and wood blocks and then with smoother, quieter asphalt. Gaslight, then electric arc lights, and finally Edison's incandescent lamps brightened the cities after dark, making law enforcement easier, stimulating nightlife, and permitting factories and shops to operate after sunset.

Urban transportation underwent enormous changes. Until the 1880s, horse-drawn cars running on tracks set flush with the street were the main means of urban public transportation. In 1860 New York City's horsecars were carrying about 100,000 passengers a day. But horsecars had serious drawbacks. Enormous numbers of horses were needed, and feeding and stabling the animals was costly. Their droppings (10 pounds per day per horse) became a major source of urban pollution. That is why the invention of the electric trolley car in the 1880s put an end to horsecar transportation. Trolleys were cheaper and less unsightly than horsecars and quieter than steam-powered trains.

A retired naval officer, Frank J. Sprague, installed the first practical electric trolley line in Richmond, Virginia, in 1887 and 1888. At once other cities seized upon the trolley. Lines soon radiated outward from the city centers, bringing commuters and shoppers from the residential districts to the business district. Without them the big-city department stores could not have flourished as they did. By 1895 some 850 lines were busily hauling city dwellers over 10,000 miles of track, and mileage tripled in the following decade. As with other new enterprises, control of street railways quickly became centralized until a few big operators controlled the trolleys of more than 100 eastern cities and towns.

Streetcars changed the character of big-city life. Before their introduction, urban communities were limited by the distances people could conveniently walk to work. The "walking city" could not easily extend more than $2\frac{1}{2}$ miles from its center. Streetcars increased this radius to 6 miles or more, which meant that the area of the city expanded enormously. Dramatic population shifts resulted as the better-off moved away from the center in search of

However noisy and unsightly their overhead rails, the electric trolleys represented a tremendous improvement in the urban environment over their waste-discharging predecessors when introduced in the 1880s.

air and space, abandoning the crumbling, jam-packed older neighborhoods to the poor. Thus economic segregation speeded the growth of ghettos. Older peripheral towns that had maintained some of the self-contained qualities of village life were swallowed up, becoming metropolitan centers. The village of Medford, Massachusetts, outside Boston, had 11,000 residents in 1890 when the first trolley line from the city center reached it. By 1905 its population had reached 23,000.

As time passed, each new area, originally peopled by rising economic groups, tended to become crowded and then to deteriorate. By extending their tracks beyond the developed areas, the streetcar companies further speeded suburban growth because they assured developers, bankers, builders, and middle-class home buyers of efficient transport to the center of town. By keeping fares low (5 cents a ride was standard) the lines enabled poor people to "escape" to the countryside on holidays. Kenneth T. Jackson traces the pattern in *Crabgrass Frontier:* "First, streetcar lines were built out to existing villages. . . . These areas subsequently developed into large communities. Second, the tracks actually created residential neighborhoods where none had existed before."

Los Angeles, according to Professor Jackson, "provides the premier example of the confluence of street railway entrepreneurs and real-estate development." Henry E. Huntington, a nephew of the railroad baron Collis P. Huntington, built his Pacific Electric Railway into a vast network of lines primarily to aid in selling homesites on lands he had purchased cheaply before the tracks were laid.

The combined activities of real estate developers, trolley operators, and efficient builders made home ownership possible for people of modest means. "For the first time in the history of the world," Jackson writes, "middle-class families . . . could reasonably expect to buy a detached home on an accessible lot in a safe and sanitary environment."

Advances in bridge design, notably the perfection of the steel-cable suspension bridge by John A. Roebling, aided the ebb and flow of metropolitan populations. The Brooklyn Bridge, described by a poet as "a weird metallic Apparition . . . the cables, like divine messages from above . . . cutting and dividing into innumerable musical spaces the nude

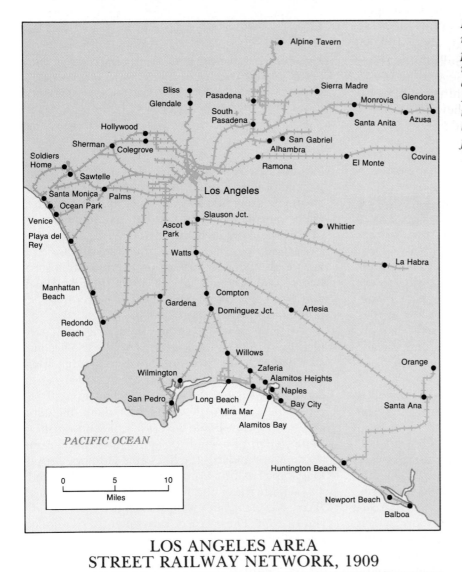

By the early 1900s, a street railway network radiated from the settled parts of central Los Angeles for 30 miles and more. Henry Huntington claimed that the Los Angeles and Pacific Electric system "extended into the open country, ahead of, and not behind, the population. . . ." Data from Fogelson, The Fragmented Metropolis.

LOS ANGELES AREA
STREET RAILWAY NETWORK, 1909

immensity of the sky," was Roebling's triumph. Completed in 1883 at a cost of $15 million, it was soon carrying more than 33 million passengers a year over the East River between Manhattan and Brooklyn.

Even the high cost of urban real estate, which spawned the tenement, produced some beneficial results in the long run. Instead of crowding squat structures cheek by jowl on 25-foot lots, architects began to build upward. The introduction of iron-skeleton construction, which freed the walls from bearing the immense weight of a tall building, was the work of a group of Chicago architects who had been attracted to the metropolis of the Middle West by opportunities to be found amid the ashes of the great fire of 1871. The group included William Le Baron Jenney, John A. Holabird, Martin Roche, John W. Root, and Louis H. Sullivan. Jenney's Home Insurance Building, completed in 1885, was the first metal-frame edifice. Height alone, however, did not satisfy these innovators; they sought a form that would reflect the structure and purpose of their buildings.

Their leader was Louis Sullivan. Architects must discard "books, rules, precedents, or any such educational impediments" and design functional buildings, he argued. A tall building "must be every inch a proud and soaring thing, rising in sheer exultation . . . from bottom to top . . . a unit without a single dissenting line." Sullivan's Wainwright Building in St. Louis and his Prudential Building in Buffalo, both completed in the early 1890s, combined beauty, modest construction costs, and efficient use of space in trailblazing ways. Soon a "race to the skies" was on in the great cities of America, and the words *skyscraper* and *skyline* entered the language.

The remarkable White City built for the Chicago World's Fair of 1893 by Daniel H. Burnham, with its broad vistas and acres of open space, led to a national City Beautiful movement, the most lasting result of which was the development of many public parks. The landscape architect Frederick Law Olmsted, designer of New York's Central Park, was a leading figure in the movement.

But efforts to relieve the congestion in slum dis-

Designed by Daniel H. Burnham for the Chicago's World Fair in 1893, "White City" inspired other architects with its ideal of uncongested and visually satisfying urban living. The results, still visible, were mixed.

tricts made little headway. In Brooklyn, Alfred T. White established Home Buildings, a 40-family model tenement in 1877; eventually he expanded the experiment to include 267 apartments. Each unit had plenty of light and air and contained its own sink and toilet. Ellen Collins developed a smaller project in Manhattan's Fourth Ward in the 1890s. These model tenements were self-sustaining, but of necessity they yielded only modest returns. The landlords were essentially philanthropists; their work had no significant impact on urban housing in the 19th century.

Leisure Activities: More Fun and Games

By bringing together large numbers of people, cities made possible many kinds of social activity difficult or impossible to maintain in rural areas. Cities remained unsurpassed as centers of artistic and intellectual life. New York was the outstanding example, as seen in its many theaters and in the founding of the American Museum of Natural History (1870), the Metropolitan Museum of Art (1870), and the Metropolitan Opera (1883), but other cities were equally hospitable to such endeavors. Boston's Museum of Fine Arts, for example, was founded in 1870, the Boston Symphony in 1881.

Of course, less sophisticated forms of recreation also flourished in the urban environment. It is only a slight exaggeration to say that crowded urban centers had a saloon on every corner; during the last third of the 19th century the number of saloons in the country tripled. Saloons were strictly male working-class institutions, usually decorated with pictures and other mementos of sports heroes, the bar perhaps under the charge of a retired pugilist.

For workingmen the saloon was a kind of club, a place to meet friends, exchange news and gossip, gamble, and eat, as well as to drink beer and whiskey. Saloons also flourished because factory owners and other employers of large numbers of workers tended to forbid the consumption of alcohol on their premises. In addition, the gradual reduction of the workday left men with more free time, which may explain why vaudeville and burlesques, the latter described by one straight-laced critic as a "disgrace-

ful spectacle of padded legs juggling and tight-laced wriggling," also proliferated.

Calvinist-inspired opposition to sports as a frivolous waste of valuable time was steadily evaporating, replaced among the upper and middle classes by the realization that games like golf and tennis were "healthy occupation[s] for mind and body." Bicycling became a fad, both as a means of getting from place to place in the ever-expanding cities and as a form of exercise and recreation.

Many of the new streetcar companies built picnic grounds and amusement parks at their outer limits. In good weather thousands seeking to relax after a hard day's work flocked to these "trolley parks" to enjoy a fresh-air meal or patronize the shooting galleries, merry-go-rounds, and "freak shows."

The postwar era also saw the first important development of spectator sports, again because cities provided the concentrations of population necessary to support them. Curious relationships developed between upper- and working-class interests and between competitive sports as pure enjoyment for players and spectators and sports as something to bet on. Horse racing had strictly upper-class origins, but racetracks attracted huge crowds of ordinary people more intent on picking a winner than on improving the breed.

Professional boxing offers an even better example. It was in a sense a hobby of the rich, who sponsored favorite gladiators, offered prizes, and often wagered large sums on the matches. But the audiences were made up overwhelmingly of young working-class males, from whose ranks most of the fighters emerged. The gambling and also the brutality of the bloody, bare-knuckle character of the fights caused many communities to outlaw boxing, a fact that added to the appeal of the sport for some.

The first widely popular pugilist was the legendary "Boston Strong Boy," John L. Sullivan, who became heavyweight champion in 1882 by disposing of one Paddy Ryan in nine rounds. Sullivan was an immensely powerful man whose idea of fighting, according to his biographer, "was simply to hammer his opponent into unconsciousness," something he did repeatedly during his ten-year reign. Sullivan became an international celebrity and made and lost large sums during this period. He was also the beneficiary of patronage in such forms as a diamond belt worth $10,000 presented to him by some of his admirers. Yet boxing remained a raffish, clandestine occupation. One of Sullivan's important fights took place in France, on the estate of Baron Rothschild, yet when it ended both he and his opponent were arrested.

Three major team games, baseball, football, and basketball, developed in something approaching their modern form during the last quarter of the century. Various forms of what became baseball were played long before that time. Organized teams, in most cases made up of upper-class amateurs, first emerged in the 1840s, but the game only became truly popular during the Civil War, when it was a major form of camp recreation for the troops.

After the war professional teams began to appear (the first, the Cincinnati Red Stockings, paid players between $800 and $1,400 for the season), and in 1876 teams in eight cities formed the National League. The American League followed in 1901. After a brief period of rivalry, the two leagues made peace in 1903, the year of the first World Series.

Organized play led to codification of the rules and improvements in technique and strategy, for example, the development of "minor" leagues, impartial umpires calling balls and strikes and ruling on close plays, the use of both catcher's masks and padded gloves, and the invention of various kinds of curves and other erratic pitches (often enhanced by "doctoring" the ball). As early as the 1870s, baseball was being called the "national game" and losing all upper-class connotations. Important games attracted crowds in the tens of thousands; betting became a problem. Despite its urban origins, its broad green fields and dusty basepaths gave the game a rural character that has only recently begun to fade.

Nobody "invented" baseball, but both football and basketball owe their present form to individuals. James Naismith's invention of basketball is undisputed. In 1891, while a student at a YMCA school, he attached peach baskets to the edge of an elevated running track in the gymnasium and drew up what are still the basic rules of the game. The first basketball was a soccer ball. The game was popular from the start, but since it was played indoors, it was not an important spectator sport until much later.

Football was not created by one person in the way that basketball was; it evolved out of English rugby. For many decades it remained almost en-

Thomas Eakins's Baseball Players Practicing, *painted in 1875, one year before the organization of the National League. The relative similarity of the batter's stance to that favored today suggests the timelessness of this national pastime.*

tirely a college sport and thus was played almost entirely by upper- and middle-class types. (Organized collegiate sports dated back to before the Civil War; the first intercollegiate matches were rowing races between Harvard and Yale students.)

The first intercollege football game occurred when Princeton defeated Rutgers in 1869, and by the 1880s college football had become extremely popular. Much of the game's modern character was the work of Walter Camp, the athletic director and football coach at Yale. Camp cut the size of teams from 15 to 11, and he invented the scrimmage line, the four-down system, and the key position of quarterback. He publicized the game in a series of books, ranging from *How to Coach a Team* (1886) to *Jack Hall at Yale* (1909). Camp's prestige was such that when he named his first All America team after the 1889 season, no one challenged his judgment. Well into the 20th century, the players that Camp selected were *the* All Americans.

Camp claimed that amateur sports like football taught the value of hard work, cooperation, and fair play. His practice was more questionable. He is known to have recruited players who could not meet Yale's academic standards and to have found means of putting money in his players' pockets. At Yale and elsewhere all the problems that emphasis on athletic achievement poses for modern institutions of higher education existed in microcosm well before 1900.

Spectator sports had little appeal to women at this time and indeed for decades thereafter. And few women participated in organized athletics. Sports were "manly" activities; a woman might ride a bicycle, play croquet and perhaps a little tennis, but to display any concentrated interest in excelling in a sport was considered unfeminine.

Religious Responses to Industrial Society

The modernization of the great cities was not solving most of the social problems of the slums. As this fact became clear, a number of urban religious leaders began to take a hard look at the situation. Traditionally, American churchmen had insisted that where sin was concerned, there were no extenuating circumstances. To the well-to-do they preached the

virtues of thrift and hard work; to the poor they extended the possibility of a better existence in the next world; to all they stressed one's responsibility for one's own behavior—and thus for one's own salvation. Such a point of view brought meager comfort to residents of slums. Consequently, the churches lost influence in the poorer sections. Furthermore, as better-off citizens followed the streetcar lines out from the city centers, their church leaders followed them.

In New York 17 Protestant congregations abandoned the depressed areas of Lower Manhattan between 1868 and 1888. Catering thereafter almost entirely to middle-class and upper-class worshipers, the pastors tended to become even more conservative. No more strident defender of reactionary ideas existed than the pastor of Brooklyn's fashionable Plymouth Congregational Church, Henry Ward Beecher. Beecher, a younger brother of Harriet Beecher Stowe, the author of *Uncle Tom's Cabin*, attributed poverty to the improvidence of laborers who, he claimed, squandered their wages on liquor and tobacco. "No man in this land suffers from poverty," he said, "unless it be more than his fault—unless it be his sin." The best check on labor unrest was a plentiful supply of cheap immigrant labor, he told President Hayes. Unions were "the worst form of despotism and tyranny in the history of Christendom."

An increasing proportion of the residents of the blighted districts were Catholics, and the Roman church devoted much effort to distributing alms, maintaining homes for orphans and old people, and other forms of social welfare. But church leaders seemed unconcerned with the social causes of the blight; they were deeply committed to the idea that sin and vice were personal, poverty an act of God. They deplored the rising tide of crime, disease, and destitution among their coreligionists, yet they failed to see the connection between these evils and the squalor of the slums. "Intemperance is the great evil we have to overcome," wrote the president of the leading Catholic charitable organization, the Society of St. Vincent de Paul. "It is the source of the misery for at least three-fourths of the families we are called upon to visit and relieve." The church, according to the historian Aaron I. Abell, "seemed oblivious to the bearing of civil legislation on the course of moral and social reform." Instead it invested much money and energy in chimerical at-

Perhaps the most widely admired of middle-class urban ministers of his day, Henry Ward Beecher also became the best known when a member of his Brooklyn congregation in 1874 charged him with adultery. A jury exonerated him.

tempts to colonize poor city dwellers in the West.

Like conservative Protestant clergymen, the Catholic hierarchy tended to be at best neutral toward organized labor. Cardinal James Gibbons spoke favorably of the Knights of Labor in 1886 after the Haymarket bombing, but he took a dim view of strikes. The clergy's attitude changed somewhat after Pope Leo XIII issued his encyclical *Rerum novarum* (1891). This statement criticized the excesses of capitalism, including the "greed of unchecked competition"; it defended the right of labor to form unions and stressed the duty of government to care for the poor. Workers were entitled to wages that would guarantee their families a reasonable and frugal comfort, Leo declared, and they committed no sin by seeking government aid to get it. Concrete action by American Catholics, however, was slow in coming, probably because of the conservatism of the clergy and the parochial concerns of lay leaders.

The conservatism of most Protestant and Catholic clergymen did not prevent some earnest preachers from working directly to improve the lot of the city poor. Some followed the path blazed by Dwight L. Moody, a lay evangelist who became famous throughout America and Great Britain in the 1870s. A gargantuan figure weighing nearly 300 pounds, Moody conducted a vigorous campaign to persuade the denizens of the slums to cast aside their sinful ways. He went among them full of enthusiasm and God's love and made an impact no less powerful than that of George Whitefield during the Great Awakening of the 18th century or Charles Grandison Finney in the first part of the 19th. The evangelists founded mission schools in the slums and tried to provide spiritual and recreational facilities for the unfortunate. They were prominent in the establishment of American branches of the Young Men's Christian Association (1851) and the Salvation Army (1880).

However, the evangelists paid little heed to the causes of urban poverty and vice, believing that faith in God would enable the poor to transcend the material difficulties of life. For a number of Protestant clergymen who had become familiar with the slums, a different approach seemed called for. Slum conditions caused the sins and crimes of the cities; the wretched human beings who committed them could not be blamed, these ministers argued. They began to preach a "Social Gospel" that focused on improving living conditions rather than on saving souls. If people were to lead pure lives, they must have enough to eat, decent homes, and opportunities to develop their talents. Social Gospelers advocated civil service reform, child labor legislation, regulation of big corporations, and heavy taxes on incomes and inheritances.

The most influential preacher of the Social Gospel was probably Washington Gladden. At first Gladden, who was raised on a Massachusetts farm, had opposed all government interference in social and economic affairs, but his experiences as a minister in Springfield, Massachusetts, and Columbus, Ohio, exposed him to the realities of life in industrial cities, and his views changed. In *Applied Christianity* (1886) and in other works he defended labor's right to organize and strike and denounced the idea that supply and demand should control wage rates. He favored factory inspection laws, strict regulation of public utilities, and other reforms.

Gladden never questioned the basic values of capitalism. By the 1890s a number of ministers had gone all the way to socialism. The Reverend William D. P. Bliss of Boston, for example, believed in the kind of welfare state envisioned by Edward Bellamy in *Looking Backward*. He founded the Society of Christian Socialists (1889) and edited a radical journal, *The Dawn*. In addition to nationalizing industry, Bliss and other Christian Socialists advocated government unemployment relief programs, public housing and slum clearance projects, and other measures designed to aid the city poor.

Nothing so well reveals the receptivity of the public to the Social Gospel as the popularity of Charles M. Sheldon's novel *In His Steps* (1896), one of America's all-time best-sellers. Sheldon, a minister in Topeka, Kansas, described what happened in the mythical city of Raymond when a group of leading citizens decided to live truly Christian lives, asking themselves, "What would Jesus do?" before adopting any course of action. Naturally the tone of Raymond's society was immensely improved, but basic social reforms followed quickly. The Rectangle, a terrible slum area "too dirty, too coarse, too sinful, too awful for close contact," became the center of a great reform effort. One of Raymond's "leading society heiresses" undertook a slum clearance project, and a concerted attack was made on drunkenness and immorality. The moral regeneration of the entire community was soon accomplished.

The Settlement Houses

Although millions read *In His Steps*, its effect, and that of other Social Gospel literature, was merely inspirational. On the practical level, a number of earnest souls began to grapple with slum problems by organizing what were known as settlement houses. These were community centers located in poor districts that provided guidance and services to all who would use them. The settlement workers, most of them idealistic, well-to-do young people, lived in the houses and were active in neighborhood affairs.

The prototype of the settlement house was London's Toynbee Hall, founded in the early 1880s;

the first American example was the Neighborhood Guild, opened on the Lower East Side of New York in 1886 by Dr. Stanton Coit. By the turn of the 20th century 100 had been established, the most famous being Jane Addams's Hull House in Chicago (1889), Robert A. Woods's South End House in Boston (1892), and Lillian Wald's Henry Street Settlement in New York (1893).

Though some men were active in the movement, the most important settlement house workers were women fresh from college—the first generation of young women to experience the trauma of having developed their capacities only to find that society offered them few opportunities to use them. The settlements provided an outlet for their hopes and energies, and they seized on it avidly. An English social reformer who visited Hull House around the turn of the century described the residents as "strong-minded energetic women, bustling about their various enterprises" and "earnest-faced self-subordinating and mild-mannered men who slide from room to room apologetically."

The settlement workers tried to interpret American ways to the new immigrants and to create a community spirit in order to teach, in the words of one of them, "right living through social relations." Unlike most charity workers, who acted out of a sense of upper-class responsibility toward the unfortunate, they expected to benefit morally and intellectually themselves by experiencing a way of life far different from their own and by obtaining "the first-hand knowledge the college classroom cannot give." Lillian Wald, a nurse by training, explained the concept succinctly in *The House on Henry Street* (1915): "We were to live in the neighborhood, . . . identify ourselves with it socially, and, in brief, contribute to it our citizenship."

Lillian Wald and other settlement workers soon discovered that practical problems absorbed most of their energies. They agitated for tenement house laws, regulation of the labor of women and children, and better schools. They employed private resources to establish playgrounds in the slums, along with libraries, classes in everything from child nutrition and home management to literature and arts and crafts, social clubs, and day-care centers. When they observed that many poor families were so occupied with the struggle to survive that they were neglecting or even abandoning their children, they tried to place the children in foster homes in the country.

In Boston, Robert A. Woods organized clubs to get the youngsters of the South End off the streets, helped establish a restaurant where a meal could be had for 5 cents, acted as an arbitrator in labor disputes, and lobbied for laws tightening up the franchises of public utility companies. In Chicago, Jane Addams developed an outstanding cultural program that included classes in music and art and an excellent "little theater" group. Hull House soon boasted a gymnasium, a day nursery, and several social clubs. Addams also worked tirelessly and effectively for improved public services and for social legislation of all kinds. She even got herself appointed garbage inspector in her ward and hounded local landlords and the garbage contractor until something approaching decent service was established.

A few critics considered the settlement houses mere devices to socialize the unruly poor by teaching them the "punctilios of upper-class propriety," but almost everyone appreciated their virtues. By the end of the century the Catholics, laggard in entering the arena of practical social reform, were joining the movement, partly because they were losing many communicants to socially minded Protestant churches. The first Catholic-run settlement house was founded in 1898 in an Italian district of New York. Two years later Brownson House in Los Angeles, catering chiefly to Mexican immigrants, opened its doors.

With all their accomplishments, the settlement houses seemed to be fighting a losing battle. "Private beneficence," Jane Addams wrote of Hull House, "is totally inadequate to deal with the vast numbers of the city's disinherited." As a tropical forest grows faster than a handful of men armed with machetes can cut it down, so the slums, fed by an annual influx of hundreds of thousands, blighted new areas more rapidly than the intrepid settlement house workers could clean up old ones. It became increasingly apparent that the wealth and authority of the state must be brought to bear in order to keep abreast of the problem.

Civilization and Its Discontents

As the 19th century died, the majority of the American people—especially the comfortably well-off, the residents of small towns, the shopkeepers, some farmers, and skilled workers—remained confirmed

This portrait of Jane Addams was completed in 1896 by Alice Kellog Tyler, who worked as an artist at Hull House.

optimists and uncritical admirers of their civilization. However, blacks, immigrants, and others who failed to share equitably in the good things of life, along with a growing number of humanitarian reformers, found little to cheer about and much to lament in their increasingly industrialized society. Giant monopolies flourished despite federal restrictions. The gap between rich and poor appeared to be widening, while the slum spread its poison and the materially successful made a god of their success. Human values seemed in grave danger of being crushed by impersonal forces typified by the great corporations.

In 1871 Walt Whitman, usually so full of extravagant praise for the American way of life, had called his fellow countrymen the "most materialistic and money-making people ever known."

I say we had best look our times and lands searchingly in the face, like a physician diagnosing some deep disease. Never was there, perhaps, more hollowness of heart than at present, and here in the United States.

By the late 1880s a well-known journalist could write to a friend: "The wheel of progress is to be run over the whole human race and smash us all." Others noted an alarming jump in the national divorce rate and an increasing taste for all kinds of luxury. "People are made slaves by a desperate struggle to keep up appearances," a Massachusetts commentator declared, and the economist David A. Wells expressed concern over statistics showing that heart disease and mental illness were on the rise. These "diseases of civilization," Wells explained, were "one result of the continuous mental and nervous activity which modern high-tension methods of business have necessitated."

Wells was a prominent liberal, but pessimism was no monopoly of liberals. A little later, Senator Henry Cabot Lodge of Massachusetts, himself a millionaire, complained of the "lawlessness" of the "modern and recent plutocrat" and his "disregard of the rights of others." Lodge spoke of "the enormous contrast between the sanguine mental attitude prevalent in my youth and that, perhaps wiser, but certainly darker view, so general today." His onetime Harvard professor, Henry Adams, was still more critical of the moneygrubbers. "All one's friends," he complained, along with church and university leaders and other educated people, "had joined the banks to force submission to capitalism."

Of course, intellectuals often tend to be critical of the world they live in, whatever its nature; Thoreau denounced materialism and the worship of progress in the 1840s as vigorously as any late-19th-century prophet of gloom. But the voices of the dissatisfied were rising. Despite the many benefits that industrialization had made possible, it was by no means clear around 1900 that the American people were really better off under the new dispensation.

Milestones

1858	English liner *Great Eastern* launched
1876	National Baseball League founded
1880	Salvation Army founded
1880s	"New immigration" begins
1882	John L. Sullivan wins heavyweight boxing championship
	Chinese Exclusion Act
1883	Brooklyn Bridge completed
1885	Foran Contract Labor Act
1887	American Protective Association founded
1888	First urban electric streetcar system
1889	Jane Addams founds Hull House
	Walter Camp's first All America football team
1890	Jacob Riis, *How the Other Half Lives*
	Calvin Woodward opens his Manual Training School
1891	Pope Leo XIII issues *Rerum novarum* encyclical
1896	Charles M. Sheldon, *In His Steps*

SUPPLEMENTARY READING

Titles marked with an asterisk have been published in paperback.

An enormous number of books deal with the social history of late-19th-century America. J. A. Garraty, **The New Commonwealth*** (1968), treats most of the subjects covered in this chapter; A. M. Schlesinger's classic study, **The Rise of the City** (1933), provides a wealth of information about social trends. See also the appropriate sections of Steven Mintz and Susan Kellogg, **Domestic Revolutions: A Social History of the American Family** (1988), and C. N. Degler, **At Odds: Women and the Family in America** (1980).

Henry Adams, **The Education of Henry Adams*** (1918), is a fascinating if highly personal view of the period, and James Bryce, **The American Commonwealth*** (1888), while primarily a political analysis, contains a great deal of information about social conditions, as does D. A. Wells, **Recent Economic Changes** (1889).

On industrial workers, see David Montgomery, **Beyond Equality*** (1967), J. E. Drucker, **Men of the Steel Rails** (1983), Walter Licht, **Working on the Railroad** (1984), and H. G. Gutman, **Work, Culture, and Society in Industrializing America*** (1977). J. A. Garraty (ed.), **Labor and Capital in the Gilded Age*** (1968), provides a convenient selection of testimony from the great 1883 Senate investigation of that subject, while David Brody, **Steelworkers in America*** (1960), and Stephan Thernstrom, **Poverty and Progress: Social Mobility in a Nineteenth-Century City** (1964), throw much light on the lives of workingmen. S. M. Rothman, **Woman's Proper Place** (1978), discusses the new job opportunities for women. Thernstrom's book **The Other Bostonians** (1973) is a brilliant analysis of social and geographic mobility and an excellent summary of work on these important topics. Businessmen's attitudes are covered in T. C. Cochran, **Railroad Leaders** (1953), and E. C. Kirkland, **Dream and Thought in the Business Community** (1956).

On immigration, see M. A. Jones, **American Immigration*** (1960), and John Higham, **Send These to Me*** (1975). Oscar Handlin, **The Uprooted*** (1951), describes the life of the new immigrants somewhat romantically but with sensitivity, while John Higham, **Strangers in the Land*** (1955), stresses the reactions of native-born Americans to successive waves of immigration. Moses Rischin, **The Promised City: New York's Jews*** (1962), Thomas Kessner, **The Golden Door: Italian and Jewish Immigrant Mobility** (1977), Humbert Nelli, **The Italians of Chicago*** (1970), Virginia Yans-McLaughlin, **Family and Community: Italian Immigrants in Buffalo** (1977), and T. N. Brown, **Irish-American Nationalism** (1966), are important monographs.

A brief interpretive history of urban development is C. N. Glaab and A. T. Brown, **A History of Urban America*** (1967). K. T. Jackson, **Crabgrass Frontier** (1985), is a pioneering history of suburban development, and J. C. Teaford, **The Unheralded Triumph** (1984), gives weight to the accomplishments of the cities as well as their inadequacies. On the growing pains of American cities, consult R. H. Bremner, **From the Depths*** (1956), Jacob Riis, **How the Other Half Lives*** (1890), and Roy Lubove, **The Progressives and the Slums** (1962). Urban architecture is discussed in J. E. Burchard and Albert Bush-Brown, **The Architecture of America*** (1961). S. B. Warner, Jr., **Streetcar Suburbs** (1962), is an interesting study of Boston's development that is full of suggestive ideas about late-19th-century growth.

On the early development of intercollegiate sports, see R. A. Smith, **Sports and Freedom: The Rise of Big-Time College Athletics** (1988). The response of religion to industrialism is discussed in H. F. May, **Protestant Churches and Industrial America*** (1949), A. I. Abell, **American Catholicism and Social Action** (1960), and Arthur Mann, **Yankee Reformers in the Urban Age*** (1954). For details of the settlement house movement, see A. F. Davis, **Spearheads for Reform** (1967), Davis's **American Heroine** (1973), a life of Jane Addams, and two classic personal accounts, Jane Addams, **Twenty Years at Hull House*** (1910), and Lillian Wald, **The House on Henry Street** (1915).

The New Immigrants

A great many immigrants in the late 1800s and early 1900s settled in large East Coast cities, especially New York. This 1886 watercolor of Baxter Street is a reasonably realistic sketch of an area in New York's infamous Five Points slum. The sketch was done for a stage set used in a comedy about Irish immigrants.

Starting in 1892, Ellis Island in New York Harbor was the processing center for immigrants. The newcomers often had to wait hours before being cleared for entry into the United States. Many were from southern and eastern Europe. Lewis Hine photographed this Italian mother and child waiting to be admitted.

Part of the processing was a medical examination. Below a doctor checks a group of women with her stethoscope. The eye chart on the back wall is in Cyrillic (the Russian alphabet).

Once cleared at Ellis Island, the immigrants often found their way to neighborhoods in New York City where people from their mother countries had already settled. Orchard St. (left) in Manhattan was a bustling shopping area for the eastern European Jewish community, with food and clothing sold out of storefronts and off pushcarts in the street. Mulberry Bend (below) was in the heart of the Italian district of Manhattan's Lower East Side.

Living conditions in the tenements that lined these streets could be appalling. The boy at lower left fills a basin at a communal faucet, which was the tenants' only source of water for cooking, laundry, and bathing.

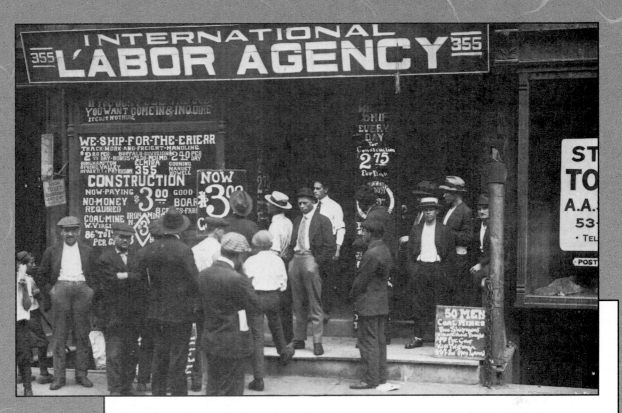

Getting a job was the first priority for immigrants, since most arrived with little money or other resources. This New York employment agency, photographed by Lewis Hine in 1910, posted available jobs in construction and coal mining in places as far away as West Virginia.

For some families the workplace was the same tenement room in which they ate and slept. The garment industry, employing a largely Jewish immigrant work force, relied on "home work" and paid workers by the garment (the piece) rather than by the hour.

Levi Strauss (1830–1902) was not a "new" immigrant, having emigrated to New York from Bavaria in 1847. He peddled clothing and household items until 1853, when he booked passage on a clipper ship bound for San Francisco. He had planned to sell dry goods to the gold prospectors, including canvas for tents and wagon covers, but he found that what the miners needed most was sturdy work clothes. So he hired a tailor to sew the canvas into trousers—he later switched to blue-dyed denim—and soon "those pants of Levi's" became famous. By the 1870s Strauss's copper-riveted Model 501 Double X blue jeans and denim overalls were an established American institution, as this ad from the period shows.

Levi Strauss's success was repeated by many of the "new" immigrants. A sampling of people who achieved their ambitions in various fields in their adopted country appears on the facing page.

Jacob Riis (1849–1914)
From Denmark in 1870.
*Journalist and photographer. Author
of* How the Other Half Lives *(1890),
an exposé of immigrant life
in the slums.*

Mother Frances Xavier Cabrini
(1850–1917)
From Italy in 1889.
*Roman Catholic saint, canonized in
1946. Founded convents, schools,
orphanages, and hospitals.*

Emma Goldman
(1869–1940)
From Russia in 1885.
*Lecturer, editor, and anarchist activist.
Founder of* Mother Earth, *anarchist journal.
See "American Lives" portrait, page 638.*

Felix Frankfurter (1882–1965)
From Austria in 1894.
*Harvard law professor, 1914–1939.
Supreme Court justice, 1939–1962.
A founder of the American Civil
Liberties Union.*

Sidney Hillman (1887–1946)
From Lithuania in 1907.
*Labor leader. President of
Amalgamated Clothing Workers of
America, 1914–1946. Active in
Roosevelt's New Deal.*

Irving Berlin (1888–1989)
From Russia in 1893.
*Songwriter. Composed nearly one
thousand songs, including "God
Bless America," "White Christmas,"
and "Alexander's Ragtime Band," his
first big hit in 1911.*

XXI

Intellectual and Cultural Trends

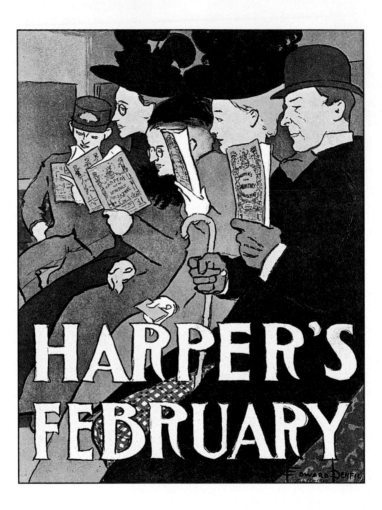

These natural ordermakers, whether amateurs or officials, came to the front immediately. There seemed to be no possibility which there was not some one there to think of, or which within twenty-four hours was not in some way provided for. . . . California education has, of course, made the thought of all possible recuperation easy.

WILLIAM JAMES, *eyewitness account of the San Francisco earthquake, 1906*

I ndustrialization altered the way Americans thought at the same time that it transformed their ways of making a living. Technological advances revolutionized the communication of ideas more drastically than they did the transportation of goods or the manufacture of steel. The materialism that permeated American attitudes toward business also affected contemporary education and literature, while Charles Darwin's theory of evolution influenced American philosophers, lawyers, and historians profoundly.

New ideas about how children should be educated and what they should be taught emerged along with new methods of communicating information to adults. As American society became more complex, the need for specialized training increased, boosting the importance of higher education. Americans began to make significant contributions both in the so-called hard sciences, such as chemistry and physics, and in relatively new soft social sciences, such as psychology, political science, and sociology. A new literary flowering comparable to the renaissance of the 1840s and 1850s occurred in the 1870s and 1880s. By the end of the 19th century America had finally emerged intellectually from the shadow of Europe.

The Pursuit of Knowledge

Improvements in public education and the needs of an increasingly complex society for every type of intellectual skill caused a veritable revolution in how knowledge was discovered, disseminated, and put to use. Observing the effects of formal education on their children, many older people were eager to experience some of its benefits. Nothing so well illustrates the desire for new information as the rise of the Chautauqua movement, founded by John H. Vincent, a Methodist minister, and Lewis Miller, an Ohio manufacturer of farm machinery. Vincent had charge of Sunday schools for the Methodist church. In 1874 he and Miller organized a two-week summer course for Sunday school teachers on the shores of Lake Chautauqua in New York. Besides instruction, they offered good meals, evening songfests around the campfire, and a relaxing atmosphere—all for $6 for the two weeks.

The 40 young teachers who attended were delighted with the program, and soon the leafy shore of Lake Chautauqua became a city of tents each summer as thousands poured into the region from all over the country. The founders expanded their offerings to include instruction in literature, science, government, and economics. Famous authorities, including, over the years, six presidents of the United States, came to lecture to open-air audiences on every subject imaginable. Eventually Chautauqua even offered correspondence courses leading over a four-year period to a diploma. Books were written specifically for the program, and a monthly magazine, *The Chautauquan*, was published.

Such success provoked imitation, and by 1900 there were about 200 Chautauqua-type organizations. Intellectual standards in these programs varied greatly; musicians (good and bad), homespun humorists, inspirational lecturers, and assorted quacks shared the platform with prominent divines and scholars. Moneymaking undoubtedly motivated many of the entrepreneurs who operated the centers, all of which, including the original Chautauqua, reflected the prevailing tastes of the American people—diverse, enthusiastic, uncritical, and shallow. Nevertheless, the movement provided opportunities for thousands seeking stimulation and intellectual improvement. Still larger numbers profited from the proliferation of public libraries. Private donors, led by the ironmaster Andrew Carnegie, contributed millions to the cause. In 1900 over 1,700 libraries in the United States had collections of more than 5,000 volumes.

Newspapers were an even more important means for disseminating information and educating the masses. Here new technology supplied the major incentive for change. The development by Richard Hoe and Stephen Tucker of the web press (1871), which printed simultaneously on both sides of paper fed into it from large rolls, and Ottmar Mergenthaler's linotype machine (1886), which cast rows of type as needed directly from molten metal, cut printing costs dramatically. Machines for making paper out of wood pulp reduced the cost of newsprint to a quarter of what it had been in the 1860s. By 1895 machines were printing, cutting, and folding 32-page newspapers at a rate of 24,000 an hour.

The telegraph and transoceanic cables wrought a similar transformation in the gathering of news. Press associations, led by the New York Associated Press, flourished; the syndicated article appeared; and a few publishers—Edward W. Scripps was the first—began to amass chains of newspapers.

Population growth and better education created an ever-larger demand for printed matter. At the same time, the integration of the economy enabled manufacturers to sell their goods all over the country. Advertising became important, and sellers soon learned that newspapers and magazines were excellent means of placing their products before millions of eyes. Advertising revenues soared just when new machines and general expansion were making publishing an expensive business. The day of the journeyman printer-editor ended. Rich men such as the railroad magnate Jay Gould and the mining tycoon George Hearst invested heavily in newspapers in the post–Civil War decades.

Rich publishers tended to be conservative, but reaching the masses meant lowering intellectual and cultural standards, appealing to emotions, and adopting popular, sometimes radical, causes. Cheap, mass-circulation papers had first appeared in the 1830s and 1840s, the most successful being the *Sun,* the *Herald,* and the *Tribune* in New York, the *Philadelphia Public Ledger,* and the *Baltimore Sun.* None of them much exceeded a circulation of 50,000 before the Civil War. The first publisher to reach a truly massive audience was Joseph Pulitzer,

a Hungarian-born immigrant who made a first-rate paper of the *St. Louis Post-Dispatch.* In 1883 Pulitzer bought the *New York World,* a sheet with a circulation of perhaps 20,000. Within a year he was selling 100,000 copies daily, and by the late 1890s the *World's* circulation regularly exceeded 1 million.

Pulitzer achieved this brilliant success by casting a wide net. To the masses he offered bold, black headlines devoted to crime (ANOTHER MURDERER TO HANG), scandal (VICE ADMIRAL'S SON IN JAIL), catastrophe (TWENTY-FOUR MINERS KILLED), society and the theater (LILY LANGTRY'S NEW ADMIRER), together with feature stories, political cartoons, comics, and pictures. For the educated and affluent he provided better political and financial coverage than the most respectable New York journals. Pulitzer made the *World* a crusader for civic improvement by attacking

John Singer Sargent's 1905 portrait of Joseph Pulitzer. Upon his death six years later, Pulitzer's will provided for the endowment of the Columbia School of Journalism and the establishment of Pulitzer Prizes for journalism, letters, and other categories.

Publishing challenger to Joseph Pulitzer in the 1890s, William Randolph Hearst, here depicted in 1906 as a member of Congress, and his newspapers remained a not always constructive force in national politics well into the 1930s.

political corruption, monopoly, and slum problems.

"The *World* is the people's newspaper," Pulitzer boasted, and in the sense that it interested men and women of every sort, he was correct. Pulitzer's methods were quickly copied by competitors, especially William Randolph Hearst, who purchased the *New York Journal* in 1895 and soon outdid the *World* in sensationalism. But no other newspaperman of the era approached Pulitzer in originality, boldness, and the knack of reaching the masses without abandoning seriousness of purpose and basic integrity.

Magazine Journalism

Growth and ferment also characterized the magazine world. In 1865 there were about 700 magazines in the country; by the turn of the century, more than 5,000. Until the mid-1880s, few of the new magazines were in any way unusual. A handful of serious periodicals, such as the *Atlantic Monthly, Harper's,* and *The Century,* staid in tone and conservative in political caste, dominated the field. Articles on current affairs, a good deal of fiction and poetry, and historical and biographical studies filled their pages. Although they had great influence, none approached a mass circulation because of the limited size of the upper-middle-class audience they aimed at. *The Century* reached a peak in the 1880s of about 250,000 when it published a series of articles on Civil War battles by famous commanders, but it could not sustain that level. A circulation of 100,000 was considered good for such magazines.

The leading publisher of magazines directed at the average citizen in the 1860s and 1870s was Frank Leslie. His periodicals bore such titles as *Frank Leslie's Chimney Corner, Frank Leslie's Illustrated Newspaper,* and *Frank Leslie's Jolly Joker.* Leslie specialized in illustrations of current events (he put as many as 34 engravers to work on a single picture in order to bring it out quickly) and on providing what he frankly admitted was "mental pabulum"—a combination of cheap romantic fiction, old-fashioned poetry, jokes, and advice columns. Some of his magazines sold as many as 300,000 copies per issue.

After about 1885 new serious magazines such as *The Forum* (1886) and *The Arena* (1889) emphasized hard-hitting articles on controversial subjects by leading experts. The weekly *Literary Digest* (1890) offered summaries of press opinion on current events, and the *Review of Reviews* (1891) provided monthly commentary on the news.

Even more startling changes revolutionized the mass-circulation field. In 1889 Edward W. Bok became editor of the *Ladies' Home Journal.* Besides advice columns ("Ruth Ashmore's Side Talks with Girls"), he offered articles on child care, gardening, and interior decorating, published fine contemporary novelists, and commissioned public figures, such as Presidents Grover Cleveland and Benjamin Harrison, to discuss important questions. He printed colored reproductions of art masterpieces—the invention of cheap photoengraving was of enormous significance in the success of mass-circulation magazines—and crusaded for women's suffrage, conservation, and other reforms. Bok did more than cater to public tastes; he created new tastes.

Bok and his many competitors reached millions

of readers. Like Pulitzer in the newspaper field, they found ways of interesting rich and poor, the cultivated and the ignorant. Using the new printing technology to cut costs and drawing heavily on advertising revenues, they sold their magazines for 10 or 15 cents a copy and still made fortunes.

Colleges and Universities

The same forces that were affecting the dissemination of information were also altering higher education and professional training. The number of colleges rose from about 350 to 500 between 1878 and 1898, and the student body roughly tripled. Despite this growth, less than 2 percent of the college-age population attended college, but the aspirations of the nation's youth were rising, and more and more parents had the financial means necessary for fulfilling them.

More significant than the expansion of the colleges were the alterations in their curricula and in the atmosphere on the average campus. In 1870 most colleges were still small, limited in their offerings, intellectually stagnant. The ill-paid professors were seldom scholars of stature. Thereafter, change came like a flood tide. State universities proliferated; the federal government's land-grant program in support of training in "agriculture and the mechanic arts," established under the Morrill Act of 1862, came into its own; wealthy philanthropists poured fortunes into old institutions and founded new ones; professional schools of law, medicine, education, business, journalism, and other specialties increased in number.

In the forefront of reform was Harvard, the oldest and most prestigious college in the country. In the 1860s it possessed an excellent faculty, but teaching methods were antiquated, and the curriculum had remained almost unchanged since the colonial period. In 1869, however, a dynamic president, the chemist Charles W. Eliot, introduced the elective system, gradually eliminating required courses and expanding offerings in such areas as modern languages, economics, and the laboratory sciences.

Eliot also encouraged the faculty to experiment with new teaching methods, and he brought in professors with original minds and new ideas. One was Henry Adams, grandson of John Quincy Adams, who made the study of medieval history a true intellectual experience. "Mr. Adams roused the spirit

of inquiry and controversy in me," one student later wrote.

Under Eliot's guidance the standards of the medical school were raised. In the law school, Christopher Columbus Langdell introduced the case method of study. In some respects Eliot went too far—the elective system encouraged superficiality and laxness in many students—but on balance he transformed Harvard from a college, "a place to which a young man is sent," to a university, a place "to which he goes."

An even more important development in higher education was the founding of Johns Hopkins in 1876. This university was one of many established in the period by wealthy industrialists; its benefactor, the Baltimore merchant Johns Hopkins, had made his fortune in the Baltimore and Ohio Railroad. Its distinctiveness, however, was due to the vision of Daniel Coit Gilman, its first president.

Gilman modeled Johns Hopkins on the German universities, where meticulous research and freedom of inquiry were the guiding principles. In staffing the institution, he sought scholars of the highest reputation, scouring Europe as well as America in his search for talent and offering outstanding men high salaries for that time—up to $5,000 for a professor, roughly ten times the income of a skilled artisan. At the same time, he employed a number of relatively unknown but brilliant younger scholars, such as Herbert Baxter Adams, whom he made an associate in history on the strength of his excellent doctoral dissertation at the University of Heidelberg. Gilman promised his teachers good students and ample opportunity to pursue their own research (which explains why so many Hopkins professors repeatedly turned down attractive offers from other universities).

Johns Hopkins specialized in graduate education. In the generation after its founding, it turned out a remarkable percentage of the most important scholars in the nation, including Woodrow Wilson in political science, John Dewey in philosophy, Frederick Jackson Turner in history, and John R. Commons in economics. The seminar conducted by Herbert Baxter Adams was particularly productive; the Adams-edited *Johns Hopkins Studies in Historical and Political Science*, consisting of the doctoral dissertations of his students, was "the mother of similar studies in every part of the United States."

The success of Johns Hopkins did not stop the migration of American scholars to Europe; more than 2,000 matriculated at German universities during the 1880s. But as Hopkins graduates took up professorships at other institutions and as scholars trained elsewhere adopted the Hopkins methods, true graduate education became possible in most sections of the country.

The example of Johns Hopkins encouraged other wealthy individuals to endow universities offering advanced work. Clark University in Worcester, Massachusetts, founded by Jonas Clark, a merchant and real estate speculator, opened its doors in 1889. Its president, G. Stanley Hall, had been a professor of psychology at Hopkins, and he built the new university in that institution's image. More important was John D. Rockefeller's creation, the University of Chicago (1892). The president of the University of Chicago, William Rainey Harper, was a brilliant biblical scholar—he received his Ph.D. from Yale at the age of 18—and an imaginative administrator.

Like Daniel Coit Gilman, Harper sought top-flight scholars for his faculty. He offered such high salaries that he was besieged with over 1,000 applications. Armed with Rockefeller dollars, he "raided" the best institutions in the nation. He decimated the faculty of the new Clark University—"an act of wreckage," the indignant President Hall complained, "comparable to anything that the worst trust ever attempted against its competitors." Chicago offered first-class graduate and undergraduate education. During its first year there were 120 instructors for fewer than 600 students, and despite fears that the mighty tycoon Rockefeller would force his social and economic views on the institution, academic freedom was the rule.

State and federal aid to higher education expanded rapidly. The Morrill Act, granting land to each state at a rate of 30,000 acres for each senator and representative, provided the endowments that gave many important modern universities, such as Illinois, Michigan State, and Ohio State, their start. While the federal assistance was earmarked for specific subjects, the land-grant institutions offered a full range of courses, and all received additional state funds. They were coeducational from the start, and most developed professional schools and experimented with extension work and summer programs.

Typical of the better state institutions was the University of Michigan, which reached the top rank among the nation's universities during the presidency of James B. Angell (1871–1909). Like Eliot at Harvard, Angell expanded the undergraduate curriculum and strengthened the law and medical schools. He encouraged graduate studies, seeking to make Michigan "part of the great world of scholars," and sought ways in which the university could serve the general community.

Important advances were made in women's higher education beginning with Vassar College, which opened its doors to 300 women students in 1865. Wellesley and Smith, both founded in 1875, completed the so-called Big Three women's colleges. These three, the already established Mount Holyoke, and Bryn Mawr (1885), Barnard (1889), and Radcliffe (1893) became known as the Seven Sisters.

The only professional careers easily available to women graduates were nursing, teaching, and the new area called social work. Nevertheless, the remarkable women that these institutions trained were conscious of their uniqueness and determined to demonstrate their capabilities. Fewer than 40 percent of the first few generations of women graduates ever married. "Sending a daughter to college," the historian William H. Chafe writes, was "like letting the genie out of the bottle."

Not all the changes in higher education were beneficial. The elective system led to superficiality; students gained a smattering of knowledge of many subjects and mastered none. Intensive graduate work often produced narrowness of outlook and research monographs on trivial subjects. Attempts to apply the scientific method in fields such as history and economics often enticed students into making smug claims to objectivity and definitiveness that from the nature of the subjects they could not even approach in their work.

The gifts of rich industrialists sometimes came with strings, and college boards of trustees tended to be dominated by businessmen who sometimes attempted to impose their own social and economic beliefs on faculty members. Few professors actually lost their positions because their views offended trustees, but at many institutions trustees exerted constant nagging pressures that limited academic freedom and scholarly objectivity. At state colleges, politicians often interfered in academic affairs, even treating professorships as part of the patronage system.

Thorstein Veblen pointed out in his caustic study *The Higher Learning in America* (1918) that "the in-

A geology field trip in the 1880s sets out from the administration building of Smith College. Along with their picks and hammers, the young women carry baskets that look as though they might contain lunch.

trusion of businesslike ideals, aims and methods" harmed the universities in countless subtle ways. Size alone—the verbose Veblen called it "an executive weakness for spectacular magnitude"—became an end in itself, and the practical values of education were exalted over the humanistic. At many institutions professors came to be regarded as mere hired hands. In 1893 the members of the faculty of Stanford University were officially classified as personal servants of Mrs. Leland Stanford, widow of the founder. This was done in good cause—the Stanford estate was tied up in probate court and the ruling made it possible to pay professors out of Mrs. Stanford's allowance for household expenses—but that such a procedure was even conceivable must have appalled the scholarly world.

As the number of college graduates increased and as colleges ceased being primarily training institutions for clergymen, the influence of alumni on educational policies began to make itself felt—not always happily. Campus social activities became more important. Fraternities proliferated. Interest in organized sports first appeared as a laudable outgrowth of the general expansion of the curriculum, but soon athletic contests were playing a role all out of proportion to their significance. After football evolved as the leading intercollegiate sport it became a source of revenue that many colleges dared not neglect. Since students, alumni, and the public demanded winning teams, college administrators stooped to subsidizing student athletes, in extreme cases employing players who were not students at all. One exasperated college president quipped that the B.A. degree was coming to mean Bachelor of Athletics. Thus higher education reflected American values, with all their strengths and weaknesses.

Scientific Advances

Much has been made of the crassness of late-19th-century American life, yet the period produced intellectual achievements of the highest quality. If the business mentality dominated society, and if the great barons of industry, exalting practicality over theory, tended to look down on the life of the mind, intellectuals, quietly pondering the problems of their generation, nonetheless created works that affected the country as profoundly as the achievements of industrial organizers like Rockefeller and Carnegie and technicians like Edison and Bell.

In pure science America produced a number of outstanding figures in these years. The giant among them, whose contributions some experts rank with those of Newton, Darwin, and Einstein, was Josiah Willard Gibbs, professor of mathematical physics at Yale from 1871 to 1903. Gibbs created an entirely new science, physical chemistry, and made possible the study of how complex substances respond to changes in temperature and pressure. Purely theoretical at the time, Gibbs's ideas led to vital advances in metallurgy and in the manufacture of plastics, drugs, and other products. Gibbs is often used to illustrate the supposed indifference of the age to its great minds, but this is hardly fair; he was a shy, self-effacing man who cared little for the spotlight or for collecting disciples. He published his major papers in the obscure *Transactions of the Connecticut Academy of Arts and Sciences.* Furthermore, he was so far ahead of his time that only a handful of specialists had a glimmering of the importance of his work.

Of lesser but still major significance was the work of Albert A. Michelson of the University of Chicago, who made the first accurate measurements of the speed of light. Michelson's research helped prepare the way for Einstein's theory of relativity; in 1907 he became the first American scientist to win a Nobel Prize.

The New Social Sciences

In the social sciences, the achievements of the leading thinkers were closely connected to the practical issues of the age. The application of the theory of evolution to every aspect of human relations, the impact of industrialization on society—such topics were of intense concern to economists, sociologists, and historians. An understanding of Darwin increased the already strong interest in studying the development of institutions and their interactions. Controversies over trusts, slum conditions, and other problems drew scholars out of their towers and into practical affairs.

Social scientists were impressed by the progress being made in the physical and biological sciences. They eagerly applied the scientific method to their own specialties, hoping thereby to arrive at objective truths in fields that were by nature essentially subjective.

Among the economists, something approaching a revolution took place in the 1880s. The classical school, which maintained that immutable natural laws governed all human behavior and used the insights of Darwin only to justify unrestrained competition and laissez faire, was challenged by a group of young economists who argued that as times changed, economic theories and laws must be modified in order to remain relevant. Richard T. Ely, another of the scholars who made Johns Hopkins a font of new ideas in the 1880s, summarized the thinking of this group in 1885. The state, Ely proclaimed, is "an educational and ethical agency whose positive aid is an indispensable condition of human progress." Laissez faire was outmoded and dangerous. Economic problems were basically moral problems; their solution required "the united efforts of Church, state and science." The proper way to study these problems was by analyzing actual conditions, not by applying abstract laws or principles.

This approach produced the so-called institutionalist school of economics, whose members made detailed, on-the-spot investigations of labor unions, sweatshops, factories, and mines. The study of institutions, they believed, would lead to both theoretical insights and practical social reform. John R. Commons, one of Ely's students at Johns Hopkins and later professor of economics at the University of Wisconsin, was the outstanding member of this school. His ten-volume *Documentary History of American Industrial Society* (1910–1911) reveals the institutionalist approach at its best.

A similar revolution struck sociology in the mid-1880s. Prevailing opinion up to that time rejected the idea of government interference with the organization of society. The influence of the English social Darwinist Herbert Spencer, who objected even to public schools and the postal system, was immense. Spencer and his American disciples, among them Edward L. Youmans, editor of *Popular Science Monthly,* twisted Darwin's ideas to mean that society could be changed only by the force of evolution, which moved with cosmic slowness. "You and I can do nothing at all," Youmans told the reformer Henry George. "It's all a matter of evolution. Perhaps in four or five thousand years evolution may have carried men beyond this state of things."

Such a point of view made little sense in America, where society was changing rapidly and the range of government social and economic activity was expanding. It was first challenged by an obscure scholar employed by the U.S. Geological Survey, Lester Frank Ward. In *Dynamic Sociology* (1883) Ward assailed the Spencerians for ignoring the possibility of "the improvement of society by cold calculation." In *The Psychic Factors of Civilization* (1893) he blasted the "law of competition." Human progress, he argued, consisted of "triumphing little by little over this law," for example, by interfering with biological processes through the use of medicines to kill harmful bacteria.

Government regulation of the economy offered another illustration of how people could control the environment. "Nothing is more obvious today," Ward wrote in 1895, "than the signal inability of capital and private enterprise to take care of themselves unaided by the state." Society must indeed evolve, but it would evolve through careful social planning. Like the new economists, Ward emphasized the practical and ethical sides of his subject. Sociologists should seek "the betterment of society," he said, "Dynamic Sociology aims at the organization of happiness." Ward's arguments yielded few concrete results before 1900, but they ultimately demolished social Darwinism and laid the theoretical basis for the modern welfare state.

Similar currents of thought influenced other social sciences. In *Systems of Consanguinity* (1871) the pioneer anthropologist Lewis Henry Morgan developed a theory of social evolution and showed how kinship relationships reflected and affected tribal institutions. The new political scientists were also evolutionists and institutionalists. The Founding Fathers, living in a world dominated by Newton's concept of the universe as an immense, orderly machine, had conceived of the political system as an impersonal set of institutions and principles—a government of laws rather than of men. Nineteenth-century thinkers (John C. Calhoun is the best example) concerned themselves with abstractions, such as states' rights, and ignored the extralegal aspects of politics, such as parties and pressure groups. In the 1880s political scientists began to employ a different approach. In his doctoral dissertation at Johns Hopkins, *Congressional Government* (1885), Woodrow Wilson analyzed the American political system. He concluded that the real locus of authority lay in the committees of Congress, which had no constitutional basis at all. Wilson was by no means a radical, but he viewed politics as a dynamic process and offered no theoretical objection to the expansion of state power. "Every means," he wrote in *The State* (1889), "by which society may be perfected through the instrumentality of government . . . ought certainly to be diligently sought."

Progressive Education

Traditionally, American teachers had emphasized the three Rs and relied on strict discipline and rote learning. Typical of the pedagogues of the period was the Chicago teacher, described by a reformer in the 1890s, who told her students firmly: "Don't stop to think; tell me what you know!" Yet new ideas were attracting attention. According to a German educator, Johann Friedrich Herbart, teachers could best arouse the interest of their students by relating new information to what they already knew; good teaching called for professional training, psychological insight, enthusiasm, and imagination, not merely facts and a birch rod. At the same time, evolutionists were pressing for a kind of education that would help children to "survive" by adapting to the demands of their environment.

Forward-looking educators seized on these ideas because dynamic social changes were making the old system increasingly inadequate. Settlement house workers discovered that slum children needed training in handicrafts, good citizenship, and personal hygiene as much as in reading and writing. They were appalled by the local schools, which suffered from the same ills—filth, overcrowding, rickety construction—that plagued the tenements and by school systems that were controlled by machine politicians who doled out teaching positions to party hacks and other untrained persons. They argued that playgrounds, nurseries, kindergartens, and adult education programs were essential in communities where most women worked and many people lacked much formal education. "We are impatient with the schools which lay all stress on reading and writing," Jane Addams declared. This type of education "fails to give the child any clew to the life about him."

The philosopher who summarized and gave direction to these forces was John Dewey, a professor at the University of Chicago. Dewey was concerned with the implications of evolution—indeed, of all science—for education. Essentially, his approach was ethical. Was the nation's youth being properly prepared for the tasks it faced in the modern world? In 1896, together with his wife Harriet, Dewey founded the Laboratory School to put his educational ideas to the test. Three years later he published *The School and Society,* describing and defending his theories.

"Education," Dewey insisted, was "the fundamental method of social progress and reform." To seek to improve conditions merely by passing laws was "futile." Moreover, in an industrial society the family no longer performed many of the educational functions it had carried out in an agrarian society. Farm children learn about nature, about work, about human character in countless ways denied to children in cities. The school can fill the gap by becoming "an embryonic community . . . with types of occupations that reflect the life of the larger society." At the same time, education should center on the child, and new information should be related to what the child already knows. Children's imaginations, energies, and curiosity are tools for broadening their outlooks and increasing their stores of information. Finally, the school should become an instrument for social reform, "saturating" children with the "spirit of service" and helping to produce a "society which is worthy, lovely, and harmonious." Education, in other words, ought to build character and teach good citizenship as well as transmit knowledge.

The School and Society created a stir, and Dewey immediately assumed leadership of what in the next generation was called progressive education. Although the gains made in public education before 1900 were more quantitative than qualitative and the philosophy dominant in most schools was not very different at the end of the century from that prevailing in Horace Mann's day, change was in the air.

Law and History

Even jurisprudence, by its nature conservative and rooted in tradition, felt the pressure of evolutionary thought and the new emphasis on studying insti-

On joining the faculty of the University of Chicago in 1894, John Dewey, a child of rural Vermont, took up the challenge of adapting American education practices and ideals to the rapidly urbanizing society that he saw all about him. His subsequent move to Columbia University's Teachers College in 1904 only reinforced his commitment to "progressive education."

tutions as they actually are. In 1881 Oliver Wendell Holmes, Jr., published *The Common Law.* Rejecting the ideas that judges should limit themselves to the mechanical explication of statutes and that law consisted only of what was written in law books, Holmes argued that "the felt necessities of the time" rather than precedent should determine the rules by which people are governed. "The life of the law has not been logic; it has been experience," he wrote. "It is revolting," he added on another occasion, "to have no better reason for a rule of law than that it was laid down in the time of Henry IV."

Holmes went on to a long and brilliant judicial career during which he repeatedly stressed the right of the people, through their elected representatives, to deal with contemporary problems in any reasonable way, unfettered by outmoded conceptions of the proper limits of government authority. Like the societies they regulated, laws should evolve as times and conditions changed, he said.

This way of reasoning caused no sudden reversal of judicial practice. Holmes's most notable opinions as a judge tended to be dissents. But his philosophy reflected the best thinking of the late 19th century, and his influence has grown with every decade of the 20th.

The new approach to knowledge did not always advance the cause of liberal reform. Historians in the graduate schools became intensely interested in studying the origins and evolution of political institutions. They concluded, after much "scientific" study of old charters and law codes, that the roots of democracy were to be found in the customs of the ancient tribes of northern Europe. This theory of the Teutonic origins of democracy, which has since been thoroughly discredited, fitted well with the prejudices of people of British stock, and it provided ammunition for those who favored restricting immigration and for those who argued that blacks were inferior beings.

Out of this work, however, came an essentially

Appointed to the Supreme Court in 1902 by his friend Theodore Roosevelt, Oliver Wendell Holmes, Jr., remained there for 29 years and seven presidents. His opinions, often in dissent, regularly called on his colleagues to exercise judicial restraint and allow elected officials to carry out their democratic responsibilities.

democratic concept, the frontier thesis of Frederick Jackson Turner, still another scholar trained at Johns Hopkins. Turner's essay "The Significance of the Frontier in American History" (1893) argued that the frontier experience, through which every section of the country had passed, had affected the thinking of the people and the shape of American institutions. The isolation of the frontier and the need during each successive westward advance to create civilization anew account, Turner wrote, for the individualism of Americans and the democratic character of their society. Nearly everything unique in our culture could be traced to the existence of the frontier, he claimed.

Life on the frontier was not as democratic as Turner believed, and his thesis certainly does not "explain" American development as completely as he said it did. Nevertheless, his work showed how important it was to investigate the evolution of institutions, and it encouraged historians to study social and economic, as well as purely political, subjects. If the claims of the new historians to objectivity and definitiveness were absurdly overstated, their emphasis on thoroughness, exactitude, and impartiality did much to raise standards in the profession. Perhaps the finest product of the new scientific school, a happy combination of meticulous scholarship and literary artistry, was Henry Adams's nine-volume *History of the United States During the Administrations of Jefferson and Madison.*

Realism in Literature

When what Mark Twain called the Gilded Age began, American literature was dominated by the romantic mood. All the important writers of the 1840s and 1850s except Hawthorne, Thoreau, and Poe were still living. Longfellow stood at the height of his fame, and the lachrymose Susan Warner—"tears on almost every page"—continued to turn out stories in the style of her popular *Wide, Wide World.* Romanticism, however, had lost its creative force; most writing in the decade after 1865 was sentimental trash pandering to the preconceptions of middle-class readers. Magazines like the *Atlantic Monthly* overflowed with stories about fair ladies worshiped from afar by stainless heroes, women coping selflessly with drunken husbands, and poor but honest youths rising through various combinations of virtue and assiduity to positions of wealth and influence. Most writers of fiction tended to ignore the eternal conflicts inherent in human nature.

The patent unreality, even dishonesty, of contemporary fiction eventually caused a reaction. The most important forces giving rise to the Age of Realism were those that were transforming every other aspect of American life: industrialism, with its associated complexities and social problems; the theory of evolution, which made people more aware of the force of the environment and the basic conflicts of existence; the new science, which taught dispassionate, empirical observation. Novelists undertook the examination of slum life, the conflict between capital and labor, and political corruption. They created multidimensional characters, depicted persons of every social class, used dialect and slang to capture the flavor of particular types, and fashioned painstaking descriptions of the surroundings into which they placed their subjects.*

Mark Twain

Easy as it was to romanticize the West, that region lent itself to the realistic approach as well. Almost of necessity, novelists writing about the West described coarse characters from the lower levels of society and dealt with crime and violence. It would have been difficult indeed to write a genteel romance about a mining camp. The outstanding figure of western literature, the first great American realist, was Mark Twain.

Twain was born Samuel L. Clemens in 1835. He grew up in Hannibal, Missouri, on the banks of the Mississippi. After mastering the printer's trade and working as a riverboat pilot, he went west to Nevada in 1861. The wild, rough life of Virginia City fascinated him, but prospecting got him nowhere, and he became a reporter for the *Territorial Enterprise*. Soon he was publishing humorous stories about the local life under the nom de plume Mark Twain. In 1865, while working in California, he wrote "The Celebrated Jumping Frog of Calaveras County," a story that brought him national recognition. A tour of Europe and the Holy Land in 1867–1868 led to *The Innocents Abroad* (1869), which made him famous.

Twain's greatness stemmed from his keen reportorial eye and ear, his eagerness to live life to the fullest, his marvelous sense of humor, and his ability to be at once in society and outside it, to love humanity yet be repelled by human vanity and perversity. He epitomized the zest and adaptability of his age and also its materialism. No contemporary pursued the almighty dollar more assiduously. An inveterate speculator, he made a fortune with his pen and lost it in foolish business ventures. He wrote tirelessly and endlessly about America and Europe, about his own times and the feudal past, about tourists, slaves, tycoons, cracker-barrel philosophers— and human destiny. He was equally at home and equally successful on the Great River of his childhood, in the mining camps, and in the eastern bourgeois society of his mature years. But every prize slipped through his fingers. Twain died a dark pessimist, surrounded by adulation yet alone, an alien and a stranger in the land he loved and knew so well.

Twain excelled every contemporary in the portrayal of character. In his biting satire *The Gilded Age* (1873) he created that magnificent mountebank Colonel Beriah Sellers, purveyor of eyewash ("the Infallible Imperial Oriental Optic Liniment") and false hopes, ridiculous, unscrupulous, but lovable. In *Huckleberry Finn* (1884), his masterpiece, his portrait of the slave Jim, loyal, patient, naive, yet withal a man, is unforgettable. When Huck takes advantage of Jim's credulity merely for his own amusement, the slave turns from him coldly and says: "Dat truck dah is trash; en trash is what people is dat puts dirt on de head er dey fren's en makes 'em ashamed." And there is Huck Finn himself, full of devilry, romantic, amoral—up to a point—and at bottom the complete realist. When Miss Watson tells him he can get anything he wants by praying for it, he makes the effort, is disillusioned, and concludes: "If a body can get anything they pray for, why don't Deacon Winn get back the money he lost on pork? . . . Why can't Miss Watson fat up? No, I says to myself, there ain't nothing in it."

Whether directly, as in *The Innocents Abroad* and in his fascinating account of the world of the river pilot, *Life on the Mississippi* (1883), or when transformed by his imagination in works of fiction such as *Tom Sawyer* (1876) and *A Connecticut Yankee in King Arthur's Court* (1889), Mark Twain always put much of his own experience and feeling into his work. A story, he told a fellow author, "must be

---

* The romantic novel did not disappear. General Lew Wallace's *Ben Hur* (1880) and Frances Hodgson Burnett's *Little Lord Fauntleroy* (1886) were best-sellers.

Mark Twain, in a photograph (left) taken five years before his death in 1910, was both a satirist of American optimism in his writings and its victim in misguided business ventures that brought him to the brink of bankruptcy. He is caricatured (right) riding his "Celebrated Jumping Frog of Calaveras County" in this 1872 cartoon by English artist Frederick Waddy.

written with the blood out of a man's heart." His innermost confusions, the clash between his recognition of the pretentiousness and meanness of human beings and his wish to be accepted by society, added depths and overtones to his writing that together with his comic genius give it lasting appeal. He could not rise above the sentimentality and prudery of his generation entirely, for these qualities were part of his nature. He never dealt effectively with sexual love, for example, and often, even in *Huckleberry Finn,* contrived to end his tales on absurdly optimistic notes that ring false after so many brilliant pages portraying life as it is. Rough and uneven like the man himself, his works catch more of the spirit of the age he named than those of any other writer.

William Dean Howells

Twain's realism was far less self-conscious than that of his longtime friend William Dean Howells. Like Twain, Howells, who was born in Ohio in 1837, had little formal education. He learned the printer's trade from his father and became a reporter for the *Ohio State Journal.* In 1860 he wrote a campaign biography of Lincoln and was rewarded with an appointment as consul in Venice. His sketches in *Venetian Life* (1866) were a product of this experience. After the Civil War he worked briefly for *The Nation* in New York and then moved to Boston, where he became editor of the *Atlantic Monthly.* In 1886 he returned to New York as editor of *Harper's.*

A long series of novels and much literary criticism poured from Howells's pen over the next 30 years. He was not at first a critic of society, being content to write about what he called the "smiling aspects" of life. Realism to Howells meant concern for the complexities of individual personalities and faithful description of the genteel, middle-class world he knew best. But he had a sharp eye, an open mind, and a social conscience. Gradually he became aware of the problems that industrialization had created. In 1885, in *The Rise of Silas Lapham*, he dealt with some of the ethical conflicts faced by businessmen in a competitive society. The harsh public reaction to the Haymarket bombing in 1886 stirred him, and he threw himself into a futile campaign to prevent the execution of the anarchist suspects. Thereafter he moved rapidly toward the left; soon he was calling himself a socialist. "After fifty years of optimistic content with 'civilization' . . . I now abhor it, and feel that it is coming out all wrong in the end, unless it bases itself anew on a real equality," he wrote. But he added immediately: "Meanwhile I wear a fur-lined overcoat, and live in all the luxury my money can buy."

Howells was more than a reformer, more than an inventor of utopias like Edward Bellamy, though he admired Bellamy and wrote a utopian novel of his own, *A Traveller from Altruria* (1894). In *A Hazard of New Fortunes* (1890) he attempted to portray the whole range of metropolitan life, weaving the destinies of a dozen interesting personalities from diverse sections and social classes. The book represents a triumph of realism in its careful descriptions of various sections of New York and the ways of life of rich and poor, in the intricacy of its characters, and in its rejection of sentimentality and romantic love. "A man knows that he can love and wholly cease to love, not once merely, but several times," the narrator says, "but in regard to women he cherishes the superstition of the romances that love is once for all, and forever."

Howells was also the most influential critic of his time. He helped bring the best contemporary foreign writers, including Tolstoy, Dostoyevski, Ibsen, and Zola, to the attention of readers in the United States, and he encouraged many important young American novelists, among them Stephen Crane, Theodore Dreiser, Frank Norris, and Hamlin Garland.

Some of these writers went beyond Howells's realism to what they called naturalism. Many, like Twain and Howells, began as newspaper reporters.

Working for a big-city daily in the 1890s was sure to teach anyone a great deal about the dark side of life. Naturalist writers believed that the human being was essentially an animal, a helpless creature whose fate was determined by environment. Their world was Darwin's world—mindless, without mercy or justice. They wrote chiefly about the most primitive emotions—lust, hate, greed. In *Maggie, A Girl of the Streets* (1893) Stephen Crane described the seduction, degradation, and eventual suicide of a young woman, all set against the background of a sordid slum; in *The Red Badge of Courage* (1895) he captured the pain and humor of war. In *McTeague* (1899) Frank Norris told the story of a brutal, dull-witted dentist who murdered his greed-crazed wife with his bare fists.

Such stuff was too strong for Howells, yet he recognized its importance and befriended the younger writers in many ways. He found a publisher for *Maggie* after it had been rejected many times, and he wrote appreciative reviews of the work of Garland and Norris. Even Theodore Dreiser, who was contemptuous of Howells's writings and considered him hopelessly middle-class in point of view, appreciated his aid and praised his influence on American literature. Dreiser's first novel, *Sister Carrie* (1900), treated sex so forthrightly that it was withdrawn after publication.

Henry James

Henry James was very different in spirit and background from the tempestuous naturalists. Born to wealth and reared in a cosmopolitan atmosphere, James spent most of his mature life in Europe, writing novels, short stories, plays, and volumes of criticism. Although far removed from the world of practical affairs, he was preeminently a realist, determined, as he once said, "to leave a multitude of pictures of my time" for the future to contemplate. He admired the European realists and denounced the "floods of tepid soap and water which under the name of novels are being vomited forth" by the romancers. "All life belongs to you," he told his fellow novelists. "There is no impression of life, no manner of seeing it and feeling it, to which the plan of the novelist may not offer a place."

While he preferred living in the cultivated surroundings of London high society, James yearned for the recognition of his fellow Americans almost as avidly as Mark Twain. However, he was incapable of modifying his rarefied, overly subtle manner of writing. Most serious writers of the time admired his books, and he received many honors, but he never achieved widespread popularity. His major theme was the clash of American and European cultures, his primary interest the close-up examination of wealthy, sensitive, yet often corrupt persons in a cultivated but far from polite society.

James dealt with social issues such as feminism and the difficulties faced by artists in the modern world, but he subordinated them to his interest in his subjects as individuals. *The American* (1877) told the story of the love of a wealthy American in Paris for a French noblewoman who rejected him because her family disapproved of his "commercial" background. *The Portrait of a Lady* (1881) described the disillusionment of an intelligent woman married to a charming but morally bankrupt man and her eventual decision to remain with him nonetheless. *The Bostonians* (1886) was a complicated and psychologically sensitive study of the varieties of female behavior in a seemingly uniform social situation.

James's reputation, greater today than in his lifetime, rests more on his highly refined accounts of the interactions of individuals and their environment and his masterful commentaries on the novel as a literary form than on his ability as a storyteller. Few major writers have been more long-winded, more prone to circumlocution. Yet few have been so dedicated to their art, possessed of such psychological penetration, or so successful in producing a large body of important work.

Realism in Art

American painters responded to the times as writers did, but with one difference: Despite the new concern for realism, the romantic tradition retained its vitality. Preeminent among the realists was Thomas Eakins, who was born in Philadelphia in 1844. Eakins studied in Europe in the late 1860s and was influenced by the great realists of the 17th century, Velázquez and Rembrandt. Returning to America in 1870, he passed the remainder of his life teaching and painting in Philadelphia.

The scientific spirit of the age suited Eakins perfectly. He mastered human anatomy; some of his finest paintings, such as *The Gross Clinic* (1875), are

graphic illustrations of surgical operations. He was an early experimenter with motion pictures, using the camera to capture exactly the attitudes of human beings and animals in action. Like his friend Walt Whitman, whose portrait is one of his greatest achievements, Eakins gloried in the ordinary. But he had none of Whitman's weakness for sham and self-delusion. His portraits are monuments to his integrity. Never would he touch up or soften a likeness to please his sitter. When the Union League of Philadelphia commissioned a canvas of Rutherford B. Hayes, Eakins showed the president working in his shirtsleeves, which scandalized the club fathers. His work was no mere mirror reflecting surface values. His study of six men bathing (*The Swimming Hole*) is a stark portrayal of nakedness; his surgical scenes catch the tenseness of a situation without descending into sensationalism.

Winslow Homer, a Boston-born painter best known for his brilliant watercolors, was also influenced by realist ideas. Homer was a lithographer as well as a master of the watercolor medium, yet he had had almost no formal training. Indeed, he was contemptuous of academicians and refused to go abroad to study. Aesthetics seemed not to concern him at all; he liked to shock people by referring to his profession as "the picture line." His concern for accuracy was so intense that in preparation for painting *The Life Line* (1884) he made a trip to Atlantic City to observe the handling of a breeches buoy. "When I have selected [a subject]," he said, "I paint it exactly as it appears."

During the Civil War, Homer worked as an artist-reporter for *Harper's Weekly,* and he continued to do magazine illustrations for some years thereafter. He roamed America, painting scenes of southern farm life, Adirondack campers, and, after about 1880, magnificent seascapes and studies of fishermen and sailors.

Homer's work contains romantic elements. His *Gulf Stream* (1899), showing a sailor on a small, broken boat menaced by an approaching waterspout and a school of sharks, and his *Fox Hunt* (1893), in which huge, ominous crows hover over a fox at bay, express his interest in the violence and drama of raw nature, a distinctly romantic theme. However, his approach, even in these works, was utterly prosaic. When some women complained about the fate of the black sailor in *Gulf Stream,* Homer wrote his dealer sarcastically: "Tell these ladies that the unfortunate Negro . . . will be rescued and returned

Thomas Eakins's interest in science was as great as his interest in art. In the early 1880s he collaborated with the photographer Eadweard Muybridge in serial-action photographic experiments and later devised a special camera for his ana-tomical studies; this is one of his pictures taken with the Marey wheel.

to his friends and home, and live happily ever after."

The outstanding romantic painter of the period was Albert Pinkham Ryder, a strange, neurotic genius haunted by the mystery and poetry of the sea. Ryder was born in New Bedford, Massachusetts, in 1847, during that city's heyday as a whaling port and spent most of his mature years in New York City, living and working in a dirty, cluttered attic studio. He typified the solitary romantic—brooding, eccentric, otherworldly, mystical. His heavily glazed paintings of dark seas and small boats "bathed in an atmosphere of golden luminosity" beneath a pale moon, weird canvases like *The Race Track* (*Death on a Pale Horse*), which shows a specter carrying a scythe riding on an empty track under an ominous sky, radiate a strange magic.

The careers of Eakins, Homer, and Ryder show that the late-19th-century American environment was not uncongenial to first-rate artists. Nevertheless, at least two major American painters aban-

doned native shores for Europe. One was James A. McNeill Whistler, whose portrait of his mother, which he called *Arrangement in Grey and Black*, is probably the most famous canvas ever painted by an American. Whistler left the United States in 1855 when he was 21 and spent most of his life in Paris and London. "I shall come to America," he announced grandly, "when the duty on works of art is abolished!"

Whistler made a profession of eccentricity, but he was a talented and versatile artist. Some of his portraits are triumphs of realism, while his misty studies of the London waterfront are thoroughly romantic in conception. Paintings such as "Whistler's Mother" represent still another expression of his talent. Spare and muted in tone, they are more interesting as precise arrangements of color and space than as images of particular objects; they had considerable influence on the course of modern art.

The second important expatriate artist was Mary Cassatt, daughter of a wealthy Pittsburgh banker

The impact of Eakins's photographic experiments (see figure on previous page) can be seen in The Swimming Hole, *painted in 1883. Eakins was then director of the Pennsylvania Academy's art school.*

and sister of Alexander J. Cassatt, who was president of the Pennsylvania Railroad around the turn of the century. She went to Paris as a tourist and dabbled in art like many conventional young socialites, then was caught up in the impressionist movement and decided to become a serious painter. Her work is more French than American and was little appreciated in the United States before the First World War. When once she returned to America for a visit, the *Philadelphia Public Ledger* reported: "Mary Cassatt, sister of Mr. Cassatt, president of the Pennsylvania Railroad, returned from Europe yesterday. She has been studying painting in Paris, and owns the smallest Pekinese dog in the world."

If Mary Cassatt was unappreciated and if Whistler had reasons for considering Americans uncul-

tured, it remains true that interest in art was considerable. Museums and art schools increased in number, and settlement house workers put on exhibitions that attracted enthusiastic crowds. Wealthy patrons gave countless commissions to portrait painters and poured fortunes into collecting. Martin A. Ryerson, with money made in lumber, bought the works of the French impressionists when few Americans understood their importance. Charles L. Freer of the American Car and Foundry Company was a specialist in oriental art. John G. Johnson, a successful corporation lawyer, covered the walls of his Philadelphia mansion with Italian primitives, accumulated before anyone else appreciated them. Other enthusiasts, notably the banker J. P. Morgan, employed experts to help them put together their collections. Nor were the advanced painters of the day rejected by wealthy patrons. Though Eakins's work was undervalued, he received many important commissions. Some of Homer's canvases commanded thousands of dollars, and so did those of the radical Whistler.

The Pragmatic Approach

It would have been remarkable indeed if the intellectual ferment of the late 19th century had not affected contemporary ideas about the meaning of life, the truth of revealed religion, moral values, and similar fundamental problems. In particular, the theory of evolution, so important in altering contemporary views of science, history, and social relations, produced significant changes in American thinking about religious and philosophical questions.

Evolution posed an immediate challenge to religion: If Darwin was correct, the biblical account of the creation was obviously untrue and the idea that the human race had been formed in God's image was highly unlikely. A bitter controversy erupted, described by President Andrew D. White of Cornell University in *The Warfare of Science with Theology in Christendom* (1896). While millions continued to believe in the literal truth of the Bible, among intellectuals, lay and clerical, victory went to the evolutionists because in addition to the arguments of the geologists and the biologists, scholars were throwing light on the historical development of the Bible, showing it to be of human rather than divine origin.

Evolution did not undermine the faith of any large percentage of the population. If the account of the Creation in Genesis could not be taken literally, the Bible remained a repository of wisdom and inspiration. Such books as John Fiske's *Outlines of Cosmic Philosophy* (1874) provided religious persons with the comforting thesis that evolution, while true, was merely God's way of ordering the universe—as the liberal preacher Washington Gladden put it, "a most impressive demonstration of the presence of God in the world."

The effects of Darwinism on philosophy were less dramatic but in the end more significant. Fixed systems and eternal verities were difficult to justify in a world that was constantly evolving. By the early 1870s a few philosophers had begun to reason that

Now widely recognized as one of America's finest impressionist painters, Mary Cassatt found her talent ignored in this country during her lifetime. She portrayed mothers and children with a grace and tenderness that (some would say) only a woman artist could convey.

ideas and theories mattered little except when applied to specifics. "Nothing justifies the development of abstract principles but their utility in enlarging our concrete knowledge of nature," wrote Chauncey Wright, secretary of the American Academy of Arts and Sciences. In "How to Make Our Ideas Clear" (1878), Wright's friend Charles S. Peirce, an amazingly versatile and talented albeit obscure thinker, argued that concepts could be fairly understood only in terms of their practical effects. Once the mind accepted the truth of evolution, Peirce believed, logic required that it accept the impermanence even of scientific laws. There was, he wrote, "an element of indeterminacy, spontaneity, or absolute chance in nature."

This startling philosophy, which Peirce called pragmatism, was presented in more understandable language by William James, brother of the novelist. James was one of the most remarkable persons of his generation. Educated in London, Paris, Bonn, and Geneva—as well as at Harvard—he studied painting, participated in a zoological expedition to South America, took a medical degree, and was a professor at Harvard successively of comparative anatomy, psychology, and philosophy. His *Principles of Psychology* (1890) may be said to have established that discipline as a modern science. His *Varieties of Religious Experience* (1902), which treated the subject from both psychological and philosophical points of view, helped thousands of readers to reconcile their religious faith with their increasing knowledge of psychology and the physical universe.

Although he was less rigorous a logician than Peirce, James's wide range and his verve and imagination as a writer made him by far the most influential philosopher of his time. He rejected the deterministic interpretation of Darwinism and all other one-idea explanations of existence. Belief in free will was one of his axioms; environment might influence survival, but so did the *desire* to survive, which existed independent of surrounding circumstances. Even truth was relative; it did not exist in the abstract but *happened* under particular circumstances. What a person thought helped to make thought occur or come true. The mind, James wrote in a typically vivid phrase, has "a vote" in determining truth. Religion was true, for example, because people were religious.

The pragmatic approach inspired much of the reform spirit of the late 19th century and even more of that of the early 20th. James's hammer blows shattered the laissez faire extremism of Herbert Spencer. In "Great Men and Their Environment" (1880) he argued that social changes were brought about by the actions of geniuses whom society had selected and raised to positions of power, rather than by the impersonal force of the environment. Such reasoning fitted the preconceptions of rugged individualists yet encouraged those dissatisfied with society to work for change. Educational reformers like John Dewey, the institutionalist school of economists, settlement house workers, and other reformers adopted pragmatism eagerly.

Yet pragmatism brought Americans face to face with somber problems. Though relativism made them optimistic, it bred insecurity, for there could be no certainty, no comforting reliance on any eternal value in the absence of absolute truth. Pragmatism also seemed to suggest that the end justified the means, that what worked was more important than what ought to be. At the time of James's death in 1910, the *Commercial and Financial Chronicle* pointed out that the pragmatic philosophy was helpful to businessmen in making decisions. By emphasizing practice at the expense of theory, the new

William James (with the beard) and his novelist brother Henry James in a warm photographic portrait taken around 1900.

philosophy encouraged materialism, anti-intellectualism, and other unlovely aspects of the American character. And what place had conventional morality in such a system? Perhaps pragmatism placed too much reliance on the free will of human beings, ignoring their capacity for selfishness and self-delusion.

The people of the new century found pragmatism a heady wine. They would quaff it freely and enthusiastically—down to the bitter dregs.

Milestones

1865 Vassar College founded ·
1869 Charles W. Eliot becomes president of Harvard
1874 Chautauqua movement begins
1876 Johns Hopkins University founded
1881 Oliver Wendell Holmes, Jr., *The Common Law*
1883 Joseph Pulitzer purchases the *New York World*

1886 Ottmar Mergenthaler invents the linotype machine
William Dean Howells becomes editor of *Harper's*
1889 Edward W. Bok becomes editor of the *Ladies' Home Journal*
1890 William James, *Principles of Psychology*
1893 Frederick Jackson Turner, "The Significance of the Frontier in American History"
1899 John Dewey, *The School and Society*

SUPPLEMENTARY READING

Titles marked with an asterisk have been published in paperback.

All the surveys of American intellectual history deal extensively with this period. See, for example, Louis Hartz, **The Liberal Tradition in America*** (1955), and Clinton Rossiter, **Conservatism in America*** (1962). P. A. Carter, **The Spiritual Crisis of the Gilded Age** (1971), and H. S. Commager, **The American Mind*** (1950), contain much interesting information, and there are useful essays on aspects of the subject in H. W. Morgan (ed.), **The Gilded Age: A Reappraisal*** (1970), Ray Ginger, **The Age of Excess*** (1965), is also stimulating.

The best treatment of the Chautauqua movement is Victoria Case and R. O. Case, **We Called It Culture** (1948). Trends in the history of journalism are discussed in B. A. Weisberger, **The American Newspaperman** (1961), George Juergens, **Joseph Pulitzer and the *New York World*** (1966), and W. A. Swanberg, **Citizen Hearst*** (1961).

On higher education, see L. R. Veysey, **The Emergence of the American University*** (1965), E. A. Green, **Mary Lyon and Mount Holyoke** (1979), Hugh Hawkins, **Pioneer: A History of the Johns Hopkins University**

(1960), and Hawkins's **Between Harvard and America: The Educational Leadership of Charles W. Eliot** (1972). Thorstein Veblen, **The Higher Learning in America*** (1918), is full of stimulating opinions.

For developments in American science, see the excellent essay by P. F. Boller, Jr., in H. W. Morgan (ed.), **The Gilded Age*** (1970). A good general introduction to the work of the social scientists is Sidney Fine, **Laissez Faire and the General-Welfare State** (1957), but see also Richard Hofstadter, **Social Darwinism in American Thought*** (1944), and Jurgen Herbst, **The German Historical School in American Scholarship** (1965). As to trends in educational theory, see L. A. Cremin, **American Education: The Metropolitan Experience** (1988). On Twain, see Justin Kaplan, **Mr. Clemens and Mark Twain*** (1966); on Howells, see E. H. Cady, **The Realist at War** (1958); on James, see Leon Edel, **Henry James*** (1953–1962).

Two good sources on pragmatism are Hofstadter's **Social Darwinism** and Bruce Kuklick, **The Rise of American Philosophy** (1977).

American Lives:
The Johnson Family of Nebraska

Settlers entering Nebraska

Jens Johnson was 22 when he emigrated to the United States from Denmark in 1849. He made his way west to Madison, Wisconsin, where he worked at odd jobs while accumulating enough money to buy a wagon, horses, and a plow. He married a young Norwegian woman in Madison. They were able to get a small farm in the western part of the state, where they began to raise a family. When the Civil War broke out, Johnson volunteered. He fought all through the war without a scratch, serving under Grant at Shiloh and Vicksburg, later under Sherman "from Atlanta to the Sea." Jens thought Grant showed little regard for his men and dismissed him as "a butcher." But he greatly admired Sherman.

Shortly after he returned to Wisconsin his wife died of tuberculosis, leaving him with four young children, all girls. He packed them into a covered wagon with all his worldly goods and set out for Nebraska, where in the northeastern part of the state, he took up a quarter section under the Homestead Act. They lived in a tent made from the cover of the wagon until he built a house.

In 1867, Johnson met Edel Maria Bille, a recently arrived Danish woman who was living with her aunt on a nearby farm, and soon persuaded her to marry him. They had four children, three of them boys. For years the family lived almost entirely on what their farm produced. They grew wheat, corn, and vegetables and raised cattle, sheep, pigs, and chickens, as well as horses. They had plenty of wood for the fire and for fencing on their own property. Wild berries for jams grew in abundance.

Jens had his wheat ground at a nearby mill, the miller doing the job in exchange for a quarter of the flour. He slaughtered an occasional cow or some pigs, kept the meat frozen in winter, then smoked or salted the rest when the warm weather came. He kept a large store of wool from his sheep, which the women used to knit stockings, mittens, and sweaters for the family.

Of course the Johnsons had to have money to buy things like sugar and coffee, or manufactured goods such as shoes, dishes, and wire for fences. To pay for these things they sold some butter and eggs, or perhaps a cow in the nearby town of Homer. It was a life of hard, endless

Family farm in northeastern Nebraska

memory, especially on learning to spell. The oldest of the Johnson boys, Alvin, remembered struggling to master the following sentence: "Bill Wright, the mill wright, can't write 'rite' right." The boys dreamed of going west; a branch of the Oregon Trail ran past the farm and canvas-topped prairie schooners were still to be seen going by in the 1870s.

In the late 1880s Jens Johnson turned management of the farm over to his three sons. They decided to change it from a self-sufficient, "farming-as-a-way-of-life" enterprise to a business. They cleared more land in order to grow more corn and oats. They raised as many hogs and cattle as possible, intending to sell them to meat packers. But the pigs were wiped out by hog cholera and chinch bugs destroyed the entire crop of oats. Eventually they began to turn a profit but, as Alvin later wrote, by 1892 they had done "more worrying than my father did in all his life."

Eventually, all the Johnsons left the farm. Two of the older girls got jobs in the Indian Service, another taught school for a time then moved to New York to study medicine at Cornell. The two younger sons became lawyers. Alvin became a college professor and eventually the founder and director of the New School for Social Research. Jens and Edel Johnson sold the farm, moved to a nearby town, then to California, where they spent their last years.

labor; even the smallest children contributed. But the Johnsons saw what they were doing not as working but as living. Time was their money, a kind, after all, that had to be spent one way or another. They had little real money, but little need for it, and everyone felt needed.

That part of Nebraska was being settled by people of many backgrounds. First the New Englanders, who had arrived during the struggle over slavery in the territories that resulted from the passage of the Kansas-Nebraska Act. Many veterans had arrived, like Jens Johnson, after the Civil War. One of his friends was a Swede who had come to America to escape a jail term for having killed a deer that was eating his crops. There was a group of Germans, including a rather odd former philosophy professor named Winkhaus, who was said to be "brain-broke" from having spent too much time thinking. The district contained settlers from Ireland too, as well as a large Danish community.

It was by no means an ideal community. The native-born settlers disliked the immigrants, for some reason especially the Danes. The Protestants distrusted the Irish because they were Catholics. The local Republican politicians waved the bloody shirt, while most of the hardworking farmers expressed contempt for the politicians, claiming that they were being governed by "a wasp's nest of crooks and scoundrels."

The only public school in the area was open from December through February. The teachers were inexperienced. Much stress was placed on

A country school

XXII

Politics: Local, State, and National

"What a pity he is so dreadfully senatorial," said Mrs. Lee. "Otherwise I rather admire him."

"Now he is settling down to his work," continued Carrington. "See how he dodges all the sharp issues. . . . What a genius the fellow has for leading a party."

HENRY ADAMS, Democracy, *1880*

The ordinary American voter does not object to mediocrity. He has a lower conception of the qualities requisite to make a statesman than those who direct public opinion in Europe have.

JAMES BRYCE, Why Great Men Are Not Chosen President, *1888*

boards of experts, once broad policies have been laid down by Congress, but in the 19th century, specialists had not yet arrived at this conclusion. Reformers could thunder self-righteously against the spoils system, but how could political parties exist without it? Young economists like Richard T. Ely and Henry Carter Adams were insisting that laissez faire was outmoded, but no one had yet devised the techniques and instruments that would have to be used if the economy was to be measured and managed effectively by a central authority. The embryonic social sciences had not even collected the statistical information necessary for efficient direction of the economy. If the politicians steered clear of the "real" issues, they did so as much out of a healthy respect for their own ignorance as out of any desire to avoid controversy.

he major American parties have nearly always avoided clear-cut stands on controversial questions in order to appeal to as wide a segment of the electorate as possible, but in the last quarter of the 19th century, their equivocations assumed abnormal proportions. This was due in part to the precarious balance of power between them: Neither dared declare itself too clearly on any question lest it drive away more voters than it attracted.

The rapid pace of social and economic change also militated against political decisiveness. No one in or out of politics had as yet devised effective solutions for many current problems. When party leaders tried to deal with the money question, they discovered that the bankers and the professional economists were as confused as the public at large. "We dabble in theories of our own and clutch convulsively at the doctrines of others," a Philadelphia banker confessed. "From the vast tract of mire by which the subject is surrounded, overlaid, and besmeared, it is almost impossible to arrive at anything like a fair estimate of its real nature." How could mere politicians act rationally or consistently in such circumstances?

The parties stumbled badly when they confronted the tariff problem because tariffs in a complex industrial economy are not susceptible to determination by counting noses. Modern experience has shown that they are better arrived at by impartial

Politicial Decision Making: Ethnic and Religious Issues

The major parties had national committees, and delegates met in national conventions every four years to select their presidential candidates and draft "platforms," but they remained essentially separate state organizations. Professionals spent far more time dealing with local people and local issues than they did thinking about tariffs and money policy and other matters of broad national concern. They had to understand how different kinds of people felt about such matters if they wanted to win their support. In many parts of the country, that meant entering a veritable maze of diverse and often conflicting interests. People's ethnic backgrounds, their religious affiliations, whether they lived in cities or on farms, how they felt about the Civil War, and countless aspects of their lives that had no apparent relationship to national political issues affected whether they voted Republican or Democratic.

The politicians of the period were not shy about explaining why people voted the way they did. Senator George Frisbie Hoar of Massachusetts, for example, offered such an analysis in an 1889 magazine article. The Republicans, he wrote, were

the men who do the work of piety and charity in our churches . . . who adminster our school systems . . . who own and till their own farms . . . who perform skilled labor . . . who went to the war . . . who paid the debt, and kept the currency sound, and saved the nation's honor.

The Democrats, he went on, were "the old slave-owner and slave-driver, the saloon-keeper, the ballot-box-stuffer, the Kuklux, the criminal class of the great cities, and men who cannot read or write."

Despite the partisan character of Hoar's analysis, it contained an element of truth; a more disinterested observer, James Bryce, wrote in *The American Commonwealth* that at least in the North, "the best people" were Republicans, whereas a "vast ignorant fluctuating mass of people" were Democrats. But if Hoar or even Bryce were correct, the Republicans would have swept the northern states at every election, which they assuredly did not.

In any case, it was (and it remains) even more difficult to discover *why* people voted one way or the other in the decades after the Civil War. People of Irish descent tended to vote Democratic, but whether they did so because they lived in cities or because they were Roman Catholics or because they believed that most Americans of British descent voted Republican was not always clear.

Plausible generalizations break down when examined closely. Northerners were Republicans, southerners Democrats; Catholics were Democrats, Protestants Republicans; German-Americans voted Democratic, Americans of Scandinavian descent Republican. All these statements and many others like them are subject to a multitude of exceptions. And of course they conflict one with another. They offer little guidance for predicting how, for example, a German Lutheran living in Tennessee would vote.

Detailed analyses of local elections in districts where people of particular religious and ethnic backgrounds lived suggest that Protestants who belonged to churches that emphasized ritual and the passive acceptance of authority tended to vote Democratic; those who worshiped in churches where the stress was on simple services, personal piety, and the importance of being "saved" usually voted Republican. Middle western German Lutherans were "ritualists," and many did tend to vote for Democrats. But as Paul Kleppner has explained in *The Cross of Culture*, "Not all German Lutherans were equally ritualistic," and numbers of them voted for Republicans.

Local and state issues also interacted with religious and ethnic backgrounds to affect political attitudes. Prohibition, public education, and other matters subject to state and local control that seemed to have little or no relation to religion were in fact questions on which voters split along religious and ethnic lines. All these tangles influenced the way political leaders devised their strategies and chose candidates for office. And how voters felt about local issues almost invariably affected how they voted in national elections.

City Government

City governments were influenced by the religious and ethnic character of the inhabitants and further complicated by the special problems of late-19th-century urban life: rapid, helter-skelter growth; the influx of European immigrants; the need to develop costly transportation, sanitation, and other public-utility systems; and the crime and corruption that the size, confusion, and anonymity incidental to urban existence fostered.

The movement to the suburbs of large numbers of middle-class city people who might have been expected to supply the political leadership needed to deal with these problems created a vacuum of sorts, a vacuum that was filled by political bosses, with their informal but powerful "machines."

The immigrants who flocked into American cities in the 1880s and early 1890s made up much of the "vast ignorant fluctuating mass" that Bryce was referring to in his description of party alignments. They were largely of peasant stock, and having come from societies unacquainted with the blessings of democracy, they had no experience with representative government. The tendency of urban workers to move frequently in search of better jobs further lessened the likelihood that they would develop political influence independently.

Furthermore, the difficulties of life in the slums bewildered and often overwhelmed newcomers, both native and foreign-born. Hopeful, but passive and naive, they could hardly be expected to take a broad view of social problems when so beset by personal ones. This enabled shrewd urban politicians—most of them in this period of Irish origin, the Irish being the firstcomers among the migrants and, according to mobility studies, more likely to stay put—to take command of the city masses and march them in obedient phalanxes to the polls.

Most city machines were loose-knit neighborhood organizations headed by ward bosses, not tightly geared hierarchical bureaucracies ruled by a single leader. "Big Tim" Sullivan of New York's Lower East Side and "Hinky Dink" Kenna of Chicago were typical of the breed. People like Sullivan and Kenna performed many useful services for what they liked to think of as their constituents. They found jobs for new arrivals and distributed food and other help to all in bad times. Anyone in trouble with the law could obtain at least a hearing from the ward boss, and often, if the crime was venial or due to ignorance, the difficulty was quietly "fixed" and the culprit was sent off with a word of caution. Sullivan provided turkey dinners for 5,000 or more derelicts each Christmas, distributed new shoes to the poor children of his district on his birthday, and arranged summer boat rides and picnics for young and old alike. At any time of year the victim of some sudden disaster could turn to the local clubhouse for help. Informally, probably without consciously intending to do so, the bosses educated the immigrants in the complexities of American civilization, helping them to leap the gulf between the almost medieval society of their origins and the modern industrial world.

The price of such aid—the bosses were not altruists—was unquestioning political support, which the bosses converted into cash. In New York, Sullivan levied tribute on gambling, had a hand in the liquor business, and controlled the issuance of peddlers' licenses. When he died in 1913, he was reputedly worth $1 million. Yet he and others like him were immensely popular; 25,000 grieving constituents followed Big Tim's coffin on its way to the grave.

Though he served a useful social function, the typical boss was not a reformer. Surveying the role of the Irish in New York City politics, the sociologist (later senator) Daniel Patrick Moynihan noted that despite their successes, the bosses "did not know what to do with power. . . . They never thought of politics as an instrument of social change."

The more visible and better-known city bosses played even less socially justifiable roles than the ward bosses. Their principal technique for extracting money from the public till was the kickback. To get city contracts, suppliers were made to pad their bills and, when paid for their work with funds from the city treasury, turn over the excess to the poli-

Thomas Nast's devastating assaults on the Tweed Ring, printed in Harper's Weekly, *helped bring about the ring's demise. In this cartoon Tweed and his fellow vultures cower under the storm against them. Tweed offered Nast a $500,000 bribe to stop the cartoon.*

ticians. Similarly, operators of streetcar lines, gas and electricity companies, and other public utilities were compelled to pay huge bribes to obtain favorable franchises.

The most notorious of the 19th-century city bosses was William Marcy Tweed, whose "Tweed Ring" extracted tens of millions of dollars from New York City during the brief period from 1869 to 1871. Tweed was swiftly jailed. More typical was Richard Croker, who ruled New York's Tammany Hall organization from the mid-1880s to the end of the century. Croker held a number of local offices, but his power rested on his position as chairman of the Tammany Hall finance committee. Although more concerned than Tweed with the social and economic services that machines provided, Croker was primarily a corrupt political manipulator; he accumulated a large fortune and owned a $200,000 mansion and a stable of racehorses, one of which was good enough to win the English Derby.

Despite their welfare work and their popularity, most bosses were essentially thieves. Efforts to romanticize them as the Robin Hoods of industrial society grossly distort the facts. However, the system developed and survived because too many middle-class city dwellers were indifferent to the fate of the poor. Except during occasional reform waves, few tried to check the rapaciousness of the politicos.

Many substantial citizens shared at least indirectly in the corruption. The owners of tenements were interested in crowding as many rent payers as possible into their buildings. Utility companies seeking franchises preferred a system that enabled them to buy favors. Honest citizens who had no selfish stake in the system and who were repelled by the sordidness of city government were seldom sufficiently concerned to do anything about it. When young Theodore Roosevelt decided to seek a political career in 1880, his New York socialite friends laughed in his face. They told him, Roosevelt wrote in his autobiography, "that politics were 'low'; that the organizations were not controlled by 'gentlemen'; that I would find them run by saloon-keepers, horse-car conductors, and the like."

Many so-called urban reformers resented the boss system mainly because it gave political power to people who were not "gentlemen" or, as one reformer put it, to a "proletarian mob" of "illiterate peasants, freshly raked from Irish bogs, or Bohemian mines, or Italian robber nests." A British visitor in Chicago struck at the root of the urban problem of the era. "Everybody is fighting to be rich," he said, "and nobody can attend to making the city fit to live in."

Republicans and Democrats

As for national politics, with the Democrats invincible in the South and the Republicans predominant in New England and most of the states beyond the Mississippi, the outcome of presidential elections was usually determined in a handful of populous states: New York (together with its satellites, New Jersey and Connecticut), Ohio, Indiana, and Illinois. The fact that opinion in these states on important questions such as the tariff and monetary policy was divided and that every imaginable religious and ethnic interest was represented in the electorate goes far to explain why the parties hesitated to commit themselves on issues. In every presidential election, Democrats and Republicans concentrated their heaviest guns on these states. Of the 18 Democrats and Republicans nominated for president in the nine elections between 1868 and 1900, only three were not from New York, Ohio, Indiana, or Illinois, and all three lost.

Partisanship was intense in these states. A story is told of a Democrat from a town in Illinois who was trying to persuade a doctor he knew to settle there. He admitted that the town already had five doctors, more than enough to care for the medical needs of the populace. But all five were Republicans. "If you come here you can commence all the Democratic practice," he assured the doctor. There are, he added sagely, "a set of public men here that will do what they can for you." Campaigns were conducted in a carnival atmosphere, entertainment being substituted for serious debate. Large sums were spent on brass bands, barbecues, uniforms, and banners. Speakers of national reputation were imported to attract crowds, and spellbinders noted for their leather lungs—this was before the day of the loudspeaker—and their ability to rouse popular emotions were brought in to address mass meetings.

With so much depending on so few, the level of political morality was abysmal. Mudslinging, character assassination, and plain lying were standard practice; bribery was routine. Drifters and other dissolute citizens were paid in cash—or more often in free drinks—to vote the party ticket. The names of persons long dead were solemnly inscribed in voting registers, their suffrages exercised by impostors. During the 1880 campaign the Democratic national chairman, hearing that the Republicans were planning to transport Kentuckians into Indiana to vote illegally in that crucial state, urged Indiana Democrats to "check this outrageous fraud." Then, perhaps seeking an easier solution to the problem, he added: "If necessary . . . keep even with them." Since, as this incident demonstrates, both parties indulged in these tactics, their efforts often canceled one another's, yet certain presidents were made and unmade in this sordid fashion.

The Men in the White House

The leading statesmen of the period showed as little interest in important contemporary questions as the party hacks who made up the rank and file of their organizations. Consider the presidents.

Rutherford B. Hayes, president from 1877 to 1881, came to office with a distinguished record. He attended Kenyon College and Harvard Law School before settling down to practice in Cincinnati. Although he had a family to support, he volunteered for service within weeks after the first shell fell on Fort Sumter. "A just and necessary war," he called it in his diary. "I would prefer to go into it if I knew I was to die . . . than to live through and after it without taking any part."

Hayes was wounded at South Mountain on the eve of Antietam, and later served under Sheridan in the Shenandoah Valley campaign of 1864. En-

tering the army as a major, he emerged a major general. In 1864 he was elected to Congress; four years later he became governor of Ohio, serving three terms altogether. The Republicans nominated him for president in 1876 because of his reputation for honesty and moderation, and his election, made possible by the Compromise of 1877, seemed to presage an era of sectional harmony and political probity.

Outwardly Hayes had a sunny disposition; inwardly, in his own words, he was sometimes "nervous to the point of disaster." Despite his geniality, he was utterly without political glamour. He played down the tariff issue whenever possible, favoring protection in principle but refusing to become a mere spokesman for local interests. On the money question he was conservative. He cheerfully approved the resumption of gold payments in 1879 and vetoed bills to expand the currency. He ac-

In this 1880 campaign lithograph by Currier & Ives, "Farmer Garfield" uses a scythe made of honesty, ability, and patriotism to cut a swath to the White House through brush infested by snakes with names like Falsehood and Malice. One snake bears the countenance of Garfield's predecessor, Hayes.

counted himself a civil service reformer, being opposed to the collection of political contributions from federal officeholders.

Since Hayes saw himself more as a caretaker than a leader, he believed that Congress should assume the main responsibility for solving national problems. One historian writes that he showed "no capacity for such large-minded leadership as might have tamed the political hordes and aroused the enthusiasm, or at least the interest, of the public."

Hayes complained about the South's failure to treat blacks decently after the withdrawal of federal troops, but he took no action. He worked harder for civil service reform yet failed to achieve the "thorough, rapid, and complete" change he had promised. In most matters, he was content to "let the record show that he had made the requests."

Hayes's successor, James A. Garfield, was cut down by an assassin's bullet four months after his inauguration. Even in that short time, however, his ineffectiveness had been demonstrated. Garfield grew up in poverty on an Ohio farm. When the Civil War broke out, he helped organize a volunteer regiment and soon proved himself an excellent battlefield commander. He fought at Shiloh and later at Chickamauga. In two years he rose from lieutenant colonel to major general. In 1863 he won a seat in Congress, where his oratorical and managerial skills brought him to prominence in the affairs of the Republican party.

Garfield was studious and industrious, and he had wide-ranging interests. His weakness was indecisiveness—what an admirer described as a "want of certainty."

He did not enjoy waving the bloody shirt, but when hard pressed politically—as when his name was linked with the Crédit Mobilier railroad scandal—he would lash out at the South in an effort to distract the voters. In theory he was inclined toward low tariffs. Nevertheless, he would not sacrifice the interests of Ohio manufacturers for a mere principle.

Similarly, though eager to improve the efficiency of the government and resentful of the "intellectual dissipation" resulting from time wasted listening to the countless appeals of office seekers, he often wilted under pressure from the spoilsmen. Only on fiscal policy did he take a firm stand: He opposed categorically all inflationary schemes.

Political patronage proved to be Garfield's undoing. The Republican party in 1880 was split into two factions, the "Stalwarts" and the "Half-Breeds." The Stalwarts, led by New York Senator Roscoe Conkling, believed in the blatant pursuit of the spoils of office. The Half-Breeds did not disagree but behaved more circumspectly, hoping to attract the support of independents. Competition for office was the main reason for their rivalry.

Garfield had been a compromise choice at the 1880 Republican convention. His election precipitated a great battle over patronage, the new president standing in a sort of no-man's-land between the factions. He did stand up to the most grasping politicians, resisting in particular the demands of Senator Conkling. By backing the investigation of a post office scandal and by appointing a Half-Breed collector of the Port of New York, he infuriated the Stalwarts. In July 1881 an unbalanced Stalwart lawyer named Charles J. Guiteau shot Garfield in the Washington railroad station. After lingering for weeks, the president died on September 19.

The assassination of Garfield elevated Chester A. Arthur to the presidency. Arthur was a New York lawyer. An abolitionist, he became an early convert to the Republican party and rose rapidly in its local councils. In 1871 Grant gave him the juiciest political plum in the country, the collectorship of the Port of New York, which he held until removed by Hayes in 1878 for refusing to keep his hands out of party politics.

The vice-presidency was the only elective position that Arthur had ever held. Before Garfield's death, he had paid little attention to questions like the tariff and monetary policy, being content to take in fees ranging upward of $50,000 a year as collector of the port and to oversee the operations of the New York customs office, with its hordes of clerks and laborers. (During Arthur's tenure, the novelist Herman Melville was employed as an "outdoor inspector" by the Custom House.) Of course, Arthur was an unblushing defender of the spoils system, though in fairness it must be said that he was personally honest and an excellent administrator.

The tragic circumstances of his elevation to the presidency sobered Arthur considerably. Although he was a genial, convivial man, perhaps overly fond of good food and flashy clothes, he comported himself with great dignity as president. He handled patronage matters with restraint, and he gave at least nominal support to the movement for civil service reform, which had been strengthened by the public's indignation at the assassination of Garfield. In 1883 Congress passed the Pendleton Act, "classifying" about 10 percent of all government jobs and creating the bipartisan Civil Service Commission to administer competitive examinations for these positions. The law made it illegal to force officeholders to make political contributions and empowered the president to expand the list of classified positions at his discretion.

Many politicians resented the new system—one senator denounced it as "un-American"—but the Pendleton Act opened a new era in government administration. The results have been summed up by the historian Ari Hoogenboom:

> An unprofessional civil service became more professionalized. Better-educated civil servants were recruited and society accorded them a higher place. . . . Local political considerations gave way in civil servants' minds to the national concerns of a federal office. Business influence and ideals replaced those of the politician.

Arthur urged the appointment of a nonpartisan commission to study tariff rates and to suggest rational reductions; when such a commission was created, he urged Congress to adopt its recommendations. He came out for federal regulation of railroads several years before the passage of the Interstate Commerce Act.

As an administrator Arthur was systematic, thoughtful, businesslike, and at the same time cheerful and considerate. Just the same, he too was a political failure. He made no real attempt to push his program through Congress, instead devoting most of his energies to a futile effort to build up his personal following in the Republican party by distributing favors. But the Stalwarts would not forgive his "desertion," and the reform element could not forget his past. At the 1884 convention the politicos shunted him aside.

The election of 1884 brought the Democrat Grover Cleveland to the White House. Cleveland grew up in western New York. After studying law, he settled in Buffalo. Though somewhat lacking in the social graces and in intellectual pretensions, he had a basic integrity that everyone recognized; when

A portrait of Grover Cleveland by the artist Anders Zorn. The well-fed look was the trademark of most politicians of that era.

a group of reformers sought a candidate for mayor in 1881, he was a natural choice. His success in Buffalo led to his election as governor of New York in 1882.

In the governor's chair his no-nonsense attitude toward public administration endeared him to civil service reformers at the same time that his basic conservatism pleased businessmen. When he vetoed a popular bill to force a reduction of the fares charged by the New York City elevated railway on the grounds that it was an unconstitutional violation of the company's franchise, his stock soared. Here was a man who cared more for principle than the adulation of the multitude, a man of courage, honest, hardworking, and eminently sound. The Democrats nominated him for president in 1884.

The election revolved around personal issues, for the platforms of the parties were almost identical. On the one hand, the Republican candidate, the dynamic James G. Blaine, had an immense following, but his reputation had been soiled by the publication of the "Mulligan letters," which connected him with the corrupt granting of congressional favors to the Little Rock and Fort Smith Railroad. On the other hand, it came out during the campaign that Cleveland, a bachelor, had fathered an illegitimate child. Instead of debating public issues, the Republicans chanted the ditty

> *Ma! Ma! Where's my pa?*
> *Gone to the White House,*
>   *Ha! Ha! Ha!*

to which the Democrats countered

> *Blaine, Blaine, James G. Blaine,*
> *The continental liar from the State of Maine.*

Blaine lost more heavily in the mudslinging than Cleveland, whose quiet courage in saying, "Tell the truth," when his past was brought to light contrasted favorably with Blaine's glib and unconvincing denials. A significant group of eastern Republicans, known as Mugwumps, campaigned for the Democrats.* However, Blaine ran a strong race against a general pro-Democratic trend; Cleveland won the election by fewer than 25,000 votes. The change of 600 ballots in New York would have given that state, and the presidency, to his opponent.

As a Democrat, Cleveland had no stomach for refighting the Civil War. Civil service reformers overestimated his commitment to their cause, for he believed in rotation in office. He would not summarily dismiss Republicans, but he thought that when they had served four years, they "should as a rule give way to good men of our party." He did, however, insist on honesty and efficiency regardless of party. As a result, he made few poor appointments.

Cleveland had little imagination and too narrow a conception of his powers and duties to be a successful president. His appearance perfectly re-

flected his character: a squat, burly man weighing well over 200 pounds, he could defend a position against heavy odds, yet he lacked flexibility. He took a fairly broad view of the powers of the federal government, but he thought it unseemly to put pressure on Congress, believing in "the entire independence of the executive and legislative branches."

Toward the end of his term Cleveland bestirred himself and tried to provide constructive leadership on the tariff question. The government was embarrassed by a large revenue surplus, which Cleveland hoped to reduce by cutting the duties on necessities and on raw materials used in manufacturing. He devoted his entire annual message of December 1887 to the tariff, thereby focusing public attention on the subject. When worried Democrats reminded him that an election was coming up and that the tariff might cause a rift in the organization, he replied simply: "What is the use of being elected or re-elected, unless you stand for something?"

The House of Representatives, dominated by southern Democrats, passed a bill reducing many duties, but the measure, known as the Mills bill, was flagrantly partisan: It slashed the rates on iron products, glass, wool, and other items made in the North and left those on southern goods almost untouched. The Republican-controlled Senate rejected the Mills bill, and the issue was left to be settled by the voters at the 1888 election.

In that contest, Cleveland obtained a plurality of the popular vote, but his opponent, Benjamin Harrison, grandson of President William Henry Harrison, carried most of the key northeastern industrial states by narrow margins, thereby obtaining a comfortable majority in the electoral college, 233 to 168.

Although intelligent and able, Harrison was too reserved to make a good politician. He did not suffer fools gladly and kept even his most important advisers at arm's length. One observer called him a "human iceberg." During the Civil War, he fought under Sherman at Atlanta and won a reputation as a stern, effective disciplinarian. In 1876 he ran unsuccessfully for governor of Indiana, but in 1881 he was elected to the Senate.

Harrison believed ardently in protective tariffs, stating firmly, if illogically, that he was against "cheaper costs" because cheaper costs seemed "necessarily to involve a cheaper man and woman under

---

* The Mugwumps considered themselves reformers, but on social and economic questions nearly all of them were very conservative. They were sound-money proponents and advocates of laissez faire. Reform to them consisted almost entirely of doing away with corruption and making the government more efficient.

PUT YOUR APPLICATION IN THE SLOT AND GET AN OFFICE.

President Benjamin Harrison swapping political office for electioneering support as depicted by a cartoonist, a practice that civil service reformers insisted corrupted national politics. In point of fact, "Little Ben" was among the least given to patronage appointments among post–Civil War presidents.

the coat." His approach to fiscal policy was conservative, though he was freehanded in the matter of veterans' pensions. He would not use "an apothecary's scale," he said, "to weigh the rewards of men who saved the country." No more flamboyant waver of the bloody shirt existed.

Harrison professed to favor civil service reform, but a biographer, Father Harry J. Sievers, admits that he fashioned a "singularly unimpressive" record on the question. He appointed the vigorous young reformer Theodore Roosevelt to the Civil Service Commission and then proceeded to undercut him systematically. Before long the frustrated Roosevelt was calling the president a "cold blooded, narrow minded, prejudiced, obstinate, timid old psalm singing Indianapolis politician."

Under Harrison, Congress distinguished itself by expending, for the first time in a period of peace, more than $1 billion in a single session. It raised the tariff to an all-time high. The Sherman Antitrust Act was passed; so was the Silver Purchase Act, authorizing the government to coin large amounts of that metal, a measure much desired by mining interests and those favoring inflation. A "force" bill providing for federal control of elections as a means of protecting the right of southern blacks to vote, a right increasingly under attack, passed the House only to be filibustered to death in the Senate.

Harrison had little to do with the fate of any of these measures. By and large he failed, as one historian has said, to give the people "magnetic and responsive leadership." The Republicans lost control of Congress in 1890, and two years later Grover Cleveland swept back into power, defeating Harrison by more than 350,000 votes.

Congressional Leaders

Among the lesser politicians of the period, the most outstanding was James G. Blaine of Maine, who served in Congress from 1863 to 1881, first in the House and then in the Senate. Blaine had many of the qualities that mark a great leader: personal dynamism, imagination, political intuition, oratorical ability, and a broad view of the national interest. President Lincoln spotted him when he was a freshman congressman, calling him "one of the brightest men in the House" and "one of the coming men of the country."

Blaine was essentially a reasonable man, a member of the moderate Republican faction during Reconstruction. He favored sound money without opposing inflexibly every suggestion for increasing the volume of the currency. He supported the protective system yet advocated reciprocity agreements to increase trade. He adopted a moderate and tolerant attitude toward the South. Almost alone among the politicians of his generation, he was deeply interested in foreign affairs. His personal warmth captivated thousands.

That Blaine, though perennially an aspirant, never became president was in part a reflection of his abilities and his participation in so many controversial affairs. Naturally, he aroused jealousies and made many enemies. But some inexplicable flaw marred his character. He had a streak of reck-

*Parodying a popular painting of the day depicting a beautiful Greek courtesan
being unveiled before Athenian statesmen,* Puck's *Bernhard Fillam drew James
G. Blaine revealed to Republican leaders in 1884. The "Mulligan letters" receive prominent display among the tattoos, and Blaine's renowned personal
magnetism is labeled as a fraud.*

lessness entirely out of keeping with his reasonable
position on most issues. He showered contempt on
civil service reformers, characterizing them as
"noisy but not numerous, . . . ambitious but not
wise, pretentious but not powerful." The scandal
of the Mulligan letters made a dark blot on his record. Blaine moved though history amid cheers and
won a host of spectacular if petty triumphs, yet his
career was barren, essentially tragic.

Roscoe Conkling's was another remarkable but
empty career. Handsome, colorful, companionable,
and dignified, Conkling served in Congress almost
continuously from 1859 to 1881 and was a great
power, dominating the complex politics of New
York for many years. Such was his prestige that two
presidents offered him a seat on the Supreme Court.
Yet no measure of importance was attached to his
name; he squandered his energies in acrimonious

personal quarrels, caring only for partisan advantage.

Dozens of other figures might be mentioned;
the following are representative types.

Congressman William McKinley of Ohio was the
most personally attractive. He was a man of simple
honesty, nobility of character, quiet warmth—and
a politician to the core. The tariff was McKinley's
special competence, the principle of protection his
guiding star. The peak of his career still lay in the
future in the early 1890s.

Another Ohioan, John Sherman, brother of the
famous Civil War general, accomplished the remarkable feat of holding national office continuously from 1855 to 1898. He had a deserved reputation for expertise in financial matters. However,
he was colorless and stiff, and altogether too willing
to compromise his beliefs for political advantage.

Sherman gave his name (and not much else) to the Antitrust Act of 1890 and to other important legislation, but in retrospect he left little mark on the history of the country despite his long service.

Thomas B. Reed, Republican congressman from Maine, was a witty, widely read man but ultraconservative and cursed with a sharp tongue that he could never curb. Reed coined the famous definition of a statesman: "a politician who is dead." When one pompous politico said in his presence that he would rather be right than president, Reed advised him not to worry, since he would never be either. In 1890 Reed was elected Speaker of the House and quickly won the nickname "Czar" because of his autocratic way of expediting business. Since the Republicans had only a paper-thin majority, the Democrats attempted to block action on partisan measures by refusing to answer to their names on quorum calls. Reed coolly ordered the clerk to re-cord them as present and proceeded to carry on the business of the House. His control became so absolute that Washington jokesters said that representatives dared not breathe without his permission. Reed had large ambitions and the courage of his convictions, but his vindictiveness kept him from exercising a constructive influence on his times.

Agricultural Discontent

The vacuity of American politics may well have stemmed from the complacency of the middle-class majority. The country was growing; no foreign enemy threatened it; the poor were mostly recent immigrants, blacks, and others with little influence, easily ignored by those in comfortable circumstances. However, one important group in society suffered increasingly as the years rolled by: the

The western land boom reached a climax on April 22, 1889, when parts of Oklahoma were opened to settlers. With a few hours, nearly 2 million acres were claimed by hordes of "boomers." This photograph was taken a few weeks later in the boom town of Guthrie, whose sign painter was working overtime.

farmers. Out of their travail came the force that finally, in the 1890s, brought American politics face to face with the problems of the age.

Immediately after the Civil War, wheat sold at nearly $1.50 a bushel, and in the early 1870s it was still worth well over a dollar. By the mid-1890s the average price stood in the neighborhood of 60 cents. Cotton, the great southern staple, which sold for more than 30 cents a pound in 1866 and 15 cents in the early 1870s, at times in the 1890s fell below 6 cents.

The tariff on manufactured goods appeared to aggravate the farmers' predicament, and so did the domestic marketing system, which enabled a multitude of middlemen to gobble up a large share of the profits of agriculture. The shortage of credit, particularly in the South, was an additional burden. Furthermore, the improvements in transportation that made it practicable for farmers in Australia, Canada, Russia, and Argentina to sell their produce in western European markets increased the competition faced by Americans seeking to dispose of surplus produce abroad.

Throughout the mid-1880s farmers on the plains had experienced boom conditions. Adequate rainfall produced bountiful harvests, credit was available, and property values rose rapidly. In the 1880s the population of Kansas increased by 43 percent, that of Nebraska by 134 percent, that of the Dakotas by 278 percent. This agricultural expansion contributed to the destruction of open-range cattle raising and changed the economy of cattle towns like Dodge City, which came to depend more on farmers than on cowboys and ranchers for business.

Speculative booms occur periodically in every frontier district; like all others, this one collapsed when settlers and investors took a more realistic look at the prospects of the region. In this case special circumstances turned the slump into a catastrophe. A succession of dry years shattered the hopes of the farmers. The downward swing of the business cycle in the early 1890s completed the devastation. Settlers who had paid more for their lands than they were worth and borrowed money at high interest rates to do so found themselves squeezed relentlessly. Thousands lost their farms and returned eastward, penniless and dispirited. The population of Nebraska increased by fewer than 4,000 persons in the entire decade of the 1890s.

The Populist Movement

The agricultural depression triggered a new outburst of farm radicalism, the Alliance movement. Alliances were organizations of farmers' clubs, most of which had sprung up during the bad times of the late 1870s. The first Knights of Reliance group was founded in 1877 in Lampasas County, Texas. As the Farmers Alliance, this organization gradually expanded in northeastern Texas, and after 1885 it spread rapidly throughout the cotton states. Alliance leaders stressed cooperation. Their co-ops bought fertilizer and other supplies in bulk and sold them at fair prices to members. They sought to market their crops cooperatively but could not raise the necessary capital from banks—with the result that some of them began to question the workings of the American financial and monetary system. They became economic and social radicals in the process. In the northern regions a similar though less influential alliance movement developed.

The alliances adopted somewhat differing policies, but all agreed that agricultural prices were too low, that transportation costs were too high, and that something was radically wrong with the nation's financial system. "There are three great crops raised in Nebraska," an angry rural editor proclaimed in 1890. "One is a crop of corn, one is a crop of freight rates, and one a crop of interest. One is produced by farmers who by sweat and toil farm the land. The other two are produced by men who sit in their offices and behind their bank counters and farm the farmers." All agreed on the need for political action if the lot of the agriculturalist was to be improved.

Although the state alliances of the Dakotas and Kansas joined the Southern Alliance in 1889, for a time local prejudices and conflicting interests prevented the formation of a single national organization. Northern farmers mostly voted Republican, southerners Democratic, and resentments created during the Civil War lingered in all sections. Cotton-producing southerners opposed the protective tariff; most northerners, fearing the competition of foreign grain producers, favored it. Railroad regulation and federal land policy seemed vital questions to northerners; financial reform loomed most important in southern eyes. Northerners were receptive to the idea of forming a third party, while southerners, wedded to the one-party system, pre-

Mary Elizabeth Lease was a prominent Populist noted for her rallying cry to "raise less corn and more hell."

ferred working to capture local Democratic machines.

The farm groups entered local politics in the 1890 elections. Convinced of the righteousness of their cause, they campaigned with tremendous fervor. The results were encouraging. In the South, Alliance-sponsored gubernatorial candidates won in Georgia, Tennessee, South Carolina, and Texas; eight southern legislatures fell under Alliance control, and 44 congressmen and 3 senators committed to Alliance objectives were sent to Washington. In the West, Alliance candidates swept Kansas and captured a majority in the Nebraska legislature and enough seats in Minnesota and South Dakota to hold the balance of power between the major parties.

Such success, coupled with the reluctance of the Republicans and Democrats to make concessions to their demands, encouraged Alliance leaders to cre-

ate a new national party. By uniting southern and western farmers, they succeeded in breaking the sectional barrier erected by the Civil War. If they could recruit industrial workers, perhaps a real political revolution could be accomplished. In February 1892, farm leaders, representatives of the Knights of Labor, and various professional reformers, some 800 in all, met at St. Louis, organized the People's, or Populist, party, and issued a call for a national convention to meet at Omaha in July.

That convention nominated General James B. Weaver of Iowa for president (with a one-legged Confederate veteran as his running mate) and drafted a platform that called for a graduated income tax and national ownership of railroads and the telegraph and telephone systems. It also advocated a "subtreasury" plan that would permit farmers to hold nonperishable crops off the market when prices were low. Under this proposal, the government would make loans in the form of greenbacks to farmers, secured by crops held in storage in federal warehouses. When prices rose, the farmers could sell their crops and repay the loans. To combat deflation further, the platform demanded the unlimited coinage of silver and an increase in the money supply "to no less than $50 per capita."

To make the government more responsive to public opinion, the Populists urged the adoption of the initiative and referendum procedures and the election of United States senators by popular vote. To win the support of industrial workers, their platform denounced the use of Pinkerton detectives in labor disputes and backed the eight-hour day and the restriction of "undesirable" immigration.

The Populists created, in the phrase of the historian Lawrence Goodwyn, "a multi-sectional institution of reform." They were not, however, revolutionaries. They saw themselves not as a persecuted minority but as a victimized majority betrayed by what would a century later be called the establishment. They were at most ambivalent about the free enterprise system, and they tended to attribute social and economic injustices not to built-in inequities in the system but to nefarious conspiracies organized by selfish interests in order to subvert the system.

The appearance of the new party was the most exciting and significant aspect of the presidential campaign of 1892, which saw Harrison and Cleveland refighting the election of 1888. The Populists put forth a host of colorful spellbinders: Tom Watson, a Georgia congressman whose temper was such that on one occasion he administered a beating to a local planter with the man's own riding crop; William A. Peffer, a senator from Kansas whose long beard and grave demeanor gave him the look of a Hebrew prophet; "Sockless Jerry" Simpson of Kansas, unlettered but full of grass-roots shrewdness and wit, a former Greenbacker and an admirer of the single-tax doctrine of Henry George; Ignatius Donnelly, the "Minnesota Sage," who claimed to be an authority on science, economics, and Shakespeare (he believed that Francis Bacon wrote the plays) and whose widely read novel, *Caesar's Column* (1891), pictured an America of the future wherein a handful of plutocrats tyrannized masses of downtrodden workers and serfs.

In the one-party South, Populist strategists sought to wean black farmers away from the ruling Democratic organization. Their competition forced the "subsidies" paid for black votes up to as much as a dollar—two days' wages. Southern black farmers had their own Colored Alliance, and even before 1892 their leaders had worked closely with the white alliances. Nearly 100 black delegates had attended the Populist convention at St. Louis. Of course, the blacks would be useless to the party if they could not vote; therefore, white Populist leaders opposed the southern trend toward disfranchising blacks and called for full civil rights for all.

Jeremiah "Sockless Jerry" Simpson speaking at a political debate in Kansas in 1892. Like many Populists, a flamboyant campaigner, Simpson earned his nickname by using the claim that he wore no socks against his well-dressed opponent for a congressional seat.

In the Northwest, the Populists assailed the "bankers' conspiracy" in unbridled terms. Ignatius Donnelly, running for governor of Minnesota, wrote another futuristic political novel, *The Golden Bottle,* and made 150 speeches, vowing to make the campaign "the liveliest ever seen" in the state.

The results proved disappointing. Tom Watson lost his seat in Congress, and Donnelly ran a poor third in the Minnesota gubernatorial race. The Populists did sweep Kansas. They elected numbers of local officials in other western states and cast over a million votes for General Weaver. But the effort to unite white and black farmers in the South failed miserably. Conservative Democrats, while continuing with considerable success to attract black voters, played on racial fears cruelly, insisting that the Populists sought to undermine white supremacy. Since most white Populists saw the alliance with blacks as at best a marriage of convenience, this argument had a deadly effect. Elsewhere, even in the old centers of the Granger movement, the party made no significant impression. Urban workers remained aloof.

By standing firmly for conservative financial policies, Cleveland attracted considerable Republican support and won a solid victory over Harrison in the electoral college, 277 to 145. Weaver's electoral vote was 22.

Showdown on Silver

One conclusion that politicians reached after analyzing the 1892 returns was that the money question, particularly the controversy over the coinage of silver, was of paramount interest to the voters. Despite the wide-ranging appeal of the Populist platform, most of Weaver's strength came from the silver-mining states. By contrast, Cleveland's strong stand for gold proved popular in the Northwest.

In truth, the issue of gold versus silver was superficial; the important question was what, if anything, should be done to check the deflationary spiral. The declining price level benefited bondholders and other people with fixed incomes and injured debtors. Industrial workers profited from deflation except during periods of depression, when unemployment rose—which helps explain why the Populists made little headway among them. Southern farmers, who were prisoners of the crop-lien system,

and farmers in the plains states were hit hard by the downward trend.

By the early 1890s, discussion of federal monetary policy revolved around the coinage of silver. Traditionally, the United States had been on a bimetallic standard. Both gold and silver were coined, the number of grains of each in the dollar being adjusted periodically to reflect the commercial value of the two metals. An act of 1792 established a 15:1 ratio—371.25 grains of silver and 24.75 grains of gold were each worth $1 at the Mint. In 1834 the ratio was changed to 16:1 and in 1853 to 14.8:1, the latter reduction in the value of gold reflecting the new discoveries in California. This ratio slightly undervalued silver. In 1861, for example, the amount of silver bullion in a dollar was worth $1.03 in the open market, so no one took silver to the Mint for coinage. However, an avalanche of silver from the mines of Nevada and Colorado gradually depressed the price until, around 1874, it again became profitable for miners to coin their bullion. Alas, when they tried to do so, they discovered that the Coinage Act of 1873, taking account of the fact that no silver had been presented to the Mint in years, had demonetized the metal.

The silver mines denounced this "Crime of '73," and inflationists, who wanted more money put into circulation regardless of its base, joined them in demanding a return to bimetallism. Conservatives, still fighting the battle against greenback paper money, resisted strongly. The result was a series of compromises. In 1878 the Bland-Allison Act authorized the purchase of $2 million to $4 million of silver a month at the market price, but this had little inflationary effect because the government consistently purchased the minimum amount. The commercial price of silver continued to fall; in 1890 its ratio to gold was 20:1. In that year the Sherman Silver Purchase Act required the government to buy 4.5 million *ounces* of silver monthly, but in the face of increasing supplies, the price of silver fell still further. The ratio reached 26:1 in 1893 and 32:1 in 1894.

The compromises satisfied no one. Silver miners grumbled because their bullion brought in only half what it had in the early 1870s. Debtors noted angrily that because of the general decline in prices, the dollars they used to meet their obligations were worth more than twice as much as in 1865. Advocates of the gold standard feared that unlimited silver coinage would be authorized, "destroying the value of the dollar." When a financial panic brought on by the collapse of the London banking house of Baring Brothers ushered in a severe industrial depression, the confidence of both silverites and "gold bugs" was further eroded.

President Cleveland believed that the controversy over silver had caused the depression by shaking the confidence of the business community and that all would be well if the country returned to a single gold standard. He summoned a special session of Congress, and by exerting immense political pressure he obtained the repeal of the Sherman Silver Purchase Act in October 1893. All that this accomplished was to split the Democratic party, its southern and western wings deserting him almost to a man.

During 1894 and 1895, while the nation floundered in the worst depression it had ever experienced, a series of events further undermined public confidence. In the spring of 1894 several "armies" of the unemployed, the most imposing led by Jacob S. Coxey, an eccentric Ohio businessman, marched on Washington to demand relief. Coxey wanted the government to undertake a program of federal public works and to authorize local communities to exchange non-interest-bearing bonds with the Treasury for $500 million in paper money, the funds to be used to hire unemployed workers to build roads. The scheme, Coxey claimed, would pump money into the economy, provide work for the jobless, and benefit the entire nation by improving transportation facilities.

When Coxey's group of demonstrators, perhaps 500 in all, reached Washington, he and two other leaders were arrested for trespassing on the grounds of the Capitol. Their followers were dispersed by club-wielding policemen. This callous treatment convinced many Americans that the government had little interest in the suffering of the people, an opinion strengthened when Cleveland, in July 1894, used federal troops to crush the Pullman strike.

The next year the Supreme Court handed down several reactionary decisions. In *United States* v. *E. C. Knight Company* it refused to employ the Sherman Antitrust Act to break up the Sugar Trust. In *Pollock* v. *Farmers' Loan and Trust Company* it invalidated a federal income tax law despite the fact that a similar measure levied during the Civil War had been upheld by the Court in *Springer* v. *United States* (1881).

Finally, the Court denied a writ of habeas corpus to Eugene V. Debs of the American Railway Union, who was languishing in prison for disobeying a federal injunction during the Pullman strike.

On top of these indications of official conservatism came a desperate financial crisis. Throughout 1894 the Treasury's supply of gold dwindled as worried citizens exchanged greenbacks (now convertible into gold) for hard money and foreign investors cashed in large amounts of American securities. The government tried to sell bonds for gold to bolster the reserve, but since most investors purchased the bonds with gold-backed paper money, in effect withdrawing gold from the Treasury and then returning it for the bonds, the gold reserve continued to melt away. Early in 1895 it touched a low point of $41 million.

At this juncture a syndicate of bankers headed by J. P. Morgan turned the tide by underwriting a $62 million bond issue, guaranteeing that half the gold would come from Europe. This caused a great public outcry; the spectacle of the nation being saved from bankruptcy by a private banker infuriated millions.

These events, together with the continuing depression, discredited the Cleveland administration. "I haven't got words to say what I think of that old bag of beef," Governor "Pitchfork Ben" Tillman of South Carolina, who had resolutely resisted the Populists in 1892, told a local audience two years later. "If you send me to the Senate, I promise I won't be bulldozed by him."

As the presidential election of 1896 approached, with the Populists demanding unlimited coinage of silver at a ratio of 16:1, the major parties found it impossible to continue straddling the money question. The Populist vote had increased by 42 percent in the 1894 congressional elections. Southern and western Democratic leaders feared that they would lose their following unless Cleveland was repudiated. Western Republicans, led by Senator Henry M. Teller of Colorado, were threatening to bolt to the Populists unless their party came out for silver coinage. After a generation of political equivocation, the major parties had to face an important issue squarely.

The Republicans, meeting to choose a candidate at St. Louis in June 1896, announced for the gold standard. "We are unalterably opposed to every measure calculated to debase our currency or impair the credit of our country," the platform declared. "We are therefore opposed to the free coinage of silver. . . . The existing gold standard must be maintained." The party then nominated Ohio's William McKinley for president. McKinley, best known for his staunch advocacy of the protective tariff yet highly regarded by labor, was expected to run strongly in the Middle West and the East.

The Democratic convention met in July at Chicago. The pro-gold Cleveland element made a hard fight, but the silverites swept them aside. The high point came when a youthful Nebraskan named William Jennings Bryan spoke for silver against gold, for western farmers against the industrial East. Bryan's every sentence provoked ear-shattering applause.

We have petitioned and our petitions have been scorned; we have entreated, and our entreaties have been disregarded; we have begged, and they have

Portraits of William Jennings Bryan with his wife and children, along with the text of the "cross of gold" speech, appeared on this typically colorful campaign poster for the 1896 campaign.

mocked when our calamity came. We beg no longer we entreat no more; we petition no more. We defy them!

The crowd responded like a great choir to Bryan's oratorical cues. "Burn down your cities and leave our farms," he said, "and your cities will spring up again as if by magic; but destroy our farms and the grass will grow in the streets of every city in the country." He ended with a marvelous figure of speech that set the tone for the coming campaign. "You shall not press down upon the brow of labor this crown of thorns," he warned, bringing his hands down suggestively to his temples. "You shall not crucify mankind upon a cross of gold!" Dramatically, he extended his arms to the side, the very figure of the crucified Christ.

The convention promptly adopted a platform calling for "the free and unlimited coinage of both silver and gold at the present legal ratio of 16 to 1" and went on to nominate Bryan, who was barely 36, for president.

This action put tremendous pressure on the Populists. If they supported Bryan, they risked losing their party identity; if they nominated another candidate, they would ensure McKinley's election. Those more concerned with immediate political advantage, especially officeholders and aspirants, took the former position. Those (mostly old Alliance members raised in the cooperative movement) who considered free silver a minor issue and a poor substitute for the subtreasury plan as an approach to the deflation problem, rejected "fusion" with the Democrats. "The Democratic idea of fusion," Tom Watson complained, is "that we play Jonah while they play whale." In part because the delegates could not find a person of stature willing to become a candidate against him, the Populist convention nominated Bryan, seeking to preserve the party identity by substituting Watson for the Democratic vice-presidential nominee, Arthur Sewall of Maine.

The Election of 1896

Never did a presidential campaign raise such intense emotions. The Republicans from the silver-mining states swung solidly behind Bryan. The gold Democrats refused to accept the decision of the Chi-

Cartoon satirizing the predicament of Democrats like New York's Governor David B. Hill, who found their party aligned with the Populists in the 1896 presidential election. More than sartorial adjustments were required of such conservative politicos.

cago convention. Cleveland professed to be "so dazed by the political situation that I am in no condition for speech or thought on the subject." Many others adopted the policy of Governor David B. Hill of New York, who said, "I am a Democrat still—very still." The extreme gold bugs, calling themselves National Democrats, nominated their own candidate, 79-year-old Senator John M. Palmer of Illinois. Palmer ran only to injure Bryan. "Fellow Democrats," he announced, "I will not consider it any great fault if you decide to cast your vote for William McKinley."

At the start the Republicans seemed to have everything in their favor. Bryan's youth and relative lack of political experience—two terms in the House—contrasted unfavorably with McKinley's distinguished war record, his long service in Congress and as governor of Ohio, and his reputation for honesty and good judgment. The severe depression operated in favor of the party out of power, although by repudiating Cleveland, the Democrats escaped much of the burden of explaining away his errors. The newspapers came out almost unanimously for the Republicans. Important Democratic papers such as the *New York World*, the *Boston Herald*, the *Baltimore Sun*, the *Chicago Chronicle*, and the *Richmond Times* supported McKinley editorially and even slanted news stories against the Democrats. The *New York Times* accused Bryan of being insane, his affliction being variously classified as "paranoia querulenta," "graphomania," and "oratorical monomania." The Democrats had very little money and few well-known speakers to fight the campaign.

But Bryan proved a formidable opponent. Casting aside tradition, he took to the stump personally, traveling 18,000 miles and making over 600 speeches. He was one of the greatest of orators. A big, handsome man with a voice capable of carrying without strain to the far corners of a great hall yet equally effective before a cluster of auditors at a rural crossroads, he projected an image of absolute sincerity without appearing fanatical or argumentative. At every major stop on his tour, huge crowds assembled. In Minnesota he packed the 10,000-seat St. Paul Auditorium, while thousands milled in the streets outside.

His energy was amazing, and his charm and good humor were unfailing. At one whistle stop, while he was shaving in his compartment, a small group outside the train began clamoring for a glimpse of him. Flinging open the window and beaming through the lather, he shook hands cheerfully with each of the admirers. Everywhere he hammered away at the money question. Yet he did not totally neglect other issues. He was defending, he said, "all the people who suffer from the operations of trusts, syndicates, and combines."

McKinley's campaign was managed by a new type of politician, Marcus Alonzo Hanna, an Ohio businessman. In a sense Hanna was a product of the Pendleton Civil Service Act. When deprived of the contributions of officeholders, the parties turned to business for funds, and Hanna was one of the first leaders with a foot in both camps. Politics fascinated him, and despite his wealth and wide interests, he was willing to labor endlessly at the routine work of political organization.

Hanna aspired to be a kingmaker and early fastened on McKinley, whose charm he found irresis-

tible, as the vehicle for satisfying his ambition. He spent about $100,000 of his own money on the pre-convention campaign. His attitude toward the candidate, one mutual friend observed, was "that of a big, bashful boy toward the girl he loves."

Before most Republicans realized how effective Bryan was on the stump, Hanna perceived the danger and sprang into action. Since the late 1880s the character of political organization had been changing. The Civil Service Act was also cutting down on the number of jobs available to reward campaign workers. At the same time, the new mass-circulation newspapers and the nationwide press associations were increasing the pressure on candidates to speak openly and often on national issues. This trend put a premium on party organization and consistency— the old political trick of speaking out of one side of the mouth to one audience and out the other to another no longer worked very well. The old military metaphors of political discourse, the terms *campaign* and *spoils* and *standard bearer*, remained, but others more businesslike became popular: *boss, machine, lobbyist.*

As the federal government became more involved in economic issues, business interests found more reason to be concerned about national elections and were more willing to spend money in behalf of candidates whose views they approved. In the campaign of 1888 the Republicans had set up a businessman's "advisory board" to raise money and stir up enthusiasm for Benjamin Harrison.

Hanna understood what was happening to politics. Certain that money was the key to political power, he raised an enormous campaign fund. When businessmen hesitated to contribute, he pried open their purses by a combination of persuasiveness and intimidation. Banks and insurance companies were "assessed" a percentage of their assets, big corporations a share of their receipts, until some $3.5 million had been collected.

Hanna disbursed these funds with efficiency and imagination. He sent 1,500 speakers into the doubtful districts and blanketed the land with 250 million pieces of campaign literature, printed in a dozen languages. "He has advertised McKinley as if he were a patent medicine," Theodore Roosevelt, never at a loss for words, exclaimed.

Incapable of competing with Bryan as a swayer of mass audiences, McKinley conducted a "front-porch campaign." This technique dated from the first Harrison-Cleveland election, when Harrison regularly delivered off-the-cuff speeches to groups of visitors representing special interests or regions in his hometown of Indianapolis. The system conserved the candidate's energies and enabled him to avoid the appearance of seeking the presidency too openly—which was still considered bad form—and at the same time allowed him to make headlines throughout the country.

Guided by the masterful Hanna, McKinley brought the front-porch method to perfection. Superficially, the proceedings were delightfully informal. From every corner of the land, groups representing various regions, occupations, and interests descended on McKinley's unpretentious frame house in Canton, Ohio. Gathering on the

Beginning with his acceptance of the presidential nomination, William McKinley mounted his campaign from his front porch in Canton, Ohio.

lawn—the grass was soon reduced to mud, the fence stripped of pickets by souvenir hunters—the visitors paid their compliments to the candidate and heard him deliver a brief speech, while beside him on the porch his aged mother and adoring invalid wife listened with rapt attention. Then there was a small reception, during which the delegates were given an opportunity to shake their host's hand.

Despite the air of informality, these performances were carefully staged. The delegations arrived on a tightly coordinated schedule worked out by McKinley's staff and the railroads, which operated cut-rate excursion trains to Canton from all over the nation. McKinley was fully briefed on the special interests and attitudes of each group, and the speeches of delegation leaders were submitted in advance. Often his secretary amended these remarks, and on occasion McKinley wrote the visitors' speeches himself. His own talks were carefully prepared, each calculated to make a particular point. All were reported fully in the newspapers. Thus without moving from his doorstep, McKinley met thousands of people from every section of the country.

These tactics worked admirably. On election day McKinley carried the East; the Middle West including even Iowa, Minnesota, and North Dakota; and the Pacific Coast states of Oregon and California. Bryan won in the South, the plains states, and the Rocky Mountain region. McKinley collected 271 electoral votes to Bryan's 176, the popular vote being 7,036,000 to 6,468,000.

The Meaning of the Election

The sharp sectional division marked the failure of the Populist effort to unite northern and southern farmers and also the triumph of the industrial part of the country over the agricultural. Business and financial interests voted solidly for the Republicans, fearing that a Democratic victory would bring economic chaos. When a Nebraska landowner tried to float a mortgage during the campaign, a loan company official wrote him: "If McKinley is elected, we think we will be in the market, but we do not care to make any investments while there is an uncertainty as to what kind of money a person will be paid back in."

Other social and economic interests were far

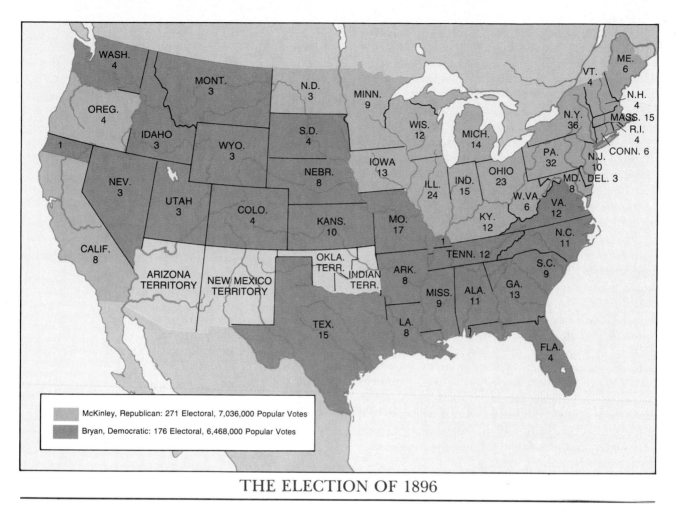

THE ELECTION OF 1896

from being united. Many thousands of farmers voted for McKinley, as his success in states such as North Dakota, Iowa, and Minnesota proved. In the East and in the states bordering the Great Lakes, the agricultural depression was not severe, and farm radicalism was almost nonexistent.

A preponderance of the labor vote also went to the Republicans. In part this resulted from the tremendous pressures that many industrialists applied to their workers. "Men," one manufacturer announced, "vote as you please, but if Bryan is elected . . . the whistle will not blow Wednesday morning." Some companies placed orders for materials subject to cancellation if the Democrats won. Yet coercion was not a major factor, for McKinley was highly regarded in labor circles. While governor of Ohio,

he had advocated the arbitration of industrial disputes and backed a law fining employers who refused to permit workers to join unions. During the Pullman strike he had sent his brother to try to persuade George Pullman to deal fairly with the strikers. He had invariably based his advocacy of high tariffs on the argument that American wage levels would be depressed if foreign goods could enter the country untaxed. Mark Hanna too had the reputation of always giving his employees a square deal. The Republicans carried nearly all the large cities, and in closely contested states such as Illinois and Ohio this made the difference between victory and defeat.

During the campaign, some frightened Republicans had laid plans for fleeing the country if Bryan were elected, and belligerent ones, such as Theodore Roosevelt, then police commissioner of New York City, readied themselves to meet the "social revolutionaries" on the battlefield. Victory sent such people into transports of joy. Most conservatives concluded that the way of life they so fervently admired had been saved for all time.

However heartfelt, such sentiments were not founded on fact. With workers standing beside capitalists and with the farm vote split, it cannot be said that the election divided the nation class against class or that McKinley's victory saved the country from revolution.

Far from representing a triumph for the status quo, the election marked the coming of age of modern America. The battle between gold and silver, which everyone had considered so vital, had little real significance. The inflationists seemed to have been beaten, but new gold discoveries in Alaska and South Africa and improved methods of extracting gold from low-grade ores soon led to a great expansion of the money supply. In any case, within two decades the system of basing the volume of currency on bullion had been abandoned. Bryan and the "political" Populists who supported him, supposedly the advance agents of revolution, were oriented more toward the past than the future; their ideal was the rural America of Jefferson and Jackson.

McKinley, for all his innate conservatism, was capable of looking ahead toward the new century. His approach was national where Bryan's was basically parochial. Though never daring and seldom imaginative, he was able to deal pragmatically with current problems. Before long, as the United States became increasingly an exporter of manufactures, he would even modify his position on the tariff. And no one better reflected the spirit of the age than Mark Hanna, the outstanding political realist of his generation. Far from preventing change, the outcome of the election of 1896 made possible still greater changes as the United States moved into the 20th century.

Milestones

1873 Congress suspends the coining of silver ("Crime of '73")
1877 Farmers Alliance movement begins
1878 Bland-Allison Act
1879 Greenback paper money made convertible into gold
1881 President Garfield assassinated
1883 Pendleton Civil Service Act
1887 Interstate Commerce Act
Cleveland's tariff message
1890 Sherman Silver Purchase Act
1892 People's (Populist) party founded
1893 Panic of 1893
1894 Coxey's Army marches to Washington to demand relief
1895 Supreme Court declares federal income tax unconstitutional (_Pollock v. Farmers' Loan and Trust Company_)
J. P. Morgan raises $62 million in gold for the Treasury
1896 William Jennings Bryan, "Cross of Gold" speech

SUPPLEMENTARY READING

Titles marked with an asterisk have been published in paperback.

The political history of this period is covered in lively and controversial fashion in Matthew Josephson, **The Politicos*** (1938), and more solidly and sympathetically in H. W. Morgan, **From Hayes to McKinley** (1969). H. U. Faulkner, **Politics, Reform, and Expansion*** (1959), treats the politics of the 1890s in some detail, and Samuel McSeveney, **The Politics of Depression: Political Behavior in the Northeast** (1972), and C. V. Woodward, **Origins of the New South*** (1951), are important regional studies. J. A. Garraty, **The New Commonwealth*** (1968), attempts to trace the changing character of the political system after 1877.

There are three superb analyses of the political system of the period written by men who studied it firsthand: James Bryce, **The American Commonwealth*** (1888), Woodrow Wilson, **Congressional Government*** (1886), and Moisei Ostrogorski, **Democracy and the Organization of Political Parties*** (1902). Morton Keller, **Affairs of State** (1977), is an interesting analysis of public life in the period. L. D. White, **The Republican Era*** (1958), is an excellent study of the government in that period. D. J. Rothman, **Politics and Power: The United States Senate*** (1966), analyzes the shifting structure of the upper house.

J. C. Teaford, **The Unheralded Triumph: City Government** (1984), B. C. Campbell, **Representative Democracy** (1980), R. J. Jensen, **The Winning of the Midwest** (1971), and Paul Kleppner, **The Cross of Culture** (1977), are important studies of the character of state and local politics.

The issues of post-Reconstruction politics are discussed in S. P. Hirshson, **Farewell to the Bloody Shirt*** (1962), Allen Weinstein, **Prelude to Populism: Origins of the Silver Issue** (1970), Irwin Unger, **The Greenback Era*** (1964), W. T. K. Nugent, **Money and American Society** (1968), Geoffrey Blodgett, **The Gentle Reformers** (1966), J. G. Sproat, **"The Best Men": Liberal Reformers in the Gilded Age** (1968), Ari Hoogenboom, **Outlawing the Spoils** (1961), and in several essays in H. W. Morgan (ed.), **The Gilded Age*** (1970).

Among biographies of political leaders, the following are especially worth consulting: Ari Hoogenboom, **The Presidency of Rutherford B. Hayes** (1988), Allan Peskin, **Garfield** (1978), F. C. Reeves, **Gentleman President: Chester A. Arthur** (1978), J. D. Doenecke, **The Presidency of James A. Garfield and Chester A. Arthur** (1981), Allan Nevins, **Grover Cleveland** (1932), H. S. Merrill, **Bourbon Leader: Grover Cleveland and the Democratic Party*** (1957), H. J. Sievers, **Benjamin Harrison** (1952–1968), H. E. Socolovsky and A. B. Spetter, **The Presidency of Benjamin Harrison** (1987), and H. W. Morgan, **William McKinley and His America** (1963).

On the farmers' problems, see F. A. Shannon, **The Farmer's Last Frontier*** (1945), J. D. Hicks, **The Populist Revolt*** (1931), and Theodore Saloutos, **Farmer Movements in the South*** (1960). Populism has been the subject of intensive study. Richard Hofstadter, **The Age of Reform*** (1955), takes a dim view of populism as a reform movement, while Norman Pollack, **The Populist Response to Industrial America** (1962), pictures it as a radical one. W. T. K. Nugent, **The Tolerant Populists** (1963), leans in Pollack's direction but is more restrained. Lawrence Goodwyn, **Democratic Promise: The Populist Movement in America** (1976), calls it "a people's movement of mass democratic aspiration." R. W. Cherny, **Populism, Progressivism, and the Transformation of Nebraska Politics** (1981), Sheldon Hackney, **Populism to Progressivism in Alabama** (1969), and Steven Hahn, **The Roots of Southern Populism** (1983), are more than local studies.

On the depression of the 1890s, consult Charles Hoffman, **The Depression of the Nineties** (1970), Carlos Schwantes, **Coxey's Army** (1985), Stanley Buder, **Pullman** (1967), and Nick Salvatore, **Eugene V. Debs** (1982). On Bryan and the election of 1896, see P. W. Glad, **The Trumpet Soundeth** (1960), R. W. Cherny, **A Righteous Cause: William Jennings Bryan** (1985), S. L. Jones, **The Presidential Election of 1896** (1964), R. F. Durden, **The Climax of Populism** (1965), and P. W. Glad, **McKinley, Bryan, and the People*** (1964). On McKinley, consult L. L. Gould, **The Presidency of William McKinley** (1980), and Herbert Croly, **Marcus Alonzo Hanna** (1912), the best life of Hanna.

XXIII

From Isolation to Empire

You furnish the pictures and I'll furnish the war.

WILLIAM RANDOLPH HEARST *to Frederic Remington, 1898*

I walked the floor of the White House night after night until midnight; and I am not ashamed to tell you, gentlemen, that I went down on my knees and prayed Almighty God for light and guidance more than one night. And one night late it came to me. . . . There was nothing left for us to do but to take them all, and to educate the Filipinos, and uplift and Christianize them.

PRESIDENT WILLIAM McKINLEY *explaining to Methodist churchmen his decision to favor annexation of the Philippine Islands, 1899*

A mericans have always been somewhat ambivalent in their attitudes toward other nations, and at no time was this more clearly the case than in the decades following the Civil War. Occupied with exploiting the West and building their great industrial machine, they gave little thought to foreign affairs. Benjamin Harrison reflected a widely held belief when he said during the 1888 presidential campaign that the United States was "an apart nation" and so it should remain. James Bryce made the same point in *The American Commonwealth.* "Happy America," he wrote, stood "apart in a world of her own . . . safe even from menace."

The historian David W. Pletcher has called the period the "awkward age" of American diplomacy, a time when the foreign service was "amateurish" and "spoils-ridden," when policy was either non-existent or poorly planned, when treaties were clumsily drafted and state secrets ill kept. "The general idea of the diplomatic service," one reporter commented at this time, "is that it is a soft berth for wealthy young men who enjoy court society." The *New York Sun,* an important newspaper, suggested in the 1880s that the State Department had "outgrown its usefulness" and ought to be abolished.

America's Divided View of the World

Late-19th-century Americans never ignored world affairs entirely. They had little direct concern for what went on in Europe, but their interest in Latin America was great and growing, in the Far East only somewhat less so. Economic developments, especially shifts in foreign commerce resulting from industrialization, strengthened this interest with every passing year. Whether one sees isolation or expansion as the hallmark of American foreign policy after 1865 depends on the part of the world one looks at.

The disdain of the people of the United States for Europe rested on several historical foundations. Faith in the unique character of American civilization—and the converse of that belief, suspicion of Europe's supposedly aristocratic and decadent society—formed the chief basis of this isolation. Bitter memories of indignities suffered during the Revolution and the Napoleonic wars and anger at the hostile attitude of the great powers toward the United States during the Civil War strengthened it, as did the dislike of Americans for the pomp and punctilio of European monarchies. Also important was the undeniable truth that the United States was practically invulnerable to European attack and at the same time incapable of mounting an offensive against any European power. In turning their backs on Europe, Americans were taking no risk and passing up few opportunities—hence their indifference.

When occasional disagreements with one or another of the great powers erupted, the United States pressed its claims hard. It insisted, for example, that Great Britain pay for the loss of some 100,000 tons of American shipping sunk by Confederate cruisers that had been built in British yards during the rebellion. Some politicians even demanded that the British pay for the entire cost of the war after the Battle of Gettysburg—some $2 billion—on the grounds that without British backing, the Confederacy would have collapsed at about that point. However, the controversy never became critical, and in 1871 the two nations signed the Treaty of Washington, agreeing to arbitrate the so-called *Alabama* claims. The next year the judges awarded the United States $15.5 million for the ships and cargoes that had been destroyed.

In the 1880s a squabble developed with Ger-

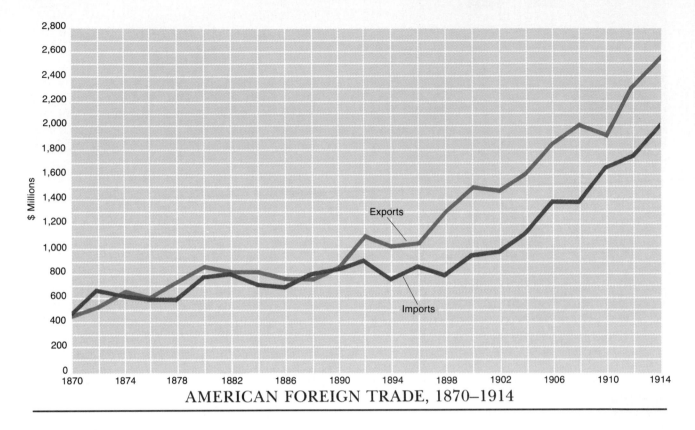

AMERICAN FOREIGN TRADE, 1870–1914

many, France, and a number of other countries over their banning of American pork products, ostensibly because some uninspected American pork was discovered to be diseased. The affair produced a great deal of windy oratory denouncing European autocracy and led to threats of economic retaliation. Congress eventually provided for the inspection of meat destined for export, and in 1891 the European nations lifted the ban. Similarly, there were repeated alarms and outbursts of anti-British feeling in the United States in connection with Great Britain's treatment of Ireland—all motivated chiefly by the desire of politicians to appeal to Irish-American voters.

Origins of the Large Policy

The nation's interests elsewhere in the world gradually increased. During the Civil War, France had established a protectorate over Mexico, installing the Archduke Maximilian of Austria as emperor.

In 1866 Secretary of State William H. Seward demanded that the French withdraw, and the government moved 50,000 soldiers to the Rio Grande. Fearing American intervention, among other reasons, the French pulled their troops out that winter, whereupon nationalist rebels seized and executed Maximilian. Shortly thereafter, at Seward's instigation, the United States purchased Alaska from Russia for $7.2 million, thereby ridding the continent of another foreign power.

That same year, 1867, the aggressive Seward acquired the Midway Islands in the western Pacific, which had been discovered in 1859 by an American naval officer, N. C. Brooks. Seward also made overtures toward annexing the Hawaiian Islands, and he looked longingly at Cuba. In 1870 President Grant submitted to the Senate a treaty annexing the Dominican Republic. He applied tremendous pressure in an effort to obtain ratification, thus forcing a "great debate" on extracontinental expansion. Expansionists stressed the wealth and resources of the country, the markets it would provide, even its "salubrious climate." But the arguments of the opposition proved more persuasive. The distance of the Dominican Republic from the continent, its crowded, dark-skinned population of what one congressman called "semi-civilized, semi-barbarous men who cannot speak our language," made annexation appear unattractive. The treaty was rejected. Prevailing opinion was well summarized by a Philadelphia newspaper: "The true interests of the American people will be better served . . . by thorough and complete development of the immense resources of our existing territory than by any rash attempts to increase it."

But the internal growth that preoccupied Americans eventually led them to look outward. By the late 1880s the country was exporting a steadily increasing share of its agricultural and industrial production. Exports, only $450 million in 1870, passed the billion-dollar mark early in the 1890s.

The character of foreign trade was also changing. Manufactures loomed ever more important among exports. American steelmakers could compete with British producers anywhere in the world. In 1900 one firm received a large order for steel plates from a Glasgow shipbuilder, and another won contracts for structural steel to be used in constructing bridges for the Uganda Railroad in British East Africa. When a member of Parliament questioned the colonial secretary about the latter deal, the secretary replied: "Tenders [bids] were invited in the United Kingdom . . . [but] one of the American tenders was found to be considerably the lowest in every respect and was therefore accepted." When American industrialists became conscious of their ability to compete with Europeans in far-off markets, they took more interest in world affairs, particularly during periods of depression, when domestic consumption fell.

Shifting intellectual currents further altered attitudes. Darwin's theories, applicable by analogy to international relations, gave the concept of manifest destiny a new plausibility. Darwinists like the historian John Fiske argued that the American government was so clearly the world's "fittest" that it was destined to spread peacefully over "every land on the earth's surface." In *Our Country* (1885) Josiah Strong found racist and religious justifications for expansionism, again based on the theory of evolution. The Anglo-Saxon race, centered now in the United States, possessed "an instinct or genius for

colonization," Strong claimed. "God, with infinite wisdom and skill is training the Anglo-Saxon race for . . . the final competition of races." Christianity, he added, had developed "aggressive traits calculated to impress its institutions upon mankind." Soon American civilization would "move down upon" Mexico and all Latin America, and "out upon the islands of the sea, over upon Africa and beyond." "Can anyone doubt," Strong asked, "that the result of this . . . will be 'the survival of the fittest'?"*

The completion of the conquest of the West encouraged Americans to consider expansion beyond the seas. "For nearly 300 years the dominant fact in American life has been expansion," declared Frederick Jackson Turner, propounder of the frontier thesis. "That these energies of expansion will no longer operate would be a rash prediction." Turner and writers who advanced other expansionist arguments were much influenced by foreign thinking. European liberals had tended to disapprove of colonial ventures, but in the 1870s and 1880s many of them were changing their minds. English liberals in particular began to talk and write about the "superiority" of English culture, to describe the virtues of the "Anglo-Saxon race," to stress a "duty" to spread Christianity among the heathen, and to advance economic arguments for overseas expansion.

European ideas were reinforced for Americans by their observations of the imperialist activities of the European powers in what would today be called underdeveloped areas. By swallowing up most of Africa and biting off bits and pieces of the crumbling empire of China, the French, British, Germans, and other colonizers inspired some Americans to advocate joining the feast before all the choice morsels had been digested. "While the great powers of Europe are steadily enlarging their colonial domination in Asia and Africa," James G. Blaine said in 1884, "it is the especial province of this country to improve and expand its trade with the nations of America." While Blaine emphasized commerce, the excitement and adventure of overseas enterprises appealed to many people even more than the economic possibilities or any sense of obligation to fulfill a supposed national, religious, or racial destiny.

---

* In later writings Strong insisted that by "fittest" he was referring to "social efficiency," not "mere strength."

Finally, military and strategic arguments were advanced to justify adopting a "large" policy. The powerful Union army had been demobilized rapidly after Appomattox; in the 1880s only about 25,000 men were under arms, their chief occupation fighting Indians in the West. Half the navy had been scrapped after the war, and the remaining ships were obsolete. While other nations were building steam-powered iron warships, the United States still depended on wooden sailing vessels.

The decrepit state of the navy vexed many of its officers and led one of them, Captain Alfred Thayer Mahan, to develop a startling theory about the importance of sea power. He explained his theory in *The Influence of Sea Power upon History* (1890) and *The Influence of Sea Power upon the French Revolution and Empire* (1892). According to Mahan, history proved that a nation with a powerful navy and the overseas bases necessary to maintain it would be invulnerable in war and prosperous in time of peace. Applied to the current American situation, this meant that in addition to building a modern fleet, the United States should obtain a string of coaling stations and bases in the Caribbean, annex the Hawaiian Islands, and cut a canal across Central America. A more extensive colonial empire might follow, but these bases and the canal they would protect were essential first steps to ensure America's future as a great power.

Writing at a time when the imperialist-minded European nations showed signs of extending their influence in South America and the Pacific islands, Mahan attracted many influential disciples. One was Congressman Henry Cabot Lodge of Massachusetts. Lodge had married into a navy family and was intimate with the head of the new Naval War College, Commodore Stephen B. Luce. He helped push through Congress in 1883 an act authorizing the building of three steel warships, and he consistently advocated expanding and modernizing the fleet. Elevated to the Senate in 1893, Lodge pressed for expansionist policies, basing his arguments on Mahan's strategic concepts. "Sea power," he proclaimed, "is essential to the greatness of every splendid people." Lodge's friend Theodore Roosevelt was another ardent supporter of the "large" policy, but he had little influence until McKinley appointed him assistant secretary of the navy in 1897.

A 1904 photograph of Admiral Alfred Thayer Mahan, a leading advocate of sea power and proponent of naval expansionism. His views found favor among such imperialist-minded Republicans as Henry Cabot Lodge and Theodore Roosevelt.

The Course of Empire in the Pacific

The interest of the United States in the Pacific and the Far East began in the late 18th century, when the first American merchant ship dropped anchor in Canton harbor. After the Treaty of Wanghia (1844), American merchants in China enjoyed many privileges, and trade expanded rapidly. Missionaries began to flock to the country; in the late 1880s, over 500 were living there.

The Hawaiian Islands were an important way station on the route to China, and by 1820 merchants and missionaries were making contacts there. As early as 1854 a movement to annex the islands existed, though it foundered because Hawaii insisted on being admitted to the Union as a state. Commodore Perry's expedition to Japan led to the signing of a commercial treaty (1858) that opened several Japanese ports to American traders.

The United States pursued a policy of cooperating with the European powers in expanding commercial opportunities in the Far East. In Hawaii the tendency was to claim a special position but to accept the fact that Europeans also had interests in the islands. This state of affairs did not change radically following the Civil War. Despite Chinese protests over the exclusion of their nationals from the United States after 1882, American commercial privileges in China were not disturbed. American influence in Hawaii increased; the descendants of missionary families, most of them engaged in raising sugar, dominated the Hawaiian monarchy. In 1875 a reciprocity treaty admitted Hawaiian sugar to the United States free of duty in return for a promise to yield no territory to a foreign power. When this treaty was renewed in 1887, the United States obtained the right to establish a naval base at Pearl Harbor. In addition to occupying Midway Island, America obtained a foothold in the Samoan Islands in the South Pacific.

During the 1890s American interest in the Pacific area steadily intensified. Conditions in Hawaii had much to do with this. The McKinley Tariff Act of 1890, discontinuing the duty on raw sugar and compensating American producers of cane and beet sugar by granting them a bounty of 2 cents a pound, struck Hawaiian sugar growers hard, for it destroyed the advantage they had gained in the reciprocity treaty. The following year the death of the complaisant King Kalakaua brought Queen Liliuokalani, a determined nationalist, to the throne. Placing herself at the head of a "Hawaii for the Hawaiians" movement, she abolished the existing constitution under which the white minority had pretty much controlled the islands and attempted to rule as an absolute monarch. The resident Americans then staged a coup. In January 1893, with the connivance of the United States minister, John L. Stevens, who ordered 150 marines from the cruiser *Boston* into Honolulu, they deposed Queen Liliuokalani and set up a provisional government. Stevens recognized their regime at once, and the new government sent a delegation to Washington to seek a treaty of annexation.

In the closing days of the Harrison administration such a treaty was negotiated and sent to the Senate, but when Cleveland took office in March,

he withdrew it. The new president disapproved of the way American troops had been used to overthrow the queen. He sent a special commissioner, James H. Blount, to Hawaii to investigate. When Blount reported that the native Hawaiians opposed annexation, the president dismissed Stevens and attempted to restore Queen Liliuokalani. Since the provisional government was by that time firmly entrenched, this could not be accomplished peacefully. Because Cleveland was unwilling to use force against the Americans in the islands, however much he objected to their actions, he found himself unable to do anything. The revolutionary government of Hawaii remained in power, independent yet eager to be annexed.

The Hawaiian debate continued sporadically over the next four years. It provided a thorough airing of the question of overseas expansion. Fears that another power—Great Britain or perhaps Japan—might step into the void created by Cleveland's refusal to act alarmed those who favored annexation. When the Republicans returned to power in 1897, a new annexation treaty was negotiated, but domestic sugar producers now threw their weight against it, and the McKinley administration could not obtain the necessary two-thirds majority in the Senate. Finally, in July 1898, after the outbreak of the Spanish-American War, Congress annexed the islands by joint resolution, a procedure requiring only a simple majority vote.

The Course of Empire in Latin America

Most of the arguments for extending American influence in the Pacific applied more strongly to Central and South America, where the United States had much larger economic interests and where the strategic importance of the region was clear. Furthermore, the Monroe Doctrine had long conditioned the American people to the idea of acting to protect national interests in the Western Hemisphere.

As early as 1869 President Grant had come out for an American-owned canal across the isthmus of Panama, in spite of the fact that the United States had agreed in the Clayton-Bulwer Treaty with Great Britain (1850) that neither nation would "obtain or maintain for itself any exclusive control" over an interoceanic canal. In 1880, when the French engineer Ferdinand de Lesseps organized a company to build a canal across the isthmus, President Hayes announced that the United States would not permit a European power to control such a waterway. "The policy of the country is a canal under American control," he announced, another blithe disregard of the Clayton-Bulwer agreement.

In 1889 a pan-American conference met in Washington to discuss hemisphere problems. Secretary of State James G. Blaine hoped to use this meeting to obtain a reciprocity agreement with the Latin American countries, for the United States was importing about three times as much from them as they were purchasing in America. However, the delegates accomplished nothing beyond the establishment of the International Bureau—later known as the Pan-American Union—to promote commercial and cultural exchange. The conference was nevertheless significant, for it marked the first effort by the United States to assume the leadership of the nations of the hemisphere.

At the Washington meeting the United States posed as a friend of peace; Blaine's proposals included a general arbitration treaty to settle hemisphere disputes. A minor disagreement with the Republic of Chile in 1891 soon demonstrated that the country could quickly be brought to the verge of war with one of its southern neighbors. Anti-*Yanqui* feeling was high in Chile, chiefly because the United States had refused to sell arms to the current government during the revolution that had brought it to power. In October a group of sailors from the U.S.S. *Baltimore* on shore leave in Valparaiso was set upon by a mob. Two of the sailors were killed and more than a dozen injured. President Harrison, furious at what he called an "insult . . . to the uniform of the United States sailors," demanded "prompt and full reparation." When the Chilean authorities delayed in supplying an appropriate apology and issued a statement that "imputed untruth and insincerity" on Harrison's part, the president sent to Congress a special message virtually inviting it to declare war. Faced with this threat, Chile backed down, offering the required apology and agreeing to pay damages to the sailors. Chile's humiliation destroyed much of the goodwill engendered by the Pan-American Conference.

When Cleveland returned to power in 1893, the possibility of trouble in Latin America seemed remote, for he had always opposed imperialistic ventures. The Latin American diplomatic colony in Washington greeted him warmly after its experience with Harrison. Yet scarcely two years later the United States was again on the verge of war in South America, this time as a result of a crisis in Venezuela, and before this issue was settled, Cleveland had made the most powerful claim to American hegemony in the hemisphere ever uttered.

The tangled borderland between Venezuela and British Guiana had long been in dispute, Venezuela demanding more of the region than it was entitled to and Great Britain submitting exaggerated claims and imperiously refusing to submit the question to arbitration. What made a crisis of the controversy was the political situation in the United States. A minor incident in Nicaragua, where the British had temporarily occupied the port of Corinto to force compensation for injuries to British subjects in that country, had alarmed American supporters of the Monroe Doctrine. Cleveland had avoided involvement, and along with his refusal to take Hawaii, the incident had angered expansionists. With his party rapidly deserting him because of his stand on the silver question and with the election of 1896 approaching, the president desperately needed a popular issue.

There was considerable latent anti-British feeling in the United States. By taking the Venezuelan side in the boundary dispute, Cleveland would be defending a weak neighbor against a great power, a position certain to evoke a popular response. "Turn this Venezuela question up or down, North, South, East or West, and it is a winner," one Democrat advised the president.

Cleveland did not resist the temptation to intervene. In July 1895 he ordered Secretary of State Richard Olney to send a near-ultimatum to the British. By occupying the disputed territory, Olney insisted, Great Britain was invading Venezuela and violating the Monroe Doctrine. Quite gratuitously, he went on to boast: "To-day the United States is practically sovereign on this continent, and its fiat is law upon the subjects to which it confines its interposition." Unless Great Britain responded promptly by agreeing to arbitration, the president would call the question to the attention of Congress.

The note threatened war, but the British ignored it for months. They did not take the United States seriously as a world power, and with reason, for the American navy, although expanding, could not hope to stand up against the British, who had 50 battleships, 25 armored cruisers, and many smaller vessels. When Lord Salisbury, the prime minister and foreign secretary, finally replied, he rejected outright the argument that the Monroe Doctrine had any status under international law and refused to arbitrate what he called the "exaggerated pretentions" of the Venezuelans.

If Olney's note had been belligerent, this reply was supercilious and sharp to the point of asperity. Cleveland was furious. On December 17, 1895, he asked Congress for authority to appoint an American commission to determine the correct line between British Guiana and Venezuela. When that had been done, he added, the United States should "resist by every means in its power" the appropriation by Great Britain of any territory "we have determined of right belongs to Venezuela." Congress responded at once, unanimously appropriating $100,000 for the boundary commission. Popular approval was almost universal.

In Great Britain, government and people suddenly awoke to the seriousness of the situation. No one wanted a war with the United States over a remote patch of tropical real estate. In Europe, Britain was concerned about German economic competition and the increased military power of that nation. In addition, Canada would be terribly vulnerable to American attack in the event of war. The immense potential strength of the United States could no longer be ignored. Why make an enemy of a nation of 70 million, already the richest industrial power in the world? To fight with the United States, the British colonial secretary realized, "would be an absurdity as well as a crime."

Great Britain agreed to arbitrate the boundary. The war scare subsided; soon Olney was talking about "our inborn and instinctive English sympathies" and offering "to stand side by side and shoulder to shoulder with England in . . . the defence of human rights." When the boundary tribunal awarded nearly all the disputed region to Great Britain, whatever ill feeling the surrender may have occasioned in that country faded away. Instead of leading to war, the affair marked the beginning of an era of Anglo-American friendship. It had the unfortunate effect, however, of adding to the long-held American conviction that the nation could get what it wanted in international affairs by threat and bluster—a dangerous illusion.

The Cuban Revolution

On February 10, 1896, scarcely a week after Venezuela and Great Britain had signed the treaty ending their dispute, General Valeriano Weyler arrived in Havana from Spain to take up his duties as governor of Cuba. His assignment to this post was occasioned by the guerrilla warfare that Cuban nationalist rebels had been waging for almost a year. Weyler, a tough and ruthless soldier, set out to administer Cuba with "a salutary rigor." He began herding the rural population into wretched "reconcentration" camps in order to deprive the rebels of food and recruits. Resistance in Cuba hardened.

The United States had been interested in Cuba since the time of John Quincy Adams and, were it not for northern opposition to adding more slave territory, might well have obtained the island in one way or another before 1860. When the Cubans revolted against Spain in 1868, considerable support for intervening on their behalf developed. Hamilton Fish, Grant's secretary of state, resisted this sentiment, and Spain managed to pacify the rebels in 1878 by promising reforms. But change was slow in coming; slavery was not abolished until 1886. The worldwide depression of the 1890s hit the Cuban economy hard, and when an American tariff act in 1894 jacked up the rate on Cuban sugar by 40 percent, thus cutting off Cuban growers from the American market, the resulting distress precipitated another revolt.

Public sympathy in the United States went to the Cubans, who seemed to be fighting for liberty and democracy against an autocratic Old World power. Most American newspapers supported the Cubans; labor unions, veterans' organizations, many Protestant clergymen, and important politicians in both major parties demanded that the United States aid the rebel cause. Rapidly increasing American investments in Cuban sugar plantations, now approaching $50 million, were endangered by the fighting and by the social chaos sweeping across the island. Cuban propagandists in the United States played on American sentiments cleverly. When reports, often exaggerated, of the cruelty of "Butcher" Weyler and the horrors of his reconcentration

Instability in Latin America led many to speculate that the United States would play an increasingly dominant role in the region. In Louis Dalrymple's 1895 cartoon, Uncle Sam wins the affections of the damsel Cuba as Spanish misrule and native insurgency lay waste to each other.

camps filtered into America, the cry for action intensified. In April 1896 Congress adopted a resolution suggesting that the revolutionaries be granted the rights of belligerents. Since this would have been akin to formal recognition, Cleveland would not go that far, but he did exert diplomatic pressure on Spain to remove the causes of the rebels' complaints, and he offered the services of his government as mediator. The Spanish rejected the suggestion.

For a time the issue subsided. The election of 1896 deflected American attention from Cuba, and then McKinley refused to take any action that might disturb Spanish-American relations. Business interests—except those with holdings in Cuba—backed McKinley, for they feared that a crisis would upset the economy, which was just beginning to pick up after the depression. In Cuba, General Weyler made some progress toward stifling rebel resistance.

American expansionists, however, continued to demand intervention, and the press, especially Joseph Pulitzer's *New York World* and William Randolph Hearst's *New York Journal*, competing fiercely to increase circulation, kept resentment alive with tales of Spanish atrocities. McKinley remained adamant. Although he warned Spain that Cuba must be pacified, and soon, his tone was friendly and he issued no ultimatum. A new government in Spain relieved the situation by recalling Weyler and promising the Cubans partial self-government. In a message to Congress in December 1897, McKinley urged that Spain be given "a reasonable chance to realize her expectations" in the island. McKinley was not insensitive to Cuba's plight—though not a rich man, he made an anonymous contribution of $5,000 to the Red Cross Cuban relief fund—but he genuinely wanted to avoid intervention.

His hopes were doomed, primarily because

Spain failed to "realize her expectations." The fighting in Cuba continued. When riots broke out in Havana in January 1898, McKinley ordered the battleship *Maine* to Havana harbor to protect American citizens.

Shortly thereafter, Hearst's *New York Journal* printed a letter written to a friend in Cuba by the Spanish minister in Washington, Dupuy de Lôme. The letter had been stolen by a spy. De Lôme, an experienced but arrogant diplomat, failed to appreciate McKinley's efforts to avoid intervening in Cuba. In the letter he characterized the president as a *politicastro*, or "small-time politician," which was a gross error, and a "bidder for the admiration of the crowd," which was equally insulting though somewhat closer to the truth. Americans were outraged, and de Lôme's hasty resignation did little to soothe their feelings.

Then, on February 15, the *Maine* exploded and sank in Havana harbor, 260 of its crew perishing in the disaster. Interventionists in the United States accused Spain of having destroyed the ship and clamored for war. The willingness of Americans to blame Spain indicates the extent of anti-Spanish opinion in the United States by 1898. No one has ever discovered what actually happened. A naval court of inquiry decided that the vessel had been sunk by a submarine mine, but it now seems more likely that an internal explosion destroyed the *Maine*. The Spanish government could hardly have been foolish enough to commit an act that would probably bring American troops into Cuba.

With admirable courage, McKinley refused to panic, but he could not resist the wishes of millions of citizens that something be done to stop the fighting and allow the Cubans to determine their own fate. Spanish pride and Cuban patriotism had taken the issue of peace or war out of the president's hands. Spain could not put down the rebellion, and it would not yield to the nationalists' increasingly extreme demands. To have granted independence to Cuba might have caused the Madrid government to fall, might even have led to the collapse of the monarchy, for the Spanish public was in no mood to surrender. The Cubans, sensing that the continuing bloodshed aided their cause, refused to give the Spanish regime room to maneuver. After the *Maine* disaster, Spain might have agreed to an armistice had the rebels asked for one, and in the resulting negotiations it might well have given up the island. The rebels refused to make the first

move. The fighting continued, bringing the United States every day closer to intervention.

The president faced a dilemma. Most business interests of the country, to which he was particularly sensitive, opposed intervention. His personal feelings were equally firm. "I have been through one war," he told a friend. "I have seen the dead piled up, and I do not want to see another." Congress, however, seemed determined to act. When he submitted a restrained report on the sinking of the *Maine,* the Democrats in Congress, even most of those who had supported Cleveland's policies, gleefully accused him of timidity. Vice-President Garret A. Hobart warned him that the Senate could not be held in check for long; should Congress declare war on its own, the administration would be discredited.

McKinley spent a succession of sleepless nights; sedatives brought him no repose. Finally, early in April, the president drafted a message asking for authority to use the armed forces "to secure a full and final termination of hostilities" in Cuba.

At the last moment the Spanish government seemed to yield; it ordered its troops in Cuba to cease hostilities. McKinley passed this information on to Congress along with his war message, but he gave it no emphasis and did not try to check the march toward war. To seek further delay would have been courageous but not necessarily wiser. Merely to stop fighting was not enough. The Cuban nationalists now insisted on full independence, and the Spanish politicians were unprepared to abandon the last remnant of their once-great American empire. If the United States took Cuba by force, the Spanish leaders might save their political skins; if they meekly surrendered the island, they were done for.

The "Splendid Little" Spanish-American War

On April 20 Congress, by joint resolution, recognized the independence of Cuba and authorized the use of the armed forces to drive out the Spanish. An amendment proposed by Senator Henry M. Teller disclaiming any intention of adding Cuban territory to the United States passed without opposition. Four days later Spain declared war on the United States.

The Spanish-American War was fought to free

624 CHAPTER XXIII FROM ISOLATION TO EMPIRE

Cuba, but the first action took place on the other side of the globe, in the Philippine Islands. Weeks earlier, Assistant Secretary of the Navy Theodore Roosevelt had alerted Commodore George Dewey, who was in command of the United States Asiatic Squadron located at Hong Kong, to move against the Spanish base at Manila if war came. Dewey had acted promptly, drilling his gun crews, taking on supplies, giving his gleaming white ships a coat of battle-gray paint, and establishing secret contacts with the Filipino nationalist leader, Emilio Aguinaldo. When word of the declaration of war reached him, he steamed from Hong Kong across the South China Sea with four cruisers and two gunboats. On the night of April 30 he entered Manila Bay, and at daybreak he opened fire on the Spanish fleet at 5,000 yards. His squadron made five passes, each time reducing the range; when the smoke had cleared, all ten of Admiral Montojo's ships had been destroyed. Not a single American was killed in the engagement.

Dewey immediately asked for troops to take and hold Manila, for now that war had been declared, he could not return to Hong Kong or put in at any other neutral port. McKinley took the fateful step of dispatching some 11,000 soldiers and additional naval support. On August 13 these forces, assisted by Filipino irregulars under Aguinaldo, captured Manila.

Meanwhile, in the main theater of operations, the United States had won a swift and total victory, though more because of the weakness of the Spanish armed forces than because of the power or efficiency of the American. When the war began, the regular army consisted of about 28,000 men. This tiny force was bolstered by 200,000 hastily enlisted volunteers. In May an expeditionary force gathered at Tampa, Florida. That hamlet was inundated by the masses

A woman recruiting officer, accompanied by a military band, urging enlistments in New York City at the outbreak of the Spanish-American War. Patriotism, at least, was not seen as gender-specific.

of men and supplies that descended on it. Entire regiments sat without uniforms or weapons while hundreds of freight cars jammed with equipment lay forgotten on sidings. Army management was abominable, rivalry between commanders a serious problem. Aggressive units like the regiment of "Rough Riders" raised by Theodore Roosevelt, now a lieutenant colonel of volunteers, scrambled for space and supplies, shouldering aside other units to get what they needed. "No words could describe . . . the confusion and lack of system and the general mismanagement of affairs here," the angry Roosevelt complained.

Since a Spanish fleet under Admiral Pascual Cervera was known to be in Caribbean waters, no invading army could safely embark until the fleet could be located. On May 29, American ships found Cervera at Santiago harbor, on the eastern end of Cuba, and established a blockade. In June a 17,000-man expeditionary force commanded by General William Shafter landed at Daiquiri, east of Santiago, and pressed quickly toward the city, handicapped more by its own bad staff work than by the enemy, though the Spanish troops resisted bravely. The Americans sweated through Cuba's torrid summer in heavy wool winter uniforms, ate "embalmed beef" out of cans, and fought mostly with old-fashioned rifles using black-powder cartridges that marked the position of each soldier with a puff of smoke whenever he pulled the trigger. On July 1 they broke through undermanned Spanish defenses and stormed San Juan Hill, the intrepid Roosevelt in the van. ("Are you afraid to stand up while I am on horseback?" Roosevelt demanded of one soldier.)

With Santiago harbor in range of American artillery, Admiral Cervera had to run the blockade. On July 3 his black-hulled ships, flags proudly flying, steamed forth from the harbor and fled westward along the coast. Like hounds after rabbits, five American battleships and two cruisers, commanded by Rear Admiral William T. Sampson and Commodore Winfield Scott Schley, ran them down. In four hours the entire Spanish force was destroyed by a hail of 8-inch and 13-inch projectiles. Damage to the American ships was superficial; only one seaman lost his life in the engagement.

The end then came abruptly. Santiago surrendered on July 17. A few days later other United States troops completed the occupation of Puerto Rico. On August 12, one day before the fall of Manila, Spain agreed to get out of Cuba and to cede Puerto Rico and the island of Guam in the Marianas to the United States. The future of the Philippines was to be settled at a formal peace conference, convening in Paris on October 1.

Developing a Colonial Policy

Although the Spanish resisted surrendering the Philippines at Paris, they had been so thoroughly defeated that they had no choice. The decision hung rather on the outcome of a conflict over policy within the United States. The war, won at so little cost militarily, produced problems far larger than those it solved.* The nation had become a great power in the world's eyes. The United States, a French diplomat wrote a few years later, "is seated at the table where the great game is played, and it cannot leave it." European leaders had been impressed by the forcefulness of Cleveland's diplomacy in the Venezuela boundary dispute and by the efficiency the navy displayed in the war. The annexation of Hawaii and other overseas bases intensified their conviction that the United States was serious about becoming a major force in international affairs.

But were the American people determined to exercise that force? The debate over taking the Philippine Islands throws much light on their attitudes. The imagination of Americans had been captured by the trappings of empire, not by its essence. It was titillating to think of a world map liberally sprinkled with American flags and of the economic benefits that colonies might bring, but most citizens were not prepared to join in a worldwide struggle for power and influence. They entered blithely upon adventures in far-off regions without facing the implications of their decision.

Since the United States (in the Teller Amendment) had abjured any claim to Cuba, even though expansionists had long desired the island, logic dictated that a similar policy be applied to the Philippines, a remote land few Americans had ever thought about before 1898. But expansionists were

---

* More than 5,000 Americans died as a result of the conflict, but fewer than 400 fell in combat. The others were mostly victims of yellow fever, typhoid, and other diseases.

As the Monroe Doctrine became more significant around the turn of the century, chauvinistic cartoonists used it to taunt European powers. In this example, from a 1901 issue of Puck, *the European chickens complain, "You're not the only rooster in South America!" to which Uncle Sam retorts, "I was aware of that when I cooped you up!"*

eager to annex the entire archipelago. Even before he had learned to spell the name, Senator Lodge was saying that "the Phillipines (*sic*) mean a vast future trade and wealth and power," offering the nation a greater opportunity "than anything that has happened . . . since the annexation of Louisiana."

President McKinley adopted a more cautious stance, but he too favored "the general principle of holding on to what we can get." A speaking tour of the Middle West in October 1898, during which he experimented with varying degrees of commitment to expansionism, convinced him that the public wanted the islands. Business opinion had shifted dramatically during the war. Business leaders were now calling the Philippines the gateway to the markets of the Far East.

The Anti-imperialists

An important minority objected strongly to the United States acquiring overseas possessions. Persons as different in interest and philosophy as the tycoon Andrew Carnegie and the labor leader Samuel Gompers, the venerable Republican Senator George Frisbie Hoar of Massachusetts and "Pitchfork Ben" Tillman, the southern Democratic firebrand, together with the writers Mark Twain and William Dean Howells, the reformers Lincoln Steffens and Jane Addams, and the educators Charles W. Eliot of Harvard and David Starr Jordan of Stanford united in opposing the annexation of the Philippines.

The anti-imperialists insisted that since no one would consider statehood for the Philippines, it would be unconstitutional to annex them. It was a violation of the spirit of the Declaration of Independence to govern a foreign territory without the consent of its inhabitants, Senator Hoar argued; by taking over "vassal states" in "barbarous archipelagoes" the United States was "trampling . . . on our own great Charter, which recognizes alike the liberty and the dignity of individual manhood."

McKinley was not insensitive to this appeal to idealism and tradition, which was the fundamental element in the anti-imperialist argument, but he rejected it for several reasons. Many people who opposed Philippine annexation were neither idealists nor constitutional purists. Partisanship led numbers of Democrats to object. Other anti-imperialists were governed by racial and ethnic prejudices, as Senator Hoar's statement indicates. They opposed not expansion as such—Carnegie, for example, was eager to have Canada added to the Union—but expansion that brought under the American flag people whom they believed unfit for American citizenship. Labor leaders particularly feared the competition of "the Chinese, the Negritos, and the Malays" who presumably would flood into the United States if the Philippines were taken.

More compelling to McKinley was the absence of any practical alternative to annexation. Public opinion would not sanction restoring Spanish authority in the Philippines or allowing some other power to have them. That the Filipinos were sufficiently advanced and united socially to form a stable government if granted independence seemed unlikely. Senator Hoar believed that "for years and for generations, and perhaps for centuries, there would have been turbulence, disorder and revolution" in the islands if they were left to their own devices.

Strangely—for he was a kind and gentle man—Hoar faced this possibility with equanimity. McKinley was unable to do so. The president searched the depths of his soul and could find no solution but annexation. Of course, the state of public feeling made the decision easier. And he probably found the idea of presiding over an empire appealing. Certainly the commercial possibilities did not escape him. In the end it was with a heavy sense of responsibility that he ordered the American peace commissioners to insist on acquiring the Philippines. To salve the feelings of the Spanish, the United States agreed to pay $20 million for the archipelago, but it was a forced sale, accepted by Spain under duress.

The peace treaty faced a hard battle in the United States Senate, where a combination of partisan politics and anticolonialism made it difficult to amass the two-thirds majority necessary for ratification. McKinley had shrewdly appointed three senators, including one Democrat, to the peace commission. This predisposed many members of the upper house to approve the treaty, but the vote was close. William Jennings Bryan, titular head of the Democratic party, could probably have prevented ratification had he urged his supporters to vote nay. Although he was opposed to taking the Philippines, he did not do so. To reject the treaty would leave the United States technically at war with Spain and the fate of the Philippines undetermined; better to accept the islands and then grant them independence. The question should be decided, Bryan said, "not by a minority of the Senate but by a majority of the people" at the next presidential election. Perplexed by Bryan's stand, a number of Democrats allowed themselves to be persuaded by the expansionists' arguments and by McKinley's judicious use of patronage; the treaty was ratified in February 1899 by a vote of 57 to 27.

The Philippine Rebellion

The national referendum that Bryan had hoped for never materialized. Bryan himself confused the issue in 1900 by making free silver a major plank in his platform, thereby driving conservative anti-imperialists into McKinley's arms. Moreover, early in 1899 the Filipino nationalists under Aguinaldo, furious because the United States would not withdraw, rose in rebellion. A savage guerrilla war resulted, one that cost far more in lives and money than the "splendid little" Spanish-American conflict.

Like all conflicts waged in tangled terrain chiefly by small, isolated units surrounded by a hostile civilian population, neither side displayed much regard for the "rules" of war. Goaded by sneak attacks and instances of cruelty to captives, American soldiers, most of whom had little respect for Filipinos to begin with, responded in kind. Civilians were rounded up, prisoners were tortured, property was

Emilio Aguinaldo, who commanded Filipino insurgents who worked with Commodore Dewey to help overthrow Spanish rule of the Philippines in 1898. He later took up arms against the United States in a brutal three-year struggle when President McKinley opposed granting independence to the islands.

destroyed. Horrible tales of rape, arson, and murder by United States troops filtered into the country, providing ammunition for the anti-imperialists. "You seem to have about finished your work of civilizing the Filipinos," Andrew Carnegie wrote angrily to one of the American peace commissioners. "About 8,000 of them have been completely civilized and sent to Heaven. I hope you like it." In fact, far more than 8,000 Filipinos lost their lives during the conflict, which raged for three years. More than 70,000 American soldiers had to be sent to the islands before the resistance was crushed, and about as many of them lost their lives as had perished in the Cuban conflict.

In 1899, before the fighting started, McKinley had sent a commission to the Philippines to study the problem. The committee attributed the revolt to the ambitions of the nationalist leaders and recommended that the Philippines be granted independence at an indefinite future date. The following year the president sent another commission, this one headed by William Howard Taft, a federal judge, to establish a government. Taft, a warmhearted, affable man, took an instant liking to the Filipinos, and his policy of encouraging them to participate in the territorial government attracted many converts. In July 1901 he became the first civilian governor of the Philippines, though the rebellion went on for many months.

Actually, McKinley's reelection in 1900 settled the Philippine question so far as most Americans were concerned. Anti-imperialists still claimed that it was unconstitutional to take over territories without the consent of the local population. Their reasoning, though certainly not specious, was unhistorical. No American government had seriously considered the wishes of the American Indians, the French and Spanish settlers in Louisiana, or the Eskimos of Alaska when it had seemed in the national interest to annex new lands.

Cuba and the United States

Nevertheless, grave constitutional questions arose as a result of the acquisitions that followed the Spanish-American War. McKinley acted with remarkable independence in handling the problems involved in expansion. He set up military governments in Cuba, Puerto Rico, and the Philippines without specific congressional authority. But eventually both Congress and the Supreme Court took a hand in shaping colonial policy. In 1900 Congress passed the Foraker Act, establishing a civil government for Puerto Rico. It did not give the Puerto Ricans either American citizenship or full local self-government, and it placed a tariff on Puerto Rican products imported into the United States.

The tariff provision was promptly challenged in the courts on the grounds that Puerto Rico was part of the United States, but in *Downes* v. *Bidwell* (1901) the Supreme Court upheld the legality of the duties. In this and other "insular cases" the reasoning of the judges was more than ordinarily difficult to follow. ("We suggest, without intending to decide, that there may be a distinction between certain natural rights enforced in the Constitution . . . and what may be termed artificial or remedial rights," the Downes opinion held.) The effect, however, was clear: The Constitution did not follow the flag; Congress could act toward the colonies almost as it pleased. A colony, one dissenting justice said, could be kept "like a disembodied shade, in an indeterminate state of ambiguous existence for an indefinite period."

While the most heated arguments raged over Philippine policy, the most difficult colonial problems concerned the relationship between the United States and Cuba, for there idealism and self-interest clashed painfully. Despite the desire of most Americans to get out of Cuba, an independent government could not easily be created. Order and prosperity did not automatically appear when the red and gold ensigns of Spain were hauled down from the flagstaffs of Havana and Santiago.

The insurgent government was feeble, corrupt, and oligarchic, the Cuban economy in a state of collapse, life chaotic. The first Americans entering Havana found the streets littered with garbage and the corpses of horses and dogs. All public services were at a standstill; it seemed essential for the United States, as McKinley said, to give "aid and direction" until "tranquillity" could be restored.

As soon as American troops landed in Cuba, trouble broke out between them and the populace. Most American soldiers viewed the ragged, half-starved insurgents as "thieving dagoes" and displayed an unfortunate race prejudice against their dark-skinned allies. The novelist Stephen Crane, who covered the war for Pulitzer's *World,* reported: "Both officers and privates have the most lively contempt for the Cubans. They despise them."

General Shafter did not help matters. He believed the Cubans "no more fit for self-government than gun-powder is for hell," and he used the insurgents chiefly as labor troops. After the fall of Santiago, he refused to let rebel leaders participate in the formal surrender of the city. This infuriated the proud and idealistic Cuban commander, General Calixto Garcia.

When McKinley established a military government for Cuba late in 1898, it was soon embroiled with local leaders. Then an eager horde of American promoters descended on Cuba in search of profitable franchises and concessions. Congress put a stop to this exploitation by forbidding all such grants as long as the occupation continued.

The problems were indeed knotty, for no strong local leader capable of uniting Cuba appeared. Even Senator Teller, father of the Teller Amendment, expressed concern lest "unstable and unsafe" elements gain control of the country. European leaders expected that the United States would eventually annex Cuba, and many Americans, including General Leonard Wood, who became military governor in December 1899, considered this the best solution. The desperate state of the people, the heavy economic stake of Americans in the region, and its strategic importance militated against withdrawal.

In the end the United States did withdraw, after doing a great deal to modernize sugar production, improve sanitary conditions, establish schools, and restore orderly administration. In November 1900 a Cuban constitutional convention met at Havana and proceeded without substantial American interference or direction to draft a frame of government. The chief restrictions imposed by this document on Cuba's freedom concerned foreign relations; at the insistence of the United States, it authorized American intervention whenever necessary "for the reservation of Cuban independence" and "the maintenance of a government adequate for the protection of life, property, and individual liberty." Cuba had to promise to make no treaty with a foreign power compromising its independence and to grant naval bases on its soil to the United States.

This arrangement, known as the Platt Amendment, was accepted, after some grumbling, by the Cubans. It had the support of most American opponents of imperialism. The amendment was a true compromise; as David F. Healy, a leading student of Cuban-American relations, has said, "It promised to give the Cubans real internal self government . . . and at the same time to safeguard American interests." In May 1902 the United States turned over the reins of government to the new republic. The next year the two countries signed a reciprocity treaty tightening the economic bonds between them.

True friendship did not result. Although American troops occupied Cuba only once, in 1906, and then at the specific request of Cuban authorities, the United States repeatedly used the threat of intervention to coerce the Cuban government. American economic penetration proceeded rapidly and without regard for the well-being of the Cuban peasants, many of whom lived in a state of peonage on great sugar plantations. Nor did their good intentions make up for the tendency of Americans to consider themselves innately superior to the Cubans and to overlook the fact that Cubans did not always wish to adopt American customs and culture. The reform program instituted during the occupation was marred by attempts to apply American standards at every step. The new schools used American textbooks that had been translated into Spanish without adapting the material to the experience of Cuban children. General Wood considered the Cubans "inert" because they showed little interest in his plans to grant a large measure of self-government to municipal authorities. He failed to understand that the people were accustomed to a centralized system with decision making concentrated in Havana. Wood complained that the Cubans were mired in "old ruts," yet the same charge might well have been leveled at him, though he was an efficient and energetic administrator.

The United States in the Caribbean

If the purpose of the Spanish-American War had been to bring peace and order to Cuba, the Platt Amendment was a logical step. The same purpose soon necessitated a further extension of the principle, for once the United States accepted the role of protector and stabilizer in part of the Caribbean, it seemed desirable, for the same economic, strategic, and humanitarian reasons, to supervise the entire region.

The Caribbean countries were economically underdeveloped, socially backward, politically unstable, and desperately poor. Everywhere, a few families owned most of the land and dominated social and political life. Most of the people were uneducated peasants, many of them little better off than slaves. Rival cliques of wealthy families struggled for power, force being the usual method of effecting a change in government. Most of the meager income of the average Caribbean state was swallowed up by the military or diverted into the pockets of the current rulers.

Cynicism and fraud poisoned relations between most of these nations and the great powers. European merchants and bankers systematically cheated their Latin American customers, who in turn frequently refused to honor their obligations. Foreign bankers floated Caribbean bond issues on outrageous terms, while revolutionary Caribbean governments annulled concessions and repudiated debts with equal disdain for honest business dealing.

Because these countries were weak, the powers tended to intervene whenever their nationals were cheated or when chaotic conditions endangered the lives and property of foreigners. In one notorious instance Germany sent two warships to Port-au-Prince, Haiti, and by threatening to bombard the town compelled the Haitian government to pay $30,000 in damages to a German citizen who had been arrested and fined for allegedly assaulting a local policeman.

In 1902, shortly after the United States had pulled out of Cuba, trouble erupted in Venezuela, where a dictator, Cipriano Castro, was refusing to honor debts owed the citizens of European nations. To force Castro to pay up, Germany and Great Britain established a blockade of Venezuelan ports and destroyed a number of Venezuelan gunboats and harbor defenses. Under American pressure the Europeans agreed to arbitrate the dispute. For the first time, European powers had accepted the broad implications of the Monroe Doctrine. The British prime minister, Arthur Balfour, went so far as to state publicly that "it would be a great gain to civilization if the United States were more actively to interest themselves in making arrangements by which these constantly recurring difficulties . . . could be avoided."

By this time Theodore Roosevelt had become president of the United States, and he quickly capitalized on the new European attitude. In 1903 the Dominican Republic defaulted on bonds totaling some $40 million. When European investors urged their governments to intervene, Roosevelt announced that under the Monroe Doctrine the United States could not permit foreign nations to intervene in Latin America. But, he added, Latin American nations should not be allowed to escape their obligations. "If we intend to say 'Hands off,' . . . sooner or later we must keep order ourselves," he told Secretary of War Elihu Root.

The president did not want to make a colony of the Dominican Republic. "I have about the same desire to annex it as a gorged boa constrictor might have to swallow a porcupine wrong-end-to," he said. He therefore arranged for the United States to take charge of the Dominican customs service—the one

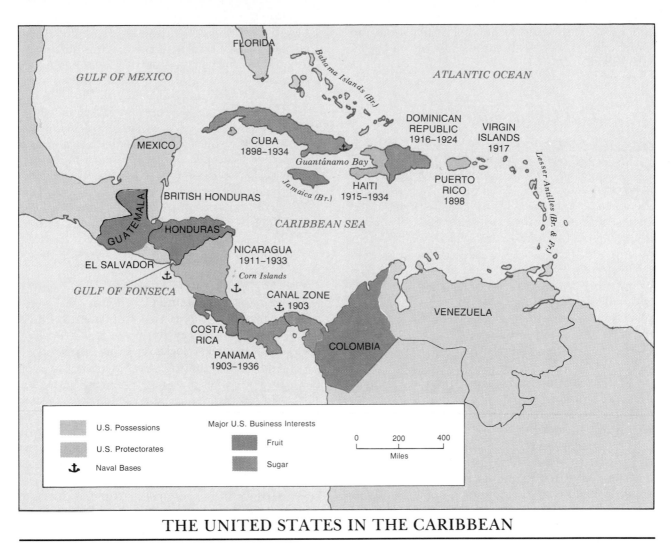

THE UNITED STATES IN THE CARIBBEAN

Puerto Rico was ceded by Spain after the Spanish-American War; the Virgin Islands were bought from Denmark; and the Canal Zone was leased from Panama. The ranges of dates following Cuba, Dominican Republic, Haiti, Nicaragua, and Panama cover those years during which the United States either had troops in occupation or, in some other way (such as financial), had a protectorate relationship with that country.

reliable source of revenue in that poverty-stricken country. Fifty-five percent of the customs duties would be devoted to debt payment, the remainder turned over to the Dominican government to care for its internal needs. Roosevelt defined his policy, known as the Roosevelt Corollary to the Monroe Doctrine, in a message to Congress in December 1904. "Chronic wrongdoing" in Latin America, he stated with his typical disregard for the subtleties of complex affairs, might require outside interven-

tion. Since, under the Monroe Doctrine, no other nation could step in, the United States must "exercise . . . an international police power."

In the short run this policy worked admirably. Dominican customs were honestly collected for the first time, and the country's finances were put in order. The presence of American warships in the area provided a needed measure of political stability. In the long run, however, the Roosevelt Corollary caused a great deal of resentment in Latin

America, for it added to nationalist fears that the United States wished to exploit the region for its own benefit.

The Open Door Policy

The insular cases, the Platt Amendment, and the Roosevelt Corollary established the framework for American policy both in Latin America and in the Far East. Coincidental with the Cuban rebellion of the 1890s, a far greater upheaval had convulsed the ancient empire of China. In 1894 and 1895 Japan easily defeated China in a war over Korea. Alarmed by Japan's aggressiveness, the European powers hastened to carve out for themselves new spheres of influence along China's coast. After the annexation of the Philippines, McKinley's secretary of state, John Hay, urged on by businessmen fearful of losing out in the scramble to exploit the Chinese market, tried to prevent the further absorption of China by the great powers.

For the United States to join in the dismemberment of China was politically impossible because of anti-imperialist feeling, so Hay sought to protect American interests by clever diplomacy. In a series of "Open Door" notes (1899) he asked the powers to agree to respect the trading rights of all countries and to impose no discriminatory duties within their spheres of influence. Chinese tariffs should continue to be collected in these areas and by Chinese officials.

The replies to the Open Door notes were at best noncommittal, yet Hay blandly announced in March 1900 that the powers had "accepted" his suggestions! Thus he could claim to have prevented the breakup of the empire and protected the right of Americans to do business freely in its territories. In reality nothing had been accomplished; the imperialist nations did not extend their political control of China only because they feared that by doing so they might precipitate a major war among themselves. Nevertheless, Hay's action marked a revolutionary departure from the traditional American policy of isolation, a bold advance into the complicated and dangerous world of international power politics.

Within a few months of Hay's announcement, the Open Door policy was put to the test. Chinese nationalists, angered by the spreading influence of

foreign governments, launched the so-called Boxer Rebellion. They swarmed into Peking and drove foreigners within the walls of their legations, which were placed under siege. For weeks, until an international rescue expedition (which included 2,500 American soldiers) broke through to free them, the fate of the foreigners was unknown. Fearing that the Europeans would use the rebellion as a pretext for further expropriations, Hay sent off another round of Open Door notes announcing that the United States believed in the preservation of "Chinese territorial and administrative entity" and in "the principle of equal and impartial trade with all parts of the Chinese Empire." This broadened the Open Door policy to include all China, not merely the European spheres of influence.

Hay's diplomacy was superficially successful. While the United States maintained no important military force in the Far East, American business and commercial interests there were free to develop and to compete with Europeans'. But once again European jealousies and fears rather than American cleverness were responsible. When the Japanese, mistrusting Russian intentions in Manchuria, asked Hay how he intended to implement his policy, he replied meekly that the United States was "not prepared . . . to enforce these views on the east by any demonstration which could present a character of hostility to any other power." The United States was being caught up in the power struggle in the Far East without having faced the implications of its actions.

In time the country would pay a heavy price for this unrealistic attitude, but in the decade following 1900 its policy of diplomatic meddling unbacked by bayonets worked fairly well. Japan attacked Russia in a quarrel over Manchuria, smashing the Russian fleet in 1905 and winning a series of battles on the mainland. Japan was not prepared for a long war, however, and suggested to President Roosevelt that an American offer to mediate would be received favorably.

Eager to preserve the nice balance in the Far East, which enabled the United States to exert influence without any significant commitment of force, Roosevelt accepted the hint. In June 1905 he invited the belligerents to a conference at Portsmouth, New Hampshire. At the conference the Japanese won title to Russia's sphere around Port Arthur and a free hand in Korea, but when they

A rendering of a multinational assault on antiforeign Chinese militants—Boxers—who held Americans captive in Peking in 1900. A detachment of American Marines is at the left of the picture.

demanded Sakhalin Island and a large money indemnity, the Russians balked. Unwilling to resume the war, the Japanese settled for half of Sakhalin and no money.

The Treaty of Portsmouth was unpopular in Japan, and the government managed to place the blame on Roosevelt, who had supported the compromise. Ill feeling against Americans increased in 1906 when the San Francisco school board, responding to local opposition to the influx of cheap labor from Japan, instituted a policy of segregating oriental children in a special school. Japan protested, and President Roosevelt persuaded the San Franciscans to abandon segregation in exchange for his pledge to cut off further Japanese immigration. He accomplished this through a "Gentlemen's Agreement" (1907) in which the Japanese promised not to issue passports to laborers seeking to come to America. Discriminatory legislation based specifically on race was thus avoided. However, the atmosphere between the two countries remained charged. Japanese resentment at American race prejudice was great; many Americans talked fearfully of the "yellow peril."

Theodore Roosevelt was preeminently a realist in foreign relations. "Don't bluster," he once said. "Don't flourish a revolver, and never draw unless you intend to shoot." In the Far East he failed to follow his own advice. He considered the situation in that part of the world fraught with peril. The Philippines, he said, were "our heel of Achilles," indefensible in case of a Japanese attack. He suggested privately that the United States ought to "be prepared for giving the islands independence . . . much sooner than I think advisable from their own standpoint."

Yet even though Roosevelt did not increase appreciably American naval and military strength in the Orient, neither did he stop trying to influence the course of events in the area, and he took no step toward withdrawing from the Philippines. He sent the fleet on a world cruise to demonstrate its might to Japan but knew well that this was mere bluff. "The 'Open Door' policy," he warned his successor, "completely disappears as soon as a powerful nation determines to disregard it." Nevertheless he allowed the belief to persist in the United States that the nation could influence the course of Far Eastern history without risk or real involvement.

The Isthmian Canal

In the Caribbean region American policy centered on building an interoceanic canal across Central America. Expanding interests in Latin America and the Far East made a canal necessary, a truth pointed up during the war with Spain by the two-month voyage of the U.S.S. *Oregon* around South America from California waters to participate in the action against Admiral Cervera's fleet at Santiago. The first step was to get rid of the old Clayton-Bulwer Treaty with Great Britain, which barred the United States from building a canal on its own. In 1901 Lord Pauncefote, the British ambassador, and Secretary of State John Hay negotiated an agreement abrogating the Clayton-Bulwer pact and giving America the right to build, and by implication fortify, a transisthmian waterway. The United States agreed in turn to maintain any such canal "free and open to the vessels of commerce and of war of all nations."

One possible canal route lay across the Colombian province of Panama, where the French-controlled New Panama Canal Company had taken over the franchise of the old De Lesseps company. Only 50 miles separated the oceans in Panama. The terrain, however, was rugged and unhealthy. Though the French company had sunk much money into the project, it had little to show for its efforts aside from some rough excavations. A second possible route ran across Nicaragua. This route was about 200 miles long but was relatively easy, since much of it traversed Lake Nicaragua and other natural waterways.

President McKinley appointed a commission to study the alternatives. It reported that the Panamanian route was technically superior but recommended building in Nicaragua because the New Panama Canal Company was asking $109 million for its assets, which the commission valued at only $40 million. Lacking another potential purchaser, the French company lowered its price to $40 million, and after a great deal of clever propagandizing by Philippe Bunau-Varilla, a French engineer with heavy investments in the company, President Roosevelt settled on the Panamanian route.

In January 1903 Secretary of State Hay negotiated a treaty with Tomás Herrán, the Colombian chargé d'affaires in Washington. In return for a 99-year lease on a zone across Panama 6 miles wide, the United States agreed to pay Colombia $10 mil-

The Panama Canal under construction. Cutting the path between the seas consumed more than 61 million pounds of dynamite and the lives of hundreds of workers, most of whom were black laborers from Barbados and Jamaica.

lion and an annual rent of $250,000. The Colombian senate, however, unanimously rejected this treaty, in part because it did not adequately protect Colombian sovereignty over Panama and in part because it hardly seemed fair that the New Panama Canal Company should receive $40 million for its frozen assets and Colombia only $10 million. The government demanded $15 million directly from the United States, plus $10 million of the company's share.

A little more patience might have produced a mutually satisfactory settlement, but Roosevelt regarded the Colombians as highwaymen who were "mad to get hold of the $40,000,000 of the Frenchmen." ("You could no more make an agreement with the Colombian rulers," Roosevelt later remarked, "than you could nail currant jelly to a wall.") When Panamanians, egged on by the French company, staged a revolution in November 1903, Roosevelt ordered the cruiser *Nashville* to Panama. Colombian government forces found themselves looking down the barrels of the guns of the *Nashville* and shortly thereafter eight other American warships. The revolution succeeded.

Roosevelt instantly recognized the new Republic of Panama. Secretary Hay and the new Panamanian minister, Bunau-Varilla, then negotiated a treaty granting the United States a zone 10 miles wide in perpetuity, on the same terms as those rejected by Colombia. Within the Canal Zone the United States could act as "the sovereign of the territory . . . to the entire exclusion of . . . the Republic of Panama." The United States guaranteed the independence of the republic. The New Panama Canal Company then received its $40 million.

Historians have condemned Roosevelt for his actions in this shabby affair, and with good reason. It was not that he fomented the revolution, for he did not. Separated from the government at Bogotá by an impenetrable jungle, the people of Panama province had long wanted to be free of Colombian rule. Since an American-built canal would bring a flood of dollars and jobs to the area, they were prepared to take any necessary steps to avoid having the United States shift to the Nicaraguan route. Nor was it that Roosevelt prevented Colombia from suppressing the revolution. He sinned, rather, in his disregard of Latin American sensibilities. He referred to the Colombians as "dagoes" and insisted smugly that he was defending "the interests of collective civilization" when he overrode their opposition to his plans. "They cut their own throats," he said. "They tried to hold us up; and too late they have discovered their criminal error."

If uncharitable, Roosevelt's analysis was not entirely inaccurate, yet it did not justify his haste in taking Panama under his wing. "Have I defended myself?" Roosevelt asked Secretary of War Root. "You certainly have, Mr. President," Root retorted. "You were accused of seduction and you have conclusively proved that you were guilty of rape." Throughout Latin America, especially as nationalist sentiments grew stronger, Roosevelt's intolerance and aggressiveness in the canal incident bred resentment and fear.

In 1921 the United States made amends by giving Colombia $25 million. Colombia in turn recognized the independence of the Republic of Panama, but Panama was independent only in name because the United States controlled the canal. Meanwhile, the first vessels passed through the canal in 1914—and American hegemony in the Ca-ribbean expanded. Yet even in that strategically vital area there was more show than substance to American strength. The navy ruled Caribbean waters largely by default, for it lacked adequate bases in the region. In 1903, as authorized by the Cuban constitution, the United States obtained an excellent site for a base at Guantanamo Bay, but before 1914 Congress appropriated only $89,000 to develop it.

The tendency was to try to influence outlying areas without actually controlling them. Roosevelt's successor, William Howard Taft, called this policy "dollar diplomacy," his reasoning being that economic penetration would bring stability to underdeveloped areas and power and profit to the United States without the government's having to commit troops or spend public funds.

Under Taft the State Department won a place for American bankers in an international syndicate engaged in financing railroads in Manchuria. When Nicaragua defaulted on its foreign debt in 1911, the department arranged for American bankers to reorganize Nicaraguan finances and manage the customs service. Although the government truthfully insisted that it did not "covet an inch of territory south of the Rio Grande," dollar diplomacy provoked further apprehension in Latin America. Efforts to establish similar arrangements in Honduras, Costa Rica, and Guatemala all failed. In Nicaragua orderly administration of the finances did not bring internal peace. In 1912 some 2,500 American marines and sailors had to be landed to put down a revolution.

Economic penetration proceeded briskly. American investments in Cuba reached $500 million by 1920, and smaller but significant investments were made in the Dominican Republic and in Haiti. In Central America the United Fruit Company accumulated large holdings in banana plantations, railroads, and other ventures. Other firms plunged heavily in Mexico's rich mineral resources.

Non-Colonial Imperial Expansion

The United States deserves fair marks for effort in its foreign relations following the Spanish-American War, barely passing marks for performance, and failing marks for results. If one defines imperialism narrowly as a policy of occupying and governing foreign lands, American imperialism lasted for an extremely short time. With trivial exceptions, all the American colonies—Hawaii, the Philippines, Guam, Puerto Rico, the Guantanamo base, and the Canal Zone—were obtained between 1898 and 1903. In retrospect it seems clear that the urge to own colonies was only fleeting; the legitimate questions raised by the anti-imperialists and the headaches connected with the management of overseas possessions soon produced a change of policy.

The objections of protectionists to the lowering of tariff barriers, the shock of the Philippine insurrection, and a growing conviction that the costs of colonial administration outweighed the profits affected American thinking. Hay's Open Door notes (which anti-imperialists praised highly) marked the beginning of the retreat from imperialism thus defined, while the Roosevelt Corollary and dollar diplomacy signaled the consolidation of a new policy. Elihu Root summarized this policy as it applied to the Caribbean nations (and by implication to the rest of the underdeveloped world) in 1905: "We do not want to take them for ourselves. We do not want any foreign nations to take them for themselves. We want to help them."

Yet imperialism can be given a broader definition. The historian William Appleman Williams, a sharp critic, has described 20th-century American foreign policy as one of "non-colonial imperial expansion." Its object was to obtain profitable American economic penetration of underdeveloped areas without the trouble of owning and controlling them. Its subsidiary aim was to encourage these countries to "modernize," that is, to remake themselves in the image of the United States. The Open Door policy, in Williams's view, was not unrealistic and by no means a failure—indeed, it was too successful. He criticized American policy not because it did not work or because it led to trouble with the powers but because of its harmful effects on underdeveloped countries.

Examined from this perspective, the Open Door policy, the Roosevelt Corollary, and dollar diplomacy make a single pattern of exploitation, "tragic" rather than evil, according to Williams, because its creators were not evil but only of limited vision. They did not recognize the contradictions in their ideas and values. They saw American expansion as beneficial to all concerned—and not exclusively in

materialistic terms. They genuinely believed that they were exporting democracy along with capitalism and industrialization.

Williams probably goes too far in arguing that American statesmen consciously planned their foreign policy in these terms. American economic interests in foreign nations expanded enormously in the 20th century, but diplomacy had relatively little to do with this. Western industrial society (not merely American) was engulfing the rest of the world, as it continues to engulf it. Yet he is correct in pointing out that western economic penetration has had many unfortunate results for the nonindustrial nations. It is also true that Americans were particularly, though not uniquely, unimpressed by the different social and cultural patterns of people in far-off lands and insensitive to the wishes of such people to develop in their own ways.

Both the United States government and American businessmen showed little interest in finding out what the people of Cuba wanted from life. They assumed that the Cubans wanted what everybody (read "Americans") wanted and, if by some strange chance this was not the case, that it was best to give it to them anyway. Dollar diplomacy had as its objectives the avoidance of violence and the economic development of Latin America; it paid small heed to how peace was maintained or how the fruits of development were distributed. The policy was self-defeating, for long-run stability depended on the support of the people, and this was seldom forthcoming.

By the eve of World War I the United States had become a world power and had assumed what it saw as a duty to guide the development of many countries with traditions far different from its own. The American people, however, did not understand what these changes involved. While they stood ready to extend their influence into distant lands, they did so blithely, with little awareness of the implications of their behavior for themselves or for other peoples. The national psychology, if such can be said to exist, remained fundamentally isolationist. Americans understood that their wealth and numbers made their nation strong and that geography made it practically invulnerable. Thus they proceeded to do what they wanted to do in foreign affairs, limited more by their humanly flexible consciences than by any rational analysis of the probable consequences. This policy seemed safe enough—in 1914.

Milestones

1850 Clayton-Bulwer Canal Treaty	Spanish-American War breaks out
1858 Commercial treaty with Japan	Battle of Manila Bay
1867 Alaska purchased from Russia	Battle of San Juan Hill
1871 Treaty of Washington, settling the	Annexation of Hawaii
Alabama claims	**1899** Open Door notes
1875 Hawaiian reciprocity treaty	**1900** Platt Amendment to the Cuban
1885 Josiah Strong, *Our Country*	constitution
1889 First Pan-American Conference	**1901** Hay-Pauncefote Canal Treaty
1890 A. T. Mahan, *The Influence of Sea*	Supreme Court decides *Insular Cases*
Power	on control of colonies
1891 *Baltimore* crisis with Chile	**1902** Venezuela bond dispute
1893 Queen Liliuokalani of Hawaii	**1904** Roosevelt Corollary to the Monroe
overthrown	Doctrine
1895 Venezuela boundary dispute	**1907** "Gentlemen's Agreement" with Japan
1898 *Maine* explodes in Havana harbor	

SUPPLEMENTARY READING

Titles marked with an asterisk have been published in paperback.

For an overview of post–Civil War diplomatic history, see Milton Plesur, **America's Outward Thrust*** (1971), and D. M. Pletcher, **The Awkward Years** (1962). J. A. S. Grenville and G. B. Young, **Politics, Strategy, and American Diplomacy: Studies in Foreign Policy** (1966), throws light on many aspects of the period. Walter La Feber, **The New Empire** (1963), presents a forceful but somewhat overstated argument on the extent of expansionist sentiment, especially on the part of American businessmen. Contemporary attitudes are reflected in Josiah Strong, **Our Country** (1885) and A. T. Mahan, **The Influence of Sea Power upon History*** (1890), provides the clearest presentation of Mahan's thesis.

On Hawaiian annexation, see Mere Tate, **The United States and the Hawaiian Kingdom** (1965). On the Spanish-American War, see D. F. Trask, **The War with Spain in 1898** (1981), H. W. Morgan, **America's Road to Empire*** (1965), E. R. May, **Imperial Democracy*** (1961), L. L. Gourd, **The Presidency of William McKinley** (1980), and Orestes Ferrara, **The Last Spanish War** (1937).

On imperialism, see David Healy, **U.S. Expansionism: The Imperialist Urge in the 1890's** (1970), E. R May, **American Imperialism: A Speculative Essay** (1968), and W. A. Williams, **The Tragedy of American Diplomacy*** (1962). R. L. Beisner, **Twelve Against Empire: The Anti-imperialists*** (1968), contains lively and thoughtful sketches of leading foes of expansion. See also E. B. Thompkins, **Anti-imperialism in the United States** (1970). For details of colonial problems, see Leon Wolff, **Little Brown Brother** (1961), and R. E. Welch, Jr., **Response to Imperialism** (1979), on the Philippines; D. F. Healy, **The United States in Cuba** (1963); and D. G. Munro, **Intervention and Dollar Diplomacy in the Caribbean** (1964). David McCullough, **The Path Between the Seas** (1977), is an excellent history of the Panama Canal. Other useful volumes include Thomas McCormick, **China Market*** (1967), H. C. Hill, **Roosevelt and the Caribbean** (1927), R. E. Osgood, **Ideals and Self-interest in America's Foreign Relations*** (1953), and G. F. Kennan, **American Diplomacy*** (1951).

American Lives:

Emma Goldman

Emma Goldman in the 1890s

In January of 1886 a 16-year-old Jewish girl named Emma Goldman arrived in New York City from St. Petersburg, Russia, where her parents ran a grocery store. As soon as she had been examined by immigration officials she hurried on to Rochester, New York, where her half-sister lived. Emma was extremely independent-minded. Her father had tried to make her get married when she was 15, saying when she protested that "all a Jewish daughter needs to know is how to prepare *gefülte* fish, cut noodles fine, and give the man plenty of children." She had flatly refused to marry. "I wanted to study, to know life, to travel," she explained years later. She had also found the harsh government of the Czar unbearable. Finally, she and an older sister left for America. Like most immigrants, they expected the United States, "the land of opportunity," to be a kind of paradise on earth.

At first Emma lived with her half-sister's family and got a job in a factory sewing coats for $2.50 a week. Since she paid her sister $1.50 a week for room and board and needed 60 cents a week for carfare, she had only 40 cents for all her other needs. But when she asked her employer for more money he simply told her to "look for work elsewhere." This she did, finding a job at another factory that paid $4 a week.

The next year she married Jacob Kirshner, another Russian immigrant, but they did not get along and were soon divorced. Then she moved to New Haven, Connecticut, where she worked in a corset factory. In 1889 she moved to New York City. There she fell in with a group of radicals, most of them either socialists or anarchists. She herself was by this time an ardent anarchist, convinced by her experiences with the darker aspects of American capitalism that *all* governments repressed individual freedom and should simply be abolished.

In New York Emma fell in love with another Russian-born radical, Alexander Berkman. They started a kind of commune with another couple, sharing everything equally. Emma worked at home sewing shirts. Alexander found a job making cigars.

Next, Goldman and Berkman moved back to New Haven, where she started a cooperative dressmaking shop. Then the couple moved to Springfield, Massachusetts, where, with Berkman's cousin, an artist, they opened a photography studio. When this business failed they borrowed $150 and opened an ice cream parlor.

Nearly all immigrants of that period retained their faith in the promise of American life even after they discovered that the streets were not paved with gold and that the people and the government were not as perfect as they had expected when they arrived. But Emma Goldman was so disappointed by the United States that she became even more radical than she had been in Czarist Russia. The harsh punishment meted out to the anarchists who were accused of the Haymarket bombing shocked her deeply.

In 1892 when she and Berkman learned of the bloody battle of Pinkertons and strikers during the Homestead steel strike, they closed the ice cream parlor and went to New York. They decided to assassinate Henry Clay Frick, the archvillain of the Homestead drama. First they tried to manufacture a bomb, but that proved to be beyond their powers. Berkman then went to Pittsburgh where, posing as a representative of an agency that provided strikebreakers, he got into

Frick's office and shot him. For this crime he was sentenced to 14 years in prison.

The next year Goldman was herself arrested and sentenced to a year in jail after making an "incendiary" speech urging unemployed workers to distrust politicians and demand government relief. Thereafter she was taken up by important native-born radicals and soon was preaching anarchism to ordinary workers rather than to other radical immigrant groups. She got to know Lillian Wald and other New York settlement workers, but while she respected their motives, she disparaged their methods. It did little good to teach the poor good table manners, she said, if they did not have enough food to eat. Next she studied nursing in Vienna for a year. When she returned, she worked as a midwife among the New York poor, an experience that made her an outspoken advocate of birth control. She also helped organize a theatrical group, managed a touring group of Russian actors, and lectured on theatrical topics.

In 1906 Goldman founded *Mother Earth*, an anarchist journal. When Alexander Berkman was released from prison later that year, she made him its editor. *Mother Earth* attacked governments, organized religion, and private property. Goldman believed in a primitive form of communism in which all would share equally and no one would have power over anyone else. She was convinced that the result would be world peace and universal prosperity.

By this time Emma Goldman had become a celebrity. As Berkman noted, she "had become a woman of the world." He was disturbed by what he called "the foreign element in the circle she had gathered around her," but it was foreign only from his still narrowly Russian immigrant's perspective. Over the next decade she campaigned for freedom of speech all over the United States and in Canada, and lectured in support of birth control. At one point she developed a joint subscription plan covering *Mother Earth* and the *American Journal of Eugenics*, a magazine that advocated the use of contraception. In 1915 she deliberately courted arrest by describing methods of contraception at public lectures before large audiences. Men, she reported, showed great interest, but women "snicker and giggle and pretend to be shocked." Eventually she was arrested, convicted, and sentenced to a brief jail term.

With Alexander Berkman in 1917

Goldman's biographer, Richard Drinnan, has described her as "one of the significant women in the years before the First World War." The outbreak of that conflict, and especially American entry in it, seemed to her a calamity beyond measure. When Congress passed a conscription act, she, Berkman, and a few other radicals organized the No-Conscription League, not so much to persuade men to resist the draft as to provide aid and comfort to anyone who did so.

After American entry into World War I, both she and Berkman were convicted of conspiring to persuade men not to register for the draft. She was sentenced to two years in federal prison and in 1919 she and Berkman were deported to Russia.

Of course "Red Emma" Goldman was not a typical American, but she was in many ways a typical American immigrant. She held on to the culture of the old country; most of her close friends in the United States were Russians. But at the same time she learned English and quickly became familiar with American ways. She worked hard and developed a number of valuable skills. Gradually she moved up the economic ladder: from sweatshop laborer, to factory work, to running a shop, to nursing, to lecturing, and to editing a magazine. And while she was critical of the government and economic system of the United States, she was a typical immigrant also in insisting that she was an American patriot. "The kind of patriotism we represent," she said during her trial in 1917, "is the kind of patriotism which loves America with open eyes."

XXIV

Progressivism: The Age of Reform

The true friend of property, the true conservative, is he who insists that property shall be the servant and not the master of the commonwealth. . . . The citizens of the United States must effectively control the mighty commercial forces which they have themselves called into being.

THEODORE ROOSEVELT, *1910*

he period bounded roughly by the end of the Spanish-American War and American entry into World War I is usually called the Progressive Era. Like all such generalizations about complex subjects, this title involves a great simplification. Whether *progressive* is taken to mean "tending toward change" or "improvement" or is merely used to suggest an attitude of mind, it was neither a unique nor a universal characteristic of the early years of the 20th century. Progressive elements had existed in earlier periods and did not disappear when the first American soldiers took ship for France. In important ways the progressivism of the time was a continuation of the response to industrialism that began after the Civil War, a response that has not ended. Historians have scoured the sources trying to define and explain the Progressive Era, without satisfying everyone. Nevertheless, the term *progressive* provides a useful de-

scription of this exciting and significant period of American history.

Roots of Progressivism

The progressives were never a single group seeking a single objective. The movement sprang from many sources. One was the fight against corruption and inefficiency in government, which began with the Liberal Republicans of the Grant era and was continued by the Mugwumps of the 1880s. The struggle for civil service reform was only the first skirmish in this battle; the continuing power of corrupt political machines and the growing influence of corporations and their lobbyists on municipal and state governments outraged thousands of citizens and led them to seek ways of purifying politics and making the machinery of government at all levels responsive to the majority rather than to special-interest groups.

Progressivism also had roots in the effort to regulate and control big business, which characterized the Granger and Populist agitation of the 1870s and 1890s. The failure of the Interstate Commerce Act to end railroad abuses and of the Sherman Antitrust Act to check the growth of large corporations became increasingly apparent after 1900. The return of prosperity after the depression of the 1890s encouraged reformers by removing the inhibiting fear, so influential in the 1896 presidential campaign, that an assault on the industrial giants might lead to the collapse of the economy.

Between 1897 and 1904 the trend toward concentration in industry accelerated. Such new giants as Amalgamated Copper (1899), U.S. Steel (1901), and International Harvester (1902) attracted most of the attention, but even more alarming were the overall statistics. In a single year (1899) more than 1,200 firms were absorbed in mergers, the resulting combinations being capitalized at $2.2 billion. By 1904 there were 318 industrial combinations in the country, with an aggregate capital of $7.5 billion. People who considered bigness inherently evil demanded that the huge new "trusts" be broken up or at least strictly controlled.

Settlement house workers and other reformers concerned about the welfare of the urban poor made up a third battalion in the progressive army. This was an area in which women made the most important contributions. The working and living conditions of slum dwellers remained abominable, and the child labor problem was particularly acute; in 1900 about 1.7 million children under the age of 16 were working full time—more than the membership of the American Federation of Labor. In addition, laws regulating the hours and working conditions of women in industry were far from adequate, and almost nothing had been done, despite the increased use of dangerous machinery in the factories, to enforce safety rules or to provide compensation or insurance for workers injured on the job. As the number of professionally competent social workers grew, the movement for social welfare legislation gained momentum.

All these tendencies may be summed up in Robert H. Wiebe's phrase, "the search for order." America was becoming more urban, more industrial, more mechanized, more centralized—in short, more complex. This trend put a premium on efficiency and cooperation. It seemed obvious to the progressives that people must become more socially minded, the economy more carefully organized.

By attracting additional thousands of sympathizers to the general cause of reform, the return of prosperity after 1896 fueled the progressive movement. Good times made the average person more tolerant and generous. So long as profits were on the rise, the average employer did not object if labor improved its position too. Middle-class Americans who had been prepared to go to the barricades in the event of a Bryan victory in 1896 became conscience-stricken when they compared their own comfortable circumstances with those of the "huddled masses" of immigrants and native poor.

Giant industrial and commercial corporations threatened not so much the economic well-being as the ambitions and sense of importance of the middle class. What owner of a small mill or shop could now hope to rise to the heights attained by Carnegie or merchants like John Wanamaker and Marshall Field? The growth of large labor organizations worried such types. In general, character and moral values seemed less influential; organizations—cold, impersonal, heartless—were coming to control business, politics, and too many other aspects of life.

This development led historian Richard Hofstadter to suggest still another explanation of the progressive movement. Numbers of moderately prosperous businessmen, together with members of the professions and other educated people, felt threatened by the increasing power and status of the new tycoons, many of them coarse, domineering, and fond of vulgar display. The antics of machine politicians who made a mockery of the traditions of duty, service, and patriotism associated with statesmanship also troubled them. Comfortably well-off, middle-level businessmen lived in what seemed like genteel poverty compared to a Rockefeller or a Morgan.

Protestant pastors accustomed to the respect and deference of their flocks found their moral leadership challenged by materialistic vestrymen who did not even pay them decent salaries. College professors worried about their institutions falling under the sway of wealthy trustees who had little interest in or respect for learning. Lawyers had been "the aristocracy of the United States," James Bryce recalled in 1905; they were now merely "a part of the great organized system of industrial and financial enterprise."

Such people could support reform measures without feeling that they were being very radical because the intellectual currents of the time harmonized with their ideas of social improvement and the welfare state. The new doctrines of the social scientists, the Social Gospel religious leaders, and the philosophers of pragmatism provided a salubrious climate for progressivism. Many of the thinkers who formulated these doctrines in the 1880s and 1890s turned to the task of putting them into practice in the new century. Their number included the economist Richard T. Ely, the philosopher John Dewey, and the Baptist clergyman Walter Rauschenbusch, who, in addition to his many books extolling the Social Gospel, was active in civic reform movements.

The Muckrakers

As the diffuse progressive army gradually formed its battalions, a new journalistic fad brought the movement into focus. For many years magazines had been publishing articles discussing current political, social, and economic problems. Henry Demarest Lloyd's first blast at the Standard Oil monopoly appeared in the *Atlantic Monthly* in 1881. Over the years the tempo and forcefulness of this

One of McClure's *most effective "muckrakers," Ida Tarbell brought to her investigative journalism the well-trained mind of an historian and the indignation of a daughter whose father was done in by the interests, specifically the Standard Oil Company.*

type of literature increased. Then, in the fall of 1902, *McClure's* began two particularly hard-hitting series of articles, one on Standard Oil by Ida Tarbell, the other on big-city political machines by Lincoln Steffens. These articles provoked much comment. When the editor, S. S. McClure, decided to include in the January 1903 issue an attack on labor gangsterism in the coal fields along with installments of the Tarbell and Steffens series, he called attention to the circumstance in a striking editorial.

Something was radically wrong with the "American character," McClure wrote. These articles showed that large numbers of American employers, workers, and politicians were fundamentally immoral. Lawyers were becoming tools of big business, judges were permitting evildoers to escape justice, the churches were materialistic, educators seemed incapable of understanding what was happening.

"There is no one left; none but all of us," McClure concluded. "We have to pay in the end."

McClure's editorial loosed a chain reaction. The issue sold out quickly. Thousands of readers found their own vague apprehensions brought into focus, some becoming active in progressive movements, more lending passive support.

Other editors jumped to adopt the McClure formula. A small army of professional writers soon flooded the periodical press with denunciations of the insurance business, the drug business, college athletics, prostitution, sweatshop labor, political corruption, and dozens of other subjects. This type of article inspired Theodore Roosevelt, with his gift for vivid language, to compare the journalists to "the Man with the Muck-Rake" in John Bunyan's *Pilgrim's Progress*, whose attention was so fixed on the filth at his feet that he could not notice the "celestial crown" that was offered him in exchange. Roosevelt's characterization grossly misrepresented the literature of exposure, but the label *muckraking* was thereafter affixed to the type. Despite its literal connotations, *muckraker* became a term of honor.

The Progressive Mind

Progressives sought to arouse the conscience of "the people" in order to "purify" American life. They were convinced that human beings were by nature decent, well-intentioned, and kind. (After all, the words *human* and *humane* have the same root.) Unlike many earlier reformers, they believed that the source of society's evils lay in the structure of its institutions, not in the weaknesses or sinfulness of individuals. Therefore local, state, and national government must be made more responsive to the will of decent citizens who stood for the traditional virtues. Then the government must act; whatever its virtues, laissez-faire was obsolete. Businessmen, especially big businessmen, must be compelled to behave fairly, their acquisitive drives curbed in the interests of justice and equal opportunity for all. The weaker elements in society—women, children, the poor, the infirm—must be protected against unscrupulous power.

Despite its fervor and democratic rhetoric, progressivism was paternalistic, moderate, and often softheaded. Typical reformers of the period oversimplified complicated issues and treated their personal values as absolute standards of truth and morality. Thus progressives often acted at cross-purposes; at times some were even at war with themselves. This accounts for the diffuseness of the movement. Cutthroat business practices were criticized by great tycoons seeking to preserve their own positions and by small operators trying to protect themselves against the tycoons. But many tycoons and small operators considered themselves progressives; the former wanted federal regulation of big business and the latter strict enforcement of the antitrust laws, both legitimate "progressive" objectives.

Many progressives who desired to improve the living standards of industrial workers rejected the proposition that workers could help themselves best by organizing powerful national unions. They found it difficult to cooperate with actual working people, who seemed to them unrefined and narrow-minded. Union leaders favored government action to outlaw child labor and restrict immigration but

adopted a laissez-faire attitude toward wages-and-hours legislation; they preferred to win these objectives through collective bargaining, thereby justifying their own existence. Many who favored "municipal socialism" (public ownership of streetcar lines, waterworks, and other local utilities) adamantly opposed national ownership of railroads. Progressives stressed individual freedom yet gave strong backing to the drive to deprive the public of its right to drink alcoholic beverages. Few progressives worked more assiduously than Congressman George W. Norris of rural Nebraska for reforms that would increase the power of the ordinary voter, such as the direct primary and popular election of senators, yet Norris characterized the mass of urban voters as "the mob."

The progressives never challenged the fundamental principles of capitalism, nor did they attempt a basic reorganization of society. They would have little to do with the socialist brand of reform. Wisconsin was the most progressive of states, but its leaders never cooperated with the Socialist party of Milwaukee. When socialists threatened to win control of Los Angeles in 1911, California progressives made common cause with reactionary groups in order to defeat them. Many progressives were anti-immigrant, and only a handful had anything to offer blacks, surely the most exploited group in American society.

A good example of the relatively limited radicalism of most progressives is offered by the experiences of progressive artists. Early in the century a number of painters, including Robert Henri, John Sloan, and George Luks, tried to develop a distinctively American style. They turned to city streets and the people of the slums for their models, and they depended more on inspiration and inner conviction than careful craftsmanship to achieve their effects.

These so-called ashcan artists were individualists, yet they supported political and social reform and were caught up in the progressive movement. Sloan was a socialist; Henri claimed to be an anarchist. Most saw themselves as rebels. But artistically the ashcan painters were not very advanced. Their idols were long-dead European masters such as Hogarth, Goya, and Daumier. They were uninfluenced by the outburst of Postimpressionist activity then taking place in Europe. To their dismay, when they included canvases by European painters

A George Luks portrait of a coal miner, 1924, an impressive example of the "ashcan" school of American painting, which typically combined working-class subject matter and social conscience.

like Matisse and Picasso in a show of their own works they put on at the 69th Regiment Armory in New York City in 1913, the Europeans got all the attention.

"Radical" Progressives: The Wave of the Future

There were, of course, some people whose views were more fundamentally radical. The hard times of the 1890s and the callous reactions of conservatives to the victims of that depression pushed many toward Marxian socialism. In 1900 the labor leader Eugene V. Debs ran for president on the Socialist ticket. He polled fewer than 100,000 votes. When he ran again four years later he got more

than 400,000. Labor leaders hoping to organize unskilled workers in heavy industry were increasingly frustrated by the craft orientation of the American Federation of Labor, and some saw in socialism a way to win rank-and-file backing.

In 1905 Debs; William "Big Bill" Haywood, of the Western Federation of Miners; Mary Harris "Mother" Jones, a former organizer for the United Mine Workers; Daniel De Leon, of the Socialist Labor party; and a few others organized a new union, the Industrial Workers of the World. The IWW was openly anticapitalist. The preamble to its constitution began: "The working class and the employing class have nothing in common."

But the IWW never attracted many ordinary workers. Haywood, its most prominent leader, was usually a general in search of an army. His forte was attracting attention to spontaneous strikes by unorganized workers, not the patient recruiting of workers and the pursuit of practical goals. Shortly after the founding of the IWW, he was charged with complicity in the murder of an antiunion governor of Colorado after an earlier strike but was acquitted. In 1912 he was closely involved in a bitter and at times bloody strike of textile workers in Lawrence, Massachusetts, which was settled with some benefit to the strikers, and in a strike the following winter and spring by silk workers in Paterson, New Jersey, that was a failure.

Other "advanced" European ideas affected the thinking and behavior of progressive intellectuals. Sigmund Freud's psychoanalytical theories attracted numbers of Americans, especially after G. Stanley Hall invited Freud and some of his disciples to lecture at Clark University in 1909. Not many progressives actually read *The Interpretation of Dreams* or any of Freud's other works, none of which was translated into English before 1909, but many picked up enough of the vocabulary of psychoanalysis to discourse impressively about the significance of slips of the tongue, sublimation, and infant sexuality.

Some saw in Freud's ideas reason to effect a "revolution of manners and morals" that would have shocked (or at least embarrassed) Freud, who was personally quite conventional. They advocated easy divorce, trial marriage, and doing away with the double standard in all matters relating to sex. They rejected Victorian reticence and what they incorrectly identified as "puritan" morality out of hand, and they called for programs of sex education, especially the dissemination of information about methods of birth control.

Most large cities boasted groups of these "bohemian" thinkers, by far the most famous being the one centered in New York City's Greenwich Village. It was, Thomas Bender writes in *New York Intellect*, "a happy collaboration of 'revolutionary' writers and artists . . . at one time or another, almost every man or woman of the Village rebellion." The dancer Isadora Duncan, the photographer Alfred Stieglitz, the novelist Floyd Dell, several of the ashcan artists, and the playwright Eugene O'Neill rubbed shoulders with Big Bill Haywood of the IWW, the anarchist Emma Goldman, the psychoanalyst A. A. Brill, the militant feminist advocate of birth control

The impact of The Silent War, *a 1906 novel by John Ames Mitchell that dealt with the growing class struggle in America, was enhanced by William Balfour-Ker's graphic illustration,* From the Depths.

Margaret Sanger, Max Eastman, editor of their organ, *The Masses*, and John Reed, a young Harvard graduate who was soon to become famous for his eyewitness account of the Russian Revolution, *Ten Days That Shook the World*.

Goldman, Haywood, Sanger, and a few others in this group were genuine radicals who sought basic changes in bourgeois society, but despite much talk, most of the Greenwich Village intellectuals displayed what their historian Leslie Fishbein calls "a highly personalistic concern" for their own interests. *The Masses* described itself as "a revolutionary and not a reform magazine . . . a magazine whose final policy is to do as it pleases." Nearly all of them came from middle-class backgrounds. They found the far-different world of the Italian and Jewish immigrants of the Village and its surrounding neighborhoods charming. But they did not become involved in the immigrants' lives the way the settlement house workers did. Their influence on their own times, therefore, was limited. "Do as I say, not as I do" is not an effective way to change minds. They are historically important, however, because many of them were genuinely creative people and because many of the ideas and practices they advocated were adopted by later generations.

The creative writers of the era, applying the spirit of progressivism to the realism they had inherited from Howells and the naturalists, tended to adopt an optimistic tone. The poet Ezra Pound, for example, at this time talked grandly of an American Renaissance and fashioned a new kind of poetry called imagism, which, while not appearing to be realistic, abjured all abstract generalizations and concentrated on concrete word pictures to convey meaning. "Little" magazines and experimental theatrical companies sprang to life by the dozen, each convinced that it would revolutionize its art. The poet Carl Sandburg, the best-known representative of the "Chicago school," denounced the local plutocrats but sang the praises of the city they had made: "Hog Butcher for the World," "City of the Big Shoulders."

Most writers eagerly adopted Freudian psychology without understanding it. Freud's teachings seemed only to mean that they should cast off the restrictions of Victorian prudery; they ignored his essentially dark view of human nature. Theirs was an "innocent rebellion," exuberant and rather muddleheaded.

Political Reform: Cities First

To most "ordinary" progressives, political corruption and inefficiency lay at the root of the evils plaguing American society, and nowhere were corruption and inefficiency more obvious than in the nation's cities. Two characteristics of urban life are its anonymity and its complexity. These qualities help explain why slavery did not flourish in cities, which was undoubtedly a good thing, but also why the above-named vices did flourish, which was not good at all. As the cities grew, their antiquated and boss-ridden administrations became more and more disgraceful. Consider the example of San Francisco. After 1901, a shrewd lawyer named Abe Ruef ruled one of the most powerful and dissolute political machines in the nation. Only one kind of paving material was used on San Francisco's streets, and Ruef was the lawyer for the company that supplied it. When the gas company asked for a rate increase of 10 cents per 100 cubic feet, Ruef, who was already collecting $1,000 a month from the company as a "retainer," demanded and got an outright bribe of $20,000. A streetcar company needed city authorization to install overhead trolley wires; Ruef's approval cost the company $85,000. Prostitution flourished, with Ruef and his henchmen sharing in the profits. There was a brisk illegal trade in liquor licenses and other favors.

Similar conditions existed in dozens of communities. For his famous muckraking series for *McClure's*, Lincoln Steffens visited St. Louis, Minneapolis, Pittsburgh, New York, Chicago, and Philadelphia and found them all riddled with corruption.

Beginning in the late 1890s progressives mounted a massive assault on dishonest and inefficient urban governments. In San Francisco a group headed by Fremont Older, a newspaperman, and Rudolph Spreckels, a wealthy sugar manufacturer, broke the machine and lodged Ruef in jail. In Toledo, Ohio, Samuel M. "Golden Rule" Jones won election as mayor in 1897 and succeeded in arousing the citizenry against the corruptionists. Other important progressive mayors were Tom L. Johnson of Cleveland, whose administration Lincoln Steffens called the best in the United States; Seth Low and later John P. Mitchell of New York; and Hazen S. Pingree of Detroit.

City reformers could seldom destroy the machines without changing urban political institutions. Some cities obtained "home rule" charters that gave them greater freedom from state control in dealing with local matters. Many created research bureaus that investigated government problems in a scientific and nonpartisan manner. A number of middle-sized communities (Galveston, Texas, was the prototype) experimented with a system that integrated executive and legislative powers in the hands of a small elected commission, thereby concentrating responsibility and making it easier to coordinate complex activities. Out of this experiment came the city manager system, under which the commissioners appointed a professional manager to administer city affairs on a nonpartisan basis. Dayton, Ohio, which adopted the plan after the town was devastated by a flood in 1913, offers the best illustration of the city manager system in the Progressive Era.

Once the political system had been made responsive to the desires of the people, the progressives hoped to use it to improve society itself. Many cities experimented with "gas and water socialism," taking over public utility companies and operating them as departments of the municipal government. Under "Golden Rule" Jones, Toledo established a minimum wage for city employees, built playgrounds and golf courses, and moderated its harsh penal code. Mayor Seth Low improved New York's public transportation system and obtained passage of the tenement house law of 1901. Mayor Tom Johnson forced a fare cut to 3 cents on the Cleveland street railways.

Political Reform: The States

To carry out this kind of change required the support of state legislatures, since all municipal government depends on the authority of a sovereign state. Such approval was often difficult to obtain—local bosses were usually entrenched in powerful state machines, and most legislatures were controlled by rural majorities insensitive to urban needs. Therefore, the progressives had to strike at inefficiency and corruption at the state level too.

During the first decade of the new century, Wisconsin, the progressive state par excellence, was transformed by Robert M. La Follette, one of the most remarkable figures of the age. La Follette was born in Primrose, Wisconsin, in 1855. He had served

Robert M. La Follette speaking to Wisconsin farmers in 1897. After six years as governor of the state, he won election to the Senate, serving four terms.

three terms as a Republican congressman (1885–1891) and developed a reputation as an uncompromising foe of corruption before being elected governor in 1900. That the people would always do the right thing if properly informed and inspired was the fundamental article of his political faith. "Machine control is based upon misrepresentation and ignorance," La Follette said. "Democracy is based upon knowledge." His own career seemed to prove his point, for in his repeated clashes with the conservative Wisconsin Republican machine, he won battle after battle by vigorous grass-roots campaigning.

Despite the opposition of railroad and lumbering interests, Governor La Follette obtained a direct primary system for nominating candidates, a corrupt practices act, and laws limiting campaign expenditures and lobbying activities. In power he became something of a boss himself. He made ruthless use of patronage, demanded absolute loyalty of his subordinates, and often stretched, or at least oversimplified, the truth when presenting complex issues to the voters.

La Follette was a consummate showman who never rose entirely above rural prejudices. He was prone to scent a nefarious "conspiracy" organized by "the interests" behind even the mildest opposition to his proposals. But he was devoted to the cause of honest government. Realizing that some state functions called for specialized technical knowledge, he used commissions and agencies to handle such matters as railroad regulation, tax assessment, conservation, and highway construction. Wisconsin established a legislative reference library to assist lawmakers in drafting bills. For work of this kind, La Follette called on the faculty of the University of Wisconsin, enticing top-notch economists and political scientists into the public service and drawing freely on the advice of such outstanding social scientists as Richard T. Ely, John R. Commons, and E. A. Ross.

The success of what became known as the Wisconsin Idea led other states to adopt similar programs. Reform administrations swept into office in Iowa and Arkansas (1901), Oregon (1902), Minnesota, Kansas, and Mississippi (1904), New York and Georgia (1906), Nebraska (1909), New Jersey and Colorado (1910). In some cases the reformers were Republicans, in others Democrats, but in all the example of Wisconsin was influential. By 1910 15 states had established legislative reference services, most of them staffed by personnel trained in Wisconsin. The direct primary system became almost universal.

Some states went beyond Wisconsin in striving to make their governments responsive to the popular will. In 1902 Oregon began to experiment with the initiative, a system by which a bill could be forced on the attention of the legislature by popular petition, and the referendum, a method for allowing the electorate to approve measures rejected by their representatives and to repeal measures that the legislature had passed. Eleven states, most of them in the West, legalized these devices by 1914.

State Social Legislation

The first state laws aimed at social problems long antedated the Progressive Era, but most were either so imprecise as to be unenforceable or, like the Georgia law "limiting" textile workers to 11 hours a day, so weak as to be ineffective. In 1874 Massachusetts restricted the working hours of women and children to ten per day, and by the 1890s many other states, mostly in the East and Middle West, had followed suit. Illinois passed an eight-hour law for women workers in 1893. A New York law of 1882 struck at the sweatshops of the slums by prohibiting the manufacture of cigars on premises "occupied as a house or residence."

As part of this trend, some states established special rules for workers in hazardous industries. In the 1890s several states limited the hours of railroad workers on the grounds that fatigue sometimes caused railroad accidents. Utah restricted miners to eight hours in 1896. In 1901 New York finally enacted an effective tenement house law, greatly increasing the area of open space on building lots and requiring toilets for each apartment, better ventilation systems, and more adequate fireproofing.

Before 1900 the collective impact of such legislation was not impressive. Powerful manufacturers and landlords often succeeded in defeating the bills or rendering them innocuous. The federal system further complicated the task of obtaining effective legislation.

The Fourteenth Amendment to the Constitution, although enacted to protect the civil rights of blacks, imposed a revolutionary restriction on the states by forbidding them to "deprive any person of life, liberty, or property without due process of law." Since much state social legislation represented new uses of police power that conservative judges considered dangerous and unwise, the Fourteenth Amendment gave them an excuse to overturn the

laws on the grounds that they deprived someone of liberty or property.

As stricter and more far-reaching laws were enacted, many judges, sensing what they took to be a trend toward socialism and regimentation, adopted an increasingly narrow interpretation of state police power. The United States Supreme Court upheld the Utah mining law of 1896 (*Holden* v. *Hardy*, 1898), but in 1905 it declared in the case of *Lochner* v. *New York* that a New York ten-hour act for bakers deprived the bakers of the liberty of working as long as they wished and thus violated the Fourteenth Amendment. Justice Oliver Wendell Holmes, Jr., wrote a famous dissenting opinion in this case. If the people of New York believed that the public health was endangered by bakers working long hours, he reasoned, it was not the Court's job to overrule them. "A constitution is not intended to embody a particular economic theory, whether of paternalism . . . or of laissez faire," Holmes said. "The word 'liberty,' in the Fourteenth Amendment, is perverted when it is held to prevent the natural outcome of a dominant opinion."

Nevertheless, the progressives continued to battle for legislation based on police power. Women played a particularly important part in these struggles. Sparked by the National Child Labor Committee, organized in 1904, reformers over the next ten years obtained laws in nearly every state banning the employment of young children and limiting the hours of older ones. Many of these laws were poorly enforced, yet when Congress passed a federal child labor law in 1916, the Supreme Court, in *Hammer* v. *Dagenhart* (1918), declared it unconstitutional.*

By 1917 nearly all the states had placed limitations on the hours of women industrial workers, and about ten had set minimum wage standards for women. But once again federal action that would have extended such regulation to the entire country did not materialize. A minimum wage law for women in the District of Columbia was overturned by the Court in *Adkins* v. *Children's Hospital* (1923).

Laws protecting workers against on-the-job accidents were also enacted by many states. Disasters like the 1911 fire in New York City, in which nearly

---

* A second child labor law, passed in 1919, was also thrown out by the Court, and a child labor amendment, submitted in 1924, failed to achieve ratification by the necessary three-quarters of the states.

150 women perished because the Triangle shirt-waist factory had no fire escapes, led to the passage of stricter municipal building codes and factory inspection acts. By 1910 most states had modified the common-law principle that a worker accepted the risk of accident as a condition of employment and was not entitled to compensation if injured unless it could be proved that the employer had been negligent. Gradually the states adopted accident insurance plans, and some began to grant pensions to widows with small children. Most manufacturers favored such measures, if for no other reason than that they regularized procedures and avoided costly lawsuits.

The passage of so much state social legislation sent conservatives scurrying to the Supreme Court for redress. Such persons believed that no government had the power to deprive either workers or employers of the right to negotiate any kind of labor contract they wished. The decision of the Supreme Court in *Lochner* v. *New York* seemed to indicate that the justices would adopt this point of view. But when an Oregon law limiting women laundry workers to ten hours a day was challenged in *Muller* v. *Oregon* (1908), Florence Kelley and Josephine Goldmark of the Consumers' League persuaded Louis D. Brandeis to defend the statute before the Court.

The Consumers' League, whose slogan was "investigate, agitate, legislate," was probably the most effective of the many women's reform organizations of the period. With the aid of League researchers, Brandeis prepared a remarkable brief stuffed with economic and sociological evidence indicating that long hours damaged both the health of individual women and the health of society. This nonlegal evidence greatly impressed the justices. "It may not be amiss," they declared, "to notice . . . expressions of opinion from other than judicial sources" in determining the constitutionality of such laws. "Woman's physical structure, and the functions she performs in consequence thereof, justify special legislation," they concluded. After 1908 the right of states to protect women, children, and workers performing dangerous and unhealthy tasks by special legislation was widely accepted. The use of the "Brandeis brief" technique to demonstrate the need for such legislation became standard practice.

Progressives also launched a massive, if ill-coordinated, attack on problems related to monopoly. The variety of regulatory legislation passed by

the states between 1900 and 1917 was almost infinite. Wisconsin created a powerful railroad commission staffed with nonpartisan experts; it enacted a graduated income tax and strengthened the state tax commission, which then proceeded to force corporations to bear a larger share of the cost of government; it overhauled the laws regulating insurance companies and set up a small state-owned life insurance company to serve as a yardstick for evaluating the rates of private companies. In 1911, besides creating an industrial commission to enforce the state's labor and factory legislation, Wisconsin progressives established a conservation commission, headed by Charles R. Van Hise, president of the University of Wisconsin.

A similar spate of legislation characterized the brief reign of Woodrow Wilson as governor of New Jersey (1911–1913). Urged on by the relentless Wilson, the legislature created a public utility commission with authority to evaluate the properties of railroad, gas, electric, telephone, and express companies and to fix rates and set standards for these corporations. The legislature enacted storage and food inspection laws, and in 1913 it passed seven bills (the "Seven Sisters" laws) tightening the state's loose controls over corporations, which had won New Jersey the unenviable reputation of being "the mother of trusts." Economic reforms in other states were less spectacular but impressive in the mass. In New York an investigation of the big life insurance companies led to comprehensive changes in the insurance laws and put Charles Evans Hughes, who had conducted the investigation, in the governor's chair. In Iowa stiff laws regulating railroads were passed in 1906. In Nebraska the legislature created a bank deposit insurance system in 1909. Minnesota levied an inheritance tax and built a harvesting machine factory to compete with the harvester trust. Georgia raised the taxes on corporations.

Political Reform in Washington

On the national level the Progressive Era saw the culmination of the struggle for women's suffrage. The shock occasioned by the failure of the Thirteenth and Fourteenth amendments to give women the vote resulted in a split among feminists. One group, the American Women's Suffrage Association, focused on the vote question alone. The more

A banner in a 1911 women's suffrage parade carries one of the longest-standing arguments in favor of women getting the vote.

radical National Women's Suffrage Association, led by Elizabeth Cady Stanton and Susan B. Anthony, concerned itself with many issues of importance to women as well as the suffrage. The NWSA put the immediate interests of women ahead of everything else. It was deeply involved in efforts to unionize women workers, yet it did not hesitate to urge women to be strikebreakers if they could get better jobs by doing so.

Aside from their lack of unity, feminists were handicapped in the late 19th century by Victorian sexual inhibitions, which most of their leaders shared. Even under the best of circumstances, dislike of male-dominated society was hard enough to separate from dislike of men. At a time when sex was an unmentionable topic in polite society and sexual feelings were often deeply repressed, some of the most militant advocates of women's rights probably did not understand their own feelings. Most feminists, for example, opposed contraception, insisting that birth control by any means other than abstinence would encourage what they called masculine lust. The Victorian idealization of female "purity" and the popular image of women as the revered guardians of home and family further confused many reformers. And the trend of 19th-century scientific thinking influenced by the Darwinian concept of biological adaptation led to the conclusion that the female personality was different from that of the male and that the differences were inherent, not culturally determined.

These ideas and prejudices enticed feminists into a logical trap. If women were morally superior to men—a tempting conclusion—giving women the vote would improve the character of the electorate. Society would benefit because politics would become less corrupt, war a thing of the past. "City housekeeping has failed," said Jane Addams of Hull House in arguing for the reform of municipal government, "partly because women, the traditional housekeepers, have not been consulted."

The trouble with this argument (aside from the fact that opponents could easily demonstrate that in states where women did vote, governments were no better or worse than elsewhere) was that it surrendered the principle of equality. In the long run this was to have serious consequences for the women's movement, though the immediate effect of the

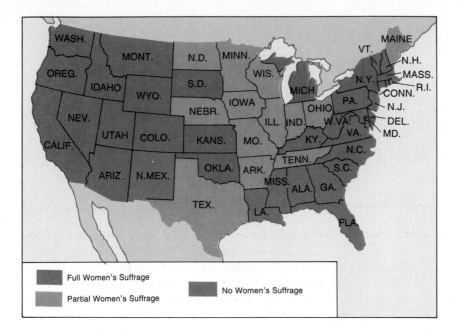

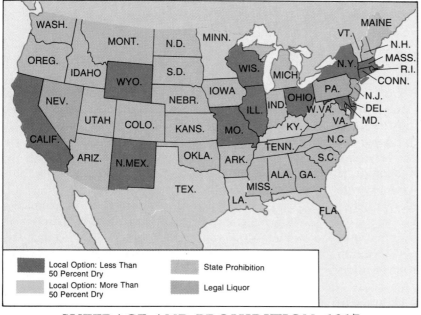

SUFFRAGE AND PROHIBITION, 1917

These maps give a sense of the state-by-state progress of women's suffrage and prohibition by 1917. The Eighteenth Amendment, enforcing national prohibition, passed in 1919; the Nineteenth Amendment, allowing women the right to vote, in 1920. Both amendments were a culmination of reform efforts before and during the Progressive Era. The original 1917 version of the temperance map referred to the three "wet" states—New Jersey, Pennsylvania, and Nevada—as "Booze States."

purity argument was probably to advance the suffragists' cause.

By the early 20th century there were signs of progress. In 1890 the two major women's groups combined as the National American Women's Suffrage Association. Stanton and Anthony were the first two presidents of the association, but new leaders were emerging, the most notable being Carrie Chapman Catt, a woman who combined superb organizing abilities and political skills with commitment to broad social reform. The NAWSA made winning the right to vote its main objective and concentrated on a state-by-state approach. By 1896 Wyoming, Utah, Colorado, and Idaho had been won over to women's suffrage.

The burgeoning of the progressive movement helped as middle-class recruits of both sexes adopted the cause. California voted for women's suffrage in 1911 after having defeated the proposal some years earlier, and several other states fell into line. For the first time, large numbers of working-class women began to agitate for the vote.

The suffragists then shifted the campaign back to the national level, the lead taken by a new organization, the Congressional Union, headed by Alice Paul. After some hesitation the NAWSA began to campaign for a constitutional amendment, which won congressional approval in 1918. By 1920 the necessary three-quarters of the states had ratified the Nineteenth Amendment; the long fight was over.

The progressive drive for political democracy also found expression in the Seventeenth Amendment to the Constitution, ratified in 1913, which required the popular election of senators. And a group of "insurgent" congressmen managed to reform the House of Representatives by limiting the power of the Speaker. During the early years of the century, operating under the system established in the 1890s by "Czar" Thomas B. Reed, Speaker Joseph G. Cannon exercised tyrannical authority, appointing the members of all committees and controlling the course of legislation. Representatives could seldom obtain the floor without obtaining the Speaker's consent. In 1910 the insurgents, led by George W. Norris, stripped Cannon of his control over the House Rules Committee. Thereafter, appointments to committees were determined by the entire membership, acting through party caucuses. This change was thoroughly progressive. "We want

the House to be representative of the people and each individual member to have his ideas presented and passed on," Norris explained.

No other important alterations of the national political system were made during the Progressive Era. Although some 20 states passed presidential primary laws, the cumbersome method of electing presidents was not changed.

Theodore Roosevelt: Cowboy in the White House

On September 6, 1901, an anarchist named Leon Czolgosz shot President McKinley during a public reception at the Pan-American Exposition at Buffalo, New York. Eight days later McKinley died and Theodore Roosevelt became president of the United States. His ascension to the presidency marked the beginning of a new era in national politics.

Although only 42, by far the youngest president in the nation's history up to that time, Roosevelt brought solid qualifications to the office. Son of a well-to-do New York merchant of Dutch ancestry, he had graduated from Harvard in 1880 and studied law briefly at Columbia, though he did not complete his degree. In addition to political experience that included three terms in the New York assembly, six years on the United States Civil Service Commission, two years as police commissioner of New York City, another as assistant secretary of the navy, and a term as governor of New York, he had been a rancher in Dakota Territory and a soldier in the Spanish-American War. He was also a well-known historian: His *Naval War of 1812* (1882), begun during his undergraduate days at Harvard, and his four-volume *Winning of the West* (1889–1896) were valuable works of scholarship, and he had written two popular biographies and other books as well. Politically, he had always been a loyal Republican. He rejected the Mugwump heresy in 1884, despite his distaste for Blaine, and during the tempestuous 1890s he vigorously denounced populism, Bryanism, and "labor agitators."

Nevertheless, Roosevelt's elevation to the presidency alarmed many conservatives, and not without reason. He did not fit their conception, based on a composite image of the chief executives from Hayes to McKinley, of what a president should be like. He seemed too undignified, too energetic, too outspoken, too unconventional. It was one thing to have operated a cattle ranch, another to have captured a gang of rustlers at gunpoint; one thing to have run a metropolitan police force, another to have roamed New York slums in the small hours to catch patrolmen fraternizing with thieves and prostitutes; one thing to have commanded a regiment, another to have killed a Spaniard personally.

Roosevelt had been a sickly child, plagued by asthma and poor eyesight, and he seems to have spent much of his adult life compensating for the sense of inadequacy that these troubles bred in him. He repeatedly carried his displays of physical stamina and personal courage, and his love of athletics and big-game hunting, to preternatural lengths. Henry Adams, who watched Roosevelt's development over the years with a mixture of fear and amusement, said that he was "pure act."

Once, while fox hunting, Roosevelt fell from his

horse, cutting his face severely and breaking his left arm. Instead of waiting for help or struggling to some nearby house to summon a doctor, he clambered back on his horse and resumed the chase. "I was in at the death," he wrote next day. "I looked pretty gay, with one arm dangling, and my face and clothes like the walls of a slaughter house." That evening, after his arm had been set and put in splints, he attended a dinner party.

Roosevelt worshiped aggressiveness and was extremely sensitive to any threat to his honor as a gentleman. When another young man showed some slight interest in Roosevelt's fiancée, he sent for a set of French dueling pistols. His teachers found him an interesting student, for he was intelligent and imaginative, if rather annoyingly argumentative. "Now look here, Roosevelt," one Harvard professor finally said to him, "let me talk. I'm running this course."

Few individuals have rationalized or sublimated

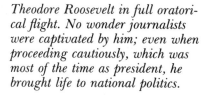

Theodore Roosevelt in full oratorical flight. No wonder journalists were captivated by him; even when proceeding cautiously, which was most of the time as president, he brought life to national politics.

their feelings of inferiority as effectively as Roosevelt, and to such good purpose. And few have been more genuinely warmhearted, more full of spontaneity, more committed to the ideals of public service and national greatness. As a political leader he was energetic and hard-driving. Conservatives and timid souls, sensing his aggressiveness even when he held it in check, distrusted Roosevelt's judgment, fearing he might go off half-cocked in some crisis. In fact his judgment was nearly always sound; responsibility usually tempered his aggressiveness.

When Roosevelt was first mentioned as a running mate for McKinley in 1900, he wrote: "The Vice Presidency is a most honorable office, but for a young man there is not much to do." As president it would have been unthinkable for him to preside over a caretaker administration devoted to maintaining the status quo. However, the reigning Republican politicos, basking in the sunshine of the prosperity that had contributed so much to their victory in 1900, distrusted anything suggestive of change.

Had Roosevelt been the impetuous hothead that conservatives feared, he would have plunged ahead without regard for their feelings and influence. Instead he moved slowly and often got what he wanted by using his executive power rather than by persuading Congress to pass new laws. His domestic program included some measure of control of big corporations, more power for the Interstate Commerce Commission, and the conservation of natural resources. By consulting congressional leaders and following their advice not to bring up controversial matters like the tariff and currency reform, he obtained a modest budget of new laws.

The Newlands Act (1902) funneled the proceeds from land sales in the West into federal irrigation projects. The Department of Commerce and Labor, which was to include a Bureau of Corporations with authority to investigate industrial combines and issue reports was established. The Elkins Railroad Act of 1903 strengthened the Interstate Commerce Commission's hand against the railroads by making the receiving as well as the granting of rebates illegal and by forbidding the roads to deviate in any way from their published rates.

Roosevelt and Big Business

Roosevelt soon became known as a trustbuster, and in the sense that he considered the monopoly prob-

Roosevelt, the trust-busting lion tamer, whips beef, oil, steel, and other trusts into shape as they emerge from their Wall Street den.

lem the most pressing issue of the times, this was accurate to an extent. But he did not believe in breaking up big corporations indiscriminately. Regulation seemed the best way to deal with large corporations because, he said, industrial giantism "could not be eliminated unless we were willing to turn back the wheels of modern progress."

With Congress unwilling to pass a stiff regulatory law, Roosevelt resorted to the Sherman Act to get at the problem. Although the Supreme Court decision in the Sugar Trust case seemed to have emasculated that law, in 1902 he ordered the Justice Department to bring suit against the Northern Securities Company.

He chose his target wisely. The Northern Securities Company controlled the Great Northern, the Northern Pacific, and the Chicago, Burlington and Quincy railroads. It had been created in 1901 after a titanic battle on the New York Stock Exchange between the forces of J. P. Morgan and James J. Hill and those of E. H. Harriman, who was associated with the Rockefeller interests. In their efforts to obtain control of the Northern Pacific, the rivals had forced its stock up to $1,000 a share, ruining many speculators and threatening to cause a panic.

Neither side could win a clear-cut victory, so they decided to put the stock of all three railroads into a holding company owned by the two groups. Since Harriman already controlled the Union Pacific and the Southern Pacific, a virtual monopoly of western railroads was effected. The public had been alarmed, for the merger seemed to typify the rapaciousness of the tycoons.

The announcement of the suit caused consternation in the business world. Morgan rushed to the White House. "If we have done anything wrong," he said to the president, "send your man to my man and they can fix it up." Roosevelt was not fundamentally opposed to this sort of agreement, but it was too late to compromise in this instance. Attorney General Philander C. Knox pressed the case vigorously, and in 1904 the Supreme Court ordered the dissolution of the Northern Securities Company.

Roosevelt then ordered suits against the meat packers, the Standard Oil Trust, and the American Tobacco Company. His stock among progressives rose, yet he had not embarrassed the conservatives in Congress by demanding new antitrust legislation.

The president went out of his way to assure cooperative corporation magnates that he was not against size per se. His Bureau of Corporations followed a policy of "obtaining hearty co-operation rather than arousing (the) antagonism of business and industrial interests." At a White House conference in 1905, Roosevelt and Elbert H. Gary, chairman of the board of U.S. Steel, reached a "gentlemen's agreement" whereby Gary promised "to cooperate with the Government in every possible way." The Bureau of Corporations would conduct an investigation of U.S. Steel, Gary allowing it full access to company records. Roosevelt in turn promised that if the investigation revealed any corporate malpractices, he would allow Gary to set matters right voluntarily, thereby avoiding an antitrust suit. He reached a similar agreement with the International Harvester Company two years later.

There were limits to the effectiveness of such arrangements. Standard Oil agreed to a similar détente and then reneged, refusing to turn over vital records to the bureau. The Justice Department brought suit against the company under the Sherman Act, and eventually it was broken up at the order of the Supreme Court. Roosevelt would have preferred a more binding kind of regulation, but when he asked for laws giving the government supervisory authority over big combinations, Congress refused to act.

Square Dealing

Roosevelt made remarkable use of his executive power during the anthracite coal strike of 1902. In June the United Mine Workers, led by John Mitchell, laid down their picks and demanded higher wages, an eight-hour day, and recognition of the union. Most of the anthracite mines were owned by railroads. Two years earlier the miners had won a 10 percent wage increase in a similar strike, chiefly because the owners feared that labor unrest might endanger the election of McKinley. Now the coal companies were dead set against further concessions; when the men walked out, they shut down their properties and prepared to starve the strikers into submission.

The strike dragged on through summer and early fall. The miners conducted themselves with great restraint, avoiding violence and offering to submit their claims to arbitration. As the price of anthracite soared with the approach of winter, sentiment in their behalf mounted.

The owners' spokesman, George F. Baer of the Reading Railroad, proved particularly inept at public relations. Baer stated categorically that God was on the side of management, but when someone suggested asking an important Roman Catholic prelate to arbitrate the dispute, he replied icily: "Anthracite mining is a business and not a religious, sentimental or academic proposition."

Roosevelt shared the public's sympathy for the miners, and the threat of a coal shortage alarmed him. Early in October he summoned both sides to a conference in Washington and urged them as patriotic Americans to sacrifice any "personal consideration" for the "general good." His action enraged the coal operators, for they believed he was trying to force them to recognize the union. They refused even to speak to the UMW representatives at the conference and demanded that Roosevelt end the

A silent procession of striking coal miners makes an orderly demonstration at Shenandoah, Pennsylvania, during the 1902 coal strike.

strike by force and bring suit against the union under the Sherman Act. Mitchell, aware of the immense prestige that Roosevelt had conferred on the union by calling the conference, cooperated fully with the president.

The attitudes of management and the union further strengthened public support for the miners. Even former president Grover Cleveland, who had used federal troops to break the Pullman strike, said that he was "disturbed and vexed by the tone and substance of the operators' deliverances." Encouraged by this state of affairs, Roosevelt took a bold step: He announced that unless a settlement was reached promptly, he would order federal troops into the anthracite regions, not to break the strike but to seize and operate the mines.

The threat of government intervention brought the owners to terms. A Cabinet member, Elihu Root, worked out the details with J. P. Morgan, whose firm had major interests in the Reading and other railroads, while cruising the Hudson River on Morgan's yacht. The miners would return to the pits, and all issues between them and the coal companies would be submitted for settlement to a commission appointed by Roosevelt. Both sides accepted the arrangement, and the men went back to work. In March 1903 the commission granted the miners a 10 percent wage increase and a nine-hour day.

To the public the incident seemed a perfect illustration of the progressive spirit—in Roosevelt's words, everyone had received a "square deal." In fact the results were by no means so clear-cut. The miners gained relatively little, and the companies lost still less, for they were not required to recognize the United Mine Workers and the commission also recommended a 10 percent increase in the price of coal, ample compensation for the increased wage costs. The president was the main winner. The public acclaimed him as a fearless, imaginative, public-spirited leader. Without calling on Congress for support, he had expanded his own authority and hence that of the federal government. His action marked a major forward step in the evolution of the modern presidency.

T.R.: President in His Own Right

By reviving the Sherman Act, settling the coal strike, and pushing moderate reforms through Congress, Roosevelt ensured that he would be reelected president in 1904. Progressives, if not yet captivated, were at least pleased by his performance. Conservative Republicans offered no serious objection. Sensing that Roosevelt had won over the liberals, the Democrats nominated a conservative, Judge Alton B. Parker of New York, and bid for the support of eastern industrialists.

This strategy failed, for businessmen continued to eye the party of Bryan with intense suspicion. They preferred, as the *New York Sun* put it, "the impulsive candidate of the party of conservatism to the conservative candidate of the party which the business interests regard as permanently and dangerously impulsive." Despite his resentment at Roosevelt's attack on the Northern Securities Company, J. P. Morgan contributed $150,000 to the Republican campaign. Other tycoons gave with equal generosity. Roosevelt swept the country, carrying even the normally Democratic border states of Maryland and Missouri.

Encouraged by the landslide and the increasing militancy of progressives, Roosevelt pressed for more reform legislation. His most imaginative proposal was a plan to make the District of Columbia a model progressive community. He suggested child labor and factory inspection laws and a slum clear-

ance program, but Congress refused to act. Likewise, his request for a minimum wage for railroad workers was rejected.

He had greater success when he proposed still another increase in the power of the Interstate Commerce Commission. Rebating remained a serious problem. With progressive state governors demanding federal action and farmers and manufacturers, especially in the Middle West, clamoring for relief against discriminatory rates, Roosevelt was ready by 1905 to make railroad legislation his major objective. The ICC should be empowered to fix rates, not merely to challenge unreasonable ones. It should have the right to inspect the private records of the railroads, since fair rates could not be determined unless the true financial condition of the roads was known.

Because these proposals struck at rights that businessmen considered sacrosanct, many congressmen balked. But Roosevelt applied presidential pressure, and in June 1906 the Hepburn bill became law. It gave the commission the power to inspect the books of railroad companies, to set maximum rates (once a complaint had been filed by a shipper), and to control sleeping car companies, owners of oil pipelines, and other firms engaged in transportation. Railroads could no longer issue passes freely—an important check on their political influence. In all, the Hepburn Act made the ICC a more powerful and more active body. Though it did not outlaw judicial review of ICC decisions, thereafter those decisions were seldom overturned by the courts.

Congress also passed meat inspection and pure food and drug legislation. In 1906 Upton Sinclair published *The Jungle,* a devastating exposé of the filthy conditions in the Chicago slaughterhouses. Sinclair was more interested in writing a socialist tract than he was in meat inspection, but his book, a best-seller, raised a storm against the packers. After Roosevelt read *The Jungle,* he sent two officials to Chicago to investigate. Their report was so shocking, he said, that its publication would "be well-nigh ruinous to our export trade in meat." He threatened to release the report, however, unless Congress acted. After a hot fight, the meat inspection bill passed. The Pure Food and Drug Act, forbidding the manufacture and sale of adulterated and fraudulently labeled products, rode through Congress on the coattails of this measure.

Before the passage of the Pure Food and Drug Act in 1906, manufacturers were free to use any ingredients they chose. Many "tonics" kept their promises of increased vigor by delivering doses of cocaine, alcohol, or other narcotics.

Roosevelt has probably received more credit than he deserves for these laws. He had never been deeply interested in pure food legislation, and he considered Dr. Harvey W. Wiley, chief chemist of the Department of Agriculture and the leader of the fight for this reform, something of a crank. He compromised with opponents of meat inspection cheerfully, despite his loud denunciations of the evils under attack. "As now carried on the (meat-packing) business is both a menace to health and an outrage on decency," he said. "No legislation that is not drastic and thoroughgoing will be of avail." Yet he went along with the packers' demand that the government pay the costs of inspection, though he believed that "the only way to secure efficiency is by the imposition upon the packers of a fee." Nevertheless, the end results were positive and in line with his conception of the public good.

To advanced liberals Roosevelt's achievements seemed limited when placed beside his professed objectives and his smug evaluations of what he had done. How could he be a reformer and a defender of established interests at the same time? Roosevelt found no difficulty in holding such a position. As one historian has said, "He stood close to the center and bared his teeth at the conservatives of the right and the liberals of the extreme left."

Tilting Left

As the progressive movement advanced, Roosevelt advanced with it. He never accepted all the ideas of what he called its "lunatic fringe," but he took steadily more liberal positions. He always insisted that he was not hostile to business interests, but when those interests sought to exploit the national domain, they had no more implacable foe. Conservation of natural resources was dear to his heart and probably his most significant achievement as president. He placed some 150 million acres of forest lands in federal reserves, and he strictly enforced the laws governing grazing, mining, and lumbering. When his opponents attached to an important appropriations bill a rider prohibiting the creation of further reserves without the approval of Congress, Roosevelt transferred an additional 17 million acres to the reserve before signing the bill. In 1908 he organized a National Conservation Conference, attended by 44 governors and 500 others, to discuss conservation matters. As a result of this meeting, most states created conservation commissions.

As Roosevelt became more liberal, conservative Republicans began to balk at following his lead. The sudden panic that struck the financial world in October 1907 speeded the trend. Government policies had no direct bearing on the panic, which began with a run on several important New York trust companies and spread to the Stock Exchange when speculators found themselves unable to borrow money to meet their obligations. In the emergency, Roosevelt authorized the deposit of large amounts of government cash in New York banks. He informally agreed to the acquisition of the Tennessee Coal and Iron Company by U.S. Steel when the bankers told him that the purchase was necessary to end the panic. In spite of his efforts, conservatives insisted on referring to the financial collapse as "Roosevelt's panic," and they blamed the president for the depression that followed on its heels.

Roosevelt, however, turned left rather than right. In 1908 he came out in favor of federal income and inheritance taxes, stricter regulation of interstate corporations, and reforms designed to help industrial workers. He denounced "the speculative folly and the flagrant dishonesty" of "malefactors of great wealth," further alienating conservative, or Old Guard, Republicans, who resented the attacks on their integrity implicit in Roosevelt's statements. When the president began criticizing the courts, the last bastion of conservatism, he lost all chance of obtaining further reform legislation. As he said himself, during his last months in office "stagnation continued to rage with uninterrupted violence."

William Howard Taft: The Listless Progressive

But Roosevelt remained popular and politically powerful. Before his term ended, he chose William Howard Taft, his secretary of war, to succeed him and easily obtained Taft's nomination. William Jennings Bryan was again the Democratic candidate. Campaigning on Roosevelt's record, Taft carried the country by well over a million votes, defeating Bryan 321 to 162 in the electoral college.

Taft was intelligent, experienced, and public-spirited; he seemed ideally suited to carry out Roosevelt's policies. Born in Cincinnati in 1857, educated at Yale, he had served as an Ohio judge, as solicitor general of the United States under Benjamin Harrison, and then as a federal circuit court judge before accepting McKinley's assignment to head the Philippine Commission in 1900. His suc-

Taft was the first presidential golfer, playing enthusiastically despite his bulk. He ended his career happily as a chief justice of the Supreme Court.

cess as civil governor of the Philippines led Roosevelt to make him secretary of war in 1904.

Taft supported the Square Deal loyally. This, together with his mentor's ardent endorsement, won him the backing of most progressive Republicans. Yet the Old Guard liked him too; although outgoing, he had none of the Roosevelt impetuosity and aggressiveness. His genial personality and his obvious desire to avoid conflict appealed to moderates.

However, Taft lacked the physical and mental stamina required of a modern chief executive. Though not lazy, he weighed over 300 pounds and needed to rest this vast bulk more than the job allowed. He liked to eat in leisurely fashion, to idle away mornings on the golf course, to take an afternoon nap. Campaigning bored him; speech making seemed a useless chore. The judicial life was his real love; intense partisanship dismayed and confused him. He was too reasonable to control a coalition and not ambitious enough to impose his will on others. He found extremists irritating and persistent people (including his wife) difficult to resist. He supported many progressive measures, but he never absorbed the progressive spirit.

Taft honestly desired to carry out most of Roosevelt's policies. He enforced the Sherman Act vigorously and continued to expand the national forest reserves. He signed the Mann-Elkins Act of 1910, which empowered the Interstate Commerce Commission to suspend rate increases without waiting for a shipper to complain and established the Commerce Court to speed the settlement of railroad rate cases. An eight-hour day for all persons engaged in work on government contracts, mine safety legislation, and several other reform measures received his approval. He even summoned Congress into special session specifically to reduce tariff duties—something that Roosevelt had not dared to attempt.

But Taft had been disturbed by Roosevelt's sweeping use of executive power. "We have got to work out our problems on the basis of law," he insisted. Whereas Roosevelt had excelled at maneuvering around congressional opposition and at finding ways to accomplish his objectives without waiting for Congress to act, Taft adamantly refused to use such tactics. His restraint was in many ways admirable, but it reduced his effectiveness.

In case after case, Taft's lack of vigor and his political ineptness led to trouble. In the matter of the tariff, he favored downward revision. When the special session met in 1909, the House promptly passed a bill that was in line with his desires. But Senate protectionists restored the high rates of the Act of 1897 on most items. A group of insurgent senators, led by Robert La Follette of Wisconsin, fought these changes desperately, producing masses of statistics to show that the proposed schedules on cotton goods, woolens, and other products were unreasonably high. They were fighting the president's battle, yet Taft did little to help them. He signed the final Payne-Aldrich measure and called it "the best (tariff) bill that the Republican party ever passed." His attitude dumbfounded the progressives.

In 1910 Taft got into difficulty with the conservationists. Though he believed in husbanding natural resources carefully, he did not like the way Roosevelt had circumvented Congress in adding to the forest reserves. He demanded, and eventually obtained, specific legislation to accomplish this purpose. The issue that aroused the conservationists concerned the integrity of his secretary of the interior, Richard A. Ballinger. A less than ardent conservationist, Ballinger returned to the public domain certain waterpower sites that the Roosevelt administration had withdrawn on the legally questionable grounds that they were to become ranger stations. Ballinger's action alarmed Chief Forester Gifford Pinchot, the darling of the conservationists. When Pinchot learned that Ballinger intended to validate the shaky claim of mining interests to a large tract of coal-rich land in Alaska, he launched an intemperate attack on the secretary.

In the Ballinger-Pinchot controversy, Taft felt obliged to support his own man. The coal lands dispute was complex, and Pinchot's charges were exaggerated. It was certainly unfair to call Ballinger "the most effective opponent the conservation policies have yet had." When Pinchot, whose own motives were partly political, persisted in criticizing Ballinger, Taft dismissed him. He had no choice under the circumstances, but a more adept politician might have found some way of avoiding a showdown.

Breakup of the Republican Party

One ominous aspect of the Ballinger-Pinchot affair was that Pinchot was a close friend of Theodore Roosevelt. After Taft's inauguration, Roosevelt had gone off to hunt big game in Africa, bearing in his baggage an autographed photograph of his protégé and a touching letter of appreciation, in which the new president said: "I can never forget that the power I now exercise was a voluntary transfer from you to me." For months, as he trudged across Africa, guns blazing, Roosevelt was out of touch with affairs in the United States. As soon as he emerged from the wilderness in March 1910, bearing more than 3,000 trophies, including 9 lions, 5 elephants, and 13 rhinos, he was caught up in the squabble between the progressive members of his party and its titular head. Pinchot met him in Italy, laden with injured innocence and a packet of angry letters from various progressives. His intimate friend Senator Henry Cabot Lodge, essentially a conservative, barraged him with messages, the gist of which was that Taft was lazy and inept and that Roosevelt should prepare to become the "Moses" who would guide the party "out of the wilderness of doubt and discontent" into which Taft had led it.

Roosevelt hoped to steer a middle course, but

Pinchot's complaints impressed him. Taft had decided to strike out on his own, he concluded. "No man must render such a service as that I rendered Taft and expect the individual . . . not in the end to become uncomfortable and resentful," he wrote Lodge sadly. Taft sensed the former president's coolness and was offended. He was egged on by his ambitious wife, who wanted him to stand clear of Roosevelt's shadow and establish his own reputation.

Perhaps the resulting rupture was inevitable. The Republican party was dividing into two factions, the progressives and the Old Guard. Forced

Political cartoonists came of age during the Progressive Era, not least because of such easily caricatured presidents as the frenetic T.R. and the outsized Taft.

THE DISPUTED CHAIR

T. R. TO TAFT: "I only lent it to you, anyway"

to choose between them, Taft threw in his lot with the Old Guard. Roosevelt backed the progressives. Speaking at Osawatomie, Kansas, in August 1910, he came out for a comprehensive program of social legislation, which he called the New Nationalism. Besides attacking "special privilege" and the "unfair money-getting" practices of "lawbreakers of great wealth," he called for a broad expansion of federal power. "The betterment we seek must be accomplished," he said, "mainly through the National Government."

The final break came in October 1911, when the president ordered an antitrust suit against U.S. Steel. Roosevelt, of course, opposed breaking up large corporations. "The effort at prohibiting all combination has substantially failed," he said in his New Nationalism speech. "The way out lies . . . in completely controlling them." Taft was prepared to enforce the Sherman Act "or die in the attempt." But what angered Roosevelt was Taft's emphasis in the suit on U.S. Steel's absorption of the Tennessee Coal and Iron Company, which Roosevelt had unofficially authorized during the panic of 1907. The government's antitrust brief made Roosevelt appear to have been either an abettor of monopoly or, far worse, a fool who had been duped by the steel corporation. Early in 1912 he declared himself a candidate for the Republican presidential nomination.

Roosevelt plunged into the preconvention campaign with typical energy. He was almost uniformly victorious in states that held presidential primaries, carrying even Ohio, Taft's home state. However, the president controlled the party machinery and entered the national convention with a small majority of the delegates. Since some Taft delegates had been chosen under questionable circumstances, the Roosevelt forces challenged the right of 254 of them to their seats. The Taft-controlled credentials committee, paying little attention to the evidence, gave all but a few of the disputed seats to the president, who then won the nomination on the first ballot.

Had Roosevelt swallowed his resentment and bided his time, Taft would almost certainly have been defeated in the election, and the 1916 Republican nomination would have been Roosevelt's for the asking. But he was understandably outraged by the ruthless manner in which the Taft "steamroller" had overridden his forces. When his leading supporters urged him to organize a third party, and

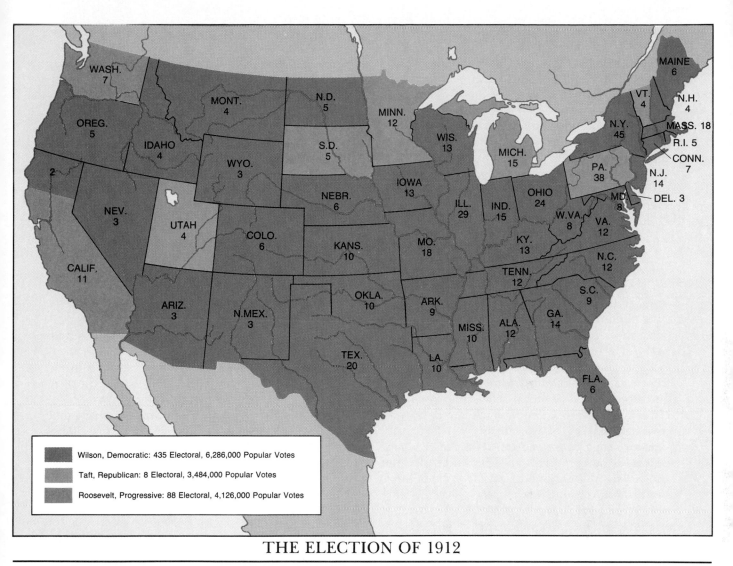

THE ELECTION OF 1912

Wilson, Democratic: 435 Electoral, 6,286,000 Popular Votes

Taft, Republican: 8 Electoral, 3,484,000 Popular Votes

Roosevelt, Progressive: 88 Electoral, 4,126,000 Popular Votes

The fourth largest vote getter in the election of 1912 was Eugene V. Debs of the Socialist party, who gained about 900,000 popular votes (or approximately 6 percent of the total popular vote), but no electoral vote.

when two of them, George W. Perkins, formerly a partner of the banker J. P. Morgan, and the publisher Frank Munsey, offered to finance the campaign, Roosevelt agreed to make the race.

In August, amid scenes of hysterical enthusiasm, the first convention of the Progressive party met at Chicago and nominated him for president. Announcing that he felt "as strong as a bull moose," Roosevelt delivered a stirring "confession of faith," calling for strict regulation of corporations, a tariff

commission, national presidential primaries, minimum wage and workers' compensation laws, the elimination of child labor, and many other reforms.

The Election of 1912

The Democrats made the most of the opportunity offered by the Republican schism. Had they nominated a conservative or allowed Bryan a fourth chance, they would probably have ensured Roosevelt's election. Instead, after battling through 46 ballots at their convention in Baltimore, they nominated Woodrow Wilson, who had achieved a remarkable liberal record as governor of New Jersey.

Although as a political scientist Wilson had criticized the status quo and taken a pragmatic approach to the idea of government regulation of the economy, he had objected strongly to Bryan's brand of politics. In 1896 he voted for the Gold Democratic party candidate for president. But by 1912, influenced partly by ambition and partly by the spirit of the times, he had been converted to progressivism. He called his brand of reform the New Freedom.

The federal government could best advance the cause of social justice, Wilson reasoned, by eradicating the special privileges that enabled the "interests" to flourish. Where Roosevelt had lost faith in competition as a way of protecting the public against monopolies, Wilson insisted that competition could be restored. The government must break up the great trusts, establish fair rules for doing business, and subject violators to stiff punishments. Thereafter, the free enterprise system would protect the public from exploitation without destroying individual initiative and opportunity. "If America is not to have free enterprise, then she can have freedom of no sort whatever," he said. Although rather vague, this argument appealed to thousands of voters who found the growing power of large corporations frightening but who hesitated to make the thoroughgoing commitment to government control of business that Roosevelt was advocating.

Roosevelt's reasoning was perhaps theoretically more sound.

Laissez faire made less sense than it had in earlier times. The complexities of the modern world seemed to call for a positive approach, a plan, the close application of human intelligence to social and economic problems. As Herbert Croly insisted in *The Promise of American Life* (1909), the time had come to employ Hamiltonian means to achieve Jeffersonian ends.

Roosevelt dismissed Wilson's New Freedom as "rural toryism," but being less drastic and more in line with American experience than the New Nationalism, it had much to recommend it. The danger that selfish individuals would use the power of the state for their own ends had certainly not disappeared, despite the efforts of progressives to make

government more responsive to popular opinion. Any considerable expansion of national power would increase the danger and probably create new difficulties. Managing so complicated an enterprise as an industrialized nation was sure to be a formidable task. Furthermore, individual freedom of opportunity merited the toleration of a certain amount of inefficiency.

To choose between the New Nationalism and the New Freedom, between the dynamic Roosevelt and the idealistic Wilson, was indeed difficult. Thousands grappled with this problem before going to the polls, but partisan politics determined the outcome of the election. Taft got the hard-core Republican vote but lost the progressive wing of the GOP to Roosevelt. Wilson had the solid support of both conservative and liberal Democrats. As a result, Wilson won an easy victory in the electoral college, receiving 435 votes to Roosevelt's 88 and Taft's 8. The popular vote was Wilson, 6,286,000; Roosevelt, 4,126,000; and Taft, 3,484,000.

If partisan politics had determined the winner, the election was nonetheless an overwhelming endorsement of progressivism. The temper of the times was shown by the 897,000 votes given Eugene Debs, who was again the Socialist candidate. Altogether, professed liberals amassed over 11 million of the 15 million ballots cast. Wilson was a minority president, but he took office with a clear mandate to press forward with further reforms.

Wilson: The New Freedom

No man ever rose more suddenly or spectacularly in American politics than Woodrow Wilson. In the spring of 1910 he was president of Princeton University; he had never held or even run for public office. In the fall of 1912 he was president-elect of the United States. Yet if his rise was meteoric, in a very real sense he had devoted his life to preparing for it. He was born in Staunton, Virginia, in 1856, the son of a Presbyterian minister. As a student he became interested in political theory, dreaming of representing his state in the Senate. He studied law solely because he thought it the best avenue to public office, and when he discovered that he did not like legal work, he took a doctorate at Johns Hopkins in political science.

For years Wilson's political ambitions appeared

WILSON: THE NEW FREEDOM

Woodrow Wilson, presiding over the 1906 Princeton commencement, with steel magnate cum *educational philanthropist Andrew Carnegie firmly in tow.*

doomed to frustration. He taught at Bryn Mawr, then at Wesleyan, finally at his alma mater, Princeton. He wrote several influential books, among them *Congressional Government* and *The State,* and achieved an outstanding reputation as a teacher and lecturer. In 1902 he was chosen president of Princeton and soon won a place among the nation's leading educators. He revised the curriculum, introducing many new subjects and insisting that students pursue an organized and integrated course of study.

He instituted the preceptorial system, which placed the students in close intellectual and social contact with their teachers. He attracted outstanding young scholars to the Princeton faculty.

In time Wilson's educational ideas and his overbearing manner of applying them got him in trouble with some of Princeton's alumni and trustees. Though his university career was wrecked, the controversies, in which he appeared to be championing democracy and progress in the face of reactionary opponents, brought him at last to the attention of the politicians. Then, in a great rush, came power and fame.

Wilson was an immediate success as president. Since Roosevelt's last year in office, Congress had been almost continually at war with the executive branch and with itself. Legislative achievements had been relatively few. Now a small avalanche of important measures received the approval of the lawmakers. In October 1913 the Underwood Tariff brought the first significant reduction of duties since before the Civil War. Food products, wool, iron and steel, shoes, agricultural machinery, and other items that could be produced more cheaply in the United States than abroad were placed on the free list. Rates on most other goods were cut substantially, the object being to equalize foreign and domestic costs. To compensate for the expected loss of revenue, the act provided for a graduated tax on personal incomes.*

Two months later the Federal Reserve Act gave the country a central banking system for the first time since Jackson destroyed the Bank of the United States. The measure divided the nation into 12 banking districts, each under the supervision of a Federal Reserve bank, a sort of bank for bankers. All national banks in each district and any state banks that wished to participate had to invest 6 percent of their capital and surplus in the reserve bank, which was empowered to exchange (the technical term is *rediscount*) paper money, called Federal Reserve notes, for the commercial and agricultural paper that member banks took in as security from borrowers. The volume of currency was no longer at the mercy of the supply of gold or any other particular commodity.

---

* The Sixteenth Amendment, ratified in February 1913, authorized the imposition of a federal income tax.

The crown and nerve center of the system was the Federal Reserve Board in Washington, which appointed a majority of the directors of the Federal Reserve banks and had some control over rediscount rates (the commission charged by the reserve banks for performing the rediscounting function). The board provided a modicum of public control over the banks, but the effort to weaken the power of the great New York banks by decentralizing the system proved ineffective. Nevertheless, a true central banking system was created.

When inflation threatened, the reserve banks could raise the rediscount rate, discouraging borrowing and thus reducing the amount of money in circulation. In bad times it could lower the rate, making it easier to borrow and injecting new dollars into the economy. Much remained to be learned about the proper management of the money supply, but the nation finally had a flexible yet safe currency.

In 1914 Congress passed two important laws affecting corporations. One created the Federal Trade Commission to replace Roosevelt's Bureau of Corporations. In addition to investigating corporations and publishing reports, this nonpartisan board could issue cease and desist orders against "unfair" trade practices brought to light through its research. The law did not define the term *unfair*, and the commission's rulings could be taken on appeal to the federal courts, but the FTC was nonetheless a powerful instrument for protecting the public against the trusts.

The second measure, the Clayton Antitrust Act, made certain specific business practices illegal, including price discrimination that tended to foster monopoly; "tying" agreements, which forbade retailers from handling the products of a firm's competitors; and the creation of interlocking directorates as a means of controlling competing companies. The act exempted labor unions and agricultural organizations from the antitrust laws and curtailed the use of injunctions in labor disputes. The officers of corporations could be held individually responsible if their companies violated the antitrust laws.

The Democrats controlled both houses of Congress for the first time since 1890 and were eager to make a good record, but Wilson's imaginative and aggressive use of presidential power was decisive. He called the legislators into special session in April 1913 and appeared before them to lay out his program; he was the first president to address Congress in person since John Adams. Then he

followed the course of administration bills closely. He had a private telephone line installed between the Capitol and the White House. Administration representatives haunted the cloakrooms and lobbies of both houses. Cooperative congressmen began to receive notes of praise and encouragement, recalcitrant ones stern demands for support, often pecked out on the president's own portable typewriter. When lobbyists tried to frustrate his plans for tariff reform by bringing pressure to bear on key senators, he made a dramatic appeal to the people. "The public ought to know the extraordinary exertions being made by the lobby in Washington," he told reporters. "Only public opinion can check and destroy it." The voters responded so strongly that the Senate passed the tariff bill substantially as Wilson desired it.

Wilson explained his success by saying, only half humorously, that running the government was child's play for anyone who had managed the faculty of a university. Responsible party government was his objective; he expected individual Democrats to support the decisions of the party majority, and his idealism never prevented him from awarding the spoils of office to city bosses and conservative congressmen, so long as they supported his program. Nor did his career as a political theorist make him rigid and doctrinaire. In practice the differences between his New Freedom and Roosevelt's New Nationalism tended to disappear. The Underwood Tariff and the Clayton Antitrust Act fitted the philosophy Wilson had expounded during the campaign, but the Federal Trade Commission represented a step toward the kind of regulated economy that Roosevelt advocated. So did the Federal Reserve system.

There were limits to Wilson's progressivism, limits imposed partly by his temperament and partly by his philosophy. He objected as strenuously to laws granting special favors to farmers and workers as to those benefiting the tycoons. When a bill was introduced in 1914 making low-interest loans available to farmers, he refused to support it. "It is unwise and unjustifiable to extend the credit of the Government to a single class of the community," he said. He considered the provision exempting unions from the antitrust laws equally unsound. Nor would he push for a federal law prohibiting child labor; such a measure would be unconstitutional, he believed. He also refused to back the constitutional amendment giving the vote to women.

By the end of 1914 the Wilsonian record, on balance, was positive but distinctly limited. The president believed that the major progressive goals had been achieved; he had no plans for further reform. Many other progressives thought that a great deal more remained to be done.

The Progressives and Minority Rights

On one important issue, race relations, Wilson was distinctly reactionary. With a mere handful of exceptions, the progressives exhibited strong prejudices against nonwhite people and against certain categories of whites as well. Many were as unsympathetic to immigrants from Asia and eastern and southern Europe as any of the "conservative" opponents of immigration in the 1880s and 1890s. The Gentlemen's Agreement excluding Japanese immigrants was reached in 1907 at the height of the progressive movement. In the same year, Congress appointed a commission headed by Senator William Dillingham of Vermont to study the immigration question. The Dillingham Commission labored for more than two years and brought forth a 41-volume report that led in 1913 to a bill restricting the number of newcomers to be admitted and reducing especially the influx from eastern and southern Europe. Only the outbreak of war in Europe in 1914, which cut immigration to a trickle, prevented the passage of this measure.

American Indians were also affected by the progressives' racial attitudes. Where the sponsors of the Dawes Act had assumed that Indians were inherently capable of adopting the ways of "civilized" people, in the progressive period the tendency was to write Indians off as fundamentally inferior and to assume that they would make second-class citizens at best. Francis Leupp, Theodore Roosevelt's commissioner of Indian affairs, put it this way in a 1905 report: "If nature has set a different physical stamp upon different races of men it is fair to assume that the variation . . . is manifested in mental and moral traits as well. . . . Nothing is gained by trying to undo nature's work." A leading muckraker, Ray Stannard Baker, who was far more sympathetic to blacks than most progressives, dismissed Indians as pathetic beings, "eating, sleeping, idling, with no more thought of the future than a white man's child."

In 1902 Congress passed the Dead Indian Land Act, which made it easier for Indians to sell allotments that they had inherited, and in 1906 another law further relaxed restrictions on land sales. Efforts to improve the education of Indian children continued, but most progressives assumed that only vocational training would benefit them. Theodore Roosevelt knew from his experiences as a rancher in Dakota Territory that Indians could be as energetic and capable as whites, but he considered these "exceptional." As for the rest, it would be many generations before they could be expected to "move forward" enough to become "ordinary citizens," Roosevelt believed. "The Indian stirred little controversy among the leading political warriors of the progressive era," a recent scholar writes.

To say that blacks did not fare well at the hands of progressives would be a gross understatement. Populist efforts to unite white and black farmers in the southern states had led to the imposition of further repressive measures. Segregation became more rigid, white opposition to black voting more monolithic. In 1900 the body of a Mississippi black was dug up by order of the state legislature and reburied in a segregated cemetery; in Virginia in 1902 the daughter of Robert E. Lee was arrested for riding in the black section of a railroad car. "Insult is being added to injury continually," a black journalist in Alabama complained. "Have those in power forgotten that there is a God?"

Many progressive women, still smarting from the insult to their sex entailed in the Fourteenth and Fifteenth amendments and eager to attract southern support for their campaign for the vote, adopted racist arguments. They contrasted the supposed corruption and incompetence of black voters with their own "purity" and intelligence. Southern progressives of both sexes argued that disfranchising blacks would reduce corruption by removing from unscrupulous white politicians the temptation to purchase black votes!

The typical southern attitude toward the education of blacks was summed up in a folk proverb: "When you educate a Negro, you spoil a good field hand." In 1910, only about 8,000 black children in the entire South were attending high schools. Despite the almost total suppression of black rights, lynchings continued to occur; between 1900 and 1914 more than 1,100 blacks were murdered by mobs, most (but not all) in the southern states. In the rare cases where local prosecutors brought the lynchers to trial, juries almost without exception brought in verdicts of not guilty.

Booker T. Washington was shaken by this trend, but he could find no way to combat it. The times were passing him by. He appealed to his white southern "friends" for help but got nowhere. Increasingly he talked about the virtues of rural life, the evils of big cities, and the uselessness of higher education for black people. By the turn of the century a number of young, well-educated blacks, most of them northerners, were breaking away from his accommodationist leadership.

Black Militancy

Wlliam E. B. Du Bois was the most prominent of the militants. Du Bois was born in Great Barrington, Massachusetts, in 1868. His father, a restless wanderer of Negro and French Huguenot stock, abandoned the family, and young William grew up on the edge of poverty. Neither accepted nor openly rejected by the overwhelmingly white community, he devoted himself to his studies, showing such brilliance that his future education was assured by scholarships: to Fisk University, then to Harvard, then to the University of Berlin. In 1895 Du Bois became the first American black to earn a Ph.D. in history from Harvard; his dissertation, *The Suppression of the African Slave Trade* (1896), remains a standard reference.

Personal success and "acceptance" by whites did not make the proud and sensitive Du Bois complacent. Outraged by white racism and the willingness of many blacks to settle for second-class citizenship, he set out to make American blacks proud of their color—"Beauty is black," he said—and of their African origins and culture.

Like Washington, Du Bois wanted blacks to lift themselves by their own bootstraps. They must establish their own businesses, run their own newspapers and colleges, write their own literature; they must preserve their identity rather than seek to amalgamate themselves into a society that offered them only crumbs and contempt. At first he cooperated with Washington, but in 1903, in an essay, "Of Mr. Booker T. Washington and Others," he subjected Washington's "attitude of adjustment and submission" to polite but searching criticism. Washington had asked blacks to give up political power, civil rights, and the hope of higher education, not realizing that "voting is necessary to modern manhood, that . . . discrimination is barbarism, and that black boys need education as well as white boys." Washington "apologizes for injustice," Du Bois charged. "He belittles the emasculating effects of caste distinctions, and opposes the higher training and ambitions of our brightest minds." Du Bois deemed this totally wrong. "The way for a people to gain their reasonable rights is not by voluntarily throwing them away."

Du Bois was not an uncritical admirer of the ordinary American black. He believed that "immorality, crime, and laziness" were common vices. Quite properly, he blamed the weaknesses of blacks on the treatment afforded them by whites, but his approach to the solution of racial problems was frankly elitist. "The Negro race," he wrote, "is going to be saved by its exceptional men," what he called the "talented tenth" of the black population. After describing in vivid detail how white mistreatment had corrupted his people, Du Bois added loftily: "A saving remnant continually survives and persists, continually aspires, continually shows itself in thrift and ability and character." As the historian Ben-

A striking likeness of W. E. B. Du Bois drawn by Winold Reiss when Du Bois was in his fifties.

jamin Quarles has said, Du Bois was "uncomfortable in the presence of the rank and file."

Whatever his prejudices, Du Bois exposed both the weaknesses of Washington's strategy and the callousness of white American attitudes. Accommodation was not working. Washington was praised, even lionized by prominent southern whites, yet when Theodore Roosevelt invited him to a meal at the White House, they exploded with indignation, and Roosevelt, although not personally prejudiced, meekly backtracked, never repeating his "mistake." He defended his record by saying, "I have stood as valiantly for the rights of the negro as any president since Lincoln," which, sad to relate, was true enough.

Not mere impatience but despair led Du Bois and a few like-minded blacks to meet at Niagara Falls in July 1905 and to issue a stirring list of demands: the unrestricted right to vote, an end to every kind of segregation, equality of economic opportunity, higher education for the talented, equal justice in the courts, and an end to trade-union discrimination. This Niagara Movement did not attract mass support, but it did stir the consciences of some whites, many of them the descendants of abolitionists, who were also becoming disenchanted by the failure of accommodation to provide blacks with real opportunity.

In 1909, the centennial of the birth of Abraham Lincoln, a group of these liberals, including the newspaperman Oswald Garrison Villard (grandson of William Lloyd Garrison), the social worker Jane Addams, the philosopher John Dewey, and the novelist William Dean Howells, founded the National Association for the Advancement of Colored People (NAACP). The organization was dedicated to the eradication of racial discrimination. Its leadership was predominantly white in the early years, but Du Bois became a national officer and the editor of its journal, *The Crisis*.

A turning point had been reached. After 1909 virtually every important leader, white and black alike, rejected the Washington approach. More and more, blacks turned to the study of their past in an effort to stimulate pride in their heritage. In 1915 Carter G. Woodson founded the Association for the Study of Negro Life and History; the following year he began editing the *Journal of Negro History*, which became the major organ for the publishing of scholarly studies on the subject.

This militancy produced few results in the Pro-gressive Era. Theodore Roosevelt behaved no differently from earlier Republican presidents; he courted blacks when he thought it advantageous, turned his back when he did not. When he ran for president on the Progressive ticket in 1912, he pursued a "lily-white" policy, hoping to break the Democrats' monopoly in the South. By trusting in "(white) men of justice and of vision," Roosevelt argued in the face of decades of experience to the contrary, "the colored men of the South will ultimately get justice."

The southern-born Wilson was actively antipathetic to blacks. During the 1912 campaign he appealed to them for support and promised to "assist in advancing the interest of their race" in every possible way. Once elected, he refused even to appoint a privately financed commission to study the race problem. Southerners dominated his administration and Congress; as a result, blacks were further degraded. No less than 35 blacks in the Atlanta post office lost their jobs. In Washington employees in many government offices were rigidly segregated, and those who objected were summarily discharged.

These actions stirred such a storm that Wilson backtracked a little. But he never abandoned his belief that segregation was in the best interests of both races. "Wilson . . . promised a 'new freedom,' " one newspaperman complained. "On the contrary we are given a stone instead of a loaf of bread." Even Booker T. Washington admitted that his people were more "discouraged and bitter" than at any time in his memory.

Du Bois, who had supported Wilson in 1912, attacked administration policy in *The Crisis*. In November 1914 the militant editor of the *Boston Guardian*, William Monroe Trotter, a classmate of Du Bois at Harvard and a far more caustic critic of the Washington approach, led a delegation to the White House to protest the segregation policy of the government. When Wilson accused him of blackmail, Trotter lost his temper, and an ugly confrontation resulted. The mood of black leaders had changed completely.

By this time the Great War had broken out in Europe. Soon its effects would be felt by every American, by blacks perhaps more than by any other group. In November 1915, a year almost to the day after Trotter's clash with Wilson, Booker T. Washington died. One era had ended; a new one was beginning.

Milestones

1890 National American Women's Suffrage
Association founded
1900 Robert La Follette elected governor of
Wisconsin
1901 President McKinley assassinated
1902 National coal strike
Oregon adopts initiative system for
proposing legislation
1904 *Northern Securities* case revives the
Sherman Antitrust Act
National Child Labor Committee
established
1905 Industrial Workers of the World
founded
1906 Hepburn Act strengthens Interstate
Commerce Commission
Upton Sinclair, *The Jungle*
1907 U.S. Steel absorbs the Tennessee Coal
and Iron Company
1908 Theodore Roosevelt convenes the
National Conservation Conference
Muller v. *Oregon* upholds the law

limiting the working hours of
women
1909 Herbert Croly, *The Promise of American
Life*
National Association for the
Advancement of Colored People
founded
1910 Ballinger-Pinchot affair
1911 Roosevelt's New Nationalism speech
1912 Roosevelt runs for president on the
Progressive party ticket
1913 Sixteenth Amendment authorizes
federal income taxes
Seventeenth Amendment provides for
direct election of U.S. senators
Underwood Tariff
Federal Reserve Act
1914 Federal Trade Commission Act
Clayton Antitrust Act
1920 Nineteenth Amendment guarantees
women the right to vote

SUPPLEMENTARY READING

Titles marked with an asterisk have been published in paperback.

The political history of the Progressive Era is surveyed in G. E. Mowry, **The Era of Theodore Roosevelt*** (1958), and A. S. Link, **Woodrow Wilson and the Progressive Era*** (1954). Important interpretations of progressivism include Richard Hofstadter, **The Age of Reform*** (1955), Gabriel Kolko, **The Triumph of Conservatism*** (1963), J. M. Cooper, Jr., **The Warrior and the Priest: Theodore Roosevelt and Woodrow Wilson** (1983), D. W. Grantham, **Southern Progressivism** (1983), and R. H. Wiebe, **Businessmen and Reform*** (1962).

The role of muckraking journalism is considered in D. M. Chalmers, **The Social and Political Ideas of the Muckrakers*** (1964), and Peter Lyon, **Success Story: The Life and Times of S. S. McClure** (1963).

On the radicals, see Leslie Fishbein, **Rebels in Bohemia** (1982), Thomas Bender, **New York Intellectuals** (1987), H. F. May, **The End of American Innocence*** (1964), and N. G. Hale, **Freud and the Americans** (1971).

State and local progressivism are considered in G. E. Mowry, **The California Progressives*** (1951), R. S. Max-

well, **La Follette and the Rise of Progressivism in Wisconsin** (1956), H. L. Warner, **Progressivism in Ohio** (1964), Sheldon Hackney, **Populism to Progressivism in Alabama** (1969), Z. L. Miller, **Boss Cox's Cincinnati*** (1968), J. D. Buenker, **Urban Liberalism and Progressive Reform** (1973), G. B. Tindall, **The Emergence of the New South** (1967), and C. V. Woodward, **Origins of the New South*** (1951). The struggle for women's suffrage is described in A.S. Kraditor, **The Ideas of the Woman Suffrage Movement*** (1981). See also W. L. O'Neill, **Everyone Was Brave: The Rise and Fall of Feminism in America*** (1969), and C. N. Degler, **At Odds** (1980). Books treating special aspects of progressivism include A. F. Davis, **Spearheads for Reform: The Social Settlements and the Progressive Movement*** (1967), Melvin Dubofsky, **When Workers Organize** (1968), Samuel Haber, **Efficiency and Uplift** (1964), James Weinstein, **The Corporate Ideal and the Liberal State** (1981), J. H. Timberlake, **Prohibition and the Progressive Movement*** (1963), Albro Martin, **Enterprise Denied: Origins** of the Decline of American Railroads (1971), Ruth Rosen, **The Lost Sisterhood** (1982), and W. L. O'Neill, **Divorce in the Progressive Era** (1967). On blacks, see C. F. Kellogg, **NAACP: A History of the National Association for the Advancement of Colored People*** (1970), E. M. Rudwick, **W. E. B. Du Bois*** (1960), and J. T. Kirby, **Darkness at the Dawning: Race and Reform in the Progressive South** (1972). On the treatment of Indians, consult F. E. Hoxie, **A Final Promise: The Campaign to Assimilate the Indians** (1984).

W. H. Harbaugh, **Power and Responsibility*** (1961), is the soundest scholarly treatment of Roosevelt's career. G. W. Chessman, **Theodore Roosevelt and the Politics of Power*** (1969), is a good brief account, and J. M. Blum, **The Republican Roosevelt*** (1954), is a brilliant analysis

of his political philosophy and his management of the presidency.

On Taft, see D. F. Anderson, **William Howard Taft: A Conservative's Conception of the Presidency** (1973), and P. E. Coletta, **The Presidency of William Howard Taft** (1973). The breakup of the Republican party and the history of the Progressive party are discussed in J. A. Garraty, **Right-hand Man: The Life of George W. Perkins** (1960).

The standard biography of Wilson, still incomplete, is A. S. Link, **Wilson** (1947–1965). Two brief biographies are J. M. Blum, **Woodrow Wilson and the Politics of Morality*** (1956), and J. A. Garraty, **Woodrow Wilson*** (1956).

Women in the Workplace

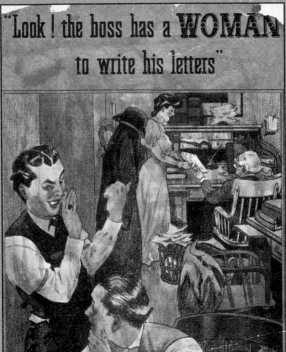

"Look! the boss has a WOMAN to write his letters"

It used to be argued that the "liberation" of American women occurred in the 1920s with the emergence of the "flapper," with her short skirts, bobbed hair, and fondness for cigarettes, alcohol, and other forms of what was quaintly described as "making whoopee." The flapper phenomenon was explained by referring to the disillusionment that affected people after the World War, and to the passage of the women's suffrage amendment, which, by giving women political power, was thought to have opened the way for the achievement of full equality.

It is now clear that flappers were the exception rather than the rule in the 1920s, that they were by no means as liberated as they and others thought, and that, in any case, the struggle for true equality of the sexes was far from over. Furthermore, much more significant changes in the lives of women were taking place at that time than those associated with what the flappers were doing, or even with the right to vote.

None of these changes was more important than the fact that increasing numbers of women were holding down full-time jobs. The trend toward taking up work outside the home began to accelerate in the prewar years and has, of course, continued into the present day. But what happened to working women in the 1920s marked a kind of turning point.

In the 1890s, a new female secretary in an office might be the butt of wisecracks from the male help (see opposite page), but more and more educated middle-class women were venturing into the world of work outside the home. This 1908 visiting nurse, climbing over the tenement rooftops of New York's Lower East Side on her way to see patients who were too sick to visit a clinic, was perhaps more venturesome than most.

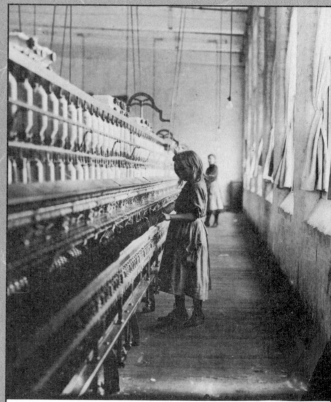

Women had, of course, worked in mills and factories and as domestics for a very long time. Working children, like the little girl tending textile machinery above, were common. Their plight was a serious concern to muckraking writers and photographers like Lewis Hine. Black women (left) often found it impossible even to get industrial jobs, and had to settle for domestic work as maids and cooks.

Many immigrant women worked in garment industry sweatshops. In 1911, the tragic fire at the Triangle Shirtwaist Co., which caused workers to leap to their deaths (top), gave impetus to labor organizations such as Women's Trade Union League and the International Ladies' Garment Workers Union (ILGWU). The Women's League sponsored demonstrations (note the sign on the right of the lower photo: "Do You Want Fire Protection? Organize") and pushed for better pay and conditions for women workers.

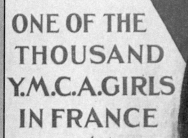

ONE OF THE
THOUSAND
Y.M.C.A.GIRLS
IN FRANCE

United
War Work
Campaign
Nov.11th to 18th

American entry into World War I brought great changes to the lives of women workers. A few went to France with YMCA units and other service organizations that ran field kitchens, hospitals, and recreation programs for American troops (above). Even privileged young women such as the Vassar College group at left took cooking lessons in a patriotic spirit, to help on the home front.

Other women took jobs formerly held by men who had
joined the army. For example,
they served as welders in munitions plants (bottom), as
streetcar conductors (lower
left), and as car cleaners on
the Northern Pacific Railroad
(right).

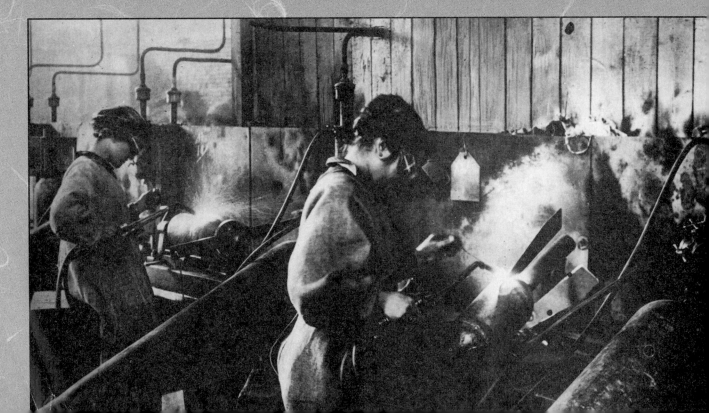

Reginald Marsh's painting Subway, 14th St. *(1930) catches the turbulent, competitive spirit of rush-hour New York in which women were no longer "protected," in the Victorian sense, from the realities of working life.*

Woodrow Wilson and the Great War

It is a fearful thing to lead this great people into war, into the most terrible and disastrous of all wars, civilization itself seeming to be in the balance. But the right is more precious than peace, and we shall fight for the things which we have always carried nearest our hearts— for democracy.

WOODROW WILSON, *War Message to Congress, April 2, 1917*

oodrow Wilson's approach to foreign relations was well intentioned and idealistic but somewhat confused. He knew that the United States had no wish to injure any foreign state and assumed that all nations would recognize this fact and cooperate. He wanted to help other countries, especially the republics of Latin America, achieve stable democratic governments and improve the living conditions of their people. Imperialism was, in his eyes, immoral. At the same time, he felt obliged to sustain and protect American interests abroad. The maintenance of the Open Door in China and the completion of the Panama Canal were as important to him as they had been to Theodore Roosevelt.

Wilson's view of nations with traditions different from those of the United States was shortsighted and provincial. His attitude resembled that of 19th-century Christian missionaries: He wanted to spread the gospel of American democracy, to lift and enlighten the unfortunate and the ignorant—but in his own way. "I am going to teach the South American republics to elect good men!" he told one British diplomat.

Missionary Diplomacy

Wilson set out to raise the moral tone of American foreign policy by denouncing dollar diplomacy. Encouraging bankers to lend money to countries like China, he said, implied the possibility of "forcible interference" if the loans were not repaid, and that would be "obnoxious to the principles upon which the government of our people rests." To seek special economic concessions in Latin America was "unfair" and "degrading." The United States would deal with Latin American nations "upon terms of equality and honor."

In certain small matters Wilson succeeded in conducting American diplomacy on this idealistic basis. He withdrew the government's support of the international consortium that was arranging a loan to develop Chinese railroads, and American bankers pulled out. When the Japanese attempted, in the notorious Twenty-one Demands (1915), to reduce China almost to the status of a Japanese protectorate, he persuaded them to modify their conditions slightly. Congress had passed a law in 1912 exempting American coastal shipping from the payment of tolls on the Panama Canal in spite of a provision in the Hay-Pauncefote Treaty with Great Britain guaranteeing that the canal would be available to the vessels of all nations "on terms of entire equality." Wilson insisted that Congress repeal the law. He also permitted Secretary of State William Jennings Bryan to negotiate conciliation treaties with 21 nations. The distinctive feature of these agreements was the provision for a "cooling off" period of one year, during which signatories agreed, in the event of a dispute, not to engage in hostilities.

Where more vital interests were concerned, Wilson sometimes failed to live up to his promises. Because of the strategic importance of the Panama Canal, he was unwilling to tolerate "unrest" anywhere in the Caribbean. Within months of his inauguration he was pursuing the same tactics that circumstances had forced on Roosevelt and Taft. The Bryan-Chamorro Treaty of 1914, which gave the United States an option to build a canal across Nicaragua, made that country virtually an American protectorate and served to maintain in power an unpopular dictator, Adolfo Díaz.

A much more serious example of missionary diplomacy occurred in Mexico. In 1911 a liberal coalition overthrew the dictator Porfirio Díaz, who had been exploiting the resources and people of Mexico for the benefit of a small class of wealthy landowners, clerics, and military men since the 1870s. Francisco Madero became president.

Madero, a wealthy landowner apparently influenced by the progressive movement in the United States, was committed to economic reform and the drafting of a democratic constitution. Unfortunately, he was weak-willed and a terrible administrator. Conditions in Mexico deteriorated rapidly, and less than a month before Wilson's inauguration, one of Madero's generals, Victoriano Huerta, seized power and had his former chief murdered. Huerta was an unabashed reactionary, but he was committed to maintaining the stability that foreign investors desired. Most of the European powers promptly recognized his government.

The American ambassador, together with important American financial and business interests in Mexico and in the United States, urged Wilson to do so too, but he refused. His sympathies were all with the government of Madero, whose murder had horrified him. "I will not recognize a government of butchers," he said. This was unconventional; nations do not ordinarily consider the means by which a foreign regime has come to power before deciding to establish diplomatic relations.

Wilson brought enormous pressure to bear against Huerta. He dragooned the British into withdrawing recognition. He dickered with other Mexican factions. He demanded that Huerta hold free elections as the price of American mediation in the continuing civil war. Huerta would not yield an inch. Indeed, he drew strength from Wilson's effort to oust him, for even his enemies resented American interference in Mexican affairs. Frustration, added to his moral outrage, weakened Wilson's judgment. He subordinated his wish to let the Mexicans solve their own problems to his desire to destroy Huerta.

The tense situation exploded in April 1914, when a small party of American sailors was arrested in the port of Tampico, Mexico. When the Mexican government refused to supply the apology demanded by the sailors' commander, Wilson fastened on the affair as an excuse for sending troops into Mexico.

The invasion took place at Veracruz, whence Winfield Scott had launched the assault on Mexico City in 1847. Instead of meekly surrendering the city, the Mexicans resisted tenaciously, suffering

Francisco "Pancho" Villa, Mexican insurrectionary, border bandit, and thorn in President Wilson's side, in 1920, after his capture by the Mexican Army.

400 casualties before falling back. This bloodshed caused dismay throughout Latin America and failed to unseat Huerta.

At this point, Argentina, Brazil, and Chile offered to mediate the dispute. Wilson accepted, Huerta also agreed, and the conferees met at Niagara Falls, Ontario, in May. Although no settlement was reached, Huerta, hard pressed by Mexican opponents, abdicated. On August 20, 1914, General Venustiano Carranza entered Mexico City in triumph.

Carranza favored representative government, but he proved scarcely more successful than the tyrant Huerta in controlling the country. One of his own generals, Francisco "Pancho" Villa, rose against him and seized control of Mexico City.

Wilson now made a monumental blunder. Villa professed to be willing to cooperate with the United States, and Wilson, taking him at his word, gave him his support. However, Villa was little more than an ambitious bandit with no other objective than personal power. Carranza, though no radical, was committed to social reform. Fighting back, he drove the Villistas into the northern provinces.

Wilson finally realized the extent of Carranza's influence in Mexico, and in October 1915 he recognized the Carranza government. Still his Mexican troubles were not over. Early in 1916 Villa, seeking to undermine Carranza by forcing the United States to intervene, stopped a train in northern Mexico and killed 16 American passengers in cold blood. Then he crossed into New Mexico and burned the town of Columbus, killing 19. Having learned his lesson, Wilson would have preferred to bear even this assault in silence, but public opinion forced him to send American troops under General John J. Pershing across the border in pursuit of Villa.

Villa proved impossible to catch. Cleverly, he drew Pershing deeper and deeper into Mexico, and this alarmed Carranza, who insisted that the Americans withdraw. Several clashes occurred between Pershing's men and Mexican regulars, and for a brief period in June 1916 war seemed imminent. Wilson now acted bravely and wisely. Early in 1917 he recalled Pershing's force, leaving the Mexicans to work out their own destiny.

Missionary diplomacy in Mexico had produced mixed but in the long run beneficial results. By opposing Huerta, Wilson had surrendered to his prejudices, yet he had also helped the real revolutionaries even though they opposed his acts. His bungling bred anti-Americanism in Mexico, but by his later restraint in the face of stinging provocations, he permitted the constitutionalists to consolidate their power.

Outbreak of the Great War

On June 28, 1914, in the Austro-Hungarian provincial capital of Sarajevo, Gavrilo Princip, a young student, assassinated the Archduke Franz Ferdinand, heir to the imperial throne. Princip was a member of the Black Hand, a Serbian terrorist organization. He was seeking to further the cause of Serbian nationalism. Instead his rash act precipitated a general European war. Within little more than a month, following a complex series of diplomatic challenges and responses, two great coalitions, the Central Powers (chiefly Germany and Aus-

tria-Hungary) and the Allied Powers (chiefly Great Britain, France, and Russia), were locked in a brutal struggle that brought one era in world history to a close and inaugurated another.

The outbreak of what contemporaries were soon to call the Great War caught Americans psychologically unprepared; few understood the significance of what had happened. President Wilson promptly issued a proclamation of neutrality and asked the nation to be "impartial in thought." Of course, no one, not even the president, had the superhuman self-control that this request called for, but the almost unanimous reaction of Americans, aside from dismay, was that the conflict did not concern them. They were wrong, for this was a world war, and Americans were sure to be affected by its outcome.

There were good reasons, aside from a failure to understand the significance of the struggle, why

Antiwar protesters marching in the May Day parade, 1916, when the war in Europe had been under way for 20 months and the entry of the United States was still opposed by most politicians.

the United States sought to remain neutral. Over a third of its 92 million inhabitants were either European-born or the children of European immigrants. Sentimental ties bound them to the lands of their ancestors. American involvement would create new internal stresses in a society already strained by the task of assimilating so many diverse groups. War was also an affront to the prevailing progressive spirit, which assumed that human beings were reasonable, high-minded, and capable of settling disputes peaceably. Along with the traditional American fear of entanglement in European affairs, these were ample reasons for remaining aloof.

Though most Americans hoped to keep out of the war, nearly everyone was partial to one side or the other. People of German or Austrian descent, about 8 million in number, and the nation's 4.5 million Irish-Americans, motivated chiefly by hatred of the British, sympathized with the Central Powers. The majority of the people, however, influenced by bonds of language and culture, preferred an Allied victory, and when the Germans launched a mighty assault across neutral Belgium in an effort to outflank the French armies, this unprovoked attack on a tiny nation whose neutrality the Germans had previously agreed to respect caused a great deal of anti-German feeling.

As the war progressed, the Allies cleverly exploited American prejudices by such devices as publishing exaggerated tales of German atrocities against Belgian civilians. A supposedly impartial study of these charges by the widely respected James Bryce, author of *The American Commonwealth*, portrayed the Germans as ruthless barbarians. The Germans also conducted a propaganda campaign in the United States, but they labored under severe handicaps and won few converts.

Freedom of the Seas

Propaganda did not basically alter American attitudes; far more important were questions rising out of trade and commerce. Under international law, neutrals could trade freely with any belligerent. Americans were prepared to do so, but because the British fleet dominated the North Atlantic, they could not. The situation was similar to the one that had prevailed during the Napoleonic wars. The British declared nearly all commodities, even food-

stuffs, to be contraband of war. They set limits on exports to neutral nations such as Denmark and the Netherlands so that those countries could not transship supplies to Germany. They forced neutral merchant ships into Allied ports in order to search them for goods headed for the enemy. Many cargoes were confiscated, often without payment. American firms that traded with the Central Powers were "blacklisted," which meant that no British subject could deal with them. When these policies caused protests in America, the British answered that in a battle for survival, they dared not adhere to old-fashioned rules of international law.

Had the United States insisted that Great Britain abandon these "illegal" practices, as the Germans demanded, no doubt it could have had its way. The British foreign secretary, Sir Edward Grey, later admitted: "The ill-will of the United States meant certain defeat. The object of diplomacy, therefore, was to secure the maximum of blockade that could be enforced without a rupture with the United States." It is ironic that an embargo, which failed so ignominiously in Jefferson's day, would have been almost instantly effective if applied at any time after 1914, for American supplies were vital to the Allies.

Though British tactics frequently exasperated Wilson, he never considered taking such a drastic step. He faced a dilemma. To allow the British to make the rules meant siding against the Central Powers. Yet to insist on the old rules (which had never been obeyed in wartime) meant siding against the Allies because that would have deprived them of much of the value of their naval superiority. Nothing the United States might do would be truly impartial.

Wilson's own sentiments made it doubly difficult for him to object strenuously to British practices. No American admired British institutions and culture more extravagantly. "Everything I love most in the world is at stake," he confessed privately to the British ambassador. A German victory "would be fatal to our form of Government and American ideals."

In any event, the immense expansion of American trade with the Allies made an embargo unthinkable. While commerce with the Central Powers fell to a trickle, that with the Allies soared from $825 million in 1914 to over $3.2 billion in 1916. An attempt to limit this commerce would have raised a storm; to have eliminated it would have

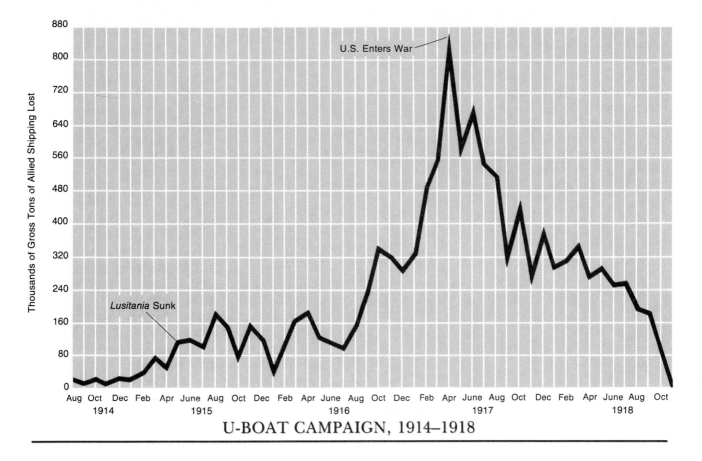

U-BOAT CAMPAIGN, 1914–1918

caused a catastrophe. Munitions makers and other businessmen did not want the United States to enter the war. Neutrality suited their purposes admirably.

Britain and France soon exhausted their ready cash and by early 1917 had borrowed well over $2 billion. Although these loans violated no principle of international law, they fastened the United States more closely to the Allies' cause.

During the first months of the Great War, the Germans were not especially concerned about neutral trade or American goods because they expected to crush the Allied armies quickly. When their first swift thrust into France was blunted along the Marne River and the war became a bloody stalemate, they began to challenge the Allies' control of the seas. Unwilling to risk their battleships and cruisers against the much larger British fleet, they resorted to a new weapon, the submarine, commonly known as the U-boat (for *Unterseeboot*).

German submarines played a role in World War I not unlike that of American privateers in the Rev-

olution and the War of 1812: They ranged the seas stealthily in search of merchant ships. However, submarines could not operate under the ordinary rules of war, which required that a raider stop its prey, examine its papers and cargo, and give the crew and passengers time to get off in lifeboats before sending it to the bottom. When surfaced, U-boats were vulnerable to the deck guns that many merchant ships carried; they could even be sunk by ramming, once they had stopped and put out a boarding party. Therefore, they commonly launched their torpedoes from below the surface without warning. The result was often a heavy loss of life on the torpedoed ships.

In February 1915 the Germans declared the waters surrounding the British Isles a zone of war and announced that they would sink without warning all enemy merchant ships encountered in the area. Since Allied vessels sometimes flew neutral flags to disguise their identity, neutral ships entering the zone would do so at their own risk. This statement was largely bluff, for the Germans had only a handful of submarines at sea; but they were feverishly building more.

Wilson—perhaps too hurriedly, considering the importance of the question—warned the Germans that he would hold them to "strict accountability" for any loss of American life or property resulting from violations of "acknowledged (neutral) rights on the high seas." He did not distinguish clearly between losses incurred through the destruction of *American* ships and those resulting from the sinking

Three weeks before the Lusitania *was torpedoed, this notice appeared in the classified sections of Washington newspapers.*

NOTICE!

TRAVELLERS intending to embark on the Atlantic voyage are reminded that a state of war exists between Germany and her allies and Great Britain and her allies; that the zone of war includes the waters adjacent to the British Isles; that, in accordance with formal notice given by the Imperial German Government, vessels flying the flag of Great Britain, or of any of her allies, are liable to destruction in those waters and that travellers sailing in the war zone on ships of Great Britain or her allies do so at their own risk.

IMPERIAL GERMAN EMBASSY
WASHINGTON, D. C., APRIL 22, 1915.

of other vessels. If he meant to hold the Germans responsible for injuries to Americans on *belligerent* vessels, he was changing international law as arbitrarily as the Germans were. Secretary of State Bryan, who opposed Wilson vigorously on this point, stood on sound legal ground when he said, "A ship carrying contraband should not rely upon passengers to protect her from attack—it would be like putting women and children in front of an army."

Correct or not, Wilson's position reflected the attitude of most Americans. It seemed barbaric to them that defenseless civilians should be killed without warning, and they refused to surrender their "rights" as neutrals to cross the North Atlantic on any ship they wished. The depth of their feeling was demonstrated when, on May 7, 1915, the submarine *U-20* sank the British liner *Lusitania* off the Irish coast. Nearly 1,200 persons, including 128 Americans, lost their lives in this catastrophe.

The torpedoing of the *Lusitania* caused as profound and emotional a reaction in the United States as that following the destruction of the *Maine* in Havana harbor. Wilson, like McKinley in 1898, was shocked, but he kept his head. He demanded that Germany disavow the sinking, indemnify the victims, and promise to stop attacking passenger vessels. When the Germans quibbled about these points, he responded with further diplomatic correspondence rather than with an ultimatum.

In one sense this was sound policy. The Germans pointed out that they had published warnings in American newspapers saying they considered the *Lusitania* subject to attack, that the liner was carrying munitions, and that on past voyages it had flown the American flag as a *ruse de guerre*. It would have been difficult politically for the German government to have backed down before an American ultimatum; however, after dragging the controversy out for nearly a year, it apologized and agreed to pay an indemnity. After the torpedoing of the French channel steamer *Sussex* in March 1916 had produced another stiff American protest, the Germans at last promised, in the *Sussex* pledge, to stop sinking merchant ships without warning.

Had Wilson forced a showdown in 1915, he would have alienated a large segment of American opinion. Even his relatively mild notes resulted in the resignation of Secretary of State Bryan, who believed it unneutral to treat German violations of international law differently from Allied violations—and Bryan reflected the feelings of thousands.*

Yet if Wilson had sought a declaration of war over the *Lusitania*, a majority of Congress and the country would probably have gone along, and in that event the dreadful carnage in Europe would have ended much sooner. This is the reasoning of hindsight, yet such a policy would have been logical, given Wilson's assumptions about the justice of the Allied cause and America's stake in an Allied victory.

In November 1915 Wilson at last began to press for increased military and naval expenditures. Nevertheless, he continued to vacillate. He dispatched a sharp note protesting Allied blacklisting of American firms, and to his confidant, Colonel Edward M. House, he called the British "poor boobs."

The Election of 1916

Part of Wilson's confusion in 1916 resulted from the political difficulties he faced in his fight for reelection. He had won the presidency in 1912 only because the Republican party had split in two. Now Theodore Roosevelt, the chief defector, had become so incensed by Wilson's refusal to commit the United States to the Allied cause that he was ready to support almost any Republican in order to guarantee the president's defeat. At the same time, many progressives were complaining about Wilson's unwillingness to work for further domestic reforms. Unless he could find additional support, he seemed likely to be defeated.

He attacked the problem by wooing the progressives. In January 1916 he appointed Louis D. Brandeis to the Supreme Court. In addition to being an advanced progressive, Brandeis was Jewish, the first American of that religion appointed to the Court. Wilson's action won him many friends among people who favored fair treatment for minority groups. In July he bid for the farm vote by signing the Farm Loan Act to provide low-cost loans based on agricultural credit. Shortly thereafter, he approved the Keating-Owen Child Labor Act, barring goods manufactured by the labor of children

under 16 from interstate commerce, and a workers' compensation act for federal employees. He persuaded Congress to pass the Adamson Act, establishing an eight-hour day for railroad workers, and he modified his position on the tariff by approving the creation of a tariff commission.

Each of these actions represented a sharp reversal. In 1913 Wilson had considered Brandeis too radical even for a Cabinet post. The new farm, labor, and tariff laws were all examples of the kind of "class legislation" he had refused to countenance in 1913 and 1914. As the historian Arthur S. Link has pointed out, Wilson was putting into effect "almost every important plank of the Progressive platform of 1912." His actions paid spectacular political dividends when Roosevelt refused to run as a Progressive and came out for the Republican nominee, Associate Justice Charles Evans Hughes. The Progressive convention then endorsed Hughes, who had compiled a fine liberal record as governor of New York, but many of Roosevelt's 1912 supporters felt that he had betrayed them and voted for Wilson.

The key issue in the campaign was American policy toward the warring powers. Wilson intended to stress preparedness, which he was now wholeheartedly supporting. However, during the Democratic convention, the delegates shook the hall with cheers whenever orators referred to the president's success in keeping the country out of the war. One spellbinder, referring to the *Sussex* pledge, announced that the president had "wrung from the most militant spirit that ever brooded above a battlefield an acknowledgement of American rights and an agreement to American demands," and the convention erupted in a demonstration that lasted more than 20 minutes. Thus "He Kept Us Out of War" became the Democratic slogan.

To his credit, Wilson made no promises. "I can't keep the country out of war," he told one member of his Cabinet. "Any little German lieutenant can put us into the war at any time by some calculated outrage." His attitude undoubtedly cost him the votes of extremists on both sides, but it won the backing of thousands of moderates.

The combination of progressivism and the peace issue placed the Democrats on substantially equal terms with the Republicans; thereafter, personal factors probably tipped the balance. Hughes was very stiff and an ineffective speaker; he offended a number of important politicians, especially in cru-

---

* Wilson appointed Robert Lansing, counselor of the State Department, to succeed Bryan.

*A Wilson campaign truck offered New York City voters a convenient summary of
the 1916 Democratic platform. The eight-hour-day plank refers to the president's
support of a federal law for railroad workers.*

cial California, where he inadvertently snubbed the popular progressive governor, Hiram Johnson; and he equivocated on a number of issues. Nevertheless, on election night he appeared to have won, having carried nearly all the East and Middle West. Late returns gave Wilson California, however, and with it victory by the narrow margin of 277 to 254 in the electoral college. He led Hughes in the popular vote, 9.1 million to 8.5 million.

The Road to War

Encouraged by his triumph, appalled by the continuing slaughter on the battlefields, fearful that the United States would be dragged into the holocaust, Wilson made one last effort to end the war by ne-

gotiation. In 1915 and again in 1916 he had sent his friend Colonel House on a secret mission to London, Paris, and Berlin to try to mediate among the belligerents. Each had proved fruitless, but, after another long season of bloodshed, perhaps the powers would listen to reason.

Wilson's own feelings were more genuinely neutral than at any other time during the war, for the Germans had stopped sinking merchant ships without warning and the British had irritated him repeatedly by their arbitrary restrictions on neutral trade. He drafted a note to the belligerents asking them to state the terms on which they would agree to lay down their arms. Unless the fighting ended soon, he warned, neutrals and belligerents alike would be so ruined that peace would be meaningless.

When neither side responded encouragingly, Wilson, on January 22, 1917, delivered a moving, prophetic speech aimed, as he admitted, at "the people of the countries now at war" more than at their governments. Any settlement imposed by a victor, he declared, would breed hatred and more wars. There must be a "peace without victory" based on the principles that all nations were equal and that every nationality group should determine its own form of government. He mentioned, albeit vaguely, disarmament and freedom of the seas, and he suggested the creation of some kind of international organization to preserve world peace. "There must be not a balance of power, but a community of power," he said, and he added, "I am speaking for the silent mass of mankind everywhere."

This noble appeal met a tragic fate. The Germans had already decided to renounce the *Sussex* pledge and unleash their submarines against all vessels headed for Allied ports. After February 1, any ship in the war zone would be attacked without warning. Possessing more than 100 U-boats, the German military leaders had convinced themselves that they could starve the British people into submission and reduce the Allied armies to impotence by cutting off the flow of American supplies. The United States would probably declare war, but the Germans believed that they could overwhelm the Allies before the Americans could get to the battlefields in force.

In *Tiger at the Gates*, the French playwright Jean Giraudoux makes Ulysses say, while attempting to stave off what he considers an inevitable war with the Trojans: "The privilege of great men is to view catastrophe from a terrace." This is not always true, but in 1917, after the German military leaders had made their decision, events moved relentlessly, almost uninfluenced by the actors who presumably controlled the fate of the world:

February 3: S.S. *Housatonic* torpedoed. Wilson announces to Congress that he has severed diplomatic relations with Germany. Secretary of State Lansing hands the German ambassador, Count von Bernstorff, his passport. *February 24:* Walter Hines Page, United States ambassador to Great Britain, transmits to the State Department an intercepted German dispatch (the "Zimmermann telegram") revealing that Germany has proposed a secret alliance with Mexico, Mex-

"*U-Boote Heraus!*" ("*U-boats go get 'em!*") A German poster aimed at encouraging their submarine crews.

ico to receive, in the event of war with the United States, "the lost territory in Texas, New Mexico, and Arizona." *February 25:* Cunard liner *Laconia* torpedoed, two American women perish. *February 26:* Wilson asks Congress for authority to arm American merchant ships. *March 1:* Zimmermann Telegram released to the press. *March 4:* President Wilson takes oath of office, beginning his second term. Congress adjourns without passing the armed ship bill, the measure having been filibustered to death by antiwar senators. Wilson characterizes the filibusterers, led by Senator Robert M. La Follette, as "a little group of willful men, representing no opinion but their own." *March 9:* Wilson, acting under his executive powers, orders the arming of American merchantmen. *March 12:* Revolutionary provisional government established in Russia. *Algonquin* torpedoed. *March 15:* Czar Nicholas II of Russia abdicates. *March 16: City of Memphis, Illinois, Vigilancia* torpedoed. *March 21: New York World,* a leading Democratic newspaper, calls for declaration of war on Germany. Wilson summons Congress to convene in a special session on April 2. *March 25:* Wilson calls up the National Guard. *April 2:* Wilson asks Congress to declare war. Germany is guilty of "throwing to the winds all scruples of humanity," he says. America must fight, not to conquer, but for "peace and justice. . . . The world must be made safe for democracy." *April 4, 6:* Congress declares war—the vote, 82–6 in the Senate, 373–50 in the House.

The bare record conceals Wilson's agonizing search for an honorable alternative to war. To admit that Germany posed a threat to the United States meant confessing that interventionists had been right all along. To go to war meant, besides sending innocent Americans to their deaths, allowing "the spirit of ruthless brutality [to] enter into the very fibre of our national life."

The president's Presbyterian conscience tortured him relentlessly. He lost sleep, appeared gray and drawn. When someone asked him which side he hoped would win, he answered petulantly, "Neither." "He was resisting," Secretary of State Lansing recorded, "the irresistible logic of events." In the end Wilson could satisfy himself only by giving intervention an idealistic purpose. The war had become a threat to humanity. Unless the United States threw its weight into the balance, western civilization itself might be destroyed. Out of the long bloodbath must come a new and better world. The war must be fought to end, for all time, war itself. Thus in the name not of vengeance and victory but of justice and humanity he sent his people into battle.

Mobilizing the Economy

America's entry into the Great War determined its outcome. The Allies were running out of money and supplies; their troops, decimated by nearly three years in the trenches, were disheartened and rebellious. In February and March 1917 U-boats sent over a million tons of Allied shipping to the bottom of the Atlantic. The outbreak of the Russian Revolution in March 1917, at first lifting the spirits of the western democracies, led to the Bolshevik takeover under Lenin. The Russian armies collapsed; by December 1917 Russia was out of the

war and the Germans were moving masses of men and equipment from the eastern front to France. Without the aid of the United States, it is likely that the war would have ended in 1918 on terms dictated from Berlin. Instead, American men and supplies helped contain the Germans' last drives and then push them back to final defeat.

It was a close thing, for the United States entered the war little better prepared to fight than it had been in 1898. The conversion of American industry to war production had to be organized and carried out without prearrangement. What the historian Harvey A. De Weerd has called "absurdly large" goals were set, far beyond what the army could use. Confusion and waste resulted. The hurriedly designed shipbuilding program was an almost total fiasco. The gigantic Hog Island yard, which employed at its peak over 34,000 workers, completed its first vessel after the war ended. Airplane, tank, and artillery construction programs, all too large to begin with, developed too slowly to affect the war. The big guns that backed up American soldiers in 1918 were made in France and Great Britain; of the 8.8 million rounds of artillery ammunition fired by American troops, only about 8,000 were manufactured in the United States. Congress authorized the manufacture of 20,000, but only a handful, mostly British-designed planes made in America, got to France.

"America," writes David M. Kennedy in *Over Here,* "was no 'arsenal of democracy' in World War I; the American doughboy in France was typically transported in a British ship, wore a steel helmet modeled on the British Tommy's, and fought with French ordnance." American pilots such as the great "ace" Captain Eddie Rickenbacker flew British Sopwiths and De Havillands or French Spads and Nieuports. Theodore Roosevelt's son Quentin was shot down while flying a Spad over Château-Thierry in July 1918.

The problem of mobilization was complicated. It took Congress six weeks of hot debate merely to decide on conscription. Only in September 1917, nearly six months after the declaration of war, did the first draftees reach the training camps, and it is hard to see how Wilson could have speeded this process appreciably. He wisely supported the professional soldiers, who insisted that he resist the appeals of politicians who wanted to raise volunteer units, even rejecting, at considerable political cost,

Theodore Roosevelt's offer to raise an entire army division.

Wilson was a forceful and inspiring war leader once he grasped what needed to be done. He displayed both determination and unfailing patience in the face of frustration and criticism. Raising an army was only a small part of the job. The Allies had to be supplied with food and munitions, and immense amounts of money had to be collected.

After several false starts Wilson placed the task in the hands of the War Industries Board (WIB). The board was given almost dictatorial power to allocate scarce materials, standardize production, fix prices, and coordinate American and Allied purchasing. Evaluating the mobilization effort raises interesting historical questions. The antitrust laws were suspended and producers were encouraged, even compelled, to cooperate with one another. Government regulation went far beyond what the New Nationalists had envisaged in 1912.

As for the New Freedom variety of laissez faire, it had no place in a wartime economy. The nation's railroads, strained by immensely increased traffic, became progressively less efficient. A monumental tie-up in December 1917 and January 1918 finally persuaded Wilson to appoint Secretary of the Treasury William G. McAdoo director-general of the railroads, with power to run the roads as a single system. McAdoo's Railroad Administration pooled all railroad equipment, centralized purchasing, standardized accounting practices, and raised wages and passenger rates.

Wilson accepted the kind of government-in-dustry agreement developed under Theodore Roosevelt that he had denounced in 1912. Prices were set by the WIB at levels that allowed large profits—U.S. Steel, for example, despite high taxes, cleared over half a billion dollars in two years. It is at least arguable that producers would have turned out just as much even if compelled to charge lower prices.

At the start of the war, army procurement was decentralized and inefficient—as many as eight bureaus were purchasing material in competition with one another. One official bought 1,200 typewriters, stacked them in the basement of a government building, and announced proudly to his superior: "There is going to be the greatest competition for typewriters around here, and I have them all."

Mobilization required close cooperation between business and the military. However, the army resisted cooperating with civilian agencies, being, as the historian Paul Koistiner writes, "suspicious of, and hostile toward, civilian institutions." Wilson finally compelled the War Department to place officers on WIB committees, and when the army discovered that its interests were not injured by the system, the foundation was laid for what was later to be known as the "industrial-military complex," the alliance between business and military leaders that was to cause so much controversy after World War II.

The history of industrial mobilization was the history of the entire home-front effort in microcosm: Prodigies were performed, but the task was so gigantic and unprecedented that a full year passed before an efficient system had been devised, and many unforeseen results occurred.

The problem of mobilizing agricultural resources was solved more quickly, and this was fortunate because in April 1917 the British had on hand only a six-week supply of food. As food administrator Wilson appointed Herbert Hoover, a mining engineer who had headed the Belgian Relief Commission earlier in the war. Acting under powers granted by the Lever Act of 1917, Hoover set the price of wheat at $2.20 a bushel in order to encourage production. He established a government corporation to purchase the entire American and Cuban sugar crop, which he then doled out to American and British refiners. To avoid rationing he organized a campaign to persuade consumers to conserve food voluntarily. One slogan ran "If U fast U beat U boats," another "Serve beans by all means."

"Wheatless Mondays" and "meatless Tuesdays" were the rule, and although no law compelled their observance, the public responded patriotically. Boy Scouts dug up backyards and vacant lots to plant vegetable gardens; chefs devised new recipes to save on scarce items; restaurants added horsemeat, rabbit, and whale steak to their menus and doled out butter and sugar to customers in minuscule amounts. Mothers pressured their children to "Hooverize" their plates. Chicago residents were so successful in making use of leftovers that the volume of raw garbage in the city declined from 12,862 tons to 8,386 tons per month.

Without subjecting its own citizens to serious inconvenience, the United States increased food ex-

Wartime belt-tightening inspired new business ventures for a few entrepreneurs. GET AC-QUAINTED—CUT DOWN YOUR MEAT BILLS AND BUY HORSE MEAT, *urges the sign at right.*

ports from 12.3 million tons to 18.6 million tons. Farmers, of course, profited greatly: Their real income went up nearly 30 percent between 1915 and 1918.

Workers in Wartime

With the army siphoning so many men from the labor market and with immigration reduced to a trickle, unemployment disappeared and wages rose. Although the cost of living soared, imposing hardships on people with fixed incomes, the boom produced unprecedented opportunities.

Americans, always a mobile people, pulled up their roots in record numbers. Disadvantaged groups, especially blacks, were particularly attracted by jobs in big-city factories. Early in the conflict, the government began regulating the wages and hours of workers building army camps and manufacturing uniforms. In April 1918 Wilson created the National War Labor Board, headed by former president Taft and Frank P. Walsh, a prominent lawyer, to settle labor disputes. The board considered more than 1,200 cases and prevented many strikes. The War Labor Policies Board, chaired by Felix Frankfurter of the Harvard Law School, set wages-and-hours

standards for each major war industry. Since these were determined in consultation with employers and representatives of labor, they speeded the unionization of workers by compelling management, even in antiunion industries like steel, to deal with labor leaders. Union membership rose by 2.3 million during the war.

However, the wartime emergency roused the public against strikers; some conservatives even demanded that war workers be conscripted just as soldiers were. While he opposed strikes that impeded the war effort, Wilson set great store in preserving the individual worker's freedom of action. It would be "most unfortunate . . . to relax the laws by which safeguards have been thrown about labor," he said. "We must accomplish the results we desire by organized effort rather than compulsion."

Trends in the steel industry reflect the improvement of the lot of labor in wartime. Wages of unskilled steelworkers more than doubled. Thousands of southern blacks flocked into the steel towns. Union organizers made inroads in many plants, and by the summer of 1918 they were preparing an all-out effort to unionize the industry. If the world was to be made safe for democracy, they argued, there must be "economic democracy [along] with political democracy."

Paying for the War

Wilson managed the task of financing the war effectively. The struggle cost the United States about $33.5 billion, not counting pensions and other postwar expenses. About $7 billion of this was lent to the Allies,* but since this money was spent largely in America, it contributed to the national prosperity.

Over two-thirds of the cost of the war was met by borrowing. Five Liberty and Victory Loan drives, spurred by advertising, parades, and other appeals to patriotism, persuaded the people to open their purses. Industrialists, eager to inculcate in their employees a sense of personal involvement in the war effort, conducted campaigns in their plants. Some went so far as to threaten "A Bond or Your Job," but more typical was the appeal of the managers of the Gary, Indiana, plant of U.S. Steel, who published bond advertisements in six languages in order to reach their immigrant workers.

In addition to borrowing, the government collected about $10.5 billion in taxes during the war. A steeply graduated income tax took more than 75 percent of the incomes of the wealthiest citizens. A 65 percent excess-profits tax and a 25 percent inheritance tax were also enacted. Thus while many individuals made fortunes out of the war, its cost was distributed far more equitably than that of the Civil War. Americans also contributed generously to philanthropic agencies engaged in war work. Most notable, perhaps, was the great 1918 drive of the United War Work Council, an interfaith religious group, which raised over $200 million mainly to finance recreational programs for the troops overseas.

Propaganda and Civil Liberties

Wilson was preeminently a teacher and preacher, a specialist in the transmission of ideas and ideals. He excelled at mobilizing public opinion and inspiring Americans to work for the better world he hoped would emerge from the war. In April 1917 he created the Committee on Public Information (CPI), headed by the journalist George Creel. Soon 75,000 speakers were deluging the country with propaganda prepared by hundreds of CPI writers. They pictured the war as a crusade for freedom and democracy, the Germans as a bestial people bent on world domination.

A large majority of the nation supported the war enthusiastically. But thousands of persons—German-Americans and Irish-Americans, for example; people of pacifist leanings such as Jane Addams, the founder of Hull House; and some who thought both sides in the war were wrong—still opposed American involvement. Creel's committee and a

In 1917 the Germania Life Insurance Building in St. Paul was renamed the Guardian Building; since Germania herself could not be disguised, down she came.

---

* In 1914 Americans owed foreigners about $3.8 billion. By 1919 Americans *were owed* $12.5 billion by Europeans alone.

number of unofficial "patriotic" groups allowed their enthusiasm for the conversion of the hesitant to become suppression of dissent. Persons who refused to buy war bonds were often exposed to public ridicule and even assault. People with German names were persecuted without regard for their views; some school boards outlawed the teaching of the German language; sauerkraut was renamed "liberty cabbage." Opponents of the war of unquestionable patriotism were subjected to coarse abuse. A cartoonist pictured Senator Robert La Follette, who opposed entering the war, receiving an Iron Cross from the German militarists, and the faculty of his own University of Wisconsin voted to censure him.

Wilson, "a friend of free speech in theory," David M. Kennedy has written, "was its foe in fact." He signed the Espionage Act of 1917, which imposed fines of up to $10,000 and jail sentences ranging to 20 years on persons convicted of aiding the enemy or obstructing recruiting, and he authorized the postmaster general to ban from the mails any material that seemed treasonable or seditious.

In May 1918, again with Wilson's approval, Congress passed the Sedition Act, which made "saying anything" to discourage the purchase of war bonds a crime, with the proviso that investment counselors could still offer "bona fide and not disloyal advice" to clients. The law also made it illegal to "utter, print, write, or publish any disloyal, profane, scurrilous, or abusive language" about the government, the Constitution, or the uniform of the army or navy. Socialist periodicals such as *The Masses* were suppressed, and Eugene V. Debs was sentenced to ten years in prison for making an antiwar speech. Ricardo Flores Magón, an anarchist, was sentenced to 20 years in jail for publishing a statement criticizing Wilson's Mexican policy, an issue that had nothing to do with the war.

These laws went far beyond what was necessary to protect the national interest. Citizens were jailed for suggesting that the draft law was unconstitutional and for criticizing private organizations like the Red Cross and the YMCA. One woman was sent to prison for writing, "I am for the people, and the government is for the profiteers."

The Supreme Court upheld the constitutionality of the Espionage Act in *Schenck* v. *United States* (1919), a case involving a man who had mailed circulars to draftees urging them to refuse to report

for induction into the army. Free speech has its limits, Justice Oliver Wendell Holmes, Jr., explained. No one has the right to cry, "Fire!" in a crowded theater. When there is a "clear and present danger" that a particular statement would threaten the national interest, it can be repressed by law. In peacetime Schenck's circulars would be permissible, but not in time of war.

The "clear and present danger" doctrine did not prevent judges and juries from interpreting the Espionage and Sedition acts broadly, and while in many instances their decisions were overturned by higher courts, this usually did not occur until after the war. The wartime hysteria far exceeded anything that happened in Great Britain and France. In 1916 the French novelist Henri Barbusse published *Le Feu (Under Fire)*, a graphic account of the horrors and purposelessness of trench warfare. In one chapter Barbusse described a pilot flying over the trenches on a Sunday, observing French and German soldiers at Mass in the open fields, each worshiping the same God. Yet *Le Feu* circulated freely in France and even won the coveted Prix Goncourt.

Wartime Reforms

The American mobilization experience was part and product of the Progressive Era. The work of the progressives at the national and state levels in expanding government functions in order to deal with social and economic problems provided precedents and conditioned the people for the all-out effort of 1917 and 1918. Social and economic planning and the management of huge business operations by public boards and committees got their first practical tests. College professors, technicians, and others with complex skills entered government service en masse. The federal government for the first time entered actively such fields as housing and labor relations.

Many progressives believed that the war was creating the sense of common purpose that would stimulate the people to act unselfishly to benefit the poor and to eradicate social evils. Patriotism and public service seemed at last united. Secretary of War Newton D. Baker, a prewar urban reformer, expressed this attitude in supporting a federal child labor law: "We cannot afford, when we are losing boys in France, to lose children in the United States."

Men and women of this sort worked for a dozen causes only remotely related to the war effort. The women's suffrage movement was brought to fruition, as was the campaign against alcohol. Both the Eighteenth Amendment, outlawing alcoholic beverages, and the Nineteenth, giving women the vote, were adopted at least in part because of the war. Reformers began to talk about health insurance. The progressive campaign against prostitution and venereal disease gained strength, winning the enthusiastic support both of persons worried about inexperienced local girls being seduced by the soldiers and of those concerned lest prostitutes lead innocent soldiers astray. One of the latter type claimed to have persuaded "over 1,000 fallen women" to promise not to go near any army camps.

The effort to wipe out prostitution around military installations was a cause of some misunderstanding with the Allies, who provided licensed facilities for their troops as a matter of course. When the premier of France graciously offered to supply prostitutes for American units in his country, Secretary Baker is said to have remarked: "For God's sake . . . don't show this to the President or he'll stop the war." Apparently Baker had a rather peculiar sense of humor. After a tour of the front in France, he assured an American women's group that life in the trenches was "far less uncomfortable" than he had thought and that not a single American doughboy was "living a life which he would not be willing to have [his] mother see him live."

Efforts by young women such as these in war gardens were meant not only to keep the boys "over there" well supplied with vegetables, but also to make those in the United States feel part of the struggle to make the world safe for democracy.

Women and Blacks in Wartime

Although a number of prominent feminists were pacifists, most supported the war enthusiastically, moved by patriotism and the belief that opposition to the war would doom their hopes of gaining the vote. They also expected that the war would open up many kinds of high-paying jobs to women. To some extent it did; about a million women replaced men in uniform, but the numbers actually engaged in war industries were small (about 6,000 found jobs making airplanes, for example), and the gains were fleeting. When the war ended, most women who were engaged in industrial work either left their jobs voluntarily or were fired to make room for returning veterans. Some women went overseas as nurses, and a few served as ambulance drivers and YMCA workers.

Most unions were unsympathetic to the idea of enrolling women, and the government did little to encourage women to do more for the war effort than prepare bandages, knit warm clothing for soldiers, participate in food conservation programs, and encourage people to buy war bonds. There was a Women in Industry Service in the Department of Labor and a Woman's Committee of the Council of National Defense, but both served primarily as window dressing for the Wilson administration. The final report of another wartime agency, issued in 1919, admitted that few women war workers had been paid as much as men and that women had been promoted more slowly than men, were not accepted by unions, and were discharged promptly when the war ended.

The wartime "great migration" of southern blacks to northern cities where jobs were available brought them important economic benefits. Actually, the emigration of blacks from the former slave states began with emancipation, but the mass exodus that many people had expected was slow to materialize. Between 1870 and 1890 only about 80,000 blacks moved to northern cities. Compared with the influx from Europe and from northern farms, this was a trivial number. The black portion of the population of New York City, for example, fell from over 10 percent in 1800 to under 2 percent in 1900.

Around the turn of the century, as the first post-slavery generation reached maturity and as south-

ern repression increased, the northward movement quickened—about 200,000 blacks migrated between 1890 and 1910. Then, after 1914, the war boom drew blacks north in a flood. Agents of northern manufacturers flocked into the Cotton Belt to recruit them in wholesale lots. "Leave the benighted land," the *Chicago Defender*, a newspaper with a considerable circulation in southern states, urged. "Get out of the South." Half a million made the move between 1914 and 1919. The black population of New York rose from 92,000 to 152,000, that of Chicago from 44,000 to 109,000, that of Detroit from 5,700 to 41,000.

Life for the newcomers was difficult; many whites resented them; workers feared them as potential strikebreakers yet refused to admit them into their unions. In East St. Louis, Illinois, where employers had brought in large numbers of blacks in an attempt to discourage local unions from striking for higher wages, a bloody riot erupted during the summer of 1917 in which nine whites and an undetermined number of blacks were killed. As in peacetime, the Wilson administration was at worst antagonistic and at best indifferent to blacks' needs and aspirations.

Nevertheless, the blacks who moved north during the war were, as a group, infinitely better off, materially and psychologically, than those they left behind. They earned good wages and were accorded at least some human rights. They were not treated by the whites as equals, or even in most cases entirely fairly, but they could vote, send their children to decent schools, and within reasonable limits do and say what they pleased without fear of humiliation or physical attack.

There were two black regiments in the regular army and a number of black national guard units when the war began, and once these outfits were brought up to combat strength, no more volunteers were accepted. Indeed, at first no blacks were conscripted; southerners in particular found the thought of giving large numbers of blacks guns and teaching them how to use them most disturbing. Blacks were, however, soon drafted, and once they were, a larger proportion of them than whites were taken. One Georgia draft board exempted more than 500 of 815 white registrants and only 6 of the 202 blacks in its jurisdiction before its members were relieved of their duties. After a riot in Texas in which black soldiers killed 17 white civilians, black recruits were dispersed among many camps for training to lessen the possibility of trouble.

In the service, all blacks were placed in segregated units. Only a handful were commissioned officers. Most, even those sent overseas, were assigned to labor battalions, working as stevedores and common laborers. But many fought and died for the country. Altogether about 200,000 served in France. There were black Red Cross nurses in France, and some blacks held relatively high posts in government agencies in Washington, the most important being Emmett J. Scott, who was special assistant for Negro affairs in the War Department.

W. E. B. Du Bois supported the war wholeheartedly. He praised Wilson for making, at last, a strong statement against lynching, which had in-

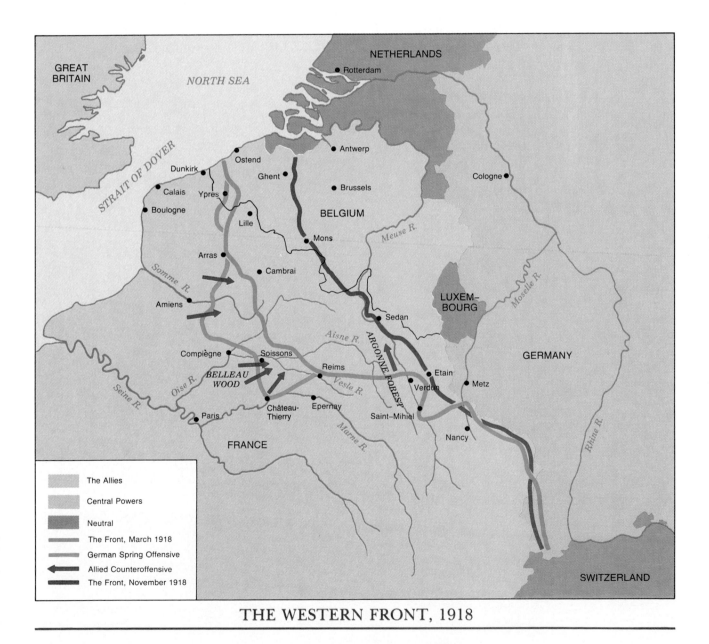

THE WESTERN FRONT, 1918

creased to a shocking extent during the previous decade. He even went along with the fact that the handful of black officer candidates were trained in a segregated camp. "Let us," he wrote in *The Crisis,* "while the war lasts, forget our special grievances and close ranks shoulder to shoulder with our fellow citizens and the allied nations that are fighting for democracy."

Many blacks condemned Du Bois's accommodationism (which he promptly abandoned when the war ended), but most saw the war as an opportunity to demonstrate their patriotism and prove their worth. For the moment the prevailing mood was one of optimism. "We may expect to see the walls of prejudice gradually crumble"—this was the common attitude of blacks in 1917 and 1918. If winning the war would make the world safe for democracy, surely blacks in the United States would be better off when it was won. Whether or not this turned out to be so was (and still is) a matter of opinion.

"Over There"

All activity on the home front had one ultimate objective: defeating the Central Powers on the bat-

American infantrymen of the 1st Division under shell fire outside Exermont, in the Ardennes Forest, France, in the waning days of the Great War.

tlefield. This was accomplished. The navy performed with special distinction. In April 1917, German submarines sank more than 870,000 tons of Allied shipping; after April 1918, monthly losses never reached 300,000 tons. The decision to send merchant ships across the Atlantic in convoys screened by destroyers made the reduction possible. Checking the U-boats was essential because of the need to transport American troops to Europe. Slightly more than 2 million soldiers made the voyage safely. Those who crossed on fast ocean liners were in little danger so long as the vessel maintained high speed and followed a zigzag course, a lesson learned from the *Lusitania*, whose captain had neglected both these precautions. Those who traveled on slower troop transports benefited from the protection of destroyers and also from the fact that the Germans concentrated on attacking supply ships. They continued to believe that inexperienced American soldiers would not be a major factor in the war.

The first units of the American Expeditionary Force (AEF), elements of the regular army commanded by General John J. Pershing, reached Paris on Independence Day in 1917. They took up positions on the front near Verdun in October. Not until the spring of 1918, however, did the "doughboys" play a significant role in the fighting, though their mere presence boosted French and British morale.

Pershing, as commander of the AEF, insisted on maintaining his troops as independent units; he would not allow them to be filtered into the Allied armies as reinforcements. This was part of a perhaps unfortunate general policy that reflected America's isolationism. (Wilson always referred to the other nations fighting Germany as "associates," not as "allies.")

In March 1918 the Germans launched a great spring offensive, their armies strengthened by thousands of veterans from the Russian front. By late May they had reached a point on the Marne River near the town of Château-Thierry, only 50 miles from Paris. Early in June the AEF fought its first major engagements, driving the Germans back from Château-Thierry and Belleau Wood.

In this fighting only about 27,500 Americans saw action, and they suffered appalling losses. Nevertheless, when the Germans advanced again in the direction of the Marne in mid-July, 85,000 Americans were in the lines that withstood their charge. Then, in the major turning point of the war, the Allied armies counterattacked. Some 270,000 Americans participated, helping to flatten the German bulge between Reims and Soissons. By late August the American First Army, 500,000 strong, was poised before the Saint-Mihiel salient, a deep extension of the German lines southeast of Verdun. On September 12 this army, buttressed by French troops, struck and in two days wiped out the salient.

Late in September began the greatest American engagement of the war. No fewer than 1.2 million doughboys drove forward west of Verdun into the Argonne Forest. For over a month of indescribable horror they inched ahead through the tangle of the Argonne and the formidable defenses of the Hindenburg line, while to the west, French and British armies staged similar drives. In this one offensive the AEF suffered 120,000 casualties. Finally, on November 1, they broke the German center and raced toward the vital Sedan-Mézières railroad. On November 11, with Allied armies advancing on all fronts, the Germans signed the armistice, ending the fighting.*

Preparing for Peace

On November 11, 1918, the fighting ended, but the shape of the postwar world remained to be determined. European society had been shaken to its foundations. Confusion reigned. People wanted peace yet burned for revenge. Millions faced starvation. Other millions were disillusioned by the seemingly purposeless sacrifices of four years of horrible war. Communism—to some an idealistic promise of human betterment, to others a commitment to rational economic and social planning, to still others a danger to individual freedom, toleration, and democracy—having conquered Russia, threatened to envelop Germany and much of the

---

* American losses in the war amounted to 112,432 dead and 230,074 wounded. More than half of the deaths, however, resulted from disease. Though severe, these casualties were trivial compared with those of the other belligerents. British Commonwealth deaths amounted to 947,000, French to 1.38 million, Russian to 1.7 million, Italian to 460,000. Among the Central Powers, Germany lost 1.8 million men, Austria-Hungary 1.2 million, Turkey 325,000. In addition, about 20 million were wounded.

defunct Austro-Hungarian Empire, perhaps even the victorious Allies. How could stability be restored? How could victory be made worth its enormous cost?

Woodrow Wilson had grasped the significance of the war while most statesmen still thought that triumph on the battlefield would settle everything automatically. As early as January 1917 he had realized that victory would be wasted if the winners permitted themselves the luxury of vengeance. Such a policy would disrupt the balance of power and lead to economic and social chaos. American participation in the struggle had not blurred his vision. The victors must build a better society, not punish those they believed had destroyed the old.

In a speech to Congress on January 8, 1918, Wilson outlined a plan, known as the Fourteen Points, designed to make the world "fit and safe to live in." The peace treaty should be negotiated in full view of world opinion, not in secret. It should guarantee the freedom of the seas to all nations, in war as in peacetime. It should tear down barriers to international trade, provide for a drastic reduction of armaments, and establish a colonial system that would take proper account of the interests of the native peoples concerned. European boundaries should be redrawn so that no substantial group would have to live under a government not of its own choosing.

More specifically, captured Russian territory should be restored, Belgium evacuated, Alsace-Lorraine returned to France, the heterogeneous nationalities of Austria-Hungary accorded autonomy. Italy's frontiers should be adjusted "along clearly recognizable lines of nationality," the Balkans made free, Turkey divested of its subject peoples, an independent Polish state (with access to the Baltic Sea) created. To oversee the new system, Wilson insisted, "a general association of nations must be formed under specific covenants for the purpose of affording mutual guarantees of political independence and territorial integrity to great and small states alike."

Wilson's Fourteen Points for a fair peace lifted the hopes of people everywhere. After the guns fell silent, however, the vagueness and inconsistencies in his list became apparent. Complete national self-determination was impossible in Europe; there were too many regions of mixed population for every group to be satisfied. Self-determination, like the war itself, fostered the spirit of nationalism that Wilson's dream of international organization, a league of nations, was designed to de-emphasize. Furthermore, the Allies had made territorial commitments to one another in secret treaties that ran counter to the principle of self-determination, and they were not ready to give up all claim to Germany's colonies. Freedom of the seas in wartime posed another problem; the British flatly refused to accept the idea. In every Allied country, millions rejected the idea of a peace without indemnities. They expected to make the enemy pay for the war, hoping, as Sir Eric Geddes, first lord of the Admiralty, said, to squeeze Germany "as a lemon is squeezed—until the pips squeak."

Wilson assumed that the practical benefits of his program would compel opponents to fall in line. He had the immense advantage of seeking nothing for his own country and the additional strength of being leader of the one important nation to emerge from the war richer and more powerful than it had been in 1914.

Yet this combination of altruism, idealism, and power was his undoing; it intensified his tendency to be overbearing and undermined his judgment. He had never found it easy to compromise. Once, when he was president of Princeton, he got into an argument over some abstract question with a professor while shooting a game of pool. To avoid acrimony, the professor finally said: "Well, Doctor Wilson, there are two sides to every question." "Yes," Wilson answered, "a right side and a wrong side." Now, believing that the fate of humanity hung on his actions, he was unyielding. Always a preacher, he became in his own mind a prophet—almost, one fears, a kind of god.

In the last weeks of the war Wilson proved to be a brilliant diplomat, first dangling the Fourteen Points before the German people to encourage them to overthrow Kaiser Wilhelm II and sue for an armistice, then sending Colonel House to Paris to persuade Allied leaders to accept the Fourteen Points as the basis for the peace. When the Allies raised objections, House made small concessions, but by hinting that the United States might make a separate peace with Germany, he forced them to agree. Under the armistice, Germany had to withdraw behind the Rhine River and surrender its submarines, together with quantities of munitions and other materials. In return it received the assurance of the Allies that the Wilsonian principles would prevail at the Paris peace conference.

Wilson then came to a daring decision: He would personally attend the conference, which convened on January 12, 1919, at Paris, as a member of the United States Peace Commission. This was a precedent-shattering step, for no president had ever left American territory while in office. (Taft, who had a summer home on the St. Lawrence River in Canada, never vacationed there during his term, believing that to do so would be unconstitutional.)

Wilson probably erred in going to Paris, but not because of the novelty or possible illegality of the act. By going, he was turning his back on obvious domestic problems. Western farmers believed that they had been discriminated against during the war, since wheat prices had been controlled while southern cotton had been allowed to rise unchecked from 7 cents a pound in 1914 to 35 cents in 1919. The administration's drastic tax program had angered many businessmen. Labor, despite its gains, was restive in the face of reconversion to peacetime conditions.

Wilson had increased his political difficulties by making a partisan appeal for the election of a Democratic Congress in 1918. Republicans, who had in many instances supported his war program more loyally than the Democrats, considered the action a gross affront. The appeal failed; the Republicans won majorities in both houses. Wilson appeared to have been repudiated at home at the very moment that he set forth to represent the nation abroad. Most important, Wilson intended to break with the isolationist tradition and bring the United States into a league of nations. Such a revolutionary change would require explanation; he should have undertaken a major campaign to convince the American people of the wisdom of this step.

Wilson also erred in his choice of the other commissioners. He selected Colonel House, Secretary of State Lansing, General Tasker H. Bliss, and Henry White, a career diplomat. These men were thoroughly competent, but only White was a Republican, and he had no stature as a politician. Since the peace treaty would have to be ratified by the Senate, Wilson should have given that body some representation on the commission, and since the Republicans would have a majority in the new Senate, a Republican senator, or someone who had the full confidence of the Republican leadership, should

have been appointed. (The wily McKinley had named three senators to the American delegation to the peace conference after the Spanish-American War.)

The Paris Peace Conference

Wilson arrived in Europe a world hero. He toured England, France, and Italy briefly and was greeted ecstatically almost everywhere. The reception tended to increase his sense of mission and to convince him, in the fashion of a typical progressive, that whatever the European politicians might say about it, "the people" were behind his program.

When the conference settled down to its work, control quickly fell into the hands of the so-called Big Four: Wilson, Prime Minister David Lloyd George of Great Britain, Premier Georges Clemenceau of France, and Prime Minister Vittorio Orlando of Italy. Wilson stood out in this group but did not dominate it. His principal advantage in the negotiations was his untiring industry. He alone of the leaders tried to master all the complex details of the task.

The 78-year-old Clemenceau cared only for one thing: French security. He viewed Wilson cynically, saying that since mankind had been unable to keep God's Ten Commandments, it was unlikely to do better with Wilson's Fourteen Points. Lloyd George's approach was pragmatic and almost cavalier. He sympathized with much that Wilson was trying to accomplish but found the president's frequent sermonettes about "right being more important than might, and justice being more eternal than force" incomprehensible. "If you want to succeed in politics," Lloyd George advised a British statesman, "you must keep your conscience well under control." Orlando, clever, cultured, a believer in international cooperation but inflexible where Italian national interests were concerned, was not the equal of his three colleagues in influence. He left the conference in a huff when they failed to meet all his demands.

The conference labored from January to May 1919 and finally brought forth the Versailles Treaty. American liberals whose hopes had soared at the thought of a peace based on the Fourteen Points found the document abysmally disappointing.

The "Big Four" at the Hotel Crillon in Paris. First row, from the left: Orlando of Italy, Lloyd George of Great Britain, Clemenceau of France, and Wilson of the United States.

The peace settlement failed to carry out the principle of self-determination completely. It gave Italy a large section of the Austrian Tyrol, though the area contained 200,000 people who considered themselves Austrians. Other German-speaking groups were incorporated into the new states of Poland and Czechoslovakia. Japan was allowed to take over the Chinese province of Shantung, and the Allies swallowed up all the German colonies in Africa and the Far East.

The victors forced Germany to accept responsibility for having caused the war—an act of senseless vindictiveness as well as a gross oversimplification—and to sign a "blank check," agreeing to pay for all damage to civilian properties and even future pensions and other indirect war costs. This reparations bill, as finally determined, amounted to $33 billion. Instead of attacking imperialism, the treaty attacked German imperialism; instead of seeking a new international social order based on liberty and democracy, it created a great-power entente designed to crush Germany and to exclude Bolshevist Russia from the family of nations. It said nothing about freedom of the seas, the reduction of tariffs, or disarmament. To those who had taken Wilson's "peace without victory" speech and the Fourteen Points literally, the Versailles Treaty seemed an abomination.

The complaints of the critics were individually reasonable, yet their conclusions were not entirely fair. The new map of Europe left fewer people on "foreign" soil than in any earlier period of history. Though the Allies seized the German colonies, they were required, under the mandate system, to render to the League of Nations annual accounts of their stewardship and to prepare the inhabitants for eventual independence. Above all, Wilson had persuaded the powers to incorporate the League of Nations in the treaty.

Wilson expected the League of Nations to make up for all the inadequacies of the Versailles Treaty. Once the League had begun to function, problems like freedom of the seas and disarmament would solve themselves, he argued, and the relaxation of trade barriers would surely follow. The League would arbitrate international disputes, act as a central body for registering treaties, and employ military and economic sanctions against aggressor nations. Each member promised (Article 10) to protect the "territorial integrity" and "political independence" of all other members. No great power could be made to go to war against its will, but Wilson emphasized that all were *morally* obligated to carry out League decisions. By any standard, Wilson had achieved a remarkably moderate peace, one full of hope for the future. Except for the war guilt clause and the heavy reparations imposed on Germany, he could be justly proud of his work.

The Senate and the League of Nations

When Wilson returned from France, he finally directed his attention to the task of winning public approval of his handiwork. A large majority of the people probably favored the League of Nations in principle, though few understood all its implications or were entirely happy with every detail. Wilson had persuaded the Allies to accept certain changes in the original draft to mollify American opposition. No nation could be forced to accept a colonial mandate, and "domestic questions" such as the Monroe Doctrine, tariffs, and immigration were excluded from League control.

Many senators found these modifications insufficient. Even before the peace conference ended, 37 Republican senators signed a round-robin, devised by Henry Cabot Lodge of Massachusetts, opposing Wilson's League and demanding that the question of an international organization be put off until "the urgent business of negotiating peace terms with Germany" had been completed. Wilson rejected this suggestion icily. Further alterations were out of the question. "Anyone who opposes me . . . I'll crush!" he told one Democratic senator. "I shall consent to nothing. The Senate must take its medicine." Thus the stage was set for a monumental test of strength between the president and the Republican majority in the Senate.

Partisanship, principle, and prejudice clashed mightily in this contest. A presidential election loomed. Should the League prove a success, the Republicans wanted to be able to claim a share of the credit, but Wilson had refused to allow them to participate in drafting the document. This predisposed all of them to favor changes. Politics aside, genuine alarm at the possible sacrifice of American sovereignty to an international authority led many Republicans to urge modification of the League covenant, or constitution. Personal dislike of Wilson

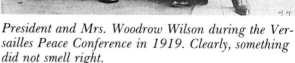

President and Mrs. Woodrow Wilson during the Versailles Peace Conference in 1919. Clearly, something did not smell right.

and his high-handed methods motivated others. Yet the noble purpose of the League made many reluctant to reject it entirely. The intense desire of the people to have an end to the long war made GOP leaders hesitate before voting down the Versailles Treaty, and they could not reject the League without rejecting the treaty.

Wilson could count on the Democratic senators almost to a man, but he had to win over many Republicans to obtain the two-thirds majority necessary for ratification. Republican opinion divided roughly into three segments. At one extreme were some dozen "irreconcilables," led by the shaggy-browed William E. Borah of Idaho, an able and kindly person of progressive leanings but an uncompromising isolationist. Borah claimed that he would vote against the League even if Jesus Christ returned to earth to argue in its behalf, and most of his followers were equally inflexible. At the other extreme stood another dozen "mild" reservationists who were in favor of the League but who hoped to alter it in minor ways, chiefly for political purposes. In the middle were the "strong" reservationists, senators willing to go along with the League only if American sovereignty were fully protected and it was made clear that their party had played a major role in fashioning the final document.

Senator Lodge, the leader of the Republican opposition, was a haughty, rather cynical, intensely partisan individual. He possessed a keen intelligence, a mastery of parliamentary procedure, and, as chairman of the Senate Foreign Relations Committee, a great deal of power. Although not an isolationist, he had little faith in the League. He also had a profound distrust of Democrats, especially Wilson, whom he considered a hypocrite and a coward. The president's pious idealism left him cold. While perfectly ready to see the country participate actively in world affairs, Lodge insisted that its right to determine its own best interests in every situation be preserved. He had been a senator since 1893 and an admirer of senatorial independence since early manhood. When a Democratic president tried to ram the Versailles Treaty down the Senate's throat, he fought him with every weapon he could muster.

A skeptical view of the League of Nations in London's Punch. *The dove of peace looks askance at Wilson's hefty olive branch, asking "Isn't this a bit thick?"*

Lodge belonged to the strong reservationist faction. His own proposals, known as the Lodge Reservations, 14 in number to match Wilson's Fourteen Points, limited the United States' obligations to the League and stated in unmistakable terms the right of Congress to decide when to honor these obligations. Some of the reservations were mere quibbles. Others, such as the provision that the United States would not endorse Japan's seizure of Chinese territory, were included mainly to embarrass Wilson by pointing up compromises he had made at Versailles. The most important reservation applied to Article 10 of the League covenant, which committed signatories to protect the political independence and territorial integrity of all member nations. Wilson had rightly called Article 10 "the heart of the Covenant." One of Lodge's reservations made it inoperable so far as the United States was concerned "unless in any particular case the Congress . . . shall by act or joint resolution so provide."

Lodge performed brilliantly, if somewhat unscrupulously, in uniting the three Republican factions behind his reservations. He got the irreconcilables to agree to them by conceding their right to vote against the final version in any event, and he held the mild reservationists in line by modifying some of his demands and stressing the importance of party unity. Reservations—as distinct from amendments—would not have to win the formal approval of other League members. In addition, the Lodge proposals dealt forthrightly with the problem of reconciling traditional concepts of national sovereignty with the new idea of world cooperation. Supporters of the League could accept them without sacrifice of principle. Wilson, however, refused to agree. "Accept the Treaty with the Lodge reservations?" the president snorted when a friendly senator warned him that he must accept a compromise. "Never! Never!"

This foolish intransigence seems almost incomprehensible in a man of Wilson's intelligence and political experience. In part his hatred of Lodge accounts for it, in part his faith in his League. His physical condition in 1919 also played a role. At Paris he had suffered a violent attack of indigestion that was probably a symptom of a minor stroke. Thereafter, many observers noted small changes in his personality, particularly increased stubbornness and a loss of good judgment. Instead of making concessions, the president set out early in September on a nationwide speaking tour to rally support for the League. Though some of his speeches were brilliant, they had little effect on senatorial opinion, and the effort drained his last physical reserves. On September 25, after an address in Pueblo, Colorado, he collapsed. The rest of the trip had to be canceled. A few days later, in Washington, he suffered a severe stroke that partially paralyzed his left side.

For nearly two months the president was almost totally cut off from affairs of state, leaving supporters of the League leaderless while Lodge maneuvered the reservations through the Senate. Gradually, popular attitudes toward the League shifted. Organized groups of Italian-, Irish-, and German-Americans, angered by what they considered unfair treatment of their native lands in the Versailles Treaty, clamored for outright rejection. The arguments of the irreconcilables persuaded many citizens that Wilson had made too sharp a break with America's isolationist past and that the Lodge Reservations were therefore necessary. Other issues connected with the reconversion of society to a peacetime basis increasingly occupied the public mind.

A coalition of Democratic and moderate Republican senators could easily have carried the treaty. That no such coalition was organized was Wilson's fault. Lodge obtained the simple majority necessary to add his reservations to the treaty merely by keeping his own party united. When the time came for the final roll call on November 19, Wilson, bitter and emotionally distraught, urged the Democrats to vote for rejection. "Better a thousand times to go down fighting than to dip your colours to dishonourable compromise," he explained to his wife. Thus the amended treaty failed, 35 to 55, the irreconcilables and the Democrats voting against it. Lodge then allowed the original draft without his reservations to come to a vote. Again the result was defeat, 38 to 53. Only one Republican cast a ballot for ratification.

Dismayed but not yet crushed, friends of the League in both parties forced reconsideration of the treaty early in 1920. Neither Lodge nor Wilson would yield an inch. Lodge, who had little confidence in the effectiveness of any league of nations, was under no compulsion to compromise. Wilson, who believed that the League was the world's best

hope, did have such a compulsion. Yet he would not compromise either.

As the British historian Robert Skidelsky has written, "The architect of the Treaty's defeat in Congress was Wilson himself." His behavior is further evidence of his physical and mental decline. Probably he was incompetent to perform the duties of his office. Had he died or stepped down, the treaty, with reservations, would almost certainly have been ratified. When the Senate balloted again in March, half the Democrats voted for the treaty with the Lodge Reservations. The others, mostly southern party regulars, joined the irreconcilables. Together they mustered 35 votes, 7 more than the one-third that meant defeat.

Demobilization

To win the war, the nation had accepted drastic regulation of the economy in order to increase production and improve social efficiency. When the war ended, the government, in Wilson's words, "took the harness off" at once, blithely assuming that the economy could readjust itself without direction. The army was hastily demobilized, pouring millions of veterans into the job market without plan. All society seemed in flux. When the War Department sent letters to the next of kin of 30,000 soldiers buried in France, 12,000 of the letters were returned as undeliverable. No person of the name on the envelope lived at the indicated address. Nearly all controls established by the War Industries Board and other agencies were dropped overnight. Billions of dollars' worth of war contracts were canceled.

Business boomed in 1919 as consumers spent wartime savings on automobiles, homes, and other goods that had been in short supply during the conflict. But temporary shortages caused inflation; by 1920 the cost of living stood at more than twice the level of 1913.

Inflation in turn produced labor trouble. The unions, grown strong during the war, struck for wage increases. Over 4 million workers, one out of five in the labor force, were on strike at some time during 1919. Work stoppages aggravated shortages, triggering further inflation and more strikes. Then came one of the most precipitous economic declines

*During the Red Scare, radical cartoonist William Gropper sharply criticized the
tactics of Attorney General Palmer. These drawings appeared in* The Liberator
*early in 1920. At left, Palmer's agents warn, "Clear the road there, boys—we got
a dangerous Red." At right, a suspect faces a loutish, unsympathetic audience.*

in American history. Between July 1920 and March
1922, prices, especially agricultural prices, plummeted. Unemployment soared. Thus the unrealistic
attitude of the Wilson government toward the complexities of economic readjustment caused considerable unnecessary strife.

The Red Scare

Far more serious than the economic losses were the
social effects of these difficulties. Everyone wanted
peace, but wartime tensions did not subside; apparently people continued to need some release for
the aggressive drives they had formerly focused on
the Germans. Most Americans found strikes frustrating and drew invidious comparisons between the
lot of the unemployed soldier who had risked his
life for a dollar a day and that of the striker who
had drawn fat wages during the war in perfect
safety.

The activities of radicals in the labor movement
led millions of Americans to associate unionism and
strikes with the new threat of communist world revolution. Although there were only a relative handful
of communists in the United States, Russia's experience persuaded many people that a tiny minority of ruthless revolutionaries could take over a

nation of millions if conditions were right. Communists appointed themselves the champions of
workers; labor unrest attracted them magnetically.
When strikes broke out, some accompanied by violence, many people interpreted them as commun-
ist-inspired preludes to revolution. Louis Wiley, an
experienced *New York Times* reporter, told a friend
at this time that anarchists, socialists, and radical
labor leaders were "joining together with the object
of overthrowing the American Government
through a bloody revolution and establishing a Bol-
shevist republic."

Organized labor in America had seldom been
truly radical. The Industrial Workers of the World
(IWW) had made little impression in most industries. But some labor leaders had been attracted to
socialism, and many Americans failed to distinguish
between the common ends sought by communists
and socialists and the entirely different methods by
which they proposed to achieve those ends. When
a general strike paralyzed Seattle in February 1919,
the fact that a procommunist had helped organize
it sent shivers down countless conservative spines.
When the radical William Z. Foster began a drive
to organize the steel industry at about this time, the
fears became more intense. In September 1919 a
total of 343,000 steelworkers walked off their jobs,
and in the same month the Boston police struck.

Violence marked the steel strike, and the suspension of police protection in Boston led to looting and fighting that ended only when Governor Calvin Coolidge (who might have prevented the strike had he acted earlier) called out the National Guard.

During the same period a handful of terrorists caused widespread alarm by attempting to murder various prominent persons, including John D. Rockefeller, Justice Oliver Wendell Holmes, Jr., and Attorney General A. Mitchell Palmer. Although the terrorists were anarchists and anarchism had little in common with communism, many citizens lumped all extremists together and associated them with a monstrous assault on society.

What aroused the public even more was the fact that most radicals were not American citizens. Wartime fear of alien saboteurs easily transformed itself into peacetime terror of foreign radicals. In place of Germany, the enemy became the lowly immigrant, usually an Italian or a Jew or a Slav and usually an industrial worker. In this muddled way, radicalism, unionism, and questions of racial and national origins combined to make many Americans believe that their way of life was in imminent danger. That few immigrants were radicals, that most workers had no interest in communism, and that the extremists themselves were faction-ridden and irresolute did not affect conservative thinking. From all over the country came demands that radicals be ruthlessly suppressed. Thus the "Red Scare" was born.

Attorney General Palmer was the key figure in the resulting purge. He had been a typical progressive, a supporter of the League of Nations and such reforms as women's suffrage and child labor legislation. But pressure from Congress and his growing conviction that the communists really were a menace led him to join the "red hunt." Soon he was saying of the radicals: "Out of the sly and crafty eyes of many of them leap cupidity, cruelty, insanity, and crime; from their lopsided faces, sloping brows, and misshapen features may be recognized the unmistakable criminal type."

In August 1919, Palmer established within the Department of Justice the General Intelligence Division, headed by J. Edgar Hoover, to collect information about clandestine radical activities. In November, Justice Department agents swooped down on the meeting places in a dozen cities of an anarchist organization known as the Union of Russian Workers. More than 650 persons, many of them unconnected with the union, were arrested, but in only 43 cases could evidence be found to justify deportation.

Nevertheless, the public reacted so favorably that Palmer, thinking now of winning the 1920 Democratic presidential nomination, planned an immense roundup of communists. He obtained 3,000 warrants, and on January 2, 1920, his agents, reinforced by local police and self-appointed vigilantes, struck simultaneously in 33 cities. Palmer's biographer, Stanley Coben, has described the "Palmer raids" vividly:

> There was a knock on the door, the rush of police. In meeting houses, all were lined up to be searched; those who resisted often suffered brutal treatment. . . . Police searched the homes of many of those arrested; books and papers, as well as many people found in these residences, were carried off to headquarters. Policemen also sought those whose names appeared on seized membership lists; they captured many of these suspects in bed or at work, searching their homes, confiscating their possessions, almost always without warrants.

About 6,000 persons were taken into custody, many of them citizens and therefore not subject to the deportation laws, many others unconnected with any radical cause. Some were held incommunicado for weeks while the authorities searched for evidence against them. In a number of cases, individuals who went to visit prisoners were themselves thrown behind bars on the theory that they too must be communists. Hundreds of suspects were jammed into filthy "bullpens," beaten, and forced to sign "confessions."

The public tolerated these wholesale violations of civil liberties because of the supposed menace of communism. Gradually, however, protests began to be heard, first from lawyers and liberal magazines, then from a wider segment of the population. No revolutionary outbreak had taken place. Of 6,000 seized in the Palmer raids, only 556 proved liable to deportation. The widespread ransacking of communists' homes and meeting places produced mountains of inflammatory literature but only three pistols.

Palmer, attempting to maintain the crusade, announced that the radicals planned a gigantic terrorist demonstration for May Day 1920. In New York and other cities, thousands of police were placed on round-the-clock duty; federal troops stood by anxiously. But the day passed without even a rowdy meeting. Suddenly Palmer appeared ridiculous. The Red Scare swiftly subsided.

The Election of 1920

Wilson still hoped for vindication at the polls in the presidential election, which he sought to make a "great and solemn referendum" on the League. He would have liked to run for a third term, but in his enfeebled condition, he attracted no support among Democratic leaders. The party nominated James M. Cox of Ohio.

Cox favored joining the League, but the election did not produce the referendum on the new organization that Wilson desired. The Republicans, whose candidate was another Ohioan, Senator Warren G. Harding, equivocated shamelessly on the issue. The election turned on other matters, largely emotional. Disillusioned by the results of the war, many Americans had had their fill of idealism. They wanted, apparently, to end the long period of moral uplift and reform agitation that had begun under Theodore Roosevelt and return to what Harding called "normalcy."

To the extent that the voters were expressing opinions on Wilson's League, their response was overwhelmingly negative. Senator Harding had been a strong reservationist, yet he swept the country, winning over 16.1 million votes to Cox's 9.1 million. In July 1921, Congress formally ended the war with the Central Powers by passing a joint resolution.

The defeat of the League was a tragedy both for Wilson, whose crusade for a world order based on peace and justice ended in failure, and for the world, which was condemned by the result to endure another still more horrible and costly war. Perhaps this dreadful outcome could not have been avoided. Had Wilson compromised and Lodge behaved like a statesman instead of a politician, America would have joined the League, but it might well have failed to respond when called on to meet its obligations. As events soon demonstrated, the League powers acted pusillanimously and even dishonorably when challenged by aggressor nations.

Yet it might have been different had the Senate ratified the Versailles Treaty. What was lost when the treaty failed in the Senate was not peace but the possibility of peace, a tragic loss indeed.

Milestones

1914 United States invades Veracruz, Mexico
War breaks out in Europe
1915 U-boat torpedoes the *Lusitania*
United States recognizes the Carranza government in Mexico
1916 Louis D. Brandeis named to the Supreme Court
Adamson Act gives railroad workers the eight-hour day
"Pancho" Villa burns Columbus, New Mexico
1917 Wilson's "Peace Without Victory" speech
Germany resumes unrestricted submarine warfare
United States declares war on the Central Powers
Herbert Hoover named Food Administrator
Bernard Baruch named head of the War Industries Board
1918 Sedition Act
Republicans gain control of both houses of Congress
Armistice ends the Great War
1919 Steel strike
Red Scare, climaxing in Palmer raids
Paris Peace Conference
Senate rejects Versailles Treaty
1920 Senate rejects Versailles Treaty

SUPPLEMENTARY READING

Titles marked with an asterisk have been published in paperback.

Wilson's handling of foreign relations is discussed in several volumes by A. S. Link: **Wilson** (1947), **Woodrow Wilson and the Progressive Era*** (1954), and **Wilson the Diplomatist*** (1957). R. H. Ferrell, **Woodrow Wilson and World War I*** (1985), is an up-to-date survey of the period. See also N. G. Levin, Jr., **Woodrow Wilson and World Politics*** (1968). Latin American affairs under Wilson are treated in D. G. Munro, **Intervention and Dollar Diplomacy in the Caribbean** (1964).

For details of America's entry into the Great War, see E. R. May, **The World War and American Isolation*** (1959), and E. H. Buehrig, **Woodrow Wilson and the Balance of Power** (1955).

The war on the home front is covered in D. M. Kennedy, **Over Here: The First World War and American Society** (1980), and more briefly in W. E. Leuchtenburg, **The Perils of Prosperity*** (1958). A good account of military preparation is H. A. De Weerd, **President Wilson Fights His War** (1968). Other useful volumes include R. D. Cuff, **The War Industries Board** (1973); Charles Gilbert, **American Financing of World War I** (1970); S. L. Vaughn, **Holding Fast the Inner Lines** (1980), which deals with the Committee on Public Information; M. I. Urofsky, **Big Steel and the Wilson Administration** (1969); Donald Johnson, **The Challenge to American Freedoms** (1963); David Brody, **Steelworkers in Amer-**ica* (1960); D. R. Beaver, **Newton D. Baker and the American War Effort** (1966); and S. W. Livermore, **Politics is Adjourned: Woodrow Wilson and the War Congress*** (1966).

On American military participation, consult De Weerd, **President Wilson Fights His War.** Laurence Stallings, **The Doughboys*** (1963), is a good popular account of the American army in France. See also F. E. Vandiver, **Black Jack: The Life and Times of John J. Pershing** (1977). On blacks in the army, see A. E. Barbeau and F. Henri, **The Unknown Soldiers** (1974).

On the peace settlement, in addition to the biographies of Wilson, consult A. J. Mayer, **Politics and Diplomacy of Peacemaking** (1967), T. A. Bailey, **Woodrow Wilson and the Lost Peace*** (1944) and **Woodrow Wilson and the Great Betrayal*** (1945), J. A. Garraty, **Henry Cabot Lodge** (1953), and Ralph Stone, **The Irreconcilables*** (1970).

On radicalism and the Red Scare, see R. K. Murray, **The Red Scare*** (1955), Stanley Coben, **A. Mitchell Palmer** (1963), David Brody, **The Steel Strike of 1919*** (1965), and R. L. Friedheim, **The Seattle General Strike*** (1965). On the election of 1920, see Wesley Bagby, **The Road to Normalcy*** (1962), Burl Noggle, **Into the Twenties** (1974), and R. K. Murray, **The Harding Era** (1969).

Postwar Society and Culture: Change and Adjustment

In the spring of '27 something bright and alien flashed across the sky. A young Minnesotan who seemed to have nothing to do with his generation did a heroic thing and for a moment people set down their glasses in the country clubs and speakeasies and thought of their old best dreams.

F. SCOTT FITZGERALD *on Lindbergh's flight to Paris*

The Great War seemed to many who lived through it a turning point in history, the real division separating the 19th from the new 20th century. Actually most of what seemed new to the people of the 1920s had begun well before 1917, and the changes they noticed were still going on. They were in the midst of new social, cultural, and economic forces, forces that were to shape their lives and those of their children and grandchildren.

Closing the Gates

Fear of Outsiders

The ending of the Red Scare did not signal the disappearance of xenophobia. It was perhaps inevitable and possibly wise that some limitation be placed on the entry of immigrants into the United States after the war. An immense backlog of prospective migrants had piled up during the conflict, and the desperate postwar economic condition of Europe led hundreds of thousands to seek better circumstances in the United States. Immigration increased from 110,000 in 1919 to 430,000 in 1920

and 805,000 in 1921, with every prospect of continuing to rise.

In 1921 Congress, reflecting widespread prejudice against eastern and southern Europeans, passed an emergency act establishing a quota system. Each year 3 percent of the number of foreign-born residents of the United States in 1910 (about 350,000 persons) might enter the country. Each country's quota was based on the number of its nationals in the United States in 1910. This meant that only a relative handful of the total would be from southern and eastern Europe. In 1924 the quota was reduced to 2 percent and the base year shifted to 1890, thereby lowering further the proportion of southern and eastern Europeans admitted.

In 1929 Congress established a system that allowed only 150,000 immigrants a year to enter the country. Each national quota was based on the supposed origins of the entire white population of the United States in 1920, not merely on the foreign-born. Here is an example of how the system worked:

$$\frac{\text{Italian quota}}{150,000} = \frac{\text{Italian-origin population, 1920}}{\text{White population, 1920}}$$

$$\frac{\text{Italian quota}}{150,000} = \frac{3,800,000}{95,500,000}$$

$$\text{Italian quota} = 6,000 \text{ (approximately)}$$

Presumably this method would preserve the status quo; in fact it heavily favored immigrants from Great Britain. The system was complicated and unscientific, for no one could determine with accuracy the "origins" of millions of citizens.

The law reduced actual immigration to far below 150,000 a year. British immigration between 1931 and 1939, for example, amounted to only 23,000 even though the annual British quota was over 65,000. Meanwhile, hundreds of thousands of southern and eastern Europeans waited for admission.

The United States had closed the gates. The National Origins Act caused the foreign-born percentage of the population to fall from about 13 percent in 1920 to 4.7 percent in 1970. Instead of an open, cosmopolitan society eager to accept, in Emma Lazarus's stirring line, the "huddled masses yearning to breathe free," America now became

709

Immigrants entering the United States through New York City's Ellis Island. When immigration to the United States surged again after the war, restrictionists moved quickly to convince Congress to reject the traditional policy of unlimited immigration in favor of strict national quotas.

committed to preserving a homogeneous, "Anglo-Saxon" population.

Distaste for immigrants from eastern Europe, many of whom were Jewish, expanded into a more general anti-Semitism in the 1920s. American Jews, whether foreign-born or native, were subject to increasing discrimination, not because they were slow in adopting American ways but because, being ambitious and hardworking as immigrants were sup-

posed to be, many of them were getting ahead in the world more rapidly than expected. Prestigious colleges like Harvard, Yale, and Columbia that had in the past admitted Jews based on their academic records now imposed unofficial but effective quotas. Medical schools also established quotas, and no matter how talented, most young Jewish lawyers and bankers could find places only in so-called Jewish firms.

New Urban Social Patterns

The census of 1920 revealed that for the first time a majority of Americans (54 million in a population of 106 million) lived in "urban" rather than "rural" places. These figures are somewhat misleading when applied to the study of social attitudes because the census classified anyone in a community of 2,500 or more as urban. Of the 54 million "urban" residents in 1920, over 16 million lived in villages and towns of fewer than 25,000 persons, and the evidence suggests strongly that a large majority of them held ideas and values more like those of rural citizens than like those of city dwellers. But the truly urban Americans, the one person in four who lived in a city of 100,000 or more—and particularly the nearly 16.4 million who lived in metropolises of at least half a million—were increasing steadily in number and influence. More than 19 million persons moved from farms to cities in the 1920s, and the population living in centers of 100,000 or more increased by about a third.

Being a city dweller meant far more than changing one's physical surroundings. It affected family structure, educational opportunities, and dozens of other aspects of human existence. Indeed, since most of the changes in the relations of husbands, wives, and children that had occurred in the 19th century were related to the fact that people were leaving farms to work in towns and cities, these trends continued and were intensified in the early 20th century as more and more people settled in urban centers. In addition, couples continued to marry more out of love and physical attraction than for social position or economic advantage or to please parents. In each successive decade, people married slightly later and had slightly fewer children.

Earlier differences between working-class and

middle-class family structures persisted. In 1920 about a quarter of the American women who were working were married, but less than 10 percent of all married women were working. Middle-class married women who worked were nearly all either childless or highly paid professionals who were able to employ servants. Most male skilled workers now earned enough to support a family in modest comfort so long as they could work steadily, but an unskilled laborer still could not. Wives in most such families helped out, usually by taking in laundry or doing piecework sewing for jobbers.

However, there were important variations in the roles of wives of different ethnic backgrounds. Those who could not speak English well had difficulty obtaining work. Italian immigrant women rarely worked outside the home even if childless. Irish-American wives often found jobs as domestics or, if better educated, as nurses, telephone operators, or clerks. Out of necessity, a far larger proportion of black women, married or single, worked than white women, but they could rarely find better-paying jobs than domestic service. Compulsory education and state child labor laws kept an increasing percentage of the children of the unskilled out of the job market into their mid-teens, but many found odd jobs, and some evaded the laws.

By the 1920s the concept of the "companionate" family had emerged. In such families, husbands and wives would deal with each other as equals, which under existing conditions meant sharing housework and child care, downplaying male authority, and stressing mutual satisfaction in sexual and other matters. They should be friends and lovers, not merely housekeepers, earners of money, and producers of children. Procreation did not have to be the main purpose of matrimony, but if there were children, they should be left as free as possible to develop in their own way; rigid discipline was limiting and therefore wrong. By contrast, advocates of companionate relationships believed that there was nothing particularly sacred about marriage; divorce should be made easier for couples that did not get along, provided they did not have children.

Much attention was given at this time to "scientific" child raising. Child-care experts (a new breed) agreed that routine medical examinations and good nutrition were of central importance, but they were divided about how the socialization and psychological development of the young should be handled. One school stressed rigid training: Children should not be spoiled by indulgence, toilet training should begin early in infancy, thumb sucking should be suppressed, too much kissing could turn male youngsters into "mama's boys." "Children are made not born," John B. Watson, a former president of the American Psychological Association who was also a vice-president of the important J. Walter Thompson advertising agency, explained in *The Psychological Care of Infant and Child* (1928). "Never hug and kiss them, never let them sit in your lap. If you must, kiss them once on the forehead when they say good night."

The other school favored a more permissive approach. Toilet training could wait; parents should pay attention to their children's expressed needs, not impose a generalized set of rules upon them. In *The Companionate Marriage* (1927), Benjamin B. Lindsey, a juvenile court judge, suggested a kind of trial marriage, a period during which a young couple could get used to each other before undertaking to raise a family. By practicing contraception, such couples could separate without doing serious damage to anyone if they decided to end the relationship. If the relationship remained firm and loving, it would become a traditional marriage, and their children would grow up in a loving environment that would help them to become warm, well-adjusted adults.

Lindsey was one among many self-appointed experts who advocated more freedom for young people and open discussion of all questions related to sex. He was most concerned about the welfare of children, whose natural sexuality, he insisted, was being stupidly repressed by Victorian prudes. Others put more emphasis on married women's rights and the injustice of the double standard. Still others were interested in breaking down 19th-century sexual taboos for all people, married or single.

The Younger Generation

All of these matters were of particular concern to young adults—the generation born around the turn of the century that had grown up before and during the Great War. That war had raised their hopes for the future and its outcome dashed them. Now the narrowness and prudery of so many of their elders and the stuffy conservatism of nearly all politicians seemed not merely old-fashioned but ludicrous. The actions of red-baiters and reactionaries led them to exaggerate the importance of their right to express themselves in bizarre ways. Their models and indeed some of their leaders were the prewar Greenwich Village bohemians.

The 1920s has been dubbed the Jazz Age, the era of "flaming youth," when young people danced to syncopated "African" rhythms, careened about the countryside in automobiles in search of pleasure and forgetfulness, and made gods of movie stars and professional athletes. This view of the period bears some resemblance to reality. "Younger people," one observer noted in 1922, were attempting "to create a way of life free from the bondage of

In his many illustrations for magazines such as Life *and* McClure's, *John Held, Jr., captured the spirit of the roaring twenties and the new sense of freedom expressed in flapper-style clothing and freer relations between the sexes.*

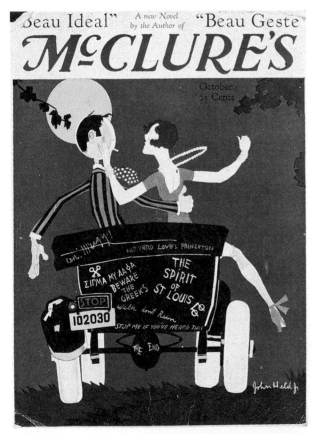

an authority that has lost all meaning." But the resemblance is only superficial; they certainly appreciated having a good time, and like any generation moving from adolescence to maturity, the young people of the 1920s were eager to understand the world and make their way in it. They were more unconventional than their grandparents primarily because they were adjusting to more profound and more rapid changes in their world than their grandparents could have imagined.

Beliefs that only the avant garde had held before the war became commonplaces. In other words, trends barely perceptible during the Progressive Era now reached avalanche proportions. This was particularly noticeable in relationships between the sexes. The historian Beth L. Bailey has shown how this relates to courtship. In the late 19th century a typical young man "paid a call" on a female friend. He met and conversed with her parents, perhaps over coffee and cookies. The couple remained at home, the parents nearby if not actually participating in what was essentially a social (one might say, public) event held in a private place.

By the 1920s paying calls was being replaced by dating; the young man called only to "pick up" his date, the two to go off, free of parental supervision, for whatever diversion they wished. Unlike a call, Professor Bailey explains, a date was "a private act in the public world."

Dating developed many conventions out of keeping with the trend toward freedom in sexual matters of which it was a part. A man asked a woman for a date because dating meant going somewhere and spending money, and the man was expected to do the transporting and pay the bill. This made the woman doubly dependent; under the old system, *she* provided the refreshments, and there was no taboo against her doing the inviting.

But there is no question that for the young people of the 1920s, relations between the sexes were becoming more relaxed and uninhibited. Respectable young women smoked cigarettes, something previously done in public only by prostitutes and bohemian types. They cast off their heavy corsets, wore lipstick and "exotic" perfumes, and shortened both their hair and their skirts, the latter rising steadily from instep to ankle to calf to knee and beyond as the decade progressed.

Freudian psychology and the more accessible ideas of the British "sexologist" Havelock Ellis reached steadily deeper into the popular psyche. According to A. A. Brill, the chief American popularizer of Freud's theories, the sex drive was irrepressible. "Love and sex are the same thing," he wrote. "The urge is there, and whether the individual desires it or no, it always manifests itself."* Since sex was "the central function of life," Ellis argued, it must be "simple and natural and pure and good." Bombarded by these exciting ideas and by erotic books and movies, to say nothing of their own inclinations, young people found casting off their inhibitions more and more tempting.

Conservatives bemoaned what they described as the breakdown of moral standards, the fragmentation of the family, and the decline of parental authority—all with some reason. Nevertheless, society was not collapsing. Much of the rebelliousness of the young, like their particular styles of dress, was faddish, in a sense a kind of youthful conformity. This was particularly true of college students, every aspect of whose extracurricular life (which was consuming a steadily larger share of most students' time and energy to begin with) was governed by elaborate rituals. In *The Damned and the Beautiful*, Paula S. Fass has shown how such matters as fraternity and sorority initiations, proms, attendance at Saturday afternoon football games, styles of dress, and college slang, seemingly aspects of independence and free choice, were nearly everywhere shaped and controlled by peer pressure.

But young people's new ways of relating to one another, while influenced by the desire to conform, were not mere fads and were not confined to people under 30. This can be seen most clearly in the birth control movement, the drive to legalize the use of contraceptives.

The "New" Woman

The young people of the 1920s were more open about sex and perhaps more sexually precocious than the young had been before the war. This does not mean that most of them engaged in sexual intercourse before marriage or that they tended to

marry earlier. Single young people might "believe in" birth control, but relatively few (at least by modern standards) had occasion to practice it. Contraception was a concern of married people, particularly married women.

The leading American proponent of birth control in the 1920s, and the person who coined the term, was Margaret Sanger, one of the less self-centered Greenwich Village bohemians. Before the war she was a political radical, a friend of Eugene Debs, Big Bill Haywood, and Emma Goldman. Gradually, however, her attention focused on the plight of the poor women she encountered while working as a nurse; many of these women were burdened by large numbers of children yet knew nothing about contraception. Sanger began to write articles and pamphlets designed to enlighten them, but when she did so she ran afoul of the Comstock Act of 1873, an antiobscenity law that banned the distribution of information about contraception from the mails. She was frequently in trouble with the law, but she was persistent to the edge of fanaticism. In 1921 she founded the American Birth Control League and two years later a research center.

The medical profession, though wary of the issue, gave some support to the birth control movement, as did the eugenicists, who claimed that unless the fecundity of "unfit" types (people others might describe simply as poor) was curbed, "race suicide" would result. Sanger accepted support wherever it could be found; by the end of the decade she was no longer on the cutting edge of the movement or even a very radical feminist. But by that time resistance to the use of contraception was crumbling. However, the Supreme Court did not determine that the right to use contraceptives was guaranteed by the Constitution until the 1960s.

Other sex-based restrictions and limitations that were of particular importance to women also seemed to be breaking down. The divorce laws had been modified in most states. More women were taking jobs, attracted by the expanding demand for clerks, typists, salespeople, receptionists, telephone operators, and similar service-oriented occupations. Over 10.6 million women were working by the end of the decade, compared to 8.4 million in 1920. The Department of Labor's Women's Bureau, outgrowth of a wartime agency, was founded in 1920 and was soon conducting investigations of the work-

---

* The historian John C. Burnham claims that Brill's "preoccupation with the grossly sexual and his insensitivity to intellectual subtleties gave much of American psychoanalysis both a sensational and simplistic tendency."

ing conditions women faced in different industries and how various laws affected them.

But most of these gains were illusory. Relaxation of the strict standards of sexual morality did not eliminate the double standard. More women worked, but most of the jobs they held were still menial or of a kind that few men wanted: domestic service, elementary school teaching, clerical work, selling behind a counter. One of the worst blows fell in 1923 when in the case of *Adkins* v. *Children's Hospital*, the Supreme Court declared a federal law that limited the hours of work for women in the District of Columbia unconstitutional.

Where they competed for jobs with men, women usually received much lower wages. Women's Bureau studies demonstrated this repeatedly, yet when the head of the bureau, Mary Anderson, tried to get employers to raise women's wages, most of them first claimed that the men had families to support, and when she reminded them that many female employees also had family responsibilities, they told her that there was a "tacit understanding" that women were to make less than men. "If I paid them the same," one employer said, "there would be a revolution." Efforts to get the American Federation of Labor to take up the issue met with failure; few of the unions in the federation admitted women.

The number of women college graduates con-

Mass-produced and mass-marketed clothing became readily available to most Americans for the first time in the 1920s, as this young saleswoman's wares attest.

tinued to expand, but the colleges placed more emphasis on subjects like home economics that seemed designed to make them better housewives rather than professional nutritionists or business executives. As one Vassar College administrator (a woman!) said, colleges should provide "education for women along the lines of their chief interests and responsibilities, motherhood and the home."

The 1920s proved disillusioning to feminists, who now paid a price for their single-minded pursuit of the right to vote in the Progressive Era. After the ratification of the Nineteenth Amendment, Carrie Chapman Catt was exultant. "We are no longer petitioners," she announced, "but free and equal citizens." Many activists, assuming the battle won, lost interest in agitating for change. They believed that the suffrage amendment had given them the one weapon needed to achieve whatever women still lacked. In fact, it soon became apparent that women did not vote as a bloc. Many, perhaps most, married women voted for the candidates their husbands supported.

When radical feminists discovered that voting did not automatically bring true equality, they founded the Women's party and began campaigning for an equal rights amendment. Their leader, Alice Paul, a dynamic if somewhat fanatical person, disdained specific goals such as disarmament, an end to child labor, and liberalized birth control. Total equality for women was the one objective. The party considered protective legislation governing the hours and working conditions of women discriminatory. This caused the so-called social feminists, who believed that children and working women needed the protection provided by such laws, to break away.

The Women's party never attracted a wide following, but only partly because of the split with the social feminists. Many of the younger radical women, like the bohemians of the Progressive Era, were primarily concerned with their personal freedom to behave as they wished; politics did not interest them. But a more important reason was that nearly all the radicals failed to see that questions of gender—the attitudes that men and women *were taught* to take toward each other, not immutable physical or psychological differences—stood in the way of true sexual equality. Many more women joined the more moderate League of Women Voters, which attempted to mobilize support for a broad spectrum of reforms, some of which had no specific connection with the interests of women as such. The entire women's movement lost momentum. The battle for the equal rights amendment persisted through the 1930s, but it was lost. By the end of that decade the movement was moribund.

Popular Culture: Movies and Radio

The postwar decade saw immense changes in popular culture. Unlike the literary flowering of the era, these changes seemed in tune with the times, not a reaction against them. This was true in part because they were products as much of technology as of human imagination.

The first motion pictures were made around 1900, but the medium only came into its own after the Great War. The early films, such as the eight-minute epic *The Great Train Robbery* (1903), were brief, action-packed, and unpretentious. Professional actors and most educated people viewed them with amused contempt. But their success was instantaneous with recent immigrants and many other slum dwellers. In 1912 there were nearly 13,000 movie houses in the United States, more than 500 in New York City alone. Many of these places were converted stores called nickelodeons because the admission charge was only 5 cents.

In the beginning the mere recording of movement seemed to satisfy the public, but success led to rapid technical and artistic improvements and consequently to more cultivated audiences. David W. Griffith's 12-reel *Birth of a Nation* (1915) was a particularly important breakthrough in both areas, though Griffith's sympathetic treatment of the Ku Klux Klan of Reconstruction days angered blacks and white liberals.

By the mid-1920s the industry, centered in Hollywood, California, was the fourth largest in the nation in capital investment. Films moved from the nickelodeons to converted theaters. So large was the audience that movie "palaces" seating several thousand people sprang up in the major cities. *Daily* ticket sales averaged more than 10 million. With the introduction of talking movies, *The Jazz Singer* (1927) being the first of significance, and color films a decade later, the motion picture reached technological maturity. Costs and profits mounted; by

Man against machine: Charlie Chaplin duels a folding Murphy bed in the film One A.M.

the 1930s, million-dollar productions were common.

Many movies were still tasteless trash catering to the prejudices of the multitude. Sex, crime, war, romantic adventure, broad comedy, and luxurious living were the main themes, endlessly repeated in predictable patterns. Popular actors and actresses tended to be either handsome, talentless sticks or so-called character actors who were typecast over and over again as heroes, villains, comedians. The stars attracted armies of adoring fans and received thousands of dollars a week for their services. Critics charged that the movies were destroying the legitimate stage (which experienced a sharp decline), corrupting the morals of youth, and glorifying the materialistic aspects of life.

Nevertheless, the motion picture made positive contributions to American culture. Beginning with the work of Griffith, filmmakers created an entirely new theatrical art, using close-ups to portray character and heighten tension and broad panoramic shots to transcend the limits of the stage. They employed, with remarkable results, special lighting effects, the fade-out, and other techniques impossible in the live theater. Movies enabled dozens of established actors to reach wider audiences and developed many first-rate new ones. As the medium matured, it produced many dramatic works of high quality. At its best the motion picture offered a breadth and power of impact superior to anything on the traditional stage.

Charlie Chaplin was the greatest film star of the era. His characterization of the sad-eyed little tramp with his toothbrush moustache and his cane, tight frock coat, and baggy trousers became famous throughout the world. Chaplin's films were superficially unpretentious; they seemed even in the 1920s old-fashioned, aimed at the lower-class audiences that had first found the movies magical. But his work proved both universally popular and enduring; he was perhaps the greatest comic artist of all time. The animated cartoon, perfected by Walt Disney, was a lesser but significant cinematic achievement; Mickey Mouse, Donald Duck, and other Disney cartoon characters gave endless delight to millions of children.

Even more pervasive than the movies in its effects on the American people was radio. Wireless transmission of sound was developed in the late 19th century by many scientists in Europe and the United States. An American, Lee De Forest, working in the decade before the Great War, devised the key improvements that made long-distance broadcasting possible. During the war radio was put to important military uses and was strictly controlled, but immediately thereafter the airwaves were thrown open to everybody.

Radio was briefly the domain of hobbyists, thousands of "hams" broadcasting in indiscriminate fashion. Even under these conditions, the manufacture of radio equipment became a big business. In 1920 the first commercial station (KDKA in Pittsburgh) began broadcasting, and by the end of 1922 over 500 stations were in operation. In 1926 the National Broadcasting Company, the first continentwide network, was created.

It took little time for broadcasters to discover the power of the new medium. When one pioneer interrupted a music program to ask listeners to phone in requests, the station received 3,000 calls in an hour. The immediacy of radio explained its tremendous impact. As a means of communicating the latest news, it had no peer; beginning with the broadcast of the 1924 presidential nominating conventions, all major public events were covered "live." Advertisers seized on radio too; it proved to be as effective a way to sell soap as to transmit news.

Advertising had mixed effects on broadcasting. The sums paid by businesses for airtime made possible elaborate entertainments performed by the finest actors and musicians, all without cost to listeners. However, advertisers hungered for mass markets. They preferred to sponsor programs of little intellectual content, aimed at the lowest tastes and utterly uncontroversial. And good and bad alike, programs were constantly interrupted by irritating pronouncements extolling the supposed virtues of one commercial product or another.

In 1927 Congress limited the number of stations and parceled out wavelengths to prevent interference. Further legislation in 1934 established the Federal Communications Commission, with power to revoke the licenses of stations that failed to operate in the public interest. But the FCC placed no effective controls on programming or on advertising practices.

The Golden Age of Sports

The extraordinary popularity of sports in the postwar period can be explained in a number of ways. People had more money to spend and more free time to fill. Radio was bringing suspenseful, play-by-play accounts of sports contests into millions of homes, thus encouraging tens of thousands to want to see similar events with their own eyes. New means of persuasion developed by advertisers to sell lipstick, breakfast cereal, and refrigerators were applied with equal success to sporting events and to the athletes who participated in them.

There had been great athletes before; indeed, probably the greatest all-around athlete of the 20th century was Jim Thorpe, a Sac and Fox Indian who won both the pentathalon and the decathalon at the 1912 Olympic Games, made Walter Camp's All America football team in 1912 and 1913, then played major league baseball for several years before becoming a pioneer founder of and player in the National Football League. But what truly made the 1920s a golden age was a coincidence—the emergence in a few short years of a remarkable collection of what today would be called superstars.

In football there was the University of Illinois's Harold "Red" Grange, who averaged over 10 yards a carry during his college career and who in one incredible quarter during the 1924 game between Illinois and Michigan carried the ball four times and scored a touchdown each time, gaining in the process 263 yards. In prize fighting, heavyweight champion Jack Dempsey, the "Manassas Mauler," knocked out a succession of challengers in bloody battles only to be deposed in 1927 by "Gentleman Gene" Tunney, who gave him a 15-round boxing lesson and then, according to Tunney's own account, celebrated by consuming "several pots of tea."

During the same years William "Big Bill" Tilden dominated tennis, winning the men's singles title every year from 1920 to 1925 along with nearly every other tournament he entered. Beginning in 1923, Robert T. "Bobby" Jones ruled over the world of golf with equal authority, his climactic achievement being his capturing of the amateur and open championships of both the United States and Great Britain in 1930.

A few women athletes dominated their sports during this Golden Age in similar fashion. In tennis

Gertrude Ederle being greased before the start of her 1926 swim across the English Channel. She not only made it, but in faster time than any of the four men who had preceded her.

Helen Wills was three times United States singles champion and the winner of the women's singles at Wimbledon eight times in the late 1920s and early 1930s. The swimmer Gertrude Ederle, holder of 18 world's records by the time she was 17, swam the English Channel on her second attempt in 1926. She was not only the first woman to do so, but she did it faster than any of the four men who had previously made it across.

However, the sports star among stars was "the Sultan of Swat," baseball's Babe Ruth.* Ruth not only dominated baseball, he changed it from a game ruled by pitchers and low scores to one where hitting was more greatly admired. Originally himself a brilliant pitcher, his incredible hitting ability made him more valuable in the outfield, where he could play every day. Before Ruth, John "Home Run" Baker was the most famous slugger; his greatest home run total was 12, achieved shortly before the World War. Ruth hit 29 in 1919 and 54 in 1920, his first year

with the New York Yankees. By 1923 he was so feared that he was given a base on balls more than half the times he appeared at the plate.

The achievements of these and other outstanding athletes had a cumulative effect. New stadiums were built, and they were filled by "the largest crowds that ever witnessed athletic sports since the fall of Rome." Record crowds paying unprecedented sums attended all sorts of events.

Football was the preeminent school sport. At many colleges football afternoons came to resemble religious rites both in their formality, with their cheerleaders and marching bands, and in the fervor of the crowds. A national magazine titled a 1928 article "The Great God Football," and the editor of a college newspaper denounced "disloyal" students who took seats in the grandstand where they could see what was happening on the field rather than encouraging the team by doing their bit in the student cheering section in the end zone.

Tens of thousands of men and women took up tennis, golf, and swimming. The turkey trot, a popular prewar dance, led in the next decade to what one historian called "an imitative swarm of hops,

* His full name was George Herman Ruth, but everyone used the nickname "Babe," given him early in his career.

wriggles, squirms, glides and gallops named after all the animals in the menagerie."

Urban-Rural Conflicts: Fundamentalism

These were buoyant times for people in tune with the times—the young, the devil-may-care, factory workers with money in their pockets, many different types. Nearly all of them were city people. However, the tensions and hostilities of the 1920s also found expression in ways related to an older rift in American society, the conflict between the urban and the rural way of life. To many among the scattered millions who tilled the soil and among the millions who lived in towns and small cities, the new city-oriented culture seemed sinful, overly materialistic, and unhealthy. To them change was something to be resented and resisted.

In Baptism in Kansas (*1928*), *John Stewart Curry viewed sympathetically the sincerity and depth of feeling that marked the revival of religious fundamentalism in much of rural America during the 1920s. Curry was a leader of the rural regionalist painters, seeking, he said, to show the "struggle of man against nature."*

Yet there was no denying its fascination. Made even more aware of the appeal of the city by radio and the automobile, farmers and townspeople coveted the comfort and excitement of city life at the same time that they condemned its vices. Rural society proclaimed the superiority of its ways at least in part to protect itself from temptation. Change, omnipresent in the postwar world, must be resisted even at the cost of individualism and freedom.

One expression of this intolerance was a resurgence of religious fundamentalism. Although it was especially prevalent among Baptists and Methodists, fundamentalism was primarily an attitude of mind, profoundly conservative, rather than a religious idea. Fundamentalists rejected the theory of evolution, indeed, all knowledge about the origins of the universe and the human race that had been discovered during the 19th century.

Urban sophisticates tended to dismiss fundamentalists as boors and hayseed fanatics, yet the persistence of old-fashioned ideas was understandable. In rural areas where educational standards were low and culture was relatively static, old ideas remained unchallenged. The power of reason, so obvious in a technologically advanced society, seemed much less obvious to rural people. Farmers, living in close contact with the capricious, elemental power of nature, tended to have more respect for the force of divine providence than city folk. Beyond this, the majesty and beauty of the King James translation of the Bible, the only book in countless rural homes, made it extraordinarily difficult for many persons to abandon their belief in its literal truth.

What made crusaders of the fundamentalists, however, was their resentment of modern urban culture. While in some cases they harassed liberal ministers, their religious attitudes had little public significance; their efforts to impose their views on public education were another matter. The teaching of evolution must be prohibited, they insisted. Throughout the early 1920s they campaigned vigorously for laws banning discussion of Darwin's theory in textbooks and classrooms.

Their greatest asset in this unfortunate crusade was William Jennings Bryan. Age had not improved the "Peerless Leader." After leaving Wilson's Cabinet in 1915, he devoted much time to religious and moral issues, but without applying himself conscientiously to the study of these difficult questions. He went about the country charging that "they"—

meaning the mass of educated Americans—had "taken the Lord away from the schools." He denounced the use of public money to undermine Christian principles, and he offered $100 to anyone who would admit to being descended from an ape. His immense popularity in rural areas assured him a wide audience, and no one came forward to take his money.

The fundamentalists won a minor victory in 1925, when Tennessee passed a law forbidding instructors in the state's schools and colleges to teach "any theory that denies the story of the Divine Creation of man as taught in the Bible." Although the bill passed both houses by big majorities, most legislators voted aye only because they dared not expose themselves to charges that they disbelieved the Bible. Educators in the state, hoping to obtain larger school appropriations from the legislature, hesitated to protest. Governor Austin Peay, an intelligent and liberal-minded man, feared to veto the bill lest he jeopardize other measures he was backing. "Probably the law will never be applied," he predicted when he signed it. Even Bryan, who used his influence to obtain passage of the measure, urged—unsuccessfully—that it include no penalties.

Upon learning of the passage of this act, the American Civil Liberties Union announced that it would finance a test case challenging its constitutionality if a Tennessee teacher would deliberately violate the statute. Urged on by friends, John T. Scopes, a young biology teacher in Dayton, reluctantly agreed and did teach that man was descended from other primates. He was arrested. A battery of nationally known lawyers came forward to defend him; the state obtained the services of Bryan himself. The so-called "Monkey Trial" became an overnight sensation.

Clarence Darrow, chief counsel for the defendant, stated the issue clearly. "Scopes isn't on trial," he said, "civilization is on trial. The prosecution is opening the doors for a reign of bigotry equal to anything in the Middle Ages. No man's belief will be safe if they win." The comic aspects of the trial obscured this issue. Big-city reporters like H. L. Mencken of the *Baltimore Evening Sun* flocked to Dayton to make sport of the fundamentalists. Scopes's conviction was a foregone conclusion; after the jury rendered its verdict, the judge fined him $100.

Nevertheless, the trial exposed both the stupidity

and the danger of the fundamentalist position. The high point came when Bryan agreed to testify as an expert witness on the Bible. In a sweltering courtroom, both men in shirtsleeves, the lanky, roughhewn Darrow cross-examined the aging champion of fundamentalism, mercilessly exposing his childlike faith and his abysmal ignorance. Bryan admitted to believing that Eve had been created from Adam's rib and that a whale had swallowed Jonah. "I believe in a God that can make a whale and can make a man and make both do what He pleases," he explained.

The Monkey Trial ended badly for nearly everyone concerned. Scopes moved away from Dayton; the judge, John Raulston, was defeated when he sought reelection; Bryan died in his sleep a few days after the trial. But fundamentalism continued to flourish, not only in the nation's backwaters but also in many cities, brought there by rural people in search of work. In retrospect, even the heroes of the Scopes trial—science and freedom of thought—seem somewhat less stainless than they did to liberals at the time. The account of evolution in the textbook used by Scopes was far from satisfactory, yet it was advanced as unassailable fact. The book also contained statements that to the modern mind seem at least as bigoted as anything that Bryan said at Dayton. In a section on the "races of man," for example, it described Caucasians as "the highest type of all . . . represented by the civilized white inhabitants of Europe and America."

Urban Rural Conflicts: Prohibition

The conflict between the countryside and the city was fought on many fronts, and in one sector the rural forces achieved a quick victory. This was the prohibition of the manufacture, transportation, and sale of alcoholic beverages by the Eighteenth Amendment, ratified in 1919. Although there were some big-city advocates of prohibition, the Eighteenth Amendment, in the words of the historian Andrew Sinclair, marked a triumph of the "Corn Belt over the conveyor belt."

The temperance movement had been important since the Age of Jackson; it was a major issue in many states during the Gilded Age, and by the Progressive Era many reformers were eager to prohibit

drinking entirely. Indeed, prohibition was a typical progressive reform, moralistic, backed by the middle class, aimed at frustrating "the interests"—in this case, the distillers.

The World War aided the prohibitionists by increasing the need for food. The Lever Act of 1917 outlawed the use of grain in the manufacture of alcoholic beverages, primarily as a conservation measure. The prevailing dislike of foreigners helped the dry cause still more, as beer drinking was associated with Germans. State and local laws had made a large part of the country dry by 1917. National prohibition became official in January 1920.

This "experiment noble in purpose," as Herbert Hoover called it, achieved a number of socially desirable results. It reduced the national consumption of alcohol from 2.6 gallons per capita in the period just before the war to under one gallon in the early 1930s. Arrests for drunkenness fell off sharply, as did deaths from alcoholism. Fewer workers squandered their wages on drink. If the drys had been willing to legalize beer and wine, the experiment might have worked. Instead, by insisting on total abstinence, they drove thousands of moderates to violate the law. Strict enforcement became impossible, especially in the cities.

In areas where sentiment favored prohibition strongly, liquor remained difficult to find. Elsewhere, anyone with sufficient money could obtain it easily. Smuggling became a major business, *bootlegger* a household word. Private individuals busied themselves learning how to manufacture "bathtub gin." Many druggists issued prescriptions for alcohol with a free hand. The manufacture of wine for religious ceremonies was legal; consumption of sacramental wine jumped by 800,000 gallons during the first two years of prohibition. The saloon disappeared, replaced by the speakeasy, a supposedly secret bar or club, operating under the benevolent eye of the local police.

That the law was often violated does not mean that it was ineffective any more than violations of laws against theft and murder mean that those laws are ineffective. Although gangsters such as Alphonse "Scarface Al" Capone of Chicago were engaged in the liquor traffic, their "organizations" existed before the passage of the Eighteenth Amendment. But prohibition widened already serious rifts in the social fabric of the country. Besides

Ben Shahn's Prohibition Alley *is a richly symbolic summary of the seamier side of the "noble experiment." Under a diagram of the workings of a still, bootleggers stack whiskey smuggled in by ship, an operation eyed by Chicago gangster Al Capone. At lower left is a victim of gang warfare; at lower right, patrons outside a speakeasy.*

undermining public morality by encouraging hypocrisy, it almost destroyed the Democratic party as a national organization; Democratic immigrants in the cities hated it, but southern Democrats sang its praises (often while continuing to drink—the humorist Will Rogers quipped that Mississippi would vote dry "as long as the voters could stagger to the polls").

The hypocrisy of prohibition had a particularly deleterious effect on politicians, a class seldom famous for candor. Congressmen catered to the demands of the powerful lobby of the Anti-Saloon League yet failed to grant adequate funds to the Prohibition Bureau. Nearly all the prominent leaders, Democrat and Republican, from Wilson and La Follette to Hoover and Franklin D. Roosevelt, equiv-

ocated shamelessly on the liquor question. By the end of the decade almost every competent observer recognized that prohibition needed at least to be overhauled, but the well-organized and powerful dry forces rejected all proposals for modifying it.

The Ku Klux Klan

The most horrible manifestation of the social malaise of the 1920s was the revival of the Ku Klux Klan. This new Klan, founded in 1915 by William J. Simmons, a former preacher, admitted only native-born white Protestants. The distrust of foreigners, blacks, Catholics, and Jews implicit in this regulation explains why it flourished in the social climate that spawned religious fundamentalism, immigration restriction, and prohibition. In 1920 two unscrupulous publicity agents, Edward Y. Clarke and Elizabeth Tyler, got control of the movement and organized a massive membership drive, diverting a major share of the initiation fees into their own pockets. In a little over a year they enrolled 100,000 recruits, and by 1923 they claimed the astonishing total of 5 million.

Simmons gave his society trappings and mystery calculated to attract gullible and bigoted persons who yearned to express their frustrations and hostilities without personal risk. Klansmen masked themselves in white robes and hoods and enjoyed a childish mumbo jumbo of magnificent-sounding titles and dogmas (kleagle, klaliff, kludd; kloxology, kloran). They burned crosses in the night, organized mass demonstrations to intimidate people they disliked, and put pressure on employers to fire black workers from better-paying jobs.

The Klan had relatively little appeal in the Northeast or in metropolitan centers in other parts of the country, but it found many members in mid-dle-sized cities and in the small towns and villages of middle western and western states like Indiana and Oregon. The scapegoats in such regions were immigrants, Jews, and especially Catholics. The rationale was an urge to return to an older, supposedly finer America and to stamp out all varieties of nonconformity. Klansmen "watched everybody," themselves safe from observation behind their masks and robes. They persecuted gamblers, "loose" women, violators of the prohibition laws, and anyone who happened to differ from them on religious questions or who belonged to a "foreign race."

The very success of the Klan led to its undoing. Factionalism sprang up, and rival leaders squabbled over the large sums that had been collected from the membership. The cruel and outrageous behavior of the organization roused both liberals and conservatives in every part of the country. And of course its victims joined forces against their tormentors. When the powerful leader of the Indiana Klan, a middle-aged reprobate named David C. Stephenson, was convicted of assaulting and causing the death of a young woman, the rank and file aban-

A Ku Klux Klan initiation ceremony, photographed in Kansas in the 1920s. During its peak influence at mid-decade, Klan endorsement was essential to political candidates in many areas of the West and Midwest. Campaigning for reelection in 1924, an Indiana congressman testifies, "I was told to join the Klan, or else."

doned the organization in droves. The Klan remained influential for a number of years, contributing to the defeat of the Catholic Alfred E. Smith in the 1928 presidential election, but it ceased to be a dynamic force after 1924. By 1930 it had only some 9,000 members.

Sacco and Vanzetti

The excesses of the fundamentalists, the xenophobes, the Klan, the red-baiters, and the prohibitionists disturbed American intellectuals profoundly. More and more they became alienated, bitter, and contemptuous of the people who appeared to control the country. Yet their alienation came at the very time that society was growing more dependent on brains and sophistication. This compounded the confusion and disillusionment characteristic of the period.

Nothing demonstrates this fact so clearly as the Sacco-Vanzetti case. In April 1920 two men in South

Braintree, Massachusetts, killed a paymaster and a guard in a daring daylight robbery of a shoe factory. Shortly thereafter, Nicola Sacco and Bartolomeo Vanzetti were charged with the crime, and in 1921 they were convicted of murder. Sacco and Vanzetti were anarchists and Italian immigrants. Their trial was a travesty of justice. The presiding judge, Webster Thayer, conducted the proceedings like a prosecuting attorney; privately he referred to the defendants as "those anarchist bastards."

The case became a cause célèbre. Prominent persons throughout the world protested, and for years Sacco and Vanzetti were kept alive by efforts to obtain a new trial. Vanzetti's quiet dignity and courage in the face of death wrung the hearts of millions. "You see me before you, not trembling," he told the court. "I never commit a crime in my life. . . . I am so convinced to be right that if you could execute me two times, and if I could be reborn two other times, I would live again and do what I have done already." When, in August 1927, the two were at last electrocuted, the disillusionment of American

Vanzetti (left) and Sacco were led into court handcuffed in April 1927 to hear the death sentence pronounced. They were electrocuted in August of that year, six years after their conviction.

intellectuals with current values was profound. Some historians, impressed by modern ballistic studies of Sacco's gun, now suspect that he, at least, may have been guilty. Nevertheless, the truth and the shame remain: Sacco and Vanzetti paid with their lives for being radicals and aliens, not for any crime.

Literary Trends

The literature of the 1920s reflects the disillusionment of the intellectuals. The prewar period had been an age of hopeful experimentation in the world of letters. But the historian Henry F. May has shown that the Progressive Era writers, along with most other intellectuals, were beginning to abandon this view by about 1912. The wasteful horrors of the World War and then the antics of the fundamentalists and the cruelty of the red-baiters and the Klan turned them into critics of society. Among the many writers shaken by the execution of Sacco and Vanzetti were the poet Edna St. Vincent Millay, the playwright Maxwell Anderson, and the novelists Upton Sinclair and John Dos Passos. After the war the poet Ezra Pound dropped his talk of an American Renaissance and wrote instead of a "botched civilization." The soldiers of the Great War, he said,

> walked eye-deep in hell
> believing in old men's lies, then unbelieving
> came home, home to a lie,
> home to deceits,
> home to old lies and new infamy . . .

Yet out of this negativism came a literary flowering of major importance. The herald of the new day was Henry Adams, whose autobiography, *The Education of Henry Adams*, was published posthumously in 1918. Adams's disillusionment long antedated the war, but his description of late-19th-century corruption and materialism and his warning that industrialism was crushing the human spirit beneath the weight of its machines appealed powerfully to those whose pessimism was newborn. Soon hundreds of bright young men and women were referring to themselves, with almost maudlin self-pity, as the "lost generation."

The symbol of the lost generation, in his own mind as well as to his contemporaries and to later critics, was F. Scott Fitzgerald. Born to modest wealth in St. Paul, Minnesota, in 1896, Fitzgerald attended Princeton and served in the army during the World War. He rose to sudden fame in 1920 when he published *This Side of Paradise,* a somewhat sophomoric novel that appealed powerfully to college students and captured the fears and confusions of the lost generation. In *The Great Gatsby* (1925), a more mature work, Fitzgerald dissected a modern millionaire—coarse, unscrupulous, jaded, in love with another man's wife. Gatsby's tragedy lay in his dedication to a woman who, Fitzgerald made clear, did not merit his passion. He lived in "the service of a vast, vulgar, meretricious beauty," and in the end he understood this himself.

The tragedy of *The Great Gatsby* was related to Fitzgerald's own. Pleasure-loving and extravagant, he squandered the money earned by *This Side of Paradise.* When *The Great Gatsby* failed to sell as well, he turned to writing potboilers. "I really worked hard as hell last winter," he told the critic Edmund Wilson, "but it was all trash and it nearly broke my heart." While some of his later work, particularly *Tender Is the Night* (1934), was first-class, he descended into the despair of alcoholism and ended his days as a Hollywood scriptwriter.

Many young American writers and artists became expatriates in the 1920s. They flocked to Rome, Berlin, and especially Paris, where they could live cheaply and escape what seemed to them the "conspiracy against the individual" prevalent in their own country. The *quartier latin* along the left bank of the Seine was a large-scale Greenwich Village in those days. Writers, artists, and eccentrics of every sort lived there. Some made meager livings as journalists, translators, and editors, perhaps turning an extra dollar from time to time by selling a story or a poem to an American magazine or a painting to a tourist.

Ernest Hemingway was the most talented of the expatriates. He had served in the Italian army during the war and been grievously wounded (in spirit as well as in body). He settled in Paris in 1922 to write. His first novel, *The Sun Also Rises* (1926), portrayed the café world of the expatriate and the rootless desperation, amorality, and sense of outrage at life's meaninglessness that obsessed so many in those years. In *A Farewell to Arms* (1929) he drew on his military experiences to describe the confusion and horror of war.

Hemingway's books were best-sellers, and he became a legend in his own time, but his style rather than his ideas explains his towering reputation. Few novelists have been such self-conscious craftsmen or as capable of suggesting powerful emotions and action in so few words. Mark Twain and Stephen Crane were his models, Gertrude Stein, a quirky, revolutionary genius, his teacher. But his style was his own, direct, simple, taut, spare:

> I went out the door and down the hall to the room where Catherine was to be after the baby came. I sat in a chair there and looked at the room. I had the paper in my coat that I had bought when I went out for lunch and I read it . . . . After a while I stopped reading and turned off the light and watched it get dark outside. (*A Farewell to Arms*)

This kind of writing, evoking rather than describing emotion, fascinated readers and inspired hundreds of imitators; it has made a permanent mark on world literature. What Hemingway had to say was of less universal interest—he was an unabashed, rather muddled romantic, an adolescent emotionally. He wrote about bullfights, hunting and fishing, violence; while he did so with masterful penetration, these themes placed limits on his work that he never transcended. The critic Alfred Kazin summed Hemingway up in a sentence: "He brought a major art to a minor vision of life."

Although neither was the equal of Hemingway or Fitzgerald, two other writers of the 1920s deserve mention: H. L. Mencken and Sinclair Lewis. Each reflected the distaste of intellectuals for the climate of the times. Mencken, a Baltimore newspaperman and founder of one of the great magazines of the era, the *American Mercury,* was a thoroughgoing cynic. He coined the world *booboisie* to define the complacent, middle-class majority, and he fired superbly witty broadsides at fundamentalists, prohibitionists and "Puritans." "Puritanism," he once said, "is the haunting fear that someone, somewhere, may be happy."

Contrasting images of two literary stars of the "lost generation": (left) F. Scott Fitzgerald as the thoughtful, introspective artist, and (right) Ernest Hemingway, sportsman and man of action.

But Mencken was never indifferent to the many aspects of American life that aroused his contempt. Politics at once fascinated and repelled him, and he assailed the statesmen of his generation with magnificent impartiality:

BRYAN: "If the fellow was sincere, then so was P. T. Barnum. . . . He was, in fact, a charlatan, a mountebank, a zany without sense or dignity."

WILSON: "The bogus Liberal. . . . A pedagogue thrown up to 1,000 diameters by a magic lantern."

HARDING: "The numskull, Gamaliel. . . . the Marion stonehead. . . . The operations of his medulla oblongata . . . resemble the rattlings of a colossal linotype charged with rubber stamps."

COOLIDGE: "A cheap and trashy fellow, deficient in sense and almost devoid of any notion of honor—in brief, a dreadful little cad."

HOOVER: "Lord Hoover is no more than a pious old woman, a fat Coolidge. . . . He would have made a good bishop."

As these examples demonstrate, Mencken's diatribes, though amusing, were not profound. In perspective he seems more a professional iconoclast than a constructive critic; like both Fitzgerald and Hemingway, he was something of a perennial adolescent. However, he consistently supported freedom of expression of every sort.

Sinclair Lewis was probably the most popular American novelist of the 1920s. Like Fitzgerald, his first major work brought him instant fame and notoriety—and for the same reason. *Main Street* (1920) portrayed the smug ignorance and bigotry of the American small town so accurately that even Lewis's victims recognized themselves; his title became a symbol for provinciality and middle-class meanness of spirit. In *Babbitt* (1922) he created an image of the businessman of the 1920s, gregarious, a "booster," blindly orthodox in his political and social opinions, a slave to every cliché, and full of loud self-confidence, but underneath the surface a bumbling, rather timid fellow who would have liked to be better than he was but dared not try.

Lewis went on to dissect the medical profession in *Arrowsmith* (1925), religion in *Elmer Gantry* (1927), fascism in *It Can't Happen Here* (1935). Although his indictment of contemporary society rivaled Mencken's in savagery, Lewis was not a cynic. Superficially

as objective as an anthropologist, he remained at heart committed to the way of life he was assaulting. His remarkable powers of observation depended on his identification with the society he described. He was frustrated by the fact that his victims, recognizing themselves in his pages, accepted his criticisms with remarkable good temper and, displaying the very absence of intellectual rigor that he decried, cheerfully sought to reform.

Lacking Mencken's ability to remain aloof, Lewis tended to value his own work in terms of its popular reception. He craved the good opinion and praise of his fellows. When he was awarded the Pulitzer Prize for *Arrowsmith,* he petulantly refused it because it had not been offered earlier. He politicked shamelessly for a Nobel Prize, which he received in 1930, the first American author to win this honor.

Lewis was preeminently a product of the 1920s. When times changed, he could no longer portray society with such striking verisimilitude; none of his later novels approached the level of *Main Street* and *Babbitt.* When critics noticed this, Lewis became bewildered, almost disoriented. He died in 1951 a desperately unhappy man.

The "New Negro"

Even more than for white liberals, the postwar reaction had brought despair for many blacks. Aside from the barbarities of the Klan, they suffered from the postwar middle-class hostility to labor (and from the persistent reluctance of organized labor to admit black workers to its ranks). The increasing presence of southern blacks in northern cities also caused conflict. Some 393,000 settled in New York, Pennsylvania, and Illinois in the 1920s, most of them in New York City, Philadelphia, and Chicago. The black population of New York City more than doubled between 1920 and 1930.

In earlier periods blacks in northern cities had tended to live together but in small neighborhoods scattered over large areas. Now the tendency was toward concentration in what came to be called ghettos. Harlem, a white middle-class residential section of New York City as late as 1910, had 50,000 blacks in 1914, 73,000 in 1920, and nearly 165,000 in 1930.

The restrictions of ghetto life produced a vicious circle of degradation. Population growth and segregation caused a desperate housing shortage; rents in Harlem doubled between 1919 and 1927. Since the average black worker was unskilled and ill paid, tenants were forced to take in boarders. Landlords converted private homes into rooming houses and allowed their properties to fall into disrepair. The process of decay was speeded by the influx of what the black sociologist E. Franklin Frazier called "ignorant and unsophisticated peasant people" from the rural South, who were inexperienced in city living. These conditions caused disease and crime rates to rise sharply.

Even in small northern cities where they made up only a tiny proportion of the population, blacks were treated badly. When Robert S. Lynd and Helen M. Lynd made their classic sociological analysis of "Middletown" (Muncie, Indiana), they discovered that although black and white children attended the same schools, the churches, the larger movie houses, and other places of public accommodation were segregated. The local YMCA had a gymnasium where high school basketball was played, but the secretary refused to allow any team with a black player to use it. Even the news in Muncie was segregated. Local papers chronicled the affairs of the black community—roughly 5 percent of the population—under the heading "In Colored Circles."

Coming after the hopes inspired by wartime gains, the disappointments of the 1920s produced a new militancy among many blacks. In 1919 W. E. B. Du Bois wrote in *The Crisis:* "We are cowards and jackasses if . . . we do not marshal every ounce of our brain and brawn to fight . . . against the forces of hell in our own land." He increased his commitment to black nationalism, organizing a series of Pan-African Conferences in an effort—futile, as it turned out—to create an international black movement.

Du Bois never made up his mind whether to work for integration or black separatism. Such ambivalence never troubled Marcus Garvey, a West Indian whose Universal Negro Improvement Association attracted hundreds of thousands of followers in the early 1920s. Garvey had nothing but contempt for whites, for light-skinned blacks like Du Bois, and for organizations such as the NAACP, which sought to bring whites and blacks together to fight segregation and other forms of prejudice. "Back to Africa" was his slogan; the black man must "work out his salvation in his motherland." (Paradoxically, Garvey's ideas won the enthusiastic sup-

port of the Ku Klux Klan and other white racist groups.)

Garvey's message was naive, but it served to build racial pride among the masses of poor and unschooled blacks. He dressed in elaborate braided uniforms, wore a plumed hat, drove about in a limousine. Both God and Christ were black, he insisted. He organized black businesses of many sorts, including a company that manufactured black dolls. He established a corps of Black Cross nurses and a Black Star steamship line to transport blacks back to Africa.

More sophisticated black leaders like Du Bois detested Garvey, whom they thought something of a charlatan. His motives are at this distance unclear, and part of his troubles resulted only from his being a terrible businessman. In 1923 his steamship line went into bankruptcy. He was convicted of defrauding the thousands of his supporters who had invested in its stock and was sent to prison. Nevertheless, his message, if not his methods, helped to create the "New Negro," proud of being black and prepared to resist both white mistreatment and white ideas. "Up you mighty race, you can accomplish what you will!"

The ghettos produced compensating advantages for blacks. One effect, not fully used until later, was to increase their political power by enabling them to elect representatives to state legislatures and to Congress and to exert considerable influence in closely contested elections. More immediately, city life stimulated self-confidence; despite their horrors, the ghettos offered economic opportunity, political rights, and freedom from the everyday debasements of life in the South. The ghetto was a black world where black men and women could be themselves.

Black writers, musicians, and artists found in the ghettos both an audience and the "spiritual emancipation" that unleashed their capacities. Jazz, the great popular music of the age, was largely the creation of black musicians working in New Orleans before the turn of the century. By the 1920s it had spread throughout the country and to most of the rest of the world. White musicians and white audiences took it up; in a way, it became a force for racial tolerance and understanding.

Jazz meant improvisation, and both players and audiences experienced in it a kind of liberation. Jazz was the music of the 1920s in part because it ex-

Beginning in the late 1930s, black artist Jacob Lawrence painted a series of powerful "picture-narratives" dealing with the black experience in America. This painting, of Southern blacks crowding onto northbound trains during World War I, is the first of a 60-panel narrative that Lawrence titled The Migration of the Negro.

pressed the desire of so many people to break with tradition and throw off conventional restraints. Surely this helps to explain why it was so important to blacks.

Harlem, the largest black city in the world, became in the 1920s a cultural capital, center of the "Harlem Renaissance." Black newspapers and magazines flourished along with theatrical companies and libraries. Du Bois opened *The Crisis* to young writers and artists, and a dozen "little" magazines sprang up. Langston Hughes, one of the best poets of the era, described the exhilaration of his first arrival in this city within a city, a "magnet" for every black intellectual and artist. "Harlem! I . . . dropped my bags, took a deep breath, and felt happy again."

With some exceptions, black writers like Hughes

did not share in the disillusionment that afflicted so many white intellectuals. The persistence of prejudice angered them and made them militant. But to be militant one must be at some level hopeful, and this they were. Sociologists and psychologists (for whom the ghettos were rich social laboratories) were demonstrating that environment rather than heredity was preventing black economic progress. Together with the achievements of creative blacks, which for the first time were being appreciated by large numbers of white intellectuals, these discoveries seemed to herald the eventual disappearance of race prejudice. The black, Alain Locke wrote in *The New Negro* (1925), "lays aside the status of beneficiary and ward for that of a collaborator and participant in American civilization." Alas, as Locke and other black intellectuals were soon to discover, this prediction, like so many made in the 1920s, did not come to pass.

The "New Era"

Despite the turmoil of the times and the dissatisfactions expressed by some of the nation's best minds, the 1920s was an exceptionally prosperous decade. Business boomed, real wages rose, unemployment declined. The United States was as rich as all Europe; perhaps 40 percent of the world's total wealth lay in American hands. Little wonder that business leaders and other conservatives described the period as a "new era."

The prosperity rested on many bases, one of which was the friendly, hands-off attitude of the federal government, which bolstered the confidence of the business community. The Federal Reserve Board kept interest rates low, a further stimulus to economic growth. Pent-up wartime demand helped to power the boom; the construction business in particular profited from a series of extremely busy years. The continuing mechanization and rationalization of industry provided a more fundamental stimulus to the economy. From heavy road-grading equipment and concrete mixers to devices for making cigars and glass tubes, from pneumatic tools to the dial telephone, machinery was replacing human hands at an ever more rapid rate. Industrial output almost doubled between 1921 and 1929 without any substantial increase in the industrial labor force. Greater use of power, especially of electricity, also encouraged expansion—by 1929 the United States was producing more electricity than the rest of the world combined.

Most important, American manufacturing was experiencing a remarkable improvement in efficiency. The method of breaking down the complex processes of production into many simple operations and the use of interchangeable parts were 19th-century innovations; in the 1920s they were adopted on an almost universal scale. The moving assembly line, which carried the product to the worker, perfected by Henry Ford in his automobile plant in the decade before World War I, speeded production and reduced costs. In ten years the hourly output of Ford workers quadrupled. The time-and-motion studies of Frederick W. Taylor, developed early in the century, were applied in hundreds of factories after the war. Taylor's method was to make careful analyses of each step and movement in the manufacturing process. Then workers would be taught exactly how best to perform each function. Taylor described his system as "enforced standardization" made possible by the "enforced cooperation" of workers. "Taylorism" alarmed some union leaders, but no one could deny the effectiveness of "scientific shop management" methods.

The Age of the Consumer

The growing ability of manufacturers to produce goods meant that great effort had to be made to create new consumer demands. Advertising and salesmanship were raised almost to the status of fine arts. Bruce Barton, one of the advertising geniuses of the era, wrote a best-selling book, *The Man Nobody Knows* (1925), in which he described Jesus as the "founder of modern business," the man who "picked up twelve men from the bottom ranks . . . and forged them into an organization that conquered the world." In 1930 no less a personage than Eleanor Roosevelt, wife of the governor of New York, gave a testimonial for a leading breakfast cereal, which had, she said, "undoubtedly played its part" in building the "robust physique" of her teenage son, John.

Producers concentrated on making their goods more attractive and on changing models frequently to entice buyers into the market. The practice of selling goods on the installment plan helped bring expensive items within the reach of the masses. Inventions and technological advances created new or improved products: radios, automobiles, electric appliances such as vacuum cleaners and refrigerators, gadgets like cigarette lighters, new forms of entertainment like motion pictures. These influences interacted in much the way the textile industry in the early 19th century and the railroad industry after the Civil War had been the "multipliers" of their times.

Undoubtedly, the automobile had the single most important impact on the nation's economy in the 1920s. Although well over a million cars a year were being regularly produced by 1916, the real expansion of the industry came after 1921. Output reached 3.6 million in 1923 and fell below that figure only twice during the remainder of the decade. By 1929 some 23 million private cars clogged the highways, an average of nearly one per family.

The auto industry gave birth to industries that manufactured tires and spark plugs and other products. It consumed immense quantities of rubber, paint, glass, nickel, and petroleum products. It triggered a gigantic road-building program: The 387,000 miles of paved roads in the United States in 1921 grew to 662,000 miles in 1929. Thousands of persons found employment in filling stations, roadside stands, and other businesses catering to the motoring public. The tourist industry profited, and the shift of population from the cities to the suburbs was accelerated.

The automobile made life more mobile yet also more encapsulated. It changed recreational patterns and family life. It created a generation of tinkerers and amateur mechanics and explorers. In addition, it profoundly affected the way Americans thought. It gave them a freedom never before imagined. The owner of the most rickety jalopy could travel farther, faster, and far more comfortably than a monarch of old with his blooded steeds and gilded coaches.

These benefits were real and priceless. But cars came to have a symbolic significance that was equally important; they gave their owners a feeling of power and status similar to that which owning a horse gave to a medieval knight. According to some authorities, the typical American cared more about owning an automobile than about owning a home.

In time there were undesirable, even dangerous results of the automotive revolution: roadside scenery disfigured by billboards, gas stations, and other enterprises aimed at satisfying the traveler's needs; horrendous traffic jams; soaring accident rates; air pollution; the neglect of public transportation, which was an important cause of the deterioration of inner cities. All these disadvantages were noticed during the 1920s, but in the springtime of the new industry they were discounted. The automobile seemed an unalloyed blessing, part toy, part tool, part symbol of American freedom, prosperity, and individualism.

According to his biographer, Allan Nevins, Henry Ford's complex personality included the characteristics of "a wry, cross-grained, brilliant adolescent." Here, on a summer outing, Ford poses as a western badman.

Henry Ford

The person most responsible for the growth of the automobile industry was Henry Ford, a self-taught mechanic from Greenfield, Michigan. Ford was not a great inventor or one of the true automobile pioneers. He was not even the first person to man-

ufacture a good low-priced car (that was the achievement of Ransom E. Olds, producer of the "Merry Oldsmobile"). He had two brilliant insights. The first was, in his words, "Get the prices down to the buying power." Through mass production, cars could be made cheaply enough to put them within reach of the ordinary citizen. In 1908 he designed the Model T Ford, a simple, tough box on wheels. In a year he proved his point by selling 11,000 Model

Ts. Thereafter, relentlessly cutting costs and increasing efficiency by installing the assembly-line system, he expanded production at an unbelievable rate. By 1925 he was turning out more than 9,000 cars a day, one approximately every 10 seconds, and the price of the Model T had been reduced to below $300.

Ford grasped the importance of high wages in stimulating output (and selling more automobiles). This was his second insight. The assembly line simplified the laborer's task and increased the pace of work; at the same time it made each worker much more productive. Jobs became boring and fatiguing, and absenteeism and labor turnover developed into serious problems. To combat this, in 1914 Ford established the $5 day, an increase of about $2 over prevailing wages. The rate of turnover in his plant fell 90 percent, and although critics charged that he recaptured his additional labor costs by speeding up the line, his policy had a revolutionary effect on wage rates. Later he raised the minimum to $6 and then to $7 a day.

Ford's profits soared along with sales; since he owned the entire company, he became a billionaire. He also became an authentic folk hero: His homespun style, his dislike of bankers and sophisticated society, and his intense individualism endeared him to millions. He stood as a symbol of the wonders of the American system—he had given the nation a marvelous convenience at a low price, at the same time enriching himself and raising the living standards of his thousands of employees.

Unfortunately, Ford had the defects of his virtues in full measure. He paid high wages but tyrannized his workers. He refused to deal with any union and employed spies to investigate the private lives of his help and gangsters and bully boys to enforce plant discipline. When he discovered a worker driving any car but a Ford, he had him dismissed. So close was the supervision in the factory that workers devised the "Ford whisper," a means of talking without moving the lips.

Success made Ford stubborn. The Model T remained essentially unchanged for nearly 20 years. Other companies, notably General Motors, were soon turning out better vehicles for very little more money. Customers, increasingly affluent and style-conscious, began to shift to Chevrolets and Chryslers. Finally, in 1927, Ford shut down all operations for 18 months in order to retool for the Model A.

His competitors rushed in during this period to fill the vacuum. Although his company continued to make a great deal of money, Ford never regained the dominant position he had held for so long.

Ford was enormously uninformed, yet—because of his success and the praise the world heaped on him—he did not hesitate to speak out on subjects far outside his area of competence, from the evils of drink and tobacco to medicine and international affairs. He developed political ambitions and published virulent anti-Semitic propaganda. He said he would not give 5 cents for all the art in the world.

While praising his talents as a manufacturer, historians have not dealt kindly with Ford the man, in part no doubt because he once said, "History is more or less the bunk."

The Airplane

Henry Ford was also an early manufacturer of airplanes, and though the airplane industry was not economically important in the 1920s, its development in that decade laid the basis for changes in life-styles and attitudes at least as momentous as those produced by the automobile. The invention of the internal combustion gasoline engine, with its extremely high ratio of power to weight, made the airplane possible, which explains why the early experiments with "flying machines" took place at about the same time that the prototypes of the modern automobile were being manufactured. Wilbur and Orville Wright made their famous flight at Kitty Hawk, North Carolina, in 1903, five years before Ford produced his Model T. Another pair of brothers, Malcolm and Haimes Lockheed, built their Model G, one of the earliest commercial planes (commercial in the sense that they used it to take passengers up at $5 a ride) in 1913.

The World War speeded the advance of airplane technology, and most of the planes built in the 1920s were intended for military use. Practical commercial air travel was long delayed. Aerial acrobats, parachute jumpers, wing walkers, and other "daredevils" who put on shows at county fairs and similar places where crowds gathered were the principal civilian aviators of the 1920s. They "barnstormed" from town to town, living the same kind of inbred, encapsulated lives that circus people did, their chief rewards being the sense of independence and pride

A boyish-looking Charles A. Lindbergh during his flying apprenticeship as a stunt pilot in 1925, two years before his solo flight across the Atlantic.

that the successful performance of their highly skilled but risky trade provided.

The great event of the decade for aviation, still an achievement that must strike awe in the hearts of reflective persons, was Charles A. Lindbergh's nonstop flight from New York to Paris in May 1927. It took more than 33 hours for Lindbergh's single-engine *Spirit of St. Louis* to cross the Atlantic, a formidable physical achievement for the pilot as well as an example of skill and courage. When the public learned that the intrepid "Lucky Lindy" was handsome, modest, uninterested in converting his new fame into cash, and a model of propriety (he neither drank nor smoked), his role as an American hero was assured. It was a role Lindbergh detested—one biographer has described him as "by nature solitary"—but could not avoid.

Lindbergh's flight enormously increased public interest in flying, but it was a landmark in aviation technology as well. The day of routine passenger flights was at last about to dawn. In July 1927, a mere two months after the *Spirit of St. Louis* touched down at Le Bourget Field in France, William E. Boeing of Boeing Air Transport began flying passengers and mail between San Francisco and Chicago, using the M-40, a plane of his own design and manufacture. Early in 1928 he changed the company name to United Aircraft and Transport. Two years later Boeing produced the first all-metal low-wing plane, and in 1933 the twin-engine 247, called

by the historian John B. Rae "the first genuinely modern transport airplane."

In retrospect the postwar era seems even more a period of transition than it appeared to most people at the time. Rarely had the old become the new so swiftly, and rarely had the two existed side by side in such profusion. Creativity and reaction, hope and despair, freedom and repression—the modern world in all its unfathomable complexity was emerging.

Milestones

1908 Henry Ford begins production of Model T automobile

1914 Ford establishes the $5 day for auto workers

1919 Eighteenth Amendment outlaws alcoholic beverages
Nineteenth Amendment grants women the vote

1920 Sinclair Lewis, *Main Street*
F. Scott Fitzgerald, *This Side of Paradise*
First commercial radio station, KDKA, begins broadcasting

1921 Margaret Sanger founds the American Birth Control League

1923 Supreme Court overturns the law limiting hours of work for women

1925 Scopes trial in Dayton, Tennessee

1926 Gertrude Ederle swims the English Channel
Ernest Hemingway, *The Sun Also Rises*

1927 Babe Ruth hits 60 home runs
Charles A. Lindbergh flies solo from New York to Paris
Sacco and Vanzetti executed
The Jazz Singer first sound motion picture
Jack Dempsey loses heavyweight boxing title to Gene Tunney

1930 Bobby Jones wins the U.S. and British amateur and open golf titles

SUPPLEMENTARY READING

Titles marked with an asterisk have been published in paperback.

A comprehensive survey of the 1920s is J. D. Hicks, **Republican Ascendancy*** (1960); W. E. Leuchtenburg, **The Perils of Prosperity*** (1958), is equally broad in coverage and more interpretive. See also Geoffrey Perrett, **America in the Twenties** (1982), P. A. Carter, **Another Part of the Twenties** (1977), and John Braeman et al. (eds.), **Change and Continuity: The Twenties** (1968). F. L. Allen, **Only Yesterday*** (1931), is a modern classic, oriented especially toward social history.

Nativism and immigration restriction are covered in M. A. Jones, **American Immigration*** (1960), and John Higham, **Strangers in the Land*** (1955). On changes in the family, see Steven Mintz and Susan Kellogg, **Domestic**

Revolutions (1988); on other social trends, see John D'Emilio and Estelle Freedman, **Intimate Matters** (1988), N. G. Hale, **Freud and the Americans** (1971), Paula Fass, **The Damned and the Beautiful** (1977), and D. M. Brown, **Setting a Course: American Women in the 1920s** (1987). The "new" woman is discussed in William Chafe, **The American Woman** (1972), S. M. Rothman, **Women's Proper Place** (1975), and Nancy Woloch, **Women and the American Experience** (1971). Women workers are dealt with in W. D. Wandersee, **Women's Work and Family Values** (1981). On popular culture, see Russell Lynes, **The Tastemakers*** (1954), Robert Sklar, **Movie-made America** (1976), S. J. Douglas, **Inventing American**

Broadcasting (1987), and P. T. Rosen, **The Modern Stentors: Radio Broadcasting and the Federal Government** (1980).

Fundamentalism is treated in N. F. Furniss, **The Fundamentalist Controversy** (1954), the Monkey Trial in Lawrence Levine, **Defender of the Faith** (1965). The most thoughtful history of prohibition is Andrew Sinclair, **Prohibition: The Era of Excess*** (1962), but see also J. R. Gusfield, **Symbolic Crusade** (1963), and N. H. Clark, **Deliver Us from Evil*** (1976). On the Klan, consult D. M. Chalmers, **Hooded Americanism*** (1965), K. T. Jackson, **The Ku Klux Klan in the City*** (1967), and A. S. Rice, **The Ku Klux Klan in American Politics** (1961).

Sacco and Vanzetti are dealt with sympathetically in all surveys of the period, but Francis Russell, **Tragedy in Dedham** (1962), casts doubt on their innocence.

For the history of blacks, see Gilbert Osofsky, **Harlem: The Making of a Ghetto*** (1965), E. D. Cronon, **Black Moses: The Story of Marcus Garvey*** (1955), and N. I. Huggins, **Harlem Renaissance*** (1971).

The literature of the 1920s is analyzed in Alfred Kazin, **On Native Grounds*** (1942), and F. J. Hoffman, **The Twenties*** (1955). On Fitzgerald, see Arthur Mizener, **The Far Side of Paradise*** (1951); on Hemingway, C. H. Baker, **Hemingway*** (1956); on Mencken, W. R. Manchester, **Disturber of the Peace*** (1951); on Lewis, Mark Schorer, **Sinclair Lewis*** (1961).

The New Era is treated in the general books on the 1920s and in E. W. Hawley, **The Great War and the Search for a Modern Order*** (1979), Daniel Horowitz, **The Morality of Spending** (1985), S. M. Jacoby, **Employing Bureaucracy** (1985), and Roland Marchand, **Advertising the American Dream** (1985).

On Henry Ford, see Allan Nevins and F. E. Hill, **Ford** (1954–1957), and Keith Sward, **The Legend of Henry Ford*** (1948). J. B. Rae, **The American Automobile Industry** (1984), J. J. Flink, **The Car Culture** (1975), and D. L. Lewis and Lawrence Goldstein (eds.), **The Automobile and American Culture** (1984), are full of interesting material.

American Painting, 1920–1960

EDWARD HOPPER *Early Sunday Morning* (1930)

Edward Hopper's aim as an artist was "the most exact transcription" of his "most intimate impressions." With concentrated simplicity, he painted an essence of the American scene, conveying an eerie sense of loneliness. He displayed little interest in foreign artistic trends.

JOHN MARIN *Sun Spots* (1920)

John Marin's watercolor **Sun Spots** shows the influence of modern French artists such as Monet and Picasso. In his cityscapes and landscapes, Marin used simplified, scattered shapes to paint nature's "warring, pushing, pulling" forces.

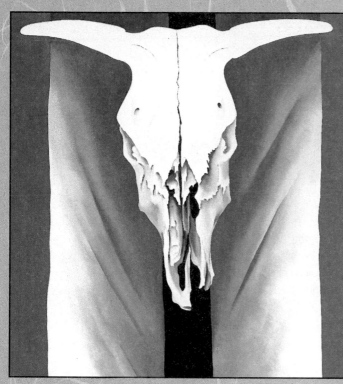

GEORGIA O'KEEFFE *Cow Skull: Red, White, and Blue* (1931)

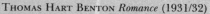

In the 1920s Georgia O'Keeffe, America's premier woman painter, moved to the southwest. Like Hopper, she ignored European influences and found her way to artistic abstraction through observation of her desert surroundings.

THOMAS HART BENTON *Romance* (1931/32)

The most controversial and probably the most influential of the so-called regional painters was Thomas Hart Benton. A violently opinionated Populist, Benton denounced the entire modern movement in painting as "dirt." His main subject was his native Missouri, as exemplified in this touching 1931 scene.

Reginald Marsh *Twenty Cent Movie*
(1936)

Mark Rothko *Number 10* (1950)

Ben Shahn *Willis Avenue Bridge* (1940)

*In the 1930s a group of artists now known as so-
cial realists used their work to probe into the lives
of ordinary people. Reginald Marsh haunted run-
down New York neighborhoods during the depression to record his impressions of bums, honky-tonks,
and subways. In* Twenty Cent Movie *(top) the
front of a seedy movie house pulses with color and
action. Ben Shahn is well-known for his powerfully
sympathetic portrayals of the abandoned, the homeless, the crippled, and the derelict (bottom).*

ROBERT MOTHERWELL *Elegy to the Spanish Republic 108* (1965/67)

WILLEM DE KOONING *Women and Bicycle* (1952/53)

Abstract expressionism burst on the art scene in the decade following 1945. Some works, such as Robert Motherwell's Elegy to the Spanish Republic *(above), used actual places and events as a starting point for abstract comment. Mark Rothko pioneered "color-field abstraction," the subtle interaction of areas of color (opposite page). Willem de Kooning, an action painter like Jackson Pollock (see page 887), did a famous series of canvases on the theme of women (right).*

JASPER JOHNS *Target with Four Faces* (1955)

Op and pop artists turned from the emotionalism of most abstract expressionism to a cool and more detached approach. Josef Albers's Homage to the Square: Apparition (*below*) was one of his long series of canvases studying the variations of color and dimension possible within one simple design. Jasper Johns, in Target with Four Faces (*left*), a precursor of pop art, used a repetitively simple and easily identified symbol, the target.

Whatever the art fashion of the moment, representational art is always in demand. The commercial uses of such work are everywhere. And serious easel painting retains a durable human appeal. The modern persistence of the realist tradition is best demonstrated by the work of Andrew Wyeth (*opposite page*), whose paintings portray in careful detail the people and places he knows best.

JOSEF ALBERS *Homage to the Square: Apparition* (1959)

Andrew Wyeth *Albert's Son* (1959)

The New Era, 1921–1933

All we can hope to assure the individual through government is liberty, justice, intellectual welfare, equality of opportunity, and stimulation to service.

HERBERT HOOVER, American Individualism, *1922*

I do not approve of stealing, but if I had to make a choice between stealing and starving, I would surely not choose to starve.

DANIEL WILLARD, *president of the Baltimore & Ohio Railroad, 1928*

T he men who presided over the government of the United States from 1921 to 1929 were Warren G. Harding of Ohio and Calvin Coolidge of Massachusetts. Harding was a newspaperman by trade, publisher of the *Marion Star,* with previous political experience as a legislator and lieutenant governor in his home state and as a United States senator. No president, before or since, looked more like a statesman; few were less suited for running the country. Coolidge was a taciturn, extremely conservative New Englander with a long record in Massachusetts politics climaxed by his inept but much admired suppression of the Boston police strike while governor. Harding referred to him as "that little fellow from Massachusetts." Coolidge preferred to follow public opinion and hope for the best. "Mr. Coolidge's genius for inactivity is developed to a very high point," the correspondent Walter Lippmann wrote. "It is a grim, determined, alert inactivity, which keeps Mr. Coolidge occupied constantly."*

---

* Coolidge was physically delicate, being plagued by chronic stomach trouble. He required 10 or 11 hours of sleep a day.

"Normalcy"

Harding won the 1920 Republican nomination because the party convention could not decide between General Leonard Wood, who represented the Roosevelt progressives, and Frank Lowden, governor of Illinois. His genial nature and lack of strong convictions made him attractive to many of the politicos after eight years of the headstrong Wilson. During the campaign he exasperated sophisticates by his ignorance and imprecision. He coined the famous vulgarism *normalcy* as a substitute for the word *normality,* referred, during a speech before a group of actors, to Shakespeare's play *Charles the Fifth,* and committed numerous other blunders. "Why does he not get a private secretary who can clothe . . . his 'ideas' in the language customarily used by educated men?" one Boston gentleman demanded of Senator Lodge, who was strongly supporting Harding. Lodge, ordinarily a stickler for linguistic exactitude, replied acidly that he found Harding a paragon by comparison with Wilson, "a man who wrote English very well without ever saying anything." A large majority of the voters, untroubled by the candidate's lack of erudition, shared Lodge's confidence that he would be a vast improvement over Wilson.

Harding has often been characterized as lazy and incompetent. In fact, he was hardworking and politically shrewd; his major weaknesses were indecisiveness and an unwillingness to offend. He turned the most important government departments over to efficient administrators of impeccable reputation: Charles Evans Hughes, the secretary of state; Herbert Hoover in the Commerce Department; Andrew Mellon in the Treasury; and Henry C. Wallace in Agriculture. He kept track of what these men did but seldom initiated policy in their areas. However, Harding gave many lesser offices, and a few of major importance, to the unsavory "Ohio Gang" headed by Harry M. Daugherty, whom he made attorney general.

The president was too kindly, too well-intentioned, and too unambitious to be dishonest. He appointed corruptionists like Daugherty, Secretary of the Interior Albert B. Fall, Director of the Mint "Ed" Scobey, and Charles R. Forbes, head of the new Veterans Bureau, out of a sense of personal obligation or because they were old friends who shared his taste for poker and liquor. Before 1921

743

Said President Harding's mother of her son's accommodating ways, "I'm only grateful Warren wasn't born a girl."

he had enjoyed officeholding; he was adept at mouthing platitudes, a loyal party man who seldom questioned the decisions of his superiors. In the lonely eminence of the White House, whence, as President Harry Truman later said, the buck cannot be passed, he found only misery. "The White House is a prison," he complained. "I can't get away from the men who dog my footsteps. I am in jail."

"Regulating" Business

Secretary of the Treasury Mellon, multimillionaire banker and master of the aluminum industry, dominated administration domestic policy. Mellon set out to lower the taxes of the rich, reverse the low-tariff policies of the Wilson period, return to the laissez faire philosophy of McKinley, and reduce the national debt by cutting expenses and administrating the government more efficiently.

In principle his program had considerable merit. Tax rates designed to check consumer spending in time of war and to raise the huge sum needed to defeat the Central Powers were undoubtedly hampering economic expansion in the early 1920s. Certain industries that had sprung up in the United States during the Great War were suffering from German and Japanese competition now that the fighting had ended. Rigid regulation necessary during a national crisis could well be dispensed with in peacetime. And efficiency and economy in government are always desirable.

Yet Mellon carried his policies to unreasonable extremes. He proposed eliminating inheritance taxes and reducing the tax on high incomes by two-thirds, but he opposed lower rates for taxpayers earning less than $66,000 a year, apparently not realizing that economic expansion required greater mass consumption as well. Freeing the rich from "oppressive" taxation, he argued, would enable them to invest more in potentially productive enterprises, the success of which would create jobs for ordinary people. Little wonder that Mellon's admirers called him the greatest secretary of the treasury since Alexander Hamilton.

Although the Republicans had large majorities in both houses of Congress, Mellon's proposals were too reactionary to win unqualified approval. Congress passed the Budget and Accounting Act (1921), creating a director of the budget to assist in preparing a unified budget and a comptroller general to audit government accounts. A general budget had long been needed; previously, Congress had dealt with the requirements of each department separately, trusting largely to luck that income and expenditures would balance at year's end. Mellon's tax and tariff program ran into stiff opposition from middle western Republicans and southern Democrats, who combined to form the so-called farm bloc. The revival of European agriculture after the World War cut the demand for American farm produce just when the increased use of fertilizers and machinery was boosting output. As in the era after the Civil War, farmers found themselves burdened with heavy debts while their income dwindled. In the decade after 1919 their share of the national income fell by nearly 50 percent. The farm bloc represented a kind of conservative populism, economic grievances combining with a general prejudice against "Wall Street financiers" and rich industrialists to unite agriculture against "the interests."

Mellon epitomized everything the farm bloc disliked. Rejecting his more extreme suggestions, it pushed through the Revenue Act of 1921, which abolished the excess-profits tax and cut the top income tax rate from 73 percent to 50 percent but raised the tax on corporate profits slightly and left inheritance taxes untouched. Three years later Congress cut the maximum income tax to 40 percent, reduced taxes on lower incomes significantly, and raised inheritance levies.

Congress also overhauled Mellon's tariff proposals. It placed heavy duties on agricultural products in 1921. The Fordney-McCumber Tariff of 1922 granted more than adequate protection to the "infant industries" (rayon, china, toys, and chemicals) yet held to the Wilsonian principle of moderate protection for most industrial products. Agricultural machinery and other items used by farmers remained on the free list.

Mellon nevertheless succeeded in balancing the budget and reducing the national debt by an average of over $500 million a year. So committed were the Republican leaders to retrenchment that they even resisted the demands of veterans, organized in the politically potent American Legion, for an "adjusted compensation" bonus. Arguing, not entirely without reason, that they had served for a pittance while war workers had been drawing down high wages, the veterans sought grants equal to $1.00 a day for their period in uniform ($1.25 for time overseas). Congress responded sympathetically, but Harding and Coolidge both vetoed bonus bills in the name of economy. Finally, in 1924, a compromise bill granting the veterans paid-up life insurance policies was passed over Coolidge's veto.

That the business community heartily approved the policies of Harding and Coolidge is not surprising. Both presidents were uncritical advocates of the business point of view. "We want less government in business and more business in government," Harding pontificated, to which Coolidge added, "The business of the United States is business." Harding and Coolidge used their power of appointment to convert regulatory bodies like the Interstate Commerce Commission and the Federal Reserve Board into pro-business agencies that ceased almost entirely to restrict the activities of the industries they were supposed to be controlling. The ICC became almost the reverse of what it had been in the Progressive Era. The Federal Trade Commission, in the words of one bemused academic, seemed to be trying to commit hara-kiri.

The Harding Scandals

At least Mellon was honest. The Ohio Gang used its power in the most corrupt way imaginable. Jesse Smith, a crony of Attorney General Daugherty, was what today would be called an influence peddler. When he was exposed in 1923, he committed suicide. Charles R. Forbes of the Veterans Bureau siphoned millions of dollars appropriated for the construction of hospitals into his own pocket. When he was found out, he fled to Europe. Later he returned, stood trial, and was sentenced to two years in prison. His assistant, Charles F. Cramer, committed suicide. Daugherty himself was implicated in the fraudulent return of German assets seized by the alien property custodian to their original owners. He escaped imprisonment only by refusing to testify on the ground that he might incriminate himself. Thomas W. Miller, the alien property custodian, was sent to jail for accepting a bribe.

The worst scandal involved Secretary of the Interior Albert B. Fall, a former senator. In 1921 Fall arranged with the complaisant secretary of the navy, Edwin Denby, for the transfer to the Interior Department of government oil reserves being held for the future use of the navy. He then leased these properties to private oil companies. Edward L. Doheny's Pan-American Petroleum Company got the Elk Hills reserve in California; the Teapot Dome reserve in Wyoming was turned over to Harry F. Sinclair's Mammoth Oil Company. When critics protested, Fall explained that it was necessary to develop the Elk Hills and Teapot Dome properties because adjoining private drillers were draining off the navy's oil. Nevertheless, in 1923 the Senate ordered a full-scale investigation, conducted by Senator Thomas J. Walsh of Montana. It soon came out that Doheny had "lent" Fall $100,000 in hard cash, handed over secretly in a "little black bag." Sinclair had given Fall over $300,000 in cash and negotiable securities.

Although the three culprits escaped conviction on the charge of conspiring to defraud the government, Sinclair was sentenced to nine months in jail for contempt of the Senate and for tampering with a jury, and Fall was fined $100,000 and given a year in prison for accepting a bribe. In 1927 the Supreme Court revoked the leases, and the two reserves were returned to the government.

The public still knew little of the scandals when,

"Thar she blows!!" proclaims the cover of the humor magazine Life's *"oil number" in March 1924, as an honest citizen prepares to harpoon the Teapot Dome conspiracy. A guilty-looking politician has bailed out and is trying to swim clear of the impending fracas.*

in June 1923, Harding left Washington on a speaking tour that included a visit to Alaska. His health was poor and his spirits were low, for he had begun to understand how his "Goddamn friends" had betrayed him. On the return trip from Alaska, he came down with what his physician, an incompetent crony whom he had made surgeon general of the United States, diagnosed as ptomaine poisoning resulting from his having eaten a tainted Japanese crab. In fact the president had suffered a heart attack. He died in San Francisco on August 2.

Few presidents have been more deeply mourned by the people at the moment of their passing. Harding's kindly nature, his very ordinariness, increased his human appeal. Three million people viewed his coffin as it crossed the country. When the scandals came to light, sadness turned to scorn and contempt. The poet e. e. cummings came closer to catching the final judgment of Harding's contemporaries than any historian has:

> the first president to be loved by his
> bitterest enemies" is dead
> the only man woman or child who wrote
> a simple declarative sentence with seven
>   grammatical
> errors "is dead"
> beautiful Warren Gamaliel Harding
> "is" dead
> he's
> "dead"
> if he wouldn't have eaten them Yapanese Craps
> somebody might hardly never not have been
>   unsorry, perhaps

Coolidge Prosperity

Had he lived, Harding might well have been defeated in 1924 because of the scandals. Vice-President Coolidge, unconnected with the troubles and not the type to surround himself with cronies of any kind, seemed the ideal person to clean out the corruptionists. After he had replaced Attorney General Daugherty with Harlan Fiske Stone, dean of the Columbia University Law School, the scandals ceased to be a serious political handicap for the Republicans.

Coolidge soon became the darling of the conservatives. His admiration for businessmen and his devotion to laissez faire knew no limit. "The man who builds a factory builds a temple," he said in all seriousness. "The Government can do more to remedy the economic ills of the people by a system of rigid economy in public expenditures than can be accomplished through any other action." Andrew Mellon, whom he kept on as secretary of the treasury, became his mentor in economic affairs.

Coolidge won the 1924 Republican nomination easily. The Democrats, badly split, required 103 ballots to choose a candidate. The southern wing, dry, anti-immigrant, pro-Klan, had fixed on William G. McAdoo, Wilson's secretary of the treasury. The eastern, urban, wet element supported Governor Alfred E. Smith of New York, child of the slums, a Catholic who had compiled a distinguished record in the field of social welfare legislation. After days

However accurate the point that his policies and those of big business were harmonious, the image of "Silent Cal" Coolidge playing a saxophone for the benefit of a Charleston-dancing "flapper" is sheer cartoonist license.

of futile politicking, the party compromised on John W. Davis, a conservative corporation lawyer closely allied with the Morgan banking interests.

Dismayed by the conservatism of Coolidge and Davis, Robert M. La Follette, backed by the farm bloc, the Socialist party, the American Federation of Labor, and numbers of intellectuals, entered the race as the candidate of a new Progressive party. The Progressives adopted a neopopulist platform calling for the nationalization of railroads, the direct election of the president, the protection of labor's right to bargain collectively, and other reforms.

The situation was almost exactly the opposite of 1912, when one conservative had run against two liberals and had been swamped. Coolidge received 15.7 million votes, Davis 8.4 million, La Follette 4.8 million. In the electoral college La Follette won only

his native Wisconsin; Coolidge defeated Davis, 382 to 136. Conservatism was clearly the dominant mood of the country.

While Coolidge reigned, complacency was the order of the day. "The country," the president reported to Congress in 1928, "can regard the present with satisfaction, and anticipate the future with optimism."

Peace Without a Sword

Presidents Harding and Coolidge handled foreign relations in much the same way as they managed domestic affairs. Harding deferred to senatorial prejudice against executive domination in the area and let his secretary of state, Charles Evans Hughes, make policy. Coolidge adopted a similar course. In directing foreign relations, they faced the obstacle of a resurgent isolationism. The same forces of war-bred hatred, postwar disillusionment, and fear of communist subversion that produced the Red Scare at home led Americans to back away from close involvement in world affairs. The bloodiness and apparent senselessness of the Great War convinced millions that the only way to be sure it would not happen again was to "steer clear" of "entanglements." That these famous words had been used by Washington and Jefferson in vastly different contexts did not deter the isolationists of the 1920s from attributing to them the same authority they gave to Scripture. Yet far-flung American economic interests and the need for both raw materials for industry and foreign markets for America's growing surpluses of agricultural and manufactured goods made close attention to and involvement in developments all over the world unavoidable.

Isolationist sentiments therefore did not deter the government from seeking to advance American interests abroad. The Open Door concept remained predominant; the State Department worked to uncover opportunities in underdeveloped countries for exporters and investors, hoping both to stimulate the American economy and to bring stability to "backward" nations. While this policy sometimes aroused local resentments because of the tendency of the United States to support entrenched elites while the masses of peasants and city workers lived in poverty, it also resulted in a further retreat from active interventionism.

The first important diplomatic event of the period revealed a great deal about American foreign policy after the World War. During the war Japan had greatly increased its influence in the Far East, especially in Manchuria, the northeastern province of warlord-dominated China. To maintain the Open Door in China, it would be necessary to check Japanese expansion. But there was little hope of restoring the old spheres of influence, which the mass of Chinese people bitterly resented. In addition, Japan, the United States, and Great Britain were engaged in expensive naval building programs, a competition none of them really wanted but from which no one dared withdraw unilaterally.

In November 1921, hoping to reach a general agreement with China, Japan, and the Europeans that would keep China open to the commerce of all and slow the armaments race, Secretary of State Hughes convened a conference in Washington. By the following February the Washington Conference had drafted three major treaties and a number of lesser agreements.

In the Five-Power Treaty, the United States, Great Britain, France, Japan, and Italy agreed to stop building battleships for ten years and to reduce their fleets of capital ships to a fixed ratio, with Great Britain and the United States limited to 525,000 tons, Japan to 315,000 tons, and France and Italy to 175,000 tons. The new ratio was expected to produce a balance of forces in the Pacific.

The Four-Power Treaty, signed by the United States, Great Britain, Japan, and France, committed these nations to respect one another's interests in the islands of the Pacific and to confer in the event that any other country launched an attack in the area.

All the conferees signed the Nine-Power Treaty, agreeing to respect China's independence and to maintain the Open Door. On the surface, this was of monumental importance to the United States, since it seemed to mean that Japan had given up its territorial ambitions on the Asian mainland and that both the Japanese and the Europeans had formally endorsed the Open Door concept.

By taking the lead in drafting these agreements, the United States regained some of the moral influence it had lost by not joining the League of Nations. The treaties, however, were uniformly toothless. The signers of the Four-Power pact agreed only to consult in case of aggression in the Pacific; they made no promises to help one another or to restrict their own freedom of action. As President Harding assured the Senate, there was "no commitment to armed force, no alliance, no written or moral obligation to join in defense."

The naval disarmament treaty said nothing about the number of other warships that the powers might build, about the far more important question of land and air forces, or about the underlying industrial and financial structures that controlled the ability of the nations to make war. In addition, the 5:5:3 ratio actually enabled the Japanese to dominate the western Pacific. It made the Philippine Islands undefendable and exposed Hawaii to possible attack. In a sense these American bases became hostages of Japan. Yet Congress was so unconcerned about Japanese sensibilities that it refused to grant any immigration quota to Japan under the National Origins Act of 1924, even though the formula as applied to other nations would have allowed only 100 Japanese a year to enter the country. The law, Secretary Hughes warned, produced in Japan "a sense of injury and antagonism instead of friendship and cooperation."

Hughes did not think war a likely result, but Japanese resentment of "white imperialism" played into the hands of the military party in that nation. Many Japanese army and navy officers considered war with the United States inevitable. "The emotional resentment against America," Akira Iriye writes in *Across the Pacific*, "was reinforced by a more sophisticated view of future Japanese-American conflict that was advocated by some army strategists."

As for the key Nine-Power Treaty, Japan did not abandon its territorial ambitions in China, and China remained so riven by conflict among the warlords and so resentful of the "imperialists" that the economic advantages of the Open Door turned out to be small indeed.

The United States entered into all these agreements without realizing their full implications and not really prepared to play an active part in Far Eastern affairs. "We have no favorites in the present dog fight in China," the head of the Far Eastern division of the State Department wrote of the civil war going on there in 1924. "They all look alike to us." The Japanese soon realized that the United States would not do much to defend its interests in China. The result, in Professor Iriye's words, was "a new image of America, as a country that delighted in moralism . . . but that was not likely to challenge Japan with force."

The Peace Movement

The Americans of the 1920s wanted peace but would neither surrender their prejudices and dislikes nor build the defenses necessary to make it safe to indulge these passions. "The people have had all the war, all the taxation, and all the military service that they want," President Coolidge announced in 1925.

Peace societies flourished, among them the Carnegie Endowment for International Peace, designed "to hasten the abolition of war, the foulest blot upon our civilization," and the Woodrow Wilson Foundation, aimed at helping "the liberal forces of mankind throughout the world . . . who intend to promote peace by the means of justice." In 1923 Edward W. Bok, retired editor of the *Ladies' Home Journal,* offered a prize of $100,000 for the best workable plan for preserving international peace. He was flooded with suggestions. Former Assistant Secretary of the Navy Franklin D. Roosevelt drafted one while recovering from an attack of infantile paralysis. Such was the temper of the times that he felt constrained to include in the preamble this statement:

We seek not to become involved as a nation in the purely regional affairs of groups of other nations, nor to give to the representatives of other peoples the right

Leaders of the Women's International League for Peace and Freedom assembled at the end of World War I to argue in favor of U.S. participation in a worldwide peace organization such as the League of Nations. Jane Addams is in front, fourth from left; at her left is Mrs. Robert La Follette, wife of the Wisconsin senator.

to compel us to enter upon undertakings calling for a leading up to the use of armed force without our full and free consent, given through our constitutional procedure.

So great was the opposition to international cooperation that the United States refused to accept membership on the World Court, although this tribunal could settle disputes only when the nations involved agreed. Probably a majority of the American people favored joining the court, but its advocates were never able to persuade two-thirds of the Senate to ratify the necessary treaty. Too many peace lovers believed that their goal could be attained simply by pointing out the moral and practical disadvantages of war.

The culmination of this illusory faith in preventing war by criticizing it came with the signing of the Kellogg-Briand Pact in 1928. The treaty was born in the fertile brain of French Foreign Minister Aristide Briand, who was eager to collect allies against possible attack by a resurgent Germany. In 1927 Briand proposed to Secretary of State Frank B. Kellogg that their countries agree never to go to war with each other. Kellogg found the idea as repugnant as any conventional alliance, but American isolationists and pacifists found the suggestion fascinating. They plagued Kellogg with demands that he negotiate such a treaty.

To extricate himself from this situation, Kellogg suggested that the pact be broadened to include all nations. Now Briand was angry. Like Kellogg, he saw how meaningless such a treaty would be, especially when Kellogg insisted that it be hedged with a proviso that "every nation is free at all times . . . to defend its territory from attack and it alone is competent to decide when circumstances require war in self-defense." Nevertheless, Briand too found public pressures irresistible. In August 1928, at Paris, diplomats from 15 nations bestowed on one another an "international kiss," condemning "recourse to war for the solution of international controversies" and renouncing war "as an instrument of national policy." Seldom has so unrealistic a promise been made by so many intelligent people. Yet most Americans considered the Kellogg-Briand Pact a milestone in the history of civilization: The Senate, habitually so suspicious of international commitments, ratified it 85 to 1.

The Good Neighbor Policy

The conflict betweeen the desire to avoid foreign entanglements and the desire to advance American economic interests is well illustrated by events in Latin America. "Yankeephobia" had long been a chronic condition south of the Rio Grande. The continued presence of marines in Central America fed this ill feeling, as did the failure of the United States to enter the League of Nations (which all but four Latin American nations had joined). Basic, of course, was the objection to being controlled by foreigners, whether directly when troops were employed or through the economic domination involved in dollar diplomacy. The immense wealth and power of the "Colossus of the North" and the feeling of most Latin Americans that the wielders of this strength had little respect for the needs and values of their southern neighbors were further causes of distrust. However, the evident desire of the United States to limit its international involvements had a gradually mollifying effect on Latin American opinion.

In dealing with this part of the world, Harding and Coolidge performed neither better nor worse than Wilson had. In the face of continued radicalism and instability in Mexico, which caused Americans with interests in land and oil rights to suffer heavy losses, President Coolidge acted with forbearance. His appointment of Dwight W. Morrow, a patient, sympathetic ambassador, resulted in an improvement in Mexican-American relations. The Mexicans were able to complete their social and economic revolution in the 1920s without significant interference by the United States.

Under Coolidge's successor, Herbert Hoover, the United States began at last to treat Latin American nations as equals. Hoover reversed Wilson's policy of trying to teach them "to elect good men." The Clark Memorandum (1930), written by Undersecretary of State J. Reuben Clark, disassociated the right of intervention in Latin America from the Roosevelt Corollary. The corollary had been an improper extension of the Monroe Doctrine, Clark declared. The right of the United States to intervene depended rather on "the doctrine of self-preservation."

The distinction seemed slight to Latin Americans, but since it seemed unlikely that the existence of the United States could be threatened in the area, it was important. By 1934 the marines who had been occupying Nicaragua, Haiti, and the Dominican Republic had all been withdrawn and the United States had renounced the right to intervene in Cuban affairs, thereby abrogating the Platt Amendment to the Cuban constitution. Unfortunately, the United States did little to try to improve social and economic conditions in the Caribbean region, so the underlying envy and resentment of "rich Uncle Sam" did not disappear.

The Totalitarian Challenge

The futility and danger of isolationism were exposed in September 1931 when the Japanese, long dominant in Chinese Manchuria, marched in an army and converted it into a puppet state they named Manchukuo. This violated both the Kellogg-Briand and Nine-Power pacts. China, now controlled by General Chiang Kai-shek, appealed to the League of Nations and to the United States for help. Neither would intervene. When League officials asked about the possibility of American cooperation in some kind of police action, President Hoover refused to consider either economic or military reprisals. The United States was not a world policeman, he said. The Nine-Power and Kellogg-Briand treaties were "solely moral instruments."

The League sent a commission to Manchuria to investigate. Henry L. Stimson, Hoover's secretary of state, announced that the United States would never recognize the legality of seizures made in violation of American treaty rights. This so-called Stimson Doctrine served only to irritate the Japanese.

In January 1932 Japan attacked Shanghai, the bloody battle marked by the indiscriminate bombing of residential districts. When the League of Nations at last officially condemned their aggressions, the Japanese withdrew from the organization and extended their control of northern China. The lesson of Manchuria was not lost on Adolf Hitler, who became chancellor of Germany on January 30, 1933.

It is easy, in surveying the diplomatic events of 1920–1929, to condemn the United States and the European democracies for their unwillingness to stand up for principles, their refusal to resist when Japan and later Germany and Italy embarked on the aggressions that led to World War II. It is also proper to place some of the blame for the troubles of the era on the same powers: They controlled much of the world's resources and were primarily interested in holding on to what they had.

War Debts and Reparations

The democracies did not take a strong stand against Japan in part because they were quarreling about other matters. Particularly divisive was the controversy over war debts—what Germany owed the Allies and what the Allies owed the United States. The United States had lent more than $10 billion to its comrades in arms. Since most of this money had been spent on weapons and other supplies in the United States, it might well have been considered part of America's contribution to the war effort. The public, however, demanded full repayment—with

A merciless France demands war reparations from Germany in this Los Angeles Times *cartoon from 1922. American aid to the German economy had little effect in the face of Germany's enormous reparations costs.*

interest. "These were loans, not contributions," Treasury Secretary Mellon firmly declared. Even when the Foreign Debt Commission scaled down the interest rate from 5 percent to about 2 percent, the total, to be repaid over a period of 62 years, amounted to more than $22 billion.

Repayment of such a sum was virtually impossible. In the first place, the money had not been put to productive use. Dollars lent to build factories or roads might be expected to earn profits for the borrower, but those devoted to the purchase of shells only destroyed wealth. Furthermore, the American protective tariff reduced the ability of the Allies to earn the dollars needed to pay the debts.

The Allies tried to load their obligations to the United States, along with the other costs of the war, on the backs of the Germans. They demanded reparations amounting to $33 billion. If this sum were collected, they declared, they could rebuild their economies and obtain the international exchange needed to pay their debts to the United States. But Germany was reluctant even to try to pay such huge reparations, and when Germany defaulted, so did the Allies.

Everyone was bitterly resentful: the Germans because they felt they were being bled white; the Americans, as Senator Hiram Johnson of California would have it, because the wily Europeans were treating the United States as "an international sucker"; the Allies because, as the French said, *l'oncle Shylock* (a play on the names Uncle Sam and Shylock, the moneylender in Shakespeare's *Merchant of Venice*) was demanding his pound of flesh with interest. "If nations were only business firms," Clemenceau wrote to President Coolidge in 1926, "bank notes would determine the fate of the world. . . . Come see the endless lists of dead in our villages."

Everyone shared the blame: the Germans because they resorted to a runaway inflation that reduced the mark to less than one trillionth of its prewar value, at least in part in hopes of avoiding their international obligations; the Americans because they refused to recognize the connection between the tariff and the debt question; the Allies because they made little effort to pay even a reasonable proportion of their obligations.

In 1924 an international agreement, the Dawes Plan, provided Germany with a $200 million loan designed to stabilize its currency. Germany agreed to pay about $250 million a year in reparations. In 1929 the Young Plan further scaled down the reparations bill. In practice, the Allies paid the United States about what they collected from Germany. Since Germany got the money largely from private American loans, the United States would have served itself and the rest of the world far better had it written off the war debts at the start. In any case, in the late 1920s Americans stopped lending money to Germany, the Great Depression struck, Germany defaulted on its reparations payments, and the Allies then gave up all pretense of meeting their obligations to the United States. The last token payments were made in 1933. All that remained was a heritage of mistrust and hostility.

The Election of 1928

Meanwhile, dramatic changes had occurred in the United States. The climax of Coolidge prosperity came in 1928. The president—somewhat cryptically, as was his wont—decided not to run again, and Secretary of Commerce Hoover, whom he detested, easily won the Republican nomination. Hoover was the intellectual leader, almost the philosopher, of the New Era. He spoke and wrote of "progressive individualism." American capitalists, he believed, had learned to curb their selfish instincts. Voluntary trade associations could create "codes of business practice and ethics that would eliminate abuses and make for higher standards."

Although stiff and uncommunicative and entirely without experience in elective office, Hoover made an admirable candidate in 1928. His roots in the Middle West and West (Iowa-born, he was raised in Oregon and educated at Stanford University in California) neatly balanced his outstanding reputation among eastern business tycoons. He took a "modern" approach to both capital and labor; businessmen should cooperate with one another and with their workers too. He opposed both union busting and trustbusting. His career as a mining engineer had given him a wide knowledge of the world, yet he had become highly critical of Europe—which disarmed the isolationists, who might otherwise have suspected that his long years abroad had made him an effete cosmopolite.

The Democrats, having had their fill of factionalism in 1924, could no longer deny the nomination to Governor Al Smith. Superficially, Smith was

Hoover's antithesis. Born and raised in New York's Lower East Side slums, affable, witty, determinedly casual of manner, he had been schooled in machine politics by Tammany Hall. Smith was a Catholic, Hoover a Quaker; Smith was a wet, whereas Hoover supported prohibition; Smith dealt easily with people of every race and nationality, while Hoover had little interest in and less knowledge of blacks and immigrants. However, like Hoover, Smith managed to combine a basic conservatism with humanitarian concern for the underprivileged. As adept in administration as Hoover, he was equally uncritical of the American capitalist system.

Unwilling to challenge the public's complacent view of Coolidge prosperity, the Democrats adopted a conservative platform. Smith appointed John J. Raskob, a wealthy automobile executive, to manage his campaign. Franklin D. Roosevelt, who ran for governor of New York at Smith's urging in 1928, charged that Hoover's expansion of the functions of the Department of Commerce had been at least mildly socialistic. This strategy failed miserably. Nothing Smith could do or say was capable of convincing many businessmen that he was a better choice than Hoover. His Catholicism, his brashness, his criticism of prohibition, his machine connections, and his urban background hurt him in rural areas, especially in the normally Democratic South.

In the election Hoover won a smashing triumph, 444 to 87 in the electoral college, 21.4 million to 14 million in the popular vote. All the usually Democratic border states and even North Carolina, Florida, and Texas went to the Republicans, along with the entire West and the Northeast save for Massachusetts and Rhode Island.

After this defeat the Democratic party appeared on the verge of extinction. Nothing could have been further from the truth. The religious question and his big-city roots had hurt Smith, but the chief reason he lost was prosperity—and the good times were soon to end. Hoover's overwhelming victory also concealed a political realignment that was taking place. Working-class voters in the cities, largely Catholic and unimpressed by Coolidge prosperity, had swung heavily to the Democrats. In 1924 the 12 largest cities had been solidly Republican; in 1928 all went Democratic. In agricultural states like Iowa, Smith ran far better than Davis had in 1924, for Coolidge's vetoes of bills designed to raise farm prices had caused considerable resentment. A new

Herbert Hoover relaxing during the 1928 presidential campaign. "That man has been offering me advice for the last five years," President Coolidge said of his Secretary of Commerce, "all of it bad."

coalition of urban workers and dissatisfied farmers was in the making.

Economic Problems

The American economic system of the 1920s had grave flaws. Certain industries did not share in the good times. The coal business, suffering from the competition of petroleum, entered a period of decline. The production of cotton and woolen cloth also lagged because of the competition of new synthetics, principally rayon. The industry began to be plagued by falling profit margins and chronic unemployment.

The movement toward consolidation in industry, somewhat checked during the latter part of the Progressive Era, resumed; by 1929 a mere 200 corporations controlled nearly half the nation's corporate assets. General Motors, Ford, and Chrysler turned out nearly 90 percent of all American cars and trucks. Four tobacco companies produced over 90 percent of the cigarettes. One percent of all financial institutions controlled 46 percent of the nation's banking business. Even retail merchandising, traditionally the domain of the small shopkeeper, reflected the trend. The A&P food chain expanded from 400 stores in 1912 to 17,500 in 1928. The Woolworth chain of five-and-ten-cent stores experienced similar growth.

Most large manufacturers, aware that bad public relations resulting from the unbridled use of monopolistic power outweighed any immediate economic gain, sought stability and "fair" prices rather than the maximum profit possible at the moment. "Regulated" competition was the order of the day, oligopoly the typical situation. The trade association movement flourished; producers formed voluntary organizations to exchange information, discuss policies toward government and the public, and "administer" prices in their industry. Usually the largest corporation, such as U.S. Steel in the iron and steel business, became the "price leader," its competitors, some themselves giants, following slavishly.

The success of the trade associations depended in part on the attitude of the federal government, for such organizations might well have been attacked under the antitrust laws. Their defenders argued that the associations made business more efficient and prevented violent gyrations of prices and production. President Harding accepted this line of reasoning. Secretary of Commerce Hoover put the facilities of his department at the disposal of the associations. "We are passing from a period of extremely individualistic action into a period of associational activities," Hoover stated. After Coolidge became president, the Antitrust Division of the Justice Department itself encouraged the trade associations to cooperate in ways that had previously been considered violations of the Sherman Act.

Even more important to the trade associations were the good times. With profits high and markets expanding, the most powerful producers could afford to share the bounty with smaller, less efficient competitors.

The weakest element in the economy was agriculture. Farm prices slumped and farmers' costs mounted. Besides having to purchase expensive machinery in order to compete, farmers confronted high foreign tariffs and in some cases quotas on the importation of foodstuffs. As crop yields per acre rose, chiefly because of the increased use of chemical fertilizers, agricultural prices fell further.

Despite the efforts of the farm bloc, the government did little to improve the situation. President Harding opposed direct aid to agriculture as a matter of principle. "Every farmer is a captain of industry," he declared. "The elimination of competition among them would be impossible without sacrificing that fine individualism that still keeps the farm the real reservoir from which the nation draws so many of the finest elements of its citizenship." During his administration Congress strengthened the laws regulating railroad rates and grain exchanges and made it easier for farmers to borrow money, but it did nothing to increase agricultural income. Nor did the high tariffs on agricultural produce have much effect. Being forced to sell their surpluses abroad, farmers found that world prices depressed domestic prices despite the tariff wall.

In 1921 George N. Peek, a plow manufacturer from Moline, Illinois, advanced a scheme to "make the tariff effective for agriculture." The federal government, Peek suggested in "Equality for Agriculture," should buy up the surplus American production of wheat.* This additional demand would cause domestic prices to rise. Then the government could sell the wheat abroad at the lower world price. It could recover its losses by assessing an "equalization fee" on the wheat farmers.

Peek's plan had flaws. If the price of staples rose, farmers would tend to increase their output. Yet this problem might have been solved by imposing production controls. It was certainly a promising idea; hundreds of organizations in the Farm Belt endorsed it. Farm bloc congressmen took it up, and in 1927 the McNary-Haugen bill was passed, only to be vetoed by President Coolidge. Although he raised a number of practical objections, Coolidge based his opposition chiefly on constitutional and philosophical grounds. "A healthy economic condition is best maintained through a free play of competition," he insisted, ignoring the fact that the scheme had been devised precisely because competition was proving unhealthy for American farmers. Congress passed a similar bill in 1928, and again Coolidge rejected it.

Thus while most economic indicators reflected an unprecedented prosperity, the boom time rested on unstable foundations. The problem was mainly

---

* He soon extended his plan to cover cotton and other staples.

one of maldistribution of resources. Productive capacity raced ahead of buying power. Too large a share of the profits were going into too few pockets. The 27,000 families with the highest annual incomes in 1929 received as much money as the 11 million with annual incomes of under $1,500, the minimum sum required at that time to maintain a family decently. High earnings and low taxes permitted huge sums to pile up in the hands of individuals who did not invest the money productively. A good deal of it went into stock market speculation, which led to the "big bull market" and eventually to the Great Depression.

The Crash of 1929

In the spring of 1928, prices on the New York Stock Exchange, already at a historic high, began to surge ahead. As the presidential campaign gathered momentum, the market increased its upward pace, stimulated by the candidates' efforts to outdo each other in praising the marvels of the American economic system. "Glamour" stocks skyrocketed— Radio Corporation of America rose from under 100 to 400 between March and November. A few conservative brokers expressed alarm, warning that most stocks were grossly overpriced. The majority scoffed at such talk. "Be a bull on America," they urged. "Never sell the United States short."

During the first half of 1929, stock prices climbed still higher. A mania for speculation swept the country, thousands of small investors putting their savings into common stocks.

In September the market wavered. Amid volatile fluctuations, stock averages eased downward. Most analysts contended that the Exchange was "digesting" previous gains. A Harvard economist expressed the prevailing view when he said that stock prices had reached a "permanently high plateau" and would soon resume their advance.

On October 24 a wave of selling sent prices spinning. Nearly 13 million shares changed hands—a record. Bankers and politicians rallied to check the decline, as they had during the panic of 1907 (see page 659). J. P. Morgan, Jr., rivaled the efforts of his father in that earlier crisis. President Hoover assured the people that "the business of the country . . . is on a sound and prosperous basis." But on October 29, the bottom seemed to drop out. More

James Rosenberg, an attorney and amateur artist, sketched this grim view of the Wall Street financial district, October 29, 1929 ("Black Tuesday"), as a Day of Judgment.

than 16 million shares were sold, prices plummeting. The boom was over.

Hoover and the Depression

The collapse of the stock market did not cause the depression; stocks rallied late in the year, and business activity did not begin to decline significantly until the spring of 1930. The Great Depression was a worldwide phenomenon caused chiefly by economic imbalances resulting from the chaos of the Great War. In the United States too much wealth had fallen into too few hands, with the result that consumers were unable to buy all the goods produced. The trouble came to a head mainly because of the easy-credit policies of the Federal Reserve Board and the Mellon tax structure, which favored the rich. Its effects were so profound and prolonged because the politicians (and for that matter the professional economists) did not fully understand what was happening or what to do about it.

The chronic problem of underconsumption operated to speed the downward spiral. Unable to rid themselves of mounting inventories, manufacturers closed plants and laid off workers, thereby causing demand to shrink further. Automobile output fell from 4.5 million units in 1929 to 1.1 million in 1932. When Ford closed his Detroit plants in 1931, some 75,000 workers lost their jobs, and the decline in auto production affected a host of suppliers and intermediaries as well.

The financial system cracked under the strain. More than 1,300 banks closed their doors in 1930, another 3,700 during the next two years. Each failure deprived thousands of persons of funds that might have been used to buy goods; when the Bank of the United States in New York City became insolvent in December 1930, all 400,000 depositors found their savings immobilized. And of course the industrial depression worsened the depression in agriculture by further reducing the demand for American foodstuffs. Every economic indicator reflected the collapse. New investments declined from $10 billion in 1929 to $1 billion in 1932, and national income fell from over $80 billion to under $50 billion in the same brief period. Unemployment, under 1 million at the height of the boom, rose to at least 13 million.

President Hoover was an intelligent man, experienced in business matters and knowledgeable in economics. Treasury Secretary Mellon believed that the economy should be allowed to slide unchecked until the cycle had found its bottom. "Let the slump liquidate itself," Mellon urged. "Liquidate labor, liquidate stocks, liquidate the farmers. . . . People will work harder, live a more moral life. Values will be adjusted, and enterprising people will pick up the wrecks from less competent people." Hoover realized that such a policy would cause unbearable hardship for millions. He rejected Mellon's advice to let the depression run its course.

Hoover's program for ending the depression evolved gradually. At first he called on businessmen to maintain prices and wages. The government should cut taxes in order to increase consumers' spendable income, institute public works programs to stimulate production and create jobs for the unemployed, lower interest rates to make it easier for businesses to borrow in order to expand, and make loans to banks and industrial corporations threatened with collapse and to homeowners unable to meet mortgage payments. The president also proposed measures making it easier for farmers to borrow money, and he suggested that cooperative farm marketing schemes designed to solve the problem of overproduction be supported by the government. He called for an expansion of state and local relief programs and urged all who could afford it to give more to charity. Above all he tried to restore public confidence. The economy was basically healthy; the depression was only a minor downturn; prosperity was "just around the corner."

In other words, Hoover rejected classical economics. Indeed, many laissez faire theorists attacked his handling of the depression. The English economist Lionel Robbins, writing in 1934, criticized Hoover's "grandiose buying organizations" and his efforts to maintain consumer income "at all costs." Numbers of "liberal" economists, however, praised the Hoover program.

Though Hoover's plans were theoretically sound, they failed to check the economic slide, in part because of curious limitations in his conception of how they should be implemented. He placed far too much reliance on his powers of persuasion and the willingness of citizens to act in the public interest without legal compulsion. He urged manufacturers to maintain wages and keep their factories in operation, but the manufacturers, under the harsh pressure of economic realities, soon slashed wages and curtailed output sharply. He permitted the Federal Farm Board (created under the Agricultural Marketing Act of 1929) to establish semipublic stabilization corporations with authority to buy up surplus wheat and cotton, but he refused to countenance crop or acreage controls. The stabilization corporations poured out hundreds of millions of dollars without checking falling agricultural prices because farmers increased production faster than the corporations could buy up the excess for disposal abroad.

Hoover resisted proposals to shift responsibility from state and local agencies to the federal government, despite the fact—soon obvious—that they lacked the resources to cope with the emergency. By 1932 the federal government, with Hoover's approval, was spending $500 million a year on public works projects, but because of the decline in state and municipal construction, the total public outlay fell nearly $1 billion below what it had been in 1930. More serious was his refusal, on constitutional grounds, to allow federal funds to be used for the relief of individuals. State and municipal agencies and private charities must take care of the needy, he contended.

Unfortunately, the depression was drying up the sources of private charities just as the demands on these organizations were expanding. State and municipal agencies were swamped at a time when their capacities to tax and borrow were shrinking. By 1932 more than 40,600 Boston families were on relief (compared with 7,400 families in 1929); in Chicago 700,000 persons—40 percent of the work force—were unemployed. Only the national government possessed the power and the credit to deal adequately with the crisis.

Yet Hoover would not act. He set up a committee to coordinate local relief activities but insisted on preserving what he called "the principles of individual and local responsibility." For the federal government to take over relief would "lead to the superstate where every man becomes the servant of the state and real liberty is lost."

Federal loans to businessmen were constitutional, he believed, because the money could be put to productive use and eventually repaid. When drought destroyed the crops of farmers in the South and Southwest in 1930, the government lent them money to buy seed and even food for their livestock, but Hoover would permit no direct relief for the farmers themselves. In 1932 he approved the creation of the Reconstruction Finance Corporation to lend money to banks, railroads, and insurance companies. The RFC represented an important extension of national authority, yet it was thoroughly in line with Hoover's philosophy. Its loans, secured by solid collateral, were commercial transactions, not gifts; the agency did almost nothing for individuals in need of relief. The same could be said of the Glass-Steagall Banking Act of 1932, which eased the tight credit situation by permitting Federal Reserve banks to accept a wider variety of commercial paper as security for loans. The public grew increasingly resentful of the president's doctrinaire adherence to principle while breadlines lengthened and millions of willing workers searched fruitlessly for jobs.

As time passed and the depression worsened, Hoover put more stress on the importance of balancing the federal budget, reasoning that since citizens had to live within their limited means in hard times, the government should set a good example. This policy was counterproductive; by reducing its expenditures, the government made the depression worse. The policy was also impossible to carry out because in fact the government's income fell precipitously, creating what the economist Herbert Stein has called "fiscal stimulation by inadvertence." By June 1931 the budget was nearly $500 million in the red.

Hoover understood the value of pumping money into a stagnant economy. He might have made a virtue of necessity. The difficulty lay in the fact that nearly all "informed" opinion believed that a balanced budget was essential to recovery. The most prestigious economists insisted on it; so did business leaders, labor leaders, and even most socialists. In 1932, when the House of Representatives refused to vote a tax increase, the Democratic Speaker compelled reconsideration of the bill by asking all "who do not want to balance the budget to rise." Not a single member did so. As late as 1939 a public opinion poll revealed that over 60 percent of the people (even 57.5 percent of the unemployed) favored reducing government expenditures in order to balance the budget. When Hoover said, "prosperity cannot be restored by raids on the public Treasury," he was mistaken, but it is equally wrong to criticize him for failing to understand what almost no one understood in the 1930s.

Hoover can, however, be faulted for allowing his anti-European prejudices to interfere with the implementation of his program. In 1930 Congress passed the Hawley-Smoot Tariff Act, which raised duties on most manufactured products to prohibitive levels. Hoover signed it cheerfully. The new tariff made it impossible for European nations to earn the dollars they needed to continue making payments on their World War I debts to the United States, and it helped bring on a financial collapse in Europe in 1931. In that year Hoover wisely proposed a one-year moratorium on all international obligations. But the efforts of Great Britain and many other countries to save their own skins by devaluing their currencies in order to encourage foreigners to buy their goods led him to blame them for the depression itself. He seemed unable to grasp what should have been obvious to a person of his intelligence: that high American tariffs made currency devaluation almost inevitable in Europe and that the curtailment of American investment on the Continent as a result of the depression had dealt a staggering blow to the economies of all the European nations.

Much of the contemporary criticism of Hoover and a good deal of that heaped on him by later historians was unfair. Yet his record as president shows that he was too rigidly wedded to a particular theory of government to cope effectively with the problems of the day. Since these problems were in a sense insoluble—no one possessed enough knowledge and intelligence to understand entirely what was wrong or enough authority to enforce the proper corrective measures—flexibility and a willingness to experiment were essential to any program aimed at restoring prosperity. Hoover lacked these qualities. He was his own worst enemy, being too uncompromising to get on well with the politicians and too aloof to win the confidence and affection of ordinary people. As Joan Hoff Wilson has noted, he refused "to backslap, fraternize with local supporters, kiss babies." He had too much faith in himself and his plans. When he failed to achieve the results he anticipated, he attracted, despite his devotion to duty and his concern for the welfare of the country, not sympathy but scorn.

Just as Republican presidents took credit for everything that went well in the 1920s, all that went wrong after the 1929 crash was blamed on their party leader.

Hitting Bottom

During the spring of 1932, as the economy sounded the depths, thousands of Americans faced starvation. In Philadelphia during an 11-day period when no relief funds were available, hundreds of families existed on stale bread, thin soup, and garbage. In the nation as a whole, only about one-quarter of the unemployed were receiving any public aid. In Birmingham, Alabama, landlords in poor districts gave up trying to collect rents, preferring, one Alabama congressman told a Senate committee, "to have somebody living there free of charge rather than to have the house . . . burned up for fuel" by scavengers. Many people were evicted, and they often gathered in ramshackle communities constructed of packing boxes, rusty sheet metal, and similar refuse on swamps, garbage dumps, and other waste-

land. People began to call these places "Hoovervilles."

Thousands of tramps roamed the countryside begging and scavenging for food. At the same time, food prices fell so low that farmers burned corn for fuel. In Iowa and Nebraska farmers organized Farm Holiday movements, refusing to ship their crops to market in protest against 31-cent-a-bushel corn and 38-cent wheat. They blocked roads and rail lines, dumped milk, overturned trucks, and established picket lines to enforce their boycott. The world seemed to have been turned upside down. Professor Felix Frankfurter of the Harvard Law School remarked only half humorously that henceforth the terms B.C. and A.D. would mean "Before Crash" and "After Depression."

The national mood ranged from apathy to resentment. In 1931 federal immigration agents and local groups in the Southwest began rounding up Mexican-Americans and deporting them. Some of those returned to Mexico had entered the United States illegally; others had come in properly. Unemployed Mexicans were ejected because they might become public charges, those with jobs because they were presumably taking bread from the mouths of citizens. "Capitalism is dying," the phi-

Unemployed veterans on the steps of the Capitol Building, Washington, July 5, 1932, where they demanded early payment of their bonus as a means of combatting the depression. Some 7000 of these "bonus marchers" were later forcibly evicted by the army from their encampment in nearby Anacostia Flats.

losopher Reinhold Niebuhr remarked in 1932, "and . . . it ought to die."

In June and July 1932 some 20,000 veterans marched on Washington to demand immediate payment of their "adjusted compensation" bonuses. When Congress rejected their appeal, 2,000 of them refused to leave, settling in a jerry-built camp of shacks and tents at Anacostia Flats, a swamp bordering the Potomac. President Hoover, alarmed, charged incorrectly that the "Bonus Army" was largely composed of criminals and radicals and sent troops into the Flats to disperse it with bayonets, tear gas, and tanks. The task was accomplished amid much confusion; fortunately, no one was killed. The protest had been aimless and not entirely justified, yet the spectacle of the United States government chasing unarmed veterans with tanks appalled the nation.

The unprecedented severity of the depression led some persons to favor radical economic and political changes. The disparity between the lots of the rich and the poor, always a challenge to democracy, became more striking and engendered considerable bitterness. "Unless something is done to provide employment," two labor leaders warned Hoover, "disorder . . . is sure to arise. . . . There is a grow-ing demand that the entire business and social structure be changed because of the general dissatisfaction with the present system."

The Communist party gained few converts among farmers and industrial workers, but a considerable number of intellectuals, alienated by the trends of the 1920s, responded positively to the communists' emphasis on economic planning and the total mobilization of the state to achieve social goals. Even the cracker-barrel humorist Will Rogers was impressed by reports of the absence of serious unemployment in Russia. "All roads lead to Moscow," the former muckraker Lincoln Steffens wrote.

Victims of the Depression

Depression is a word used by economists but also by psychologists, and the depression of the 1930s had profound psychological effects on its victims as well as the obvious economic ones. Almost without exception, people who lost their jobs first searched energetically for new ones, but when they remained unemployed for more than a few months, they sank gradually into apathy. E. Wight Bakke, a Yale sociologist who interviewed hundreds of unemployed men in the United States and England during the depression, described the final stage of decline as "permanent readjustment," by which he meant that the long-term jobless simply gave up. The settlement house worker Lillian Wald came to a similar conclusion. Unemployed people at her famous Henry Street settlement, she noticed, had lost both "ambition and pride."

Simple discouragement alone does not explain why so many of the jobless reacted this way. People who had worked all their adult lives often became ashamed of themselves when they could not find a job. Professor Bakke reported that half the unemployed people in New Haven that he interviewed never applied for public assistance no matter how desperate their circumstances. A purely physiological factor was often involved as well. When money ran low, people had to cut down on relatively expensive foods like fruit, meat, and dairy products. In New York City, for example, milk consumption fell by a million quarts a day. In nutritional terms they consumed more carbohydrates and less food rich in energy-building vitamins and proteins. Listlessness (another word for apathy) often resulted.

This psychological depression helps explain why the unemployed were not, in general, very radical. There were meetings and protest marches and also

strikes, but the former were usually organized by people who were not themselves unemployed, and strikers, almost by definition, are people who are refusing to work, not those who have no job to quit. According to the historian Charles H. Trout, when radicals tried to organize protests among unemployed men in Boston, the men "did not take to the streets or plead for a revision of the system, but instead throngs milled outside the Municipal Employment Bureau in the Micawber-like hope that something would turn up."

The depression affected the families of the jobless in many ways. It caused a dramatic drop in the birthrate, from 27.7 per 1,000 population in 1920 to 18.4 per 1,000 in the early 1930s, the lowest in American history. Sometimes it strengthened family ties. Some unemployed men spent more time with their children and helped their wives with cooking and housework. Others, however, became impatient when their children demanded attention, refused to help around the house, sulked, or took to drink.

The influence of wives in families struck by unemployment tended to increase, and in this respect women suffered less psychologically from the depression. They were usually too busy trying to make ends meet to become apathetic. But the way they

A bread line in Chicago. The Great Depression, an English observer said, "outraged and baffled" the nation that took it as "an article of faith . . . that America, somehow, was different from the rest of the world."

used this influence varied. Some wives were sympathetic, others scornful when the "breadwinner" came home with empty hands. When the wife of an unemployed man managed to find a job, the result could be either gratitude and pride or bitter resentment on the man's part, resentment or a sense of liberation on the woman's.

Children often caused strains in families. Parental authority declined when there was less money available to supply children's needs. Some youngsters became angry when their allowance was cut or when told that they could not have something that they particularly wanted. Some adolescents found part time jobs to help out. Others refused to go to school. The truest generalization about the effects of the depression on family relations is probably the most obvious one: Where relationships were close and loving, they became stronger; where they were not, the results could be disastrous.

The Election of 1932

As the end of his term approached, President Hoover seemed to grow daily more petulant and pessimistic. The depression, coming after 12 years of Republican rule, probably ensured a Democratic victory in any case, but his attitude as the election neared alienated many voters and turned defeat into rout.

Confident of victory, the Democrats chose Governor Franklin Delano Roosevelt of New York as their presidential candidate. Roosevelt owed his nomination chiefly to his success as governor. Under his administration, New York had led the nation in providing relief for the needy and had enacted an impressive program of old-age pensions, unemployment insurance, and conservation and public power projects. In 1928, while Hoover was carrying New York against Smith by a wide margin, Roosevelt won election by 25,000 votes. In 1930 he swept the state by a 700,000-vote majority, double the previous record. He also had the advantage of the Roosevelt name (he was a distant cousin of the inimitable T.R.), and his sunny, magnetic personality contrasted favorably with that of the glum and colorless Hoover.

Roosevelt was far from being a radical. Although he had supported the League of Nations while campaigning for the vice-presidency in 1920, during the ensuing decade he had not seriously challenged the basic tenets of Coolidge prosperity. He never had much difficulty adjusting his views to prevailing attitudes. For a time he even served as head of the American Construction Council, a trade association. Indeed, his life before the depression gave little indication that he understood the aspirations of ordinary people or had any deep commitment to social reform.

Roosevelt was born to wealth and social status in Dutchess County, New York, in 1882. Pampered in childhood by a doting yet domineering mother, he was educated at the exclusive Groton School and then at Harvard, where he proceeded, as his biographer Frank Freidel has written, "from one extracurricular triumph to another." Ambition as much as the desire to render public service motivated his career in politics; even after an attack of polio in 1921 left him badly crippled in both legs, he refused to abandon his hopes for high office. During the 1920s he was a hardworking member of the liberal wing of his party. He supported Smith for president in 1924 and 1928.

To some observers Roosevelt seemed rather a lightweight intellectually. When he ran for the vice-presidency, the *Chicago Tribune* commented: "If he is Theodore Roosevelt, Elihu Root is Gene Debs, and Bryan is a brewer." Twelve years later many critics judged him too irresolute, too amiable, too eager to please all factions to be a forceful leader. Herbert Hoover thought he was "ignorant but well-meaning," and the political analyst Walter Lippmann, in a now-famous observation, called him "a pleasant man who, without any important qualifications for the job, would very much like to be President."

Despite his physical handicap—he could walk only a few steps, and then only with the aid of steel braces and two canes—Roosevelt was a marvelous campaigner. He traveled back and forth across the country, radiating confidence and good humor even when directing his sharpest barbs at the Republicans. Like every great political leader, he took as much from the people as he gave them, understanding the causes of their confusion, sensing their needs. "I have looked into the faces of thousands of Americans," he told a friend. "They have the frightened look of lost children. . . . They are saying: 'We're caught in something we don't understand; perhaps this fellow can help us out.' "

Voters responded in a similar manner. "The people," one member of the Hoover administration

A vigorous-looking Franklin D. Roosevelt campaigning for the presidency in 1932. His vice-presidential running mate, John N. Garner, and the conveniently placed post, allowed the handicapped candidate to stand when greeting voters along the way.

noted, "seem to be lifting eager faces to Franklin Roosevelt, having the impression that he is talking intimately to them." But this man then added: "I am glad of his enthusiasm and buoyance but it cannot escape the sense that he really does not understand the full meaning of his own recitations."

Roosevelt soaked up information and ideas from a thousand sources—from professors like Raymond Moley and Rexford Tugwell of Columbia, from politicians like the Texan vice-presidential candidate John N. Garner, from social workers, businessmen, and lawyers. To those seeking specific answers to the questions of the day, he was seldom satisfying. On such vital matters as farm policy, the tariff, and government spending, he equivocated, contradicted himself, or remained silent.

Aided by hindsight, historians have discovered portents of much of his later program in his campaign speeches. These pronouncements, buried among dozens of conflicting generalities, often passed unnoticed at the time. He said, for example:

> If starvation and dire need on the part of any of our citizens make necessary the appropriation of additional funds which would keep the budget out of balance, I shall not hesitate to . . . ask the people to authorize the expenditure of that additional amount.

In the same speech, however, he called for steep cuts in federal spending and a balanced budget, and he castigated Hoover for presiding over "the greatest spending administration in peace time in our history."

Nevertheless, Roosevelt's basic position was unmistakable. There must be a "re-appraisal of values," a "new deal." Instead of adhering to conventional limits on the extent of federal power, the government should do whatever was necessary to protect the unfortunate and advance the public good. Lacking concrete answers, Roosevelt advocated a point of view rather than a plan: "The country needs bold, persistent experimentation. It is common sense to take a method and try it. If it fails, admit it frankly and try another. But above all, try something."

The popularity of this approach was demonstrated in November. Hoover, who had lost only eight states in 1928, won only six, all in the Northeast, in 1932. Roosevelt amassed 22.8 million votes to Hoover's 15.8 million and carried the electoral college, 472 to 59.

During the interval between the election and Roosevelt's inauguration in March 1933, the Great Depression reached its nadir. The holdover "lame duck" Congress, last of its kind, proved incapable of effective action.* President Hoover, perhaps understandably, hesitated to institute changes without the cooperation of his successor. Roosevelt, for equally plausible reasons, refused to accept responsibility before assuming power officially. The nation, curiously apathetic in the face of so much suffering, drifted aimlessly, like a sailboat in a flat calm.

---

* The Twentieth Amendment (1933) provided for convening new Congresses in January instead of the following December. It also advanced the date of the president's inauguration from March 4 to January 20.

Milestones

1921 Budget and Accounting Act Washington Disarmament Conference	**1929** New York Stock Exchange crash ends "big bull market"
1922 Fordney-McCumber Tariff protecting "infant industries"	Young Plan further reduces German reparations
1923 President Harding dies; Coolidge becomes president	**1930** Clark Memorandum renounces the Roosevelt Corollary to the Monroe Doctrine
Teapot Dome and other "Harding scandals" exposed	Hawley-Smoot Tariff raises duties on foreign manufactures
1924 Dawes Plan restructures German reparations payments	**1931** Japanese invade Manchuria Hoover Moratorium on war debts
National Origins Act establishes immigration quotas	**1932** Bonus Marchers in Washington dispersed by troops
1927 McNary-Haugen farm relief bill vetoed by President Coolidge	Reconstruction Finance Corporation created
1928 Kellogg-Briand Treaty outlaws war as "an instrument of national policy"	Franklin D. Roosevelt elected president

SUPPLEMENTARY READING

Titles marked with an asterisk have been published in paperback.

The political history of the 1920s is surveyed in J. D. Hicks, **Republican Ascendancy*** (1960), and R. K. Murray, **The Politics of Normalcy*** (1973), and more fully in Murray, **The Harding Era** (1969). See also E. W. Hawley, **The Great War and the Search for a Modern Order*** (1979). The labor history of the postwar decade is discussed in Irving Bernstein, **The Lean Years*** (1960), and R. H. Zieger, **Republicans and Labor** (1969).

The best brief biography of Harding is Andrew Sinclair, **The Available Man*** (1965); and D. R. McCoy, **Calvin Coolidge: The Quiet President** (1967), is the best life of Coolidge. David Burner, **The Politics of Provincialism: The Democratic Party in Transition*** (1968), discusses the evolution of the Democratic party in the 1920s. R. F. Himmelberg, **The Origins of the National Recovery Act*** (1976), is good on the trade associations.

Diplomatic developments are summarized in Selig Adler, **The Uncertain Giant*** (1965). See also Akira Iriye, **After Imperialism** (1965) and **Across the Pacific** (1967), and T. H. Buckley, **The United States and the Washington Conference** (1970). Charles De Benedetti, **Origins of the Modern American Peace Movement** (1978) deals effectively with antiwar sentiment, and J. H. Wilson, **American Business and Foreign Policy*** (1971), is an important study of American interest in foreign markets in the 1920s.

On isolationism, see R. A. Divine, **The Reluctant Belligerent** (1965) and **The Illusion of Neutrality** (1962), and Manfred Jonas, **Isolationism in America** (1966). On Latin American relations, see I. F. Gellman, **Good Neighbor Diplomacy** (1979).

Farm discontent is covered in Theodore Saloutos and J. D. Hicks, **Twentieth-Century Populism: Agricultural Discontent in the Middle West*** (1951), and G. C. Fite, **George N. Peek and the Fight for Farm Parity** (1954). On the election of 1928, see Oscar Handlin, **Al Smith and His America** (1958), and E. A. Moore, **A Catholic Runs for President** (1956).

For details on the stock market crash, see Robert Sobel, **The Great Bull Market*** (1968), and J. K. Galbraith, **The Great Crash*** (1961). Hoover's role is analyzed in A. U. Romasco, **The Poverty of Abundance*** (1965), M. L. Fausold, **The Presidency of Herbert Hoover** (1985), Joan Hoff Wilson, **Herbert Hoover: Forgotten Progressive*** (1975), and A. M. Schlesinger, Jr., **The Crisis of the Old Order** (1957). L. V. Chandler, **America's Greatest Depression*** (1970), is a good introduction to the economic problems, but see also C. H. Trout, **Boston, the Great Depression, and the New Deal** (1977), M. A. Bernstein, **The Great Depression** (1987), and J. A. Garraty, **The Great Depression*** (1986), which puts American developments in world perspective.

XXVIII

The New Deal, 1933–1941

I have been having an interesting time here. . . . Washington seems much more intelligent and cheerful than under any recent Administration, but . . . nothing really makes much sense, because Roosevelt has no real policy.

EDMUND WILSON, *critic, 1934*

The royalists of the economic order have conceded that political freedom was the business of government, but they have maintained that economic slavery was nobody's business.

FRANKLIN D. ROOSEVELT, *1936*

A s the date of Franklin Roosevelt's inauguration approached, the banking system disintegrated—no word less strong portrays the extent of the collapse. Starting in the rural West and spreading to major cities like Detroit and Baltimore, a financial panic swept the land. Depositors lined up before the doors of even the soundest institutions, desperate to withdraw their savings. Hundreds of banks were forced to close. In February, to check the panic, the governor of Michigan declared a "bank holiday," shutting every bank in the state for eight days. Maryland, Kentucky, California, and a number of other states followed suit; by inauguration day, four-fifths of the states had suspended all banking operations.

The Hundred Days

Something drastic had to be done. The most conservative business leaders were as ready for government intervention as the most advanced radicals. Partisanship, though not disappearing, was for once subordinated to broad national needs. A sign of this change came in February, even before Roosevelt took office, when Congress submitted the Twenty-first Amendment, putting an end to prohibition, to the states. Before the year was out the necessary three-quarters of the states had ratified it. The prohibition era was over.

But it was unquestionably Franklin D. Roosevelt who provided the spark that reenergized the American people. His inaugural address, delivered in a raw mist beneath dark March skies, reassured the country and at the same time stirred it to action. "The only thing we have to fear is fear itself." "Our true destiny is not to be ministered unto but to minister to ourselves and to our fellow men." "This Nation asks for action, and action now." "I assume unhesitatingly the leadership of this great army of our people." Many such lines punctuated the brief address, which concluded with a stern pledge:

> In the event that Congress shall fail . . . I shall not evade the clear course of duty that will then confront me. I shall ask the Congress for the one remaining instrument to meet the crisis—broad Executive power to wage a war against the emergency.

The inaugural captured the heart of the country; almost half a million letters of congratulation poured into the White House. When Roosevelt summoned Congress into special session on March 9, the legislators outdid one another to enact his proposals into law. "I had as soon start a mutiny in the face of a foreign foe as . . . against the program of the President," one representative declared. In the following "Hundred Days" (Congress adjourned on June 16), an impressive body of legislation was placed on the statute books. Opposition, in the sense of an organized group committed to resisting the administration, simply did not exist.

Roosevelt had the power and the will to act but no comprehensive plan of action. He and his eager congressional collaborators proceeded in a dozen directions at once, sometimes wisely, sometimes not, often at cross-purposes with themselves and one another. One of the first administration measures was the Economy Act, which reduced the salaries of federal employees by 15 percent and cut various veterans' benefits. Such belt-tightening measures could only make the depression worse.

Although Roosevelt never entirely got over the urge to economize in hard times, most of the New Deal programs were designed to stimulate the economy. Untangling the national financial mess was the most immediate task. On March 5 Roosevelt declared a nationwide bank holiday and placed an embargo on the exportation of gold. Within hours after it convened, Congress passed an emergency banking bill confirming these measures, outlawing the hoarding of gold, and giving the president broad power over the operations of the Federal Reserve system.

To explain the complexities of the banking problem to the public, Roosevelt delivered the first of his "fireside chats" over a national radio network. "I want to talk for a few minutes with the people of the United States about banking," he explained. His warmth and steadiness reassured millions of listeners. A plan for reopening the banks under Treasury Department licenses was devised, and soon most of them were functioning again, public confidence in their solvency restored. This solved the immediate problem, but inadvertently (or so it seemed) it also determined that banks should remain private institutions; many experts were urging that the banks be nationalized, a step that would probably have been easily accomplished at that critical moment. Reform, not revolutionary change, had been decided on at the very start of Roosevelt's presidency.

In April, Roosevelt took the country off the gold standard, hoping thereby to cause prices to rise. Before the session ended, Congress established the Federal Deposit Insurance Corporation (FDIC) to guarantee bank deposits. It also forced the separation of investment banking and commercial banking concerns while extending the power of the Federal Reserve Board over both types of institutions, and it created the Home Owners Loan Corporation (HOLC) to refinance mortgages and prevent foreclosures. It passed a Federal Securities Act requiring promoters to make public full financial information

Well-wishers greet the president at Warm Springs, Georgia, in 1933. The Roosevelt "magic," unfeigned and inexhaustible, amazed his associates. "I have never had contact with a man who was loved as he is," reported Secretary of the Interior Harold L. Ickes.

about new stock issues and giving the Federal Trade Commission the right to regulate such transactions.*

After Congress adjourned, the government began buying gold on the open market. When this policy failed to push up the price of gold, Congress in January 1934 passed the Gold Reserve Act, which gave the president the power to fix the price of gold by proclamation. Roosevelt promptly set the price at $35 an ounce, an increase of about 40 percent.

The National Recovery Administration

Problems of unemployment and industrial stagnation had high priority during the Hundred Days. Congress appropriated $500 million for relief of the needy, and it created the Civilian Conservation Corps to provide jobs for men between the ages of 18 and 25 in reforestation and other conservation projects. To stimulate industry, Congress passed one of its most controversial measures, the National Industrial Recovery Act (NIRA). Besides establishing the Public Works Administration with authority to spend $3.3 billion, this law permitted manufacturers to draw up industrywide codes of "fair business practices." Under the law producers could agree to raise prices and limit production without violating the antitrust laws. The law gave workers the protection of minimum wage and maximum hours regulations and guaranteed them the right "to organize and bargain collectively through representatives of their own choosing," an immense stimulus to the union movement.

The NIRA was a variant on the idea of the corporate state. This concept envisaged a system of industrywide organizations of capitalists and workers (supervised by the government) that would resolve conflicts internally, thereby avoiding wasteful economic competition and dangerous social clashes. It was an outgrowth of the trade association idea, although Hoover, who had supported voluntary associations, denounced it because of its compulsory aspects. It was also similar to experiments being carried out by the fascist dictator Benito Mussolini

in Italy and by the Nazis in Adolf Hitler's Germany. It did not, of course, turn America into a fascist state, but it did herald an increasing concentration of economic power in the hands of interest groups, both industrialists' organizations and labor unions.

The act created a government agency, the National Recovery Administration (NRA), to supervise the drafting and operation of the business codes. Drafting posed difficult problems, first because each industry insisted on tailoring the agreements to its special needs and second because most manufacturers were unwilling to accept all the provisions of Section 7a of the law dealing with the rights of labor. While thousands of employers agreed to the pledge "We Do Our Part" in order to receive the Blue Eagle symbol of NRA, many were more interested in the monopolistic aspects of the act than in boosting wages and encouraging unionization. In practice, the codes were drawn up by the largest manufacturers in each industry.

The effects of NIRA were both more and less than the designers of the system had intended. In a sense it tried to accomplish the impossible—to change the nature of business ethics and control the everyday activities of millions of individual enterprises. At the practical level, it did not end the depression. There was a brief upturn in the spring of 1933, but the expected revival of industry did not take place; in nearly every case the dominant producers in each industry used their power to raise prices and limit production rather than to hire more workers and increase output.

Beginning with the cotton textile code, however, the agreements succeeded in doing away with the centuries-old problem of child labor in industry. They established the principle of federal regulation of wages and hours and led to the organization of thousands of workers, even in industries where unions had seldom been significant. Within a year John L. Lewis's United Mine Workers expanded from 150,000 members to half a million. About 100,000 automobile workers joined unions, as did a comparable number of steelworkers.

Labor leaders used the NIRA to persuade workers that the popular president wanted them to join unions—something of an overstatement. In 1935, because the conservative and craft-oriented AFL had displayed little enthusiasm for enrolling unskilled workers on an industrywide basis, John L. Lewis, together with officials of the garment trade

---

* In 1934 this task was transferred to the new Securities and Exchange Commission, which was given broad authority over the activities of stock exchanges.

unions, formed the Committee for Industrial Organization (CIO) and set out to rally workers in each of these mass-production industries into one union without regard for craft lines, a far more effective method of organization. The AFL expelled these unions, however, and in 1938 the CIO became the Congress of Industrial Organizations. Soon it rivaled the AFL in size and importance.

The Agricultural Adjustment Administration

Roosevelt was more concerned about the plight of the farmers than that of any other group because he believed that the nation was becoming overcommitted to industry. The Agricultural Adjustment Act of May 1933, combined compulsory restrictions on production with government subsidies to growers of wheat, cotton, tobacco, pork, and a few other staple crops. The money for these payments was raised by levying processing taxes on middlemen such as flour millers. The object was to lift agricultural prices to "parity" with industrial prices, the ratio in most cases being based on the levels of 1909–1914, when farmers had been reasonably prosperous. In return for withdrawing part of their land from cultivation, farmers received "rental" payments from the Agricultural Adjustment Administration (AAA).

Since the 1933 crops were growing when the law was passed, Secretary of Agriculture Henry A. Wallace, son of Harding's secretary of agriculture and himself an experienced farmer and plant geneticist, decided to pay farmers to destroy the crops in the field. Cotton planters plowed up 10 million acres, receiving $100 million in return. Six million baby pigs and 200,000 pregnant sows were slaughtered. Such ruthlessness appalled observers, particularly when they thought of the millions of hungry Americans who could have eaten all that pork.

Thereafter, limitation of acreage proved sufficient to raise some agricultural prices considerably. Tobacco farmers benefited, and so did those who raised corn and hogs. The price of wheat also rose, though more because of bad harvests than the AAA program. But dairy farmers and cattlemen were hurt by the law, as were the railroads (which had less freight to haul) and, of course, consumers. Many

farmers insisted that NRA was raising the cost of manufactured goods more than AAA was raising the prices they received for their crops. "While the farmer is losing his pants to his creditors," one Iowan complained, "NRA is rolling up his shirt. [Soon] we'll have a nudist colony."

A far more serious weakness of the program was its failure to assist tenant farmers and sharecroppers, many of whom lost their livelihoods completely when owners took land out of production to obtain AAA payments. Yet acreage restrictions and mortgage relief helped thousands. The law was a remarkable attempt to bring order to the chaotic agricultural economy. One New Deal official called it "the greatest single experiment in economic planning under capitalist conditions ever attempted by a democracy in times of peace." This was an overstatement. The AAA was a drastic change of American policy, but foreign producers of coffee, sugar, tea, rubber, and other staples had adopted the same techniques of restricting output and subsidizing growers well before the United States did.

The Tennessee Valley Authority

Another striking achievement of the Hundred Days was the creation of the Tennessee Valley Authority (TVA). During World War I the government had constructed a hydroelectric plant at Muscle Shoals, Alabama, to provide power for factories manufacturing synthetic nitrate explosives. After 1920, farm groups and public power enthusiasts, led by Senator George W. Norris of Nebraska, had blocked administration plans to turn these facilities over to private capitalists, but their efforts to have the site operated by the government had been defeated by presidential vetoes.

Roosevelt wanted to have the entire Tennessee Valley area incorporated into a broad experiment in social planning. Besides expanding the hydroelectric plants at Muscle Shoals and developing nitrate manufacturing in order to produce cheap fertilizers, he envisioned a coordinated program of soil conservation, reforestation, and industrialization.

Over the objections of private power companies, led by Wendell L. Willkie of the Commonwealth and Southern Corporation, Congress passed the TVA Act in May 1933. This law created a board authorized to build dams, power plants, and trans-

THE NEW DEAL SPIRIT

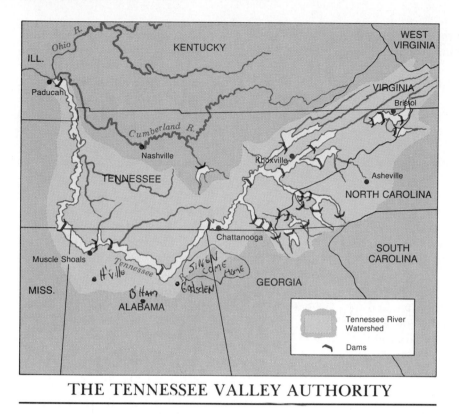

THE TENNESSEE VALLEY AUTHORITY

mission lines and to sell fertilizers and electricity to individuals and local communities. The board could undertake flood control, soil conservation, and reforestation projects and improve the navigation of the river. TVA never became the comprehensive regional planning organization some of its sponsors had anticipated, but it improved the standard of living of millions of inhabitants of the valley. In addition to producing electricity and fertilizers and providing a "yardstick" whereby the efficiency—and thus the rates—of private power companies could be tested, it took on other functions, ranging from the eradication of malaria to the development of recreational facilities.

The New Deal Spirit

By the end of the Hundred Days the country had made up its mind about Roosevelt's New Deal, and despite the vicissitudes of the next decade, it never really changed it. A large majority labeled the New Deal a solid success. Considerable recovery had taken place, but more basic was the fact that Roo-

sevelt, recruiting an army of forceful officials to staff the new government agencies, had infused his administration with a spirit of bustle and optimism. Dozens of people who lived through those stirring times have left records that reveal the New Deal spirit. The director of the presidential Secret Service unit, returning to the White House on inauguration day after escorting Herbert Hoover to the railroad station, found the executive mansion "transformed during my absence into a gay place, full of people who oozed confidence."

"Come at once to Washington," Senator Robert La Follette, Jr., son of "Fighting Bob," telegraphed Donald Richberg, an old Theodore Roosevelt progressive. "Great things are under way." "I have been in a constant spin of activity," another New Dealer wrote a friend. "I feel as if I were alive all over, and that this cockeyed world is taking us somewhere." Justice Harlan Fiske Stone of the Supreme Court recorded: "Never was there such a change in the transfer of government."

Although Roosevelt was not much of an intellectual, his openness to suggestion made him eager to draw on the ideas and energies of experts of all sorts. New Deal agencies soon teemed with college professors and young lawyers without political experience.

The New Deal lacked any consistent ideological base. Though the so-called Brains Trust (a group headed by Raymond Moley, a Columbia political scientist, that included Columbia economists Rexford G. Tugwell and Adolf A. Berle, Jr., and a number of others) attracted a great deal of attention, theorists never impressed Roosevelt. His New Deal drew on the old populist tradition, as seen in its antipathy to bankers and its willingness to adopt schemes for inflating the currency; on the New Nationalism of Theodore Roosevelt in its dislike of competition and its de-emphasis of the antitrust laws; and on the ideas of social workers trained in the Progressive Era. Techniques developed by the Wilsonians also found places in the system: Louis D. Brandeis had considerable influence on Roosevelt's financial reforms, and New Deal labor policy grew directly out of the experience of the War Labor Board of 1917–1918.

Within the administrative maze that Roosevelt created, rival bureaucrats battled to enforce their views. The "spenders," led by Tugwell, clashed with advocates of strict economy, who gathered around Lewis Douglas, director of the budget. Blithely disregarding logically irreconcilable differences, Roosevelt mediated between the factions. Washington became a battleground for dozens of special interest groups: the Farm Bureau Federation, the unions, the trade associations, the silver miners. William E. Leuchtenburg has described New Deal policy as "interest-group democracy"; another historian, Ellis W. Hawley, called it "counterorganization" policy aimed at creating "monopoly power" among groups previously unorganized, such as farmers and industrial workers. While, as Leuchtenburg says, the system was superior to that of Roosevelt's predecessors—who had allowed one interest, big business, to predominate—it slighted the unorganized majority. NRA aimed frankly at raising the prices paid by consumers of manufactured goods; the AAA processing tax came ultimately from the pocketbooks of ordinary citizens.

The Unemployed

At least 9 million persons were still without work in 1934 and hundreds of thousands of them were in real need. Here is the recollection of Malcolm Little, later famous as the radical black leader Malcolm X.

UNEMPLOYMENT AND FEDERAL ACTION, 1929–1941

Unemployment of non-farm workers reached nearly 40 percent by early 1933. The Federal Employment Relief Act (FERA) of May 1933 was followed by the Civil Works Administration (CWA) later that year, and in turn by the Works Progress Administration (WPA) in April of 1935.

By 1934, we really began to suffer. This was about the worst depression year, and no one we knew had enough to eat or live on. . . . There was a bakery where, for a nickel, a couple of us children would buy a tall flour sack of day-old bread and cookies. . . . But there were times when there wasn't even a nickel and we would be so hungry we were dizzy. My mother would boil a big pot of dandelion greens and we would eat that.

Yet the Democrats confounded the political experts, including their own, by increasing their already large majorities in both houses of Congress in the 1934 elections. All the evidence indicates that most of the jobless continued to support the administration. Their loyalty can best be explained by Roosevelt's unemployment policies.

In May 1933 Congress had established the Federal Emergency Relief Administration and given it $500 million to be dispensed through state relief organizations. Roosevelt appointed Harry L. Hopkins, an eccentric but brilliant and dedicated social worker, to direct the FERA. Hopkins insisted that the unemployed needed jobs, not handouts. In November he persuaded Roosevelt to create the Civil Works Administration, and within a month he put more than 4 million persons to work building and repairing roads and public buildings, teaching, dec-

orating the walls of post offices with murals, and applying their special skills in dozens of other ways.

The cost of this program frightened Roosevelt—Hopkins spent about $1 billion in less than five months—and he soon abolished the CWA. But an extensive public works program was continued throughout 1934 under FERA. Despite charges that many of the projects were "boondoggles," thousands of roads, bridges, schools, and other structures were built or refurbished.

After the 1934 elections, Roosevelt committed himself to the Hopkins approach. In May 1935 he put Hopkins in charge of the Works Progress Administration (WPA). By the time this agency was disbanded in 1943 it had spent $11 billion and found employment for 8.5 million persons. Besides building public works, the WPA developed the Federal Theater Project, which put thousands of actors, directors, and stagehands to work; the Federal Writers' Project, which turned out valuable guidebooks, collected local lore, and published about 1,000 books and pamphlets; and the Federal Art Project, which employed needy painters and sculptors. In addition, the National Youth Administration created part-time jobs for more than 2 million high school and college students.

WPA did not reach all the unemployed. At no

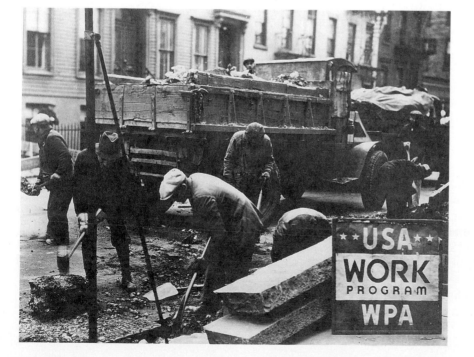

Otherwise unemployed workers removing curbstones in a street-widening project. WPA undertakings extended from carving nature trails in wilderness regions of the Far West to constructing bridges in the heart of New York City.

time during the New Deal years did unemployment fall below 10 percent of the work force, and in some places it was much higher. Unemployment in Boston, for instance, ranged between 20 and 30 percent throughout the 1930s. Like so many New Deal programs, WPA did not go far enough, chiefly because Roosevelt could not escape his fear of unbalancing the budget drastically. Halfway measures did not provide the massive stimulus the economy needed. The president also hesitated to undertake projects that might compete with private enterprises for fear of offending business. Yet his caution did him no good politically; the business interests he sought to placate were becoming increasingly hostile to the New Deal.

Literature in the Depression

Some American novelists found Soviet communism attractive and wrote "proletarian" novels in which ordinary workers were the heroes, and stylistic niceties gave way to the rough language of the street and the factory. Most of these books were of little artistic merit, and none achieved great commercial success. The best of the depression writers avoided the party line, though they were critical of many aspects of American life. One was John Dos Passos, author of the trilogy *U.S.A.* (1930–1936).

Dos Passos came from a well-to-do family of Portuguese descent. He was educated at Harvard and drove an ambulance in France during the Great War. *U.S.A.* was a massive intricately constructed work with an anticapitalist and deeply pessimistic point of view. It portrayed American society between 1900 and 1930 in broad perspective, interweaving the stories of five major characters and a galaxy of lesser figures. Throughout the narrative Dos Passos scattered capsule sketches of famous people, ranging from Andrew Carnegie and William Jennings Bryan to the movie idol Rudolph Valentino and the architect Frank Lloyd Wright. He included "newsreel" sections recounting events of the period and "camera eye" sections in which he revealed his personal reactions to the passing parade.

Dos Passos's method was relentless, cold, methodical—utterly realistic. He had no sympathy for his characters or their world. *U.S.A.* was a monument to the despair and anger of liberals confront-

ing the Great Depression. After the depression, however, Dos Passos rapidly abandoned his radical views.

The novel that best portrayed the desperate plight of the millions impoverished by the depression was *The Grapes of Wrath* (1939) by John Steinbeck, which described the fate of the Joads, an Oklahoma farm family driven by drought and bad times to abandon their land and become migratory laborers in California. Steinbeck captured the patient bewilderment of the downtrodden, the brutality bred of fear that characterized their exploiters, and the furious resentments of the radicals of the 1930s. He depicted the parching blackness of the Oklahoma dust bowl, the grandeur of California, the backbreaking toil of the migrant fruit pickers, and the ultimate indignation of a people repeatedly degraded. "In the eyes of the hungry there is a growing wrath. In the souls of the people the grapes of wrath are filling and growing heavy, growing heavy for the vintage."

Like so many other writers of the decade, Steinbeck was an angry man. "There is a crime here that goes beyond denunciation," he wrote. He had the compassion that Dos Passos lacked, and this quality raised *The Grapes of Wrath* to the level of great tragedy. In other works, such as *Tortilla Flat* (1935) and *The Long Valley* (1938), Steinbeck described the life of California cannery workers and ranchers with moving warmth without becoming overly sentimental.

Although his work was less political than that of Dos Passos or Steinbeck, Thomas Wolfe, a passionate, intensely troubled young man of vast but undisciplined talents, sought to describe the kaleidoscopic character of American life, the limitless variety of the nation. "I will know this country when I am through as I know the palm of my hand, and I will put it on paper and make it true and beautiful," he boasted.

During the last ten years of his short life Wolfe wrote four novels: *Look Homeward, Angel* (1929), *Of Time and the River* (1935), and two published posthumously, *The Web and the Rock* (1939) and *You Can't Go Home Again* (1940). All were autobiographical and to some extent repetitious, for he was an unabashed egoist. Nevertheless, he was a superb interpreter of contemporary society. He crammed his pages with unforgettable vignettes—a train hurtling across the New Jersey meadows in the dark, a young woman clutching her skirt on a windswept corner, a group of derelicts huddled for shelter in a public toilet on a frigid night. And no writer caught more clearly the frantic pace and confusion of the great cities, the despair of the depression, the divided nature of human beings, their fears and hopes, their undirected, uncontrollable energy.

William Faulkner, probably the finest modern American novelist, responded to the era in still another way. Born in 1897, within a year of Fitzgerald and Hemingway, like Wolfe he attained literary maturity only in the 1930s. After service in the Canadian air force in World War I, he returned to his native Mississippi, working at a series of odd jobs and publishing relatively inconsequential poetry and fiction. Suddenly, between 1929 and 1932, he burst into prominence with four major novels: *The Sound and the Fury, As I Lay Dying, Sanctuary,* and *Light in August.*

Faulkner created a local world, Yoknapatawpha County, and peopled it with some of the most remarkable characters in American fiction—among

Accepting the Nobel Prize in literature, Faulkner spoke of a lifelong attempt "to create out of the materials of the human spirit something which did not exist before."

"I am completely partisan," Steinbeck wrote. "Every effort I can bring to bear is . . . at the call of the common working people."

them the Sartoris family, typical of the old southern aristocracy worn down at the heels, and the Snopes clan, shrewd, unscrupulous, boorish representatives of the new day. He pictured the South's poverty and its pride, its dreadful racial problem, the guilt and obscure passions plaguing white and black alike. No contemporary excelled him as a commentator on the multiple dilemmas of modern life. His characters are possessed, driven to pursue high ideals yet weighted down with their awareness of their inadequacies and their sinfulness. They are imprisoned in their surroundings, no matter how they may strive to escape them. The French novelist Simone de Beauvoir caught this aspect of Faulkner's work when she wrote that he "offered us a glimpse of fascinating depths . . . in those secret, shameless fires that rage in the bellies of men and women alike."

Faulkner, like Dos Passos, was essentially a pessimist. His characters continually experienced emotions too intense to be bearable, often too profound and too subtle for the natures he had given them. Nevertheless, his stature was beyond question, and unlike so many other novelists of the period, he maintained a high level in his later years. He was awarded the 1949 Nobel Prize for literature.

The Extremists

Roosevelt's moderation provoked extremists both on the left and on the right. The most formidable was Louisiana's Senator Huey Long, the "Kingfish." Raised on a farm in northern Louisiana, Long was successively a traveling salesman, a lawyer, state railroad commissioner, governor, and, after 1930, United States senator. By 1933 he ruled Louisiana with the absolutism of an oriental monarch. Long was controversial in his day, and so he has remained. He was certainly a demagogue. Yet the plight of all poor people concerned him deeply. More important, he tried to do something about it.

Long did not question segregation or white supremacy, nor did he suggest that Louisiana blacks should be allowed to vote. He used the word *nigger* with total unself-consciousness, even when addressing northern black leaders. But he treated black-baiters with scathing contempt. When Hiram W. Evans, imperial wizard of the Ku Klux Klan, announced his intention to campaign against him in Louisiana, Long told reporters: "Quote me as saying that that Imperial bastard will never set foot in Louisiana, and that when I call him a sonofabitch I am not using profanity, but am referring to the circumstances of his birth."

As a reformer, Long stood in the populist tradition; he hated bankers and "the interests." He believed that poor people, regardless of color, should have a chance to earn a decent living and get an education. His arguments were simplistic, patronizing, possibly insincere, but effective. "Don't say I'm working for niggers," he told one northern journalist. "I'm for the poor man—all poor men. Black and white, they all gotta have a chance. . . . 'Every Man a King'—that's my slogan."

Raffish, totally unrestrained, yet shrewd—a fellow southern politician called him "the smartest lunatic I ever saw"—Long had supported the New Deal at the start. But partly because he thought Roosevelt too conservative and partly because of his

Senator Huey Long in a typical energetic speaking pose. Both his politics and his flamboyant, grass-roots style were in the Populist tradition.

own ambition, he soon broke with the administration. While Roosevelt was probably more hostile to the big financiers than to any other interest, Long denounced him as "a phoney" and a stooge of Wall Street. "I can take him," he boasted in a typical sally. "His mother's watching him, and she won't let him go too far, but I ain't got no mother left, and if I had, she'd think anything I said was all right."

By 1935 Long's "Share Our Wealth" movement had a membership of over 4.6 million. His program called for the confiscation of family fortunes of more than $5 million and a tax of 100 percent on incomes of over $1 million a year. The money would be used to buy every family a "homestead" (a house, a car, and other necessities) and provide an annual family income of $2,000 to $3,000, plus old-age pensions, educational benefits, and veterans' pensions. As the 1936 election approached, he planned to organize a third party to split the liberal vote. He assumed that the Republicans would win the election and so botch the job of fighting the depression that he could sweep the country in 1940.

Less powerful than Long but more widely influential was Father Charles E. Coughlin, the "Radio Priest," a genial Irishman of Canadian birth. Coughlin in 1926 began broadcasting a weekly religious message over station WJR in Detroit. His mellifluous voice and orotund rhetoric won him a huge national audience, and the depression gave him a secular cause. In 1933 he had been an eager New Dealer, but his dislike of New Deal financial policies—he believed that inflating the currency would end the depression—and his need for ever more sensational ideas to hold his radio audience led him to turn against the New Deal. By 1935 he was calling Roosevelt a "great betrayer and liar."

Although Coughlin's National Union for Social Justice was especially appealing to Catholics, it attracted people of every faith, particularly in the lower-middle-class districts of the big cities. Some of his talks caused more than a million people to send him messages of congratulation; contributions amounting to $500,000 a year flooded his headquarters. Coughlin attacked bankers, New Deal

Father Charles Coughlin, the "Radio Priest," whose weekly program reached 30–45 million listeners nationwide, photographed in Detroit as he promoted his National Union for Social Justice.

planners, Roosevelt's farm program, and the alleged sympathy of the administration for communists and Jews, both of which Coughlin denounced in his weekly talks. His program resembled fascism more than any leftist philosophy, but he posed a threat, especially in combination with Long, to the continuation of Democratic rule.

Another rapidly growing movement alarmed the Democrats in 1934 and 1935: Dr. Francis E. Townsend's campaign for "old-age revolving pensions." Townsend, a retired California physician, colorless and low-key, had an oversimplified and therefore appealing "solution" to the nation's troubles. The pitiful state of thousands of elderly persons, whose job prospects were even dimmer than those of the mass of the unemployed, he found shocking. He advocated paying every person 60 years of age and over a pension of $200 a month, the only conditions being that the pensioners not hold jobs and that they spend the entire sum within 30 days. Their purchases, he argued, would stimulate production, thereby creating new jobs and revitalizing the economy. A stiff transactions tax, collected whenever any commodity changed hands, would pay for the program.

Economists quickly pointed out that with about 10 million persons eligible for the Townsend pensions, the cost would amount to $24 billion a year—roughly half the national income. But among the elderly the scheme proved extremely popular. Townsend Clubs, their proceedings conducted in the spirit of revivalist camp meetings, flourished everywhere, and the *Townsend National Weekly* reached a circulation of over 200,000. Although most Townsendites were anything but radical politically, their plan, like Long's Share Our Wealth scheme, would have revolutionized the distribution of wealth in the country. The movement marked the emergence of a new force in American society. With medical advances lengthening the average life span, the percentage of old people in the population was rising. The breakdown of close family ties in an increasingly mobile society now caused many of these citizens to be cast adrift to live out their last years poor, sick, idle, and alone.

With the possible exception of Long, the extremists had little understanding of practical affairs. (It could be said that Townsend knew what to do with money but not how to get it and Coughlin knew how to get money but not what to do with it.) Collectively they represented a threat to Roosevelt; their success helped to make the president see that he must move boldly to restore good times or face serious political trouble in 1936.

Political imperatives had much to do with his decision, and the influence of Justice Brandeis and his disciples, notably Felix Frankfurter, was great. They urged Roosevelt to abandon his pro-business programs, especially NRA, and stress restoring competition and taxing corporations more heavily. The fact that most businessmen were turning away from him encouraged the president to accept this advice; so did the Supreme Court's decision in *Schechter* v. *United States* in May 1935, which declared the National Industrial Recovery Act unconstitutional. (The case involved the provisions of the NRA Live Poultry Code; the Court voided the act on the grounds that Congress had delegated too much legislative power to the code authorities and that the defendants, four brothers engaged in slaughtering chickens in New York City, were not engaged in interstate commerce.)

The Second New Deal

Existing laws had failed to end the depression. Extremists were luring away some of Roosevelt's supporters, and conservatives had failed to appreciate his moderation. The voters, heartened by the partial success of early New Deal measures, had responded

by further increasing the Democrats' control of Congress in the 1934 elections and were clamoring for further reforms. But the Supreme Court had declared many key New Deal measures unconstitutional. For these many reasons, Roosevelt in June launched what historians call the Second New Deal.

There followed the "Second Hundred Days," one of the most productive periods in the history of American legislation. The National Labor Relations Act—commonly known as the Wagner Act—restored the labor guarantees wiped out by the Schechter decision. It gave workers the right to bargain collectively and prohibited employers from interfering with union organizational activities in their factories. The National Labor Relations Board (NLRB) was established to supervise plant elections and designate successful unions as official bargaining agents when a majority of the workers approved. It was difficult to force some big corporations to bargain "in good faith," as the law required, but the NLRB could conduct investigations of employer practices and issue cease and desist orders when "unfair" activities came to light.

The Social Security Act of August 1935 set up a system of old-age insurance, financed partly by a tax on wages (paid by workers) and partly by a tax on payrolls (paid by employers). It created a state-federal system of unemployment insurance, similarly financed. Liberal critics considered this social security system inadequate because it did not cover agricultural workers, domestics, self-employed per-

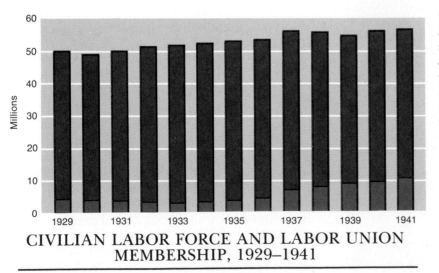

CIVILIAN LABOR FORCE AND LABOR UNION
MEMBERSHIP, 1929–1941

The green portion of the vertical bars represents the number of civilian labor force workers in unions, as against the total work force. Union membership more than doubled in the years from 1937 to 1941, from less than 5 million to more than 10 million.

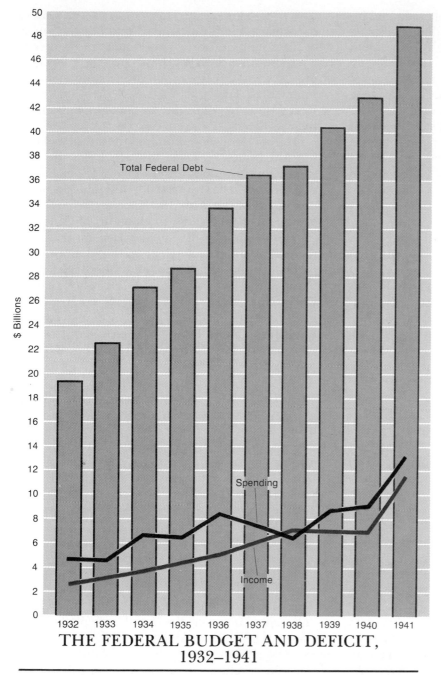

THE FEDERAL BUDGET AND DEFICIT,
1932–1941

The gap between the blue (income) line and the red (spending) line shows the deficit each year for the ten years between 1932 and 1941, and the bars show how the total debt increased to almost $43 billion by 1941. According to Keynes, such deficits help to stimulate a lagging economy.

sons, and some other groups particularly in need of its benefits. Health insurance was not included, and because the size of pensions depended on the amount earned, the lowest-paid workers could not count on much support after reaching the age of 65. Yet the law was of major significance. Over the years the pension payments were increased and the classes of workers covered expanded.

Among other important laws enacted at this time were a new banking act and a public utility act. The former strengthened the control of the Federal Reserve Board (renamed the Board of Governors) over member banks and over commercial credit and interest rates. The Public Utility Holding Company Act outlawed the pyramiding of control of gas and electricity companies through the use of holding companies and gave federal commissions the power to regulate the rates and financial practices of these companies. The hotly debated "death sentence" clause of this law provided for the dismemberment of all utility complexes more than twice removed from the actual operating companies and authorized the Securities and Exchange Commission to break up smaller ones that could not demonstrate that their existence served some socially useful purpose.

The Rural Electrification Administration (REA), created by executive order, also began to function during this remarkable period. REA lent money at low interest rates to utility companies and to farmer cooperatives interested in bringing electricity to rural areas. When REA went into operation, only one farm in ten had electricity; by 1950 only one in ten did not.

Another important measure was the Wealth Tax Act of August 1935, which, while not the "soak the rich" measure both its supporters and its opponents claimed, raised taxes on large incomes considerably. Estate and gift taxes were also increased. Stiffer taxes on corporate profits reflected the Brandeis group's desire to penalize corporate giantism. Much of the opposition to other New Deal legislation arose from the fact that after these changes in the tax laws were made, the well-to-do had to bear a larger share of the cost of *all* government activities.

Whether the Second New Deal was more radical than the First depends largely on the vantage point from which it is considered. Measures like the Social Security Act had greater long-range effect on American life than the legislation of the first Hundred Days but were fundamentally less revolutionary than laws like the National Industrial Recovery Act and the Agricultural Adjustment Act, which attempted to establish a planned economy. As Arthur M. Schlesinger, Jr., has observed:

> Where the First New Deal contemplated government, business, and labor marching hand in hand toward a brave new society, the Second New Deal proposed to revitalize the tired old society. . . . The First New Deal characteristically told business what it must do. The Second New Deal characteristically told business what it must *not* do.

This distinction escaped most of Roosevelt's critics, particularly the businessmen, who felt the impact of his assault on existing conditions most directly. Even if in theory NIRA threatened the free enterprise system, it was less objectionable to manufacturers than laws that increased their taxes and forced them to contribute to old-age pensions for their workers.

Herbert Hoover epitomized the attitude of conservatives when he called the New Deal "the most stupendous invasion of the whole spirit of Liberty that the nation has witnessed." Undoubtedly, many opponents of the New Deal sincerely believed that it was undermining the foundations of American freedom. The cost of the New Deal also alarmed them. By 1936 some members of the administration had fallen under the influence of the British economist John Maynard Keynes, who argued that the world depression could be conquered if governments would deliberately unbalance their budgets by reducing interest rates and taxes and increasing expenditures in order to stimulate consumption and investment.

Roosevelt never accepted Keynes's theories; he conferred with the economist in 1934 but could not grasp the "rigmarole of figures" with which Keynes deluged him. Nevertheless, the imperatives of the depression forced him to spend more than the government was collecting in taxes; thus he adopted in part the Keynesian approach. Conservative businessmen considered him financially irresponsible, and the fact that deficit spending seemed to be good politics made them seethe with rage.

The Election of 1936

The election of 1936 loomed as a showdown. "America is in peril," the Republican platform declared. The GOP candidate, Governor Alfred M. Landon of Kansas, was a former follower of Theodore Roosevelt, a foe of the Ku Klux Klan in the 1920s, and a believer in government regulation of business. But he was a poor speaker, colorless, and handicapped by the reactionary views of many of his backers. Against Roosevelt's charm and political astuteness, Landon's arguments—chiefly that he could administer the government more efficiently than the president—made little impression. He won the support of some anti–New Deal Democrats, among them two former presidential candidates, Al Smith and John W. Davis, but this was not enough.

The radical fringe put a third candidate in the field, Congressman William Lemke of North Dakota, who ran on the Union party ticket. Father Coughlin, denouncing Roosevelt as the "dumbest man ever to occupy the White House," rallied his National Union for Social Justice behind Lemke; Francis Townsend also supported him. However, the extremists were losing ground by 1936. Huey Long had fallen victim to an assassin in September 1935, and his organization was taken over by a blatantly demagogic rightist, Gerald L. K. Smith. The New Deal, Smith said in 1936, was led by "a slimy group of men culled from the pink campuses of America." The Townsendites fell under a cloud because of rumors that some of their leaders had their fingers in the organization's treasury. Father Coughlin's slanderous assaults on Roosevelt caused a backlash; a number of American Catholic prelates denounced him, and the Vatican issued an unofficial but influential rebuke. Lemke got only 892,000 votes.

Roosevelt did not win in 1936 because of the inadequacies of his foes. Having abandoned his efforts to hold the businessmen, whom he now denounced as "economic royalists," he appealed for the votes of workers and the underprivileged. The new labor unions gratefully poured thousands of dollars into the campaign to reelect him. Black voters switched to the Democratic party in record numbers. Farmers liked Roosevelt because of his evident concern for their welfare. When the Supreme Court declared the Agricultural Adjustment Act unconstitutional (*United States* v. *Butler*, 1936), he immediately rushed through a new law, the Soil Conservation and Domestic Allotment Act, which accomplished the same objective by paying farmers to divert land from commercial crops to soil-building plants like clover and soybeans. Countless elderly persons backed Roosevelt out of gratitude for the Social Security Act. Homeowners were grateful for his program guaranteeing mortgages—eventually about 20 percent of all urban private dwellings were refinanced by the Home Owners Loan Corporation—and for the Federal Housing Administration, which, beginning in 1934, made available low-cost, long-term loans for modernizing old buildings and constructing new ones. A modest upturn, which raised industrial output to the levels of

1930, played into Roosevelt's hands. For the first time since 1931, U.S. Steel was showing a profit.

On election day the country gave the president a tremendous vote of confidence. He carried every state but Maine and Vermont. The Republicans elected only 89 members of the House of Representatives, and their strength in the Senate fell to 16, an all-time low. Both Roosevelt's personality and his program had captivated the land. He seemed irresistible, the most powerfully entrenched president in the history of the United States.

Roosevelt and the "Nine Old Men"

On January 20, in his second inaugural, Roosevelt spoke of the plight of millions of citizens "denied the greater part of what the very lowest standards of today call the necessities of life." A third of the nation, he added without exaggeration, was "ill-housed, ill-clad, ill-nourished." He interpreted his landslide victory as a mandate for further reforms, and with his prestige and his immense congressional majorities, nothing appeared to stand in his way—nothing, that is, except the Supreme Court.

Throughout Roosevelt's first term the Court had stood almost immovable against increasing the scope of federal authority and broadening the general power of government, state as well as national, to cope with the exigencies of the depression. Of the nine justices, only Louis Brandeis, Benjamin N. Cardozo, and Harlan Fiske Stone viewed the New Deal sympathetically. Four others—James C. McReynolds, Willis Van Devanter, Pierce Butler, and George Sutherland—were intransigent reactionaries. Chief Justice Charles Evans Hughes and Justice Owen J. Roberts, though more open-minded, tended to side with the reactionaries on many questions.

Much of the early New Deal legislation, pushed through Congress at top speed during the Hundred Days, had been drafted without proper regard for the Constitution. Even the liberal justices considered the National Industrial Recovery Act unconstitutional (the Schechter decision was a unanimous one). The Court had also voided the federal Guffey-Snyder Act, establishing minimum wages in the coal industry, and a New York minimum wage law, thereby creating, as Roosevelt remarked, a "no man's land" where neither national nor state government could act. The conservative majority had adopted what Roosevelt called a "horse-and-buggy" interpretation of the commerce clause of the Constitution, closing off one of the most important avenues for expanding federal power.

Worse, the reactionaries on the Court seemed governed by no consistent constitutional philosophy; they tended to limit the police power of the states when wages-and-hours laws came before them and to interpret it broadly when state laws restricting civil liberties were under consideration. In 1937 all the major measures of the Second Hundred Days appeared doomed. The Wagner Act had little chance of winning approval, experts predicted. Lawyers were advising employers to ignore the Social Security Act, so confident were they that the Court would declare it unconstitutional.

In a New York Herald Tribune *cartoon titled "No Boost for the Administration Make-up Department," a court-packing wolf in the sheep's clothing of a court "reform" bill acts surprised when halted by a gun-toting Senate.*

Facing this situation, Roosevelt decided to ask Congress to shift the balance on the Court by increasing the number of justices, thinly disguising the purpose of his plan by making it part of a general reorganization of the judiciary. A member of the Court reaching the age of 70 would have the option of retiring at full pay. Should such a justice choose not to retire, the president was to appoint an additional justice, up to a maximum of six, in order to ease the burden of work for the aged jurists who remained on the bench.

Roosevelt knew that this measure would run into resistance, but he expected that the huge Democratic majorities in Congress could override any opposition and that the public would back him solidly. No astute politician had erred so badly in estimating the effects of an action since Stephen A. Douglas introduced the Kansas-Nebraska bill in 1854.

Although polls showed the public fairly evenly divided on the "court-packing" bill, the opposition was vocal and influential. To the expected denunciations of conservatives were added the complaints of liberals fearful that the principle of court packing might in the future be used to subvert civil liberties. What, Senator Norris asked, would have been the reaction if a man like Harding had proposed such a measure? Opposition in Congress was immediate and intense; many who had cheerfully supported every New Deal bill came out against the plan. The press denounced it, and so did most local bar associations. Chief Justice Hughes released a devastating critique; even the liberal Brandeis—the oldest judge on the Court—rejected the bill out of hand. And many voters felt that Roosevelt had tried to trick them. The 1936 Democratic platform had spoken only of a possible amendment "clarifying" the Court's power, and Roosevelt had studiously avoided the issue during the campaign.

For months Roosevelt stubbornly refused to concede defeat, but in July 1937, he had to yield. Minor administrative reforms of the judiciary were enacted, but the size of the Court remained unchanged.

The struggle did save the legislation of the Second New Deal. Alarmed by the threat to the Court, Justices Hughes and Roberts, never entirely committed to the conservative position, beat a strategic retreat on a series of specific issues. While the debate was raging in Congress, they sided with the liberals in upholding first a minimum wage law of the state of Washington that was little different from the New York act the Court had recently rejected, then the Wagner Act, then the Social Security Act. In May, Justice Van Devanter retired, and Roosevelt replaced him with Senator Hugo Black of Alabama, a New Dealer. The conservative justices thereupon gave up the fight, and soon Roosevelt was able to appoint enough new judges to give the Court a large pro–New Deal majority. No further measure of significance was declared unconstitutional during his presidency.

The Court fight hurt Roosevelt severely. His prestige never fully recovered. Conservative Democrats who had feared to oppose him because of his supposedly invulnerable popularity took heart and began to join with the Republicans on key issues. When the president summoned a special session of Congress in November 1937 and submitted a program of "must" legislation, not one of his bills was passed.

The New Deal Winds Down

The Court fight marked the beginning of the end of the New Deal. Social and economic developments contributed to its decline, and the final blow originated in the area of foreign affairs. With unemployment high, wages low, and workers relatively powerless against their employers, most Americans had liked New Deal labor legislation and sympathized with the industrial unions whose growth it stimulated. The NRA, the Wagner Act and the CIO's organizing of such industries as steel and automobiles changed the power structure within the economy. What amounted to a revolution in the lives of wage earners had occurred. Aside from the obvious changes—higher wages, shorter hours, paid vacations, insurance of various kinds—unionization had meant fair methods of settling disputes about work practices and a measure of job security based on seniority for tens of thousands of workers. The CIO in particular had done much to increase the influence of labor in politics and to bring blacks and other minorities into the labor movement.

In 1937 a series of "sit-down strikes" broke out, beginning at the General Motors plant in Flint, Michigan. Striking workers barricaded themselves inside the factories; when police and strikebreakers tried to dislodge them, they drove them off with

A group of sit-down strikers inside the Chevrolet plant in Flint, Michigan, looking out. They are hanging a "G-M stool" in effigy. The sign directly above the dummy reminds fellow workers: "Don't Scab."

barrages of soda bottles, tools, spare parts, and crockery. The tolerant attitude of the Roosevelt administration assured the strikers that the government would not intervene. "It is illegal," Roosevelt said of the General Motors strike, "but shooting it out . . . [is not] the answer. . . . Why can't those fellows in General Motors meet with the committee of workers?" Fearful that all-out efforts to clear their plants would result in the destruction of expensive machinery, most employers capitulated to the workers' demands. All the automobile manufacturers but Henry Ford quickly came to terms with the United Automobile Workers.

The major steel companies, led by U.S. Steel, recognized the CIO and granted higher wages and a 40-hour workweek. The auto and steel unions alone boasted more than 725,000 members by late 1937; other CIO units conquered numerous industries, including rubber and textiles. These gains and the aggressive way in which the unions pursued their objectives gave many members of the middle class second thoughts about the fairness of labor's demands. Sit-down strikes, the disregard of unions for the "rights" of nonunion workers, and the violence that accompanied some strikes seemed to some not merely unreasonable but a threat to social order. The enthusiasm of such people for all reform cooled rapidly.

While the sit-down strikes and the Court fight were going on, the New Deal suffered another heavy blow. Business conditions had been gradually improving since 1933. Heartened by the trend, Roosevelt, who had never fully grasped the importance of government spending in stimulating recovery, cut back sharply on the relief program in June 1937, with disastrous results. Between August and October the economy slipped downward like sand through a chute. Stock prices plummeted; unemployment rose by 2 million; industrial production slumped. This "Roosevelt recession" further damaged the president's reputation, and for many months he aggravated the situation by adopting an almost Hoover-like attitude. "Everything will work out all right if we just sit tight and keep quiet," he actually said.

While the president hesitated, rival theorists within his administration warred. The Keynesians, led by WPA head Harry Hopkins, Marriner Eccles of the Federal Reserve, and Secretary of the Interior Harold Ickes, clamored for stepped-up government spending. The conservatives, led by Treasury Secretary Henry Morgenthau, Jr., advocated retrenchment. Perhaps confused by the conflict, Roosevelt seemed incapable of decisive action. When Keynes offered him "some bird's eye impressions" of the recession in February 1938, urging "large scale recourse to . . . public works and other investments aided by Government funds," Roosevelt sent him only a routine acknowledgment drafted by Morgenthau.

In April 1938 Roosevelt finally committed himself to heavy deficit spending. At his urging Congress passed a $3.75 billion public works bill. Two major pieces of legislation were also enacted at about this time. A new AAA program in February 1938 set marketing quotas and acreage limitations for growers of staples like wheat, cotton, and tobacco and authorized the Commodity Credit Corporation

to lend money to farmers on their surplus crops. The surpluses were to be stored by the government; when prices rose, farmers could repay the loans, reclaim their produce, and sell it on the open market, thereby maintaining an "ever-normal granary."

The second measure, the Fair Labor Standards Act, abolished child labor and established a national minimum wage of 40 cents an hour and a maximum workweek of 40 hours, with time and a half for overtime. Although the law failed to cover many of the poorest-paid types of labor, its passage meant wage increases for 750,000 workers. In later years many more classes of workers were brought within its protection, and the minimum wage was repeatedly increased.

These measures further alienated conservatives without dramatically improving economic conditions. The resistance of many Democratic congressmen to additional economic and social "experiments" hardened. As the 1938 elections approached, Roosevelt decided to go to the voters in an effort to strengthen party discipline and reenergize the New Deal. He singled out a number of conservative Democratic senators, notably Walter F. George of Georgia, Millard F. Tydings of Maryland, and "Cotton Ed" Smith of South Carolina, and tried to "purge" them by backing other Democrats in the primaries.

The purge failed. Southern voters liked Roosevelt but resented his interference in local politics. Smith dodged the issue of liberalism by stressing the question of white supremacy, Tydings emphasized Roosevelt's "invasion" of Maryland. In Georgia the president's enemies compared his campaign against George to General Sherman's march across the state during the Civil War. All three senators were easily renominated and then reelected in November. In the nation at large, the Republicans made important gains for the first time since Roosevelt had taken office. The Democrats maintained nominal control of both houses of Congress, but the conservative coalition, though unable to muster the votes to do away with accomplished reforms, succeeded in blocking additional legislation.*

---

* The so-called conservative coalition was never a well-organized group. Its membership shifted from issue to issue; it had no real leaders and no long-range plans.

Significance of the New Deal

After World War II broke out in 1939, the Great Depression was swept away on a wave of orders from the beleaguered European democracies. For this prosperity, Roosevelt received much undeserved credit. His New Deal had not returned the country to full employment. Despite the aid given the jobless, the generation of workers born between 1900 and 1910 who entered the 1930s as unskilled laborers had their careers permanently stunted by the depression. Far fewer rose to middle-class status than at any time since the 1830s and 1840s. Roosevelt's willingness to experiment with different means of combating the depression made sense because no one really knew what to do; however, his uncertainty about the ultimate objectives of the New Deal was counterproductive. He vacillated between seeking to stimulate the economy through deficit spending and trying to balance the budget; between a narrow "America first" economic nationalism and a broad-gauged international approach; between regulating monopolies and trustbusting; between helping the underprivileged and bolstering the al-

ready strong. At times he acted on the assumptions that the United States had a "mature" economy and that the major problem was overproduction. At other times he appeared to think that the answer to the depression was more production. He could never make up his mind whether to try to rally liberals to his cause without regard for party or to run the government as a partisan leader, conciliating the conservative Democrats.

Roosevelt's fondness for establishing new agencies to deal with specific problems vastly increased the federal bureaucracy, indirectly added to the influence of lobbyists, and made it more difficult to monitor government activities. His cavalier attitude toward constitutional limitations on executive power, which he justified as being necessary in a national emergency, set in motion trends that so increased the prestige and authority of the presidency that the balance among the executive, legislative, and judicial branches was threatened.

Yet these are criticisms after the fact; they ignore what one historian has called the "sense of urgency and haste" that made the New Deal "a mixture of accomplishment, frustration, and misdirected ef-

The proliferation of federal agencies during the New Deal inspired cartoonists. In this example, Swift's Gulliver is tied down by the Lilliputian Brain Trusters.

fort." On balance, the New Deal had an immense constructive impact. By 1939 the country was committed to the idea that the federal government should accept responsibility for the national welfare and act to meet specific problems in every necessary way. What was most significant was not the proliferation of new agencies or the expansion of federal power; these were continuations of trends already a century old when the New Deal began. The importance of the "Roosevelt revolution" was that it removed the issue from politics. "Never again," the Republican presidential candidate was to say in 1952, "shall we allow a depression in the United States."

Because of New Deal decisions, many formerly unregulated areas of American life became subject to federal authority: the stock exchange, agricultural prices and production, labor relations, old-age pensions, relief of the needy. If the New Deal failed to end the depression, it effected changes that have—so far, at least—prevented later economic declines from becoming catastrophes. By encouraging the growth of unions, the New Deal probably helped workers obtain a larger share of the profits of industry. By putting a floor under the income of many farmers, it checked the decline of agricultural living standards, though not that of the agricultural population. The social security program, with all its inadequacies, lessened the impact of bad times on an increasingly large proportion of the population and provided immense psychological benefits to all.

Among other important social changes, the TVA and the New Deal rural electrification program made farm life literally more civilized. Urban public housing, though never undertaken on a massive scale, helped rehabilitate some of the nation's worst slums. Government public power projects, such as the giant Bonneville and Grand Coulee dams in the Pacific Northwest, were only the most spectacular part of a comprehensive New Deal program to develop the nation's natural resources. Exploitation of the natural resources of the West was checked, and a start was made toward the proper national management of the land and water of the region, along with its petroleum, lumber, and other resources. The NIRA and later labor legislation forced employers to reexamine their role in American life and to become more socially conscious. The WPA art and theater programs widened the horizons of

millions. All in all, the spirit of the New Deal heightened the people's sense of community, revitalized national energies, and stimulated the imagination and creative instincts of countless citizens.

Women New Dealers: The Network

Largely because of the influence of Eleanor Roosevelt and Molly Dewson, head of the Women's Division of the Democratic National Committee and a major force in that party, the Roosevelt administration employed far more women in positions of importance than any earlier one. Secretary of Labor Frances Perkins was the first woman appointed to a Cabinet post, but she was no token choice, having been active in labor relations for more than 20 years as secretary of the Consumers' League during the

Workers at the Carnegie Steel Company plant in Pittsburgh give a warm welcome to Frances Perkins, FDR's secretary of labor. She had been a prominent social worker and reformer in the Progressive Era.

progressive period, as a factory inspector immediately after the war, and as a member and then chair of the New York State Industrial Commission. As secretary of labor she helped draft New Deal labor legislation and kept Roosevelt informed on various labor problems outside the government.

In addition to Perkins, there were dozens of other women New Dealers. Molly Dewson and Eleanor Roosevelt headed an informal but effective "network"—women in key posts who kept in touch constantly, always seeking to place reform-minded women in government jobs. (According to the historian William Chafe, "Washington seemed like a perpetual convention of social workers as women . . . [took] on government assignments.") Dewson also won a larger influence for Democratic women in conventions and campaigns and a larger share of the spoils that came with victory. Between 1932 and 1938 the number of women postmasters increased by 50 percent.

As for Eleanor Roosevelt, through her newspaper column, "My Day," and as a speaker on public issues, she became a major force in her own right, both as a politician and as a stateswoman. She perceived herself, the historian Tamara Hareven has written, as "an ombudsman with the increasingly bureaucratized and impersonal (federal) government." Her influence on her husband and thus on the New Deal was large, especially in the area of civil rights, where the administration needed constant prodding.

She was particularly identified with efforts to obtain better treatment for blacks, in and out of government. The *Chicago Defender,* an influential black newspaper, noted that she "stood like the Rock of Gibraltar against pernicious encroachments on the rights of minorities." (A disgruntled southerner made the same point differently: "She goes around telling the Negroes they are as good as anyone else.")

Blacks During the New Deal

The shift of black voters from the Republican to the Democratic party during the New Deal years was one of the most dramatic and significant in American history. The cause was not the depression itself, although it hit blacks especially hard. In 1932, when things were at their worst, fewer blacks de-

fected from the Republican party than the members of any other traditionally Republican group. Four years later, however, blacks voted for Roosevelt in overwhelming numbers.

Blacks supported the New Deal for the same reasons that whites did, but how the New Deal affected blacks in general and racial attitudes specifically are more complicated questions. Claiming that he dared not antagonize southern congressmen, whose votes he needed for his recovery programs, Roosevelt did nothing about civil rights before 1941 and little thereafter.

Many of the early New Deal programs treated blacks as second-class citizens. They were often paid at lower rates than whites under NRA codes (and so joked sardonically that NRA stood for "Negro Run Around" and "Negroes Ruined Again"). The early farm programs shortchanged black tenant farmers and sharecroppers. Blacks got far fewer appointments in the Civilian Conservation Corps than their numbers warranted, and those who were accepted were assigned to all-black camps. TVA developments were rigidly segregated, and almost no blacks got jobs in TVA offices. New Deal urban housing projects inadvertently but nonetheless effectively increased the concentration of blacks in particular neighborhoods. The Social Security Act, by excluding agricultural laborers and domestic servants, did nothing for hundreds of thousands of poor black workers or for Mexican-American farmhands in the Southwest. In 1939 unemployment was twice as high among blacks as among whites, and whites' wages were double the level of blacks' wages.

The fact that members of racial minorities got less than they deserved did not keep most of them from becoming New Dealers: Half a loaf was more than any American government had given blacks since the time of U. S. Grant. As one black minister explained, "[Negroes] have never been so crazy as to wait for things to be perfect."

Aside from the direct benefits, blacks profited in other ways. Secretary of the Interior Harold L. Ickes appointed Charles Forman as a special assistant assigned "to keep the government honest when it came to race." In 1936 Roosevelt appointed Mary McLeod Bethune, founder of Bethune-Cookman College, as head of the Division of Negro Affairs in the National Youth Administration (NYA), a post that enabled her to develop educational and oc-

Black sharecroppers evicted from their tenant farms were photographed by Arthur Rothstein along a Missouri road in 1939. Rothstein was one of a group of outstanding photographers who created a unique "sociological and economic survey" of the nation between 1936 and 1942 under the aegis of the Farm Security Administration.

cupational training programs for disadvantaged black youngsters. Bethune, along with Forman, another black lawyer in Ickes's department, named William Hastie, and a few others made up an informal "Black Cabinet" that lobbied throughout the Washington bureaucracy on behalf of better opportunities for blacks.

In the labor movement, the new CIO unions recruited black members, and this was particularly significant because these unions were organizing industries—steel, automobiles, and mining, among others—that employed large numbers of blacks. Thus while black Americans suffered horribly during the depression, New Deal efforts to counteract its effects brought them some relief and a measure of hope. And this became increasingly true with the passage of time. During Roosevelt's second term, blacks found far less to criticize than in his first.

A New Deal for Indians

As in many other matters, New Deal policy toward American Indians built on early trends but carried them further. During the Harding and Coolidge administrations, more Indian land had passed into the hands of whites, and agents of the Bureau of Indian Affairs had tried to suppress any element of Indian culture that they considered "pagan" or "lascivious." In 1924 Congress finally granted citizenship to all Indians, but whites still generally agreed that Indians should be treated as wards of the state. Assimilation had failed; indeed, tribal cultures had proved remarkably enduring. Indian languages and religious practices, patterns of family life, arts and crafts—all had resisted generations of efforts to "civilize" the tribes.

Government policy took a new direction in 1933

when President Roosevelt named John Collier commissioner of Indian affairs. In the 1920s Collier had studied the Indians of the Southwest and was appalled by what he had learned. He became executive secretary of the American Indian Defense Association and in 1925 editor of a reform-oriented magazine, *American Indian Life.* By the time he was appointed commissioner, the depression had reduced about a third of the 320,000 Indians living on reservations to penury.

Collier was convinced that something should be done to revive the spirits of these people. He favored a pluralistic approach, seeking to help the Indians preserve their ancient cultures but also (somewhat contradictorily) to help them earn more money and make use of modern medical advances and modern techniques of soil conservation. He was particularly eager to encourage the revival of tribal governments that could function as community service centers and represent the Indians in dealings with the federal bureaucracy.

In part because of Collier's urging, Congress passed the Indian Reorganization Act of 1934. This law did away with the Dawes Act allotment system and enabled Indians to establish tribal governments with powers like those of cities, and it encouraged, but did not require, Indians to return individually owned lands to tribal control. In various ways about 4 million of the 90 million acres of Indian land lost under the allotment system were returned to the tribes. In addition, Harry Hopkins made special efforts to see that needy Indians who were not living on reservations got relief aid. There was also a special Indian division of the Civilian Conservation Corps that organized work for Indians right on their reservations.

New Deal Indian policy was controversial among Indians as well as among other groups. Some critics charged Collier with trying to turn back the clock. Others attacked him as a segregationist and claimed that he was trying to restore "pagan" religious practices and convert the Indians to communism. Still others objected to his employing professional anthropologists with supposedly "advanced" ideas.

In truth the problem was more complicated than Collier had imagined. Indians who owned profitable allotments, such as those in Oklahoma who held valuable oil and mineral rights, did not relish turning their land over to tribal control. In New Mexico, the Navajos, whose lands had relatively little com-

mercial value, nonetheless voted decisively against going back to the communal system. All told, 77 of 269 tribes voted against communal holdings. Nevertheless, like so many of its programs, the New Deal's Indian policy marked an important and necessary shift of perspective, a bold effort to deal constructively with a long-standing national problem.

The Role of Roosevelt

How much of the credit for New Deal policies belongs personally to Franklin D. Roosevelt is debatable. He had little to do with many of the details and some of the broad principles behind the New Deal. His knowledge of economics was skimpy, his understanding of many social problems superficial, his political philosophy distressingly vague. The British leader Anthony Eden described him as "a conjurer, skillfully juggling with balls of dynamite, whose nature he failed to understand," and the historian David Brody writes perceptively of Roosevelt's "unreflective acceptance" of the basic structure of American society.

Nevertheless, every aspect of the New Deal bears the brand of Roosevelt's remarkable personality. Brain Truster Rexford Tugwell has left one of the best-balanced judgments of the president. "Roosevelt was not really very much at home with ideas," Tugwell explained. He preferred to stick with what he already knew. But he was always open to new facts, and something within him "forbade inaction when there was something to be done." Roosevelt's political genius constructed the coalition that made the program possible; his humanitarianism made it a reform movement of major significance. Although considered by many a terrible administrator because he encouraged rivalry among his subordinates, assigned different agencies overlapping responsibilities, failed to discharge many incompetents, and frequently put off making difficult decisions, he was in fact one of the most effective chief executives in the nation's history. His seemingly haphazard practice of dividing authority among competing administrators unleashed the energies and sparked the imagination of his aides, which gave the ponderous federal bureaucracy a remarkable flexibility and élan.

Like Andrew Jackson, Roosevelt maximized his role as leader of all the people. His informal bi-

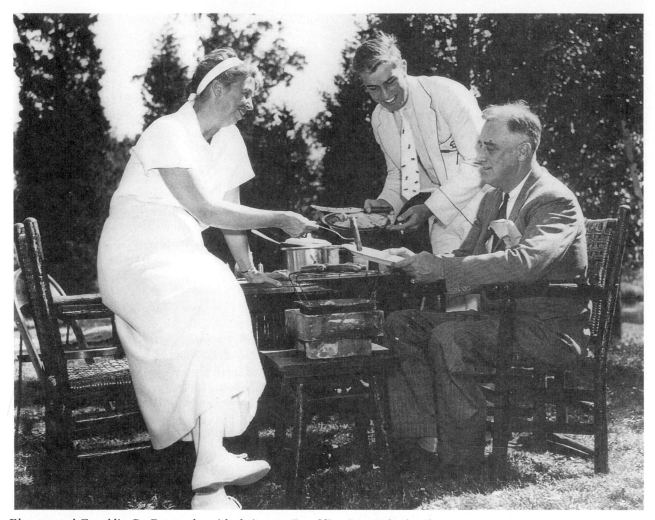

Eleanor and Franklin D. Roosevelt, with their son, Franklin, Jr., at the family home in Hyde Park, New York. While the Roosevelts' family life was far from idyllic, White House reporters generally respected their right to privacy.

weekly press conferences kept the public in touch with developments and him in tune with popular thinking. He made the radio an instrument for communicating with the masses in the most direct way imaginable: His fireside chats convinced millions that he was personally interested in each citizen's life and welfare, as in a way he was. At a time when the size and complexity of the government made it impossible for any one person to direct the nation's destiny, Roosevelt managed the minor miracle of personifying that government to 130 million people. Under Hoover, a single clerk was able to handle the routine mail that flowed into the office of the president from ordinary citizens. Under Roosevelt, the task required a staff of 50.

While the New Deal was still evolving, contemporaries recognized Roosevelt's right to a place beside Washington, Jefferson, and Lincoln among the great presidents. The years have not altered their judgment. Yet as his second term drew toward its close, some of his most important work still lay in the future.

The Triumph of Isolationism

Franklin Roosevelt was at heart an internationalist, but his highest priority was to end the depression, and like most world leaders in the 1930s, he placed revival of his own country's limping economy ahead of general world recovery. In April 1933 he took the United States off the gold standard, hoping that devaluing the dollar would make it easier to sell American goods abroad. The following month a World Economic Conference was held in London. Delegates from 64 nations sought ways to increase world trade, perhaps by a general reduction of tariffs and the stabilization of currencies. After flirting with the idea of currency stabilization, Roosevelt threw a bombshell into the conference by announcing that the United States would not return to the gold standard. His decision increased international ill feeling, and the conference collapsed. The German financier Hjalmar Schacht announced smugly that Roosevelt was adopting the maxim of the great *Führer,* Adolf Hitler: "Take your economic fate in your own hands."

Against this background, vital changes in American foreign policy took place. Unable to persuade the country to take positive action against aggressors, internationalists like Secretary of State Stimson had begun in 1931 to work for a discretionary arms embargo law, to be applied by the president in time of war against whichever side had broken the peace. By early 1933 Stimson had obtained Hoover's backing for an embargo bill, as well as the support of President-elect Roosevelt. First the munitions manufacturers and then the isolationists pounced on it, and in the resulting debate it was amended to make the embargo apply impartially to *all* belligerents.

Instead of providing an effective if essentially negative weapon for influencing international affairs, a blanket embargo would intensify America's ostrichlike isolationism. Stimson's policy would have permitted arms shipments to China but not to Japan, which might have discouraged the Japanese from attacking. As amended, the embargo would have automatically applied to both sides, thus removing the United States as an influence in the conflict. While Roosevelt accepted the change, the internationalists in Congress did not, and when they withdrew their support, the measure died.

The attitude of the munitions makers, who opposed both forms of the embargo, led to a series of studies of the industry. The most important was a Senate investigation (1934–1936) headed by Gerald P. Nye of North Dakota. Nye was convinced that "the interests" had conspired to drag America into World War 1; his investigation was more an inquisition than an honest effort to discover what American bankers and munitions makers had been doing

between 1914 and 1918. The committee's staff, ferreting through subpoenaed records, uncovered sensational facts about the lobbying activities and profits of various concerns. The Du Pont company's earnings, for example, had soared from $5 million in 1914 to $82 million in 1916. When one senator suggested to Irénée Du Pont that he was displaying a somewhat different attitude toward war than most citizens, Du Pont replied coolly: "Yes; perhaps. You were not in the game, or you might have a different viewpoint."

Munitions makers had profited far more from neutrality than from American participation in the war, but the Nye report convinced millions of citizens that the bankers who had lent the Allies money and the "merchants of death" who had sold them arms had tricked the country into war and that the "mistake" of 1917 must never be repeated.

While the Nye committee labored, Walter Millis published *The Road to War: America, 1914–1917* (1935). In this best-seller Millis advanced the thesis that British propaganda, the heavy purchases of American supplies by the Allies, and Wilson's differing reactions to violations of neutral rights by Germany and Great Britain had drawn the United States into a war it could and should have steered clear of. Thousands found Millis's logic convincing.

These developments led in 1935 to what the historian Robert A. Divine has called the "triumph of isolation." The danger of another world war mounted steadily as Germany, Italy, and Japan repeatedly resorted to force to achieve their expansionist aims. In March 1935 Hitler instituted universal military training. In May, Mussolini massed troops in Italian Somaliland, using a trivial border clash as a pretext for threatening the ancient kingdom of Ethiopia.

Congress responded by passing the Neutrality Act of 1935, which forbade the sale of munitions to all belligerents whenever the president should proclaim that a state of war existed. Americans who took passage on belligerent ships after such a proclamation had been issued would do so at their own risk. Roosevelt would have preferred a discretionary embargo or no new legislation at all, but he dared not arouse the ire of the isolationists by vetoing the bill.

In October 1935 Italy invaded Ethiopia, and Roosevelt invoked the new neutrality law. Secretary of State Cordell Hull asked American exporters to support a "moral embargo" on the sale of oil and

College campuses in the 1930s were often the scenes of organized protests against any governmental action that might increase the possibility of the United States going to war again. The faculty and students of the University of Chicago, pictured here in a 1937 demonstration, were particularly vocal in their isolationist sentiments.

other products not covered by the act. His plea was ignored; oil shipments to Italy tripled between October and January. Italy quickly overran and annexed Ethiopia. In February 1936 Congress passed a second neutrality act forbidding all loans to belligerents.

The next summer, civil war broke out in Spain. The rebels, led by the reactionary General Francisco Franco and strongly backed by Italy and Germany, sought to overthrow the somewhat leftist Spanish Republic. Here, clearly, was a clash between democracy and fascism, and the neutrality laws did not apply to civil wars. However, Roosevelt now became more fearful of involvement than some isolationists. (Senator Nye, for example, favored selling arms to the Spanish government.) The president believed that American interference might cause the conflict in Spain to become a global war, and he was wary of antagonizing the substantial number of American Catholics who were sympathetic to the Franco regime. He warned the Glenn L. Martin aircraft company that selling warplanes to the Spanish Republic "would not be in line with the policy of this government," and at his urging Congress passed another neutrality act broadening the arms embargo to cover civil wars.

Isolationism now reached its peak. A public opinion poll revealed in March 1937 that 94 percent of the people thought American policy should be directed at keeping out of all foreign wars rather than trying to prevent wars from breaking out. In April, Congress passed still another neutrality law. It continued the embargo on munitions and loans, forbade Americans to travel on belligerent ships, and gave the president discretionary authority to place the sale of other goods to belligerents on a cash-and-carry basis. In theory this would preserve the nation's profitable foreign trade without the risk of war; in fact it played into the hands of the aggressors. While German planes and cannons were turning the tide in Spain, the United States was denying the hard-pressed Spanish loyalists even a case of cartridges.

"With every surrender the prospects of a European war grow darker," Claude G. Bowers, the American ambassador to Spain, warned. The *New York Herald Tribune* pointed out that the neutrality legislation was literally reactionary—designed to keep the United States out of the war of 1914–1918, not the conflict looming on the horizon. President Roosevelt, in part because of domestic problems such as the Supreme Court packing struggle and

An American volunteer joining the Loyalist ranks in Spain in 1937. Although the American government remained officially neutral during the Spanish Civil War, hundreds of Americans joined the Lincoln Brigade to help the leftist Loyalists against General Franco and his fascist allies.

the wave of sit-down strikes and in part because of his own vacillation, seemed to have lost control over the formulation of American foreign policy. The American people, like wild creatures before a forest fire, were rushing in blind panic from the conflagration.

War Again in Europe

There were limits beyond which Americans would not go. In July 1937 the Japanese again attacked China, pressing ahead on a broad front. Roosevelt believed that invoking the neutrality law would only help the well-armed Japanese. Taking advantage of the fact that neither side had formally declared war, he allowed the shipment of arms and supplies to both sides.

Then the president went further. Speaking at Chicago in October, he condemned nations—he mentioned none by name—who were "creating a state of international anarchy and instability from which there is no escape through mere isolation or neutrality." The way to deal with "the epidemic of

world lawlessness" was to "quarantine" it. Evidently Roosevelt had no specific plan in mind; nevertheless, the quarantine speech produced a windy burst of isolationist rhetoric that forced him to back down. "It's a terrible thing," he said, "to look over your shoulder when you are trying to lead—and to find no one there."

Roosevelt came gradually to the conclusion that resisting aggression was more important than keeping out of war, but when he did, his fear of the isolationists led him at times to be less than candid in his public statements. Hitler's annexation of Austria in March 1938 caused him deep concern. The Nazis' vicious anti-Semitism had caused many of Germany's 500,000 Jewish citizens to seek refuge abroad. Now 190,000 Austrian Jews were under Nazi control. When Roosevelt learned that the Germans were burning synagogues, expelling Jewish children from schools, and otherwise mistreating innocent people, he said that he "could scarcely believe that such things could occur." But public opinion opposed changing the immigration law so that more refugees could be admitted, and the president did nothing.

In September 1938 Hitler demanded that Czechoslovakia cede the German-speaking Sudetenland region to the Reich. British prime minister Neville Chamberlain and French premier Edouard Deladier, in a conference with Hitler at Munich, yielded to Hitler's threats and promises and persuaded the Czechs to surrender the Sudetenland. Roosevelt failed again to speak out. But when the Nazis seized the rest of Czechoslovakia in March 1939, Roosevelt called for "methods short of war" to demonstrate America's determination to resist the aggressor.

When Hitler threatened Poland in the spring of 1939, demanding the free city of Danzig and the Polish Corridor separating East Prussia from the rest of Germany, and again when Mussolini invaded Albania, Roosevelt urged Congress to repeal the 1937 neutrality act so that the United States could sell arms to Britain and France in the event of war.

Congress refused. "Captain," Vice-President Garner told Roosevelt after counting noses in the Senate, "you haven't got the votes," and the president, perhaps unwisely, accepted this judgment and did not press the issue.

In August 1939 Germany and Russia signed a

A 1938 German poster glorifying Adolf Hitler with the slogan: "One people, one nation, one leader."

nonaggression pact, prelude to their joint assault on Poland. On September 1 Hitler's troops invaded Poland, at last provoking Great Britain and France to declare war. Roosevelt immediately summoned Congress into special session and again asked for repeal of the arms embargo. In November, in a vote that followed party lines closely, the Democratic majority pushed through a law permitting the sale of arms and other contraband on a cash-and-carry basis. Short-term loans were authorized, but American vessels were forbidden to carry any products to the belligerents. Since the Allies controlled the seas, cash-and-carry gave them a tremendous advantage.

The German attack on Poland effected a basic change in American thinking. Keeping out of the war remained an almost universal hope, but preventing a Nazi victory became the ultimate, if not always conscious, objective of many citizens. In

Roosevelt's case it was perfectly conscious, though he dared not express his feelings candidly because of isolationist strength in Congress and the country. He moved slowly, responding to rather than directing the course of events.

Cash-and-carry did not stop the Nazis. Poland fell in less than a month; then, after a winter lull that cynics called the "phony war," Hitler loosed his armored divisions. Between April 9 and June 22 he taught the world the awful meaning of *Blitzkrieg:* "lightning war." Denmark, Norway, the Netherlands, Belgium, and France were successively overwhelmed. The British army, pinned against the sea at Dunkirk, saved itself from annihilation only by fleeing back across the English Channel. After the French submitted to his harsh terms on June 22, Hitler controlled nearly all of western Europe.

Roosevelt responded to these disasters in a number of ways. In the fall of 1939, reacting to warnings from Albert Einstein and other scientists that the Germans were trying to develop an atomic bomb, he committed federal funds to a top secret atomic energy program. Even as the British and French were falling back, he sold them, without legal authority, surplus government arms. When Italy entered the war against France, the president called the invasion a stab in the back. During the first five months of 1940 he asked Congress to appropriate over $4 billion for national defense. To strengthen national unity, he named Henry L. Stimson secretary of war* and another Republican, Frank Knox, secretary of the navy.

After the fall of France, Hitler attempted to bomb and starve the British into submission. The epic air battles over England during the summer of 1940 ended in a decisive defeat for the Nazis, but the Royal Navy, which had only about 100 destroyers, could not control German submarine attacks on shipping. Far more destroyers were needed. In this desperate hour, Prime Minister Winston Churchill, who had replaced Chamberlain in May 1940, asked Roosevelt for 50 old American destroyers to fill the gap.

The navy had 240 destroyers in commission and more than 50 under construction. But direct loan or sale of the vessels would have violated both international and American laws. Any attempt to obtain new legislation would have aroused fears that

---

* Stimson had held this post from 1911 to 1913 in the Taft Cabinet.

the United States was going down the path that had led it into World War I. Long delay if not outright defeat would have resulted. Roosevelt therefore arranged to "trade" the destroyers for six British naval bases in the Caribbean. In addition, Great Britain leased bases in Bermuda and Newfoundland to the United States.

The destroyers-for-bases deal was one of Roosevelt's masterful achievements as a statesman and as a politician. It helped save Great Britain, and at the same time it circumvented isolationist prejudices, since the president could present it as a shrewd bargain that bolstered America's defenses. A string of island bastions in the Atlantic was more valuable than 50 old destroyers.

Lines were hardening throughout the world. In September 1940, despite last-ditch isolationist resistance, Congress enacted the first peacetime draft in American history. Some 1.2 million draftees were summoned for one year of service, and 800,000 reservists were called to active duty. That same month Japan signed a mutual-assistance pact with Germany and Italy. This Rome-Berlin-Tokyo axis fused the conflicts in Europe and Asia, turning the struggle into a global war.

A Third Term for FDR

In the midst of these events the 1940 presidential election took place. Why Roosevelt decided to run for a third term is a much-debated question. Partisanship had something to do with it, for no other Democrat seemed so likely to carry the country. Nor would the president have been human had he not been tempted to hold on to power, especially in such critical times. His conviction that no one else could keep a rein on the isolationists was probably decisive. In any case, he was easily renominated. Vice-President Garner, who had become disenchanted with Roosevelt and the New Deal, did not seek a third term; at Roosevelt's dictation, the party chose Secretary of Agriculture Henry A. Wallace to replace him.

The leading Republican candidates were Senator Robert A. Taft of Ohio, son of the former president, and District Attorney Thomas E. Dewey of New York, who had won fame as a "racket buster" and political reformer. Taft was considered conservative and lacking in political glamour; Dewey, barely 38, seemed too young and inexperienced.

Instead the Republicans nominated the darkest of dark horses, Wendell L. Willkie of Indiana, the utility magnate who had led the fight against the TVA in 1933.

Despite his political inexperience and Wall Street connections, Willkie, an energetic, charming, openhearted man, made an appealing candidate. His rough-hewn rural manner (one Democrat called him "a simple, barefoot Wall Street lawyer") won him wide support in farm districts. Willkie had difficulty, however, finding issues on which to oppose Roosevelt. Good times were at last returning. The New Deal reforms were too popular and too much in line with his own thinking to invite attack. He believed as strongly as the president that America could no longer ignore the Nazi threat.

In the end Willkie focused his campaign on Roosevelt's conduct of foreign relations. A preponderance of the Democrats favored all-out aid to Britain, while most Republicans still wished to avoid foreign entanglements. But the crisis was causing many persons to shift sides. Among interventionists, organizations like the Committee to Defend America by Aiding the Allies, headed by Republican William Allen White, and the small but influential Century Group contained members of both parties. So did the isolationist America First Committee, led by Robert E. Wood of Sears, Roebuck and the famous aviator Charles A. Lindbergh.

Wendell Willkie, just after his nomination by the Republican party for the presidency in 1940. Combining rural beginnings, Wall Street success, and a disarming grin, he gave hope of being a more formidable challenger to FDR than Alf Landon had been four years earlier.

While rejecting the isolationist position, Willkie charged that Roosevelt intended to make the United States a participant in the war. "If you reelect him," he told one audience, "you may expect war in April 1941," to which Roosevelt retorted (disingenuously, since he knew he was not a free agent in the situation), "I have said this before, but I shall say it again and again and again: Your boys are not going to be sent into any foreign wars." In November, Roosevelt carried the country handily, though by a smaller majority than in 1932 or 1936. The popular vote was 27 million to 22 million, the electoral count 449 to 82.

The Undeclared War

The election encouraged Roosevelt to act more boldly. When Prime Minster Winston Churchill informed him that the cash-and-carry system would no longer suffice because Great Britain was rapidly exhausting its financial resources, he decided at once to provide the British with whatever they needed. Instead of proposing to lend them money, a step certain to evoke memories of the vexatious war debt controversies, he devised the lend-lease program, one of his most ingenious and imaginative creations.

First he delivered a fireside chat that stressed the evil intentions of the Nazis and the dangers that a German victory would create for America. Aiding Britain should be looked at simply as a form of self-defense. "As planes and ships and guns and shells are produced," he said, American defense experts would decide "how much shall be sent abroad and how much shall remain at home." Encouraged by favorable public response to the radio talk, Roosevelt went to Congress in January 1941 with a plan calling for the expenditure of $7 billion for war materials that the president could sell, lend, lease, exchange, or transfer to any country whose defense he deemed vital to that of the United States. After two months of debate, Congress gave him what he had asked for.

Although the wording of the Lend-Lease Act obscured its immediate purpose, the saving of Great Britain, the president was frank in explaining his plan. He did not minimize the dangers involved, yet his mastery of practical politics was never more in evidence. To counter Irish-American prejudices against the English, he pointed out that the Irish Republic would surely fall under Nazi domination if Hitler won the war. He coupled his demand for heavy military expenditures with his enunciation of the idealistic "Four Freedoms"—freedom of speech, freedom of religion, freedom from want, and freedom from fear—for which, he said, the war was being fought.

After the enactment of lend-lease, aid short of war was no longer seriously debated. The American navy began to patrol the North Atlantic, shadowing German submarines and radioing their locations to British warships and planes. In April 1941 United States forces occupied Greenland; in May the president declared a state of unlimited national emergency. After Hitler invaded the Soviet Union in June, Roosevelt moved slowly, for anti-Soviet feeling in the United States was intense.* But it was obviously to the nation's advantage to help any country that was resisting Hitler's armies. In November $1 billion in lend-lease aid was put at the disposal of the Russians.

Meanwhile, the Americans occupied Iceland in July 1941, and Congress extended the draft law in August—by the margin of a single vote in the House of Representatives. In September the German submarine *U-652* fired a torpedo at the destroyer *Greer* in the North Atlantic. The *Greer,* which had provoked the attack by tracking *U-652* and flashing its position to a British plane, avoided the torpedo and dropped 19 depth charges in an effort to sink the submarine.

Roosevelt (nothing he ever did provided more ammunition for his critics) announced that the *Greer* had been innocently "carrying mail to Iceland." He called the U-boats "the rattlesnakes of the Atlantic" and ordered the navy to "shoot on sight" any German craft in the waters south and west of Iceland and to convoy merchant vessels as far as that island. After the sinking of the destroyer *Reuben James* on October 30, Congress voted to allow the arming of American merchant ships and to permit them to carry cargoes to Allied ports. For all practical purposes, though not yet officially, the United States had gone to war.

---

* During the 1930s Russia took a far firmer stand against the fascists than any other power, but after joining Hitler in swallowing up Poland, it attacked and defeated Finland during the winter of 1939–1940 and annexed the Baltic states. These acts practically destroyed the small communist movement in the United States.

Milestones

New Deal Agencies

1933 Civilian Conservation Corps (CCC)
Federal Emergency Relief
Administration (FERA)
Agricultural Adjustment
Administration (AAA)
Tennessee Valley Authority (TVA)
Home Owners Loan Corporation
(HOLC)
National Recovery Administration
(NRA)
Federal Deposit Insurance
Corporation (FDIC)
Public Works Administration (PWA)

Civil Works Administration (CWA)
1934 Securities and Exchange Commission
(SEC)
Federal Communications Commission
(FCC)
Federal Housing Administration
(FHA)
1935 Works Progress Administration
(WPA)
Resettlement Administration (RA)
Rural Elecrification Administration
(REA)
National Youth Administration (NYA)
National Labor Relations Board
(NLRB)

SUPPLEMENTARY READING

Titles marked with an asterisk have been published in paperback.

Of the many biographies of Roosevelt, see especially Frank Freidel, **Franklin D. Roosevelt** (1990), and J. M. Burns, **Roosevelt: The Lion and the Fox*** (1956). On Eleanor Roosevelt, see J. P. Lash, **Eleanor and Franklin*** (1971), and Lois Scharf, **Eleanor Roosevelt: First Lady of American Liberalism** (1987). J. T. Patterson, **Congressional Conservatism and the New Deal*** (1967), is a solid study of congressional politics. On the Brains Trust, see E. A. Rosen, **Hoover, Roosevelt, and the Brains Trust** (1977).

Useful special studies of the New Deal include M. H. Leff, '**The Limits of Symbolic Reform: The New Deal and Taxation** (1984), Richard Lowitt, **The New Deal in the West** (1984), V. L. Perkins, **Crisis in Agriculture: The AAA and the New Deal** (1969), D. E. Conrad, **The Forgotten Farmers** (1965), E. W. Hawley, **The New Deal and the Problem of Monopoly*** (1966), Roy Lubove, **The Struggle for Social Security** (1968), J. D. Matthews, **The Federal Theatre** (1967), C. H. Trout, **Boston, the Great Depression, and the New Deal** (1977), Barbara Blumberg, **The New Deal and the Unemployed** (1979), B. F. Schwartz, **The Civil Works Administration** (1984), Irving Bernstein, **Turbulent Years** (1970), J. S. Olson, **Saving Capitalism** (1988), and Sidney Fine, **Sit Down: The General Motors Strike** (1969). On constitutional questions,

see P. L. Murphy, **The Constitution in Crisis Times*** (1972).

For the activities of the "radical fringe," consult D. R. McCoy, **Angry Voices: Left-of-Center Politics in the New Deal Era** (1958), and D. H. Bennett, **Demagogues in the Depression** (1969). On Huey Long, see T. H. Williams, **Huey Long: A Biography** (1969). On blacks during the 1930s, see Raymond Wolters, **Negroes and the Great Depression*** (1970), N. J. Weiss, **Farewell to the Party of Lincoln** (1983), and Harvard Sitkoff, **A New Deal for Blacks*** (1978); on women, see W. H. Chafe, **The American Woman*** (1972), and Susan Ware, **Beyond Suffrage: Women in the New Deal** (1981) and **Partner and I** (1987), a life of Molly Dewson. On New Deal Indian policy, see K. R. Philip, **John Collier's Crusade for Indian Reform** (1977) and J. S. Olson and Raymond Wilson, **Native Americans in the 20th Century** (1984).

On isolationism and the events leading to the United States' entering the Second World War, see R. A. Divine, **The Reluctant Belligerent*** (1965), brief but comprehensive, and **The Illusion of Neutrality*** (1962), Waldo Heinrichs, **Threshold of War*** (1988), T. R. Fehrenbach, **F.D.R.'s Undeclared War** (1967), W. S. Cole, **Roosevelt and the Isolationists** (1983), and W. F. Kimball, **The Most Unsordid Act** (1969), on lend-lease.

XXIX

War and Peace

BRUTUS: *I do believe that these applauses are*
For some new honours that are heaped on Caesar.

CASSIUS: *Why, man, he doth bestride the narrow world*
Like a Colossus . . .

WILLIAM SHAKESPEARE, Julius Caesar

ONE GI: *Now we have the world by the tail.*

ANOTHER: *Now we are all sons of bitches.*

A-bomb test site blockhouse, Alamogordo, N.M., July 16, 1945

B y December 1941 the United States was in fact at war, but it is hard to see how a formal declaration could have come about had it not been for Japan. Japanese-American relations had worsened steadily after Japan resumed its war on China in 1937. As they extended their control, the invaders systematically froze out American and other foreign business interests. They declared that the Open Door policy was obsolete. Roosevelt retaliated by lending money to China and asking American manufacturers not to sell airplanes to Japan. In July 1940 Congress placed exports of aviation gasoline and certain types of scrap iron to Japan under a licensing system; in September all sales of scrap were banned. After the creation of the Rome-Berlin-Tokyo axis, Roosevelt extended the embargo to include machine tools and other items. The Japanese pushed ahead relentlessly despite the economic pressures.

The Road to Pearl Harbor

Neither the United States nor Japan wanted war. Roosevelt considered Germany a far the more dangerous enemy and was alarmed by the possibility of engaging in a two-front war. In the spring of 1941 Secretary of State Hull conferred in Washington with the Japanese ambassador, Kichisaburo Nomura, in an effort to resolve their differences. Hull showed little appreciation of the political and military situation in the Far East. He demanded that Japan withdraw from China and promise not to attack the Dutch and French colonies in Southeast Asia. How he expected to get Japan to give up its conquests without either making concessions or going to war is not clear.

Japan might well have accepted limited annexations in the area in return for the removal of American trade restrictions, but Hull seemed bent on converting the Japanese to pacifism by exhortation. He insisted on total withdrawal, to which even the moderates in Japan would not agree. When Hitler invaded the Soviet Union, thereby removing the threat of Russian intervention in the Far East, Japan decided to occupy Indochina even at the risk of war with the United States. Roosevelt retaliated in July 1941 by freezing Japanese assets in the United States and clamping an embargo on oil.

Now the war party in Japan assumed control. Nomura was instructed to tell Hull that his country would refrain from further expansion if the United States and Great Britain would cut off all aid to China and lift the economic blockade. Japan promised to pull out of Indochina once "a just peace" had been established with China. When the United States rejected these demands, the Japanese prepared to assault the Dutch East Indies, British Malaya, and the Philippines. To immobilize the United States Pacific Fleet, they planned a surprise aerial raid on the Hawaiian naval base at Pearl Harbor.

An American cryptanalyst, Colonel William F. Friedman, had cracked the Japanese diplomatic code; the government therefore had good reason to believe that war was imminent. But in the hectic rush of events, both military and civilian authorities failed to make effective use of the information collected. They expected the blow to fall somewhere in Southeast Asia, possibly in the Philippines.

The garrison at Pearl Harbor was alerted against "a surprise aggressive move in any direction." The commanders there, Admiral Husband E. Kimmel and General Walter C. Short, believing an attack impossible, took precautions only against Japanese sabotage. Thus when planes from Japanese aircraft carriers swooped down on Pearl Harbor on the morning of December 7, they found easy targets. In less than two hours they reduced the Pacific Fleet to a smoking ruin: two battleships destroyed, six others heavily battered, nearly a dozen lesser vessels put out of action. More than 150 planes were wrecked; over 2,300 servicemen were killed and 1,100 wounded.

Never had American arms suffered a more devastating or shameful defeat. The official blame was placed chiefly on Admiral Kimmel and General Short. They might well have been more alert, but responsibility for the disaster was widespread. Military and civilian officials in Washington had failed to pass on all that they knew to Hawaii or even to one another. Further, the crucial intelligence about the coming attack that the code breakers provided was mixed with masses of other information and was extremely difficult to evaluate.

On December 8 Congress declared war on Japan. Formal war with Germany and Italy was still not inevitable—isolationists were far more ready to resist the "yellow peril" in Asia than to fight in Europe. The Axis powers, however, honored their treaty obligations to Japan and on December 11 declared war on the United States. America was now fully engaged in the great world conflict.

Mobilizing the Home Front

War placed immense strains on the American economy and produced immense results. About 15 million men and women entered the armed services; they, and in part the millions more in Allied uniforms, had to be fed, clothed, housed, and supplied with equipment ranging from typewriters and paper clips to rifles and grenades, tanks and airplanes. Congress granted wide emergency powers to the president. It refrained from excessive meddling in administrative problems and in military strategy. However, though the Democrats retained control of both houses throughout the war, their margins were relatively narrow. A coalition of conservatives in both parties frequently prevented the president from having his way and exercised close control over expenditures.

Roosevelt was an inspiring war leader but not a very good administrator. Any honest account of the war on the home front must reveal glaring examples of confusion, inefficiency, and pointless bickering. The squabbling and waste characteristic of the early New Deal period made relatively little difference— what mattered then was raising the nation's spirits and keeping people occupied; efficiency was less than essential, however desirable. In wartime the nation's fate, perhaps that of the entire free world, depended on delivering weapons and supplies to the battlefronts.

The confusion attending economic mobilization can easily be overstressed. Nearly all Roosevelt's basic decisions were sensible and humane: to pay a large part of the cost of the war by collecting taxes rather than by borrowing and to base taxation on ability to pay, to ration scarce raw materials and consumer goods, and to regulate prices and wages. If these decisions were not always translated into action with perfect effectiveness, they always operated in the direction of efficiency and the public good.

Roosevelt's greatest accomplishment was his inspiring of businessmen, workers, and farmers with a sense of national purpose. In this respect his function duplicated his earlier role in fighting the depression, and he performed it with even greater success.

A sense of tremendous economic expansion caused by the demands of war can most easily be grasped by examining official statistics of production. In 1939 the United States was still mired in the Great Depression. The gross national product amounted to about $91.3 billion. In 1945, after allowing for changes in the price level, it was $166.6 billion. More specifically, manufacturing output nearly doubled, and agricultural output rose 22 percent. In 1939 the United States turned out fewer than 6,000 airplanes; in 1944, more than 96,000. Shipyards produced 237,000 tons of vessels in 1939, 10 million tons in 1943.

Wartime experience proved that the Keynesian economists were correct in saying that government spending would spark economic growth. About 8 million people were unemployed in June 1940. After Pearl Harbor, unemployment practically disappeared, and by 1945 the civilian work force had increased by nearly 7 million. Military mobilization had begun well before December 1941, by which time 1.6 million men were already under arms. Economic mobilization proceeded much more slowly, mainly because the president refused to centralize authority. For months after Pearl Harbor various civilian agencies squabbled with the military over everything from the allocation of scarce raw materials to the technical specifications of weapons. Roosevelt refused to settle these conflicts as only he could have.

The War Economy

Yet by early 1943 the nation's economic machinery had been converted to a wartime footing and was functioning smoothly. Supreme Court Justice James F. Byrnes resigned from the Court to become a sort of "economic czar." His Office of War Mobilization had complete control over the issuance of priorities and over prices. Rents, food prices, and wages were strictly regulated, and items in short supply were rationed to consumers. Wages and prices had soared during 1942, but after April 1943 they leveled off. Thereafter the cost of living scarcely changed until controls were lifted after the war.

Expanded industrial production together with conscription caused a labor shortage that increased the bargaining power of workers. At the same time, the national emergency required some limitation on the workers' right to take advantage of this power. After Pearl Harbor, Roosevelt created a National War Labor Board to arbitrate disputes and stabilize wage rates, and he banned all changes in wages without NWLB approval. In the "Little Steel" case in July 1942, the NWLB laid down the rule that wage increases should not normally exceed 15 percent of the rates of January 1941, a figure roughly in line with the increase in the cost of living since that date.

Prosperity and stiffer government controls added significantly to the strength of organized labor; indeed, the war had more to do with institutionalizing industrywide collective bargaining than the New Deal period. As workers recognized the benefits of union membership, they flocked into the organizations. Strikes declined sharply, but some crippling work stoppages did occur. In May 1943 the government seized the coal mines after John L. Lewis's United Mine Workers walked out of the pits. This strike led Congress to pass, over Roosevelt's veto, the Smith-Connally War Labor Disputes Act,

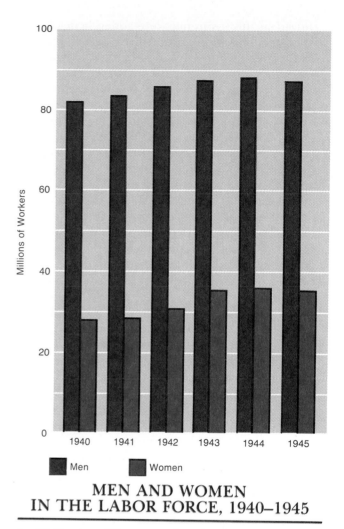

MEN AND WOMEN IN THE LABOR FORCE, 1940–1945

In 1940, about 75 percent of workers in the labor force—82 million—were men, and the other 25 percent—28 million—were women. By the end of World War II, in 1945, nearly 8 million more women had entered the work force, as against 5 million more men. The balance of the labor force had shifted to roughly 70 percent men, 30 percent women.

which gave the president the power to take over any war plant threatened by a strike and outlawed strikes against seized plants. Although strikes continued to occur—the loss in hours of labor zoomed to 38 million in 1945—when Roosevelt asked for a labor draft law, Congress refused to go along.

Wages and prices remained in fair balance. Overtime work fattened paychecks, and a new stress in labor contracts on paid vacations, premium pay for night work, and various forms of employer-subsidized health insurance were added benefits. The war effort had almost no adverse effect on the standard of living of the average citizen, a vivid demonstration of the productivity of the American economy. The manufacture of automobiles ceased, and pleasure driving became next to impossible because of gasoline rationing, but most civilian activities went on much as they had before Pearl Harbor. Because of the need to conserve cloth, skirts were shortened, cuffs disappeared from men's trousers, and the vest passed out of style. Plastics replaced metals in toys, containers, and other products. Although items such as meat, sugar, and shoes were rationed, they were doled out in amounts adequate for the needs of most persons. Americans had both guns and butter; belt-tightening of the type experienced by the other belligerents was unnecessary.

The federal government spent twice as much money between 1941 and 1945 as in its entire previous history. This made heavy borrowing necessary. The national debt, which stood at less than $49 billion in 1941, increased by more than that amount each year between 1942 and 1945 and totaled nearly $260 billion when the war ended. However, more than 40 percent of the total was met by taxation, a far larger proportion than in any earlier war.

This policy helped to check inflation by siphoning off money that would otherwise have competed for scarce consumer goods. Heavy excise taxes on amusements and luxuries further discouraged spending, as did the government's war bond campaigns, which persuaded patriotic citizens to lend part of their income to Uncle Sam. High taxes on incomes (up to 94 percent) and on excess profits (95 percent), together with a limit of $25,000 a year after taxes on salaries, convinced the people that no one was profiting inordinately from the war effort.

The income tax, which had never before touched the mass of white-collar and industrial workers, was extended downward until nearly everyone had to pay it. To ensure efficient collection of the relatively small sums paid by most persons, Congress adopted the payroll-deduction system proposed by Beardsley Ruml, chairman of the Federal Reserve Bank of New York. Employers withheld the taxes owed by workers from their paychecks and turned the money over to the government.

The steeply graduated tax rates combined with a general increase in the income of workers and farmers effected a substantial shift in the distribution of wealth in the United States. The poor became richer, while the rich, if not actually poorer, collected a smaller proportion of the national income. The wealthiest 1 percent of the population had received 13.4 percent of the national income in 1935 and 11.5 percent in 1941. In 1944 this group received 6.7 percent.

War and Social Change

Enormous social effects stemmed from this shift, but World War II altered the patterns of American life in so many ways that it would be wrong to ascribe the transformations to any single source. Never was the population more fluid. The millions who put on uniforms found themselves transported first to training camps in every section of the country and then to battlefields scattered from Europe and Africa to the far reaches of the Pacific. Burgeoning new defense plants drew other millions to places like Hanford, Washington, and Oak Ridge, Tennessee, where great atomic energy installations were constructed, and to the aircraft factories of California and other states. As in earlier periods, the trend was from east to west, from south to north, and from countryside to the cities. The population of California increased by more than 50 percent in the 1940s, that of other far western states almost as much.

During the war, marriage and birth rates rose steeply. A kind of backlog existed because many people had been forced to put off marrying and having children for financial reasons during the Great Depression. Now wartime prosperity put an end to that problem at the same time that large numbers of young couples were feeling the need to put down roots when the husbands were going off to risk death in distant lands. The population of the United States had increased by only 3 million during the depression decade of the 1930s; during the next *five* years it rose by 6.5 million.

Minorities in Time of War: Blacks, Hispanics, and Indians

The war affected black Americans in many ways. Several factors operated to improve their lot. One was their own growing tendency to demand fair treatment. Another was the reaction of Americans to Hitler's murder of millions of Jews, an outgrowth of his doctrine of "Aryan" superiority. These barbarities compelled millions of white citizens to reexamine their views about race. If the nation expected blacks to risk their lives for the common good, how could it continue to treat them as second-class citizens? Black leaders pointed out the inconsistency between fighting for democracy abroad and ignoring it at home. "We want democracy in Alabama," the NAACP announced, and this argument too had some effect on white thinking.

Blacks in the armed forces were treated more fairly than they had been in World War I. They were enlisted for the first time in the air force and the marines, and they were given more responsible positions in the army and navy. The army commissioned its first black general. Some 600 black pilots won their wings. Altogether about a million served, about half of them overseas. The extensive and honorable performance of these units could not be ignored by the white majority. However, segregation in the armed services was maintained, and black soldiers were often provided with inferior recreational facilities and otherwise mistreated in and around army camps, especially those in the South. In 1943 William Hastie, the former New Dealer who

was serving as an adviser on racial matters to Secretary of War Stimson, resigned in protest because of the "reactionary policies and discriminatory practices of the Army and Air Force in matters affecting Negroes."

Economic realities operated significantly to the advantage of black civilians. More of them had been unemployed in proportion to their numbers than any other group; now the labor shortage brought employment for all. More than 5 million blacks moved from rural areas to cities between 1940 and 1945 in search of work. At least a million of these found defense jobs in the North and on the West Coast. The black population of Los Angeles, San Francisco, Denver, Buffalo, Milwaukee, and half a dozen other important cities more than doubled in that brief period. The migrants were mostly forced to live in dreadful urban ghettos, but their very concentration (and the fact that outside the South blacks could vote freely) made them important politically.

These gains failed to satisfy black leaders. The NAACP, which increased its membership from 50,000 in 1940 to almost 405,000 in 1946, adopted a more militant stance than in World War I. Discrimination in defense plants seemed far less tolerable than it had in 1917 and 1918. A. Philip Ran-

Though assigned to segregated units, black servicemen were not limited to the infantry or enlisted ranks. Here are five graduates of the Advanced Flying School, Tuskegee, Alabama, just before receiving their commissions in 1942 as second lieutenants in the Army Air Corps.

dolph, president of the Brotherhood of Sleeping Car Porters, organized a march of blacks on Washington in 1941 to demand equal opportunity for black workers. Fearing possible violence and the wrath of southern congressmen, Roosevelt tried to persuade Randolph to call off the march. "It would make the country look bad" and "help the Germans," he claimed. But Randolph persisted, and Roosevelt finally agreed to issue an order prohibiting discrimination in plants with defense contracts. He also set up the Fair Employment Practices Committee to see that the order was carried out. Executive Order 8802 was poorly enforced, but it opened up better jobs to some workers and led many employers to change their hiring practices.

Prejudice and mistreatment did not cease. In areas around defense plants, white resentment of the black "invasion" mounted. By 1943 50,000 new black residents had crowded into Detroit. A wave of strikes disrupted production at U.S. Rubber and several former automobile plants where white workers laid down their tools to protest the hiring of blacks. In June a race riot marked by looting and bloody fighting broke out. It went on for three days, and by the time federal troops finally restored order, 25 blacks and 9 whites had been killed. Other race riots erupted in New York and many other cities.

In Los Angeles the attacks were on Mexican-born "zoot suiters," gangs whose "uniforms" were broad-brimmed fedoras, long coats, and pegged trousers. Wartime employment needs resulted in a reversal of the depression policy of forcing Mexicans out of the Southwest, and many thousands flocked north in search of work. Most had to accept menial jobs, but work was plentiful and they, as well as resident Spanish-speaking Americans, experienced rising living standards.

Some of the young Hispanics in the Los Angeles region formed gangs. They had money in their pockets and their behavior (like their costume) was not always as circumspect as local residents would have preferred. A grand jury undertook an investigation, and the Los Angeles City Council even debated banning the wearing of zoot suits. In 1943 rioting broke out when sailors on shore leave, apparently resenting these prosperous-appearing foreign civilians, began roaming the area attacking anyone they could find wearing a zoot suit.

There were at least understandable reasons why white city dwellers resented the black and Hispanic

The zoot-suit fashion favored by Mexican gang members originated in urban black neighborhoods and became a national fad during the war. The zoot suiter here, photographed in 1943, lacks the requisite wide-brimmed fedora, and so reveals his slicked hairstyle—also part of the uniform.

newcomers, although these did not justify the way the whites acted. But the mindless revulsion and flagrant contempt of so many and the willingness of white leaders to tolerate such behavior at a time when national unity was so necessary were particularly frustrating. For example, blood plasma from blacks and whites was kept separately even though the two "varieties" were indistinguishable and the process of storing plasma had been devised by a black doctor, Charles Drew.

Blacks became increasingly embittered. Roy Wilkins, head of the NAACP, put it this way in 1942: "No Negro leader with a constituency can face his members today and ask full support for the war in the light of the atmosphere the government has created." Many black newspaper editors were so critical of the administration that conservatives demanded that they be indicted for sedition.

Roosevelt would have none of that, but the militants annoyed him; he felt that they should hold their demands in abeyance until the war had been won. Apparently he failed to realize the depth of black anger, and in this he was no different from the majority of whites. A revolution was in the making, yet in 1942 a poll revealed that a solid majority of whites still believed that black Americans were satisfied with their place in society. The riots of 1943 undoubtedly disabused some of them of this illusion.

Concern about national unity did lead to a reaction against the New Deal policy of encouraging Indians to preserve their ancient cultures and develop self-governing communities. There was even talk of going back to the allotment system and trying to "assimilate" Indians into the larger society. John Collier resigned as commissioner of Indian affairs in disgust in 1945.

In fact, the war encouraged assimilation in several ways. More than 24,000 Indians served in the armed forces, an experience that brought them in contact with new people, new places, and new ideas. Many thousands more left the reservations to work in defense industries in cities all over the country.

The Treatment of German-, Italian-, and Japanese-Americans

However, while World War II affected the American people far more drastically than World War I had, it produced much less intolerance and fewer examples of the repression of individual freedom of opinion. People seemed able to distinguish between Italian fascism and Italian-Americans and between the government of Nazi Germany and Americans of German descent in a way that had escaped their parents. The fact that few Italian-Americans

Identification tags hung from the collars of the Mochida children as they posed with their parents for photographer Dorothea Lange. The date was May 8, 1942, and the family was awaiting transportation to a detention camp from their home in Hayward, California.

admired Mussolini and that nearly all German-Americans were vigorously anti-Nazi helps explain this. So does the fact that both groups were well organized and prepared to use their considerable political power if necessary to protect themselves against abuse.

But the underlying public attitude was more important. Americans went to war in 1941 without illusions and without enthusiasm, determined to win but expecting only to preserve what they had. They therefore found it easier to tolerate dissent, to view the dangers they faced realistically, and to concentrate on the real foreign enemy without venting their feelings on domestic scapegoats. The nation's 100,000 conscientious objectors met with little hostility.

The one flagrant example of intolerance was the relocation of the West Coast Japanese in internment camps in Wyoming, Arizona, and other interior states. About 110,000 Americans of Japanese ancestry, the majority of them native-born U.S. citizens, were rounded up and sent off against their will. Not one was accused of sabotage or being an enemy agent.

The Japanese were properly indignant but also baffled, in some cases hurt more than angry. "We didn't feel Japanese. We felt American," one woman, the mother of three small children, recalled many years later. "When I think back to the internment, I want to call it a concentration camp, but it wasn't." A fisherman remembered that besides his nets and all his other equipment, he had to leave behind a "brand-new 1941 Plymouth." "We hadn't done anything wrong. We obeyed the laws," he told an interviewer. "I lost everything." Then he added, almost plaintively, "But I don't blame anyone. It was a war."

The government's excuse was fear that some of the Japanese *might* be disloyal. In this connection it must not be forgotten that the Japanese had attacked Pearl Harbor without warning, without even threatening war unless certain demands were met, something even the Nazis had not done before they marched into Poland. Nevertheless, racial prejudice (the "yellow peril") and frustration at not being able to strike a quick blow at Japan in retaliation had much to do with the callous decision of the government to force people into camps without specific evidence that any of them posed a danger to American security. The Supreme Court upheld the re-

location order in *Korematsu* v. *United States* (1944), but in *Ex parte Endo* it forbade the internment of loyal Japanese-American citizens. Unfortunately, the latter decision was not handed down until December 1944.

Women's Contribution to the War Effort

With economic activity on the rise and millions of men going off to war, a sudden need for women workers developed. The trends of the 1920s—more women workers and more of them married—accelerated. By 1944 fully 6.5 million additional women had entered the work force, and at the peak of war production in 1945, more than 19 million women were employed. Additional thousands were serving in the armed forces: 100,000 in the Women's Auxiliary Army Corps (WACS), others in navy, marine and air corps auxiliaries.

At first there was considerable resistance to what was happening. About one husband in three objected in principle to his wife taking a job. Many employers in so-called heavy industry and in other fields traditionally dominated by men doubted that women could handle such tasks.

Unions frequently made the same point, usually without much evidence. A Seattle official of the International Brotherhood of Boilermakers and Iron Shipbuilders said of women job applicants: "They don't understand. . . . If one of these girls pressed the trigger on the yard rivet guns, she'd be going one way and the rivet the other." This was perhaps reasonable, though many women were soon doing "men's work" in the shipyards. But the Seattle taxicab union objected to women drivers on the ground that "drivers are forced to do things and go places that would be embarrassing for a woman to do."

These male attitudes lost force in the face of the escalating demand for labor. That employers usually did not have to pay women as much as men made them attractive, as did the fact that they were not subject to the draft. A breakthrough occurred when the big Detroit automobile manufacturers agreed to employ women on their wartime production lines. Soon women were working not only as riveters and cab drivers but also as welders, machine tool operators, and in dozens of other occupations formerly the exclusive domain of men.

Women welders beveling armor plate on tank bodies, photographed in 1943 by Margaret Bourke-White of Life.

Women took wartime jobs for many reasons other than the obvious economic ones. Patriotism, of course, was important, but so were the excitement of entering an entirely new world, the desire for independence, even loneliness. "It's thrilling work, and exciting, and something women have never done before," one woman reported. She was talking about driving a taxi.

Black women workers had a particularly difficult time, employers often hesitating to hire them because they were black, black men looking down on them because they were women. But the need for willing hands was infinite. Sybil Lewis of Sapula, Oklahoma, went to Los Angeles and found a job as a waitress in a black restaurant. Then she responded to a notice of a training program at Lockheed Aircraft, took the course, and became a riveter making airplane gas tanks. When an unfriendly foreman gave her a less attractive assignment, she moved on to Douglas Aircraft. By 1943 she was working as a welder in a shipyard.

Few wartime jobs were easy, and for women there were special burdens, not the least of which was the prejudice of many of the men they worked with. For married women there was housework to do after a long day. One War Manpower Commission bureaucrat figured out that Detroit defense plants were losing 100,000 woman-hours a month because of employees taking a day off to do the family laundry. Although the government made some effort to provide day-care facilities, there were never enough; this was one reason why relatively few women with small children entered the labor market during the war.

The war also affected the lives of women who did not take jobs. Families by the hundreds of thousands pulled up stakes and moved to the centers of war production, such as Detroit and southern California. Housing was always in short supply in these areas, and while the men went off to the familiar surroundings of yard and factory, their wives had to cope with cramped quarters, ration books, the absence of friends and relatives, the problems encountered by their children in strange schools and playgrounds, in some situations even with outdoor toilets. With so many people living among strangers and in unstable circumstances, it is not surprising that crime, juvenile delinquency, and prostitution increased, as indeed they did in other parts of the country too.

Newlywed wives of soldiers and sailors (known generally as "war brides") often followed their husbands to training camps, where life could be as difficult as it was around defense plants. Those who did not faced other problems—adjusting to being married without having had much experience of marriage, loneliness, worry. Whatever their own behavior, war brides quickly learned that society applied a double standard to infidelity, especially when it involved a man presumably risking his life in some far-off land. There was a general relaxation of sexual inhibitions, part of a decades-long trend accelerated by the war. So many hasty marriages, followed by long periods of separation, also brought a rise in divorces from about 170 per 1,000 marriages in 1941 to 310 per 1,000 in 1945.

Of course, "ordinary" housewives also had to deal with shortages, ration books, and other inconveniences during the war. In addition, most took on other duties and bore other burdens, such as tending "victory gardens" and preserving their harvests, using crowded public transportation when there was no gas for the car, mending and patching old clothes when new ones were unavailable, participating in salvage drives, and doing volunteer work for hospitals, the Red Cross, or various civil defense and servicemen's centers.

Allied Strategy: Europe First

Only days after Pearl Harbor, Prime Minister Churchill and his military chiefs met in Washington with Roosevelt and his advisers. In every quarter of the globe, disaster threatened. The Japanese were gobbling up the Far East. Hitler's armies, checked outside Leningrad and Moscow, were preparing for a massive attack in the direction of Stalingrad, on the Volga River. German divisions under General Erwin Rommel were beginning a drive across North Africa toward the Suez Canal. U-boats were taking a heavy toll in the North Atlantic. British and American leaders believed that eventually they could muster enough force to smash their enemies, but whether or not the troops already in action could hold out until this force arrived was an open question.

The decision of the strategists was to concentrate first against the Germans. Japan's conquests were in remote and, from the Allied point of view, relatively unimportant regions. If Russia surrendered, Hitler might well be able to invade Great Britain, thus making his position in Europe impregnable by depriving the United States of a base for a counterattack.

But how to strike at Hitler? American leaders wanted a second front in France, at least by 1943, and the Russians, with their backs to the wall and bearing the full weight of the German war machine, heartily agreed. Churchill, however, was more concerned with protecting Britain's overseas possessions than with easing the pressure on the Soviet Union. He advocated instead air bombardment of German industry combined with an attempt to drive the Germans out of North Africa, and his argument carried the day.

During the summer of 1942 Allied planes began to bomb German cities. In a crescendo through 1943 and 1944, British and American bombers pulverized the centers of Nazi might. Though air attacks did not destroy the German armies' capacity to fight, they hampered war production, tangled communications, and brought the war home to the German people in awesome fashion. Humanitarians deplored the heavy loss of life among the civilian population, but the response of the realists was that Hitler had begun indiscriminate bombing, and victory depended on smashing the German war machine.

In November 1942 an Allied army commanded by General Dwight D. Eisenhower struck at French North Africa. After the fall of France, the Nazis had set up a puppet regime in the parts of France not occupied by their troops, with headquarters at Vichy in central France. This collaborationist Vichy government controlled French North Africa. But the North African commandant, Admiral Jean Darlan, promptly switched sides when Eisenhower's forces landed. After a brief show of resistance, the French surrendered.

The Allies were willing to do business with Darlan despite his record as a collaborationist. This angered General Charles de Gaulle, who had organized a government in exile immediately after the collapse of France and who considered himself the true representative of the French people. Many Americans agreed with de Gaulle, but the arrangement with Darlan paid large dividends. Eisenhower was able to press forward quickly against the Germans. In February 1943 at Kasserine Pass in the

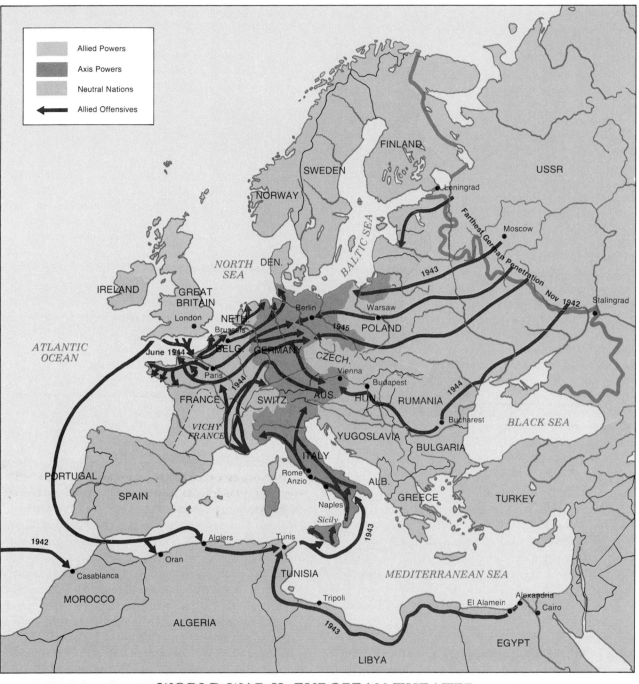

WORLD WAR II, EUROPEAN THEATER

desert south of Tunis, American tanks met Rommel's Afrika Korps. The battle ended in a standoff, but with British troops closing in from their Egyptian bases to the east, the Germans were soon trapped and crushed. In May, after Rommel had been recalled to Germany, his army surrendered.

In July 1943, while air attacks on Germany continued and the Russians slowly pushed the Germans

One of Life *photographer Robert Capa's first "pictures of victory"—American troops entering the Sicilian town of Monreale on their way up the Italian peninsula in 1943.*

back from the gates of Stalingrad, the Allies invaded Sicily from Africa. In September they advanced to the Italian mainland. Mussolini had already fallen from power, and his successor, Marshal Pietro Badoglio, surrendered. However, the German troops in Italy threw up an almost impregnable defense across the rugged Italian peninsula. The Anglo-American army inched forward, paying heavily for every advance. Monte Cassino, halfway between Naples and Rome, did not fall until May 1944, Rome not until June, and months of hard fighting still remained before the country was cleared of Germans. The Italian campaign was an Allied disappointment even though it weakened the enemy.

Germany Overwhelmed

By the time the Allies had taken Rome, the mighty army needed to invade France had been collected in England under Eisenhower's command. On D

day, June 6, 1944, the assault forces stormed ashore at five points along the coast of Normandy, supported by a great armada and thousands of planes and paratroops. Against fierce but ill-coordinated German resistance, they established a beachhead; within a few weeks a million troops were on French soil.

Thereafter victory was assured, though nearly a year of hard fighting lay ahead. In August the American Third Army under General George S. Patton, an eccentric but brilliant field commander, erupted southward into Brittany and then veered east toward Paris. Another Allied army invaded France from the Mediterranean in mid-August and advanced rapidly north. Free French troops were given the honor of liberating Paris on August 25. Belgium was cleared by British and Canadian units a few days later. By mid-September the Allies were fighting on the edge of Germany itself.

The front now stretched from the Netherlands along the borders of Belgium, Luxembourg, and

France all the way to Switzerland. If the Allies had mounted a massive assault at any one point, as the British commander, Field Marshal Bernard Montgomery, urged, the struggle might have been brought to a quick conclusion. While the two armies were roughly equal in size, the Allies had complete control of the air and 20 times as many tanks as the foe. The pressure of the advancing Russians on the eastern front made it difficult for the Germans to reinforce their troops in the west. But General Ei-

senhower believed a concentrated attack too risky. He prepared instead for a general advance.

While he was regrouping, the Germans on December 16 launched a counterattack, planned by Hitler himself, against the Allied center in the Ardennes Forest. The Germans hoped to break through to the Belgian port of Antwerp, thereby splitting the Allied armies in two. The plan was foolhardy and therefore unexpected, and it almost succeeded. The Germans drove a salient ("the

Once into Germany, the Third Army advanced so quickly in the spring of 1945 that it came upon military installations almost without warning. The photograph here is of General Dwight D. Eisenhower inspecting the condition of the concentration camp at Gotha, Germany, where slain inmates had been left unburied by their fleeing captors.

bulge") about 50 miles into Belgium. But once the element of surprise had been overcome, their chance of breaking through to the sea was lost. Eisenhower concentrated first on preventing them from broadening the break in his lines and then on blunting the point of their advance. By late January 1945 the old line had been reestablished.

The Battle of the Bulge cost the United States 77,000 casualties and delayed Eisenhower's offensive, but it exhausted the Germans' last reserves. The Allies then pressed forward to the Rhine, winning a bridgehead on the far bank of the river on March 7. Thereafter, another German city fell almost daily. With the Russians racing westward against crumbling resistance, the end could not be long delayed.

As the Americans drove swiftly forward they began to overrun Nazi concentration camps where millions of Jews had been murdered. Word of this Nazi holocaust in which no less than 6 million people were slaughtered had reached the United States much earlier. At first the news had been dismissed as propaganda, then discounted as grossly exaggerated. Hitler was known to hate Jews and to have persecuted them, but that he could order the murder of millions of innocent people, even children, seemed beyond belief. By 1943, however, the truth could not be denied.

Little could be done about those already in the camps, but there were thousands of refugees in occupied Europe who might have been spirited to safety. President Roosevelt declined to make the effort; he even refused to bomb the Auschwitz death camp in Poland or the rail lines used to bring victims to its gas chambers on the grounds that the destruction of German soldiers and military equipment took precedence over any other objective. Thus when American journalists entered the camps with the advancing troops, saw the heaps of still unburied corpses, and talked with the emaciated survivors, their reports caused a storm of protest.

Why Roosevelt acted as he did has never been satisfactorily explained. In any case, it was far too late to save more than a handful. In April, American and Russian forces made contact at the Elbe River. A few days later, with Russian shells reducing his capital to rubble, Hitler, by then probably insane, took his own life in his Berlin air raid shelter. On May 8 Germany surrendered.

The Naval War in the Pacific

Defeating Germany first had not meant abandoning the Pacific region entirely to the Japanese. While armies were being trained and material accumulated for the European struggle, much of the available American strength was diverted to maintaining vital communications in the Far East and preventing further Japanese expansion.

The navy's aircraft carriers had escaped destruction at Pearl Harbor, a stroke of immense good fortune, because without most tacticians realizing it, the airplane had revolutionized naval warfare. Commanders discovered that carrier-based planes were far more effective against warships than the heaviest naval artillery because of their greater range and more concentrated firepower. Battleships made excellent gun platforms from which to pound shore installations and support land operations, but against other vessels aircraft were of prime importance.

This truth was demonstrated in May 1942 in the Battle of the Coral Sea. Having captured an empire in a few months without the loss of any warship larger than a destroyer, the Japanese believed the war already won. This led them to overextend themselves.

The Coral Sea lies northeast of Australia and south of New Guinea and the Solomon Islands. Mastery of these waters would cut Australia off from Hawaii and thus from American aid. Admiral Isoroku Yamamoto had dispatched a large fleet of troopships screened by many warships to attack Port Moresby, on the southern New Guinea coast. On May 7 and 8 planes from the American carriers *Lexington* and *Yorktown* struck the convoy's screen, sinking a small carrier and damaging a large one. Superficially, the battle seemed a victory for the Japanese, for their planes mortally wounded the *Lexington* and sank two other ships, but the transports had been forced to turn back—Port Moresby was saved. Although large numbers of cruisers and destroyers took part in the action, none came within sight or gun range of an enemy ship. All the destruction was wrought by carrier aircraft.

Encouraged by the Coral Sea "victory," Yamamoto decided to force the American fleet into a showdown battle by assaulting Midway Island, west of Hawaii. His armada never reached its destination.

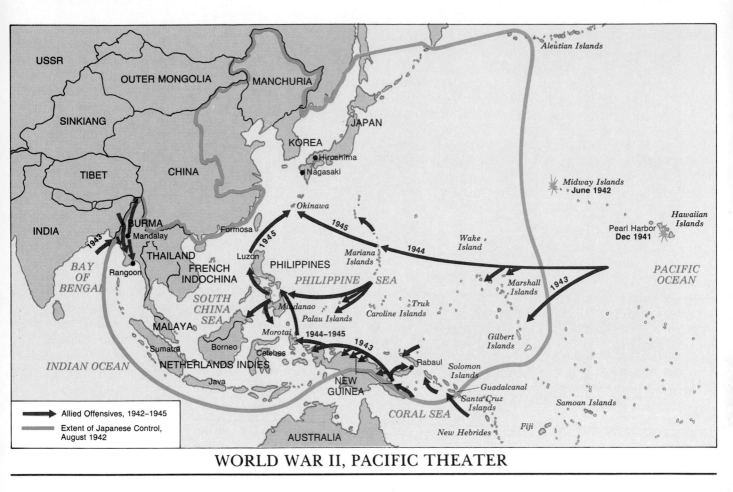

WORLD WAR II, PACIFIC THEATER

Between June 4 and 7 control of the central Pacific was decided entirely by air power. American dive bombers sent four large carriers to the bottom. About 300 Japanese planes were destroyed. The United States lost only the *Yorktown* and a destroyer. Thereafter the initiative in the Pacific war shifted to the Americans, but victory came slowly and at painful cost.

American land forces were under the command of Douglas MacArthur, a brilliant but egocentric general whose judgment was sometimes distorted by his intense concern for his own reputation. Mac-Arthur was in command of American troops in the Philippine Islands when the Japanese struck in December 1941. After his heroic but hopeless defense of Manila and the Bataan peninsula, President Roosevelt had him evacuated by PT boat to escape capture.

Thereafter MacArthur was obsessed with the idea of personally leading an American army back to the Philippines. Although many strategists believed that the islands should be bypassed in the drive on the Japanese homeland, in the end Mac-Arthur convinced the Joint Chiefs of Staff, who determined strategy. Two separate drives were undertaken, one from New Guinea toward the Philippines under MacArthur, the other through the central Pacific toward Tokyo under Admiral Chester W. Nimitz.

Island Hopping

Before commencing this two-pronged advance, the Americans had to eject the Japanese from the Solomon Islands in order to protect Australia from a

The often hand-to-hand combat required to dislodge the Japanese from entrenched positions on Pacific islands such as Bougainville, pictured here, prompted American military strategists to predict that a successful invasion of Japan itself would take 2 years and 2 million American lives.

flank attack. Beginning in August 1942, a series of land, sea, and air battles raged around Guadalcanal Island in this archipelago. Once again American air power was decisive, though the bravery and skill of the ground forces that actually won the island must not be underemphasized. American pilots, better trained and with tougher planes, had a relatively easier task. They inflicted losses five to six times heavier on the enemy than they sustained themselves. Japanese air power disintegrated progressively during the long battle, and this in turn helped the fleet to take a heavy toll of the Japanese navy. By February 1943 Guadalcanal had been secured.

In the autumn of 1943 the American drives toward Japan and the Philippines got under way at last. In the central Pacific campaign the Guadalcanal action was repeated on a smaller but equally bloody scale from Tarawa in the Gilbert Islands to Kwajalein and Eniwetok in the Marshalls. The Japanese soldiers on these islands fought like the Spartans at Thermopylae for every foot of ground. They had to be blasted and burned from tunnels and concrete pillboxes with hand grenades, flamethrowers, and dynamite. They almost never surrendered. But Admiral Nimitz's forces were in every case victorious. By midsummer of 1944 this arm of the American advance had taken Saipan and Guam in the Marianas. Now land-based bombers were within range of Tokyo.

Meanwhile, MacArthur was leapfrogging along the New Guinea coast toward the Philippines. In October 1944 he made good his promise to return to the islands, landing on Leyte, south of Luzon. Two great naval clashes in Philippine waters, the Battle of the Philippine Sea (June 1944) and the Battle for Leyte Gulf (October 1944), completed the destruction of Japan's sea power and reduced its air force to a band of fanatical suicide pilots called *kamikazes,* who tried to crash bomb-laden planes against American warships and airstrips. The *ka-*

mikazes caused much damage but could not turn the tide. In February 1945 MacArthur liberated Manila.

The end was now inevitable. B-29 Superfortress bombers from the Marianas rained high explosives and firebombs on Japan. The islands of Iwo Jima and Okinawa, only a few hundred miles from Tokyo, fell to the Americans in March and June 1945. But such was the tenacity of the Japanese soldiers that it seemed possible that it would take another year of fighting and a million more American casualties to subdue the main Japanese islands.

"The Shatterer of Worlds"

At this point came the most controversial decision of the entire war, and it was made by a newcomer on the world scene. In November 1944 Roosevelt had been elected to a fourth term, easily defeating Thomas E. Dewey. Instead of renominating Henry A. Wallace for vice-president, whom conservatives considered too radical, the Democratic convention had nominated Senator Harry S Truman of Missouri, a reliable party man well liked by professional politicians. Suddenly, in April 1945, President Roosevelt died of a cerebral hemorrhage. Thus it was Truman, a man painfully conscious of his limita-

tions yet equally aware of the power and responsibility of his office, who had to decide what to do when a mere three months later American scientists placed in his hands a new and awful weapon, the atomic bomb.

After Roosevelt had responded to Albert Einstein's warning in 1939, government-sponsored atomic research had proceeded rapidly, especially after the establishment of the so-called Manhattan Project in May 1943. The manufacture of the element plutonium at Hanford, Washington, and of uranium 235 at Oak Ridge, Tennessee, continued along with the design and construction of a transportable atomic bomb at Los Alamos, New Mexico, under the direction of J. Robert Oppenheimer. Almost $2 billion was spent before a successful bomb was exploded at Alamogordo, in the New Mexican desert, on July 16, 1945. As that first mushroom cloud formed over the desert, Oppenheimer recalled the prophetic words of the *Bhagavad Gita*: "I am become death, the shatterer of worlds."

Should a bomb with the destructive force of 20,000 tons of TNT be employed against Japan? By striking a major city, its dreadful power could be demonstrated convincingly, yet doing so would bring death to tens of thousands of Japanese civilians. Many of the scientists who had made the bomb

Hiroshima's Museum of Science and Industry was reduced to a skeleton in the atomic bomb blast. City officials decided to preserve the wreckage as a memorial.

now argued against its use. Others suggested alerting the Japanese and then staging a demonstration explosion at sea, but that idea was discarded because of concern that the bomb might fail to explode. Even General Eisenhower and General MacArthur had reservations about the need to use the weapon.

Truman was torn between his awareness that the bomb was "the most terrible thing ever discovered" and his hope that using it "would bring the war to an end." The bomb might cause a revolution in Japan, might lead the emperor to intervene, might even persuade the military to give up. Considering the hundreds of thousands of Americans who would surely die in any conventional invasion of Japan and influenced by a desire to end the Pacific war before the Soviet Union could intervene effectively and thus claim a role in the peacemaking, the president chose to go ahead.

The moral soundness of Truman's decision has been debated ever since. There is no doubt that hatred of the Japanese had something to do with the decision. What is often forgotten by those who deplore it is the fact that even though the immediate result was the death of many thousands of innocent Japanese civilians, far more Japanese would have died—many more than the Americans who would have perished—if Japan had been invaded.

In any case, on August 6 the Superfortress *Enola Gay* dropped an atomic bomb on Hiroshima, killing about 78,000 persons (including 20 American prisoners of war) and injuring nearly 100,000 more out of a population of 344,000. Over 96 percent of the buildings in the city were destroyed or damaged. Three days later, while the stunned Japanese still hesitated, a second atomic bomb, the only other one that had so far been assembled, blasted Nagasaki. This second drop was far less defensible morally, but it had the desired result. On August 15 Japan surrendered.

Thus ended the greatest war in history. Its cost was beyond calculation. No accurate count could be made even of the dead; we know only that the total was in the neighborhood of 20 million. As in World War I, American casualties—291,000 killed in battle and 671,000 wounded—were smaller than those of the other major belligerents. About 7.5 million Russians died in the war, 3.5 million Germans, 1.2 million Japanese, and 2.2 million Chinese; Britain and France, despite much smaller populations, suffered losses almost as large as the United States'. And far

more than in World War I, American resources, human and material, had made victory possible.

No one could account the war a benefit to humanity, but in the late summer of 1945 the future looked bright. Fascism had been annihilated. Successful wartime diplomatic dealings among Roosevelt, Churchill, and Joseph Stalin, the Soviet dictator, encouraged the hope that the communists were prepared to cooperate in rebuilding Europe. In the United States isolationism had disappeared; the message of Wendell Willkie's best-selling *One World*, written after a globe-circling tour made by the 1940 Republican presidential candidate at the behest of President Roosevelt in 1942, appeared to have been absorbed by the majority of the people.

Out of the death and destruction had come technological developments that seemed to herald a better world as well as a peaceful one. Enormous advances in the design of airplanes and the development of radar (which some authorities think was more important than any weapons system in winning the war) were about to revolutionize travel and the transportation of goods. Improvements in surgery and other medical advances gave promise of saving millions of lives, and the development of penicillin and other antibiotics, which had greatly reduced the death rate among troops, would perhaps banish all infectious disease.

Above all, there was the power of the atom. The force that seared Hiroshima and Nagasaki could be harnessed to serve peaceful needs, the scientists promised, with results that might free humanity forever from poverty and toil. The period of reconstruction would be prolonged, but with all the great powers adhering to the new United Nations charter, drafted at San Francisco in June 1945, international cooperation could be counted on to ease the burdens of the victims of war and help the poor and underdeveloped parts of the world toward economic and political independence. Such at least was the hope of millions in the victorious summer of 1945.

Wartime Diplomacy

That hope was not to be realized, in large part because of a conflict that developed between the Soviet Union and the western allies. During the course of World War II every instrument of mass persuasion in the country had been directed at convincing the people that the Russians were fighting America's battle as well as their own. Even before Pearl Harbor, former Ambassador Joseph E. Davies wrote in his best-selling *Mission to Moscow* (1941) that the communist leaders were "a group of able, strong men" with "honest convictions and integrity of purpose" who were "devoted to the cause of peace for both ideological and practical reasons." Communism was based "on the same principle of the 'brotherhood of man' which Jesus preached." Stalin possessed great dignity and charm, combined with much wisdom and strength of character, Davies said. "His brown eye is exceedingly kind and gentle. A child would like to sit in his lap and a dog would sidle up to him." In another book published in 1941 the journalist Walter Duranty described Stalin (who had ruthlessly executed hundreds of his former comrades) as "remarkably long-suffering in his treatment of various oppositions."

During the war Americans with as different points of view as General Douglas MacArthur and Vice-President Henry A. Wallace took strongly pro-Soviet positions, and American newspapers and magazines published many laudatory articles about Russia. *Life* reported that Russians "think like Americans." In 1943 *Time* named Stalin its "Man of the Year." The film *Mission to Moscow*, a whitewash of the dreadful Moscow treason trials of the 1930s based on Ambassador Davies's book, portrayed Stalin as a wise, grandfatherly type, puffing comfortably on an old pipe. In *One World* (1943), Wendell Willkie wrote glowingly of the Russian people, their "effective society," and their simple, warmhearted leader. When he suggested jokingly to Stalin that if he continued to make progress in improving the education of his people he might educate himself out of a job, the dictator "threw his head back and laughed and laughed," Willkie recorded. "Mr. Willkie, you know I grew up a Georgian peasant. I am unschooled in pretty talk. All I can say is I like you very much."

These views of the character of Joseph Stalin were naive, to say the least, but the identity of interests of the United States and the Soviet Union was very real during the war. Russian military leaders conferred regularly with their British and American counterparts and fulfilled their obligations scrupulously.

The Soviets repeatedly expressed a willingness to cooperate with the Allies in dealing with postwar problems. Russia was in January 1942 one of the 26 signers of the Declaration of the United Nations, in which the Allies promised to eschew territorial aggrandizement after the war, to respect the right of all peoples to determine their own form of government, to work for freer trade and international economic cooperation, and to force the disarmament of the aggressor nations.*

In May 1943 the Soviet Union dissolved the Comintern, its official agency for the promulgation of world revolution. The following October, during a conference in Moscow with Secretary of State Cordell Hull and British Foreign Minister Anthony Eden, Soviet Foreign Minister V. M. Molotov joined in setting up the European Advisory Commission to divide Germany into occupation zones after the war. At a conference held in Teheran, Iran, that December, Roosevelt, Churchill, and Stalin discussed plans for a new league of nations. When Roosevelt described the kind of world organization he envisaged, the Russian dictator offered a number of constructive suggestions.

Between August and October 1944, Allied representatives met at Dumbarton Oaks, outside Washington, D.C. The chief Russian delegate, Andrei A. Gromyko, opposed limiting the use of the veto by the great powers on the future United Nations Security Council, but he did not take a deliberately obstructionist position. At another meeting, held at Yalta in the Crimean region of the Soviet Union in February 1945, Stalin joined Roosevelt and Churchill in the call for a conference to be held in April at San Francisco to draft a charter for the United Nations. "We argued freely and frankly across the table," Roosevelt reported later. "But at the end, on every point, unanimous agreement was reached. I may say we achieved a unity of thought and a way of getting along together." Privately Roosevelt characterized Stalin as "a very interesting man" whose rough exterior clothed an "old-fashioned elegant European manner." He referred to him almost affectionately as "that old buzzard" and on one occasion called him "Uncle Joe" to his face. At Yalta, Stalin gave Roosevelt a portrait photograph, with a long Cyrillic inscription in his small, tight hand.

---

* These were the principles first laid down in the so-called Atlantic Charter, drafted by Roosevelt and Churchill at a meeting on the U.S.S. *Augusta* off Newfoundland in August 1941.

While the powers argued at length over the form of the UN charter at the 50-nation San Francisco Conference, they conducted the debates in an atmosphere of optimism and international amity. Each UN member received a seat in the General Assembly, a body designed for discussion rather than action. The locus of authority in the new organization resided in the Security Council, "the castle of the great powers." This consisted of five permanent members (the United States, the Soviet Union, Great Britain, France, and China) and six others elected for two-year terms.

The Council was charged with responsibility for maintaining world peace, but any great power could block UN action whenever it wished to do so. The United States insisted on this veto power as strongly as the Soviet Union did. In effect the charter paid lip service to the Wilsonian ideal of a powerful international police force, but it incorporated the limitations that Henry Cabot Lodge had proposed in his 1919 reservation to Article 10 of the League Covenant, which relieved the United States from the obligation of enforcing collective security without the approval of Congress.

The Cold War Under Way

Long before the war in Europe ended, however, the Allies had clashed over important policy matters. Since later world tensions developed from decisions made at this time, an understanding of the disagreements is essential for evaluating several decades of history. Unfortunately, complete understanding is not yet possible, if it ever will be, which explains why the subject remains controversial.

Much depends on one's view of the postwar Soviet system. If the Soviet government under Stalin was bent on world domination, events of the so-called Cold War fall readily into one pattern of interpretation. If Russia, having bravely and at enormous cost endured an unprovoked assault by the Nazis, was seeking only to protect itself against the possibility of another invasion, these events are best explained differently. Because the United States has opened nearly all its diplomatic records, we know a great deal about how American foreign policy was formulated and about the mixed motives and mistaken judgments of American leaders. This helps explain why many scholars have been critical of

American policy and the "cold warriors" who made and directed it. The Soviet Union, in stark contrast, has excluded historians from its archives, and consequently we know little about the motivations and inner workings of Soviet policy. Was Russia "committed to overturning the international system and to endless expansion in pursuit of world dominance?" Daniel Yergin asks in *Shattered Peace*. Only access to Soviet records can provide an answer to this vitally important question.

The Soviets resented the British-American delay in opening up a second front. They were fighting for survival against the full power of the German armies; any invasion, even an unsuccessful one, would have relieved some of the pressure. Roosevelt and Churchill would not move until they were ready, and Stalin had to accept their decision. At the same time, Stalin never concealed his determination to protect his country against future attack by extending its western frontier after the war. He warned the Allies repeatedly that he would not tolerate any anti-Soviet government along Russia's western boundary.

Most Allied leaders, including Roosevelt, admitted privately during the war that the Soviet Union would annex territory and possess preponderant power in eastern Europe after the defeat of Germany, but they never said this publicly. They believed that free governments could somehow be created in countries like Poland and Bulgaria that the Soviets would trust enough to leave to their own devices. "The Poles," Winston Churchill said early in 1945, "will have their future in their own hands, with the single limitation that they must honestly follow . . . a policy friendly to Russia. This is surely reasonable."

However reasonable, Churchill's statement was impractical. The Polish question was a terribly difficult one. The war, after all, had been triggered by the German attack on Poland; the British in particular felt a moral obligation to restore that nation to its prewar independence. During the war a Polish government in exile was set up in London, and its leaders were determined—especially after the discovery in 1943 of the murder of some 5,000 Polish officers several years earlier at Katyn, in Russia, presumably by the Soviet secret police—to make no concessions to Soviet territorial demands. Public opinion in Poland (and indeed in all the states along Russia's western frontier) was not so much anti-

Soviet as anti-Russian. Yet the Soviet Union's legitimate interests (to say nothing of its power in the area) could not be ignored.

Yalta and Potsdam

At the Yalta Conference, Roosevelt and Churchill agreed to Soviet annexation of large sections of eastern Poland. In return they demanded that free elections be held in Poland itself. "I want this election to be . . . beyond question," Roosevelt told Stalin. "It should be like Caesar's wife." In a feeble attempt at a joke he added: "I did not know her but they said she was pure." Stalin agreed, almost certainly without intending to keep his promise. The elec-

tions were never held; Poland was run by a pro-Soviet puppet regime.

Stalin apparently could not understand why his allies were so concerned about the fate of a small country remote from their strategic spheres. That they professed to be concerned seemed to him an indication that they had some secret, devious purpose. He could see no difference (and "revisionist" American historians agree with him) between the Soviet Union's dominating Poland and maintaining a government there that did not reflect the wishes of a majority of the Polish people and the United States' dominating many Latin American nations and supporting unpopular regimes within them. Roosevelt, however, was worried about the political effects that Soviet control of Poland might have in

Churchill, Roosevelt, and Stalin photographed at the week-long Yalta conference in February 1945. By April 1945, Roosevelt was dead.

the United States. Polish-Americans would be furious if the United States allowed the Russians to control their homeland.

Had Roosevelt described the difficulties to the Poles and the rest of the American people more frankly, their reaction might have been less angry. In any case, when he realized that Stalin was going to act as he pleased, Roosevelt was irate. "We can't do business with Stalin," he said shortly before his death in April 1945. "He has broken every one of the promises he made at Yalta." In July 1945, following the surrender of Germany, the new president, Harry Truman, met with Stalin and Churchill at Potsdam, outside Berlin.* They agreed to try the Nazi leaders as war criminals, made plans for exacting reparations from Germany, and confirmed the division of the country into four zones to be occupied separately by American, Russian, British, and French troops. Berlin, deep in the Soviet zone, had itself been split into four sectors. Stalin rejected all arguments that he loosen his hold on eastern Europe, and Truman (who received news of the successful testing of the atomic bomb while at Potsdam) made no concessions, but he was impressed by Stalin. The dictator was "smart as hell," he wrote in his diary. "Stalin was an SOB," the plainspoken president explained to some officers while returning to the United States from Potsdam on the cruiser *Augusta*. Then he added: "Of course he thinks I'm one too."

On both sides suspicions were mounting, positions hardening. Yet all the advantages seemed to be with the United States. Was this not, as Henry Luce, the publisher of *Time* had declared, the "American century," an era when American power and American ideals would shape the course of events the world over? Besides its army, navy, and air force and its immense industrial potential, alone among the nations the United States possessed the atomic bomb. When Stalin's actions made it clear that he intended to control eastern Europe and to exert influence elsewhere in the world, most Americans first reacted somewhat in the manner of a mastiff being worried by a yapping terrier: Their resentment was tempered by amazement. It took time for them to realize that the war had caused a fundamental change in international politics. The

United States might be the strongest country in the world, but the western European nations, victor and vanquished alike, were reduced to the status of second-class powers. The Soviet Union, by contrast, had regained the influence it had held under the czars and lost as a result of World War I and the Communist Revolution.

Milestones

1941 Roosevelt creates Fair Employment practices Committee (FEPC)
Japanese attack Pearl Harbor
1942 West Coast Japanese ordered to relocation camps
Fall of the Philippines
Battle of the Coral Sea
Battle of Midway
American troops invade North Africa
1943 Manhattan Project to make atomic bomb
Race riots in Detroit and Los Angeles
Invasion of Italy
Teheran Conference
1944 Allied invasion of Normandy, France
Liberation of Paris
Battle of the Bulge
1945 Yalta Conference
San Francisco Conference to draft UN Charter
Germany surrenders (V-E Day)
Capture of Okinawa
Atomic bomb tested at Alamogordo, New Mexico
Potsdam Conference
Atomic bombs dropped on Hiroshima and Nagasaki, Japan
Japan surrenders (V-J Day)

---

* Clement R. Attlee replaced Churchill during the conference after his Labour party won the British elections.

SUPPLEMENTARY READING

Titles marked with an asterisk have been published in paperback.

On prewar American-Japanese relations, see Akira Iriye, **After Imperialism** (1965), and on Pearl Harbor, G. W. Prange, **At Dawn We Slept** (1981), and Roberta Wohlstetter, **Pearl Harbor: Warning and Decision*** (1962). C. C. Tansill, **Back Door to War** (1952), and C. A. Beard, **President Roosevelt and the Coming of the War** (1948), are interesting interpretations by isolationists, while L. C. Gardner, **Economic Aspects of New Deal Diplomacy*** (1971), is a critical scholarly analysis. Iriye's **Power and Culture: The Japanese-American War** (1981) looks at the war in the Pacific from both sides.

The home front is discussed in Richard Polenberg, **War and Society*** (1972), A. M. Winkler, **Home Front U.S.A.** (1988), and David Brinkley, **Washington Goes to War** (1988). H. M. Harris et al. (eds.), **The Homefront** (1984), contains a sampling of reminiscences by people in all walks of life. Social trends are covered in Steven Mintz and Susan Kellogg, **Domestic Revolutions*** (1988). The effect of the war on blacks is discussed in Ulysses Lee, **The Employment of Negro Troops** (1966), N. A. Wynn, **The Afro-American and the Second World War**

(1976), D. J. Capeci, Jr., **Race Relations in Wartime Detroit** (1984), and A. R. Buchanan, **Black Americans in World War II** (1977). On the relocation of the Japanese, see Roger Daniels, **Concentration Camps USA: Japanese Americans and World War II** (1971), and Peter Irons, **Justice at War** (1984). The effects of the war on women are described in Karen Anderson, **Wartime Women** (1981), and S. M. Hartmann, **The Home Front and Beyond** (1982).

A. R. Buchanan, **The United States in World War II** (1964), provides an excellent overall survey of the military side of the conflict. S. E. Morison, **The Two-Ocean War*** (1963), deals with the naval side of the war. See also Stephen Ambrose, **Eisenhower** (1983), and D. S. Wyman, **The Abandonment of the Jews** (1984).

Wartime diplomacy is discussed in J. L. Gaddis, **The United States and the Origins of the Cold War*** (1972), Gar Alperovitz, **Atomic Diplomacy*** (1965), Martin Sherwin, **A World Destroyed** (1975), and Gaddis Smith, **American Diplomacy During the Second World War*** (1965).

XXX

The American Century

In the councils of government, we must guard against the acquisition of unwarranted influence, whether sought or unsought, by the military-industrial complex. The potential for the disastrous rise of misplaced power exists and will persist.

PRESIDENT DWIGHT D. EISENHOWER, *1961*

I n late 1945 most Americans were probably more concerned with what was happening at home than with foreign developments, and no one was more aware of this than Harry Truman. When he received the news of Roosevelt's death, he claimed that he felt as though "the moon, the stars, and all the planets" had suddenly fallen on him. Although he could not have been quite as surprised as he indicated (Roosevelt was known to have been in extremely poor health), he was acutely conscious of his own limitations.

Truman was born in Missouri in 1884. After service with a World War I artillery unit, he opened a men's clothing store in Kansas City. The store failed in the postwar depression. Truman then became a minor cog in the political machine of Democratic boss Tom Pendergast. In 1934 he was elected to the United States Senate, where he proved to be a loyal but obscure New Dealer. He first attracted national attention during World War II when his

"watchdog" committee on defense spending, working with devotion and efficiency, saved the government immense sums. This led to his nomination and election as vice-president.

As president, Truman sought to carry on in the Roosevelt tradition. Curiously, he was at the same time humble and cocky, idealistic and cold-bloodedly political. He adopted liberal objectives only to pursue them sometimes by rash, even repressive means. Too often he insulted opponents instead of convincing or conciliating them. Complications tended to confuse him, in which case he either dug in his heels or struck out blindly, usually with unfortunate results. On balance, however, he was a strong and in many ways a successful chief executive.

The Postwar Economy

Nearly all the postwar leaders were worried by the possibility of a serious postwar depression, and nearly all accepted the necessity of employing federal authority to stabilize the economy and speed national development. The Great Depression and the successful application of the theories of John Maynard Keynes during the war had convinced Democrats and Republicans alike that it was possible to prevent sharp swings in the business cycle and therefore to do away with serious unemployment by monetary and fiscal manipulation. "The agents of government must . . . put a brake at certain points where boom forces develop . . . and support purchasing power when it becomes unduly depressed," the newly created Council of Economic Advisers reported.

When World War II ended, nearly everyone wanted to demobilize the armed forces, remove wartime controls, and reduce taxes. Yet everyone also hoped to prevent any sudden economic dislocation, to check inflation, and to make sure that goods in short supply were fairly distributed. Neither the politicians nor the public was able to reconcile these conflicting objectives. No group seemed willing to limit its own demands in the general interest. Labor wanted price controls retained but wage controls lifted; industrialists wished to raise prices and to keep the lid on wages. Farmers wanted subsidies but opposed price controls and the extension of social security benefits to agricultural workers.

In this difficult situation President Truman failed to win either the confidence of the people or the support of Congress. On the one hand, he proposed a comprehensive program of new legislation that included a public housing scheme, aid to education, medical insurance, civil rights guarantees, a higher minimum wage, broader social security coverage, additional conservation and public power projects patterned after TVA, increased aid to agriculture, and the retention of anti-inflationary controls. On the other hand, he ended rationing and other controls and signed a bill cutting taxes by some $6 billion. Whenever opposition to his plans developed, he vacillated between compromise and inflexibility.

Yet the country weathered the reconversion period with remarkable ease. The pent-up demand for homes, automobiles, clothing, washing machines, and countless other products, backed by the war-enforced savings of millions of people, kept factories operating at capacity. Economists had feared that the flood of millions of veterans into the job market would cause serious unemployment. But when the veterans returned (more than 60,000 of them accompanied by foreign brides), few found themselves unoccupied for long. Because of the boom, the demand for labor was large and growing. In addition, the government made an unprecedented educational opportunity available to veterans. Instead of a general bonus, which would have stimulated consumption and inflation, in 1944 Congress passed the GI Bill of Rights, which made subsidies available to veterans so that they could continue their education, learn new trades, or start new businesses. Nearly 8 million veterans took advantage of the education and training grants, greatly to their long-term advantage, and thus to the country's.

Cutting taxes and removing price controls did cause a period of rapid inflation. Food prices rose more than 25 percent between 1945 and 1947, which led to demands for higher wages and a wave of strikes (nearly 5,000 in 1946 alone). Inflation and labor unrest helped the Republicans win control of both houses of Congress in 1946 for the first time since the 1920s. High on the Republican agenda was the passage of a new labor relations act. Labor leaders tended to support the Democrats, for they remembered gratefully the Wagner Act and other help given them by the Roosevelt administration

during the labor-management struggles of the 1930s. In 1943 the CIO had created a political action committee to mobilize the labor vote.

But the strikes of 1946 had alienated many citizens because they delayed the satisfaction of the demand for consumer goods. They even led President Truman, normally sympathetic to organized labor, to seize the coal mines, threaten to draft railroad workers, and ask Congress for other special powers to prevent national tie-ups.

This was the climate when in June 1947 the new Congress passed the Taft-Hartley Act over President Truman's veto. The measure outlawed both the closed shop (a provision written into many labor contracts requiring new workers to join the union before they could be employed) and secondary boycotts and strikes called as a result of disputes between unions over the right to represent workers. Most important, it authorized the president to seek court injunctions to prevent strikes that in his opinion endangered the national interest. The injunctions would hold for 80 days—a "cooling-off" period during which a presidential fact-finding board could investigate and make recommendations. If the dispute remained unresolved after 80 days, the president was to recommend "appropriate action" to Congress.

The Taft-Hartley Act made the task of unionizing unorganized industries more difficult, but it did not seriously hamper existing unions. Though it outlawed the closed shop, it permitted union shop contracts, which forced new workers to join the union after accepting employment.

Postwar Society: The Baby Boomers

The trend toward early marriage and larger families begun during the war continued and indeed accelerated when the conflict ended. In one year, 1946, more than 10 percent of all the single females in the country over the age of 14 got married. The birthrate had been under 20 per 1,000 population in the 1930s. It exceeded 25 in most years between 1946 and 1956.

Most servicemen had idealized the joys of domesticity while abroad, and they and their wives and sweethearts were eager to concentrate on "making a home and raising a family" now that the war had

Returning veterans and their growing families needed homes; wartime earnings and veterans' mortgages made possible their financing; developers were ready to build them. One result was the construction of hundreds of thousands of single-family homes laid out in massive tracts.

ended. People sought security after the strains and dangers of the war years, but they faced the future hopefully, encouraged by the booming economy and the sudden profusion of consumer goods. This satisfaction with the marital state was reflected in a slackening in the divorce rate. At the same time, perhaps because of the omnipresent signs of material progress and the confusion produced by rapid change, people tended to be conformists, looking over their shoulders, so to speak, rather than tackling life head on.

The period was marked by "a reaffirmation of domesticity," Elaine Tyler May writes in *Homeward Bound: American Families in the Cold War Era*. "Childlessness was considered deviant, selfish, and pitiable. . . . Nearly everyone believed that family togetherness, focused on children, was the mark of a successful and wholesome personal life." In 1955 a University of Michigan psychologist completed a study of 300 middle-class couples conducted over two decades. A large percentage of the women queried were college graduates. Some had apparently gone to college primarily to find a mate with a good future, but others had cheerfully sacrificed plans

for a professional career because "the right man" had come along. Of these, most had few regrets. "Marriage has opened up far more avenues of interest than I ever would have had without it," one reported.

Encouraged by magazines like the *Ladies' Home Journal* and *Woman's Home Companion*, which were full of articles on aspects of the subject, and by films that described the trials and triumphs of family life, many college-educated women made a "career" of home management and child development, claiming that this gave them satisfactions unavailable in the business and professional worlds.

The men of this generation also professed to have found fulfillment in family life. They tended to stress such things as the satisfactions gained by taking on the responsibilties that marriage and fatherhood entailed; they mentioned "the incentive to succeed" and the "motivation for intensive effort" produced by such responsibilties. For many men, however, these responsibilities provided a refuge from the competitive corporate world where they earned their living. The need to subordinate one's personal interests, even one's taste in clothes, to the requirements of "the organization," described in William Whyte's *Organization Man* (1956) and in novels like Sloan Wilson's *Man in the Gray Flannel Suit* (1955), caused strains that could best be relieved in the warmth and security of one's family. Wives were also directly affected by this pressure, since an executive's spouse was also expected to conform to corporate standards.

Blue-collar workers and clerical employees were not subjected to these pressures, but studies reveal that they did not differ in their attitudes toward marriage and child rearing. "The vast changes . . . are pervasive," two demographers concluded. "Social and economic variables . . . such as race, ethnic status, education and residence, do not indicate differences with respect to trends in fertility."

Government policies buttressed the inclinations of the people. Income tax deductions encouraged taxpayers to have children and to borrow money to purchase houses and furniture. Having a large family became a kind of national objective. "I'd like six kids," one husband reported. "It just seems like a minimum production goal." Life was family-centered, and family life was child-centered. Doctor Benjamin Spock's *Baby and Child Care* (1946), bible of the postwar generation, which sold well over 20 million copies in 20-odd years, was not as "permissive" as has often been suggested. Spock insisted that raising children called for professional skills. Responding blindly to children's desires was wrong. But he certainly emphasized the importance of loving care. "Children raised in loving families want to learn, want to conform, want to grow up," he explained.

The Containment Policy

While ordinary people seemed to concentrate almost compulsively on their personal affairs, foreign policy issues continued to vex the Truman presidency. Repeatedly, Stalin made it clear that he had no intention even of consulting with western leaders about his domination of eastern Europe, and he seemed intent on extending his power deep into war-devastated central Europe. The Soviet Union also controlled Outer Mongolia, parts of Manchuria, and northern Korea, and it had annexed the Kurile Islands and regained the southern half of Sakhalin Island from Japan. It was fomenting trouble in Iran. By January 1946 Truman had decided to stop "babying" the Russians. "Only one language do they understand," he noted in a memorandum. "How many divisions have you?"

American and Russian attitudes stood in sharp confrontation when the control of atomic energy came up for discussion in the UN. Everyone recognized the threat to human survival posed by the atomic bomb. In November 1945 the United States suggested allowing the UN to supervise all nuclear energy production, and the General Assembly promptly created the Atomic Energy Commission to study the question. In June 1946 Commissioner Bernard Baruch offered a plan for the eventual outlawing of atomic weapons. A system would be set up under which UN inspectors could operate without restriction anywhere in the world to make sure that no country was making bombs clandestinely. When, at an unspecified date, the system had been established, the United States would destroy its stockpile of bombs.

Most Americans thought the Baruch plan magnanimous and some considered it positively foolhardy; the Soviets simply rejected it. They would neither permit UN inspectors in the Soviet Union nor surrender their veto power over Security Council actions dealing with atomic energy. They demanded that the United States destroy its bombs at once.

"What struck most observers," the historian John Lewis Gaddis has written, "was the utter imperviousness of Stalin's regime to the gestures of restraint and goodwill that emanated from the West." Unwilling under the circumstances either to trust the Russians or to surrender what they considered their "winning weapon," the American leaders refused to agree. The resulting stalemate increased international tension.

Postwar cooperation had failed. By early 1946 a new policy was emerging. Many minds contributed to its development, but the key ideas were provided by George F. Kennan, a scholarly Foreign Service officer. Kennan had been stationed for five years in Russia and was a close student of Soviet history. He believed that the Soviet leaders saw the world as divided into socialist and capitalist camps separated by irreconcilable differences. Nothing the United States might do, however conciliatory, would reduce Soviet hostility, Kennan claimed. The nation should therefore accept this hostility as a fact of life and either resist Russian aggression firmly wherever it appeared or wait for time to bring about some change in Soviet policy.

Kennan's second alternative seemed both irresponsible and dangerous, whereas "getting tough with Russia" would find wide popular support. According to polls, a substantial majority considered American policy "too soft." During 1946 the Truman administration gradually adopted a tougher stance. The decisive policy shift came early in 1947 as a result of a crisis in Greece. Local Greek communists, waging a guerrilla war against the monarchy, were receiving aid from communist Yugoslavia and Bulgaria. Great Britain was assisting the monarchists but could no longer afford this drain on its resources. In February 1947 the British informed President Truman that they would have to cut off further aid to Greece.

The news came as a shock to American policy makers because the British predicament forced them to confront the fact that their European allies had not been able to rebuild their war-weakened economies. Russia's "Iron Curtain" (a phrase invented by Winston Churchill) seemed about to ring down on another nation. That the Greek government was reactionary appeared to them less im-

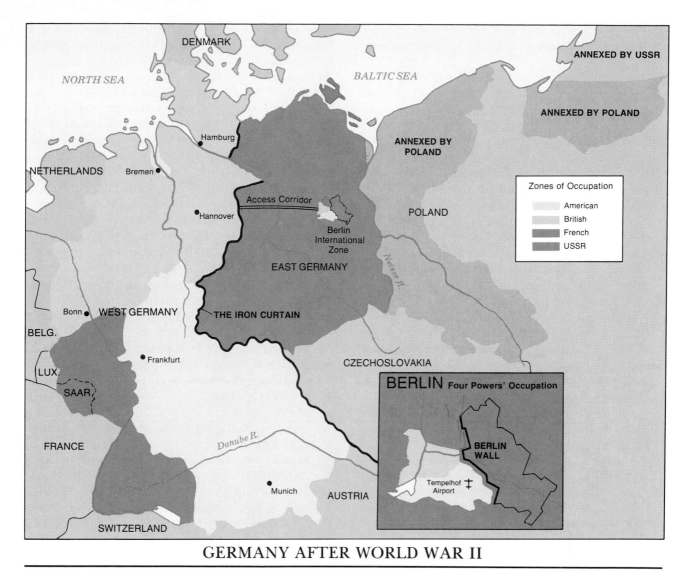

GERMANY AFTER WORLD WAR II

West Germany was created out of the merged French, British, and U.S. zones in 1947, as was West Berlin. The Russian zone became East Germany. The Berlin Wall was built later, in 1961, to keep an estimated 700 people a day from fleeing from East to West Germany.

portant than that it was threatened by communist forces. Truman therefore asked Congress to approve what became known as the Truman Doctrine. If Greece or Turkey fell to the communists, he said, all the Middle East might be lost. To prevent this "unspeakable tragedy," he asked for $400 million for military and economic aid for Greece and Turkey. "It must be the policy of the United States to support free peoples who are resisting attempted

subjugation by armed minorities or by outside pressures," he said.

By exaggerating the consequences of inaction and by justifying his request on ideological grounds, Truman attained his objective. But by not limiting his request to the specific problem posed by the situation in Greece, Truman caused considerable concern in many countries. And once official sanction was given to the communism-versus-democracy approach to foreign relations, foreign policy began to dominate domestic policy and to become more rigid.

The communist threat loomed large. With western Europe, in the words of Winston Churchill (the great phrasemaker of the era), "a rubble-heap, a charnel house, a breeding-ground of pestilence and hate," the entire continent seemed in danger of falling into communist hands without the Soviet Union raising a finger to speed the process. For humane reasons as well as for political advantage, the United States felt obliged to help these nations regain some measure of economic stability.

How might this be done? George Kennan provided an answer in an anonymous article in the July 1947 issue of *Foreign Affairs,* "The Sources of Soviet Conduct." Russian diplomacy, he wrote, moves inexorably along a prescribed path, "like a persistent toy automobile wound up and headed in a given direction, stopping only when it meets with some unmoveable force." A policy of "longterm, patient but firm and vigilant containment" based on the "application of counter-force" was the best means of dealing with Soviet pressures. The Cold War might be "a duel of infinite duration," Kennan admitted. It could be won if, without bluster, America maintained its own strength and convinced the communists that it would resist aggression firmly in any quarter of the globe.

The Marshall Plan

Although he approved its purpose, Kennan disagreed with the psychology of the Truman Doctrine, which seemed to him essentially defensive as well as vulnerable to criticism by anti-imperialists. He proposed a broad program to finance European economic recovery, the aid to be offered even to Russia if the Soviets would contribute some of their own resources to the cause. The Europeans themselves should work out the details, America providing the money, materials, and technical advice.

George C. Marshall, army chief of staff during World War II and now secretary of state, formally suggested this program, which became known as the Marshall Plan, in a Harvard commencement speech on June 5, 1947. "Hunger, poverty, desperation, and chaos" were the real enemies of freedom and democracy, Marshall said. The need was to restore "the confidence of the European people in the economic future of their own countries. . . . The program should be a joint one, agreed to by a number, if not all European nations."

The European powers seized eagerly upon Marshall's suggestion. They set up the 16-nation Committee for European Economic Cooperation, which soon submitted plans calling for up to $22.4 billion in American aid. After protracted debate, much influenced by a communist coup in Czechoslovakia in February 1948, which drew still another country behind the Iron Curtain, Congress appropriated over $13 billion for the program. Results exceeded all expectations. By 1951 western Europe was booming.

Whether the policy makers realized it or not, containment and the Marshall Plan were America's response to the power vacuum created in Europe by the debilitating effects of the war. Just as the Soviet Union extended its influence over the eastern half of the continent, the United States extended its influence in the west. Both powers were driven by insecurity—worry that the other was seeking world domination. A more accurate description of the situation would note that ignorance more than insecurity explains their worries.

In any case, the Marshall Plan formed the basis for western European economic recovery and political cooperation. In March 1948 Great Britain, France, Belgium, the Netherlands, and Luxembourg signed an alliance aimed at social, cultural, and economic collaboration. The western nations abandoned their understandable but counterproductive policy of crushing Germany economically. They instituted currency reforms in their zones and announced plans for creating a single West German republic with a large degree of autonomy.

These decisions further alarmed the Russians. In June they retaliated by closing off surface access to Berlin from the west. For a time it seemed that the Allies must either fight their way into the city or abandon it to the communists. Unwilling to adopt either alternative, Truman decided to fly supplies through the air corridors leading to the capital from Frankfurt, Hanover, and Hamburg. American C-47 and C-54 transports shuttled back and forth in weather fair and foul, carrying enough food, fuel, and other goods necessary to maintain more than 2 million West Berliners. The Berlin Airlift put the

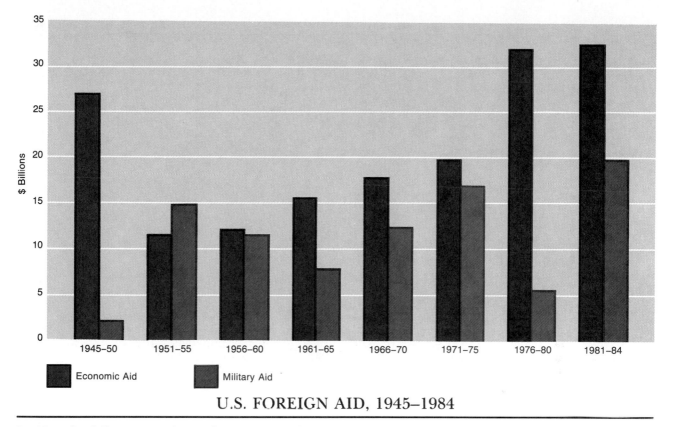

U.S. FOREIGN AID, 1945–1984

In 1945 the dollar was worth over four times its value in 1984, so in unin-flated dollars U.S. foreign aid has lessened over the years, especially during the decade 1971–1980. Even so, the total amount of U.S. foreign assistance from 1945 to 1984 was more than $280 billion.

Soviets in an uncomfortable position; if they were determined to keep supplies from West Berlin, they would have to begin the fighting. They were not prepared to do so. In May 1949 they lifted the blockade.

Containment, some of its advocates argued, required the development of a powerful military force. In May 1948 Republican Senator Arthur H. Vandenberg of Michigan, a prewar leader of the isolationists who had been converted to internationalism largely by President Roosevelt's solicitous attention to his views, introduced a resolution stating the "determination" of the United States "to exercise the right of individual or collective self-defense . . . should any armed attack occur affecting its national security." The Senate approved this resolution by a vote of 64 to 4, proof that iso-lationism had ceased to be an important force in American politics.

Dealing with Japan and China

Containment worked well in Europe, at least in the short run; in the Far East, where the United States lacked powerful allies, it was both more expensive and less effective. V-J Day found the Far East a shambles. Much of Japan was a smoking ruin. In China chaos reigned; nationalists under Chiang Kai-shek dominated the south, communists under Mao Tse-tung controlled the northern countryside, and Japanese troops still held most northern cities.

President Truman acted decisively and effectively with regard to Japan, unsurely and with un-

American cargo plane flying in supplies to West Berlin, after Soviet authorities in the surrounding East Germany closed off road and rail access to the city. The airlift remained in operation for nearly a year until the blockade was lifted in May 1949.

fortunate results where China was concerned. Even before the Japanese surrendered, he had decided not to allow the Soviet Union any significant role in the occupation of Japan. The four-power Allied Control Council was established, but American troops commanded by General MacArthur governed the country.

MacArthur displayed exactly the proper combination of imperiousness, tact, and intelligence needed to accomplish his purposes. The Japanese, revealing the same remarkable adaptability that had made possible their swift westernization in the second half of the 19th century, accepted political and social changes that involved universal suffrage and parliamentary government, the encouragement of labor unions, the breakup of large estates and big industrial combines, and the de-emphasis of the importance of the emperor. Japan lost its far-flung island empire and all claim to Korea and the Chinese mainland. Japan emerged economically strong, politically stable, and firmly allied with the United States.

The difficulties in China were probably insurmountable. Few Americans appreciated the latent power of the Chinese communists. When the war ended, Truman tried to bring Chiang's nationalists and Mao's communists together. He sent General Marshall to China to seek a settlement, but neither Chiang nor Mao would make significant concessions. Mao was convinced—correctly, as time soon proved—that he could win all of China by force, while Chiang, presiding over a corrupt and incompetent regime, grossly exaggerated his popularity among the Chinese people. In January 1947 Truman recalled Marshall and named him secretary of state. Soon thereafter civil war erupted in China.

The Election of 1948

In the spring of 1948 President Truman's fortunes were at low ebb. Public opinion polls suggested that a majority of the people considered him incompetent or worse. The Republicans seemed sure to win the 1948 presidential election, especially if Truman was the Democratic candidate. Governor Dewey, who again won the Republican nomination, ran confidently, even complacently, certain that he would carry the country with ease.

Truman's position seemed hopeless because he had alienated both southern conservatives and northern liberals. The southerners were particularly distressed because in 1946 the president had established the Committee on Civil Rights, which had recommended antilynching and anti-poll-tax legislation and the creation of a permanent Fair Employment Practices Commission. When, despite the objections of administration delegates, the Democratic convention adopted a strong civil rights plank, the southern delegates walked out. Southern conservatives then founded the States' Rights ('Dixiecrat') party and nominated J. Strom Thurmond of South Carolina for president.

As for the liberals, in 1947 a group of them had founded Americans for Democratic Action (ADA) and sought an alternative candidate for the 1948 election. A faction led by former vice-president Henry A. Wallace, which believed Truman's containment policy a threat to world peace, organized a new Progressive party and nominated Wallace. Most members of ADA, however, thought Wallace too pro-Soviet; in the end the organization supported Truman. Yet with two minor candidates sure to cut into the Democratic vote, the president's chances seemed minuscule.

Promising to "give 'em hell," Truman launched an aggressive "whistle-stop" campaign. Traveling by rail,* he made several hundred informal but hard-hitting speeches. He excoriated the "do-nothing" Republican Congress, which had rejected his program and passed the Taft-Hartley Act, and he warned labor, farmers, and consumers that if Dewey won, Republican "gluttons of privilege" would do away with all the gains of the New Deal years.

Millions were moved by his arguments and by his courageous fight against great odds. The success of the Berlin Airlift during the presidential campaign helped him considerably, as did disaffection among normally Republican middle western farmers. The Progressive party fell increasingly into the hands of communist sympathizers, driving away many liberals who might otherwise have supported Wallace. Dewey's smug, lackluster campaign failed to attract independents. The president was thus able to reinvigorate the New Deal coalition, and he won an amazing upset victory on election day. He col-

---

* The term *whistle stop* referred to rural stations where trains stopped only on signal.

In 1948 the strongly Republican Chicago Daily Tribune *guessed its post-election editions before all the returns were in. For Truman, it was the perfect climax to his hard-won victory.*

lected 24.1 million votes to Dewey's 21.9 million, the two minor candidates being held to about 2.3 million. In the electoral college his margin was a thumping 303 to 189. In his speech conceding defeat, Dewey, a man not noted for wit, remarked ruefully: "Thought I heard the voice of the people. Must have been some other noise."

Truman's victory gave the ADA considerable influence over what the president called his Fair Deal program. ADA leaders took a middle-of-the-road approach, well described in a book by Arthur M. Schlesinger, Jr., *The Vital Center* (1949), which left room for individualism and social welfare, government regulation of the economy, and the encouragement of private enterprise. The approach fitted well with Cold War conditions, which favored both massive military output and continued expansion of the supply of civilian goods. Economic growth would solve all problems, social as well as material. Through growth, the poor could be helped without taking from the rich. The way to check inflation, for example, was not by freezing prices, profits, or wages but by expanding production.

However, relatively little of Truman's Fair Deal was enacted into law. Congress approved a federal housing program and measures increasing the minimum wage and social security benefits, but these were merely extensions of New Deal legislation.

Containing Communism Abroad

During Truman's second term the confrontation between the United States and the Soviet Union, and more broadly between what was seen as "democracy" and "communism," dominated the headlines and occupied a major part of the attention of the president and most other government officials. To strengthen ties with the European democracies, in April 1949 the North Atlantic Treaty was signed in Washington. The United States, Great Britain, France, Italy, Belgium, the Netherlands, Luxembourg, Denmark, Norway, Portugal, Iceland, and Canada* agreed "that an armed attack against one or more of them in Europe or North America shall be considered an attack against them all" and that in the event of such an attack, each would take

---

* In 1952 Greece and Turkey joined the alliance, and in 1954 West Germany was admitted.

"individually and in concert with the other Parties, such action as it deems necessary, including the use of armed force." No more entangling alliance could be imagined, yet the Senate ratified this treaty by a vote of 82 to 13. The pact established the North Atlantic Treaty Organization (NATO). Disturbed by the news, released in September 1949, that the Soviet Union had produced an atomic bomb, Congress appropriated $1.5 billion to arm NATO. In 1951 General Eisenhower was recalled to active duty and placed in command of NATO forces.

The success of containment was not without its price; every move evoked a Russian response. The Marshall Plan led to the seizure of Czechoslovakia; the buildup of West Germany led to the Berlin blockade; the creation of NATO led to the eastern European military alliance known as the Warsaw Pact. Both sides contributed by their actions and their continuing suspicions to the heightening of Cold War tensions.

In Asia the effort to contain communism exploded into war. By the end of 1949 Mao Tse-tung's communist armies had administered a crushing defeat to the nationalists. The remnants of Chiang Kai-shek's forces fled to the island of Formosa, now called Taiwan. The "loss" of China to communism strengthened right-wing opponents of internationalism in the Republican party. They and other critics charged that Truman had not backed the nationalists strongly enough and that he had stupidly underestimated Mao's dedication to the cause of world revolution. Despite superficial plausibility, neither charge made much sense. American opinion would not have supported military intervention, and such intervention would unquestionably have alienated the Chinese people. That any American action could have changed the outcome in China is unlikely. The United States probably gave the nationalists too much aid rather than too little.

The attacks of his critics aroused Truman's combativeness and led him into serious miscalculations elsewhere in Asia. After the war the province of Korea was taken from Japan and divided at 38° north latitude into the Democratic People's Republic, backed by the Soviet Union, and the Republic of Korea, backed by the United States and the UN. Both powers withdrew their troops from the peninsula, the Russians leaving behind a well-armed local force while the Republic of Korea's army was small and ill trained.

Hot War in Korea

American strategists, while seeking to "contain" communism in the Far East, had decided that military involvement on the Asiatic mainland was impracticable. America's first line of defense was to be its island bases in Japan, Taiwan, and the Philippines. In January 1950 Dean Acheson, who had succeeded Marshall as secretary of state, deliberately excluded Korea from what he described as the "defensive perimeter" of the United States in Asia. "We cannot scatter our shots equally all over the world," Acheson explained to the Senate Foreign Relations Committee. It was up to the South Koreans, backed by the UN, to protect themselves. This the Koreans were unable to do; when North Korean armored divisions struck suddenly across the 38th parallel in June 1950, they quickly routed the defenders.

At this point President Truman exhibited his finest qualities: decisiveness and courage. Whatever the actual importance of South Korea to the United States, if the blatant North Korean attack were not resisted, more serious aggressions seemed sure to follow. With the backing of the UN Security Council (but without asking Congress to declare war), he sent American planes into battle.* Ground troops soon followed.

Nominally the Korean War was a struggle between the invaders and the United Nations. General MacArthur, placed in command, flew the blue UN flag over his headquarters, and 16 nations supplied troops for his army. However, more than 90 percent of the forces employed were American. At first the North Koreans pushed them back rapidly, but by the beginning of September a front was stabilized around the port of Pusan, at the southern tip of Korea. Then MacArthur executed a brilliant amphibious flanking maneuver, striking at the west coast city of Inchon, about 50 miles south of the 38th parallel. Outflanked, the North Koreans retreated in disorder. By October the battlefront had moved north of the old boundary.

General MacArthur now proposed the conquest of North Korea, the bombing of "privileged sanctuaries" on the Chinese side of the Korean border,

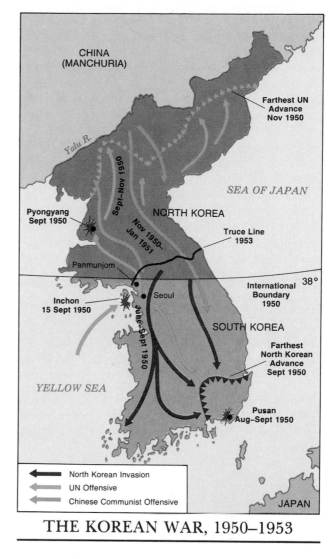

THE KOREAN WAR, 1950–1953

and the redeployment of Chinese Nationalist troops on the mainland. Less sanguine military officials balked at taking on China but urged occupying North Korea to protect the future security of the south. Most of Truman's civilian advisers, led by George Kennan, opposed any advance beyond the 38th parallel, fearing intervention not only by the Red Chinese but by the Russians as well. "When we start walking inland from the tip of Korea, we have about a 10,000 mile walk if we keep going," Kennan pointed out. "We are going to have to stop somewhere."

Faced with conflicting advice, Truman authorized MacArthur to advance as far as the Yalu River,

---

* Russia, which could have vetoed this action, was at the moment boycotting the Security Council because the UN had refused to give the Mao Tse-tung regime China's seat on that body.

the boundary between North Korea and China, but to avoid war with China or the Soviet Union at all cost. It was a momentous and unfortunate decision, an example of how power, once unleashed, so often gets out of hand. As the advance progressed, ominous rumblings came from north of the Yalu. Foreign Minister Chou En-lai warned that the Chinese would not "supinely tolerate seeing their neighbors being savagely invaded by imperialists." Chinese "volunteers" began to turn up among the captives taken by UN units.

Alarmed, Truman flew to Wake Island, in the Pacific, to confer with MacArthur, but the general assured him that the Chinese would not dare to intervene. If they did, MacArthur added, his army would crush them easily; the war would be over by Christmas.

Seldom has a general miscalculated so badly. On November 26 a total of 33 Chinese divisions suddenly smashed through the center of MacArthur's line. Overnight a triumphant advance became a disorganized retreat. MacArthur now spoke of the "bottomless well of Chinese manpower" and justified his earlier confidence by claiming, not without reason, that he was fighting "an entirely new war."

The UN army rallied south of the 38th parallel, and by the spring of 1951 the front had been stabilized. MacArthur then urged that he be permitted to bomb Chinese installations north of the Yalu. He also suggested a naval blockade of the coast of China and the use of Chinese Nationalist troops in Korea. When Truman rejected these proposals on the grounds that they would lead to a third world war, MacArthur, who tended to ignore the larger polit-

Photographer David Douglas Duncan was with the First Marine Division in Korea when it was virtually isolated by the sudden Red Chinese offensive in November 1950. Conducting in frigid weather what the military historian S. L. A. Marshall called "the greatest fighting withdrawal of modern history," the marines broke out to safety.

ical aspects of the conflict, attempted to rouse Congress and the public against the president by criticizing administration policy openly. Truman ordered him to be silent, and when the general persisted, the president removed him from command.

At first the Korean "police action" had been popular in the United States, but as the months passed and the casualties mounted, many citizens became disillusioned and angry. The war had brought into the open a basic political (or better, psychological) disadvantage of the containment policy: Its object was not victory but balance; it involved apparently unending tension without the satisfying release of an action completed. To Americans accustomed to triumph and fond of oversimplifying complex questions, containment seemed, as its costs in blood and dollars mounted, a monumentally frustrating policy.

But in time the fundamental correctness of Truman's policy and his decision to remove MacArthur became apparent. Military men backed the president almost unanimously. General Omar N. Bradley, chairman of the Joint Chiefs of Staff, said that a showdown with the Chinese "would involve us in the wrong war, at the wrong place, at the wrong time and with the wrong enemy." In June 1951 the communists agreed to discuss an armistice in Korea, and though the negotiations dragged on, with interruptions, for two years while thousands more died along the static battlefront, both MacArthur and talk of bombing China subsided.

The Communist Issue at Home

The frustrating Korean War highlighted the paradox that at the pinnacle of its power, the influence of the United States in world affairs was declining. Its monopoly of nuclear weapons had been lost. China had passed into the communist orbit. Elsewhere in Asia and throughout Africa, new nations, formerly colonial possessions of the western powers, were adopting a neutralist position in the Cold War. Despite the billions poured into armaments and foreign aid, the safety and even the survival of the country seemed far from assured.

Internal as well as external dangers loomed. Alarming examples of communist espionage in Canada, in Great Britain, and in the United States itself convinced many citizens that clever conspirators were everywhere at work undermining American security. Both the Republicans and conservative Democratic critics of Truman's domestic policies were charging that he was "soft" on communists.

There were never more than 100,000 communists in the United States, and party membership plummeted after the start of the Cold War. However, the possibility that a handful of spies could do enormous damage fueled a kind of panic that could be used for partisan purposes. In 1947, hoping to defuse the communists-in-government issue by being more zealous in pursuit of spies than his critics, Truman established the Loyalty Review Board to check up on government employees. The program made even sympathy for a long list of vaguely defined "totalitarian" or "subversive" organizations grounds for dismissal. Persons so charged were not allowed to cross-examine their accusers. During the following ten years about 2,700 government workers were discharged, only a relative handful of them for legitimate reasons. A much larger number resigned.

In 1948 Whittaker Chambers, an editor of *Time* who had formerly been a communist, charged that Alger Hiss, president of the Carnegie Endowment for International Peace and a former State Department official, had been a communist in the 1930s. Hiss denied the charge and sued Chambers for libel. Chambers then produced microfilms purporting to show that Hiss had copied classified documents for dispatch to Moscow. Hiss could not be indicted for espionage because of the statute of limitations; instead he was charged with perjury. His first trial resulted in a hung jury, his second, ending in January 1950, in conviction and a five-year jail term.

The Hiss case fed the fears of those who believed in the existence of a powerful communist underground in the United States. The disclosure in February 1950 that a respected British scientist, Klaus Fuchs, had betrayed atomic secrets to the Russians heightened these fears, as did the arrest and conviction of his American associate, Harry Gold, and two other American traitors, Julius and Ethel Rosenberg, on the same charge.

Although they were obviously not major spies and the information they revealed was not impor-

The lean, well-dressed diplomat Alger Hiss (right) being asked to identify the frumpy, ex-communist spy Whittaker Chambers (left) by the chief counsel of the House Un-American Activities Committee hearings in 1948. Hiss denied knowing Chambers; Chambers insisted that he had been a colleague in treason.

tant, the Rosenbergs were executed, to the consternation of many liberals in the United States and elsewhere. However, information gathered by other spies had speeded the Soviet development of nuclear weapons. This fact encouraged some Republicans to press the communists-in-government issue hard.

McCarthyism

On February 9, 1950, an obscure senator, Joseph R. McCarthy of Wisconsin, casually introduced this theme in a speech before the Women's Republican Club of Wheeling, West Virginia: "The reason we find ourselves in a position of impotency," he stated, "is not because our only powerful potential enemy has sent men to invade our shores, but rather because of the traitorous actions of those who have been treated so well by this nation." The State Department, he added, was "infested" with communists. "I have here in my hand a list of 205—a list of names that were known to the Secretary of State as

being members of the Communist Party and who nevertheless are still working and shaping . . . policy."*

McCarthy had no shred of evidence to back up these statements, as a Senate committee headed by the conservative Democrat Millard Tydings of Maryland soon demonstrated. He never exposed a single spy or secret American communist. One reporter quipped that McCarthy could not tell Karl Marx from Groucho. But thousands of people were too eager to believe him to listen to reason. Within a few weeks he was the most talked-about person in Congress. Inhibited neither by scruples nor by logic, he lashed out in every direction, attacking international experts like Professor Owen Lattimore of Johns Hopkins and diplomats such as John S. Service and John Carter Vincent, who were already under attack for having courageously pointed out

---

* McCarthy was speaking from rough notes, and no one made an accurate record of his words. The exact number mentioned has long been in dispute. On other occasions he said there were 57 and 81 "card-carrying communists" in the State Department.

the deficiencies of the Chiang Kai-shek regime during the Chinese civil war.

When McCarthy's victims indignantly denied his charges, he distracted the public with still more sensational accusations directed at other innocents. Even General Marshall, whose patriotism was beyond question, was subject to McCarthy's abuse. The general, he said, was "steeped in falsehood," part of a "conspiracy so immense and an infamy so black as to dwarf any previous venture in the history of man."

McCarthy was totally unscrupulous. The "big lie" was his most effective weapon; the enormity of his charges and the status of his targets convinced thousands that there must be *some* truth to what he was saying. Nevertheless, his crude tactics would have failed if the public had not been so worried about communism. The worries were caused by the reality of Soviet military power, the attack on Korea, the loss of the nuclear monopoly, and the stories about spies. Having been plunged again into the tensions of international conflicts so soon after World War II, when they had expected to relax and enjoy life, heightened the concern of many citizens and added an irrational element to their fears.

In the 1950 election campaign McCarthy "invaded" Maryland to campaign against Senator Tydings, who was running for reelection. Tydings was defeated, and two years later William Benton of Connecticut, who had introduced a resolution calling for McCarthy's expulsion from the Senate, also failed reelection after McCarthy campaigned against him. Both would probably have lost in any case for reasons unrelated to the communism issue, but thereafter fainthearted congressmen who detested McCarthy dared not incur his wrath. Large numbers of Republicans found the temptation to take advantage of his voter appeal irresistible.

Dwight D. Eisenhower

As the 1952 presidential election approached, Truman's popularity was again at a low ebb. Senator McCarthy attacked him relentlessly for his handling of the Korean conflict and his "mistreatment" of General MacArthur. In choosing their candidate, the Republicans passed over the twice-defeated Dewey and their most prominent leader, Senator Robert A. Taft of Ohio, an outspoken conservative, and nominated General Dwight D. Eisenhower.

Eisenhower's popularity did not grow merely out of his achievements in World War II. Although a West Pointer (class of 1915), he struck most persons as anything but warlike. After the bristly, combative Truman, his genial tolerance and evident desire to avoid controversy proved widely appealing. Eisenhower's reluctance to seek political office reminded the country of George Washington, while his seeming ignorance of current political issues was no more a handicap to his campaign than the similar ignorance of Jackson and Grant in their times. People "liked Ike" because of his personality—he radiated warmth and sincerity—and because his management of the Allied armies promised that he would be equally competent as head of the complex federal government. His promise during the campaign to go to Korea if elected to try to bring the war to an end was a political masterstroke.

The Democrats nominated Governor Adlai E. Stevenson of Illinois, whose grandfather had been vice-president under Grover Cleveland. Stevenson's unpretentiousness was appealing, and his witty, urbane speeches captivated intellectuals. In retrospect, however, it is clear that he had not the remotest chance of defeating the popular Eisenhower. Disillusionment with the Korean War and a widespread belief that the Democrats had been too long in power were added handicaps. His foes turned his strongest assets against him, denouncing his humor as frivolity, characterizing his appreciation of the complexities of life as self-doubt, and tagging his intellectual followers "eggheads," an appellation that effectively caricatured the balding, slope-shouldered, somewhat endomorphic candidate. "The eggheads are for Stevenson," one Republican pointed out, "but how many eggheads are there?" There were far too few to carry the country, as the election revealed. The result was a Republican landslide: Eisenhower received almost 34 million votes to Stevenson's 27 million, and in the electoral college his margin was 442 to 89.

In office, Eisenhower was the antithesis of Truman. The Republicans had charged the Democratic administration with being wasteful and extravagant. Eisenhower planned to run his administration on sound business principles and to eschew increases in the activities of the federal government. He spoke scornfully of "creeping socialism," called for more local control of government affairs, and promised to reduce federal spending in order to balance the budget and cut taxes. He believed that by battling with Congress and pressure groups over the details of legislation, his immediate predecessors had sacrificed part of their status as chief representative of the American people. Like Washington, he tried to avoid being caught up in narrow partisan conflicts. Like Washington, he was not always able to do so.

Having successfully managed the complexities of military administration, Eisenhower used the same kind of staff system as president. He gave his Cabinet officers more responsibility than many other presidents because he did not like to devote time and energy to administrative routine. This did not mean that he was lazy or politically naive. He knew that if he left too many small decisions to others, they would soon be controlling, if not actually making, the large decisions as well.

Although conservative, Eisenhower was neither a reactionary nor a fool. He hoped to balance the federal budget and lower taxes, but he was unwilling to do away with existing social and economic legislation or to cut back on military expenditures. Some economists claimed that he reacted too slowly in dealing with business recessions and that he showed insufficient concern for speeding the rate of national economic growth. Yet he adopted an almost Keynesian approach to economic problems; that is, he tried to check downturns in the business cycle by stimulating the economy. In his memoir *Mandate for Change* (1963) he wrote of resorting to "preventative action to arrest the downturn (of 1954) before it might become severe" and of being ready to use "any and all weapons in the federal arsenal, including changes in monetary and credit policy, modifications of the tax structure, and a speed-up in the construction of . . . public works" to accomplish this end.

Eisenhower approved the extension of social security to an additional 10 million persons; created the Department of Health, Education, and Welfare and the St. Lawrence Seaway project; and in 1955 came out for federal support of schools and a highway construction act that eventually produced a 40,000-mile network of superhighways covering every state in the Union.

Eisenhower's somewhat doctrinaire belief in decentralization and private enterprise reduced the effectiveness of his social welfare measures, but on balance, he proved to be an excellent politician. He knew how to be flexible without compromising his basic values. His "conservatism" became first "dynamic conservatism" and then "progressive moderation." He summarized his attitude by saying that he was liberal in dealing with individuals but conservative "when talking about . . . the individual's pocketbook." He hoped to strengthen the moderate faction of his party, but despite his extraordinary popularity, he did not succeed in persuading many right-wing Republicans that this was a good idea.

The Eisenhower-Dulles Foreign Policy

After the 1952 election Eisenhower kept his pledge to go to Korea. His trip produced no immediate result, but the truce talks, suspended before the election, were resumed. In July 1953, perhaps influenced by a hint that the United States might use "tactical" atomic bombs in Korea, the communists agreed to an armistice. Korea remained divided. Containment had proved extremely expensive; the United States had suffered more that 135,000 casualties, including 33,000 dead. Yet aggression had been confronted and fought to a standstill.

The American people, troubled and uncertain, counted on Eisenhower to find a way to employ the nation's immense strength constructively. The new president shared the general feeling that a change of tactics in foreign affairs was needed. He counted on Congress and his secretary of state to solve the practical problems.

Given this attitude, his choice of John Foster Dulles as secretary of state seemed inspired. Dulles's experience in diplomacy dated to 1907, when he had served as secretary to the Chinese delegation at the Second Hague Conference.* Later he had a small place among the army of experts advising Wilson at the Versailles Conference. More recently he had been a representative of the United States in the UN General Assembly. "With my understanding of the intricate relationships between the peoples of the world and your sensitiveness to the

---

* The delegation was headed by Dulles's grandfather, John W. Foster, who had been secretary of state under Benjamin Harrison. An uncle, Robert Lansing, had been Woodrow Wilson's secretary of state during the First World War.

Dulles during a 1956 press conference at which he rejected suggestions by Russia and India that the United States suspend further hydrogen bomb tests. His stance and gesture project his "hard line" approach.

political considerations involved," he told Eisenhower, "we will make the most successful team in history."

Dulles combined amazing energy and strong moral convictions—"there is no way to solve the great perplexing international problems except by bringing to bear on them the force of Christianity," he insisted. His objectives were magnificent; his strategy was grandiose. Instead of waiting for the communist powers to make a move and then "containing" them, the United States should put more emphasis on nuclear bombs and less on conventional weapons. Such a "New Look" would prevent the United States from being caught up in "local" conflicts like the Korean war and both save money and inspire international respect. Potential enemies would know that "massive retaliation" would be the fate of any aggressor. With the communists im-

mobilized by this threat, positive measures aimed at "liberating" eastern Europe and "unleashing" Chiang Kai-shek against the Chinese mainland would follow. Dulles professed great faith in NATO, but he believed that if America's allies lacked the courage to follow its lead, the nation would have to undertake an "agonizing reappraisal" of its commitments to them.

Thus Dulles envisioned a policy broader, more economical, and more aggressive than Truman's. By concentrating on nuclear deterrents and avoiding "brushfire" wars in remote regions, the country could increase its security and dramatically reduce the cost of defense.

Despite his determination, energy, and high ideals, Dulles failed to make the United States a more effective force in world affairs. Most of Dulles's other schemes were quite unrealistic. "Unleashing" Chiang Kai-shek against the Chinese communists would have been like matching a Pekingese against a tiger. "Liberating" Russia's European satellites would have involved a third world war. When East German workers rioted in June 1953 and again when the Hungarians revolted in 1956, no help was forthcoming from America. Above all, massive retaliation made little sense when the Soviet Union possessed nuclear weapons as powerful as those of the United States. In November 1952 America had won the race to make a hydrogen bomb, but the Russians duplicated this feat the following August. Thereafter the only threat behind massive retaliation was the threat of human extinction. Actually, the awesome force of hydrogen bombs, the smallest of which dwarfed the bomb dropped on Hiroshima, provided both powers with a true deterrent. Willy nilly, nuclear power had established itself as a formidable force for world peace.

McCarthy Self-destructs

Dulles's saber-rattling tactics were badly timed as well as impractical. While he was planning to avert future Koreas, the Soviet Union was shifting its approach. Stalin died in March 1953, and after a period of internal conflict within the Kremlin, Nikita Khrushchev emerged as the new master of Russia. Despite his blunderbuss style, Khrushchev set out to obtain his objectives by indirection. He appealed to the antiwestern prejudices of countries just emerging from the yoke of colonialism, offering them economic aid and pointing to Soviet achievements in science and technology, such as the launching of *Sputnik,* the first satellite (1957), as proof that communism would soon "bury" the capitalist system without troubling to destroy it by force. The Soviet Union was the friend of all peace-loving nations, he insisted.

Khrushchev was a master hypocrite, yet he was a realist too. While Dulles, product of a system that made a virtue of compromise and tolerance, insisted that the world must choose between American good and Russian evil, Khrushchev, trained to believe in the incompatibility of communism and capitalism, began to talk of "peaceful coexistence."

Dulles failed to win the confidence of America's allies or even that of the State Department. Senator McCarthy moderated his attacks on the Department not a jot when it came under the control of his own party. In 1953 its overseas information program received his special attention. He denounced Voice of America broadcasters for quoting the works of "controversial" authors and sent Roy M. Cohn, youthful special counsel of his Committee on Governmental Operations, on a mission to Europe to ferret out subversives in the United States Information Service.

Dulles did not come to the defense of his people. Instead he seemed determined to out-McCarthy McCarthy in his zeal to get rid of "undesirables" of all sorts. He sanctioned the discharge of nearly 500 State Department employees, not one of whom was proved to have engaged in subversive activities. People were let go merely because they were suspected of being homosexuals, the argument being that they might be blackmailed into giving state secrets to the communists. By making such "concessions" to McCarthy, Dulles hoped to end attacks on the administration's foreign policy. The tactic failed; its only result was to undermine the morale of Foreign Service officers.

But McCarthy finally overreached himself. Early in 1954 he turned his guns on the army. After a series of charges and countercharges, he accused army officials of trying to blackmail his committee and announced a broad investigation. The resulting Army-McCarthy hearings, televised across the country, proved the senator's undoing. For weeks his dark scowl, his blind combativeness, and his disregard for every human value stood exposed for

Senator Joseph McCarthy conferring with his aide, Roy M. Cohn, during the 1954 televised hearings into alleged communist infiltration of the army. McCarthy's bullying tactics and evidence that he had tried to secure preferred treatment from the army for another aide cost him most of the popular support and political clout his outspoken anti-communism had earlier won him.

millions to see. When the hearings ended in June 1954 after some million words of testimony, his spell had been broken.

The Senate, with President Eisenhower quietly applying pressure behind the scene, at last moved to censure him in December 1954. This reproof completed the destruction of his influence. Although he continued to issue statements and wild charges, the country no longer listened. In 1957 he died of cirrhosis of the liver.

Asian Policy After Korea

While the final truce talks were taking place in Korea, new trouble was erupting far to the south in French Indochina. Since December 1946 nationalist rebels led by the communist Ho Chi Minh had been harassing the French in Vietnam, one of three puppet kingdoms (the others were Laos and Cambodia) fashioned by France in Indochina after the defeat of the Japanese in World War II. When Communist China recognized the rebels, who were known as the Vietminh, and began supplying them with arms, President Truman, applying the containment policy, countered with economic and military assistance to the French. When Eisenhower succeeded to the presidency, he continued and expanded this assistance.

Early in 1954 Ho Chi Minh's troops trapped and beseiged a French army in the remote stronghold of Dien Bien Phu. Facing the loss of 20,000 soldiers, France asked the United States to commit its air force to the battle. Eisenhower, after long deliberation, refused. Although the likelihood of communist control of Vietnam worried him, his desire to avoid any taint of imperialism was reinforced by his military judgment. The idea of using American air strikes, he believed, was "just silly." The communists were "secreted all around in the jungle. How are we, in a few air strikes, to defeat them?"

In May the French garrison at Dien Bien Phu surrendered, and in July, while the United States watched from the sidelines, France, Great Britain, Russia, and China signed an agreement at Geneva dividing Vietnam along the 17th parallel. France withdrew from the area. The northern sector became the Democratic Republic of Vietnam, controlled by Ho Chi Minh; the southern sector remained in the hands of the emperor, Bao Dai. An election to settle the future of all Vietnam was scheduled for 1956.

When it seemed likely that the communists would win that election, Ngo Dinh Diem, a conservative anticommunist, overthrew Bao Dai and became president of South Vietnam. The United States supplied his government liberally with aid. The planned election was never held, and Vietnam remained divided into two nations.

Dulles responded to the diplomatic setback in Vietnam by establishing the Southeast Asia Treaty Organization (SEATO) in September 1954, but only three Asian nations—the Philippine Republic, Thailand, and Pakistan—joined this alliance.* At the same time, the unleashed Chiang Kai-shek was engaging in a meaningless artillery duel with the Chinese communists from the tiny nationalist-held islands of Quemoy and Matsu, which lay in the shadow of the mainland. When it was suggested that the United States join in the fight, Eisenhower refused on the ground, sensible but inconsistent

---

* The other signatories were Great Britain, France, the United States, Australia, and New Zealand.

with Dulles's rhetoric, that intervention might set off an atomic war.

The Middle East Cauldron

Within a year the world teetered once again on the brink of war, this time in the Middle East. American policy in that region, aside from the ubiquitous problem of restraining Russian expansion, was influenced by the huge oil resources of Iran, Iraq, Kuwait, and Saudi Arabia—about 60 percent of the world's known reserves—and by the conflict between the new Jewish state of Israel (formerly the British mandate of Palestine) and its Arab neighbors. Although he tried to woo the Arabs, President Truman had consistently placed support for Israel before other considerations in the Middle East.

Angered by the creation of Israel, the surrounding Arab nations tried to destroy the country. (The Israeli question had the same impact on Arab emotions that the "bloody shirt" had had on Republicans after the Civil War.) Though badly outnumbered, the Israelis were better organized and better armed than the Arabs and drove them off with relative ease. With them departed nearly a million Palestinian Arabs, thereby creating a desperate refugee problem in nearby countries. Truman's support of Israel and the millions of dollars contributed to the new state by American Jews caused much Arab resentment of the United States.

Dulles and Eisenhower tried to redress the balance by de-emphasizing American support of Israel. In 1952 a revolution in Egypt had overthrown the dissolute King Farouk. Colonel Gamal Abdel Nasser emerged as the strongman of Egypt. The United States was prepared to lend Nasser money to build a huge dam on the Nile at Aswan. The dam was to be the key to an Egyptian irrigation program and a vast source of electric power. However, the Eisenhower administration would not sell Egypt arms. The communists would. For this reason Nasser drifted toward the communist orbit. In May 1956 he established diplomatic relations with Red China.

When Eisenhower then decided not to finance the Aswan Dam, Nasser responded by nationalizing the Suez Canal. This move galvanized the British and French. Influenced by Dulles's argument that Egypt could be made an ally by cajolery, the British had acceded in 1954 to Nasser's demand that they evacuate their military base at Suez. Now their traditional "lifeline" to the Orient was at Egypt's mercy. In conjunction with the French, and without consulting the United States, the British decided to take back the canal by force. The Israelis, alarmed by repeated Arab hit-and-run raids along their borders, also attacked Egypt.

Events moved swiftly. Israeli armored columns crushed the Egyptian army in the Sinai peninsula in a matter of days. France and Britain occupied Port Said, at the northern end of the canal. Nasser blocked the canal by sinking ships in the channel. In the UN the Soviet Union and the United States introduced resolutions calling for a cease-fire. Both were vetoed by Britain and France.

Then Khrushchev threatened to send "volunteers" to Egypt and launch atomic missiles against France and Great Britain if they did not withdraw. Eisenhower also demanded that the invaders pull out of Egypt. In London large crowds demonstrated against their own government. On November 6, only nine days after the first Israeli units invaded Egypt, British prime minister Anthony Eden, haggard and shaken, announced a cease-fire. Israel withdrew its troops. The crisis subsided as rapidly as it had arisen.

The United States had adhered to its principles and won a measure of respect in the Arab countries. But at what cost! Its major allies had been humiliated. Their ill-timed attack had enabled Russia to recover much of the prestige lost as a result of its brutal suppression of a Hungarian revolt which had broken out a week before the Suez fiasco. Eden and French premier Guy Mollet were claiming with considerable plausibility that Dulles's futile attempt to win Arab friendship without abandoning Israel had placed them in a dilemma and that the secretary had behaved dishonorably or at least disingenuously in handling the Egyptian problem.

The bad feeling within the western alliance soon passed. When Russia seemed likely to profit from its "defense" of Egypt in the crisis, the president in January 1957 announced the Eisenhower Doctrine, which stated that the United States was "prepared to use armed force" anywhere in the Middle East against "aggression from any country controlled by international communism." In practice, the Eisenhower Doctrine amounted to little more than a restatement of the containment policy.

Eisenhower and the Russians

In Europe the Eisenhower and Dulles policies differed little from those of Truman. When Eisenhower announced his plan to rely more heavily on nuclear deterrents, the Europeans drew back in alarm, believing that in any atomic showdown they were sure to be destroyed. Khrushchev's talk of peaceful coexistence found receptive ears, especially in France.

Eisenhower therefore yielded to European pressures for a diplomatic summit conference with the Russians. In July 1955 Eisenhower, Prime Minister Eden, and a new French premier, Edgar Faure, had met at Geneva with Khrushchev and his then coleader, Nikolai Bulganin, to discuss disarmament and the reunification of West and East Germany. The meeting produced no specific agreement, but with the Russians beaming cheerfully for the cameramen and talking of peaceful coexistence and with Eisenhower pouring martinis and projecting his famous charm, observers noted a softening of tensions that was dubbed the "spirit of Geneva."

In 1956 Eisenhower was reelected, defeating Adlai Stevenson even more decisively than he had in 1952. Despite their evident satisfaction with their leader, however, the mood of the American people was sober. Hopes of pushing back the Soviet Union with clever stratagems and moral fervor were fading. America's first successful earth satellite, launched in January 1958, brought cold comfort, for it was much smaller than the earth-circling Russian *Sputniks*.

In 1957 Dulles underwent surgery for abdominal cancer, and in April 1959 he had to resign. The next month he was dead. Eisenhower had never avoided making decisions in the foreign policy area, but now he personally took over much of the actual conduct of diplomacy. The key to his approach was restraint; he exercised commendable caution in every crisis. Like U. S. Grant, he was a soldier who hated war. From Korea through the crises over Indochina, Hungary, and Suez, he avoided risky new commitments. His behavior, like his temperament, contrasted sharply with that of the aggressive, oratorically perfervid Dulles.

Amid the tension that followed the Suez crisis, the belief persisted in many quarters that the spirit of Geneva could be revived if only a new summit meeting could be arranged. World opinion was insistent that the great powers stop making and testing nuclear weapons, for every test explosion was contaminating the atmosphere with radioactive debris that threatened the future of all life. Unresolved controversies, especially the argument over divided Germany, might erupt at any moment into a globe-shattering war.

Neither the United States nor the Soviet Union dared ignore these dangers; each therefore adopted a more accommodating attitude. In the summer of 1959 Vice-President Richard M. Nixon visited the Soviet Union and his opposite number, Vice Premier Anastas I. Mikoyan, toured the United States. Although Nixon's visit was marred by a heated argument with Khrushchev about the virtues of their respective systems, conducted before a gaping crowd in the kitchen of a model American home that had been set up at a Moscow fair, the results of the exchanges raised hopes that a summit conference would prove profitable.

In September, Khrushchev came to America. His cross-country tour had its full share of comic contretemps—when denied permission to visit Disneyland because authorities feared they could not protect him properly on the grounds, the heavy-handed Khrushchev accused the United States, only half humorously, of concealing rocket launching pads there. But the general effect of his visit seemed salutary. At the end of his stay, he and President Eisenhower agreed to convene a new four-power summit conference.

The meeting never took place. On May 1, 1960, high over Sverdlovsk, an industrial center deep in the Soviet Union, an American U-2 reconnaissance plane was shot down by antiaircraft fire. The pilot of the plane, Francis Gary Powers, survived the crash, and he confessed to being a spy. His cameras contained aerial photographs of Soviet military installations. When Eisenhower assumed full responsibility for the mission, Khrushchev accused the United States of "piratical" and "cowardly" acts of aggression. The summit conference was canceled.

Latin America Aroused

Events in Latin America compounded Eisenhower's difficulties. During World War II the United States, needing Latin American raw materials, had sup-

Vice-President Richard M. Nixon and Soviet leader Nikita Khrushchev engaged in their "kitchen debate" over the future of capitalism at a Moscow trade fair in 1959. Though this encounter did little to advance U.S.-Soviet relations, it established Nixon's credentials as a tough negotiator.

plied its southern neighbors liberally with economic aid. In the period following victory, an era of amity and prosperity seemed assured. A hemispheric mutual defense pact was signed at Rio de Janeiro in September 1947, and the following year the Organization of American States came into being. In the OAS, decisions were reached by a two-thirds vote; the United States had neither a veto nor any special position.

But as the Cold War progressed, the United States neglected Latin American questions. Economic problems plagued the region, and in most nations reactionary governments reigned. Radical Latin Americans accused the United States of supporting cliques of wealthy tyrants, while conservatives blamed lack of sufficient American economic aid for the plight of the poor.

Eisenhower, eager to improve relations, stepped up economic assistance. Resistance to communism nonetheless continued to receive first priority. In 1954 the government of Jacobo Arbenz Guzman in Guatemala began to import Soviet weapons. The United States promptly dispatched arms to the neighboring state of Honduras. Within a month an army led by an exiled Guatemalan officer marched into the country from Honduras and overthrew Arbenz. Elsewhere in Latin America, Eisenhower, as Truman had before him, continued to support regimes that were kept in power by the local military.

The depth of Latin American resentment of the United States became clear in the spring of 1958, when Vice-President Nixon made what was supposed to be a goodwill tour of South America. Everywhere he was met with hostility. In Lima, Peru, he was mobbed; in Caracas, Venezuela, students kicked his shiny Cadillac and pelted him with eggs and stones. He had to abandon the remainder of his trip. For the first time the American people gained some inkling of Latin American feelings and the social and economic troubles that lay behind them.

That there was no easy solution to Latin American problems was demonstrated by events in Cuba. In 1959 a revolutionary movement headed by Fidel Castro overthrew Fulgencio Batista, one of the most noxious of the Latin American dictators. Eisenhower recognized the Castro government at once, but the Cuban leader soon began to criticize the United States in highly colored speeches. He confiscated American property without providing adequate compensation, suppressed civil liberties, and entered into close relations with the Soviet Union. After he negotiated a trade agreement with the Soviet Union in February 1960, which enabled the Russians to obtain Cuban sugar at bargain rates, the United States retaliated by prohibiting the importation of Cuban sugar into America.

Khrushchev then announced that if the United

Fidel Castro and his military advisers in the mountains of Cuba in 1957. His guerrilla assaults on the corrupt regime of Fulgencio Batista and identification of his cause with social justice won Castro the acclaim of many throughout Latin America and some support among Americans.

States intervened in Cuba, he would defend the country with atomic weapons. "The Monroe Doctrine has outlived its time," Khrushchev warned. Shortly before the end of his second term, Eisenhower broke off diplomatic relations with Cuba.

The Politics of Civil Rights

During Eisenhower's presidency a major change occurred in the legal status of American blacks. Eisenhower had relatively little to do with this change, which was part of a broad shift in attitudes toward the rights of minorities in democracies. After 1945 the question of racial equality took on special importance because of the ideological competition with communism. Evidence of color prejudice in the United States damaged the nation's image, particularly in Asia and Africa, where the United States and the Soviet Union were competing for influence. An awareness of foreign criticism of American racial attitudes, along with resentment that almost a century after the Emancipation Proclamation they were still second-class citizens, produced a growing militancy among American blacks. At the same time, fears of communist subversion in the United States led to the repression of the rights of many whites, culminating in the excesses of McCarthyism. Both these aspects of the civil rights question divided Americans along liberal and conservative lines.

As we have seen, the World War II record of the federal government on civil rights was mixed. As early as 1940, in the Smith Act, Congress made it illegal to advocate or teach the overthrow of the government by force or to belong to an organization with this objective. A dead letter during the era of Soviet-American cooperation, the law was used in the Truman era to jail the leaders of the American Communist party. The Supreme Court upheld its constitutionality in *Dennis et al.* v. *United States* (1951), in effect modifying the "clear and present danger" test established in the Schenck case of 1919 (see page 692).

In 1950 Congress passed the McCarran Internal Security Act, which made it unlawful "to combine, conspire or agree with any other person to perform any act that would substantially contribute to the establishment . . . of a totalitarian dictatorship." The law required every "Communist-front organization" to register with the attorney general. Members of front organizations were barred from defense work and from traveling abroad. Aliens who had even been members of any "totalitarian party" were denied admission to the United States, a foolish provision that prevented many anticommunists behind the Iron Curtain from fleeing to America; even a person who had belonged to a communist youth organization was kept out by its terms.

As for blacks, besides setting up the Committee on Civil Rights and beginning to desegregate the armed forces, Truman sought to establish a permanent fair employment practices commission, but Congress did not enact the necessary legislation. Under Eisenhower, while the McCarthy hysteria reached its peak and declined, the government compiled a spotty record on civil rights. The search for subversive federal employees continued.

The most glaring instance of the administration's catering to anticommunist extremists was the refusal to grant security clearance to J. Robert Oppenheimer, one of the fathers of the atomic bomb, on the grounds that he had associated with communists and communist sympathizers. The reasoning was based on the preposterous supposition that Oppenheimer could be denied access to discoveries that he already knew about because he had helped to make them.

On the positive side, Eisenhower completed the integration of the armed forces and appointed a civil rights commission. But he was temperamentally incapable of a frontal assault on the racial problem. This was accomplished by the Supreme Court, which interjected itself into the civil rights controversy in dramatic fashion in 1954.

Under pressure of litigation sponsored by the National Association for the Advancement of Colored People, the Court had been gradually undermining the "separate but equal" principle laid down in *Plessy* v. *Ferguson* in 1896. First it ruled that in graduate education, segregated facilities must be truly equal. In 1938 it ordered a black admitted to the University of Missouri law school because no law school for blacks existed in the state. This decision gradually forced some southern states to admit blacks to advanced programs. "You can't build a cyclotron for one student," the president of the University of Oklahoma confessed when the Court, in 1948, ordered Oklahoma to provide equal facilities. Two years later, when Texas actually attempted to fit out a separate law school for a single black applicant, the Court ruled that truly equal education could not be provided under such circumstances.

In 1953 President Eisenhower appointed California's Governor Earl Warren Chief Justice of the United States.* Convinced that the Court must take the offensive in the cause of civil rights, Warren succeeded in welding his associates into a unit on the question.

In 1954 an NAACP-sponsored case, *Brown* v. *Board of Education of Topeka,* came up for decision. The NAACP lawyer, Thurgood Marshall, challenging the "separate but equal" doctrine, submitted a mass of sociological evidence to show that the mere fact of segregation made equal education impossible and did serious psychological damage to both black children and white. Speaking for a unanimous Court, Warren reversed the Plessy decision. "In the field of public education, the doctrine of 'separate but equal' has no place," he declared. "Separate educational facilities are inherently unequal." The next year the Court ordered the states to proceed "with all deliberate speed" in integrating their schools.

Despite these decisions, few districts in the southern and border states seriously tried to integrate their schools. Two months after the ruling, white citizens' councils dedicated to all-out opposition had sprung up throughout the South. When the school board of Clinton, Tennessee, integrated the local high school in September 1956, a mob organized by a northern fanatic rioted in protest, shouting, "Kill the niggers!" and destroying the property of blacks. The school was kept open with the help of the National Guard until segregationists blew up the building with dynamite. In Virginia the governor announced a plan for "massive resistance" to integration that denied state aid to local school systems that wished to desegregate. When the University of Alabama admitted a single black woman in 1956, riots broke out. University officials forced the student to withdraw and then expelled her when she complained more forcefully than they deemed proper.

President Eisenhower thought equality for blacks could not be obtained by government edict. "I am convinced that the Supreme Court decision set back progress in the South at least fifteen years,"

he remarked to one of his advisers. "The fellow who tries to tell me you can do these things by force is just plain nuts." However, in 1957 events compelled him to act. When the school board of Little Rock, Arkansas, opened Central High School to a handful of black students, the governor of the state, Orval M. Faubus, called out the National Guard to prevent them from attending. Unruly crowds taunted the students and their parents.

Eisenhower could not ignore the direct flouting of federal authority. After the mayor of Little Rock sent him a telegram saying, in part, "SITUATION IS OUT OF CONTROL AND POLICE CANNOT DISPERSE THE MOB" he dispatched 1,000 paratroopers to Little Rock and summoned 10,000 National Guardsmen to federal duty. The black students then began to attend class. A token force of soldiers was stationed at Central High for the entire school year to protect them.

Extremist resistance strengthened the determination of blacks and many northern whites to make the South comply with the desegregation decision. Besides pressing cases in the federal courts, leaders of the movement organized a voter registration drive among southern blacks. As a result, the administration introduced what became the Civil Rights Act of 1957. It authorized the attorney general to obtain injunctions to stop election officials from interfering with blacks seeking to register and vote. The law also established a civil rights commission with broad investigatory powers and a civil rights division in the Department of Justice. Enforcing this Civil Rights Act was another matter. A later study of a typical county in Alabama revealed that between 1957 and 1960 more than 700 blacks with high school diplomas were rejected as unqualified by white election officials when they sought to register.

The Supreme Court under Chief Justice Warren did not limit itself to protecting the rights of black people. Its decision in *Yates* v. *United States* (1957) reinstated the "clear and present danger" principle that had been undermined in the Dennis case upholding the Smith Act ban on merely "advocating" the overthrow of the government by force. The rights of persons accused of crimes were enlarged in *Gideon* v. *Wainright* (1963), providing free legal counsel for indigent defendants, *Escobedo* v. *Illinois* (1964), requiring the police to inform accused persons of their right to remain silent, and *Miranda* v. *Arizona* (1966), giving the accused the right to have

---

* Eisenhower first offered the post to John Foster Dulles, but he declined on the grounds that he was too old to start a new career.

Angry jeers from whites rain down on Elizabeth Eckford, one of the first black students to arrive for registration at Little Rock's Central High School in 1957. State troops turned black students away from the school until President Eisenhower overruled the state decision and called in the National Guard to enforce integration.

a lawyer present while being questioned by the authorities.

In *Baker* v. *Carr* (1962), *Lucas* v. *Colorado* (1964), and other decisions, the Court put an end to unequal representation in state and local legislative bodies, thus establishing the principle known as "one man, one vote." In a much different area, the Court in *Griswold* v. *Connecticut* (1965) struck down a Connecticut statute banning the use of contraceptives on the ground that it violated individuals' right of privacy.

The Election of 1960

As the end of his second term approached, Eisenhower somewhat reluctantly endorsed Vice-President Nixon as the Republican candidate to succeed him. Richard Nixon had skyrocketed to national prominence by exploiting the public fear of communist subversion. "Traitors in the high councils

of our government," he charged in 1950, "have made sure that the deck is stacked on the Soviet side of the diplomatic tables." In 1947 he was an obscure young congressman from California; in 1950 he won a seat in the Senate; two years later Eisenhower chose him as his running mate.

Whether Nixon believed what he was saying at this period of his career is not easily discovered; with his "instinct for omnidirectional placation," he seemed wedded to the theory that politicians should slavishly represent their constituents' opinions rather than hold to their own views. Frequently he appeared to count noses before deciding what he thought. He projected an image of almost frantic earnestness, yet he pursued a flexible course more suggestive of calculation than sincerity.

Reporters generally had a low opinion of Nixon, and independent voters seldom found him attractive. He was always controversial, distrusted by liberals even when he supported liberal measures. But his defense of American values in his confrontation with Khrushchev at the Moscow Fair had won him much praise.

The Democrats nominated Senator John Fitzgerald Kennedy of Massachusetts, with his chief rival at the convention, Lyndon Johnson of Texas, the Senate majority leader, as his running mate. Kennedy was the son of Joseph P. Kennedy, a wealthy businessman and promoter who had served as ambassador to Great Britain under Franklin Roosevelt. As a PT boat commander in World War II, John Kennedy was severely injured in action. In 1946 he was elected to Congress. Besides wealth, intelligence, good looks, and charm, Kennedy had the advantage of his war record and his Irish-Catholic ancestry, the latter a particularly valuable asset in heavily Catholic Massachusetts. After three terms in the House, he moved on to the Senate in 1952 by defeating Henry Cabot Lodge, Jr. (Lodge's grandfather, Wilson's inveterate foe, had beaten Kennedy's maternal grandfather and namesake for the Senate in 1916.)

After his landslide reelection in 1958, only Kennedy's religion seemed to limit his political future. No Catholic had ever been elected president, and the defeat of Alfred E. Smith in 1928 had convinced most students of politics (including Smith) that none ever would be elected. Nevertheless, influenced by Kennedy's victories in the Wisconsin and West Virginia primaries, the latter establishing him as an effective campaigner in a predominantly Protestant region, the Democratic convention nominated him.

Kennedy had not been a particularly liberal congressman. He was friendly with Richard Nixon and admitted frankly that he liked Senator Joseph McCarthy and thought that "he may have something" in his campaign against supposed communists in government. However, as a presidential candidate, he sought to appear more forward-looking. He stressed his youth and "vigor" (a favorite word) and promised to open a "new frontier" for the country. Nixon ran on the Eisenhower record, which he promised to extend in liberal directions.

A series of televised debates between the candidates, observed by some 70 million viewers, helped Kennedy by enabling him to demonstrate his maturity and mastery of the issues. Although both candidates laudably avoided it, the religious issue was important. His Catholicism helped Kennedy in eastern urban areas but hurt him in many farm districts and throughout the West. Kennedy's victory, 303 to 219 in the electoral college, was

paper-thin in the popular vote, 34,227,000 to 34,109,000.

Although Kennedy was rich, white, and a member of the upper crust by any definition, his was a victory of minority groups (Jews, blacks, and blue-collar "ethnics" as well as Catholics gave him overwhelming support) over the "traditional" white Protestant majority, which went as heavily for Nixon as it had four years earlier for Eisenhower.

Kennedy's New Frontier

Kennedy made a striking and popular president. He projected an image of originality and imaginativeness combined with moderation and good sense. He appointed two Republicans to his Cabinet. He further flouted convention by making his younger brother Robert F. Kennedy attorney general. (When critics objected to this appointment, the president responded with a quip, saying that he had "always thought it was a good thing for a young attorney to get some government experience before going out into private practice.")

Kennedy had a genuinely inquiring mind. He kept up with dozens of magazines and newspapers and consumed books of all sorts voraciously. He invited leading scientists, artists, writers, and musicians to the White House. On one occasion when he had invited a number of Nobel Prize winners to the White House, he called the group "the most extraordinary collection of talent . . . that has ever been gathered together at the White House with the possible exception of when Thomas Jefferson dined alone." This was typical political bunkum, but just as Jefferson had sought to teach Americans to value the individual regardless of status, Kennedy seemed intent on teaching the country to respect its most talented minds.

Kennedy was determined to change the direction in which the nation was moving. He hoped to revitalize the economy and extend the influence of the United States abroad. His inaugural address was a call for commitment: "Ask not what your country can do for you," he said. "Ask what you can do for your country." But he was neither a Woodrow Wilson nor a Franklin Roosevelt when it came to bending Congress to his will. Perhaps he was too amiable, too diffident and conciliatory in his approach. A coalition of Republicans and conservative southern Democrats resisted his plans for federal aid to ed-

Vice-President Richard M. Nixon and Senator John F. Kennedy during one of the three televised debates of the 1960 presidential campaign. An effective debater from his college days, Nixon had welcomed the opportunity to take on the less experienced junior senator from Massachusetts before 70,000,000 viewers. It was a mistake.

ner, cutting taxes, easing credit, and expanding public works programs. However, liberal economists argued that it was not employing the Keynesian medicine in large enough doses. At first Kennedy rejected proposals for increasing government spending in order to stimulate consumer spending. But in January 1963 the economist Walter Heller persuaded him to try a different approach. If personal and corporate income taxes were lowered, Heller argued, the public would have more money to spend on consumer goods and corporations could invest in new facilities for producing these goods. Federal expenditures need not be cut because the increase in economic activity would raise private and corporate incomes so much that tax revenues would rise even as the tax rate was falling.

Although the prospect of lower taxes was tempting, Kennedy's call for reductions of $13.5 billion ran into strong opposition. Republicans and conservative Democrats thought the reasoning behind the scheme too complex and theoretical to be practicable. It went nowhere.

ucation, for urban renewal, for a higher minimum wage, for medical care for the aged.

The president reacted mildly, almost ruefully, when opponents in Congress blocked proposals that in his view were reasonable and moderate. He seemed to doubt at times that the cumbersome machinery of the federal government could be made to work. Even to some of his warmest supporters he sometimes appeared strangely paralyzed, unwilling either to exert strong pressure on Congress or to appeal to public opinion. Pundits talked of a "deadlock of democracy" in which party discipline had crumbled and positive legislative action had become next to impossible.

During the presidential campaign Kennedy had promised "to get the country moving again." The relatively slow growth of the economy in the Eisenhower years had troubled some economists. Three recessions occurred between 1953 and 1961, each marked by increases in unemployment. Moreover, in the later years of Eisenhower's presidency the rate of inflation began to rise.

During the recessions the Eisenhower administration reacted in the orthodox Keynesian man-

The Cuban Crises

Kennedy's curious lack of determined leadership also marred his management of foreign affairs, particularly during his first year in office. He hoped to reverse the Truman-Eisenhower policy of backing reactionary regimes merely because they were anticommunist. Recognizing that American economic aid could accomplish little in Latin America unless accompanied by internal reforms, he organized the Alliance for Progress, which committed the Latin Americans to land reform and economic development projects with the assistance of the United States. At the first sign of pro-Soviet activity in any Latin American country, however, he tended to overreact. Critics have described his behavior toward Latin America as a mixture of "overambitious idealism" and "pointless obsessiveness" about security.

His most serious blunder involved Cuba. Anti-Castro exiles were eager to organize an invasion of their homeland, reasoning that the Cuban masses would rise up against Castro as soon as "democratic" forces provided a standard they could rally to. Under Eisenhower the Central Intelligence Agency had begun training some 2,000 of these men in Central America.

Kennedy was of two minds about this plan. Secretary of State Dean Rusk and a few of his other advisers opposed it, as did J. William Fulbright, the chairman of the Senate Foreign Relations Committee, who said, "The Castro regime is a thorn in the flesh but it is not a dagger in the heart." But after much soul-searching, Kennedy authorized the attack. The exiles were given American weapons, but no planes or warships were committed to the secret operation.

The invaders struck on April 17, 1961, landing at the Bay of Pigs, on Cuba's southern coast. But the Cuban people failed to support them, and they were soon pinned down and forced to surrender. Since America's involvement could not be disguised, the affair exposed the country to all the criticism that a straightforward assault would have produced, without accomplishing the overthrow of Castro. Worse, it made Kennedy appear impulsive as well as unprincipled. Castro soon acknowledged that he was a Marxist and tightened his connections with the Soviet Union. For his part, Kennedy imposed an economic blockade on Cuba, and he appears to have gone along with a CIA attempt to assassinate Castro.

In June, Kennedy met with Premier Khrushchev in Vienna. During their discussions he evidently failed to convince the Russian that he would resist pressure with determination. In August, Khrushchev abruptly closed the border between East and West Berlin and erected an ugly wall of concrete blocks and barbed wire across the city to stop the exodus of dissident East Germans. When Kennedy did not order American forces in Berlin to tear down the wall, the Soviet leader found further reason to believe he could pursue aggressive tactics with impunity. Resuming the testing of nuclear weapons, he exploded a series of gigantic hydrogen bombs, one with a power 3,000 times that of the bomb that had devastated Hiroshima.

When the Russians resumed nuclear testing, Kennedy followed suit. He expanded the American space program,* vowing that an American would land on the moon within ten years, and called on Congress for a large increase in military spending. At the same time, he pressed forward along more constructive lines by establishing the Agency for International Development to administer American economic aid throughout the world and the Peace Corps, an organization that effectively mobilized American idealism and technical skills to help developing nations.

These actions had no observable effect on the Russians. In 1962 Khrushchev devised the boldest and most reckless challenge of the Cold War—he moved military equipment and thousands of Soviet technicians into Cuba. American intelligence reports revealed that in addition to planes and conventional weapons, guided missiles were being imported and launching pads were being constructed on Cuban soil. U-2 reconnaissance planes photographed these sites, and by mid-October, Kennedy had proof that the missile sites were approaching completion.

The president faced a dreadful decision. When he confronted Soviet Foreign Minister Andrei Gromyko, Gromyko insisted that only "defensive" (antiaircraft) missiles were being installed. But even if this were true, allowing the construction of missile sites so close to the United States was politically unacceptable, especially after the Bay of Pigs fiasco.

Kennedy decided that he must take strong action. On October 22 he went before the nation on television. The Soviet buildup was "a deliberately provocative and unjustified change in the status quo," he said. The navy would stop and search all vessels headed for Cuba and turn back any containing "offensive" weapons. Kennedy called on Khrushchev to dismantle the missile bases and remove from the island all weapons capable of striking the United States. Any Cuban-based nuclear attack would result, he warned, in "a full retaliatory response upon the Soviet Union."

For days, while the world held its breath, work on the missile bases continued. Then Khrushchev backed down. He withdrew the missiles and cut back his military establishment in Cuba to modest proportions. Kennedy then lifted the blockade.

Critics have argued that Kennedy overreacted to the Soviet missiles. There was no evidence that the Russians were planning an attack, and in any case they already had missiles in Siberia capable of striking American targets. The Cuban missiles

---

* Russian superiority in space was gradually reduced. In April 1961 the cosmonaut Yuri Gagarin orbited the earth; in August another Russian circled the globe 17 times. The first American to orbit the earth, John Glenn, made his voyage in February 1962. In 1965 the United States kept a two-man Gemini craft in orbit two weeks, effecting a rendezvous between it and a second Gemini.

U.S. United Nations Ambassador Adlai Stevenson (seated right) in the U.N. Security Council displaying aerial photographs of missile installations in Cuba in the midst of the Cuban Missile Crisis in October 1962. Until this moment, the Soviet delegate, Valerian Zorin (seated, third from left), had denied the existence of Soviet missiles in the western hemisphere. He could do so no longer.

might be seen as a deterrent against a possible attack on the Soviet Union by United States missiles in Europe, and by demanding their withdrawal, Kennedy risked triggering a nuclear holocaust as much as Khrushchev. Yet he probably had no choice once the existence of the sites was known to the public. (In some respects this is the most frightening aspect of the crisis.)

For better or worse, Kennedy's firmness in the missile crisis repaired the damage done his reputation by thc Bay of Pigs affair. It also led to a lessening of Soviet-American tensions. Khrushchev agreed to the installation of a telephone "hot line" between the White House and the Kremlin so that in any future crisis the leaders of the two nations could be in instant communication. Although the arms race continued unabated, in 1963 nearly 100 nations, including all the major powers except France and China, signed a treaty banning the testing of nuclear weapons in the atmosphere.

Tragedy in Dallas

Although his domestic policies were making little progress in Congress and the economy remained in rather poor shape, Kennedy retained his hold on public opinion. In the fall of 1963 most observers believed he would easily win a second term. Then,

while visiting Dallas, Texas, on November 22, he was shot in the head by an assassin, Lee Harvey Oswald, and died almost instantly.

This senseless murder shocked the world and precipitated an extraordinary series of events. Oswald had fired on the president with a rifle from an upper story of a warehouse. No one saw him pull the trigger. He was apprehended largely because, in his demented state, he killed a policeman later in the day in another part of the city. He denied his guilt, but a mass of evidence connected him with the crime. Before he could be brought to trial, however, he was himself murdered by one Jack Ruby, the owner of a Dallas nightclub, while being transferred, in the full view of television cameras, from one place of detention to another.

This amazing incident, together with the fact that Oswald had defected to Russia in 1959 and then returned to the United States, convinced many people that some nefarious conspiracy lay at the root of the tragedy. Oswald, the argument ran, was a pawn, his murder designed to keep him from exposing the masterminds who had engineered the assassination. An investigation by a special commission headed by Chief Justice Earl Warren came to the conclusion that Oswald acted alone, yet doubts persisted in many minds.

Kennedy's election had seemed to mark the beginning of a new era in American history. Instead,

Jacqueline Kennedy and Robert F. Kennedy returning from the Arlington Cemetery on November 26, 1963, following the burial of President John F. Kennedy. Not since Lincoln's funeral had there been such an intense display of public grief over the loss of a political leader.

his assassination marked the end of an old one. Whatever their strengths and weaknesses, the three postwar presidents had achieved, at minimum, the respect of nearly everyone. There were critics who felt that the job was too big for Truman, others who considered Eisenhower a political amateur and Kennedy too much a showman. But as was true of most of their predecessors, their honesty and patriotism seemed beyond question. This was not to be said of their immediate successors.

Milestones

1944 GI Bill of Rights	UN counterattack in Korea driven back by Red Chinese army
1945 Roosevelt dies; Truman becomes president	**1953** New Look foreign policy
1946 Benjamin Spock, *Baby and Child Care*	Korean War armistice
Baruch plan for control of atomic energy	**1954** Army-McCarthy hearings
1947 Taft-Hartley Act	Siege of Dien Bien Phu; French withdraw from Vietnam
Truman Doctrine	Supreme Court orders school desegregation (*Brown* v. *Board of Education*)
"X" (George Kennan), "Sources of Soviet Conduct"	
Marshall Plan proposed	**1956** Suez crisis
Loyalty Review Board	**1957** National Guard used to desegregate Little Rock high school
1948–	Civil Rights Commission
1949 Berlin Airlift	**1960** U-2 affair
1949 North Atlantic Treaty Organization (NATO) established	United States breaks diplomatic relations with Cuba
1950 North Korea invades South Korea	**1961** Bay of Pigs affair
Alger Hiss convicted of perjury	**1962** Cuban Missile Crisis
Senator McCarthy charges that the State Department is riddled with communists	**1963** President Kennedy assassinated

SUPPLEMENTARY READING

Titles marked with an asterisk have been published in paperback.

A good summary of the Cold War is T. G. Paterson, *On Every Front: The Making of the Cold War** (1979), which makes an effort to explain Soviet motives and tactics objectively. See also two books by J. L. Gaddis, **Strategies of Containment** (1982) and **The Long Peace** (1987). More critical of American policy are Walter La Feber, **America, Russia, and the Cold War*** (1968), and Daniel Yergin, **Shattered Peace** (1977). Harry Truman's **Memoirs*** (1955–1956) contain much useful information.

Postwar domestic politics is treated in W. L. O'Neill, **Riding High*** (1986), and two works by A. L. Hamby, **The Imperial Years** (1976) and **Beyond the New Deal: Harry S Truman and American Liberalism*** (1973). Interpretive works useful for understanding the period include A. M. Schlesinger, Jr., **The Vital Center*** (1949), R. E. Neustadt, **Presidential Power*** (1960), and J. M. Burns, **The Deadlock of Democracy*** (1963).

Biographical material on postwar political leaders is voluminous. On Truman, see D. R. McCoy, **The Presidency of Harry S Truman** (1984), and R. J. Donovan, **Conflict and Crisis** (1977). S. E. Ambrose's two-volume biography **Eisenhower** (1983–1984) is the fullest scholarly treatment of Dwight Eisenhower.

Among many analyses and evaluations of American foreign policy, G. F. Kennan's writings stand out, both as primary sources and as interpretations. See his **Memoirs*** (1969, 1972), **Realities of American Foreign Policy*** (1954), and **Russia and the West under Lenin and Stalin*** (1961).

On Truman's foreign policy, see Donovan's **Conflict and Crisis** and M. J. Hogan, **The Marshall Plan** (1987). W. P. Davison, **The Berlin Blockade** (1958), is also useful.

On the Korean War, consult Clay Blair, **Forgotten War: America in Korea** (1988).

McCarthyism and the Hiss case are covered in David Caute, **The Great Fear** (1978), Allen Weinstein, **Perjury: The Hiss-Chambers Case** (1978), and Robert Griffith, **The Politics of Fear*** (1970).

Economic trends are considered in Herbert Stein, **The Fiscal Revolution in America*** (1969). On labor, consult Philip Taft, **Organized Labor in American History** (1964), E. L. Dayton, **Walter Reuther** (1958), and R. H. Zieger, **John L. Lewis** (1988). On agriculture, see A. J. Matusow, **Farm Policies and Politics in the Truman Years*** (1970).

Eisenhower's own view of his presidency can be found in D. D. Eisenhower, **Mandate for Change*** (1963) and **Waging Peace** (1965). Herbert Parmet, **Eisenhower and the American Crusades** (1972), is a balanced account of his two administrations. See also C. C. Alexander, **Holding the Line: The Eisenhower Era** (1975). Dulles's views are discussed in M. A. Gun, **John Foster Dulles** (1972). The diplomacy of the Eisenhower era is also discussed in R. A. Divine, **Eisenhower and the Cold War*** (1981). For postwar constitutional issues, see P. L. Murphy, **The Constitution in Crisis Times*** (1972). Richard Kluger, **Simple Justice*** (1976), is an excellent account of *Brown* v. *Board of Education.*

On Kennedy, consult H. S. Parmet, **Jack: The Struggles of John F. Kennedy** (1980) and **JKF: The Presidency of John F. Kennedy** (1983), together a fair-minded account. A. M. Schlesinger, Jr., **A Thousand Days*** (1965), and Theodore Sorensen, **Kennedy*** (1965), are rich in eyewitness detail but extremely pro-Kennedy.

The Best of Times, the Worst of Times

The obstruction of justice thing is a [expletive deleted] hard thing to prove in court.

PRESIDENT RICHARD M. NIXON, *April 16, 1973*

A shot of President Johnson using his hands to emphasize a point while speaking to reporters conveys the talkative, intense, persuasive nature of the man.

Lyndon Baines Johnson

John F. Kennedy's death made Lyndon B. Johnson president. The two had never been close. When Kennedy offered Johnson the vice-presidency at the 1960 Democratic convention, he had expected him to refuse. (When Johnson accepted, the chagrined Kennedy said to his brother Robert: "Don't worry Bobby, nothing's going to happen to me.") From 1949 until his election as vice-president Johnson had been a senator and, for most of that time, Senate Democratic leader. Early on he had displayed what one adviser called an extraordinary "capacity for manipulation and seduction." He could be both heavy-handed and subtle, and also devious, domineering, persistent, and obliging. Many people swore by him; few had the fortitude to swear at him. Above all he knew what to do with political power. "Some men," he said, "want power so they can strut around to 'Hail to the Chief.' . . . I wanted it to use it."

On taking office as president, Johnson benefited from the sympathy of the world and from the shame felt by many who had opposed Kennedy's proposals for political or selfish reasons. Sensing the public mood, he took advantage of it by pushing hard for Kennedy's programs. Early in his career he had voted against a bill making lynching a federal crime and had opposed bills outlawing state poll taxes and establishing a federal fair employment practices commission. But after he became important in national affairs, he consistently championed racial equality. "Civil rightsers are going to have to wear sneakers to keep up with me," he now boasted.

Bills that had long been buried in committee sailed through Congress. Early in 1964 Kennedy's tax cut was passed, and the resulting economic stimulus caused a boom of major dimensions. A few months later, an expanded version of another Kennedy measure became law, the Civil Rights Act of 1964.

"We Shall Overcome"

Kennedy's original approach to the race question had been exceedingly cautious. He did not integrate the National Guard, for example, because he was afraid that if he did, southern Guard units would withdraw. His lack of full commitment dismayed many who were concerned about the persistence of racial discrimination in the country. But seemingly without plan, a grass-roots drive for equal treatment had sprung up among southern blacks themselves.

It began during the Eisenhower administration in the tightly segregated city of Montgomery, Alabama. On the evening of Friday, December 1, 1955, Rosa Parks boarded a bus on her way home from her job as a seamstress at the Montgomery Fair department store. She dutifully took a seat toward the rear as law and custom required. After white workers and shoppers had filled the forward section the driver ordered her to give up her place. Parks, who was also secretary of the Montgomery NAACP chapter, refused. She had decided, she later recalled, that "I would have to know once and for all what rights I had as a human being and a citizen."

Rosa Parks was arrested. Over the weekend, leaders of the blacks of Montgomery organized a boycott. "Don't ride the bus . . . Monday," their mimeographed notice ran. "If you work, take a cab, or share a ride, or walk." Monday dawned bitter cold, but the boycott was a total success. The black people of Montgomery, writes Taylor Branch in his stirring account of the boycott in *Parting the Waters*, "were turning the City Bus Lines into a ghost fleet."

Most Montgomery blacks could not afford to miss even one day's wages, so the protracted struggle to get to work was difficult to maintain. Black-owned taxis reduced their rates sharply, and when the city declared this illegal, car pools were quickly organized. But few blacks owned cars—nearly everyone who did volunteered, but there were never more than 350 available to carry more than about 10,000 people back and forth to their jobs every day. Nevertheless, the boycott went on.

Late in February the Montgomery authorities obtained indictments of 115 leaders of the boycott, but this move backfired because it focused national attention on the situation. A young clergyman, Martin Luther King, Jr., a gifted speaker who was emerging as the leader of the boycott, became an overnight celebrity; money poured in from all over the country to support the movement. Finally, after more than a year, the Supreme Court ruled that the segregation law was unconstitutional. Montgomery had to desegregate its public transportation system.

This success had encouraged blacks elsewhere in the South to band together against the caste system. A new organization, the Southern Christian Leadership Conference, headed by King, moved to the forefront of the civil rights movement. Other organizations joined the struggle, notably the Congress of Racial Equality (CORE), which had been founded in 1942.

In February 1960 four black students in Greensboro, North Carolina, sat down at a lunch counter in a Woolworth five-and-ten and refused to leave when they were denied service. Their "sit-in" sparked a national movement; students in dozens of other southern towns and cities copied the Greensboro blacks' example. By the end of 1961 over 70,000 persons had participated in sit-ins. Still another new organization, the Student Nonviolent Coordinating Committee (SNCC), was founded by black college students to provide a focus for the sit-in movement and conduct voter registration drives in the South, actions that more than any other aroused the fury of southern segregationists.

In May 1961 black and white foes of segregation organized a "freedom ride" to test the effectiveness of federal regulations prohibiting discrimination in interstate transportation. Boarding buses in Washington, they traveled across the South, heading for New Orleans. In Alabama they ran into bad trouble. At Anniston racists set fire to their bus, and in Birmingham they were assaulted by a mob. But violence did not stop the freedom riders. Other groups descended on the South, many deliberately seeking arrest in order to test local segregation ordinances in the courts. Repeatedly these actions resulted in the breaking down of racial barriers.

Integrationists like Martin Luther King, Jr., attracted an enormous following, but some blacks, contemptuous of white prejudices, were urging their fellows to reject "American" society and all it stood for. Black nationalism became a potent force. Elijah Muhammad, leader of the Black Muslim movement, disliked whites so intensely that he demanded that a part of the United States be set aside for the exclusive use of blacks. He urged his followers to be industrious, thrifty, and abstemious—and to view all whites with suspicion and hatred.

"This white government has ruled us and given us plenty hell, but the time has arrived that you taste a little of your own hell," Elijah Muhammad said. "There are many of my poor black ignorant brothers

Calling for black separatism, Malcolm X told an interviewer in 1964, "The Negro [must] develop his character and his culture in accord with his own nature."

. . . preaching the ignorant and lying stuff that you should love your enemy. What fool can love his enemy?" Another important Black Muslim, Malcolm X, put it this way in a 1960 speech: "For the white man to ask the black man if he hates him is just like the rapist asking the raped, or the wolf asking the sheep, 'Do you hate me?' " "If someone puts a hand on you," he advised blacks on another occasion, "send him to the cemetery."

Pushed by all these developments, President Kennedy reluctantly began to change his policy. But while the administration gave lip service to desegregation and encouraged activists' efforts to register black voters in the South, when confrontations arose, the president hesitated, arguing that it was up to state officials to enforce the law.

Ordinary black southerners (even schoolchildren) became increasingly impatient. In the face of brutal repression by local police, many adopted King's tactic of nonviolent protest. After leading a series of demonstrations in Birmingham, Alabama,

in 1963, King was thrown in jail. When local white clergymen, presumably sympathetic to the blacks' objectives, nonetheless urged them to cease their "untimely" protests, which, they claimed, "incite hatred and violence," King wrote his now-famous "Letter from Birmingham Jail," which contained this moving explanation of why he and his followers were unwilling to wait any longer for justice.

> When you have seen hate-filled policemen curse, kick, brutalize and even kill your black brothers and sisters with impunity; when you see the vast majority of your twenty million Negro brothers smothering in an airtight cage of poverty in the midst of an affluent society; when you suddenly find your tongue twisted and your speech stammering as you seek to explain to your six-year-old daughter why she can't go to the public amusement park that has just been advertised on television . . . when you take a cross-country drive and find it necessary to sleep night after night in the uncomfortable corners of your automobile because no motel will accept you; when you are humiliated day in and day out by nagging signs reading "white" and "colored": when your first name becomes "nigger" and your middle name becomes "boy" . . . then you will understand why we find it so difficult to wait.

The brutal repression of the Birmingham demonstrations brought a flood of recruits and money to the protesters' cause. Finally Kennedy gave his support to a comprehensive new civil rights bill that made racial discrimination in hotels, restaurants, and other places of public accommodation illegal and gave the attorney general the power to bring suits on behalf of individuals in order to speed up the lagging school desegregation movement. The measure also authorized agencies of the federal government to withhold federal funds from state-administered programs that failed to treat people of all races equally.

When this bill ran into stiff opposition in Congress, blacks organized a demonstration in Washington, attended by 200,000 people. At this gathering, King delivered his "I Have a Dream" address, looking forward to a time when racial prejudice no longer existed and people of all religions and colors could join hands and say, "Free at last! Free at last!"

Kennedy had sympathized with the purpose of the Washington gathering but feared it would make passage of the civil rights bill more difficult rather than easier. As in other areas, he was not a forceful advocate of his own proposals.

The Great Society

As finally passed, the Civil Rights Act outlawed discrimination by employers against blacks and also against women. It broke down the last legal barriers to black voting in the southern states and outlawed formal racial segregation of all sorts. Johnson's success in steering this and other Kennedy measures through Congress convinced him that he could be a reformer in the tradition of Franklin Roosevelt. He declared war on poverty and set out to create a "great society" in which poverty no longer existed.

During the New Deal, Franklin Roosevelt was accused of exaggeration when he said that one-third of the nation was "ill-housed, ill-clad, ill-nourished." In fact Roosevelt had underestimated the extent of poverty when he made that statement in 1937. Wartime economic growth reduced the percentage of poor people in the country substantially, but in 1960 between 20 and 25 percent of all American families—about 40 million persons—were living below the poverty line, a government standard of minimum subsistence based on income and family size.

That so many millions could be poor in a reputedly affluent society was deplorable but not difficult to explain. In any community a certain number of persons cannot support themselves because of physical incapacity, low intelligence, or psychological difficulties. There were also in the United States entire regions, the best known being the Appalachian area, that had been bypassed by economic development and no longer provided their inhabitants with adequate economic opportunities.

Moreover, prosperity and advancing technology had changed the definition of poverty. Things like telephones, radios, and electric refrigerators, unknown to the most affluent Americans of the 1860s, were necessities a century later. But as living standards rose, so did job requirements. A strong back and a willingness to work no longer guaranteed that the possessor could earn a decent living. Technology was changing the labor market. Educated workers with special skills and good verbal abilities could easily find well-paid jobs. Persons who had no special skills or were poorly educated could often find nothing.

Certain less obvious influences were at work too. Poverty tends to be more prevalent among the old and the young than among those in the prime of life; in the postwar decades these two groups were growing more rapidly than any other. Social security payments amounted to less than the elderly needed to maintain themselves decently, and some of the poorest workers, such as agricultural laborers, were not covered by the system at all. Unemployment was twice as high among youths in their late teens as in the nation as a whole and far higher among young blacks than among young whites.

As the middle class moved to the suburbs, poverty became, in the words of Michael Harrington, whose book *The Other America* (1962) did much to call attention to the problem, "less visible" to the well-meaning citizens whose energies had to be mobilized if it was to be eradicated. Many poor people were becoming alienated from society. In earlier times most of the poor were recent immigrants, believers in the American dream of rags to riches, strivers who accepted their low status as temporary. The modern poor, many studies indicated, tended to lack motivation; they felt trapped by their condition and gave up.

Poverty exacted a heavy price, both from its victims and from society. Statistics reflected the relationship between low income and bad health. Only about 4 percent of people from middle-income families were chronically ill, whereas more than 16 percent of poor families were so afflicted. Mental illness varied inversely with income, as did alcoholism, drug addiction, and crime.

Johnson's war on poverty had two objectives: to give poor people the opportunity to improve themselves and to provide them with direct assistance of various kinds. The first took the form of the Economic Opportunity Act of 1964. This law created a melange of programs, among them the Job Corps, similar to the New Deal Civilian Conservation Corps, a community action program to finance local efforts; an educational program for small children; a work-study program for college students; and a system for training the unskilled unemployed and for lending money to small businesses in poor areas. The Economic Opportunity Act combined the progressive concept of the welfare state with the conservative idea of individual responsibility. The government would support the weak and disadvantaged by giving them a fair chance to make it on their own.

Buttressed by this and other legislative triumphs, Johnson sought election as president in his own right in 1964. He achieved this ambition in unparalleled fashion. His championing of civil rights won him the almost unanimous support of blacks; his economy drive attracted the well-to-do and the business interests; his war on poverty held the allegiance of labor and other elements traditionally Democratic. His southern antecedents counterbalanced his liberalism on the race question in the eyes of many white southerners.

The Republicans played into his hands by nominating a conservative, Senator Barry M. Goldwater of Arizona. A large majority of the voters found Goldwater out of date on economic questions and dangerously aggressive on foreign affairs. During the campaign Democrats told a joke that went something like this:

(Goldwater is president. An aide rushes into his office.)

AIDE: Mr. President, the Russians have just launched an all-out nuclear attack on us. Their missiles will strike in fifteen minutes. What shall we do?
GOLDWATER: Have all the wagons form a circle.

In November, Johnson won a sweeping victory, collecting over 61 percent of the popular vote and carrying all the country except Goldwater's Arizona and five states in the Deep South. Quickly he pressed ahead with his Great Society program. In January 1965 he proposed a compulsory hospital insurance system for all persons over the age of 65, known as Medicare. As amended by Congress, the Medicare Act combined hospital insurance for retired people (funded by social security taxes) with a voluntary plan to cover doctors' bills (paid for in part by the government). The law also provided for grants to the states to help pay the medical expenses of poor people below the retirement age of 65. This part of the system was called Medicaid.

Next Congress passed the Elementary and Secondary Education Act. This measure supplied federal funds to school districts, the money to be devoted to improving the education of poor children. The theory was that children from city slums and impoverished rural areas tended to be "educationally deprived" and thus in need of extra help. The act was especially close to President Johnson's heart, having taught school in a Mexican-American district after graduating from college. To focus attention on it (and for obvious political purposes), he went back to his Texas birthplace to sign it, delivering a homily on education as the steppingstone to fame

A class for Spanish-speaking children of migrant workers in Salinas, California, funded by the federally supported Head Start Program. Launched in 1964 at President Johnson's urging, it was one of the most successful "Great Society" initiatives.

and fortune. Related to the Education Act was a program for poor preschool children, known as Head Start. This program was designed to prepare the children for elementary school. It also contributed incidentally to improving the health of the children by providing medical examinations and good meals.

Other laws passed at Johnson's urging in 1965 and 1966 dealt with support for the arts and for scientific research, highway safety, crime control, slum clearance, clean air, and the preservation of historic sites. Of particular significance was the Immigration Act of 1965, which did away with the national-origin system of admitting newcomers. Instead, 290,000 persons a year were to be admitted, priorities being based on such grounds as skill and the need for political asylum. The law also placed a limit of 120,000 persons a year on immigration from countries in the Western Hemisphere. Previously, immigration from these countries had been unrestricted.

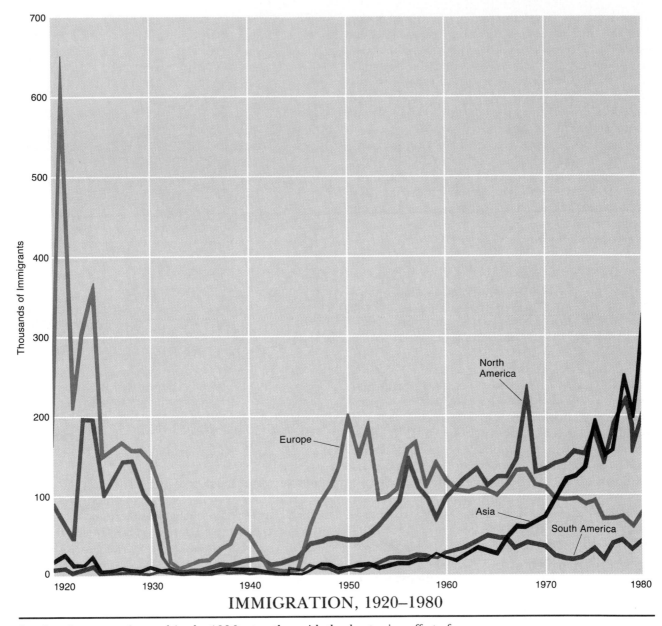

IMMIGRATION, 1920–1980

*Immigration quotas imposed in the 1920s, together with the dampening effect of
the depression years and World War II, meant that up to 1980, immigration had
still not reached its pre–World War I levels, in spite of the post-1960 influx from
Asia and North America. Canada, Mexico, Central America, and the West Indies
are included in the North American category.*

The Great Society program was one of the most
remarkable outpourings of important legislation in
American history. The results, however, were
mixed. Head Start and a related program to help
students in secondary schools prepare for college
were unqualified successes. But the 1965 Education
Act proved a disappointment. Too many local
school districts found ways of using the federal
money to cover their ordinary expenses, and the
sums actually devoted to programs for the poor
failed to improve most students' performances significantly. Medicare and Medicaid certainly provided good medical treatment for millions of people, but since the patients no longer paid most of

the bills, doctors, hospitals, and drug companies were able to raise fees and prices without fear of losing business. Medical costs escalated far more rapidly than the rate of inflation.

The Job Corps, which was designed to help poor people get better-paying jobs by providing them with vocational training, was an almost total failure. The cost of the training was high, relatively few trainees completed the courses, and of those who did, few found jobs in which they could make use of their new skills. On balance, the achievements of the Great Society were far short of what President Johnson had promised.

The War in Vietnam

In the fall of 1967 President Lyndon Johnson seemed to have every intention of running for a second full term. Whether he would be reelected was not clear, but that any Democrat could prevent this shrewd and powerful politician from being nominated seemed out of the question. Nevertheless, within a few months opposition to him had become so bitter that he withdrew as a candidate. The cause of this opposition was his handling of a conflict on the other side of the world—the war in Vietnam.

When Vietnam was divided following the defeat of the French in 1954, a handful of American military "advisers" were sent there to train a South Vietnamese army. As time passed, more American aid and "advice" were dispatched in a futile effort to establish a stable government. Pro-communist forces, now called the Vietcong, soon controlled large sections of the country, some almost within sight of the capital city of Saigon.

Gradually the Vietcong, drawing supplies from North Vietnam and indirectly from China and the Soviet Union, increased in strength. In response, more American money and more military advisers were sent to bolster Ngo Dinh Diem's regime. By the end of 1961 there were 3,200 American military men in the country; by the time Kennedy was assassinated, the American military presence had risen to more than 16,000 and 120 American soldiers had been killed.

Shortly before Kennedy's death, a group of South Vietnamese generals overthrew Diem and killed him. The following summer, after announcing that North Vietnamese gunboats had fired on

American destroyers in the Gulf of Tonkin, President Johnson demanded, and in an air of crisis obtained, an authorization from Congress to "repel any armed attack against the forces of the United States and to prevent further aggression."

With this blank check, and buttressed by his sweeping defeat of Goldwater in the 1964 presidential election, Johnson sent more troops to South Vietnam and authorized air attacks against targets in both South and North Vietnam.

At first the American ground troops were supposed to be merely teachers and advisers of the South Vietnamese army. Then they were said to be there to defend air bases, with the understanding that they would return fire if they were attacked. Next came word that the troops were being used to assist South Vietnamese units when they came under enemy fire. In fact the Americans were soon attacking the enemy directly, mounting search-and-destroy missions aimed at clearing the foe from villages and entire sections of the country.

Johnson's escalation of the American commitment occurred piecemeal and apparently without plan. At the end of 1965 some 184,000 Americans were in the field; a year later, 385,000; after another year, 485,000. By the middle of 1968 the number exceeded 538,000. Each increase was met by corresponding increases from the other side. Russia and China sent no combat troops but stepped up their aid, and thousands of North Vietnamese regulars filtered across the 17th parallel to join the Vietcong insurgents. As the scope of the action broadened, the number of American casualties rose. The United States was engaged in a full-scale war, one that Congress never declared.

Hawks and Doves

From the beginning, the war divided the American people sharply. Defenders of the president's policy, called *hawks*, emphasized the nation's moral responsibility to resist aggression and what President Eisenhower had called the domino theory. The domino theory was based on an analogy with the western powers' failure to resist Hitler before 1939. It predicted that if the communists were allowed to "take over" Vietnam, they would soon take its neighbors, then their neighbors, and so on until all Asia had been conquered. The United States was not an aggressor in Vietnam, the hawks insisted, and they

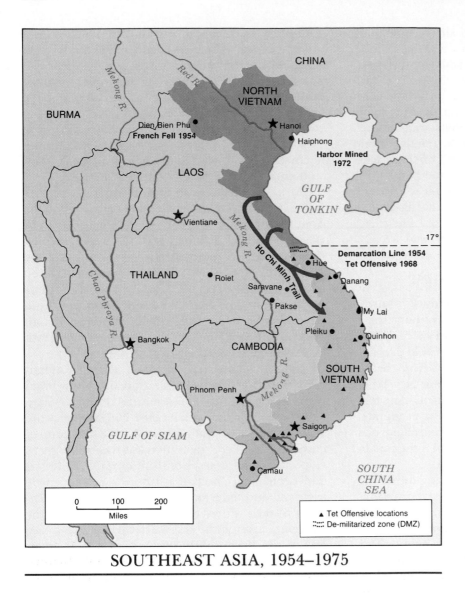

SOUTHEAST ASIA, 1954–1975

stressed Johnson's oft-expressed willingness to negotiate a general withdrawal of "foreign" forces
from the country, which the communists repeatedly
rejected.

American opponents of the war, called *doves,*
argued that the struggle between the South Vietnamese government and the Vietcong was a civil
war in which Americans should not meddle. They
stressed the repressive character of the South Vietnamese government as proof that the war was not
a contest between democracy and communism.
They objected to the massive aerial bombings (more
explosives were dropped on Vietnam between 1964
and 1968 than on Germany and Japan combined

in World War II); to the use of napalm and other
chemicals such as the defoliants that were sprayed
on forests and crops, which wreaked havoc among
noncombatants; and to the killing of civilians by
American troops. In his capacity as chairman of the
Foreign Relations Committee, Senator Fulbright
had introduced the Gulf of Tonkin Resolution in
1964. By 1967 he was calling the war "unnecessary
and immoral," American participation in it a "false
and dangerous dream of an imperial destiny."

The doves discounted the domino theory, pointing both to the growing communist split into Chinese and Russian camps and to the traditional hostility of all Vietnamese to the Chinese, which they

claimed made Chinese expansion into Southeast Asia unlikely. And they deplored the heavy loss of American lives—over 40,000 dead by 1970. The cost of the war, which came to exceed $20 billion a year, was still another reason the doves opposed it. In large part because so many people objected to the war, Johnson refused to ask Congress to raise taxes to pay for it. The deficit forced the government to borrow huge sums, which caused interest rates to soar, adding to the upward pressure on prices.

Although Johnson's financial policies were shortsighted, if not outrightly irresponsible, and although his statements about the war were often lacking in candor, he and his advisers believed that they were defending freedom and democracy. "If I got out of Vietnam," the President said, "I'd be doing exactly what Chamberlain did in World War II. I'd be giving a big fat reward for aggression."

What became increasingly clear as time passed and the costs mounted was that military victory was impossible. Yet American leaders were extraordinarily slow to grasp this fact. Repeatedly they advised the president that one more escalation (so many more soldiers, so many more air raids) would break the enemy's will to resist. The smug arrogance bred by America's brief postwar monopoly of nuclear weapons persisted in some quarters long after the monopoly had been lost.

Kennedy's decision to authorize the Bay of Pigs invasion was an example of this, but as late as 1965 McGeorge Bundy, President Johnson's special assistant for national security affairs, apparently told an interviewer (he later claimed to have been misunderstood) that "the United States was the locomotive at the head of mankind, and the rest of the world the caboose." And like the proverbial donkey plodding after the carrot on the stick, Johnson repeatedly followed the advice of hawks like Bundy.

For a long time, as opinion polls demonstrated, a majority of the American people believed he was correct. Patriotism and pride, along with the costly lessons of 1931–1939 and a stubborn refusal to admit that a mistake had been made, held them to this course.

The Election of 1968

Gradually the doves increased in number. Even some of the president's hawkish advisers were turning against the war. As they did, Johnson became

almost paranoid. Critics, he said privately, were "out to get me." But as late as the fall of 1967, opposition remained disorganized. It was especially vehement on college campuses, some students objecting because they thought the United States had no business intervening in the Vietnam conflict, others because they feared being drafted, still others because so many students were obtaining educational deferments while young men who were unable to attend college were being conscripted. Then, in November 1967, Senator Eugene McCarthy of Minnesota, low-key, rather introspective, never a leading figure in the upper house, announced that he was a candidate for the 1968 Democratic presidential nomination. Opposition to the war was his issue.

Preventing Johnson from being renominated seemed on the surface impossible. Aside from the difficulty of defeating a "reigning" president, there were the domestic achievements of Johnson's Great Society program: the health insurance program for retired people, greatly expanded federal funding of education and public housing, to say nothing of the Civil Rights Act. Even Senator McCarthy took his chances of being nominated so lightly that he did not trouble to set up a real organization. He entered the campaign only to "alleviate . . . this sense of political helplessness." Someone, he decided, must step forward to put the Vietnam question before the voters.

Suddenly, early in 1968, on the heels of the latest announcement by the American military that the communists were about to crack, North Vietnam and Vietcong forces launched a general offensive to correspond with their Lunar New Year (Tet). Striking 39 of the 44 provincial capitals, many other towns and cities, and every American base, they caused chaos throughout South Vietnam. They held Hue, the old capital of the country, for weeks. To root them out of Saigon the Americans had to level large sections of the city. Elsewhere the destruction was total, an irony highlighted by the remark of an American officer after the recapture of the village of Ben Tre: "It became necessary to destroy the town to save it."

The Tet offensive was essentially a series of raids; the communists did not expect to hold the cities indefinitely, and they did not. Their losses were enormous. Nevertheless, the psychological impact in South Vietnam and in the United States made Tet a clear victory for the North. American

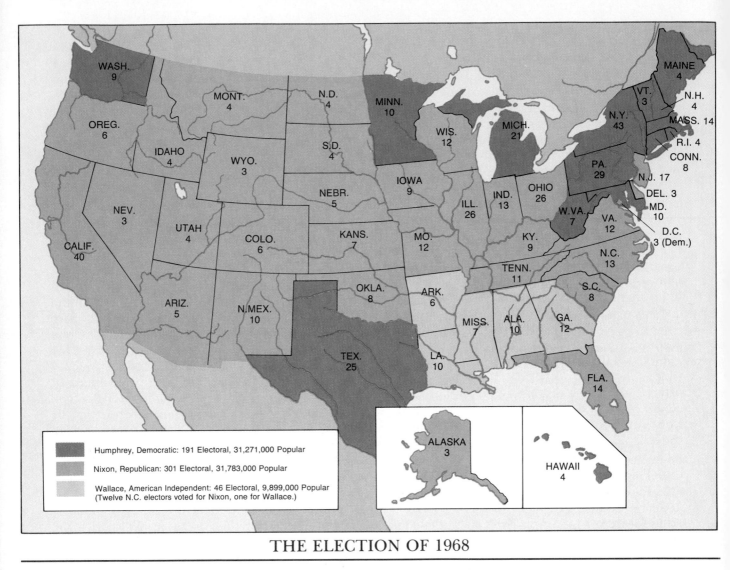

THE ELECTION OF 1968

pollsters reported an enormous shift of public opinion against further escalation of the fighting. When the commander of American forces, General William C. Westmoreland, described Tet as a communist defeat and when it came out that the administration was considering sending an additional 206,000 American troops to South Vietnam, McCarthy, campaigning before the first primary in New Hampshire, suddenly became a formidable figure. Thousands of students and other volunteers flocked to the state to ring doorbells in his behalf. On election day he polled 42 percent of the Democratic vote.

The political situation was monumentally con-

fused. Before the primary, former attorney general Robert F. Kennedy, brother of the slain president, had refused either to seek the Democratic nomination or to support McCarthy, though he disliked Johnson intensely and was opposed to his policy in Vietnam. McCarthy's strong showing caused Kennedy to change his mind. Had he done so earlier, McCarthy might have withdrawn in his favor, for Kennedy had powerful political and popular support. After New Hampshire, McCarthy understandably decided to remain in the contest.

Compounding this confusion, President Johnson suddenly withdrew from the race. Vice-President Hubert H. Humphrey then announced his candidacy, though not until it was too late for him to enter the primaries. Kennedy carried the primaries in Indiana and Nebraska. McCarthy won in Wisconsin and Oregon. In the climactic contest in California, Kennedy won by a small margin. However, immediately after his victory speech at a Los Angeles hotel, he was assassinated by Sirhan Sirhan, a young Arab nationalist who had been incensed by Kennedy's support of Israel. In effect, Kennedy's death assured the nomination of Humphrey; most professional politicians distrusted McCarthy, who seemed a diffident and aloof politician.

The contest for the Republican nomination was far less dramatic, though its outcome, the nomination of Richard M. Nixon, would have been hard to predict a few years earlier. After losing to Kennedy in 1960, he ran unsuccessfully for governor of California in 1962, then moved to New York City and joined a prominent law firm. But he remained active in Republican affairs, making countless speeches and attending political meetings throughout the country. In 1964 he campaigned hard for Goldwater. When no other Republican developed extensive support as the 1968 election approached, Nixon entered the race, swept the primaries, and won an easy first-ballot victory at the Republican convention.

Nixon then astounded the country and dismayed liberals by choosing Governor Spiro T. Agnew of Maryland as his running mate. Agnew was a political unknown. ("Spiro who?" jokesters asked.) He had been elected governor by defeating a segregationist Democrat, but after the rioting in Baltimore following the murder of Martin Luther King, Jr., he had criticized Maryland blacks for not restraining the militants. Nixon chose him primarily to attract southern votes.

Placating the South seemed necessary because Governor George C. Wallace of Alabama was making a determined bid to win enough electoral votes for his American Independent party to prevent any candidate's obtaining a majority. Wallace was flagrantly antiblack and anti-intellectual. (College professors were among his favorite targets. In attacking them he used such worn images as "ivory tower folks with pointed heads" and, more inventive, people without "sense enough to park a bicycle straight.") He seemed sure to attract substantial southern and conservative support. He denounced federal "meddling," the "coddling" of criminals, and the forced

A protester at the Democratic convention in July 1968, being led away by Chicago policemen. Unruly opposition to the process by which Democrats settled on Hubert H. Humphrey as the party's nominee for the presidency, and the heavy-handed response of Mayor Richard Daley to these protests, persuaded many voters that the fate of the republic would be safer in Republican hands.

desegregation of schools. Nixon's choice of Agnew appeared to be an effort to appeal to the groups that Wallace attracted.

This Republican strategy heightened the tension surrounding the Democratic convention, which met in Chicago in late August. Humphrey delegates controlled the convention. The vice-president had a solid liberal record on domestic issues, but he had supported Johnson's Vietnam policy with equal solidity. Voters who could not stomach the Nixon-Agnew ticket and who opposed the war faced a difficult choice. Several thousand activists representing a dozen groups, advocating tactics ranging from orderly demonstrations to civil disobedience to indiscriminate violence, descended on Chicago to put pressure on the delegates to repudiate the Johnson Vietnam policy.

In the tense atmosphere that resulted, the party

hierarchy overreacted. The mayor of Chicago, Richard J. Daley, whose ability to influence election results had been demonstrated often, ringed the convention hall with policemen to protect it from disruption. This was a reasonable precaution in itself. Inside the building the delegates nominated Humphrey and adopted a war plank satisfactory to Johnson. Outside, however, provoked by the abusive language and violent behavior of radical demonstrators, the police tore into the protesters, in Norman Mailer's graphic phrase "like a chain saw cutting into wood," while millions watched on television in fascinated horror.

At first the mayhem in Chicago seemed to benefit Nixon by strengthening the convictions of many voters that the tougher treatment of criminals and dissenters that he and Agnew were calling for was necessary. Those who were critical of the Chicago police tended to blame Humphrey, whom Mayor Daley supported.

Nixon campaigned at a deliberate, dignified pace. He made relatively few public appearances, relying instead on carefully arranged television interviews and taped commercials prepared by an advertising agency. He stressed firm enforcement of the law and his desire "to bring us together." As to Vietnam, he would "end the war and win the peace," by just what means he did not say. Agnew, in his blunt, coarse way, assaulted Humphrey, the Democrats, and left-wing dissident groups. (Critics who remembered Nixon's own political style in the era of Joseph McCarthy called Agnew "Nixon's Nixon.")

The Democratic campaign was badly organized. Humphrey was subjected to merciless heckling from antiwar audiences. He seemed far behind in the early stages. Shortly before election day, President Johnson helped him greatly by suspending air attacks on North Vietnam, and in the long run the Republican strategy helped too. Black voters and the urban poor had no practical choice but to vote Democratic. Gradually Humphrey gained ground, and on election day the popular vote was close: Nixon slightly less than 31.8 million, Humphrey nearly 31.3 million. Nixon's electoral college margin, however, was substantial—301 to 191. The remaining 46 electoral votes went to Wallace, whose 9.9 million votes came to 13.5 percent of the total. Despite Nixon's triumph, the Democrats retained control of both houses of Congress.

Nixon as President

When he took office in January 1969, Richard Nixon projected an image of calm and deliberate statesmanship; he introduced no startling changes, proposed no important new legislation. The major economic problem he faced, inflation, was primarily a result of the heavy military expenditures and easy-money policies of the Johnson administration. Nixon cut federal spending and balanced the 1969 budget, while the Federal Reserve Board forced up interest rates in order to slow the expansion of the money supply. The object was to reduce the rate of economic growth without causing heavy unemployment or precipitating a recession (the word *depression* had apparently passed out of the vocabulary of economists). Even its supporters admitted that this policy would check inflation only slowly, and when prices continued to rise, there was mounting uneasiness. Labor unions demanded large wage increases. The problem was complicated by mounting deficits in the United States' balance of trade with foreign nations, the product of an overvaluation of the dollar that encouraged Americans to buy foreign goods.

In 1970 Congress passed a law giving the president power to regulate prices and wages. Nixon had opposed this legislation, but in the summer of 1971 he decided to use it. First he announced a 90-day price and wage freeze (Phase I) and placed a 10 percent surcharge on imports. Then he set up a pay board and a price commission with authority to limit wage and price increases when the freeze ended (Phase II). These controls did not check inflation completely—and they angered union leaders, who felt that labor was being shortchanged—but they did slow the upward spiral. A 7.9 percent devaluation of the dollar in December 1971 helped the economy by making American products more competitive in foreign markets.

In handling other domestic issues, the president was less firm, sometimes even confused. He advocated a bold plan for a minimum income for poor families, which alarmed his conservative supporters and got nowhere in Congress. Hoping to strengthen the Republican position in that body, he adopted a so-called southern strategy of seeking the support of southern conservative Democrats. He checked further federal efforts to force school desegregation on reluctant local districts, and he set out to add what he called "strict constructionists" to the Supreme Court, which he believed had swung too far to the left in such areas as race relations and the rights of persons accused of committing crimes.

When Chief Justice Earl Warren retired in June 1969, Nixon was eager to divert the Court from the strong civil rights positions that it had taken during the Warren years. To replace Warren he chose a conservative, Warren E. Burger. The Senate ratified the appointment of Burger, but when Nixon sought to fill the seat of Justice Abe Fortas, who had resigned under fire after it came out that he had accepted fees from questionable sources while on the bench, with another conservative, Judge Clement F. Haynsworth, Jr., of South Carolina, the Senate rejected him on political grounds. The angry president then submitted the name of Judge G. Harrold Carswell of Florida. He also was turned down because of his alleged racist attitudes and his mediocre record on the bench.

In the face of a mass of evidence, Nixon refused to believe that the nominations were rejected for the reasons stated; he declared that "no southern conservative" could run the "liberal" Senate gauntlet successfully, and to prevent the Senate from proving him wrong he nominated a liberal, Harry A. Blackmun of Minnesota. Blackmun won the unanimous approval of the Senate. Although the Burger Court was less liberal than the Warren Court, it was far from being as conservative as Nixon apparently wanted. In 1972 it declared that the death penalty, as currently used, was a cruel and unusual punishment and thus in violation of the Eighth Amendment, and in 1973 it struck down state antiabortion legislation.

"Vietnamizing" the War

Whatever his difficulties on the domestic front, Nixon considered the solution of the Vietnam problem his chief task. When the war in Southeast Asia first burst upon American consciousness in 1954, he had favored military intervention in keeping with the containment policy. As controversy over American policy developed, he had supported most of the actions of Presidents Kennedy and Johnson. During the 1968 campaign he played down the Vietnam issue. Though he insisted he would end the war on "honorable" terms if elected, he suggested nothing very different from what Johnson was doing.

In office, Nixon proposed a phased withdrawal of all non–South Vietnamese troops, to be followed by an internationally supervised election in South Vietnam. The North Vietnamese rejected this scheme and insisted that the United States withdraw its forces unconditionally. Their intransigence left the president in a difficult position. Probably the majority of Americans considered his proposal eminently fair. With equal certainty, a majority was unwilling to increase the scale of the fighting to compel the communists to accept it, and as the war dragged on, costs in lives and money rising, the desire to extricate American troops from the conflict intensified. However, large numbers of Americans would not face up to the consequences of gratifying this desire: ending the war on the communists' terms. Nixon could not compel the foe to negotiate meaningfully, yet every passing day added to the strength of antiwar sentiment, which, as it expressed itself in ever more emphatic terms, in turn led to deeper divisions in the country.

The president responded to the dilemma by trying to build up the South Vietnamese armed forces so that American troops could pull out without the communists overrunning South Vietnam. He shipped so many planes to the Vietnamese that they came to have the fourth largest air force in the world. The trouble with this strategy of "Vietnamization" was that for 15 years the United States had been trying without success to make the South Vietnamese capable of defending themselves. For complicated reasons—the incompetence, corruption, and reactionary character of the Saigon regime probably being the most important—South Vietnamese troops had seldom displayed much enthusiasm for the tough jungle fighting at which the North Vietnamese and the Vietcong excelled. Nevertheless, efforts at Vietnamization were stepped up, and in June 1969 Nixon announced that he would soon reduce the number of American soldiers in Vietnam by 25,000. In September he promised that an additional 35,000 men would be withdrawn.

These steps did not quiet American protesters. On October 15 a national antiwar demonstration, Vietnam Moratorium Day, organized by students, produced an unprecedented outpouring all over the country. This massive display produced one of Vice-

President Agnew's most notorious blasts of adjectival invective: He said that the moratorium was an example of "national masochism" led by "an effete corps of impudent snobs who characterize themselves as intellectuals." A few days later he called on the country to "separate" radical students from society "with no more regret than we should feel over discarding rotten apples from a barrel," which at least had a quality of terseness that most of Agnew's pronouncements lacked.

A second Moratorium Day brought a crowd estimated at 250,000 to Washington to march past the White House. The president was unmoved. He could not be influenced by protests, he insisted, and during one of the Washington demonstrations he passed the time watching a football game on television. On November 3 he defended his policy in a televised speech. He stressed the sincerity of his peace efforts, the unreasonableness of the communists, the responsibility of the United States to protect the South Vietnamese people from communist reprisals and to honor its international commitments. He announced that he planned to remove all American ground forces from Vietnam. The next day, reporting a flood of telegrams and calls supporting his position, he declared that a "si-

lent majority" of the American people approved his course.

For a season, events appeared to vindicate Nixon's position. A gradual slowing of military activity in Vietnam had reduced American casualties to what those who did not find the war morally unbearable considered "tolerable" levels. Troop withdrawals continued in an orderly fashion. A new lottery system for drafting men for military duty eliminated some of the inequities in the selective service law.

But the war continued. Early in 1970 revelations that in 1968 an American unit had massacred civilians, including dozens of women and children, in a Vietnamese hamlet known as My Lai, revived the controversy over the purposes of the war and its corrosive effects on those who were fighting it. The American people, it seemed, were being torn apart by the war: one from another according to each one's interpretation of events, many within themselves as they tried to balance the war's horrors against their pride, their dislike of communism, and their unwillingness to turn their backs on their elected leader.

Not even Nixon's most implacable enemy could find reason to think that he wished the war to go on. Its human, economic, and social costs could only vex his days and threaten his future reputation. When he reduced the level of the fighting, the communists merely waited for further reductions. When he raised it, many of his own people denounced him. If he pulled out of Vietnam entirely, other Americans would be outraged.

Perhaps his error lay in his unwillingness to admit his own uncertainty, something the greatest presidents—one thinks immediately of Lincoln and Franklin Roosevelt—were never afraid to do. Facing a dilemma, he tried to convince the world that he was firmly in control of events, with the result that at times he seemed more like a high school valedictorian declaiming sententiously about the meaning of life than the mature statesman he so desperately wished to be. Thus he heightened the tensions he sought to relax—in America, in Vietnam, and elsewhere.

Even after the necessarily high-casualty "search and destroy" offensive strategy favored by President Johnson's military advisers gave way in 1969 to a more cautious use of American infantry units by President Nixon's commanders, combat deaths continued as "Vietnamization" proceeded.

The Cambodian "Incursion"

Late in April 1970 Nixon announced that Vietnamization was proceeding more rapidly than he had

An Ohio National Guard skirmish line of gas-masked troops advances up a hill on the campus of Kent State University, May 4, 1970. A moment later the guardsmen turned and fired on student antiwar demonstrators, killing four.

hoped, that communist power was weakening, that within a year another 150,000 American soldiers would be extracted from Vietnam. A week later he announced that military intelligence had indicated that the enemy was consolidating its "sanctuaries" in neutral Cambodia and that he was therefore dispatching thousands of American troops to destroy these bases.* He was in fact escalating the war. He even resumed the bombing of targets in North Vietnam. "You've got to electrify people with bold decisions," he told the Joint Chiefs of Staff. "Let's go blow the hell out of them."

To foes of the war, Nixon's decision seemed so appallingly unwise that some of them began to fear that he had become mentally unbalanced. The contradictions between his confident statements about Vietnamization and his alarmist description of powerful enemy forces poised like a dagger 30-odd miles from Saigon did not seem the product of a reasoning mind. His failure to consult congressional leaders or many of his advisers before drastically altering his policy, the critics claimed, was unconstitutional and irresponsible. His insensitive response to the avalanche of criticism that descended on him further disturbed observers.

Students took the lead in opposing the invasion

of Cambodia. Young people had been prominent in the opposition to the war from early in the conflict. Some objected to war in principle. Many more believed that this particular war was wrong because it was being fought against a small country on the other side of the globe where America's vital interests did not seem to be threatened. As the war dragged on and casualties mounted, student opposition to the draft became intense.

Nixon's shocking announcement triggered many campus demonstrations. One college where feeling ran high was Kent State University in Ohio. For several days students there clashed with local police; they broke windows and caused other damage to property. When the governor of Ohio called out the National Guard, angry students pelted the soldiers with stones. During a noontime protest on May 4 the Guardsmen, who were poorly trained in crowd control, suddenly opened fire. Four students were killed, two of them women who were merely passing by on their way to class.

While the nation reeled from this shock, two black students at Jackson State University were killed by Mississippi state policemen. A wave of student strikes followed, closing down hundreds of colleges, including many that had seen no previous unrest. Moderate students by the tens of thousands had joined with the radicals.

The almost unanimous condemnation of the invasion and of the way it had been planned shook

---

* American planes had been bombing Cambodia for some time, but this fact was not known to the public (or to Congress) until 1973.

Nixon hard. He backtracked, pulling American ground troops out of Cambodia quickly. But he did not change his Vietnam policy, and in fact the Cambodian uproar apparently stiffened his determination. As American ground troops were withdrawn, he stepped up air attacks. The balance of forces remained in uneasy equilibrium through 1971. But late in March 1972 the North Vietnamese again mounted a series of assaults throughout South Vietnam. The president responded with heavier bombing, and he ordered the approaches to Haiphong and other northern ports sown with mines to cut off the communists' supplies.

Détente

But in the midst of these aggressive actions, Nixon and his principal foreign policy adviser, Henry Kissinger, devised a bold and ingenious diplomatic offensive. Abandoning a lifetime of treating communism as a single worldwide conspiracy aimed at destroying capitalism, he was persuaded by Kissinger to deal with Russia and China as separate powers. If each dealt separately with the United States, they would have to deal differently one with the other as well.

First Nixon sent Kissinger secretly to China and the Soviet Union to prepare the way for summit meetings with the communist leaders. Both the Chinese and the Russians agreed to the meetings. Then, in February 1972, Nixon and Kissinger, accompanied by a small army of reporters and television crews, flew to Beijing. After much dining, sightseeing, posing for photographers, and consultation with Chinese officials, Nixon agreed to support the admission of China to the United Nations and to develop economic and cultural exchanges with the Chinese. Although these results appeared small, Nixon's visit, ending more than 20 years of adamant

President and Mrs. Nixon dining with Chinese Communist officials in Beijing in February 1972. Even Nixon's harshest critics conceded that his initiative in reopening U.S.-China relations was a diplomatic master stroke.

American refusal to accept the reality of the Chinese revolution, marked a dramatic reversal; as such it was hailed in the United States and elsewhere in the world.

In May, Nixon and Kissinger flew to Moscow. This trip also produced striking results. The mere fact that it took place while war still raged in Vietnam was remarkable. More important, however, the meeting resulted in the first Strategic Arms Limitation Treaty (SALT). The two powers agreed to stop making nuclear ballistic missiles and to reduce the number of antiballistic missiles in their arsenals to 200. Nixon also agreed to permit large sales of American grain to the Russians.

Nixon and Kissinger called the new policy *détente,* a French term meaning "relaxation of tensions." Détente lowered the cost of containment for the United States because it meant being more accommodating, which would reduce conflict, and making it easier to play one communist power off against the other. SALT did not end the production of atomic weapons, but such was the worldwide fear of a nuclear holocaust that any check on American and Russian arms production was regarded as encouraging. That both China and the Soviet Union had been willing to work for improved relations with the United States before America withdrew from Vietnam was also significant.

This fact, plus the failure of their offensive to overwhelm South Vietnam, led the North Vietnamese to make diplomatic concessions in the interest of getting the United States out of the war. Kissinger began negotiating seriously with their representatives in Paris in the summer of 1972. By October the draft of a settlement had been hammered out that provided for a cease-fire, the return of American prisoners of war, and the withdrawal of United States forces from Vietnam. Shortly before the presidential election, Kissinger announced that peace was "at hand."

Nixon Triumphant

A few days later President Nixon was reelected, defeating the Democratic candidate, Senator George McGovern of South Dakota, in a landslide—521 electoral votes to 17. McGovern carried only Massachusetts and the District of Columbia.

McGovern's campaign had been hampered by divisions within the Democratic party and by his tendency to advance poorly thought-out proposals, such as his scheme for funneling money directly to the poor, and his rather bumbling oratorical style. What was probably his worst blunder came after the discovery that the vice-presidential candidate he had chosen, Senator Thomas Eagleton of Missouri, had in the past undergone electroshock treatments following serious psychological difficulties. After some backing and filling, which left many voters with the impression that he was indecisive, McGovern forced Eagleton to withdraw. Sargent Shriver, former head of the Peace Corps, took Eagleton's place on the ticket.

The Eagleton affair hurt McGovern badly. Nevertheless, Nixon understandably interpreted his convincing triumph as an indication that the people approved of everything for which he stood. He had won over hundreds of thousands of voters who had supported Democrats in earlier elections. The "solid South" was again solid, but this time solidly Republican. Nixon's southern strategy of reducing the pressure for school desegregation and otherwise restricting federal efforts in behalf of blacks had a powerful attraction to northern blue-collar workers as well. They, and many people smarting from the repeated setbacks the country had experienced in Vietnam and resentful of what they considered the unpatriotic tactics of the doves, also approved of Nixon's refusal to pull out of Vietnam.

Suddenly Nixon loomed as one of the most powerful and successful presidents in American history. His bold attack on inflation, his tough-minded handling of the foreign trade question, even his harsh Vietnamese policy suggested decisiveness and self-confidence, qualities he had often seemed to lack. His willingness, despite his long history as a militant cold warrior, to negotiate with the communist nations in order to arrive at a détente that would lessen world tensions indicated a new flexibility and reasonableness. His landslide victory appeared to demonstrate that a large majority of the people approved of his way of tackling the major problems of the times.

His first reaction was to try to extract more favorable terms from the Vietnamese communists. Announcing that they were not bargaining in good faith over the remaining details of the peace treaty, he resumed the bombing of North Vietnam in December 1972, this time sending the mighty B-52s directly over Hanoi and other cities. The destructiveness of the attacks was great, but their effect-

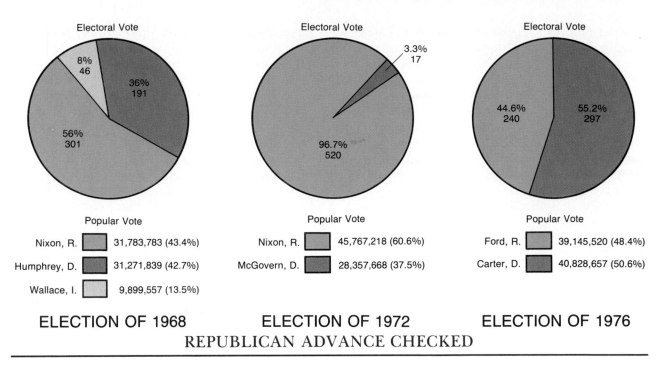

Electoral Vote

8%
46
36%
191
56%
301

Popular Vote

Nixon, R.		31,783,783 (43.4%)
Humphrey, D.		31,271,839 (42.7%)
Wallace, I.		9,899,557 (13.5%)

ELECTION OF 1968

Electoral Vote

3.3%
17
96.7%
520

Popular Vote

| Nixon, R. | | 45,767,218 (60.6%) |
| McGovern, D. | | 28,357,668 (37.5%) |

ELECTION OF 1972

Electoral Vote

44.6%
240
55.2%
297

Popular Vote

| Ford, R. | | 39,145,520 (48.4%) |
| Carter, D. | | 40,828,657 (50.6%) |

ELECTION OF 1976

REPUBLICAN ADVANCE CHECKED

iveness as a means of forcing concessions from the North Vietnamese was at best debatable, and they led for the first time to the loss of large numbers of the big strategic bombers.

Nevertheless, both sides had much to gain from ending the war. In January 1973 a settlement was finally reached. The North Vietnamese retained control of large sections of the South, and they agreed to release American prisoners of war within 60 days. When this was accomplished, the last American troops were pulled out of Vietnam. More than 57,000 Americans had died in the long war, and over 300,000 more had been wounded. The cost had reached a staggering $150 billion.

Whatever the price, the war was over for the United States, and Nixon took the credit for having ended it. He immediately turned to domestic issues, determined, he made clear, to change the direction in which the nation had been moving for decades. He sought on the one hand to strengthen the power of the presidency vis-à-vis Congress and on the other to decentralize administration by encouraging state and local management of government programs. He announced that he intended to reduce the interference of the federal government in the affairs of individuals. People should be more self-reliant, he said, and he denounced what he called "per-

missiveness." Overconcern for the interests of blacks and other minorities must end. Criminals should be punished "without pity." No person or group should be coddled by the state.

These aims brought Nixon into conflict with liberal congressmen of both parties, with the leaders of minority groups, and with people concerned about the increasing power of the executive. The conflict came to a head over the president's anti-inflation policy. After his second inauguration he ended Phase II price and wage controls and substituted Phase III, which depended on voluntary "restraints" (except in the areas of food, health care, and construction). This approach did not work. Prices soared in the most rapid inflation since the Korean War. In an effort to check the rise, Nixon set a rigid limit on federal expenditures; to keep within the limit, he cut back or abolished a large number of social welfare programs, and he reduced federal grants in support of science and education. He even impounded (refused to spend) funds already appropriated by Congress for purposes he disapproved.

Impoundment created a furor on Capitol Hill, and when Congress failed to override his vetoes of bills challenging his policy, it appeared that Nixon was in total command. The White House staff, headed by H. R. Haldeman ("the Prussian") and John Ehrlichman, dominated the Washington bureaucracy like princes of the blood or oriental viziers and dealt with legislators as though they were lackeys or eunuchs. When asked to account for their actions, they took refuge behind the shield of "executive privilege," the doctrine, never before applied so broadly, that discussions and communications within the executive branch were confidential and therefore immune from congressional scrutiny. Critics began to grumble about a new "imperial presidency." No one seemed capable of checking Nixon at any point.

The Watergate Break-in

On March 19, 1973, James McCord, a former FBI agent accused of burglary, wrote a letter to the judge presiding at his trial. His act precipitated a series of disclosures that disrupted and then destroyed the Nixon administration.

McCord had been employed during the 1972 presidential campaign as a security officer of the Committee to Re-elect the President (CREEP). At about 1 A.M. on June 17, 1972, he and four other men had broken into Democratic party headquarters at the Watergate, an apartment house and office building complex in Washington. The burglars were members of an unofficial surveillance group known as "the plumbers." Nixon had formed this group in 1971 after the so-called Pentagon Papers, a secret report on government policy in Vietnam, had been leaked to the press. The plumbers had been caught rifling files and installing electronic eavesdropping devices.

Two other Republican campaign officials were soon implicated in the affair. Their arrest aroused suspicions that the Republican party was behind the break-in. Nixon denied this. "I can say categorically," he announced on June 22, "that no one on the White House staff, no one in this Administration presently employed, was involved in this very bizarre incident." Most people evidently took the president at his word, and the affair did not materially affect the election. When brought to trial early in 1973, most of the defendants pleaded guilty.

McCord, who did not, was convicted by the jury. Before Judge John J. Sirica imposed sentences on the culprits, however, McCord wrote his letter. High

Republican officials had known about the burglary in advance and had persuaded most of the defendants to keep their connection secret, McCord claimed. Perjury had been committed during the trial.

The truth of McCord's charges swiftly became apparent. The head of CREEP, Jeb Stuart Magruder, and President Nixon's lawyer, John W. Dean III, admitted their involvement. Dean claimed in testimony before a special Senate Watergate investigation committee headed by Sam Ervin, Jr., of North Carolina, that Nixon had participated in efforts to cover up the affair. Among the disclosures that emerged over the following months were these:

That the acting director of the FBI, L. Patrick Gray, had destroyed documents related to the case.

That large sums of money had been paid the burglars at the instigation of the White House to ensure their silence.

That agents of the Nixon administration had burglarized the office of a psychiatrist, seeking evidence against one of his patients, Daniel Ellsberg, who had been charged with leaking the Pentagon papers to *The New York Times*. (This disclosure led to the immediate dismissal of the charges against Ellsberg by the presiding judge.)

That the CIA had, perhaps unwittingly, supplied equipment used in this burglary.

That CREEP officials had attempted to disrupt the campaigns of leading Democratic candidates during the 1972 primaries in a number of illegal ways.

That a number of corporations had made large contributions to the Nixon reelection campaign in violation of federal law.

That E. Howard Hunt, one of the Watergate criminals, had earlier forged State Department documents in an effort to make it appear that President Kennedy had been implicated in the assassination of President Ngo Dinh Diem of South Vietnam.

That the Nixon administration had placed wiretaps on the telephones of some of its own officials as well as on those of reporters critical of its policies without first obtaining authorization from the courts.

These revelations led to the discharge of John Dean and to the resignations of most of Nixon's closest advisers, including Haldeman, Ehrlichman, and Attorney General Richard Kleindienst. They also raised the question of the president's personal connection with the scandals. This he steadfastly denied. He insisted that he would investigate the Watergate affair thoroughly and see that the guilty were punished. He refused, however, to allow investigators to examine White House documents, again on grounds of executive privilege, which he continued to assert in very broad terms.

In the teeth of Nixon's denials, John Dean, testifying under oath before the Ervin committee, stated flatly and in circumstantial detail that the president had been closely involved in the Watergate cover-up. (Before testifying, Dean consulted with the conservative Senator Barry Goldwater. When he explained what he was going to say, Goldwater replied: "Hell, I'm not surprised. That goddamn Nixon has been lying all of his life.") Dean had been a persuasive witness, but—unlike Goldwater—many people were reluctant to believe that a president could lie so cold-bloodedly to the entire country. Therefore, when it came out during later hearings of the Ervin committee that the president had systematically made secret tape recordings of White House conversations and telephone calls, the disclosure caused a sensation. It seemed obvious that these tapes would settle the question of Nixon's involvement once and for all. Again he refused to allow access to the evidence.

One result of the scandals and of Nixon's attitude was a precipitous decline in his standing in public opinion polls. Calls for his resignation, even for impeachment, began to be heard. Yielding to pressure, he agreed to the appointment of an "independent" special prosecutor to investigate the Watergate affair, and he promised the appointee, Professor Archibald Cox of the Harvard Law School, full cooperation.

Cox swiftly aroused the president's ire by seeking access to White House records, including the tapes. When Nixon refused to turn over the tapes, Cox obtained a subpoena from Judge Sirica ordering the president to do so. The administration appealed and lost in the appellate court. Then, while the case was headed for the Supreme Court, Nixon ordered the new attorney general, Elliot Richardson, to dismiss Cox. Both Richardson, who had promised the Senate during his confirmation hearings that the special prosecutor would have a free hand, and his chief assistant, William Ruckelshaus, resigned rather than do so. The solicitor general, Robert H. Bork, third-ranking officer of the Justice Department, carried out Nixon's order.

Garry Trudeau and his politically biting cartoon strip Doonesbury *enlivened the Vietnam and Watergate* years. Doonesbury *became the first cartoon strip to win a Pulitzer Prize. (Ron Ziegler was President Nixon's press secretary.)*

These events, which occurred on Saturday, October 20, were promptly dubbed the Saturday Night Massacre. They caused an outburst of public indignation. Congress was bombarded by thousands of letters and telegrams demanding the president's impeachment. The House Judiciary Committee, headed by Peter W. Rodino, Jr., of New Jersey, began an investigation to see if enough evidence for impeachment existed.

Once again Nixon backed down. He agreed to turn over the tapes to Judge Sirica with the understanding that relevant materials could be presented to the grand jury investigating the Watergate affair, but that nothing would be revealed to the public. He then named a new special prosecutor, Leon Jaworski, and promised him access to whatever White House documents he needed. However, it soon came out that some of the tapes were missing and that an important section of another had been deliberately erased.

More Troubles

The nation had never before experienced such a series of morale-shattering crises. While the seemingly unending complications of Watergate were unfolding during 1973, a number of unrelated disasters struck. First, pushed by a shortage of grains resulting from massive Russian purchases authorized by the administration as part of its détente with the Soviet Union, food prices shot up; for example, wheat went from $1.45 a bushel to over $5.00. Nixon imposed another price freeze, which led to shortages, and when the freeze was lifted, prices resumed their steep ascent.

Then Vice-President Agnew (defender of law and order, foe of permissiveness) was accused of income tax fraud and of having accepted bribes while county executive of Baltimore and governor of Maryland. After vehemently denying all the charges for two months, Agnew, to escape a jail term, admitted in October that he had been guilty of tax evasion and resigned as vice-president. He was fined $10,000 and placed on three years' probation, and the Justice Department published a 40,000-word description of his wrongdoings.

Under the new Twenty-fifth Amendment, President Nixon nominated Gerald R. Ford of Michigan as vice-president, and he was confirmed by Congress. Ford had served continuously in Congress since 1949, as minority leader since 1964. His positions on public issues were close to Nixon's; he was an internationalist in foreign affairs and both a conservative and a convinced Republican partisan on domestic issues.

Not long after the Agnew fiasco, Nixon, responding to charges that he had paid almost no income taxes during his presidency, published his 1969–1972 returns. They showed that he had paid only about $1,600 in two years during which his income had exceeded half a million dollars. Although Nixon claimed that his returns were perfectly legal—he had taken huge deductions for the gift of some of his vice-presidential papers to the National Archives—the legality of his deductions, to say nothing of their propriety, was questionable. Combined with charges that millions of dollars of public funds had been spent on improvements for his private residences in California and Florida, the tax issue further eroded his reputation, so much so that he felt obliged, during a televised press conference, to assure the audience: "I am not a crook."

The Oil Crisis

Still another disaster followed as a result of the new war that broke out in October 1973 between Israel and the Arab states. The fighting, though bloody, was brief and inconclusive; a truce was soon arranged under the auspices of the United States and the Soviet Union. But in an effort to force western nations to compel Israel to withdraw from lands held since the Six-Day War of 1967, the Arabs cut off oil shipments to the United States, Japan, and most of western Europe. A worldwide energy crisis ensued.

The immediate shortage resulting from the Arab oil boycott was ended by the patient diplomacy of Henry Kissinger, whom Nixon had made secretary of state at the beginning of his second administration. After weeks of negotiating in the spring of 1974, first with Egypt and Israel, then with Syria and Israel, he obtained a tentative agreement, which involved Israel's withdrawal from some of the territory it had occupied in the 1967 war. The Arab nations then lifted the boycott.

A revolution had taken place. From the middle of the 19th century until after World War II, the United States had produced far more oil than it could use. However, the phenomenal expansion of oil consumption that occurred after the war soon absorbed the surplus. By the late 1960s American car owners were driving more than a trillion miles a year. Petroleum was being used to manufacture nylon and other synthetic fibers as well as paints, insecticides, fertilizers, and many plastic products. Oil and natural gas became the principal fuels for home heating. Natural gas in particular was used increasingly in factories and electric utility plants, because it was less polluting than coal and most other fuels. The Clean Air Act of 1965 speeded the process of conversion from coal to gas by countless

Gas stations all over the country began running out of gas in 1973; the shortage worsened through the winter and into 1974.

industrial consumers. Because of these developments, at the outbreak of the 1973 Arab-Israeli war the United States was importing one-third of its oil.

In 1960 the principal oil exporters—Venezuela, Saudi Arabia, Kuwait, Iraq, and Iran—had formed a cartel, the Organization of Petroleum Exporting Countries. For many years OPEC had been unable to control the world price of oil, which, on the eve of the 1973 war, was about $3.00 a barrel. The success of the Arab oil boycott served to unite the members of OPEC, and when the boycott was lifted, they boldly announced that the price was going up to $11.65 a barrel.

The announcement caused consternation throughout the industrial world. Soaring prices for oil meant soaring prices for everything made from petroleum or with petroleum-powered machinery. In the United States gasoline prices doubled over-

night, and the trend of all prices rose at a rate of more than 10 percent a year. This double-digit inflation, which afflicted nearly all the countries of the world, added considerably to President Nixon's woes.

The Judgment: "Expletive Deleted"

Meanwhile, special prosecutor Jaworski continued his investigation of the Watergate scandals, and the House Judiciary Committee pursued its study of the impeachment question. In March 1974 a grand jury indicted Haldeman, Ehrlichman, former attorney general John Mitchell, who had been head of CREEP at the time of the break-in, and four other White House aides for conspiring to block the Watergate investigation. The jurors also named Nixon an "unindicted co-conspirator," Jaworski having informed them that their power to indict a president was constitutionally questionable. Judge Sirica thereupon turned over the jury's evidence against Nixon to the Judiciary Committee. Then both the Internal Revenue Service and a joint congressional committee, having separately audited the president's income tax returns, announced that most of his deductions had been unjustified. The IRS assessed him nearly half a million dollars in taxes and interest, which he agreed to pay.

In an effort to check the mounting criticism, Nixon late in April released edited transcripts of the tapes he had turned over to the court the previous November. If he had expected the material to convince the public that he had been ignorant of the attempt to cover up the administration's connection with Watergate, he was sadly mistaken. In addition to much incriminating evidence, the transcripts provided a fascinating and to most persons shocking view of how he conducted himself in private. His repeated use of foul language, so out of keeping with his public image, offended millions. The phrase "expletive deleted," inserted in place of words considered too vulgar for publication in family newspapers, became a catchphrase overnight. Nixon appeared to be ignorant of the simplest legal principles. In conversations he seemed confused, indecisive, and devoid of concern for the public interest. The publication of the transcripts led even some of his strongest supporters to demand that he resign. And once the Judiciary Committee obtained the actual tapes, it became clear that the White House transcripts were in crucial respects inaccurate. Much material prejudicial to the president's case had been suppressed.

Yet impeaching a president seemed so drastic a step that many people felt that more direct proof of Nixon's involvement in the cover-up was necessary. Nixon insisted that all the relevant information was contained in these tapes; he adamantly refused to turn over others to the special prosecutor or the Judiciary Committee.

With the defendants in the Watergate case demanding access to tapes that they claimed would prove their innocence, Jaworski was compelled either to obtain them or to risk having the charges dismissed on the ground that the government was withholding evidence. He therefore subpoenaed 64 additional tapes. Nixon, through his lawyer James St. Clair, refused to obey the subpoena. Swiftly the case of *United States* v. *Richard M. Nixon* went to the Supreme Court.

In the summer of 1974 the Watergate drama reached its climax. The Judiciary Committee, following months of study of the evidence behind closed doors, decided to conduct its deliberations in open session. While millions watched on television, 38 members of the House of Representatives debated the charges. The discussions revealed both the thoroughness of the investigation and the soul-searching efforts of the representatives to render an impartial judgment. Three articles of impeachment were adopted. They charged the president with obstructing justice, misusing the powers of his office, and failing to obey the committee's subpoenas. On the first two, many of the Republicans on the committee joined with the Democrats in voting aye, a clear indication that the full House would vote to impeach.

On the eve of the debates, the Supreme Court had ruled unanimously that the president must turn over the 64 subpoenaed tapes to the special prosecutor. Executive privilege had its place, the Court stated, but no person, not even a president, could "withhold evidence that is demonstrably relevant in a criminal trial." For reasons that soon became obvious, Nixon seriously considered defying the Court. Only when convinced that to do so would make his impeachment and conviction certain—and would compel his lawyer, St. Clair, to withdraw from the case—did he agree to comply.

He would not, however, resign. Even if the

President Nixon, with his daughter Tricia at his side, announcing his resignation on August 8, 1974. His subsequent remarks to his staff, rambling, often incoherent and self-pitying, revealed a broken man.

House impeached him, he was counting on his ability to hold the support of at least 34 senators (one-third plus one of the full Senate) to escape conviction. But events were passing beyond his control. The 64 subpoenaed tapes had to be transcribed and analyzed; following the Supreme Court decision, Judge Sirica pointedly ordered St. Clair to prepare his material promptly.

Incredibly, up to this time, St. Clair had not listened to the tapes; Nixon had assured him that they contained no relevant evidence and had refused to allow him to judge the accuracy of this statement for himself. Now St. Clair had to listen, and when he did, Nixon's fate was sealed. Three recorded conversations between the president and H. R. Haldeman on June 23, 1972 (less than a week after the break-in and only one day after Nixon had assured the nation that no one in the White House had been involved in the affair), proved conclusively that Nixon had tried to obstruct justice by engaging the CIA in an effort to persuade the FBI not to follow up leads in the case on the spurious basis that national security was involved.

The president's defenders had all along insisted not so much that he was innocent as that solid proof of his guilt had not been demonstrated. Where, in the metaphor of the moment, was the "smoking

DEPRESSION, PROSPERITY, AND INFLATION, 1921–1985

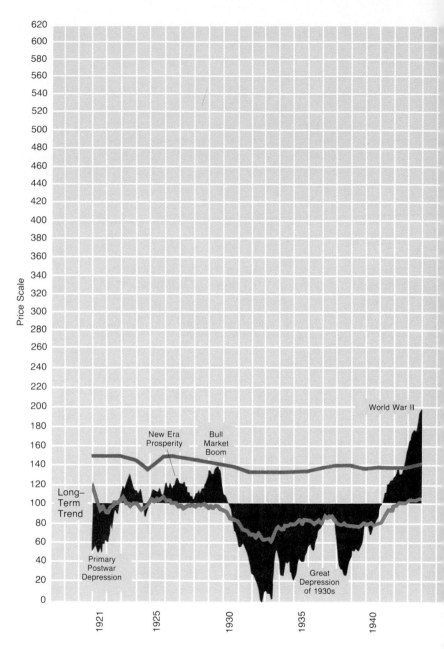

Here is the third of three price graphs. The price scale on the left axis applies to the blue line; it shows wholesale prices as they have varied around the long-term trend line of 100. Prices were much below normal during the Great Depression of the 1930s and were held down by price controls during World War II, but since then they have skyrocketed, especially during OPEC oil cartel petroleum price hikes in the 1970s. On the right axis scale is the price of a gallon of gas; the green curve reflects OPEC's inflationary influence.

gun"? they asked. That weapon had now been found, and it bore the unmistakable fingerprints of President Richard M. Nixon.

Exactly what happened in the White House after St. Clair listened to the Nixon-Haldeman conversations is not yet known. The president's chief advisers pressed him to release the material at once and admit that he had erred in holding it back. This he did on August 5; that in so doing he specifically admitted that he had withheld information from his

lawyer suggests that St. Clair, whose professional reputation was at stake, had played a major role. When they read the new transcripts, all the Republican members of the Judiciary Committee who had voted against the impeachment articles reversed themselves. Understandably, they felt betrayed; they had accepted the president's assurances that all the evidence was in, and they had gone on record before millions of eyes in his defense. The last remnants of Nixon's congressional support

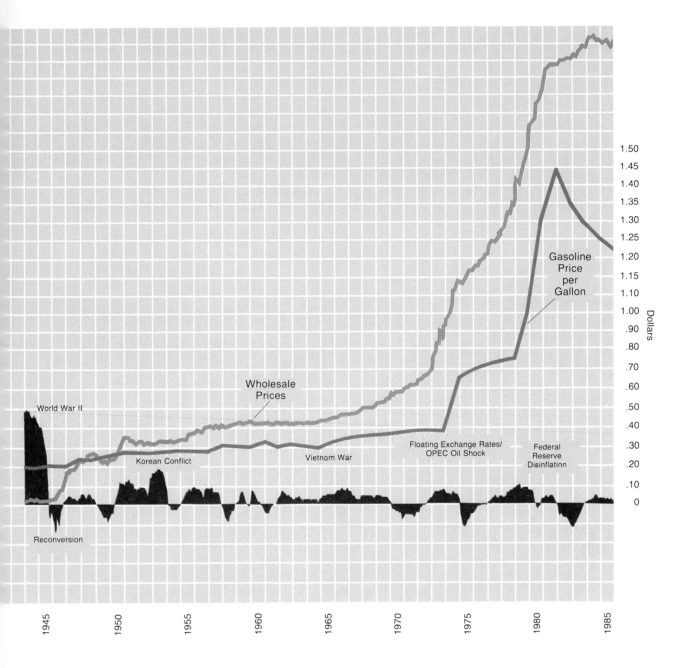

crumbled. Republican leaders told him categorically that the House would impeach him and that no more than a handful of senators would vote to acquit him.

The Meaning of Watergate

On August 8 Nixon announced his resignation. "Dear Mr. Secretary," his terse official letter to the secretary of state ran, "I hereby resign the Office of President of the United States. Sincerely, Richard Nixon." The resignation took effect at noon on August 9, when Gerald Ford was sworn in as president.

The meaning of "Watergate" became immediately the subject of much speculation. Whether Nixon's crude efforts to dominate Congress, to crush or inhibit dissent, and to subvert the electoral process would have permanently altered the American political system had they succeeded is beyond knowing. However, the orderly way in which these efforts were checked suggests that the system would have survived in any case.

Nixon's own drama is and must remain one of the most fascinating and enigmatic episodes in American history. Despite his fall from the heights because of personal flaws, his was not a tragedy in the Greek sense. When he finally yielded power, he seemed without remorse or even awareness of his transgressions. Although he enjoyed the pomp and circumstance attendant on his high office and trumpeted his achievements to all the world, he was devoid of the classic hero's pride. Did he really intend to smash all opposition and rule like a tyrant, or was he driven by lack of confidence in himself? His stubborn aggressiveness and his overblown view of

executive privilege may have reflected a need for constant reassurance that he was a mighty leader, that the nation accepted his right to exercise authority. One element in his downfall, preserved for posterity in videotapes of his television appearances, was that even while he was assuring the country of his innocence most vehemently, he did not look like a victim of the machinations of overzealous supporters. Perhaps at some profound level he did not want to be believed.

This explanation of Richard Nixon, however tentative, is at least comforting—it makes him appear less menacing. If it is correct, Americans can deplore the injuries he inflicted on society and still feel for him a certain compassion.

Milestones

1942 Congress of Racial Equality (CORE) founded
1955–
1956 Montgomery, Alabama, bus boycott
1956 Southern Christian Leadership Conference founded
1960 Student Nonviolent Coordinating Committee (SNCC) founded
1961 Freedom Riders "invade" the South
1963 President Ngo Dihn Diem of South Vietnam assassinated
    Martin Luther King, Jr., "Letter from Birmingham Jail"
1964 Gulf of Tonkin Resolution leads to escalation of Vietnam War
    Civil Rights Act
    Economic Opportunity Act
1965 Immigration Act ends national origins system
    Medicare Act
    Elementary and Secondary Education Act
    Clean Air Act
1968 Communist Tet offensive in South Vietnam
    American troop strength in Vietnam reaches 538,000
    Lyndon Johnson withdraws as presidential candidate

1969 Nixon announces "Vietnamization" of the war
1970 Nixon announces "incursion" in Cambodia
    Demonstrating antiwar students killed at Kent State and Jackson State universities
1971 Nixon freezes prices
1972 Break-in at Democratic headquarters in Washington, D.C.
    Nixon and Kissinger visit China and the Soviet Union
    Strategic Arms Limitation Treaty (SALT)
1973 House Judiciary Committee begins impeachment hearings
    Vice-President Spiro Agnew resigns
    Last American troops withdraw from South Vietnam
    Nixon fires special prosecutor Archibald Cox (Saturday Night Massacre)
1973–
1974 Arab oil boycott
1974 Supreme Court orders release of Nixon's White House tapes
    Nixon resigns; Gerald R. Ford becomes president

SUPPLEMENTARY READING

Titles marked with an asterisk have been published in paperback.

On Lyndon Johnson and the Johnson era, see J. F. Heath, **Decade of Disillusionment** (1980), and A. J. Matusow, **The Uraveling of America*** (1984). W. M. O'Neill, **Coming Apart: An Informal History of the 1960s*** (1971), and Geoffrey Hodgson, **America in Our Time** (1976), deal more broadly with the period. E. F. Goldman, **The Tragedy of Lyndon Johnson*** (1969), Doris Kearns, **Lyndon Johnson and the American Dream*** (1976), George Reedy, **Lyndon Johnson** (1982), and R. N. Goodwin, **Remembering America** (1988), are valuable memoirs.

To trace civil rights developments, consult Taylor Branch, **Parting the Waters*** (1988), David Garrow, **Bearing the Cross** (1981), Richard Kluger, **Simple Justice** (1975), Martin L. King, Jr., **Stride Toward Freedom*** (1958), and Malcolm X, **Autobiography** (1966).

On the election of 1968, T. H. White, **The Making of the President, 1968*** (1969), is lively and entertaining, while Joe McGinniss, **The Selling of the President, 1968*** (1969), is a fascinating account of the Republican advertising and television campaign. The best biography of Nixon is Stephen Ambrose, **Nixon** (1987–1989). Garry Wills, **Nixon Agonistes*** (1970), is a thoughtful though unfriendly analysis. See also R. S. Litwak, **Détente and the Nixon Doctrine** (1984), William Safire, **Before the Fall** (1975), and Rowland Evans, Jr., and R. D. Novak, **Nixon in the White House*** (1971). White's **Making of the President, 1972*** (1973) and **Breach of Faith: The Fall of Richard Nixon** (1975) are useful if not entirely satisfying.

The literature on the war in Vietnam is enormous. Stanley Karnow, **Vietnam: A History** (1983), is a straightforward narrative account, but see also A. J. Rotter, **The Path to Vietnam** (1987), Melvin Small, **Johnson, Nixon, and the Doves** (1988), Neil Sheehan, **A Bright and Shining Lie** (1988), Günter Lewy, **America in Vietnam*** (1980), Frances FitzGerald, **Fire in the Lake*** (1972), and David Halberstam, **The Best and the Brightest*** (1972); this last contains a mass of detail on the evolution of American policy, based on extensive interviews. William Shawcross, **Side-Show: Kissinger, Nixon, and the Destruction of Cambodia*** (1979), is extremely critical, and Norman Mailer, **The Armies of the Night*** (1968), is a vivid account of an antiwar demonstration in Washington.

R. S. Litwak, **Détente and the Nixon Doctrine** (1984), is a useful study of U.S.-Russian relations in the Nixon era, and Henry Kissinger's memoirs, **White House Years** (1979) and **Years of Upheaval** (1982), are important though, like most such works, self-serving.

A convenient summary of the almost infinite complexities of the Watergate affair is *New York Times* (ed.), **The End of a Presidency*** (1974), but see also Carl Bernstein and Robert Woodward, **All the President's Men*** (1974) and **Final Days*** (1976), J. W. Dean, **Blind Ambition*** (1976), and Leon Jaworski, **The Right and the Power*** (1976).

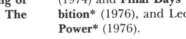

Society in Flux, 1945–1980

There's a time when the operation of the machine becomes so odious, makes you so sick at heart, that you can't take part. . . . You've got to indicate to the people that run it, the people who own it, that unless you're free, the machine will be prevented from working at all.

MARIO SAVIO, *student, University of California, 1964*

I'm not saying that women leaders would eliminate violence. We are not more moral than men; we are only uncorrupted by power so far.

GLORIA STEINEM, *1970*

Despite Lyndon Johnson's extravagant style and his landslide defeat of Barry Goldwater in the 1964 presidential election, the tone of his inaugural address in January 1965 was uncharacteristically restrained. The nation was "prosperous, great, and mighty," he said, but "we have no promise from God that our greatness will endure." He was obviously thinking of the enormous changes that were occurring in the country. He spoke of "this fragile existence," and he warned the people that they lived "in a world where change and growth seem to tower beyond the control, and even the judgment of men."

A Dynamic Society

The population was expanding rapidly. During the depressed 1930s it had increased by 9 million; in the 1950s it rose by more than 28 million, in the 1960s by another 24 million, and in the 1970s by 24 million more. Population experts observed startling shifts within this expanding mass. The westward movement had by no means ended with the closing of the frontier in the 1890s. One indication of this was the admission of Hawaii and Alaska to the Union in 1959. More significant was the growth of the Sunbelt—Florida and the states of the Southwest. California added more than 5 million to its population between 1950 and 1960, and in 1963 it passed New York to become the most populous state in the Union. Nevada and Arizona were expanding at an even more rapid rate.

The climate of the Southwest was particularly attractive to older people, especially after the perfection of mass-produced room air conditioners, and the population growth reflected the prosperity that enabled pensioners and other retired persons to settle there. At the same time, the area attracted millions of young workers, for it became the center of the aircraft and electronics industries and the government's atomic energy and space programs. These industries displayed the best side of modern capitalism: high wages, comfortable working conditions, complex and efficient machinery, and the marriage of scientific technology and commercial utility.

Advances in transportation and communication added to geographic mobility. In the postwar decades the automobile entered its golden age. In the booming 1920s, when the car became an instrument of mass transportation, about 31 million autos were produced by American factories. During the 1950s some 58 million rolled off the assembly lines; during the 1960s fully 77 million. Gasoline use increased accordingly. The more mobile population drove farther in more reliable and more comfortable vehicles over smoother and less congested highways. And the new cars were heavier and more powerful than their predecessors. Gasoline consumption first reached 15 billion gallons in 1931; it soared to 35 billion gallons in 1950 and to 92 billion in 1970. A new business, the motel industry (the word, *motel*, typically American, was a combination of *motor* and *hotel*), developed to service the millions of tourists and businessmen who burned all this fuel on their travels.

The development of the interstate highway system, begun under Eisenhower in 1956, was a major cause of increased mobility. The new roads did far more than facilitate long-distance travel; they accelerated the shift of population to the suburbs and the consequent decline of inner-city districts.

Despite the speeds that cars maintained on them, the new highways were much safer than the old roads. The traffic death rate per mile driven fell steadily, almost entirely because of the interstates.

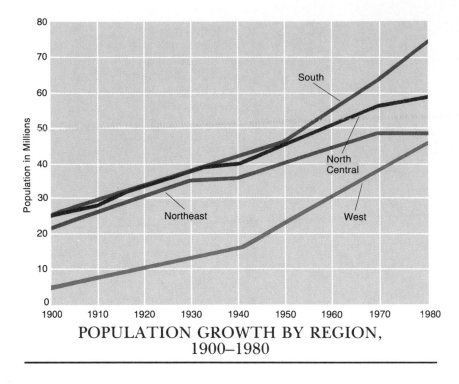

The total population of the United States in 1980 was 226.5 million. During the decade 1971–1980, the West was the fastest growing region, the Northeast the slowest. The South had been the largest region since the 1950s, but it also grew 20 percent during the 1970s, owing to migration to the Sunbelt. The North Central region increased only 4 percent in this same period.

POPULATION GROWTH BY REGION, 1900–1980

However, the environmental impact of the system was frequently severe. Elevated roads cut ugly swaths through cities, and the cars they carried released tons of noxious exhaust fumes into urban air. Hillsides were gashed, marshes filled in, forests felled, all in the name of speed and efficiency.

Although commercial air travel had existed in the 1930s and had profited from wartime technical advances in military aircraft, it truly came of age when the first jetliner—the Boeing 707, built in Seattle, Washington—went into service in 1958. Almost immediately jets came to dominate long-distance travel, to the detriment of railroad and steamship passenger service.

Television

Another important postwar change was the advent of television as a means of mass communication. Throughout the 1950s the public bought TV receivers at a rate of 6 to 7 million annually; by 1961 there were 55 million in operation, receiving the transmissions of 530 stations. During the 1960s the National Aeronautics and Space Agency (NASA)

began launching satellites capable of transmitting television pictures to earth, and the American Telephone and Telegraph Company orbited private commercial satellites that could relay television programs from one continent to another.

Television combined the immediacy of radio with the visual impact of films, and it displayed most of the strengths and weaknesses of both in exaggerated form. It swiftly became indispensable to the political system, both for its coverage of public events and as a vehicle for political advertising. Its handling of the events following President Kennedy's assassination, of national conventions and inaugurations, and of other news developments made history come alive for tens of millions. It brought sports events before the viewer vividly, attracting enormous audiences and producing so much money in advertising revenue that the economics of professional sports was revolutionized. Team franchises were bought and sold for tens of millions, and star players commanded salaries in the hundreds of thousands, eventually in the millions.

Some excellent drama was presented, especially on the National Educational Television network,

Astronaut Edwin Aldrin on the moon, July 1969. Reflected in his helmet visor are flight commander Neil Armstrong, who took this picture, and part of their spacecraft. Television enabled some 600 million people to see the historic event.

along with many filmed documentaries. "Sesame Street," a children's program presented on the educational network, won international recognition for its entertainment value and for its success in motivating underprivileged children. Commercial television indirectly improved the level of radio broadcasting by siphoning off much of the mass audience; more radio time was devoted to serious discussion programs and to classical music, especially after the introduction of frequency modulation (FM) transmissions.

The entertainment offered by most television stations was generally abominable; Newton Minow of the FCC called it a "vast wasteland." The lion's share of television time was devoted to uninspired and vulgar serials, routine variety shows, giveaway and quiz programs designed to reveal and revel in the ignorance of the average citizen, and reruns of old movies cut to fit rigid time periods and repeatedly interrupted at climactic points by "commercials." Most sets had poor accoustic qualities, which made them inferior instruments for listening to music. Serious discussion programs were too often relegated to inconvenient times, and there were not enough of them. Yet children found television fascinating, remaining transfixed before the screen when—their elders said—they should have been out of doors or curled up with a book.

Still another dubious virtue of television was its capacity for influencing the opinions and feelings of viewers. The insistent and strident claims of advertisers punctuated every program with monotonous regularity. Politicians discovered that no other device or method approached television as a means of reaching large numbers of voters with an illusion of intimacy. Since television time was expensive, only candidates who possessed or had access to huge sums could afford to use the medium—a dangerous state of affairs in a democracy. In time Congress clamped a lid on campaign expenditures, but this action did not necessarily reduce the amounts spent on television, with its capacity to reach so many people.*

"A Nation of Sheep"

Another postwar change was the marked broadening of the middle class. In 1947 only 5.7 million American families had what might be considered middle-class incomes—enough to provide something for leisure, entertainment, and cultural activities as well as for life's necessities. By the early 1960s more than 12 million families, about a third of the population, had such incomes. As they prospered, middle-class Americans became more culturally homogeneous and broader-gauged in their interests.

The percentage of immigrants in the population declined steadily; by the mid-1960s over 95 percent of all Americans were native-born. This trend contributed to social and cultural uniformity. So did the rising incomes of industrial workers and the changing character of their labor. By 1962 about 90 percent of all industrial workers enjoyed such fringe benefits as paid vacations and medical insurance at least partly financed by their employers, and nearly 70 percent participated in pension plans. The growth of pension funds made the union officials who managed them powers in the financial world. The merger in 1955 of the two great labor federations, the AFL and the CIO, added to the prestige of all union labor as well as to the power of the new organization.

As blue-collar workers invaded the middle class by the tens of thousands, they moved to suburbs previously reserved for junior executives, shopkeepers, and the like. They shed their work clothes for business suits. They took up golf. In sum, they adopted values and attitudes commensurate with their new status—which helps explain the growing conservatism of labor unions. During the Great Depression, when they were underdogs of sorts, the

unions fought for social justice. In the 1960s many union workers seemed more interested in preserving their gains against the ravages of inflation and taxation than they were in social reform.

Religion in Changing Times

Sociologists and other commentators on contemporary affairs found in the expansion of the middle class another explanation of the tendency of the country to glorify the conformist. They attributed to this expansion the blurring of party lines in politics, the national obsession with moderation and consensus, the complacency of so many Americans, and their tendency, for example, to be at once more interested in churchgoing than with the philosophic aspects of religion.

Organized religion traditionally deals with eternal values, but it is always influenced by social, cultural, and economic developments. Never has this been more true in America than in the decades after World War II. All the major faiths, despite their differences, were affected. Immediately after the war the prosperity and buoyant optimism of the period led to an expansion of religious activity. The Catholic church alone built over 1,000 new schools and more than 100 hospitals along with countless new churches. By 1950 the Southern Baptists had enrolled nearly 300,000 new members and built some 500 churches for them to worship in, and the historian Arthur Hertzberg estimates that between 1945 and 1965, Jews spent at least $1 billion building 1,000 synagogues, "the largest building boom in the history of American Jews."

But while most faiths prospered materially, the faithful tended to accept the world as it was. In *Catholic, Protestant, Jew* (1955), Will Herberg argued that in America, religious toleration had become routine. President Eisenhower lent authority to this argument when he said: "Our government makes no sense unless it is founded on a deeply felt religious faith—and I don't care what it is." According to a Gallup poll taken shortly after the war, nearly everyone in America believed in God. However, another poll revealed that many people were woefully ignorant of religious history and doctrine. Large numbers of Christians, for example, were unable to tell pollsters the name of any of the four Gospels. Professor Herberg reports that groups at

---

* The government now provides substantial public funds to major candidates in presidential elections.

typical suburban synagogues "were much more likely to discuss current events, or busy themselves with bowling, than to study the Bible."

Church and state were by law and the Constitution separate institutions, yet acts of Congress and state legislatures frequently had indirect effects on every aspect of organized religion. New Deal welfare legislation took on a large part of a burden previously borne by church groups. The expansion of higher education resulting from the G.I. Bill introduced millions of young adults to new ideas and appeared to make people somewhat more tolerant of the beliefs of others, religious beliefs included. However, studies showed that better-educated people tended to be less involved in the formal aspects of organized religion, and some became interested in "exotic" nonwestern faiths, such as Zen Buddhism. Both these trends seemed alarming to the leaders of the established religious groups, in part because they reflected an "education gap" separating religious liberals from religious conservatives.

Unlike prewar critics who had attacked "rugged individualism," many post–New Deal social critics, alarmed by the conformity of the 1950s, urged people to be more individualistic. In *The Lonely Crowd* (1950), David Riesman drew a distinction between old-fashioned "inner-directed" people and new "other-directed" conformists who were group-centered, materialistic, and generally accommodating rather than tough and uncompromising. William Whyte's best-seller *The Organization Man* (1956) and Sloan Wilson's novel *The Man in the Gray Flannel Suit* (1955) dealt with the same phenomenon. These writers did not concern themselves directly with religion, but they were reacting to problems that also affected thoughtful religious leaders. One prominent divine complained of "the drive toward a shallow and implicitly compulsory common creed," a "religion-in-general, superficial and syncretistic, destructive of the profounder elements of faith."

The civil rights movement is another illustration of a political and social issue that had important religious implications. Many militant blacks (Malcolm X was an example) were attracted to Islam by its lack of racial bias. Among those in the public eye who became Muslims were the heavyweight champion boxer Cassius Clay, who changed his name to Mohammed Ali, and Lew Alcindor, the basketball star, who became Kareem Abdul Jabbar. All the "conventional" churches played significant roles in the fight for racial justice that erupted after the Supreme Court outlawed segregation. The enormous outpouring produced by Martin Luther King, Jr.'s March on Washington in 1963 was swelled by many clergymen, and their example put pressure on both church hierarchies and ordinary members to become civil rights activists. Shocking photographs of police dogs being used to "subdue" demonstrating Catholic nuns on another occasion converted uncounted thousands to the struggle. The controversy over America's role in the Vietnam War had similar effects.

All the social changes of the period had religious ramifications. Feminists objected to male domination of most Christian churches and called for the ordination of female ministers and priests; some religious leaders supported the feminists, but conservatives rejected their ideas out of hand. Every aspect of the sexual revolution (see pp. 901ff), from the practice of couples living together openly outside marriage to the tolerance of homosexuality and pornography to the legalization of abortion, caused shock waves in the religious community.

Scientific and technological developments also affected both religious values and the way people worshiped. Darwin's theory of evolution had had social effects as well as directly religious ones in the 19th and early 20th centuries, and these were to some extent still unresolved. Many religious groups still believed in the biblical explanation of Creation and sought to have "Creation theory" taught in the schools.

On another level, the prestige of secular science gave it a kind of religious aspect disturbing to some church leaders. Medical advances that some people marveled at, such as in vitro fertilization of human eggs, organ transplants, and the development of machines capable of keeping terminally ill people alive indefinitely, seemed to others "against nature" and indeed sacrilegious. More generally, the public was divided about the ultimate value of scientific progress. Controversies over the use of atomic energy in peace and war and over the conservation of natural resources all had religious aspects.

Radio and television had more direct effects on organized religion. The "Radio Priest" of the New Deal era, Father Charles Coughlin, was the prototype of a new kind of clergyman that flourished in the postwar period. The airwaves enabled rhetorically skilled preachers to reach millions with

California minister Robert Schuller, here televising his "Hour of Power" program from his church in Garden Grove, was one of many "televangelists" who created devoted and financially sustaining congregations through their nationally broadcast television ministries. His particular appeal is suggested in the title of one of his books: Positive Prayer for Power-Filled Living.

emotionally charged messages on religious topics and also on political and social questions. The most successful in the postwar years were the leaders of evangelical protestant sects, and by the 1960s they had mastered television. Whereas most postwar revivalists, the most famous being Billy Graham, stressed interdenominational cooperation, in the 1970s a more militant, fundamentalist type emerged. These TV preachers tended to found churches and educational institutions of their own and to use radio and television to raise money to support them, but they were extremely conservative both in their religious and in their political, social, and moral views. This brought them into conflict with many other developments of the period.

Literature and Art

For a time after World War II the nation seemed on the verge of a literary outburst comparable to the one that followed World War I. A number of excellent novels based on the military experiences of young writers appeared, the most notable being *The Naked and the Dead* (1948) by Norman Mailer and *From Here to Eternity* (1951) by James Jones. Unfortunately, a new renaissance did not develop. The most talented younger writers rejected materialist values but preferred to bewail their fate rather than rebel against it. Jack Kerouac, founder of the "beat" (for *beatific*) school, reveled in the chaotic description of violence, perversion, and madness. At the other extreme, J. D. Salinger, perhaps the most popular writer of the 1950s and the particular favorite of college students—*The Catcher in the Rye* (1951) sold nearly 2 million copies in hardcover and paperback editions—was an impeccable stylist, witty, contemptuous of all pretense; but he too wrote about people entirely wrapped up in themselves.

In *Catch-22* (1955), the book that replaced *The Catcher in the Rye* in the hearts of college students, Joseph Heller produced a war novel that was farcical and an indignant denunciation of the stupidity and waste of warfare. In *The Victim* (1947), *The Adventures of Augie March* (1953), and many other novels, Saul Bellow described characters possessed of their full share of eccentricities and weaknesses without losing sight of the positive side of modern life. Bellow won many literary awards, including a Nobel Prize.

All these novelists and a number of others whose books were of lesser quality were widely read. Year after year sales of books increased, despite much talk about how television and other diversions were undermining the public's interest in reading. Sales of paperbacks, first introduced in the United States in 1939 by Pocket Books, reached enormous proportions. By 1965 about 25,000 titles were in print, and sales were approaching 1 million copies a day.

Cheapness and portability only partly accounted for the popularity of paperbacks. Readers could purchase them in drugstores, bus terminals, and supermarkets as well as in bookstores. Teachers, delighted to find out-of-print volumes easily available, assigned hundreds of them in their classes. And there was a psychological factor at work, the paperback became fashionable. People who rarely bought hardcover books purchased weighty volumes of literary criticism, translations of the works of obscure foreign novelists, specialized historical monographs, and difficult philosophical treatises now that they were available in paper covers.

The expansion of the book market, like so many

other changes, was not an unalloyed benefit even for writers. It remained difficult for unknown authors to earn a decent living. Publishers tended to concentrate their interest and their money on authors already popular and on books aimed at a mass audience. Even among successful writers of unquestioned ability, the temptations involved in large advances and in book club contracts and movie rights diverted many from making the best use of their talents.

American painters were affected by the same forces that influenced writers. In the past the greatest American artists had been shaped by European influences. This situation changed dramatically after World War II with the emergence of abstract expressionism, or action painting. This "New York school" was led by Jackson Pollock (1912–1956), who composed huge abstract designs by laying his canvas on the floor of his studio and drizzling paint on it directly from tube or pot in a wild tangle of color.

The abstract expressionists were utterly subjective in their approach to art. "The source of my painting is the Unconscious," Pollock explained. "I am not much aware of what is taking place; it is only after that I see what I have done." Pollock tried to produce not the representation of a landscape but, as the critic Harold Rosenberg put it, "an inner landscape that is part of himself."

Untutored observers found the abstract expressionists crude, chaotic, devoid of interest. The swirling, dripping chaos of the followers of Pollock, the vaguely defined planes of color favored by Mark Rothko and his disciples, and the sharp spatial confrontations composed by the painters Franz Kline, Robert Motherwell, and Adolph Gottlieb required too much verbal explanation to communicate their meaning to the average observer. Viewed in its social context, however, abstract expressionism, like so much of modern literature, reflected the estrangement of the artist from the world of the atomic bomb and the computer, a revolt against contemporary mass culture with its unthinking acceptance of novelty for its own sake.

The experimental spirit released by the abstract expressionists led to op (for *optical*) art, which employed the physical impact of pure complementary colors to produce dynamic optical effects. Even within the rigid limitations of severely formal designs composed of concentric circles, stripes,

Jackson Pollock's "drip" paintings rejected all traditional techniques and representational subjects, resulting in a purely abstract expression. The title of this large 1950 canvas—it is about 17 by 9 feet—is Autumn Rhythm.

squares, and rectangles, such paintings appeared to be constantly in motion, almost alive.

Op was devoid of social connotations; another variant, pop art, playfully yet often with acid incisiveness satirized many aspects of American culture: its vapidity, its crudeness, its violence. The painters Jasper Johns, Roy Lichtenstein, and Andy Warhol created portraits of mundane objects such as flags, comic strips, soup cans, and packing cases. Op and pop art reflected the mechanized aspects of life; the painters made use of technology in their work—for example, they enhanced the shock of vibrating complementary colors by using fluorescent paints. Some artists imitated newspaper photograph techniques by fashioning their images of sharply defined dots of color. Others borrowed from contemporary commercial art, employing spray guns, stencils, and masking tape to produce flat, hard-edged effects. The line between op and pop was frequently crossed, as in Robert Indiana's *Love,* which was reproduced and imitated on posters, Christmas cards, book jackets, buttons, rings, and even a postage stamp.

Color and shape as ends in themselves, stark and often on a heroic scale, typified the new styles. Color-field painters covered vast planes with flat, sometimes subtly shaded hues. Frank Stella, one of the most universally admired of the younger artists, composed complicated bands and curves of color on enormous, eccentrically shaped canvases. To an unprecedented degree, the artist's hand—the combination of patience and skill that had characterized traditional art—was removed from painting.

The pace of change in artistic fashion was dizzying—far more rapid than changes in literature. Aware that their generation was leading European artists instead of following them gave both artists and art lovers a sense of participating in events of historic importance.

As with literature, the effects of such success were not all healthy. Successful artists became national personalities, a few of them enormously rich. For these, each new work was exposed to the glare of publicity, sometimes with unfortunate results. Too much attention, like too much money, could be distracting, even corrupting, especially for young artists who needed time and obscurity to develop their talents. "Schools" rose and fell in rapid order,

Along with Andy Warhol, Roy Lichtenstein is recognized as a master of pop art.

it seemed, at the whim of one or another influential critic or dealer. Being different was more highly valued than aesthetic quality or technical skill. No matter how outlandish, the newest thing attracted respectful attention. The idea of the avant-garde as a revolt of creative minds against the philistinism of the middle class no longer had meaning, despite the fact that the existence of an expanding middle class made the commercial success of modern art possible.

Two Dilemmas

The many changes of the era help to explain why President Johnson expressed so much uncertainty in his inaugural address. Looking at American society more broadly, two dilemmas seem to have confronted people in the 1960s. One was that progress was often self-defeating. Reforms and innovations instituted with the best of motives often made things worse rather than better. Instances of this dilemma, large and small, are so numerous as to defy summary. DDT, a powerful chemical developed to kill insects that were spreading disease and destroying valuable food crops, proved to have lethal effects on birds and fish—and perhaps indirectly on human beings. Goods manufactured to make life fuller and happier (automobiles, detergents, electric power) produced waste products that disfigured the land and polluted air and water. Cities built in order to bring culture and comfort to millions became pestholes of crime, poverty, and depravity.

Change occurred so fast that experience (the recollection of how things had been) tended to become less useful and sometimes even counterproductive as a guide for dealing with current problems. Foreign policies designed to prevent wars, devised on the basis of knowledge of the causes of past wars, led, because the circumstances were different, to new wars. Parents who sought to transmit to their children the accumulated wisdom of their years found their advice rejected, often with good reason, because that wisdom had little application to the problems their children had to face.

The second dilemma was that modern industrial society placed an enormous premium on social cooperation, at the same time undermining the individual citizen's sense of being essential to the proper functioning of society. The economy was as complicated as a fine watch; a breakdown in any one sector had ramifications that spread swiftly to other sectors. Yet specialization had progressed so far that individual workers had little sense of the importance of their personal contributions and thus felt little responsibility for the smooth functioning of the whole. Effective democratic government required that all voters be knowledgeable and concerned, but few could feel that their individual voices had any effect on elections or public policies. The exhaust fumes of millions of automobiles poisoned the air, but it was difficult to expect the single motorist to accept the inconvenience of leaving the car in the garage when such restraint would have no measurable effect on pollution overall. "One person just can't feel that she's doing anything," a frustrated teenager wrote. "I can use soap instead of detergent . . . but what good do I feel I'm doing when there are people next door having a party with plastic spoons and paper plates?"

People tried to deal with this dilemma by joining groups; then the groups became so large that members felt as incapable of influencing them as they did of influencing the larger society. The groups were so numerous and had so many conflicting objectives that instead of making citizens more socially minded, they often made them more self-centered. The organization—union, club, party, pressure group—was a potent force in society. Yet few organizations were really concerned with the common interest, though logic required that the common interest be regarded if individuals or groups were to achieve their special interests.

These dilemmas produced a paradox. The United States was the most powerful nation in the world, its people the best educated, the richest, and probably the most energetic. American society was technologically advanced and dynamic; American traditional values were idealistic, humane, democratic. Yet the nation seemed incapable of mobilizing its resources intelligently to confront the most obvious challenges, its citizens unable to achieve much personal happiness or identification with their fellows, the society helpless in trying to live up to its most universally accepted ideals.

In part the paradox was a product of the strengths of the society and the individuals who made it up. The populace as a whole was more sophisticated. People were more aware of their immediate interests, less willing to suspend judgment and follow leaders or to look on others as better qualified to decide what they should do. They belonged to the "me generation"; they knew that they lived in a society and that their lives were profoundly affected by that society, but they had trouble feeling that they were part of a society.

President Johnson recognized the problem. He hoped to solve it by establishing a "consensus" and building his Great Society. No real consensus emerged; American society remained fragmented, its members divided against one another and often among themselves. Awareness of the complexities and contradictions of life and human institutions was a mark of increasing maturity but also a source of uncertainty and insecurity.

The Costs of Prosperity

The vexing character of modern conditions could be seen in every aspect of life. The economy, after decades of hectic expansion, accelerated still more rapidly. The gross national product approached a trillion dollars, but inflation was becoming increasingly serious. Workers were under constant pressure to demand raises—which only served to drive prices still higher. Socially the effect was devastating; it became impossible to expect workers to see inflation as a social problem and to restrain their personal demands. Putting their individual interests before those of the whole, they were prepared to disrupt the economy regardless of social cost. Even public employees traditionally committed to a no-strike policy because they worked for the entire community—teachers, garbage collectors, firefighters, the police—succumbed to this selfish, if understandable, way of looking at life.

Economic expansion resulted in large measure from technological advances, and these too proved to be mixed blessings. As we have seen, World War II needs stimulated the development of materials such as plastics, nylon, and synthetic rubber and such electronic devices as radar and television. After the war these products came into their own. Plastics invaded field after field—automobile parts, building materials, adhesives, packaging materials.

In 1951 scientists began to manufacture electricity from nuclear fuels; in 1954 the first atomic-powered ship, the submarine *Nautilus,* was launched. Although the peaceful use of atomic energy remained small compared to other sources of power, its implications were immense. Equally significant was the invention of the electronic computer, which revolutionized the collection and storage of records, solved mathematical problems beyond the scope of the most brilliant human minds, and speeded the work of bank tellers, librarians, billing clerks, statisticians—and income tax collectors.

Computers lay at the heart of industrial automation, for they could control the integration and adjustment of the most complex machines. In automobile factories they made it possible to produce entire engine blocks automatically. In steel mills molten metal could be poured into molds, cooled, rolled, and cut into slabs without the intervention of a human hand, the computers locating defects and adjusting the machinery to correct them far more accurately than the most skilled steelworker, and in a matter of seconds. Taken in conjunction with a new oxygen smelting process six or eight times faster than the open-hearth method, computer-controlled continuous casting promised to have an impact on steelmaking as great as that of the Bessemer process in the 1870s.

The material benefits of technology commonly had what the microbiologist René Dubos described as "disastrous secondary effects, many of which are probably unpredictable." The consumption of petroleum necessary to produce power soared and began to outstrip supplies, threatening shortages that would disrupt the entire economy. The burning of this fuel released immeasurable tons of smoke and other polluting gases into the atmosphere, endangering the health of millions. "Life is enriched by one million automobiles," Dubos noted, "but can be made into a nightmare by one hundred million."

The vast outpouring of flimsy plastic products and the increased use of paper, metal foil, and other disposable packaging materials seemed about to bury the country beneath mountains of trash. The commercial use of nuclear energy also caused problems. Scientists insisted that the danger from radiation was insignificant, but the possibility of accidents could not be eliminated entirely, and the safe disposal of radioactive wastes became increasingly difficult.

Even an apparently ideal form of scientific advance, the use of commercial fertilizers to boost food output, had unfortunate side effects. Phosphates

As environmental issues became more prominent, shots like this view of raw sewage being dumped into the Niagara River appeared more often in the popular press. This photo was taken by Alfred Eisenstaedt for Life *in 1968.*

washed from farmlands into streams sometimes upset the ecological balance and turned the streams into malodorous death traps for aquatic life. Above all, technology increased the capacity of the earth to support people. As population increased, production and consumption increased, exhausting supplies of raw materials and speeding the pollution of air and water resources. Where would the process end? Viewed from a world perspective, it was obvious that the population explosion must be checked or it would check itself by pestilence, war, starvation, or some combination of these scourges. Yet how to check it?

New Racial Turmoil

President Johnson and most of those who supported his policies expected that the 1964 Civil Rights Act, the Economic Opportunity Act, Medicare and Medicaid, and the other elements in the War on Poverty would produce an era of racial peace and genuine social harmony—the Great Society that everyone wanted. The change that occurred in the thinking of the black radical Malcolm X seemed a straw in the wind. In 1964 Malcolm left the Black Muslims

and founded his own Organization of Afro-American Unity. While continuing to stress black self-help and the militant defense of black rights, he now saw the fight for racial equality as part of a larger struggle for all human rights. "What we do . . . helps all people everywhere who are fighting against oppression," he said. Yet as in so many other aspects of modern life, progress itself created new difficulties. Early in 1965 Black Muslim fanatics, furious at his defection, assassinated Malcolm X while he was making a speech in favor of racial harmony.

The assassination was an act of vengeance, not of social protest. More significant was the fact that official white recognition of past injustices was making blacks more insistent that all discrimination be ended. The very process of righting past wrongs gave them the strength to fight more vigorously. Black militancy, building steadily during World War II and thereafter, had long been ignored by the white majority; in the mid-1960s it burst forth so powerfully that the most smug and obtuse white citizens had to accept its existence.

Even Martin Luther King, Jr., the standard-bearer of nonviolent resistance, became more demanding. A few weeks after Malcolm's death, King led a march from Selma, Alabama, to Montgomery as part of a campaign to force Alabama authorities to allow blacks to register to vote. His marchers were brutally assaulted by state policemen who wielded clubs and tossed canisters of tear gas. Liberal opinion was shocked as never before. Thousands of people descended on Selma to demonstrate their support for the black cause.

The Student Nonviolent Coordinating Committee, which had been born out of the struggle for racial integration, had become by late 1964 a radical organization openly scornful of integration and interracial cooperation. Many student reformers had been radicalized by the threats and open violence they had experienced while trying to register rural blacks and organize schools for black children in the South and by the slowness of the Kennedy administration to work all-out for racial justice. The slogan of the radicals was "Black Power," an expression that was given national currency by Stokely Carmichael, chairman of SNCC. Carmichael, West Indian by birth, had grown up in Harlem. In the early 1960s he had worked ceaselessly for black rights in the South, and as a result he had spent considerable time in southern jails. By 1964, though still willing to work with black moderates such as King, he was adamantly opposed to cooperating with white civil rights activists of any stripe. "The time for white involvement in the fight for equality has ended," Carmichael announced in 1966. "If we are to proceed toward true liberation, we must set ourselves off from white people." Since whites "cannot relate to the black experience," the movement "should be black-staffed, black-controlled, and black-financed."

"Integration is a subterfuge for the maintenance of white supremacy," Carmichael said on another occasion. Blacks should have their own schools, their own businesses, their own political parties, their own (African) culture.

Black Power caught on swiftly among militants. This troubled white liberals because people like Carmichael refused "to discriminate between degrees of inequity" among whites. Liberals feared that Black Power would antagonize white conservatives. They argued that since blacks made up only about 11 percent of the population, any attempt to obtain racial justice through the use of naked power was sure to fail.

Meanwhile, black anger erupted in a series of destructive urban riots. The most important occurred in Watts, a ghetto of Los Angeles, in August 1965. A trivial incident—police officers halted a motorist who seemed to be drunk and attempted to give him a sobriety test—brought thousands into the streets. The neighborhood almost literally exploded: For six days Watts was swept by fire, looting, and bloody fighting between local residents and 15,000 National Guardsmen, called up to assist the police. Order was restored only after 34 persons had been killed, more than 850 wounded, and 3,100 arrested. Property damage in Watts came to nearly $200 million.

The following summer saw similar outbursts in New York, Chicago, and other cities. In 1967 further riots broke out. In Newark, New Jersey, 25 were killed in a July outburst that lasted four days. In Detroit a few days later, what may have been the worst race riot since the Civil War erupted. The death toll in Detroit came to 43, and looting and arson assumed anarchic proportions. Then, in April 1968, the revered Martin Luther King, Jr., was murdered in Memphis, Tennessee, by a white man, James Earl Ray.* Blacks in more than 100 cities swiftly unleashed their anger in paroxysms of burning and looting. White opinion was shocked and profoundly depressed. King's death appeared to destroy the hope that his doctrine of pacific appeal to reason and right could solve the racial problem.

Public fear and puzzlement led to many investigations of the causes of the riots, the most important being that of the commission headed by Governor Otto Kerner of Illinois, which President Johnson appointed following King's murder. The conclusions of most of the studies were complex but fairly clear. Race riots had a long history in the United States, but the outbursts of the 1960s were different. Earlier troubles usually began with attacks by whites that led to black counterattacks. Riots of the Watts type were begun by blacks. Although much white-owned property was destroyed, the fighting was mostly between blacks and law enforcement officers trying to control them. White citizens tended to avoid the centers of trouble, and blacks seldom ranged outside their own neighborhoods.

---

* Ray fled to England but was apprehended, extradited, convicted, and sentenced to 99 years in prison.

The rioters were expressing frustration and despair; their resentment was directed more at the social system than at individuals. As the Kerner commission put it, the basic cause was an attitude of mind, the "white racism" that deprived blacks of access to good jobs, crowded them into slums, and, for the young in particular, eroded all hope of escape from such misery. Ghettos bred crime and depravity—as slums always have—and the complacent refusal of whites adequately to invest money and energy in helping ghetto residents, or even to acknowledge that the black poor deserved help, made the modern slum unbearable. While the ghettos expanded, middle-class whites tended more and more to flee to the suburbs or to call on the police "to maintain law and order," a euphemism for cracking down hard on deviant black behavior no matter how obvious the connection between that behavior and the slum environment.

The victims of racism employed violence not so much to force change as to obtain psychic release; it was a way of getting rid of what they could not stomach, a kind of vomiting. Thus the concentration of the riots in the ghettos themselves, the smashing, Samson-like, of the source of degradation even when this meant self-destruction. When fires broke out in black districts, the firefighters who tried to extinguish them were often showered with bottles and bricks and sometimes shot at, while above the roar of the flames and the hiss of steam rose the apocalyptic chant, "Burn, baby, burn!"

The most frightening aspect of the riots was their tendency to polarize society along racial lines. Advocates of Black Power became more determined to separate themselves from white influence; they exasperated white supporters of school desegregation by demanding schools of their own. Extremists formed the Black Panther party and collected weapons to resist the police. "Shoot, don't loot," the radical H. Rap Brown advised all who would listen. The Panthers demanded public compensation for injustices done to blacks in the past, pointing out that following World War II, West Germany had made payments to Jews to make up for Hitler's persecutions. In 1968 they nominated Eldridge Cleaver for president. Although Cleaver was a convict on parole, he was an articulate and intelligent man whose autobiographical *Soul on Ice,* written in prison, had attracted much praise.

Middle-class city residents often resented what

1968 Olympic gold and silver medal winners, T. Smith and J. Carlos, making the gloved salute of "black power" during the televised award ceremonies and the playing of the national anthem in Mexico City. Both athletes were removed from the team, but not before making their point.

seemed the favoritism of the federal government and state and local administrations, which sought through so-called affirmative action to provide blacks with new economic opportunities and social benefits. Efforts to desegregate ghetto schools by busing children out of their local neighborhoods was a particularly bitter cause of conflict.

These developments caused a powerful white backlash. Persons already subjected to the pressures caused by inflation, specialization, and rapid change that were undermining social solidarity and worried by the sharp rise in urban crime rates and welfare costs found black radicalism infuriating. In the face of the greatest national effort in history to aid them, blacks, they said, were displaying not merely ingratitude but contempt.

The Unmeltable Ethnics

The struggles of blacks for equality went hand in hand with those of Mexican-Americans, principally in the Southwest. After World War I, thousands of Mexicans flocked into the region. They could do so legally because the restrictive immigration legislation of the 1920s did not apply to Western Hemisphere nations. When the Great Depression struck, Mexican-Americans were the first to suffer—about half a million were either deported or persuaded to return to Mexico in the 1930s. But during World War II and again between 1948 and 1965, federal legislation encouraged the importation of *braceros* (temporary farm workers), and many other Mexicans entered the country illegally. The latter were known as *mojados,* or "wetbacks," because they often slipped across the border by swimming the Rio Grande. Many of these Mexicans, and other Spanish-speaking people, including the thousands from the territory of Puerto Rico who could immigrate to the mainland legally in unlimited numbers, settled in the great cities, where low-paying but usually steady work was available. They lived in slums called *barrios,* as segregated, crowded, and crime ridden as the black ghettos.

Spanish-speaking residents of the Southwest, and to a lesser degree those in the big eastern cities, were for a time largely apolitical; they tended to accept their fate with resignation, to mind their own business, to make little trouble. But in the early 1960s a new spirit of resistance arose. Leaders of the new movement called themselves Chicanos. The Chicanos demanded better schools for their children and easier access to higher education. They urged their fellows to take pride in their traditions and culture, to demand their rights, to organize themselves politically. As with the blacks, the dominant middle-class majority adjusted itself to Chicano demands grudgingly and very slowly.

One Chicano nationalist group, Alianza ("the alliance"), led by Reies Lopez Tijerina, tried to secede from New Mexico, an act that brought it into confrontation with the army and ended with Tijerina in prison. Another, the Crusade for Justice, headed by Rodolfo "Corky" Gonzales, a professional boxer, poet, and politician, focused on achieving social reforms and setting up political action groups. Its slogan, *"Venceremos,"* was Spanish for Martin Luther King's pledge: We shall overcome.

The Mexican-American founder of the National Farm Workers Association and later head of the United Farm Workers Organizing Committee, César Chávez successfully organized migrant workers throughout California in the early 1960s and later a nationwide boycott against California grape producers.

The Chicano leader with the widest influence was César Chávez, who concentrated on what was superficially a more limited goal—organizing migrant farm workers into unions. Chávez grew up in migrant camps in California; he had no schooling beyond the seventh grade. After serving in the navy during World War II, he went to work for the Community Service Organization, a group seeking to raise the political consciousness of the poor and to develop self-help programs for them. Chávez became general director of the CSO but resigned in 1962 because he felt that it was not devoting enough attention to the plight of migrant workers. He then founded the National Farm Workers' Association, later known as the United Farm Workers' Organizing Committee.

In 1965 the grape pickers in his union in Delano, California, struck for higher wages and union recognition. Chávez, seeing in the strike an opportunity to attack the very structure of the migrant labor system, turned it into a nationwide crusade. Avoiding violence, he enlisted the support of church leaders; he organized sit-ins, a march on the state capital, and then a national consumer boycott of grapes. He demonstrated convincingly that migrant workers could be unionized and that the demands of minorities for equal treatment did not necessarily lead to separatism and class or racial antagonism.

Nevertheless, racial controversies continued.

The struggles of black people for equal treatment in the 1950s and 1960s radicalized many Indians. These militants referred to themselves as Native Americans, not Indians. They used the term "Red Power" as the blacks spoke of Black Power and referred to more conservative colleagues as "Uncle Tomahawks." The National Indian Youth Council and later the American Indian Movement (AIM) demanded the return of lands taken illegally from their ancestors. They called for self-determination and a concerted effort to revive tribal cultures, even the use of peyote, a mind-altering controlled substance, in religious ceremonies,* and they organized a pan-Indian movement to advance the cause. Paradoxically, this policy brought them into conflict with traditionalist Indians devoted to local autonomy. (At least 40 Indian languages are still spoken.)

Some AIM leaders sought total separation from the United States; they envisaged setting up states within states such as the Cherokees had established in Georgia in Jacksonian days. In 1973 radicals occupied the town of Wounded Knee, South Dakota (site of one of the most disgraceful massacres of Indians in the 19th century), and held it at gunpoint for weeks. While traditionalists resisted the militants, liberal white opinion proved to be generally sympathetic. In 1975 Congress passed the Indian Self-determination Act, which gave individual tribes much greater control over such matters as education, welfare programs, and law enforcement.

Militant ethnic pride characterized the behavior of other racial minorities and of many white Americans too. Blacks donned dashikis and other African garments and wore their hair in natural "Afro" styles. Italian-Americans, Polish-Americans, and descendants of other "new immigrant" groups eagerly studied their histories in order to preserve their cultures and where necessary revive dying traditions. The American melting pot, some historians now argued, had not amalgamated the immigrant strains as completely as had been thought. Ethnic diversity became for some an end to be desired, despite the possibility that differences might as easily inspire conflict as harmonious adjustment.

For white ethnics, the concern for origins was in part nostalgic and romantic. As the number of,

Navajo Indians protesting the federal government's intervention in an intertribal land dispute in Arizona. Disputes between Native Americans and government agencies occurred not only in the Southwest but in Maine and on Cape Cod as well.

say, Greek-Americans who had ever seen Greece declined, the appeal of Greek culture and the sense that some Greek-Americans had of belonging to a distinct cultural group increased. For blacks, whose particular origins were obscured by the catastrophe of slavery, awareness of their distinctiveness was more important. Racial pride was a reflection of the new black militancy and the progress that blacks had made in the postwar period. A black man sat on the Supreme Court (Thurgood Marshall, tactician of the fight for school desegregation). President Johnson had named the first black to a Cabinet post (Robert Weaver, secretary of housing and urban development). The first black since reconstruction (Edward W. Brooke of Massachusetts) was elected to the United States Senate in 1966. A number of large cities, including Atlanta, Georgia, elected black mayors.

The color line was broken in major league baseball in 1947, and soon all professional sports were open to black athletes. Whereas the reign of black heavyweight boxing champion Jack Johnson (1908–1915) had inspired an open search for a "white hope" to depose him, and whereas the next black champion, Joe Louis (1937–1949), was accepted by whites because he "knew his place" and was "well behaved," it was possible for champion Muhammad Ali to be a hero to both white and black boxing fans despite his often bizarre behavior, his militant ad-

---

* The California Supreme Court upheld the right to use peyote in this way in *People* v. *Woody* (1964).

vocacy of racial equality, and his adoption of the Muslim religion.

Their achievements and advances aside, black Americans had found real self-awareness. The attitude of mind that ran from the lonely Denmark Vesey to Frederick Douglass and to W. E. B. Du Bois had become the black consensus.

Rethinking Public Education

Young people were in the forefront in both the fight for the rights of blacks and the women's liberation movement. In a time of uncertainty and discontent, full of conflict and dilemma, youth was affected more strongly than the older generations, and it reacted more forcefully. No institution escaped its criticisms, not even the vaunted educational system, which, youth discovered, poorly suited its needs. This was still another paradox of modern life, for American public education was probably the best (it was certainly the most comprehensive) in the world.

After World War I, under the impact of Freudian psychology, the emphasis in elementary education shifted from using the schools as instruments of social change, as John Dewey had recommended, to using them to promote the emotional development of the students. "Child-centered" educators played down academic achievement in favor of "adjustment." It probably stimulated the students' imaginations and may possibly have improved their psychological well-being, but observers soon noted that the system produced poor work habits and fuzzy thinking and fostered plain ignorance. Although "educationists" insisted that they were not abandoning traditional academic subjects, they surely de-emphasized them. "We've built a sort of halo around reading, writing, and arithmetic," one school principal charged.

The demands of society for rigorous intellectual achievement made this distortion of progressive education increasingly less satisfactory. Following World War II, critics began a concerted assault on the system. The leader of the attack was James B. Conant, former president of Harvard. His book *The American High School Today* (1959) sold nearly half a million copies, and his later studies of teacher education and the special problems of urban schools also attracted wide attention.

Conant flayed the schools for their failure to teach English grammar and composition effectively, for neglecting foreign languages, and for ignoring the needs of both the brightest and the slowest of their students. He insisted that teachers' colleges should place subject matter above educational methodology in their curricula.

The success of the Soviet Union in launching the first artificial satellite, *Sputnik,* in 1957 increased the influence of critics like Conant because it dealt a healthy blow to American overconfidence. To match the Russian achievement, the United States needed thousands of engineers and scientists, and the schools were not turning out enough graduates prepared to study science and engineering at the college level. Suddenly the schools were under enormous pressure, for with more and more young people desiring to go to college, the colleges were raising their admission standards. The traditionalists thus gained the initiative, and academic subjects enjoyed revived prestige. The National Defense Education Act of 1958 supplied a powerful stimulus by allocating funds for upgrading work in the sciences, foreign languages, and other subjects and for expanding guidance services and experimenting with television and other new teaching devices.

Concern for improving the training of the children of disadvantaged minority groups (Mexican-Americans, Puerto Ricans, Indians, blacks) pulled the system in a different direction. Many of these children lived in horrible slums, often in broken homes. They lacked the incentives and training that middle-class children received in the family. Many did poorly in school, in part because they were poorly motivated, in part because the system was poorly adapted to their needs. But catering to the needs of such children threatened to undermine the standards being set for other children. In the cities, where blacks and other minorities were becoming steadily more numerous, many schools failed to serve adequately either the disadvantaged or those fairly well off. Added to the strains imposed by racial conflicts, the effect was to create the most serious crisis American public education had ever faced.

The post-*Sputnik* stress on academic achievement profoundly affected higher education too. Prestige institutions such as Harvard, Yale, Columbia, Stanford, and a dozen other colleges and universities, able to pick and choose among floods of

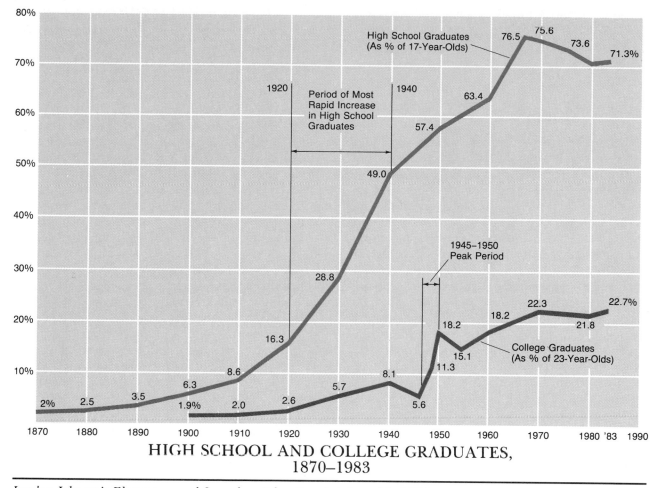

80%

High School Graduates
(As % of 17-Year-Olds)

76.5   75.6   73.6   71.3%

70%

1920   1940

Period of Most
Rapid Increase
in High School
Graduates

63.4

60%

57.4

50%

49.0

40%

30%

1945–1950
Peak Period

28.8

22.3   22.7%

18.2

20%

16.3   18.2   21.8

15.1

College Graduates
(As % of 23-Year-Olds)

11.3

8.6   8.1

10%

6.3   5.7   5.6

2%   2.5   3.5   2.0   2.6

1.9%

1870 1880 1890 1900 1910 1920 1930 1940 1950 1960 1970 1980 '83 1990

HIGH SCHOOL AND COLLEGE GRADUATES, 1870–1983

Lyndon Johnson's Elementary and Secondary Education Act, passed in 1965, was a landmark in the century-long expansion of high school education and directly influenced college education in the United States. The most rapid increase in high school graduates occurred between 1920 and 1940, but the number of graduates as a percentage of all people age 17 was greatest in 1967. The peak period for college graduates, 1945 to 1950, reflects the GI Bill after World War II.

applicants, became training centers for the intellectual elite. The federal and state governments, together with private philanthropic institutions such as the Carnegie Corporation and the Ford Foundation, poured millions of dollars into dormitory and classroom construction, teacher education, and scholarship funds. At the graduate level, the federal government's research and development program, administered by the National Science Foundation, provided billions of dollars for

laboratories, equipment, professors' salaries, and student scholarships.

At the same time, population growth and the demands of society for specialized intellectual skills caused American colleges to burst at the seams. Enrollment had risen rapidly after the war, mostly because of the G.I. Bill; by 1950 there were 2.6 million students in American colleges and universities. Yet 20 years later the total had risen to 8.6 million, a decade after that to about 12 million. To bridge the gap between high school and college, two-year junior colleges proliferated. Almost unknown before 1920, there were 1,300-odd junior colleges in the 1980s.

Students in Revolt

For a time after the war, higher education expanded with remarkable smoothness. The veterans, more mature and eager to make up for lost time, concentrated on their studies, and younger students tended to follow their lead. But in the 1960s the mood changed. The members of this college generation had grown up during the postwar prosperity and had been trained by teachers who were, by and large, New Deal liberals. They had been told that government was supposed to regulate the economy in the general interest, help the weak against the strong, and protect the liberties of all its citizens. It seemed to many students not to be performing these functions. Modern industrial society with its "soulless" corporations, its computers, and its almost equally unfeeling human bureaucracies provided them with material comforts and social advantages, but it made them feel insignificant and powerless. Their advantages also made them feel guilty when they thought about the millions of Americans who did not have them. The existence of poverty in a country as rich as the United States seemed intolerable, race prejudice both stupid and evil. Yet the government seemed incapable of attacking these disgraceful conditions head on. Still worse in their eyes, the response of their elders to McCarthyism appeared contemptible—craven cowardice of the worst sort—and dangerous. In the age of the atom, rabid anticommunism might end in nuclear war.

All these influences were encapsulated in a manifesto put forth by a small group of students at a meeting of Students for a Democratic Society (SDS) held at Port Huron, Michigan, in 1962. "We are the people of this generation . . . looking uncomfortably to the world we inherit," their Port Huron Statement began. Their main concerns were racial bigotry, the atomic bomb, and the "disturbing paradoxes" associated with these concerns. How to reconcile the contradictions between the idea that "all men are created equal" with "the facts of Negro life in the South and the big cities of the North" and between the declared peaceful intentions of the gov-

ernment and its huge "economic and military investments in the Cold War." Too many people and too many institutions, concentrating on preserving what they own and can command, "have closed their minds to the future."

The SDS statement outlined a somewhat vague list of goals, including ending the "political party stalemate," making corporations "publicly responsible," and allocating national resources on the basis of "social needs." The chief technique advanced to accomplish these objectives was "participatory democracy," getting people involved in small groups where individuals could have an impact. "We would replace power rooted in possession, privilege, or circumstance by power and uniqueness rooted in love."

SDS grew rapidly, powered by rising college enrollments, protest against the escalation of the war in Vietnam, and a seemingly unending list of local campus issues. Radical students generally had little tolerance for injustice, and their dissatisfaction often found expression in public protests. The first great student outburst convulsed the University of California at Berkeley in the fall of 1964. Angry students, many veterans of the 1964 fight for black rights in the South, staged sit-down strikes in university buildings to protest the prohibition of political canvassing on the campus. What came to be known as the Free Speech movement disrupted the institution over a period of weeks. Hundreds were arrested, the state legislature threatened reprisals, the faculty became involved in the controversy, and the crisis led to the resignation of the president of the University of California, Clark Kerr.

On campus after campus in the late 1960s SDS organized sit-ins and employed other disruptive tactics. Frequently professors and administrators played into the radicals' hands, being so offended by their methods and manners that they refused to recognize the legitimacy of some of their demands.

At Columbia in 1968, SDS and black students occupied university buildings and refused to leave unless a series of "nonnegotiable" demands (concerning such matters as the university's involvement in secret military research and its relations with minority groups living in the Columbia neighborhood) were met. When, after long delays, President Grayson Kirk called in the police to clear the buildings, a riot broke out in which dozens of students, some of them innocent bystanders, were clubbed and

*Student sit-ins kept professors and staff from gaining access to their offices on
many campuses. A typical incident was photographed at a "liberated building"
on the Columbia University campus in April 1968.*

beaten. General student revulsion at the use of the
police led to Kirk's resignation and the enactment
of many university reforms.

Equally significant in altering the student mood
was the frustration that so many of them felt with
traditional aspects of college life. Regulations that
students had formerly merely grumbled about
evoked determined, even violent opposition. Dissidents denounced rules that restricted their personal lives, such as prohibitions on the use of alcohol
and the banning of members of the opposite sex
from dormitories. They complained that required
courses inhibited their intellectual development.
They demanded a share in the government of their

institutions, long the private preserve of administrators and professors.

Beyond their specific complaints, the radicals
refused to put up with anything they considered
wrong. The knotty social problems that made their
elders gravitate toward moderation led these students to become intransigent absolutists. The line
between right and wrong became as sharply defined
as the edge of a ruler. Racial prejudice was evil: It
must be eradicated. War in a nuclear age was insane:
Armies must be disbanded. Poverty amid plenty was
an abomination: End poverty now. To the counsel
that evil can be eliminated only gradually, that misguided persons must be persuaded to mend their

ways, that compromise was the path to true progress, they responded with scorn. Extremists among them, observing the flaws in American civilization, adopted a nihilistic position—the only way to deal with a "rotten" society was to destroy it; reform was impossible, constructive compromise corrupting.

Critics found the radical students infantile, old-fashioned, and authoritarian—infantile because they refused to tolerate frustration or delay, old-fashioned because their absolutist ideas had been exploded by several generations of philosophers and scientists, and authoritarian because they rejected majority rule. As time passed, SDS was plagued by factional disputes. Radical women in the movement, for example, claimed that it was run by male chauvinists; women who sought some say in policy matters, one of them has written, were met with "indifference, ridicule, and anger."

By the end of the 1960s SDS had lost much of its influence with the general student body. Nevertheless, it had succeeded in focusing attention on genuine social and political weaknesses both on the campuses and in the larger world.

Black students influenced the academic world in a variety of ways. Almost without exception, the colleges tried to increase black enrollments by their use of scholarship funds and by lowering academic entrance requirements when necessary to compensate for the poor preparation many black students had received in the schools. This did not mean that the black students were satisfied with college life. Most were not. They tended to keep to themselves and usually had little to do with the somewhat elitist SDS. But they demanded more control over all aspects of their education than white's typically did. They wanted black studies programs taught and administered by blacks. Achievement of these goals was difficult because of the shortage of black teachers and because professors—including most black professors—considered student control of appointments and curricula unwise and in violation of the principles of academic freedom. Nevertheless, the general academic response to black demands was accommodating; if "confrontations" occurred, they were usually resolved by negotiation. Unlike white radical students, blacks tended to confine their demands to matters directly related to local conditions. Although generalization is difficult, probably the majority of academics drew a distinction between black radicals, whose actions they found understandable even when they could not in conscience

approve of them, and white radicals, most of whom they thought self-indulgent or emotionally disturbed.

The Counterculture

Some young people, known generally as hippies, were so unattracted by the modern world that they retreated from it, finding refuge in communes, drugs, and mystical religions, often wandering aimlessly from place to place. During the 1960s and 1970s groups of them could be found in every big city in the United States and Europe. Some hippies, like the poet Allen Ginsberg, one of their "elder statesmen," and the novelist Ken Kesey, were genuinely creative people. Ginsberg's dark, desperate masterpiece, *Howl*, written in 1955, is perhaps the most widely read poem of the postwar era, certainly a work of major literary significance. *Howl* begins: "I saw the best minds of my generation destroyed by madness, starving hysterical naked," and goes on to describe the wanderings and searchings of these "angelheaded hipsters," a "lost battalion of platonic conversationalists . . . seeking jazz or sex or soup" in Houston, "whoring in Colorado," and "investigating the F.B.I. in beards and shorts" in California, all the while denouncing "the narcotic tobacco haze of Capitalism." *Howl* ends with Ginsberg's indignant, almost frantic assault on that "sphinx of cement and aluminum" the fire god Moloch, the devourer of children.

Others, however, such as the Youth International Party members ("Yippies") Abbie Hoffman and Jerry Rubin, are best described as professional iconoclasts. (In 1968 the group went through the motions of nominating a pig named Pigassus for president.) And most hippies were simply unwilling to confront the two dilemmas of contemporary existence described above (see p. 889).

The hippies developed a "counterculture" so directly opposite to the way of life of their parents' generation as to suggest to critics that they were still dominated by the culture they rejected. They wore old blue jeans and (it seemed) any nondescript garments they happened to find at hand. Male hippies wore their hair long and grew beards. Females avoided makeup, bras, and other devices more conventional women used to make themselves attractive to men. Both sexes rejected the old Protestant ethic; being part of the hippie world meant not caring about money, material goods, or power over other people. Love was more important than money or influence, feelings more significant than thought, natural things superior to anything manufactured.

Most hippies resembled the radicals in their political and social opinions. They were disgusted by the dishonesty and sordid antics of many politicians, horrified by the brutality of Vietnam, appalled by racism, contemptuous of the smugness they encountered in the colleges and universities. They believed in conservation, freedom of expression, tolerance, and peace.

But they rejected activism, being almost totally apolitical. Theirs was a world of folk songs and blaring acid rock music, of "be ins," casual sex, and drugs. Their slogan, "Make love, not war," was a general pacifist pronouncement, not a specific crit-

Woodstock, New York, August 1969, where half a million people gathered in open and mostly muddy fields for three days of "Peace and Music." Both, despite bad weather and no facilities, prevailed for the most part.

icism of events in Vietnam, although Vietnam surely had a great deal to do with their underlying pessimism. Indeed, passivity was with them a philosophy, almost a principle. At rock concerts they listened where earlier generations had danced. Hallucinogenic drugs heightened users' "experiences" while they were in fact in a stupor; witness the LSD user's proviso "Tune in, turn on, drop out." Another hippie motto, "Do your own thing," can only work in social situations if no one does anything. Hippie communes were a far cry from the busy centers of social experimentation of the pre–Civil War Age of Reform.

Charles Reich, a professor at Yale, praised the hippie view of the world in *The Greening of America* (1970), dignifying it with the title, "Consciousness III." Reich's Consciousness I was the do-it-yourself, laissez faire approach to life—having "more faith in winning than in love," while Consciousness II was the psychology of "liberal intellectuals" and "members of the Communist Party, U.S.A." and the Kennedys—marked by faith in institutional solutions to problems. Reich taught a course called "Individualism in America." One semester he had over 500 students, not one of whom failed. According to the *Yale Course Guide,* published by students, Professor Reich "thinks kids are neat and what can be bad about someone telling you how the system and the older generation have warped and destroyed things for us?"

The Sexual Revolution

Young people made the most striking contribution to the revolution that took place in the late 1960s in public attitudes toward sexual relationships. Here change came with startling swiftness. Almost overnight, it seemed in retrospect, conventional ideas about premarital sex, contraception and abortion, homosexuality, pornography, and a host of related matters were openly challenged. Probably the behavior of the majority of Americans did not alter radically. But the majority's beliefs and practices were no longer automatically acknowledged as the only valid ones. It became possible for individuals to espouse different values and to behave differently with at least relative impunity. Actions that in one decade would have led to social ostracism or even to imprisonment were in the next decade accepted almost as a matter of course.

Surely among the most startling changes to occur in the 1970s and 1980s has been the willingness of homosexuals to make public their sexual preferences in the course of demanding for themselves full legal standing.

The causes of this revolution were complex and interrelated; one change led to others. More efficient methods of birth control and antibiotics that cured venereal disease removed the two principal practical arguments against sex outside marriage; with these barriers down, many people found their moral attitudes changing. Almost concurrently, Alfred C. Kinsey's *Sexual Behavior in the Human Male* (1948), which was based on thousands of confidential interviews with persons from nearly every walk of life, revealed that where sex was concerned, large numbers of Americans did not practice what they preached. Premarital sex, marital infidelity, homosexuality, and various forms of perversion were, Kinsey's figures showed, far more common than most persons had suspected.

Sexual Behavior in the Human Male shocked many people, and Kinsey's research methods were criticized by some experts. When he published *Sexual Behavior in the Human Female* in 1958, a book that demonstrated that the sexual practices of women were as varied as those of men, he was subjected to a storm of abuse and deprived of the foundation support that had financed his research.

Nevertheless, Kinsey has aptly been called "the Marx of the sexual revolution." Once it became possible to look at sex in primarily physical terms and to accept the idea that one's own urges might not be as uncommon as one had been led to believe, it became much more difficult to object to any sexual activity practiced in private by consenting adults.

Homosexuals, for example, began openly to admit their feelings and to demand that the heterosexual society cease harassing and discriminating against them.

That the sexual revolution in its many aspects served useful functions was beyond dispute. Reducing irrational fears and inhibitions was liberating for many persons of both sexes, and it tended to help young people form permanent associations on the basis of deeper feelings than their sexual drives. Women surely profited from the new freedom, just as a greater sharing of family duties by husbands and fathers opened men's lives to many new satisfactions.

But like other changes, the revolution produced new problems, and some of its results were at best ambiguous. For young people, sexual freedom could be very unsettling; sometimes it generated social pressures that propelled them into relationships they were not yet prepared to handle, with grave psychological results. Equally perplexing was the rise in the number of illegitimate births. Easy cures did not eliminate venereal disease; on the contrary, the relaxation of sexual taboos produced what public health officials called a veritable epidemic of gonorrhea, a frightening increase in the incidence of syphilis, and the emergence of a deadly new disease, acquired immune deficiency syndrome (AIDS).

Exercising the right to advocate and practice previously forbidden activities involved subjecting people who found those activities offensive—still a large proportion of the population—to embarrassment and even acute emotional distress. Some people believed pornography to be ethically wrong, and most feminists considered it degrading to women. Abortion raised difficult legal and moral questions. Such questions exacerbated already serious social conflicts.

Women's Liberation

Sexual freedom also contributed to the revival of the women's rights movement. For one thing, freedom involved a more drastic revolution for women than for men. Effective methods of contraception obviously affected women more directly than men, and the new attitudes heightened women's awareness of the way the old sexual standards and patterns of family living had restricted their entire existence. In fact the two movements interacted in innumerable ways, some clear, others obscure. Concern for better job opportunities and for equal pay for equal work, for example, fed the demand for day-care centers for children.

Still another cause of the new drive for women's rights was concern for improving the treatment of minorities. Participation in and the mere observation of the civil rights movement encouraged American women, as it frequently had in earlier times, to speak out more forcefully for their own rights. Just as white people had callously demeaned and dominated black people until forced to desist by the victims of their prejudice, so, feminists argued, they were being demeaned and dominated by a male-oriented society and must fight back.

During the immediate postwar period, the women's movement had been relatively quiescent. However, pressures were mounting because social and economic conditions were changing. When the war ended, women who had taken jobs because of the labor shortage were expected and in many cases compelled to surrender them to veterans and return to their traditional roles as housewives and mothers. Some did, as the sharp increase in marriage and birth rates in the late 1940s and early 1950s indicates. In 1940 about 15 percent of American women in their early thirties were unmarried, in 1965 only 5 percent. Many, however, did not meekly return to the home, and many of those who did contin-

Betty Friedan, author of The Feminine Mystique, *spearheaded women's rights demonstrations like the National Women's Strike in August 1970. The strike called on women to boycott four consumer products whose advertising the protesters considered insulting to women.*

ued to hold down jobs in order to help pay for their veteran-husbands' war-interrupted educations. Other women went to work to counterbalance the onslaughts of inflation, still others (some married, some not) simply because they enjoyed the money and the independence that jobs made possible. Between 1940 and 1960 the proportion of women workers doubled, and thereafter it increased still more rapidly. The rise was particularly swift among married women, and the difficulties faced by anyone trying to work while having to perform household duties increased the resentment of these workers.

Married or single, more numerous or not, women workers still faced job discrimination of many kinds. In nearly every occupation they were paid less than men who did the same work. Many interesting jobs that they were capable of holding were either closed to them entirely or doled out on the basis of some illogical and often unwritten quota system. In challenging occupations where they could find employment, they were rarely given a chance to rise to positions of leadership. Many women objected to this state of affairs even in the 1950s; in the 1960s their protest erupted into an organized and vociferous demand for change.

One of the leaders of the new women's movement was Betty Friedan. In *The Feminine Mystique* (1963), Friedan argued that advertisers, popular magazines, and other opinion-shaping forces were undermining the capacity of women to use their intelligence and their talents creatively by a pervasive and not very subtle form of brainwashing designed to convince them of the virtues of domesticity. This Friedan deplored. She argued that without understanding why, thousands of women living supposedly happy lives were experiencing vague but persistent feelings of anger and discomfort. "The only way for a woman . . . to know herself as a person is by creative work of her own," she wrote. A "problem that had no name" was stifling women's potential.

The Feminine Mystique was what later came to be known as "consciousness raising" for thousands of women. Over a million copies were quickly sold. Back in 1922 a committee of physicians and social scientists had queried 1,000 middle-class women about their personal lives. To the question "Is your married life a happy one?" only 116 had answered no. But after her book came out, Friedan was deluged by hundreds of letters from women who had thought their feelings of unease and depression despite their "happy" family life to be both unique to themselves and unreasonable. Many now determined to expand their horizons by taking jobs or resuming their education.

Friedan had assumed that if able women acted with determination, employers would recognize their abilities and stop discriminating against them. This did not happen. In 1966 she and other feminists founded the National Organization for Women. Copying the tactics of black activists, NOW called for equal employment opportunities and equal pay as civil rights. "The time has come for a new movement toward true equality for all women in America and toward a fully equal partnership of the sexes," the leaders announced. "The silken cur-

tain of prejudice and discrimination against women" in government, industry, the professions, religion, education, "and every other field of importance" must be drawn back. In 1967 NOW came out for an equal rights amendment to the Constitution, for changes in the divorce laws, and for the legalization of abortion, the right of "control of one's body."

By 1967, however, many younger feminists were arguing that NOW was not radical enough. They deplored its hierarchical structure, its lobbying activities, its stress on attracting celebrities, its imitation of conventional pressure-group tactics. Equality of the two sexes smacked of "separate but equal" to these women, and indeed, many of them had been first radicalized by the struggle against racial segregation.

Typical was Kate Millett, whose *Sexual Politics* (1970) became a best-seller. Millett called for a "sexual revolution" to do away with "traditional inhibitions and taboos." She denounced male supremacy, which she described as "the institution of patriarchy," and drew a distinction between the immutable biological differences between men and women, and gender, how men and women relate to one another socially and culturally, which are learned ways of behaving and thus capable of change. For example, Millett said that people must stop thinking of words like *violent* and *efficiency* as male characteristics and *passive* and *tenderness* as female.

The radicals gathered in small consciousness-raising groups to discuss questions as varied as the need for government child-care centers, how best to denounce the annual Miss America contests, and lesbianism. They held conferences and seminars and published magazines, the most widely known being *Ms.*, edited by Gloria Steinem. Academics among them organized women's studies programs at dozens of colleges. One course on women's health led to a handbook, *Our Bodies, Ourselves* (1973), which went through many editions.

Some radical feminists advocated raising children in communal centers and doing away with marriage as a legal institution. "The family unit is a decadent, energy-absorbing, destructive, wasteful institution," one prominent feminist declared. Others described marriage as "legalized rape." Some rejected heterosexuality as a matter of principle.

The militants attacked all aspects of the standard

An anti-abortion or, as its adherents preferred, a "Right to Life" rally opposing the 1973 Supreme Court ruling upholding the right of a woman to terminate a pregnancy. Defenders of abortion, or of "Freedom of Choice," have been no less willing to take to the barricades when they sense a possible change in federal policy on this highly charged issue.

image of the female sex. Avoiding the error of the Progressive Era reformers who had fought for the vote by stressing differences between the sexes (the supposed purity and high moral character of women), they insisted on total equality. Clichés such as "the fair sex" and "the weaker sex" made them see red. They insisted that the separation of "Help Wanted—Male" and "Help Wanted—Female" classified ads in newspapers violated the Civil Rights Act of 1964, and they demanded that men bear as much of the burden of caring for their children, cooking, and housework as women traditionally did. They took courses in self-defense in order to be able to protect themselves from muggers, rapists, and casual mashers. They denounced the use of masculine words like *chairman* (favoring *chairperson*) and

of such terms as *mankind* and *men* to designate people in general.* They substituted *Ms.* for both *Miss* and *Mrs.* on the grounds that the language drew no such distinction between unmarried and married men.

The most radical of the feminists went beyond denouncing "male supremacy." As Todd Gitlin puts it in *The Sixties: Years of Hope, Days of Rage,* they attacked "not just capitalism, but men." In *The Dialect of Sex* (1970), Shulamith Firestone suggested

---

* The difficulty here was that this form of discrimination was built into the structure of the language. Even the word *woman* derives from the Anglo-Saxon *wif-mann,* "wife of a man." Efforts to avoid the use of masculine words in general references led to such awkward expressions as *his/her* and *(s)he.*

that childbearing (not merely child rearing) should be the responsibility of society, not of individuals, arguing that new technology made this possible.

At the other extreme, many women rejected the position even of moderate feminists like Betty Friedan. Conservatives rallied behind Phillis Schlafly to campaign against the equal rights amendment. After the Supreme Court declared in *Roe* v. *Wade* (1973) that women had a constitutional right to have an abortion during the early stages of pregnancy, a vigorous right-to-life movement dedicated to over-

turning the decision sprang up. But few people escaped being affected by the women's movement. The presence of women in new roles—as television commentators, airline pilots, police officers—did not prove that a large-scale shift in employment patterns had taken place. Yet even the most unregenerate male seemed to recognize that the balance of power and influence between the sexes had been altered. Clearly, the sexual revolution was not about to end, the direction of change in relationships not to be turned back.

Milestones

1948	Alfred C. Kinsey, *Sexual Behavior in the Human Male*		accused of crimes (*Gideon* v. *Wainright*)
1950	David Riesman, *The Lonely Crowd*	**1964**	Free Speech movement at University of California
1954	Launching of U.S.S. *Nautilus*, first atomic-powered ship	**1965**	Malcolm X murdered
1955	Allen Ginsberg, "Howl" AFL and CIO merge		César Chávez organizes boycott to support grape pickers
1956	William Whyte, *The Organization Man*	**1965–1967**	Riots in ghettos
		1966	National Organization for Women (NOW) founded
1957	Russians launch first *Sputnik* Supreme Court reinstates "clear and present danger" standard in First Amendment cases (*Yates* v. *United States*)	**1968**	Student strike at Columbia University broken by police Martin Luther King, Jr., assassinated
1958	National Defense Education Act	**1969**	American astronauts land on the moon
1962	Students for a Democratic Society's Port Huron Statement	**1970**	Kate Millett, *Sexual Politics*
1963	Betty Friedan, *The Feminine Mystique* Supreme Court guarantees free legal counsel for indigents	**1973**	Supreme Court guarantees right to abortion in early stages of pregnancy (*Roe* v. *Wade*)
		1975	Indian Self-determination Act

SUPPLEMENTARY READING

Titles marked with an asterisk have been published in paperback.

J. F. Heath, **Decade of Disillusionment: The Kennedy-Johnson Years** (1980), and A. J. Matusow, **The Unraveling of America*** (1984), contain material related to this chapter, as do W. M. O'Neill, **Coming Apart: An Informal History of the 1960s*** (1971), and Godfrey Hodgson,

America in Our Time (1976). Todd Gitlin, **The Sixties: Years of Hope, Days of Rage** (1987) is an "insider's" account.

Population trends are described in C. Taeuber and I. B. Taeuber, **The Changing Population of the United**

States (1958), the movement to the suburbs in K. T. Jackson, **Crabgrass Frontier*** (1985). On television, see David Marc, **Demographic Vistas: Television in American Culture** (1984), Barbara Matusow, **The Evening Stars** (1988), and G. A. Steiner, **The People Look at Television** (1963). Daniel Hoffman (ed.), **Harvard Guide to Contemporary American Writing** (1979), contains convenient discussions of postwar literature. Morris Dickstein, **Gates of Eden: American Culture in the Sixties** (1977), is part history, part literary criticism, part memoir. Modern art is discussed in Barbara Rose, **American Art Since 1900*** (1967).

For the causes and character of the poverty and urban problems that led Johnson to devise his Great Society program, see Michael Harrington, **The Other America*** (1962), and Oscar Lewis, **La Vida: A Puerto Rican Family in the Culture of Poverty*** (1966).

On the black radicals, see Malcolm X, **Autobiography*** (1966), Stokely Carmichael and C. V. Hamilton, **Black Power*** (1967), and Eldridge Cleaver, **Soul on Ice*** (1967). Other important books on race relations include Taylor Branch, **Parting the Waters** (1988), on the career of Martin Luther King Jr.; Clayborne Carson, **In Struggle: SNCC and the Black Awakening of the 1960s** (1981); and August Meier and Elliott Rudwick, **CORE: A Study in the Civil Rights Movement*** (1973). M. S. Meier and Feliciano Rivera, **The Chicanos*** (1972), provides a sympathetic discussion of the problems and aspirations of Mexican-Americans, but see also Joan London and Henry Anderson, **So Shall Ye Reap: The Story of César Chávez and the Farm Workers Movement** (1970), A. F. Corwin, **Immigrants—and Immigrants** (1978), and J. R. Garcia, **Operation Wetback** (1980). The revived interest in ethnicity is discussed in Michael Novak, **The Rise of the Unmeltable Ethnics** (1972), and Thomas Sowell, **Ethnic America** (1981).

Educational trends are discussed in Martin Mayer, **The Schools*** (1961), J. B. Conant, **The American High School Today*** (1959), and Robert Coles, **Children of Crisis*** (1967). On militancy among college students, see Kenneth Kenniston, **Young Radicals** (1968), S. M. Lipset and P. G. Altbach (eds.), **Students in Revolt** (1969), Roger Kahn, **The Battle of Morningside Heights** (1970), and Kirkpatrick Sale, **SDS** (1973). James Miller reprints the SDS Port Huron Statement in **"Democracy in the Streets"** (1987). See also Irwin Unger, **The Movement: A History of the American New Left** (1974), and Theodore Roszak, **The Making of a Counter-Culture** (1969).

The literature on the women's movement is voluminous and difficult to evaluate. In addition to W. H. Chafe, **The American Woman*** (1972) and **Women and Equality*** (1977), see Betty Friedan, **The Feminine Mystique*** (1963), Jo Freeman, **The Politics of Women's Liberation** (1975), S. M. Rothman, **Woman's Proper Place** (1978), and Sara Evans and H. C. Boyte, **Free Spaces** (1986).

For postwar religious trends, see Robert Wuthnow, **The Restructuring of American Religion** (1988), Arthur Hertzberg, **The Jews in America** (1989), and Will Herberg, **Catholic, Protestant, Jew** (1955).

America's Changing Environment

Travelers in the American West were overawed by the majestic beauty of places like Yosemite, in California. The above scene was painted by German-born artist Albert Bierstadt in 1865 shortly after Yosemite became a state park.

By the late 1800s, conservation had become a political issue. President Theodore Roosevelt and the naturalist John Muir, shown left riding through a redwood forest in California in 1903, represented two approaches to the question. Roosevelt favored controlled exploitation of the land in ways that would replenish natural resources. "The preservation of our forests," he declared, "is an imperative business necessity." Muir's contrary insistence on conservation as an end in itself finally led to a falling out between the two men. Above, a modern protester objects to the commercialization of Yellowstone National Park.

In the summer of 1988, a mammoth forest fire raged through more than half of Yellowstone National Park's 2.2 million acres (left). Ironically, the fire was the indirect result of a new environmental consciousness. For decades rangers sought to snuff out fires, whether caused by careless campers or by lightning, as quickly as possible. In the 1970s, officials decided to let naturally occurring fires burn. But the long accumulation of brush and decaying wood made the forest a tinderbox and the 1988 conflagration resulted. Nevertheless, the forest quickly began to recover. With spring, wildflowers daubed the charred landscape with pink and yellow, soon to be followed by shrubs and seedlings (below).

The untamed beauty of the "new" continent enchanted European settlers. "The country," William Penn stated with Quaker understatement in 1683, "in its soil, air, water, seasons, and produce . . . is not to be despised." But the seemingly limitless resources of America encouraged wasteful exploitation. Farmers were notoriously prodigal, manufacturers and miners even more so.

In the Progressive Era, however, the federal government and the states began to protect the environment, mainly by putting forests and other lands in parks and reserves. But only in the 1960s did a strong environmental protection movement appear. Rachel Carson's *Silent Spring* (1962) explained how pesticides such as DDT endangered wildlife. After the massive Earth Day rallies of 1970, environmentalists focused on the threats to health posed by food additives, carcinogenic pollutants, and toxic wastes.

Pollution accompanied settlement everywhere in the West. In his prototypical Western novel, The Virginian (1903), Owen Wister describes this scene in Wyoming: "We passed the ramparts of Medicine Bow—thick heaps and fringes of tin cans, and shelving mounds of bottles cast out of the saloons." The photograph above shows Pike's Peak, Colorado, in the 1890s. By the 1960s, places like the automobile graveyard at right marred the beauty of the landscape.

Today, disposal of solid waste is a pressing problem in many communities. New York City's only working landfill, which receives 25,000 tons of garbage per day and will soon be the highest point on the East Coast south of Maine, is not unique. The one at left, in Portland, Oregon is also running out of room.

910

Concern about dependence on foreign energy resulted in the exploitation of the oil resources of Alaska despite fears of the impact of development on the fragile Arctic environment. In March 1989, the worst fears of the environmentalists were realized when an Exxon tanker ran aground near the oil port of Valdez (shown at center in 1940), spilling 11 million gallons of crude oil into Prince William Sound. The spill, the biggest in American history, killed thousands of birds and sea animals. At left, workers assist in the much-criticized clean-up effort; top right, a rescued sea otter recuperates.

New technologies are helping to make waste products and other alternative sources of energy cost effective. Above a crane feeds garbage into the furnace of a steam turbine in Bridgeport, Connecticut. The turbine, which burns 2500 tons of waste daily, supplies electricity to towns in Fairfield County. At right, solar panels power a public telephone in Mystic, Connecticut.

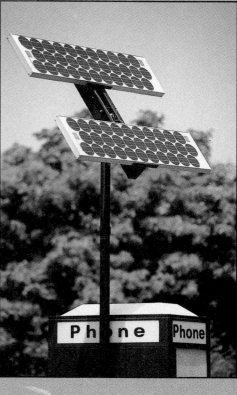

In northern California, 300 wind turbines have turned a former cattle ranch into a hillside "wind farm." The electricity produced by the windmills is sold to Pacific Gas and Electric, saving approximately 60,000 barrels of oil per year.

Florida's Everglades was once among the richest natural habitats in the United States (above). Wetland habitats are critical to many species but rapid development in south Florida has diverted water from the region, causing the sawgrass and Mangrove swamp to shrink dramatically. At left, a view of the Everglades from the Tamiami Trail.

Many current environmental issues—global warming, acid rain, and ozone depletion—demand transnational solutions. Pollutants from factories in the Middle West have caused acid rain along the East Coast of both the United States and Canada. Over time acid rain can kill marine life and even trees. The photograph at right shows acid rain damage on Mt. Mitchell in North Carolina.

Our Times

*Shucks, I don't think [Jerry Ford] can chew gum and walk at the
same time. . . . He's a nice fellow, but he spent too much time
playing football without a helmet.*

LYNDON B. JOHNSON

Call me Jimmy.

PRESIDENT JAMES EARL CARTER, *1977*

*[Reagan] has contributed a spirit of good will and grace to the
Presidency and American life generally.*

SENATOR EDWARD M. KENNEDY, *1986*

*America is never wholly herself unless she is engaged in high moral
principle. We as a people have such a purpose today. It is to make
kinder the face of the nation and gentler the face of the world.*

PRESIDENT GEORGE BUSH, *1989*

T he country greeted the accession of Gerald Ford to the presidency with a collective sigh of relief. Most observers considered Ford unimaginative, certainly not brilliant. But he was hardworking and—most important under the circumstances—his record was untouched by scandal. Although he was an almost automaton-like Republican partisan, nearly all the Democrats in Congress liked him. He was Nixon's opposite as a person, gregarious and open, and he stated repeatedly that he took a dim view of Nixon's high-handed way of dealing with Congress. He insisted that the president and Congress must work together in the nation's interest. Being a most ordinary person, earnest but limited, Ford appeared unlikely to venture beyond conventional limits or to act rashly. This was what nearly everyone wanted of the president in the wake of Nixon.

Ford as President

Ford, who unlike any earlier vice-president had been appointed rather than elected to that post, obviously desired to live up to public expectations. Yet he was soon embroiled in controversy and subject to considerable criticism, not all of it partisan. At the outset he roused widespread resentment by pardoning Nixon for whatever crimes he had committed in office, even any, if such existed, that had not yet come to light. Not many Americans wanted to see the ex-president lodged in jail, but pardoning him seemed both illogical and incomprehensible when he had admitted no guilt and had not yet been officially charged with any crime. (Nixon's instant acceptance of the pardon while claiming to have done no wrong was also illogical, but not incomprehensible.)

Ugly rumors of a "corrupt bargain" arranged before Nixon resigned, similar to that supposedly made by John Quincy Adams and Henry Clay in the 1820s, were soon circulating, for the pardon seemed grossly unfair. Why should Nixon go scot-free when his chief underlings, Mitchell, Haldeman, and Erlichman, were being brought to trial for their part in the Watergate scandal? (All three were eventually convicted and jailed.)

Ford displayed inconsistency and apparent incompetence in managing the economy. He announced that inflation was the major problem and asked patriotic citizens to signify their willingness to fight it by wearing WIN buttons (Whip Inflation Now). Almost immediately the economy entered a precipitous slump. Production fell and the unemployment rate rose above 9 percent. The president was forced to ask for tax cuts and other measures aimed at stimulating business activity. While pressing for these measures, he continued to fulminate against spending money on social programs designed to help the urban poor. The economic problems were difficult and Ford was handicapped by the fact that the Democrats had solid control of Congress, but his performance was at best inept.

That Ford would never act rashly proved to be an incorrect assumption. In the spring of 1975 North Vietnamese forces increased their attacks in South Vietnam. Dispirited, short of guns and ammunition, and incompetently led, the South Vietnamese armies fell back, then fled headlong, then dissolved. As the communists advanced, tens of

"My fellow Americans, our long national nightmare is over," Gerald Ford announced as he succeeded Richard Nixon in August 1974. Ford's candor and humility reassured a public wearied by the "dirty tricks" and "executive privilege" of the Watergate years.

thousands of South Vietnamese asked for asylum in the United States, and about 140,000 were successfully evacuated. Thousands more were callously abandoned, although their earlier collaboration with the Americans made their situation in a communist-controlled Vietnam precarious. Ford had always taken a hawkish position on the Vietnam War. As the military situation deteriorated, he urged Congress to pour more arms into the South to stem the North Vietnamese advance. The legislators flatly refused to do so, and late in April Saigon fell. The long Vietnam War was finally over.

Two weeks earlier local communists of a particularly radical persuasion had overturned the pro-American regime in Cambodia. On May 12 Cambodian naval forces seized the American merchant ship *Mayaguez* in the Gulf of Siam. President Ford, apparently frustrated by his inability to prevent the communists from taking over South Vietnam and Cambodia, reacted to the seizure without fully investigating the situation or allowing the new regime time to respond to his perfectly proper demand that the *Mayaguez* and its crew be freed. He ordered marine units to attack Tang Island, where the captured vessel had been taken. The assault succeeded in that the Cambodians released the *Mayaguez* and its crew of 39, but 38 marines died in the operation. Since the Cambodians had released the ship before the marines struck, Ford's reflexive response was probably unnecessary, although it was popular with a majority of Americans.

After some hesitation Ford decided to seek the Republican presidential nomination in 1976. He was opposed by ex-governor Ronald Reagan of California, a movie actor turned politician who was the darling of the Republican right wing. Reagan's campaign was well organized and well financed. He was an excellent speaker, where Ford proved somewhat bumbling on the stump. The contest was close, both candidates winning important primaries and gathering substantial blocs of delegates in non-primary states. At the convention in August, Ford obtained a slim majority. That he did not win easily, possessed as he was of the advantage of incumbency, made his chances of election in November appear slim.

In the meantime the Democrats had chosen James Earl Carter, a former governor of Georgia, as their candidate. Carter's rise from almost total obscurity was even more spectacular than that of George McGovern in the 1972 campaign and was made possible by the same forces: television, the democratization of the delegate-selection process, and the absence of a dominant leader among the Democrats.

Carter had been a naval officer and a substantial peanut farmer and warehouse owner before entering politics. He was elected governor of Georgia in 1970. While governor he won something of a reputation as a southern public official who treated black citizens fairly. (He hung a portrait of Martin Luther King, Jr., in his office.) Carter's political style was informal—he preferred to be called Jimmy.

During the campaign for delegates he turned his inexperience in national politics to advantage, emphasizing his lack of connection with the Washington establishment rather than apologizing for it. He repeatedly called attention to his integrity and deep religious faith. "I'll never lie to you," he promised voters, a pledge that no candidate would have bothered to make before Nixon's disgrace.

Carter entered nearly all the Democratic primaries and campaigned hard in non-primary states. Running against many different candidates, he won few decisive victories, but he accumulated delegates steadily and went to the convention in New York City in July with a solid majority.

When the final contest began, Carter had a large lead. Most of it soon evaporated. Reagan supporters among the Republicans swung behind Ford, and the prestige of the presidency was another asset. Both candidates were vague with respect to issues, a situation that hurt Carter particularly because he had made so much of honesty and straight talk. Ford stressed the need to control inflation, Carter high unemployment. Three televised debates between the candidates attracted huge audiences without generating a trend toward either candidate.

As election day approached, pollsters predicted an extremely close contest, and they were right: Carter won, 297 electoral votes to 241, having carried most of the South, including Texas, and a few large industrial states. A key element in his victory was the fact that he got an overwhelming majority of the black vote (partly on his record in Georgia, partly because Ford had been unsympathetic toward the demands of the urban poor). He also ran well in districts dominated by labor union members and throughout the South. The public's wish to punish the party of Richard Nixon was probably a further reason for his victory.

The Carter Presidency

Carter shone brightly in comparison with Nixon, and he seemed more forward-looking and imaginative than Ford. He tried to give a tone of democratic simplicity and moral fervor to his administration. After delivering his inaugural address, he walked with his wife Rosalynn and their small daughter Amy in the parade from the Capitol to the White House instead of riding in a limousine.

Jimmy Carter's informality was the perfect emblem of a post-Watergate reaction against the "imperial presidency." Yet, despite his image, Carter insisted on making many decisions—even minor ones—himself. This habit made it easy for voters to hold him personally responsible for failures.

He enrolled Amy, a fourth grader, in a largely black Washington public school. For his first talk on television he wore a sweater instead of a coat and tie, an advertisement for both his informality and the need to conserve energy by turning down thermostats. Soon after taking office he held a "call-in"; for two hours he answered questions phoned in by people from all over the country.

Carter's actual administration of his office did not go nearly so well. He put so many Georgians in important posts that his administration took on a most parochial character. Six of seven top White House aides came from his home state, as did his attorney general, the director of the Office of Management and Budget, the ambassador to the United Nations, and many lesser officials. Most of these people, like their boss, had little or no experience in national affairs. The administration developed a reputation for submitting complicated proposals to Congress with great fanfare and then failing to follow them up. Whatever matter Carter was considering at the moment seemed to absorb him totally—other urgent matters were allowed to drift.

This tendency frequently caused him to shift policies sharply when he returned to matters he had put aside. One journalist counted seven distinct changes of approach in Carter's economic policy in three years. While running for office he had emphasized the need to restrain inflation, but early in 1977 he came out for a $50 income tax rebate for individuals that would almost surely have caused prices to rise. When that idea ran into stiff congressional resistance, Carter turned to something else. And so it went.

In the face of so much frustration it was perhaps only human that Carter tended to blame others for his troubles. In a heralded television speech he described a national malaise that had sapped the people's energies and undermined civic pride. Although there was some truth in this observation, the effect was to make the president seem both ineffective and petulant.

Cold War or Détente?

In foreign affairs Carter announced that he intended to deal with all nations in a fair and humane way, putting defense of "basic human rights" before all other concerns. He cut off aid to Chile and Argentina because of human rights violations, but said little about what was going on in a long list of other repressive nations. He also negotiated treaties with Panama that provided for the gradual transfer of the isthmian canal to that nation and guaranteed its neutrality; in 1978, after long debate, the Senate ratified the treaties.

The president also intended to carry forward the Nixon-Kissinger policy of détente. He ended official American recognition of Taiwan, and in January 1979 the first exchange of ambassadors with the People's Republic of China took place. Maintaining good relations with the Soviet Union was more difficult, partly because while Secretary of State Cyrus Vance supported détente, Carter's national security adviser, Zbigniew Brzezinski, was strongly anti-Russian. (In his memoirs Vance complained of Brzezinski's "visceral anti-Sovietism," and another critic writes of his "rigid, simplified, Sovi-

Egypt's president Anwar Sadat, Jimmy Carter, and Israeli prime minister Menachem Begin clasp hands after the signing of the Camp David Agreement in 1978. Carter's active role in the peace negotiations showed his hands-on approach to the presidency.

etcentric view of the world.") Carter fluctuated between the two approaches yet seemed blissfully unaware of his ambivalence. He could complain about Soviet human rights violations and the need to strengthen NATO one day, and praise the idea of a new arms limitation agreement the next. The Russians certainly treated dissidents harshly, but they considered the president's frequent sermons on the subject politically motivated and out of keeping with his talk about détente.

In 1979 another Strategic Arms Limitation Treaty (SALT II) was signed with the Soviet Union, but the following winter the Soviet Union sent troops into Afghanistan in order to overthrow a government of which it disapproved. Carter denounced the invasion and warned the Russians that he would use force if they invaded any of the countries bordering the Persian Gulf. He stopped shipments of American grain and technologically advanced products, such as computers, to the Soviet Union, and he withdrew the SALT treaty, which he had sent to the Senate for ratification. He also refused to allow American athletes to compete in the Olympic games, which were held in the summer of 1980 in Moscow, and he began a new arms buildup.

Carter's one striking diplomatic achievement was the so-called Camp David Agreement with Israel and Egypt. Avoiding war in the Middle East was crucial because war in that part of the world was likely to result in the cutting off of oil supplies from the Arab nations. In September 1978 the president of Egypt, Anwar Sadat, and Prime Minister Menachem Begin of Israel came to the United States at Carter's invitation to negotiate a peace treaty ending the state of war that had existed between their two countries for many years. For two weeks they conferred at Camp David, the presidential retreat outside the capital, and Carter's mediation had much to do with their successful negotiations. In the treaty Israel promised to withdraw from territory captured from Egypt during the "six-day" war of 1967. Egypt in turn recognized Israel as a nation, the first Arab country to do so.

A Time of Troubles

Carter had promised to fight inflation by reducing government spending and balancing the budget, and to stimulate the economy by cutting taxes, policies that sounded (and in fact were) very much like those of Nixon and Ford. He advanced an admirable if complicated plan for conserving energy and reducing the dependence of the United States on OPEC oil. It involved raising the tax on gasoline and imposing a new tax on "gas guzzlers," cars that got relatively few miles per gallon. But in typical fashion he did not press for these measures, and he waffled on the important question of deregulating the price of American crude oil until late in his term.

For reasons that were not entirely Carter's fault, national self-confidence was at a low ebb. The crises of the Cold War had subsided and the hot war in Vietnam was over, but the United States had lost a considerable portion of its international prestige. To a degree this was unavoidable. The very success of American policies after World War II had something to do with the decline of American influence in the world. The Marshall Plan, for example, enabled the nations of western Europe to rebuild their economies; thereafter they were less dependent on outside aid, and in the course of pursuing their own interests they sometimes adopted policies that did not seem to be in the best interests of the United States. Under American occupation, Japan rebuilt its shattered economy. By the 1960s and 1970s it had become one of the world's leading manufacturing nations, its exporters providing fierce competition in markets previously dominated by Americans.

Similarly, to the extent that American aid to underdeveloped countries had improved their economies, they were more likely to act independently and not necessarily in ways that benefited the United States. On the other hand, when American aid was ineffective or used to bolster unpopular local regimes, American prestige also suffered. And the failure of the United States to achieve its objectives in the Vietnam War had a debilitating effect on its influence abroad long after the war ended.

At home the decay of the inner sections of the great cities was a continuing cause of concern. The older cities seemed almost beyond repair. Carter visited the South Bronx section of New York City in 1977. He was shocked to see block after block of rubble and rows of empty, fire-blackened buildings. He pledged that the federal government would clean up and rebuild this wasteland, but when his term ended that part of the South Bronx and similar parts of many cities remained barren ruins.

Crime rates were high in the inner cities, public transportation dilapidated and expensive, other city services undermanned and inefficient, the schools crowded, students' performances poor. Blacks, Hispanics, and other minorities made up a large percentage of the population in decaying urban areas. That they had to live in such surroundings made a mockery of the commitment of the civil rights legislation of the 1960s and Lyndon Johnson's Great Society program to treat all people equally and improve the lives of the poor.

Double-digit Inflation

The most disturbing problem that vexed the nation in the Carter years was soaring inflation. Prices had been rising for an unprecedentedly long period and in recent years at an unprecedentedly rapid pace. In 1971 an inflation rate of 5 percent had so alarmed President Nixon that he had imposed a price freeze. In 1979 a 5 percent rate would have seemed almost deflationary—the actual rate was nearly 13 percent.

Double-digit inflation had a devastating effect on the poor, the retired, and others who were living on fixed incomes. However, the squeeze that price increases put on these unfortunates was only part of the damage done. Inflation discouraged people from making long-term investments, and as time passed and the rate of inflation increased, it caused many to stop saving entirely. People began to anticipate inflation. They bought goods they did not really need, and without much regard for cost, on the assumption that whatever today's price, tomorrow's would be higher still. This behavior increased demand and thereby pushed prices up still more. Put differently, when the interest paid by savings banks was lower than the inflation rate, it seemed foolish to save money.

At another level, a kind of "flight from money" began. Well-to-do individuals transferred their assets from cash to durable goods such as land and houses, gold, works of art, jewelry, rare postage stamps, and other "collectibles." Interest rates rose rapidly as lenders demanded higher returns to compensate for expected future inflation.

Congress raised the minimum wage to help low-paid workers cope with inflation. It pegged social security payments to the cost of living index in an effort to protect retirees. Thereafter, when prices rose social security payments went up automatically. The poor and the pensioners got some immediate relief, but the laws made balancing the federal budget more difficult and the increased spending power of the recipients caused further upward pressure on prices. Inflation seemed to be feeding upon itself, and the price spiral seemed unstoppable.

The federal government made matters worse in several ways. People's wages and salaries rose in response to inflation, but their taxes went up more rapidly because large dollar incomes put them in higher tax brackets. This "bracket creep" caused resentment and frustration among middle-class families. There were "taxpayer revolts" as many people turned against long-accepted but expensive government programs for aiding the poor. Inflation also increased the government's need for money. Year after year it spent more than it received in taxes. By thus unbalancing the budget it pumped billions of dollars into the economy, and by borrowing to meet the deficits and pushing up interest rates, it increased the costs of all businesses that had to borrow.

The Carter Recession

In this situation Carter was more a bystander than a leader; he had little to suggest that was different from the policies of Nixon and Ford. In 1978 he proposed voluntary wage and price guidelines in another effort to slow inflation. Unions and manufacturers responded fairly well, but the guidelines did not apply to the prices that were going up most rapidly: oil, houses, and food. Finally, Carter named a conservative banker, Paul A. Volcker, as chairman of the Federal Reserve Board. Volcker belonged to the conservative monetarist school of economics, which taught that the way to check inflation was to limit the growth of the money supply. Under his direction the Board adopted a tight-money policy, which caused already high interest rates to soar.

High interest rates hurt all borrowers, but they were especially damaging to the automobile and housing industries because most car and home buyers borrow a large portion of the purchase price. American car manufacturers were already experiencing hard times because of the competition of

The Iranian crisis produced striking visual images that appeared worldwide in the press and on TV. These militants burned the American flag a few days after they seized the American Embassy.

Japanese and European automobiles, which gave better gasoline mileage and were seemingly better built than most American vehicles. Tens of thousands of automobile workers, among the highest paid workers in American industry, were out of work. Soaring mortgage rates had a similar effect on the sale of homes. The housing slump meant unemployment for thousands of carpenters, brick-

layers, and other construction workers and bankruptcy for many builders. Double-digit interest rates also hurt small businesses seeking to expand. Savings and loan institutions were especially hard hit because they were saddled with countless mortgages made when rates were as low as four and five percent. Now they had to pay much more than that to hold deposits and offer even higher rates to attract new money.

The Iranian Crisis: Origins

By the autumn of 1979 Carter's standing in public opinion polls was extremely low—barely one respondent in four approved of his handling of the office. He had failed to provide the fresh point of view and the firm leadership that he had promised in the 1976 campaign. His chances of being elected to a second term seemed dim.

At this point a dramatic upheaval in the Middle East revived his prospects. On November 4, 1979, about 400 armed Muslim militants broke into the American Embassy compound in Teheran, Iran, and took everyone within the walls captive. The seizure came as a surprise, but it had roots that ran far back in Iranian history. During World War II Great Britain, Russia, and later the United States occupied Iran and forced its pro-German shah into exile, replacing him with his 22-year-old son, Muhammad Reza Pahlavi. Quarreling between Russia and the western allies over influence in Iran was one of the first of the many Cold War clashes; it resulted in Russian withdrawal in 1946. In the early 1950s when liberal and nationalist elements in Iran led by premier Muhammad Mossadegh sought to reduce the power of the Anglo-Iranian Oil Company, American mediators engineered a compromise that increased the price Iran received for its petroleum.

Mossadegh was a liberal by Iranian standards but by western standards somewhat eccentric. He carried out much public business from his bed, went about in pink pajamas, broke into tears at the slightest provocation. In 1953 a CIA coup (Operation Ajax), presumably designed to prevent the nationalization of Iranian petroleum resources and the abolition of the monarchy, resulted in his overthrow. (When the plan for Operation Ajax was shown to Secretary of State Dulles, he said with relish: "So this is how we get rid of that madman Mossadegh!")

As historian James A. Bill explains, the fall of Mossadegh "bought twenty-five more years for the Pahlavi dynasty and enabled the international oil industry to export at favorable terms 24 billion barrels of oil during this period." It turned most Iranians against the United States and shah Reza Pahlavi, however, and that led to the shah's purchase of enormous amounts of American arms. "He'll buy anything that flies," one American official explained.

In 1972 President Nixon gave the shah permission to buy any nonnuclear weapon in the American arsenal and the shah, whose oil-based wealth was almost unlimited, proceeded to load up on sophisticated F-14 and F-15 fighters and other arms. Over the years he spent billions and Iran became the most powerful military force in the region. While running for president Jimmy Carter had criticized Nixon's arms sales to Iran, but in office, in typical fashion, he reversed himself, even selling the shah F-16 fighters and several expensive AWACs, observation planes equipped with ultra-sophisticated radar.

Although Iran was an enthusiastic member of the OPEC cartel, the shah was for obvious reasons a firm friend of the United States. Iran seemed, as President Carter said in 1977, "an island of stability" in the troubled Middle East. The appearance of stability was deceptive because of the shah's unpopularity. He suppressed liberal opponents brutally. At the same time, his attempts to introduce western ideas and technology in Iran caused economic disruption and angered conservatives. Muslim religious leaders were particularly offended by such "radical" policies as the shah's tentative efforts to improve the position of women in Iranian society. Because his American-supplied army and his American-trained secret police kept the shah in power, his opponents hated the United States almost as much as they hated their autocratic ruler.

Throughout 1977 riots and demonstrations convulsed Iran. When soldiers fired on protesters, the bloodshed caused more unrest; that unrest caused more bloodshed. Over 10,000 civilians were killed, many times that number wounded. In 1978 the whole country seemed to rise against the shah. Finally, in January 1979, he was forced to flee. A revolutionary government headed by a revered religious leader, the Ayatollah Ruhollah Khomeini, who had recently returned to Iran in triumph after a long exile in France, assumed power.

Khomeini denounced the United States, the "Great Satan" whose support of the shah, he said, had caused the Iranian people untold suffering. When President Carter allowed the shah, who had been living in Mexico, to come to the United States for medical treatment, the Iranian revolutionaries were convinced that an attempt would be made to restore him to his throne. The seizure of the Teheran embassy resulted.

The Iranian Crisis: Carter's Dilemma

The militants announced that the captive Americans would be held as hostages until the United States returned the shah to Iran for trial as a traitor. They also demanded that the shah's vast wealth be confiscated and surrendered to the Iranian government. Of course President Carter rejected these demands. (He had no choice in the matter; deporting the shah, who had entered the United States legally, and confiscating his property were not possible under American law.) Instead he froze Iranian assets in the United States and banned trade with Iran until the hostages were freed.

Carter wanted to rescue the hostages, but there seemed to be no way to do so. Even going to war would surely result in their execution—and the deaths of others as well. He gave some consideration to blockading Iranian ports in order to force their release, but that could have no immediate effect and it might alarm the Arab states and lead to another cutoff of Middle Eastern oil. And there was always the danger of Soviet intervention.

The American public and most foreign observers approved of the president's restraint. If he made any mistake, it was a consequence of his habit of focusing on one matter at a time. This exaggerated the importance of the hostage issue. Some critics believed that Carter was playing into the hands of the Iranians by calling attention to the fact that they could hold the mighty United States at bay.

A stalemate developed. The Iranians released the women and black captives, but the others, more than 50 in number, were subjected to countless indignities and in some cases were physically abused.

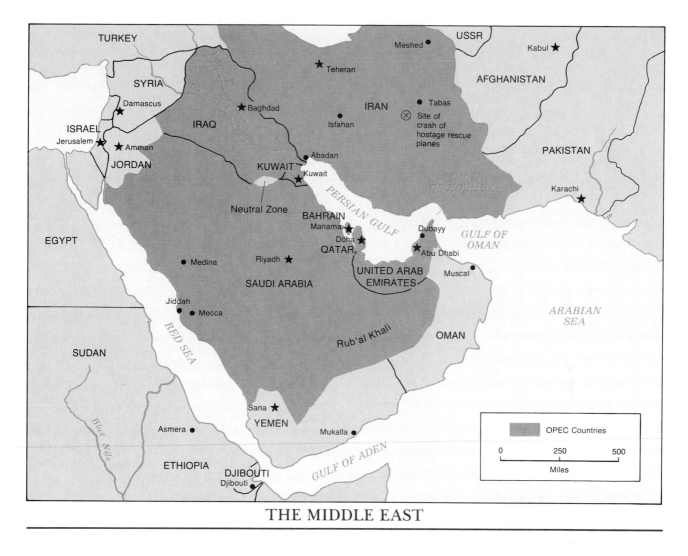

THE MIDDLE EAST

Months passed. Even after the shah, who was terminally ill with cancer, left the United States for Panama, the Iranians remained adamant.

The crisis produced a remarkable emotional response in the United States. For the first time since the Vietnam War the entire country agreed on something. One result of this was a revival of Carter's political fortunes. Before the attack on the Teheran embassy, Senator Edward M. Kennedy of Massachusetts, youngest brother of John F. Kennedy, had decided to run against Carter in the Democratic presidential primaries. He seemed a likely winner until the seizure of the hostages, but that event caused the public to rally around the president. Carter took clever political advantage of the

national concern. He refused to campaign in the primaries, insisting (without good reason) that the crisis made his constant presence in Washington essential.

Nevertheless the hostages languished in Iran. An intense debate raged within the administration about whether or not to attempt to rescue them, Brzezinski urging Carter "to lance the boil," Secretary Vance advising patience. In April 1980 Carter finally ordered a team of marine commandos flown into Iran in Sea Stallion helicopters in a desperate attempt to free them. The raid was a fiasco. Several helicopters broke down. While the others were gathered at a desert rendezvous south of Teheran, Carter called off the attempt. In the confusion of a night departure there was a crash and eight commandos were killed. The Iranians made political capital of the incident, gleefully displaying on television the wrecked aircraft and captured American equipment.

Unlike Carter's earlier actions, the raid was widely criticized. (Even before it began Secretary of State Cyrus Vance had quietly resigned on the ground that it was almost sure to result in many casualties and that if it succeeded the Iranians would only seize other Americans in the country.) And so the stalemate continued. In July 1980 the shah, who had moved from Panama to Egypt, died. It made no difference to the Iranians.

The Election of 1980

Despite the failure of the raid, Carter beat Kennedy decisively in the most important primaries without stirring from the White House. He had more than enough delegates at the Democratic convention to win nomination on the first ballot. His Republican opponent in the campaign that followed was Ronald Reagan, the former governor of California who had almost defeated Gerald Ford for the nomination in 1976. At 69, Reagan was the oldest person ever nominated for president by a major party. However, his age was not a serious handicap in the campaign; he was physically trim and vigorous and seemed no older than most other prominent politicians.

Reagan had grown up a New Deal Democrat, but during and immediately after World War II he became disillusioned with liberalism. He denounced government inefficiency and high taxation. As president of the Screen Actors' Guild he attacked the influence of communists in the movie industry. After his movie career ended (he always insisted that he had not been typed as "the nice guy who didn't get the girl"), Reagan did publicity for General Electric until 1960, then worked for various conservative causes. He campaigned for Barry Goldwater during the 1964 presidential contest. Two years later he was elected governor of California.

Reagan was a controversial governor, in part because, despite his professed conservatism and his emphasis on economy, government spending in California increased dramatically during his term. Despite or perhaps because of this shift, he was easily reelected in 1970.

The 1980 presidential campaign ranks among the most curious in American history. One of Reagan's opponents at the Republican convention, Congressman John Anderson of Illinois, refused to accept defeat and ran for president as an independent. He did so, he announced, because he thought both Carter and Reagan had little genuine popular support.

Indeed, many citizens appeared unable to decide whom to vote for. Of those who expressed a preference, many did so without enthusiasm. Anderson's problem was that he too inspired relatively little enthusiasm among voters. "None of the above" seemed the true desire of many citizens as they contemplated the list of candidates.

Both Carter and Reagan spent much time explaining why the other was unsuited to be president. Carter defended his record, though without much conviction. Reagan denounced criminals, drug addicts, and all varieties of immorality, and spoke in support of patriotism, religion, family life, and other "old-fashioned" virtues, which won him the enthusiastic backing of fundamentalist religious sects and other conservative groups. He also promised to transfer some functions of the federal government to the states, reduce spending and cut taxes, insisting at the same time that the budget could be balanced and inflation sharply reduced.

Reagan's tendency to depend on popular magazine articles, half-remembered conversations, and other informal sources for his economic "facts" reflected a mental imprecision that alarmed his critics, but his sunny disposition and his "laid-back" style compared favorably with Carter's personality. The president seemed tight-lipped and tense even when flashing his habitual toothy smile. A television debate between Carter and Reagan pointed up their personal differences, but Reagan's question to the audience, "Are you better off now than you were four years ago?" had more effect on the election than any policy he said he would pursue.

Because so many people said they were undecided, the contest seemed close—"too close to call," most experts said on election eve. It did not turn out that way. The voting was light, but those who cast ballots gave Reagan over 43 million votes to Carter's 35 million and Anderson's 5.6 million. Dissatisfaction with the Carter administration seems to have determined the result. The Republicans also gained control of the Senate and cut deeply into the Democratic majority in the House of Representatives.

Carter devoted his last weeks in office to the continuing hostage crisis. War had broken out between Iran and Iraq in September. The additional strain on an Iranian economy already shattered by revolution raised hopes that Ayatollah Khomeini would release the captive Americans. Iran needed both the assets Carter had frozen and spare parts for its American-made planes and tanks. With Algeria acting as intermediary, American and Iranian diplomats worked out an agreement. Reagan avoided involvement in the negotiations, but to put pressure on the Iranians he announced that he opposed paying "ransom" for "people who have been kidnapped by barbarians." Perhaps fearing that the new president might take some drastic action, Iran at last agreed to release the hostages in return for its assets in the United States. After 444 days in captivity, the 52 hostages were set free on January 20, the day Reagan was inaugurated.

Ronald Reagan rode to the White House in part on promises of reining in the federal government. "It's not my intention to do away with government," Reagan declared in his 1981 inaugural address. "It's rather to make it work—work with us, not over us; to stand by our side, not ride on our back."

Reagan as President

Despite his amiable, unaggressive style, Reagan acted rapidly and with determination once in office. He hoped to change the direction in which the country was moving by turning many functions of the federal government over to the states and relying more on individual initiative; the marketplace, not bureaucratic regulations, should govern most economic decisions. At the same time, Reagan called for greatly increased military expenditures. He believed that the Soviet Union had taken advantage of the relaxation of international tensions associated with détente to gain military superiority over the United States.

Cutting taxes was his first priority. He asked Congress to lower income taxes by 30 percent over three years and he demanded steep reductions in federal spending, focused chiefly on social services such as student loans and welfare payments and food stamps that went to poor people. He promised that despite these cuts he would maintain a "safety net" under the poor to protect them from real deprivation, and he insisted that in the long run they and everyone else would benefit from his program.

Reagan's tax policy was based on what was known as "supply-side economics." He claimed that

since the tax cut would leave people with more money, they would invest in productive ways rather than spend the excess on consumer goods, and that the new investment would result in increased production, more jobs, prosperity, and therefore more income for the government despite the lower tax rates. There was a superficial similarity between this argument and the reasoning behind the successful tax cut proposed by President Kennedy in 1963 and engineered by President Johnson in 1964. However, the danger of inflation was much greater in 1981. Many congressmen hesitated, but the mandate of Reagan's big election victory was hard to resist.

In August 1981 Reagan displayed his determination in convincing fashion when the nation's air traffic controllers went on strike despite the fact that they were forbidden by law to do so. Reagan ordered them to return to work. Most of the controllers, feeling that their demands were just and that the airlines could not operate without them, refused to obey this order. Reagan therefore discharged all 11,400 of them and began a crash program to train replacements. Even after the strike collapsed, the president refused to rehire the strikers. The air traffic controllers' union was destroyed.

An event unrelated to economic policy added greatly to the president's popularity. On March 30, while leaving a Washington hotel, he was shot in the chest by one John W. Hinckley, Jr.* Although he was seriously wounded, Reagan reacted coolly and with his usual self-deprecating style. When he was wheeled into the operating room for emergency surgery, he told the team of doctors before going under the anesthetic that he hoped they were all Republicans. Later he complained of his bad luck— he had been wearing a brand new suit and now it was ruined. It was hard to oppose such bravery and good humor. That he made a swift and total recovery despite his age further increased the admiration of the country.

Helped by the votes of conservative Democrats, Reagan won congressional approval of a Budget Reconciliation Act that reduced government expenditures on domestic programs by $39 billion. But Congress resisted reducing the politically popular "entitlement" programs, such as Social Security and Medicare, which accounted for about half of the budget. Congress also enacted most of the tax cuts the president had asked for, lowering individual income taxes by 25 percent over three years. Since the percentage was the same for everyone, high-income taxpayers received a disproportionately large share of the savings. Business taxes were liberalized, and capital gains, gift, and inheritance levies were reduced. To further encourage investment, the law authorized anyone with earned income to invest up to $2,000 per year in an individual retirement account (IRA). This money, and the interest or dividends it earned, would not be taxed until the individual retired.

Reagan also eliminated many government regulations affecting businesses. Long and complicated antitrust suits against International Business Machines and American Telephone and Telegraph, two of the largest corporations in the country, were dropped.

"Reaganomics," as administration policy was called, was certainly not a new theory. Carter had also advocated tax cuts, reduced federal spending, and the tight money policy adopted by Chairman

---

* Two security officers and Reagan's press secretary were also wounded by Hinckley.

Paul Volcker of the Federal Reserve Board. During his term the airlines were freed from control by the Civil Aeronautics Board. But Reagan's supply-side economics was old-fashioned to the point of being antique. It differed little from the policy conservative economists had favored in the Great Depression, which critics had derided as the "trickle-down" theory. As the economist James Tobin said in 1981, "old doctrines and policies, new forty years ago," were to be replaced by "new doctrines and policies, old forty years ago."

Tobin and most other economists did not think that Reaganomics would work. By December 1982 the economy was in a full-scale recession. More than 10 percent of the work force was unemployed. The combination of lower tax rates, soaring military expenditures without a corresponding reduction in domestic spending, and a slumping economy was further unbalancing the budget. In 1983 the federal deficit topped $195 billion, up from $59 billion only three years earlier, and it continued to expand thereafter. Month after month the Treasury was forced to borrow billions and its needs kept interest rates high.

Only the fact that inflation was slowing brightened the gloomy picture. Several causes contributed to this much-desired result. High unemployment and the economic slowdown gradually reduced consumer demand for goods and services. People began to worry about the future, and that weakened the inflationary psychology that had led them to spend in anticipation of further price increases. Most significant were the declining prices of gasoline and other petroleum products. Conservation and increased production by non-OPEC countries such as Mexico, Norway, and Great Britain gradually turned chronic shortages into an oil glut. The oil "shocks" of 1973 and 1979 had caused other prices to soar; the glut caused them to fall, though much less abruptly. All in all, the rate of inflation fell from more than 12 percent to less than 4 percent by 1984. When inflation moderated, the Federal Reserve Board relaxed its tight money policy. Interest rates then declined somewhat, making it easier to finance the purchase of homes and automobiles. The new lower tax rates left people with more spendable income for all kinds of purchases. Business began to pick up. Unemployment, while still high, fell below 8 percent in 1984.

But the recovery did not lead to much new business investment. People seemed to be spending their additional income on consumer goods. Together with the federal deficits caused by the large increase in military expenditures, this spending also prevented interest rates from going down as far as economists had hoped they would when inflation slackened.

Many of Reagan's advisers urged him to reduce the military budget and seek some kind of tax increase in order to bring the government's income more in line with its outlays. However, the president insisted that the military buildup was necessary because of the threat to world peace posed by the Soviet Union. He called Russia an "evil empire" and pursued a hard-line anticommunist foreign policy nearly everywhere. With the reluctant support of the governments of the western democracies, where many citizens feared Soviet retaliation against their countries, he installed new nuclear cruise missiles in Europe. Claiming that in Central America the communists were supplying arms to the left-wing Sandinista government of Nicaragua and encouraging communist rebels in El Salvador, he sought to undermine the Nicaraguan regime and bolster the conservative government of El Salvador. He also used American troops to overthrow a Cuban-backed regime on the tiny Caribbean island of Grenada.

In 1982 the continuing turmoil in the Middle East plunged the Reagan administration into a new crisis. Israel had invaded Lebanon to destroy PLO units that were staging raids on northern Israeli settlements from bases there. Israeli troops easily overran much of the country, but in the process the Lebanese government disintegrated and fighting broke out among Lebanese Christians and various Muslim sects. In an effort to end the bloodshed, Reagan agreed to send American troops to serve as part of an international peacekeeping force. Essentially their role was to act as a buffer between the occupying Israelis and the contending Lebanese units in and around Beirut. Before long, however, Israel pulled its troops back to southern Lebanon. Then the peacekeeping units came under fire from the different Lebanese factions. Soon the Americans were reduced to maintaining control of the Beirut airport, where they were under almost constant shelling.

At this point it would probably have been wise to withdraw, but Reagan believed that American prestige was at stake. Tragedy resulted in October 1983 when a fanatical Muslim crashed a truck loaded with explosives into a building at the airport housing American marines. The building collapsed, killing 239 marines. Early the next year, prestige or no, Reagan removed the entire American peacekeeping force from Lebanon.

Four More Years

Being a sitting president with an extraordinarily high standing in public opinion polls, Reagan was nominated for a second term at the 1984 Republican convention without opposition. The leading Democratic candidate was Walter Mondale of Minnesota, who had been vice-president under Carter. He was opposed in the primaries by half a dozen others, but only Senator Gary Hart of Colorado and the Reverend Jesse Jackson, a black civil rights activist, developed much support in the primaries. Hart aimed his campaign chiefly at younger voters; he claimed to offer "new ideas," and he accused Mondale of catering to "special-interest groups" such as organized labor. Jackson had little chance of winning, but being an excellent speaker as well as the first black to make a serious run for the presidential nomination of a major party, he roused the enthusiasm of millions of blacks. Tens of thousands of them responded to his appeal that they register and vote in the coming election.

The contest was fairly close between Mondale and Hart, but by the time of the Democratic convention, Mondale had a majority of the delegates. He was nominated on the first ballot. He then electrified the country by choosing Representative Geraldine Ferraro of New York as his running mate. Being an Italian-American and a Catholic, Ferraro was expected to appeal to conservative Democrats who had supported Reagan in 1980, but Mondale undoubtedly chose her chiefly because she was a woman—Democrats expected that she would win the votes of many Republican women and that her selection would counter the claims that Mondale was unimaginative and overly cautious.

Reagan began the campaign with several important advantages. He was especially popular among religious fundamentalists and other social conservatives and these groups were increasingly vocal. President Nixon had spoken of them as a "silent majority." By 1980 the kind of people he was

Walter Mondale and Geraldine Ferraro held a press conference in Minnesota shortly after the Democratic nominating convention in July of 1984.

referring to were no longer silent. Fundamentalist TV preachers were almost all fervent Reaganites and the most successful of them were collecting tens of millions of dollars annually in contributions from viewers. One of these, the Reverend Jerry Falwell, founded Moral Majority in 1979 and set out to create a new political movement. "Americans are sick and tired of the way the amoral liberals are trying to corrupt our nation," Falwell announced in 1979.

During the first Reagan administration Moral Majority had become a powerful political force. Falwell was against drugs, the "coddling" of criminals, homosexuality, communism, and abortion, all things that Reagan also disliked. While not openly antiblack, he disapproved of forced busing and a number of other government policies designed to help blacks and other minorities. Of course, Walter Mondale was also against many of the things that Falwell and his followers denounced, but Reagan was against them all. In addition, Reagan was in favor of government aid to private schools run by church groups, something dear to the hearts of Moral Majority types despite the constitutional principle of separation of church and state.

But Moral Majority, despite its name, was far from being an actual majority. Reagan's support was much more broadly based. Thousands of working people and an enormous percentage of white southerners, types that had been solidly Democratic during the New Deal and beyond, now voted Republican. Many younger northern Democrats who had voted in the primaries for Hart voted for Reagan in the general election. The president's personality was another important plus—voters continued to admire his informal yet firm style, and his stress on patriotism and other "old-fashioned" virtues. He was a confirmed optimist, telling the voters over and over that things were getting better and that four more years of Republican leadership would make them better still.

The tendency of voters to support a sitting president when the economy was on the rise was still another advantage. Inflation eased, unemployment fell to a bit over 7 percent, investment finally picked up, and inflation remained low. Interest rates were moving down slowly but steadily.

From the start Mondale emphasized the difficulties that he saw ahead for the nation. The president's economic policies, he said, hurt the poor, women, and minorities. Mondale also tried to focus attention on the huge increase in the federal deficit that Reagan's policies had produced, and he accused the president of misleading the public by saying that he would not raise taxes if reelected.

These were conventional campaign tactics. But Mondale, in a daring move, announced in his acceptance speech at the Democratic convention that he would raise taxes if elected. This promise, most unusual for a person running for office, was another attempt to counter his reputation for political caution.

Most polls showed Reagan far in the lead when the campaign began, and this remained true throughout the contest. Optimism and opportunity were his catchwords. Mondale, he said, "sees America wringing her hands. We see America using her hands. He sees America divided by envy. . . . We see an America inspired and uniting for opportunity."

This tactic proved effective. Nothing Mondale or Ferraro did or said affected the president's popularity. Bad news, even his own mistakes, had so little effect on his standing that people began to call him "the Teflon president." On election day he got nearly 60 percent of the popular vote and lost only in Minnesota, Mondale's home state, and in the District of Columbia. His electoral college margin was overwhelming, 523 to 13.

Of all the elements in the New Deal coalition, only the blacks, who voted solidly for Mondale, remained loyal, and their unity may have had something to do with the shift of so many white Democrats to Reagan. The Democratic strategy of nominating a woman for vice-president was a fail-

ure; far more women voted for Reagan than for the Mondale-Ferraro ticket. Reagan's triumph, like the two landslide victories of Dwight Eisenhower in the 1950s, was a personal one. The Republicans made only minor gains in the House of Representatives and actually lost two seats in the Senate.

"The Reagan Revolution"

Reagan's agenda for his second term closely resembled that of his first. In foreign affairs, he ran into continuing congressional resistance to his requests for military support for his anticommunist crusade. His anti-Soviet policies, and particularly his belligerent rhetoric, attracted no better than lukewarm support among all but the most fervent American anticommunists. This was particularly true after Mikhail S. Gorbachev became the Russian premier in March 1985. Gorbachev seemed far more moderate and flexible than his predecessors. (He was certainly more concerned about public opinion in the western democracies, which he cultivated assiduously.) He began to encourage political debate and criticism in the Soviet Union—the policy known as *glasnost*—and sought to stimulate the stagnant Russian economy by decentralizing administration and rewarding individual enterprise (*perestroika*).

Gorbachev also announced that he would continue to honor the unratified SALT II agreement,

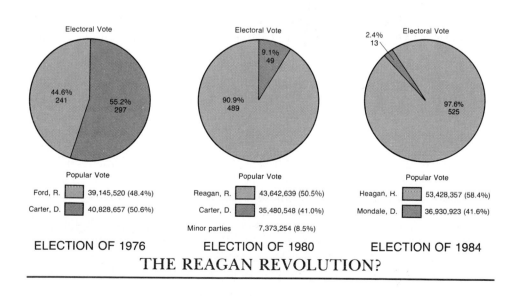

ELECTION OF 1976

	Electoral Vote
44.6% 241	55.2% 297

Popular Vote

| Ford, R. | 39,145,520 (48.4%) |
| Carter, D. | 40,828,657 (50.6%) |

ELECTION OF 1980

Electoral Vote
9.1% 49
90.9% 489

Popular Vote

Reagan, R.	43,642,639 (50.5%)
Carter, D.	35,480,548 (41.0%)
Minor parties	7,373,254 (8.5%)

ELECTION OF 1984

Electoral Vote
2.4% 13
97.6% 525

Popular Vote

| Reagan, R. | 53,428,357 (58.4%) |
| Mondale, D. | 36,930,923 (41.6%) |

THE REAGAN REVOLUTION?

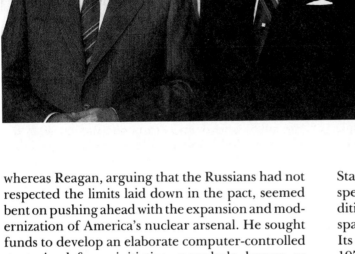

The arms cuts made at the 1988 Moscow summit showed how Ronald Reagan's ideas about the "evil empire" had changed. Yet Reagan was surprised to find that Mikhail Gorbachev believed "the communist propaganda he's grown up hearing about our country"— above all, that business dominates the government.

whereas Reagan, arguing that the Russians had not respected the limits laid down in the pact, seemed bent on pushing ahead with the expansion and modernization of America's nuclear arsenal. He sought funds to develop an elaborate computer-controlled strategic defense initiative, popularly known as "Star Wars," that would supposedly be capable of destroying enemy missiles in outer space where they could do no damage. Despite his insistence that Star Wars would be a defensive system, the Russians objected to it vociferously.

When he realized that the Russians were eager to come to some agreement limiting nuclear weapons, the president gradually abandoned his talk about Russia being an "evil empire." In October 1986 he met with Mikhail Gorbachev in Iceland in search of an agreement on arms control. This "summit" got nowhere, partly because Reagan was determined to push Star Wars and partly because he apparently did not understand the implications of nuclear disarmament for western Europe. The Europeans, fearing Soviet superiority in conventional weapons, were horrified by the thought of *total* nuclear disarmament. The Iceland setback, however, proved to be temporary and in 1988 at a second summit, Reagan and Gorbachev signed a treaty eliminating medium-range nuclear missiles.

Reagan nevertheless persisted in pressing for the

Star Wars defense-in-space system. After NASA's spectacular Apollo program, which sent six expeditions to the moon between 1969 and 1972, the space agency's prestige was beyond measurement. Its Skylab orbiting space station program (1973–1974) was equally successful. Next, shortly after the beginning of Reagan's first term, the manned space shuttle Columbia, launched by rocket power, was able, after orbiting for several days, to return to earth intact, gliding on its stubby, swept-back wings to an appointed landing strip. Columbia and other shuttles were soon transporting satellites into space for the government and private companies, and its astronauts were conducting military and scientific experiments of great importance.

Congress, however, boggled at the enormous estimated cost of Star Wars, which some feared would mount into the trillions of dollars. Costs aside, the idea of relying for national defense on the complex technology involved in controlling machines in outer space suffered a further setback in 1986, when the space shuttle Challenger exploded shortly after takeoff, killing its seven-member crew. This disaster put a stop to the program until the cause had been discovered and complex engineering changes made. Finally, in 1989 the shuttles began to fly again.

The president was more successful in winning

public support for his get-tough-with-terrorists policy. In October 1985, four Arabs seized control of the Italian cruise ship *Achille Lauro* in the eastern Mediterranean. After killing an elderly Jewish-American tourist and tossing his body into the sea, they surrendered to Egyptian authorities on condition that they be provided with safe passage to Libya on an Egyptian airliner.

The terrorist chose Libya because the president of that nation, Muammar al-Qaddafi, was a bitter enemy of Israel and the United States and an open supporter of terrorist activities. To stop them, Reagan ordered Navy F-14 jets to intercept the airliner. The jets forced the Egyptian pilot to land in Italy instead of Libya and the terrorists were taken into custody.

Then, after a Libyan-planned bombing of a West German club frequented by American servicemen, Reagan launched an air strike against Libyan bases from airfields in Great Britain. This attack alarmed Europeans, but in America the public responded enthusiastically. The president's popularity reached an all-time high.

Reagan's basic domestic objectives—to reduce the scope of federal activity, particularly in the social welfare area, to lower income taxes, and to increase the strength of the armed forces—did not change in his second term. Despite the tax cuts already made, congressional leaders of both parties agreed to the Income Tax Act of 1986, which reduced the top levy on personal incomes from 50 percent to 28 percent and the tax on corporate profits from 46 percent to 34 percent. "When I think of coming here with the tax rate at 70 percent and ending my first term under 30 percent, it's amazing," one delighted Republican senator told reporters.

Liberal members of Congress, remembering how the voters had reacted to Mondale's talk about *increasing* taxes, had found it politically difficult to oppose the measure. But the existing tax system was extremely complicated and full of "loopholes" benefiting particular interest. The new law did away with most of the tax shelters and special credits that corporations and well-to-do individuals had used to reduce their tax bills. The law also relieved six million low-income people from paying any federal income tax at all.

The objective of the law was a system that required people with similar incomes to pay roughly equal taxes. But it also undermined the principle of progressive taxation, the practice, dating back to the first income tax enacted after the adoption of the Sixteenth Amendment in 1913, of requiring high-income people to pay a larger *percentage* of their income than those with smaller incomes. The new law set only two rates: 15 percent on taxable incomes below $29,750 for families, and 28 percent on incomes above this limit. A family with a taxable income of $30,000 would pay at the same rate as one with $300 million, should any such exist.

In this and other ways, the government, in the words of economist Peter Passell, "ceased acting as a buffer against the vicissitudes of capitalism." Whatever the overall effect on the nation's economy (which continued to expand throughout Reagan's presidency) the new tax system did not prevent the gap between rich and poor from widening. At the end of his second term the standard of living of the

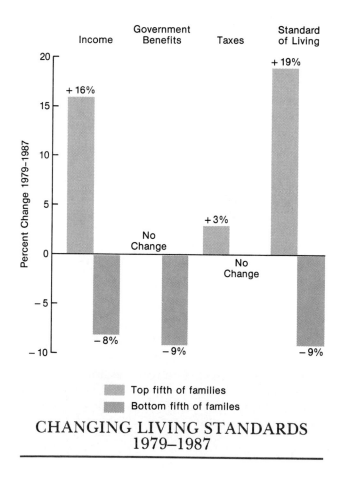

CHANGING LIVING STANDARDS
1979–1987

poorest fifth of the population (40 million people) was 9 percent lower than it had been in 1979, while that of the wealthiest fifth had risen about 20 percent.

Reagan advanced another of his objectives more gradually, but with effects likely to be long-lasting. This was his appointment of conservatives to federal judgeships. During his first year in office he appointed Sandra Day O'Connor to the Supreme Court. Justice O'Connor was the first woman ever appointed to the Court, but she was also conservative on most constitutional questions. When Chief Justice Warren C. Burger resigned in 1986 Reagan replaced him with Associate Justice William H. Rehnquist, probably the most conservative member of the Supreme Court, and he filled the vacancy with Antonin Scalia, an even more conservative judge. After the resignation of Associate Justice Lewis F. Powell in 1987, the President nominated Robert Bork, the man who, while Nixon's Solicitor General, had discharged the Watergate special prosecutor, Archibald Cox. Bork was both conservative and rigidly doctrinaire. After protracted hearings, the Senate refused to confirm him and eventually the appointment went to a less controversial but by no means liberal judge, David Kennedy. By 1988 Reagan had appointed well over half of the members sitting on the federal bench.

Change and Uncertainty

If the "Reagan Revolution" seemed to have triumphed, powerful forces were at work that no individual or party could effectively control. For one thing, the makeup of the American people, always in a state of flux, was changing at a rate approaching that of the early 1900s when the "new" immigration was at its peak. In the 1970s, after the Immigration Act of 1965 had put an end to the national origins concept, more than 4 million immigrants entered the country; the vast majority of these newcomers came from Asia and Latin America. This trend continued; of the 601,000 who arrived in 1986, nearly 500,000 were from these regions. In addition, uncounted thousands entered the country illegally, most crossing the long, sparsely settled border with Mexico.

Some of the immigrants were refugees fleeing from repressive regimes in Vietnam, Cuba, Haiti, and Central America, and nearly all were poor. Most were hardworking and law-abiding, but some became public charges and others lawbreakers. Most tended, like their predecessors, to crowd together in ethnic neighborhoods. Spanish could be heard more often than English in sections of Los Angeles, New York, Miami, and many other cities.

No strong demand for immigration restrictions

The most recent wave of immigrants has changed the face of America's cities just as earlier ethnic groups did. Street scenes from Union City, New Jersey, and Berkeley, California, reveal strong Hispanic—in this case Cuban—and Vietnamese influences (facing page).

developed, perhaps because so many Americans were themselves the children of immigrants. However, conservatives found it appalling that so many people could enter the country illegally and even Americans sympathetic to the "undocumented aliens" agreed that control was desirable. Finally, in 1986, Congress passed a law offering amnesty to illegal immigrants with long residency in the country and penalizing employers who hired illegal immigrants in the future. Many persons legalized their status under the new law, but the influx of illegal immigrants continued. Problems developed because some employers refused to hire anyone with a foreign accent on the ground that they might be "illegals" bearing false papers.

There were other trends that deeply disturbed thousands of Americans. The postwar population explosion and the subsequent decline in the birth rate made pressure on the social security system inevitable when the "baby boomers" reached retirement age in the early 21st century. More immediately, the traditional family consisting of a husband and wife and their children, the man a "breadwinner," the woman a "housewife and mother," seemed in danger of ceasing to be the norm. An ever-larger number of families were headed by single parents, in most cases by women. A disproportionate number of these families were black, and many were poor. Between 1979 and 1987, the number of single-parent families living below the poverty line increased by 46 percent.

Year after year more than 1.1 million marriages ended in divorce. The tendency of couples to live together without getting married continued, helping to explain why the number of illegitimate births rose steadily. So did the number of abortions—from 763,000 in 1974 after abortion was legalized to an average of 1.3 million a year in the 1980s.

The Reagan administration devoted much effort to reducing the amount of crime in the country, but despite the fact that the number of persons confined in prisons reached an all-time high, little progress was made. A campaign against illegal drugs resulted in many arrests, but the drugs remained widely available. Cocaine became available in a cheap, smokable, and especially addictive form called "crack," causing a problem of epidemic proportions.

The drug problem was part of a larger and still more threatening one, the spread of a deadly new disease, acquired immune deficiency syndrome (AIDS). AIDS was caused by a virus that destroyed the body's immune system, exposing the victim to a host of deadly diseases. It was uniformly fatal. Since it was transmitted by the exchange of bodily fluids, intravenous drug users (who frequently shared needles) and homosexuals were its chief victims. But since it was a venereal disease, the possibility of its spreading through the general population was a constant danger.

Other massive social and economic changes that were difficult to control were also occurring. One was the continuing shift of employment opportunities from the production of goods to the production of services—from raising wheat and manufacturing steel to advertising, banking, and recordkeeping. This meant a shift from blue- to white-collar work, which called for more better-educated workers than were currently available and increasing joblessness for the unskilled. Union membership had been falling since long before Reagan became president, but by 1985 it was down to about 19 percent of the work force, in large part because white-collar workers were difficult to organize. Furthermore, by producing goods in Asia and Latin America where labor costs were low, "multinational" manufacturing companies could avoid tariff barriers and often make larger profits than would be possible in the United States, but with harmful effects on American workers.

The Merger Movement

Another worrisome trend was the merger movement, which saw often unrelated companies swallowing up one another in unprecedented fashion. The movement began under President Carter, but Reagan's abandonment of strict enforcement of the antitrust laws encouraged the trend. The merger movement was also encouraged by the federal tax structure; corporations had to pay taxes on stock dividends, which were treated as distributed profits. But the interest paid on corporate bonds was a business expense and thus a tax deduction. In 1989 Time Inc. borrowed $13.9 billion to purchase Warner Communications, thus forming one of the world's largest publishing concerns. This combination would never have been permitted by earlier administrations and would have been financially unprofitable if Time were forced to raise the money by issuing new stock.

Piratical corporate "raiders" raised cash by issuing high-interest bonds secured by the assets of the company purchased. A shrewd broker, Michael Milkin of the firm of Drexel Burnham Lambert, emerged as the "king" of this "junk bond" business by convincing banks, corporations, and well-heeled investors that the extremely high interest paid by these bonds compensated for the risks involved.

The system made it possible for a small company or even a single entrepreneur to buy a giant corporation. In 1985 Ronald Perelman, an aggressive entrepreneur who had recently obtained control of Pantry Pride, a supermarket chain with a net worth of about $145 million, managed to take over the cosmetics and health-care firm of Revlon, the net worth of which exceeded $1 billion. One deal often led to another. In 1985 the R. J. Reynolds Tobacco Company purchased the food conglomerate Nabisco for $4.9 billion. Three years later this new giant, RJR Nabisco, was itself taken over by Kohlberg, Kravis, Roberts and Company for $24.9 billion.

Still another economic trend that defied national control was the fluctuating price of petroleum. The falling price of oil during Reagan's presidency eased inflationary pressures and helped speed recovery in the United States, but cheaper oil dealt a devastating blow to the economy of the Southwest, a region where support of Reagan's policies was particularly strong. Lower oil prices also forced oil-producing countries in and out of OPEC to cut back on their imports of manufactured goods. Mexico was particularly hard hit. The situation there was so serious that Mexico could not even pay the interest on its debts without obtaining further loans.

Many American banks suffered heavy losses when domestic and foreign oil-related loans went sour. But oil could also go up in price for reasons unrelated to events that any single nation could control, in which case it would have adverse effects on the economy.

A similar situation developed in the nation's agricultural heartland. In the 1970s, a time of rising agricultural prices, farmers borrowed heavily to expand output. With the price of land and farm products soaring, it seemed safe to do so. In 1985 about half the farmers in the country were in debt and interest payments on their debts came to $21 billion.

By that time inflation had slowed to a crawl because of the tight money policy, and world agricultural prices were falling. Between 1982 and 1986 the value of American wheat exports fell from $8 billion to between $3 and $4 billion. For many debt-ridden farmers, this meant bankruptcy. More generally, the popularity of the Reagan tax reductions and the president's refusal to consider any change in course on this subject meant that the federal government continued to run at a huge deficit; the shortfall rose from $179 billion in 1985 to more than $220 billion in 1986.

The Iran-contra Arms Deal

All these matters were partly beyond human control, or at least beyond what seemed practicable under the American political system. Overall, they diminished the effectiveness of the Reagan administration, but they did not seriously undermine it. That was the result of two self-inflicted wounds involving American policy in Central America and the Middle East.

The Central American problem resulted from a revolution in Nicaragua, where in 1979 leftist rebels had overthrown the dictatorial regime of Anastasio Somoza. Because the victorious "Sandinista" government turned out to be Marxist oriented (and supported by both Cuba and the Soviet Union) President Reagan was determined to force it from power. He backed anti-Sandinista elements in Nicaragua known as the "contras" (*contra* is Spanish for against) and in 1981 persuaded Congress to provide these "freedom fighters" with arms.

However, the contras made little progress and many Americans feared that aiding them would lead, as it had in Vietnam, to the use of American troops in the fighting. In October 1984, in the Boland Amendment, Congress banned further military aid to the rebels. The president then sought to persuade other countries and private American

Oliver North's poise and earnestness while testifying before a congressional committee investigating the Iran-contra affair prompted an outpouring of sympathy from the American people. Thousands sent telegrams and letters of support, and many included money to help "Ollie" cover the cost of his defense.

groups to help the contras (as he put it) to keep "body and soul together."

In the Middle East, a bloody war had been raging between Iran and Iraq since 1980. The chief interest of the United States in the conflict was to make sure that it did not cause the flow of Middle Eastern oil to the West to be cut off. But public opinion in the country was particularly hostile toward the Iranians. Memories of the hostage crisis of the Carter years did not fade, and Iran was widely believed to be responsible for the fact that a number of Americans were being held hostage by terrorists in Lebanon. Reagan was known to oppose any bargaining with terrorists. Nevertheless, he was eager to find some way to free the captive Americans. During 1985 he made the fateful decision to allow the indirect shipment of arms to Iran by way of Israel, his hope being that this would result in the hostages being released. When this did not happen, he went further, and in January 1986 he authorized the secret sale of American weapons directly to the Iranians.

The arms sale was arranged by Marine Colonel Oliver North, an aide of Reagan's national security adviser, Admiral John Poindexter. North was already in charge of the administration's effort to supply the Nicaraguan contras indirectly. With Poindexter's knowledge, he used $12 million of the profit from the Iranian sales to provide weapons for the contras, in plain violation of the congressional ban on such aid. North prepared a memorandum describing the transaction for Poindexter to show Reagan, but Poindexter testified under oath that he did not do so, in order, he claimed, to spare the president possible embarrassment.

News of the sales to Iran and of the use of the profits to supply the contras came to light in November 1986 and of course caused a sensation. Poindexter resigned, Colonel North was fired from his job with the security council, a special prosecutor, Lawrence E. Walsh, was appointed to investigate the affair, and both a presidential committee and a joint congressional committee began investigations. Reagan insisted that he knew nothing about the aid to the contras, but according to polls, a majority of the people did not believe him, and critics pointed out that if he was telling the truth it meant that he had not been able to control his own administration.

In May 1989 North was found guilty of destroying government documents in order to mislead Congress and obstruct its work; the following April Poindexter was convicted of five felonies, including conspiracy and lying to Congress, and was sentenced to six months in jail. Although he remained personally popular, President Reagan's influence with Congress and his reputation as a political leader plummeted. Critical comments by reporters ranged from "disengaged" and "gravely uninformed" to "out to lunch." Even earlier the Democratic elder statesman Clark Clifford described him as an "amiable dunce," and Martin Anderson, Reagan's chief economic adviser, admitted that the president "made decisions like an ancient king or a Turkish pasha, passively letting his subjects serve him."

The Election of 1988

The decline of Reagan's influence was also related to his status as a "lame duck" president entering the last year of his tenure. In both the major political parties, attention turned to the choice of presidential candidates.

After a shaky start, Reagan's vice-president, George Bush, ran away with the Republican primaries and won the nomination easily. The Democratic race was more complicated by far. So many candidates entered the field that the average citizen found it hard to tell them apart. Wits began to call the Democratic hopefuls "the seven dwarfs," referring to both their lack of distinguishing qualities and their lack of distinction.

Gradually, however, the field shrank and the race settled down to a contest between Governor Michael S. Dukakis of Massachusetts and the black leader Jesse Jackson. Jackson took consistently more liberal positions than any of the other candidates. He proposed to reduce military spending sharply and invest the savings in improving education, health care, and other social services. As in his earlier campaign, Jackson had the nearly unanimous support of blacks, but he also attracted a larger percentage of white Democrats than in 1984.

Dukakis stressed his record as an efficient manager—the Massachusetts economy was booming. Unlike the charismatic Jackson, who was an extraordinarily effective speaker, Dukakis was low-key, and an uninspired orator. But his campaign was well organized and well financed. Without overwhelming the opposition, he accumulated delegates steadily and by the end of the primary season he had a solid majority.

The chief remaining uncertainty involved the selection of Dukakis's running mate. Jackson professed to want the post, but Dukakis selected a con-

In the 1988 campaign, Michael Dukakis blasted the Republicans for favoring the rich, but avoided identifying himself as a liberal. "If anyone tells you that the American dream belongs only to the privileged few and not to all of us," Dukakis declared, "you tell them that the Reagan era is over."

servative senator, Lloyd Bentsen of Texas. When Jackson, swallowing his disappointment, gave the ticket his support in a rousing speech, the convention became a Democratic love feast.

The resulting campaign was another matter. In his capacity as vice-president, Bush had been accused by critics of being a "wimp"—a weak, bloodless kind of person who slavishly accepted every Reagan policy. As candidate for president, he set out to destroy this impression and he did so without rejecting the conservative Reagan philosophy. He attacked Dukakis savagely, charging him with coddling criminals because of a Massachusetts law granting furloughs to prisoners serving life sentences for murder. Dukakis had vetoed a Massachusetts bill compelling students to recite the pledge of allegiance because he believed it violated the constitutional guarantee of free speech. Brushing aside the constitutional issue, Bush denounced the veto repeatedly, claiming that it was a sign of Dukakis's poor judgment, if not of his lack of patriotism.

Dukakis conducted a curiously lifeless campaign. He stressed "competence," his supposed leadership qualities and his administrative abilities, but he avoided speaking out strongly for the liberal social policies that every Democratic presidential candidate since Franklin Roosevelt had supported. Consequently he found himself more often than not on the defensive against Bush's emotionally charged attacks.

On the other hand, Bush's choice of Senator Dan Quayle of Indiana as his running mate proved embarrassing to the Republicans. Although Quayle was an ardent supporter of military preparedness, it came out that he had avoided the Vietnam draft by enrolling in the Indiana National Guard, and the charge that he had used the influence of his wealthy family to get in the Guard was hard to refute. More seriously, he proved rather slow-witted in political debate, and it was difficult for Bush to explain why he had selected him.

As the campaign progressed, neither presidential candidate aroused much enthusiasm among voters, but polls indicated that Bush was gradually pulling away from his Democratic opponent. On election day he won handily, garnering 54 percent of the vote and carrying the Electoral College, 426 electoral votes to Dukakis's 112.

The End of the Cold War

Once in office, President Bush softened his tough tone, saying in his inaugural address that he hoped to "make kinder the face of the nation and gentler the face of the world." He also displayed a more traditional command of the workings of government and the details of current events than his predecessor, which was reassuring to persons put off by Reagan's lack of interest in the details of government. At the same time he pleased right-wing "Reagan loyalists" by his opposition to abortion and gun control, and by calling for a constitutional amendment prohibiting the burning of the American flag. His standing in the polls soared from high to astronomic.

One important reason for this was the flood of good news from abroad. The reforms instituted in the Soviet Union by Gorbachev led to demands for similar liberalization by the peoples of all of the Soviet Union's East European satellites, and Gorbachev responded by announcing that the Soviet Union would not use force to keep communist governments in power in these nations. Swiftly the peoples of Poland, Hungary, Czechoslovakia, Bulgaria, Romania, and East Germany did away with the repressive regimes that had ruled them throughout the postwar era and moved toward more democratic forms of government. Except in Romania, where the dictator Nicolae Ceausescu was seized, tried, and summarily executed by revolutionary leaders, all of these fundamental changes were carried out peacefully and in an orderly manner.

Almost overnight the international political climate changed. Soviet-style communism had been discredited. The Warsaw Pact was no longer a significant force in European international politics, and without it a Soviet attack anywhere on the continent was almost unthinkable. The cold war was over at last.

With pro-democratic forces in power in East Germany, demand for reunification with West Germany quickly emerged. The infamous Berlin Wall was torn down, talks were begun that seemed certain to lead to unification. This development alarmed the Russians, many Poles, and also all members of NATO, because an enlarged Germany would, on its own, approach superpower status. But given the new spirit of national self-determination, German unification seemed unavoidable.

The United States had nothing to do with the East European upheavals, but President Bush profited from them immensely. In truth, he handled the rapidly changing situation well, expressing moral support for new governments (and in the case of some, providing modest amounts of financial assistance), but refraining from trying to embarrass the Russians. His policy won the support of leaders in both the Republican and Democratic parties.

More controversial was the president's decision to send troops into Panama to overthrow General Manuel Noriega, who had refused to yield power even when his figurehead presidential candidate was defeated in a national election. Noriega was under indictment in the United States for drug trafficking, and after temporarily seeking refuge in the Vatican embassy in Panama, he surrendered to the American forces and was taken to the United States to stand trial.

At a summit meeting in Washington in June 1990 Bush and Gorbachev signed agreements reducing American and Russian stockpiles of long-range nuclear missiles by 30 percent and eliminating chemical weapons. They also announced plans for further cuts in weaponry, and President Bush agreed to the relaxation of barriers against trade with the Soviet Union, a measure designed to help the limping Russian economy.

Bush thus accomplished the objective of the invasion. However, Latin Americans were alarmed by

Most Americans supported George Bush's decision to invade Panama in order to overthrow and arrest General Manuel Noriega. Yet the Panama invasion left unanswered questions—about the total number of civilians killed, and about Noriega's long tenure as an employee of the CIA.

The opening, and then destruction, of the Berlin Wall drove home the astonishing changes taking place in Eastern Europe in 1989. When the euphoria passed, however, the United States faced new uncertainties about the status of a reunited Germany and the role of NATO—and America—in Europe.

the way the United States had used force in the region; the fact that far more Panamanian civilians than armed supporters of Noriega were killed and wounded in the affair also led to much criticism. The president's popularity, however, was not affected.

The president also benefited from the ending of the conflict between the Sandinistas and the contras in Nicaragua although, as in Eastern Europe, he did not contribute much to its solution. For the first time in that small nation's history, a free presidential election was held. The result was a victory for middle-of-the-road democratic forces. In April 1990 the new president, Violeta Chamorro, took office without incident.

Domestic Problems and Possibilities

Bush's approach to domestic issues was also politically effective, but it aroused a great deal of criticism even among Republicans. In general, he substituted words for action, urged voluntarism rather than new legislation in dealing with problems. During the presidential campaign he made a politically popular promise not to raise taxes if elected and in office he recommitted himself to that objective; in fact he proposed reducing the tax on capital gains, a measure that would increase revenues briefly but cost the government billions in the long run. No one enjoys paying taxes; the difficulty was that the national debt was huge and rapidly increasing. Dealing with it by reducing nonmilitary expenditures was extremely difficult, and what was known as the "peace dividend" expected to result from the relaxation of international tensions was slow in materializing.

Moreover, unforeseen needs for *more* expenditures were constantly arising. Nearly everyone favored extending aid to Poland and other Eastern European countries struggling to revive their stagnant economies. The invasion of Panama had been expensive and the cost of repairing the damage and helping the new government get on its feet was also substantial.

Larger still were the sums needed to bail out the invalid savings and loan industry. The combination of Reagan-inspired bank deregulation, inflation, and rising interest rates had led many savings and loan institutions to lend money recklessly. A large number invested huge sums in risky "junk" bonds that paid high interest rates and in questionable real estate ventures. In booming states such as Texas, Florida, and California such policies led to disaster when the economy cooled. In some cases the bankers had been little better than thieves, but their depositors were innocent victims and in any case their deposits were insured. The government (meaning the general public) had to make good, and the price was enormous. Shortly after his inauguration Bush estimated the cost at $30 billion. Within months estimates had risen to $130 billion and some economists predicted that, with interest charges, the cost might reach $500 billion.

Logic would suggest that if the tax burden had been roughly proportional to the needs of society when President Bush was elected, these unplanned but legitimate expenses justified and indeed required a tax increase. But Bush refused to be influenced by such logic and the Democrats were unwilling to press for new revenues unless he would agree. One indirect result of the no-new-taxes policy was to strain the resources of state governments, which had to assume burdens previously borne by Washington.

Another result was the tendency of the Bush administration to settle for half measures even when addressing matters the president considered important. Bush professed to be concerned about Jap-

anese domination of the electronics industry, yet he cut back support of research on high-definition television, semiconductors, and similar projects. He called himself the "education president" and he recognized the government's obligation to tackle the drug problem, to protect the environment, and to support efforts to discover a cure for AIDS. In all of these matters, however, critics (not all of them Democrats) believed the sums budgeted by the administration were too small.

The Imponderable Future

If historians can locate suitable records and other sources about a past event, they are able to explain, or at least make plausible guesses about, what it was and why it happened at that time, no matter how remote. Historians are also probably better than most other people at explaining how things got to be the way they are at any present moment. This is because events have causes and results, and these are things that historians are trained to study and understand. But historians are no better than anyone else at predicting the future. Results, quite obviously, come after the events that cause them; it takes time for them to unfold, which means that "at present," even the most hardworking and intelligent historians do not know anything important about what the future will bring.

Another way of putting this is to point out that in the modern world just about everything that happens is in some way related to everything else that is going on. There are far too many things happening (all producing results of some kind) for anyone to sort out which of them is going to have what effect on events that will happen tomorrow, let alone next year or in the 21st century. "Then" (whether tomorrow or next year or the 21st century) historians will be able to study those particular events that interest them and puzzle out their chief causes—but not "now."

Yet "now" is where we happen to be, and thus this book, so full of events and their causes and results, must end inconclusively. No one knows what will happen next. But of course not knowing what will happen next is one of the main reasons life is so interesting.

Milestones

1974 President Ford issues blanket pardon
to Richard Nixon
1975 End of the war in Vietnam
1978 Camp David Agreement between
Israel and Egypt
Paul A. Volcker named chairman of
Federal Reserve Board
1979 Sandinistas overthrow Somoza
government in Nicaragua
The Reverend Jerry Falwell founds
Moral Majority
American interest rates exceed 10
percent
United States recognizes People's
Republic of China
Shah forced to flee Iran; Ayatollah
Khomeini rules nation
Radical students seize U.S. Embassy in
Iran and hold occupants as hostages
1980 Commando raid designed to free
hostages in Iran aborted
1981 American hostages in Iran released
Reagan appoints Sandra Day
O'Connor to Supreme Court
Tax Reform Act lowers rates and
eliminates loopholes

1984 Boland Amendment bans military aid
to Nicaraguan contras
1985 Mikhail Gorbachev becomes premier
of Soviet Union
President Reagan proposes Strategic
Defense Initiative ("Star Wars")
plan
1986 American "retaliatory" air raid on
Libya
Reagan-Gorbachev summit meeting in
Iceland
Immigration Act grants amnesty to
long-term illegal aliens
Secret Iran-contra arms deal exposed
1987 Senate rejects nomination of Robert
Bork to Supreme Court
1988 American-Soviet treaty bans medium-
range missiles
1989 Gorbachev allows Eastern European
nations to establish independent
democratic governments
Oliver North convicted of destroying
documents and obstructing
Congress
1990 John Poindexter convicted of
conspiracy and lying to Congress

SUPPLEMENTARY READING

Authoritative works on recent history are hard to find. On Gerald Ford, see Clark Mollenhoff, **The Man Who Pardoned Nixon** (1976), Richard Reeves, **A Ford, Not a Lincoln** (1975), and Ford's autobiography, **A Time to Heal** (1979). Betty Ford's frank autobiography **The Times of My Life** (1978) is a cut above most such memoirs.

For the Carter years see Betty Glad, **Jimmy Carter in Search of the Great White House** (1980), which is critical of Carter's style and actions. Zbigniew Brzezinski, **Power and Principle** (1983), discusses the foreign policy of the administration, while James A. Bill, **The Eagle and the Lion** (1988), and Michael Ledeen and William Lewis, **Debacle** (1981), cover the Iranian hostage crisis.

Books dealing with Reagan and his administration include Hedrick Smith, **Reagan, the Man, the President** (1980), Robert Dallek, **Ronald Reagan: The Politics of Symbolism** (1984), and Rowland Evans and Robert No-

vak, **The Reagan Revolution** (1981). D. A. Stockman, **The Triumph of Politics** (1986), contains a frank discussion of administration fiscal policies. Of the memoirs by insiders, Martin Anderson, **Revolution** (1988), is favorable to Reagan and D. T. Regan, **For the Record** (1988), is critical. Peggy Noonan, **What I Saw at the Revolution** (1990), is both insightful and amusing. For the Reagan foreign policy, see J. J. Girkpatrick, **Dictatorships and Double Standards** (1982), and Strobe Talbott, **The Russians and Reagan** (1984). W. S. Cohen and G. J. Mitchell, **Men of Zeal** (1988), describes the congressional Iran-contra hearings.

Contrasting views of recent conservative trends are provided by Alan Crawford, **Thunder on the Right** (1980), and Richard Viguerie, **The New Right** (1981). See also John Kater, **Christians on the Right** (1982).

The Declaration of Independence

When in the Course of human events, it becomes necessary for one people to dissolve the political bands which have connected them with another, and to assume among the Powers of the earth, the separate and equal station to which the Laws of Nature and of Nature's God entitle them, a decent respect to the opinions of mankind requires that they should declare the causes which impel them to the separation.

We hold these truths to be self-evident, that all men are created equal, that they are endowed by their Creator with certain unalienable Rights, that among these are Life, Liberty and the pursuit of Happiness. That to secure these rights, Governments are instituted among Men, deriving their just powers from the consent of the governed, That whenever any Form of Government becomes destructive of these ends, it is the Right of the People to alter or to abolish it, and to institute new Government, laying its foundation on such principles and organizing its powers in such form, as to them shall seem most likely to effect their Safety and Happiness. Prudence, indeed, will dictate that Governments long established should not be changed for light and transient causes; and accordingly all experience hath shown, that mankind are more disposed to suffer, while evils are sufferable, than to right themselves by abolishing the forms to which they are accustomed. But when a long train of abuses and usurpations, pursuing invariably the same Object evinces a design to reduce them under absolute Despotism, it is their right, it is their duty, to throw off such Government, and to provide new Guards for their future security.—Such has been the patient sufferance of these Colonies; and such is now the necessity which constrains them to alter their former Systems of Government. The history of the present King of Great Britain is a history of repeated injuries and usurpations, all having in direct object the establishment of an absolute Tyranny over these States. To prove this, let Facts be submitted to a candid world.

He has refused his Assent to Laws, the most wholesome and necessary for the public good.

He has forbidden his Governors to pass Laws of immediate and pressing importance, unless suspended in their operation till his Assent should be obtained; and when so suspended, he has utterly neglected to attend to them.

He has refused to pass other Laws for the accommodation of large districts of people, unless those people would relinquish the right of Representation in the Legislature, a right inestimable to them and formidable to tyrants only.

He has called together legislative bodies at places unusual, uncomfortable, and distant from the depository of their Public Records, for the sole purpose of fatiguing them into compliance with his measures.

He has dissolved Representative Houses repeatedly, for opposing with manly firmness his invasions on the rights of the people.

He has refused for a long time, after such dissolutions, to cause others to be elected; whereby the Legislative Powers, incapable of Annihilation, have returned to the People at large for their exercise; the State remaining in the mean time exposed to all the dangers of invasion from without, and convulsions within.

He has endeavoured to prevent the population of these States; for that purpose obstructing the Laws of Naturalization of Foreigners; refusing to pass others to encourage their migration hither, and raising the conditions of new Appropriations of Lands.

He has obstructed the Administration of Justice, by refusing his Assent to Laws for establishing Judiciary Powers.

He has made Judges dependent on his Will alone, for the tenure of their offices, and the amount and payment of their salaries.

He has erected a multitude of New Offices, and sent hither swarms of Officers to harass our People, and eat out their substance.

He has kept among us, in times of peace, Standing Armies without the Consent of our legislature.

He has affected to render the Military independent of and superior to the Civil Power.

He has combined with others to subject us to a jurisdiction foreign to our constitution, and unacknowledged by our laws; giving his Assent to their acts of pretended legislation:

For quartering large bodies of armed troops among us:

For protecting them, by a mock Trial, from Punishment for any Murders which they should commit on the Inhabitants of these States:

For cutting off our Trade with all parts of the world:

For imposing taxes on us without our Consent:

For depriving us in many cases, of the benefits of Trial by Jury:

For transporting us beyond Seas to be tried for pretended offences:

For abolishing the free System of English Laws in a neighbouring Province, establishing therein an Arbitrary government, and enlarging its Boundaries so as to render it at once an example and fit instrument for introducing the same absolute rule into these Colonies:

For taking away our Charters, abolishing our most valuable Laws, and altering fundamentally the Forms of our Governments:

For suspending our own Legislature, and declaring themselves invested with Power to legislate for us in all cases whatsoever.

He has abdicated Government here, by declaring us out of his Protection and waging War against us.

He has plundered our seas, ravaged our Coasts, burnt our towns, and destroyed the lives of our people.

He is at this time transporting large armies of foreign mercenaries to compleat the works of death, desolation and tyranny, already begun with circumstances of Cruelty & perfidy scarcely paralleled in the most barbarous ages, and totally unworthy the Head of a civilized nation.

He has constrained our fellow Citizens taken Captive on the high Seas to bear Arms against their Country, to become the executioners of their friends and Brethren, or to fall themselves by their Hands.

He has excited domestic insurrections amongst us, and has endeavoured to bring on the inhabitants of our frontiers, the merciless Indian Savages, whose known rule of warfare, is an undistinguished destruction of all ages, sexes and conditions.

In every stage of these Oppressions We have Petitioned for Redress in the most humble terms: Our repeated Petitions have been answered only by repeated injury. A Prince, whose character is thus marked by every act which may define a Tyrant, is unfit to be the ruler of a free People.

Nor have We been wanting in attention to our British brethren. We have warned them from time to time of attempts by their legislature to extend an unwarrantable jurisdiction over us. We have reminded them of the circumstances of our emigration and settlement here. We have appealed to their native justice and magnanimity, and we have conjured them by the ties of our common kindred to disavow these usurpations, which, would inevitably interrupt our connections and correspondence. They too have been deaf to the voice of justice and of consanguinity. We must, therefore, acquiesce in the necessity, which denounces our Separation, and hold them, as we hold the rest of mankind, Enemies in War, in Peace Friends.

We, therefore, the Representatives of the united States of America, in General Congress, Assembled, appealing to the Supreme Judge of the world for the rectitude of our intentions, do, in the Name, and by Authority of the good People of these Colonies, solemnly publish and declare, That these United Colonies are, and of Right ought to be Free and Independent States; that they are Absolved from all Allegiance to the British Crown, and that all political connection between them and the State of Great Britain, is and ought to be totally dissolved; and that as Free and Independent States, they have full Power to levy War, conclude Peace, contract Alliances, establish Commerce, and to do all other Acts and Things which Independent States may of right do. And for the support of this Declaration, with a firm reliance on the Protection of Divine Providence, we mutually pledge to each other our Lives, our Fortunes and our sacred Honor.

John Hancock,

Josiah Bartlett, Wm Whipple, Saml Adams, John Adams, Robt Treat Paine, Elbridge Gerry, Steph. Hopkins, William Ellery, Roger Sherman, Samel Huntington, Wm Williams, Oliver Wolcott, Matthew Thornton, Wm Floyd, Phil Livingston, Frans Lewis, Lewis Morris, Richd Stockton, Jno Witherspoon, Fras Hopkinson, John Hart, Abra Clark, Robt Morris, Benjamin Rush, Benja Franklin, John Morton, Geo Clymer, Jas Smith, Geo. Taylor, James Wilson, Geo. Ross, Caesar Rodney, Geo Read, Thos M:Kean, Samuel Chase, Wm Paca, Thos Stone, Charles Carroll of Carrollton, George Wythe, Richard Henry Lee, Th. Jefferson, Benja Harrison, Thos Nelson, Jr., Francis Lightfoot Lee, Carter Braxton, Wm Hooper, Joseph Hewes, John Penn, Edward Rutledge, Thos Heyward, Junr., Thomas Lynch, Junor., Arthur Middleton, Button Gwinnett, Lyman Hall, Geo Walton.

The Constitution of the United States

We the people of the United States, in Order to form a more perfect Union, establish Justice, insure domestic Tranquility, provide for the common defence, promote the general Welfare, and secure the Blessings of Liberty to ourselves and our Posterity, do ordain and establish this CONSTITUTION for the United States of America.

ARTICLE I

Section 1. All legislative Powers herein granted shall be vested in a Congress of the United States, which shall consist of a Senate and House of Representatives.

Section 2. The House of Representatives shall be composed of Members chosen every second Year by the People of the several States, and the Electors in each State shall have the Qualifications requisite for Electors of the most numerous Branch of the State Legislature.

No Person shall be a Representative who shall not have attained to the Age of twenty-five Years, and been seven Years a Citizen of the United States, and who shall not, when elected, be an Inhabitant of that State in which he shall be chosen.

Representatives and direct Taxes shall be apportioned among the several States which may be included within this Union, according to their respective Numbers, which shall be determined by adding to the whole Number of free Persons, including those bound to Service for a Term of Years, and excluding Indians not taxed, three fifths of all other Persons. The actual Enumeration shall be made within three Years after the first Meeting of the Congress of the United States, and within every subsequent Term of ten Years, in such Manner as they shall by Law direct. The Number of Representatives shall not exceed one for every thirty Thousand, but each State shall have at Least one Representative; and until such enumeration shall be made, the State of New Hampshire shall be entitled to chuse three, Massachusetts eight, Rhode-Island and Providence Plantations one, Connecticut five, New-York six, New Jersey four, Pennsylvania eight, Delaware one, Maryland six, Virginia ten, North Carolina five, South Carolina five, and Georgia three.

When vacancies happen in the Representation from any State, the Executive Authority thereof shall issue Writs of Election to fill such Vacancies.

The House of Representatives shall chuse their Speaker and other Officers; and shall have the sole Power of Impeachment.

Section 3. The Senate of the United States shall be composed of two Senators from each State, chosen by the Legislature thereof, for six Years; and each Senator shall have one Vote.

Immediately after they shall be assembled in Consequence of the first Election, they shall be divided as equally as may be into three Classes. The Seats of the Senators of the first Class shall be vacated at the Expiration of the second Year, of the second Class at the Expiration of the fourth Year, and of the third Class at the Expiration of the sixth Year, so that one-third may be chosen every second Year; and if Vacancies happen by Resignation, or otherwise, during the Recess of the Legislature of any State, the Executive thereof may make temporary Appointments until the next Meeting of the Legislature, which shall then fill such Vacancies.

No Person shall be a Senator who shall not have attained to the Age of thirty Years, and been nine Years a Citizen of the United States, and who shall not, when elected, be an Inhabitant of that State in which he shall be chosen.

The Vice President of the United States shall be President of the Senate, but shall have no vote, unless they be equally divided.

The Senate shall chuse their other Officers, and also a President pro tempore, in the absence of the Vice President, or when he shall exercise the Office of the President of the United States.

The Senate shall have the sole Power to try all Impeachments. When sitting for that purpose, they shall be on Oath or Affirmation. When the President of the United States is tried, the Chief Justice shall preside: And no person shall be convicted without the Concurrence of two thirds of the Members present.

Judgment in Cases of Impeachment shall not extend further than to removal from Office, and disqualification to hold and enjoy any Office of honor, Trust, or Profit under the United States: but the Party convicted shall nevertheless be liable and subject to Indictment, Trial, Judgment, and Punishment, according to Law.

Section 4. The Times, Places and Manner of holding

Elections for Senators and Representatives, shall be prescribed in each state by the Legislature thereof; but the Congress may at any time by Law make or alter such Regulations, except as to the Places of Chusing Senators.

The Congress shall assemble at least once in every Year, and such Meeting shall be on the first Monday in December, unless they shall by Law appoint a different Day.

Section 5. Each House shall be the Judge of the Elections, Returns and Qualifications of its own Members, and a Majority of each shall constitute a Quorum to do Business; but a smaller number may adjourn from day to day, and may be authorized to compel the Attendance of absent Members, in such Manner, and under such Penalties, as each House may provide.

Each House may determine the Rules of its Proceedings, punish its Members for disorderly Behavior, and, with the Concurrence of two thirds, expel a Member.

Each House shall keep a Journal of its Proceedings, and from time to time publish the same, excepting such Parts as may in their Judgment require Secrecy; and the Yeas and Nays of the Members of either House on any question shall, at the Desire of one fifth of those Present, be entered on the Journal.

Neither House, during the Session of Congress, shall, without the Consent of the other, adjourn for more than three days, nor to any other Place than that in which the two Houses shall be sitting.

Section 6. The Senators and Representatives shall receive a Compensation for their Services, to be ascertained by Law, and paid out of the Treasury of the United States. They shall in all Cases, except Treason, Felony, and Breach of the Peace, be privileged from arrest during their Attendance at the Session of their respective Houses, and in going to and returning from the same; and for any Speech or Debate in either House, they shall not be questioned in any other Place.

No Senator or Representative shall, during the Time for which he was elected, be appointed to any civil Office under the Authority of the United States, which shall have been created, or the Emoluments whereof shall have been increased, during such time; and no Person holding any Office under the United States shall be a Member of either House during his continuance in Office.

Section 7. All Bills for raising Revenue shall originate in the House of Representatives; but the Senate may propose or concur with Amendments as on other bills.

Every Bill which shall have passed the House of Representatives and the Senate, shall, before it become a Law, be presented to the President of the United States; If he approve he shall sign it, but if not he shall return it, with his Objections, to that House in which it shall have originated, who shall enter the Objections at large

on their Journal, and proceed to reconsider it. If after such Reconsideration two thirds of that House shall agree to pass the bill, it shall be sent, together with the objections, to the other House, by which it shall likewise be reconsidered, and if approved by two thirds of that House, it shall become a Law. But in all such Cases the Votes of both Houses shall be determined by Yeas and Nays, and the Names of the Persons voting for and against the Bill shall be entered on the Journal of each House respectively. If any Bill shall not be returned by the President within ten Days (Sundays excepted) after it shall have been presented to him, the Same shall be a Law, in like Manner as if he had signed it, unless the Congress by their Adjournment prevent its Return, in which Case it shall not be a Law.

Every Order, Resolution, or Vote to which the Concurrence of the Senate and House of Representatives may be necessary (except on a question of Adjournment) shall be presented to the President of the United States; and before the Same shall take Effect, shall be approved by him, or being disapproved by him, shall be repassed by two thirds of the Senate and House of Representatives, according to the Rules and Limitations prescribed in the Case of a Bill.

Section 8. The Congress shall have Power To lay and collect Taxes, Duties, Imposts and Excises, to pay the Debts and provide for the common Defence and general Welfare of the United States; but all Duties, Imposts and Excises shall be uniform throughout the United States;

To borrow money on the credit of the United States;

To regulate Commerce with foreign Nations, and among the several States, and with the Indian Tribes;

To establish an uniform Rule of Naturalization, and uniform Laws on the subject of Bankruptcies throughout the United States;

To coin Money, regulate the Value thereof, and of foreign Coin, and fix the Standard of Weights and Measures;

To provide for the Punishment of counterfeiting the Securities and current Coin of the United States;

To establish Post Offices and post Roads;

To promote the Progress of Science and useful Arts, by securing for limited Times to Authors and Inventors the exclusive Right to their respective Writings and Discoveries;

To constitute Tribunals inferior to the Supreme Court;

To define and punish Piracies and Felonies committed on the high Seas, and Offences against the Law of Nations;

To declare War, grant Letters of Marque and Reprisal, and make Rules concerning Captures on Land and Water;

To raise and support Armies, but no Appropriation of Money to that Use shall be for a longer Term than two Years;

To provide and maintain a Navy;

To make Rules for the Government and Regulation of the land and naval forces;

To provide for calling forth the Militia to execute the Laws of the Union, suppress Insurrections and repel Invasions;

To provide for organizing, arming, and disciplining the Militia, and for governing such Part of them as may be employed in the Service of the United States, reserving to the States respectively, the Appointment of the Officers, and the Authority of training the Militia according to the discipline prescribed by Congress;

To exercise exclusive Legislation in all Cases whatsoever, over such District (not exceeding ten Miles square) as may, by Cession of particular States, and the acceptance of Congress, become the Seat of Government of the United States, and to exercise like Authority over all Places purchased by the Consent of the Legislature of the State in which the Same shall be, for the Erection of Forts, Magazines, Arsenals, dock-Yards, and other needful Buildings;—And

To make all Laws which shall be necessary and proper for carrying into Execution the foregoing Powers, and all other Powers vested by this Constitution in the government of the United States, or in any Department or Officer thereof.

Section 9. The Migration or Importation of such Persons as any of the States now existing shall think proper to admit, shall not be prohibited by the Congress prior to the Year one thousand eight hundred and eight, but a tax or duty may be imposed on such Importation, not exceeding ten dollars for each Person.

The privilege of the Writ of Habeas Corpus shall not be suspended, unless when in Cases of Rebellion or Invasion the public Safety may require it.

No Bill of Attainder or ex post facto Law shall be passed.

No capitation, or other direct, Tax shall be laid unless in Proportion to the Census or Enumeration herein before directed to be taken.

No Tax or Duty shall be laid on Articles exported from any State.

No Preference shall be given by any Regulation of Revenue to the Ports of one State over those of another: nor shall Vessels bound to, or from, one State, be obliged to enter, clear, or pay Duties in another.

No Money shall be drawn from the Treasury, but in Consequence of Appropriations made by Law; and a regular Statement and Account of the Receipts and Expenditures of all public Money shall be published from time to time.

No Title of Nobility shall be granted by the United States: And no Person holding any Office of Profit or Trust under them, shall, without the Consent of the Congress, accept of any present, Emolument, Office, or Title, of any kind whatever, from any King, Prince, or foreign State.

Section 10. No State shall enter into any Treaty, Alliance, or Confederation; grant Letters of Marque and Reprisal; coin Money; emit Bills of Credit; make any Thing but gold and silver Coin a Tender in Payment of Debts; pass any Bill of Attainder, ex post facto Law, or Law impairing the Obligation of Contracts, or grant any Title of Nobility.

No State shall, without the Consent of the Congress, lay any Imposts or Duties on Imports or Exports, except what may be absolutely necessary for executing its inspection Laws: and the net Produce of all Duties and Imposts, laid by any State on Imports or Exports, shall be for the Use of the Treasury of the United States; and all such Laws shall be subject to the Revision and Control of the Congress.

No State shall, without the Consent of Congress, lay any duty of Tonnage, keep Troops, or Ships of War in time of Peace, enter into any Agreement or Compact with another State, or with a foreign Power, or engage in War, unless actually invaded, or in such imminent Danger as will not admit of delay.

ARTICLE II

Section 1. The executive Power shall be vested in a President of the United States of America. He shall hold his Office during the Term of four years, and, together with the Vice President, chosen for the same Term, be elected, as follows:

Each State shall appoint, in such Manner as the Legislature thereof may direct, a Number of Electors, equal to the whole Number of Senators and Representatives to which the State may be entitled in the Congress; but no Senator or Representative, or Person holding an Office of Trust or Profit under the United States, shall be appointed an Elector.

The Electors shall meet in their respective States, and vote by Ballot for two persons, of whom one at least shall not be an Inhabitant of the same State with themselves. And they shall make a List of all the Persons voted for, and of the Number of Votes for each; which List they shall sign and certify, and transmit sealed to the Seat of the Government of the United States, directed to the President of the Senate. The President of the Senate shall, in the Presence of the Senate and House of Representatives, open all the Certificates, and the Votes shall then be counted. The Person having the greatest Number of Votes shall be the President, if such Number be a Majority of the whole Number of Electors appointed; and if there be more than one who have such Majority, and have an equal Number of Votes, then the House of Representatives shall immediately chuse by Ballot one of them for President; and if no Person have a Majority, then from the five highest on the List the said House shall in like Manner chuse the President. But in chusing the President, the votes shall be taken by States, the Representation from each State having one Vote; a quorum for this Purpose shall consist of a Member or Members from two-thirds of the States, and a Majority of all the States shall be necessary to a Choice. In every Case, after the Choice of the President, the Person having the greatest Number of Votes of the Electors shall be the Vice President. But if there should remain two or more who have equal votes, the Senate shall chuse from them by Ballot the Vice President.

The Congress may determine the time of chusing the Electors, and the Day on which they shall give their Votes; which Day shall be the same throughout the United States.

No person except a natural-born Citizen, or a Citizen of the United States, at the time of the Adoption of this Constitution, shall be eligible to the Office of President; neither shall any Person be eligible to that Office who shall not have attained to the Age of thirty-five years, and been fourteen Years a Resident within the United States.

In Case of the Removal of the President from Office, or of his Death, Resignation, or Inability to discharge the Powers and Duties of the said Office, the same shall devolve on the Vice President, and the Congress may by Law provide for the Case of Removal, Death, Resignation, or Inability, both of the President and Vice President, declaring what Officer shall then act as President, and such Officer shall act accordingly, until the disability be removed, or a President shall be elected.

The President shall, at stated Times, receive for his Services a Compensation, which shall neither be increased nor diminished during the Period for which he shall have been elected, and he shall not receive within that Period any other Emolument from the United States, or any of them.

Before he enter on the execution of his Office, he shall take the following Oath or Affirmation:—"I do solemnly swear (or affirm) that I will faithfully execute the Office of President of the United States, and will, to the best of my Ability, preserve, protect, and defend the Constitution of the United States."

Section 2. The President shall be Commander in Chief of the Army and Navy of the United States, and of the Militia of the several States, when called into the actual Service of the United States; he may require the Opinion, in writing, of the principal Officer in each of the executive Departments, upon any subject relating to the Duties of their respective Offices, and he shall have Power to Grant Reprieves and Pardons for Offences against the United States, except in Cases of Impeachment.

He shall have Power, by and with the Advice and Consent of the Senate, to make Treaties, provided two thirds of the Senators present concur; and he shall nominate, and by and with the Advice and Consent of the Senate, shall appoint Ambassadors, other public Ministers and Consuls, Judges of the supreme Court, and all other Officers of the United States, whose Appointments are not herein otherwise provided for, and which shall be established by Law: but the Congress may by Law vest the Appointment of such inferior Officers, as they think proper, in the President alone, in the Courts of Law, or in the Heads of Departments.

The President shall have Power to fill up all Vacancies that may happen during the Recess of the Senate, by granting Commissions which shall expire at the End of their next Session.

Section 3. He shall from time to time give to the Congress Information of the State of the Union, and recommend to their Consideration such Measures as he shall judge necessary and expedient; he may, on extraordinary occasions, convene both Houses, or either of them, and in Case of Disagreement between them, with respect to the Time of Adjournment, he may adjourn them to such Time as he shall think proper; he shall receive Ambassadors and other public Ministers; he shall take Care that the Laws be faithfully executed, and shall Commission all the Officers of the United States.

Section 4. The President, Vice President and all civil Officers of the United States, shall be removed from Office on Impeachment for, and Conviction of, Treason, Bribery, or other high Crimes and Misdemeanors.

ARTICLE III

Section 1. The judicial Power of the United States, shall be vested in one supreme Court, and in such inferior Courts as the Congress may from time to time ordain and establish. The Judges, both of the supreme and inferior Courts, shall hold their Offices during good Behaviour, and shall, at stated Times, receive for their Services, a Compensation, which shall not be diminished during their Continuance in Office.

Section 2. The judicial Power shall extend to all Cases, in Law and Equity, arising under this Constitution, the Laws of the United States, and treaties made, or which shall be made, under their Authority;—to all Cases affecting ambassadors, other public ministers and consuls;—to all cases of admiralty and maritime Jurisdiction;—to Controversies to which the United States shall be a Party;—to Controversies between two or more States;—between a State and Citizens of another State;—between

THE CONSTITUTION OF THE UNITED STATES

Citizens of different States,—between Citizens of the same State claiming Lands under Grants of different States, and between a State, or the Citizens thereof, and foreign States, Citizens or Subjects.

In all Cases affecting Ambassadors, other public Ministers and Consuls, and those in which a State shall be Party, the supreme Court shall have original Jurisdiction. In all the other Cases before mentioned, the supreme Court shall have appellate Jurisdiction, both as to Law and Fact, with such Exceptions, and under such Regulations as the Congress shall make.

The trial of all Crimes, except in Cases of Impeachment, shall be by Jury; and such Trial shall be held in the State where the said Crimes shall have been committed; but when not committed within any State, the Trial shall be at such Place or Places as the Congress may by Law have directed.

Section 3. Treason against the United States, shall consist only in levying War against them, or in adhering to their Enemies, giving them Aid and Comfort. No Person shall be convicted of Treason unless on the testimony of two Witnesses to the same overt Act, or on Confession in open Court.

The Congress shall have power to declare the Punishment of Treason, but no Attainder of Treason shall work Corruption of Blood, or Forfeiture except during the Life of the Person attained.

ARTICLE IV

Section 1. Full Faith and Credit shall be given in each State to the public Acts, Records, and judicial Proceedings of every other State. And the Congress may by general Laws prescribe the Manner in which such Acts, Records and Proceedings shall be proved, and the Effect thereof.

Section 2. The Citizens of each State shall be entitled to all Privileges and Immunities of Citizens in the several States.

A Person charged in any State with Treason, Felony, or other Crime, who shall flee from Justice, and be found in another State, shall on demand of the executive Authority of the State from which he fled, be delivered up, to be removed to the State having Jurisdiction of the crime.

No Person held to Service or Labour in one State, under the Laws thereof, escaping into another, shall, in Consequence of any Law or Regulation therein, be discharged from such Service or Labour, but shall be delivered up on Claim of the Party to whom such Service or Labour may be due.

Section 3. New States may be admitted by the Congress into this Union; but no new State shall be formed or erected within the Jurisdiction of any other State; nor any State be formed by the Junction of two or more States, or parts of States, without the Consent of the Legislatures of the States concerned as well as of the Congress.

The Congress shall have Power to dispose of and make all needful Rules and Regulations respecting the Territory or other Property belonging to the United States; and nothing in this Constitution shall be so construed as to Prejudice any Claims of the United States, or of any particular State.

Section 4. The United States shall guarantee to every State in this Union a Republican Form of Government, and shall protect each of them against Invasion; and on Application of the Legislature, or the Executive (when the Legislature cannot be convened) against domestic Violence.

ARTICLE V

The Congress, whenever two-thirds of both Houses shall deem it necessary, shall propose Amendments to this Constitution, or, on the Application of the Legislatures of two-thirds of the several States, shall call a Convention for proposing Amendments, which, in either Case, shall be valid to all Intents and Purposes, as part of this Constitution, when ratified by the Legislatures of three-fourths of the several States, or by Conventions in three-fourths thereof, as the one or the other Mode of Ratification may be proposed by the Congress; Provided that no Amendment which may be made prior to the Year One thousand eight hundred and eight shall in any Manner affect the first and fourth Clauses in the Ninth Section of the first Article; and that no State, without its Consent, shall be deprived of its equal Suffrage in the Senate.

ARTICLE VI

All Debts contracted and Engagements entered into, before the Adoption of this Constitution, shall be as valid against the United States under this Constitution, as under the Confederation.

This Constitution, and the Laws of the United States which shall be made in Pursuance thereof; and all Treaties made, or which shall be made, under the Authority of the United States, shall be the supreme Law of the Land; and the Judges in every State shall be bound thereby, any Thing in the Constitution or Laws of any State to the Contrary notwithstanding.

The Senators and Representatives before mentioned, and the Members of the several State Legislatures, and all executive and judicial Officers, both of the United States and of the several States, shall be bound by Oath or Affirmation to support this Constitution; but no religious Test shall ever be required as a qualification to any Office or public Trust under the United States.

ARTICLE VII

The Ratification of the Conventions of nine States shall be sufficient for the Establishment of this Constitution between the States so ratifying the same.

Done in Convention by the Unanimous Consent of the States present the Seventeenth Day of September in the Year of our Lord one thousand seven hundred and Eighty seven, and of the Independence of the United States of America the Twelfth. In Witness whereof We have hereunto subscribed our Names.

Go. Washington, *President and deputy from Virginia; Attest* William Jackson, *Secretary; Delaware:* Geo. Read,* Gunning Bedford, Jr., John Dickinson, Richard Bassett, Jaco. Broom; *Maryland:* James McHenry, Daniel of St. Thomas' Jenifer, Danl. Carroll; *Virginia:* John Blair, James Madison, Jr.; *North Carolina:* Wm. Blount, Richd. Dobbs Spaight, Hu Williamson; *South Carolina:* J. Rutledge, Charles Cotesworth Pinckney, Charles Pinckney, Pierce Butler; *Georgia:* William Few, Abr. Baldwin; *New Hampshire:* John Langdon, Nicholas Gilman; *Massachusetts:* Nathaniel Gorham, Rufus King; *Connecticut:* Wm. Saml. Johnson, Roger Sherman;* *New York:* Alexander Hamilton; *New Jersey:* Wil. Livingston, David Brearley, Wm. Paterson, Jona. Dayton; *Pennsylvania:* B. Franklin,* Thomas Mifflin, Robt. Morris,* Geo. Clymer,* Thos. FitzSimons, Jared Ingersoll, James Wilson, Gouv. Morris.

Articles in Addition to, and Amendment of, the Constitution of the United States of America, Proposed by Congress, and Ratified by the Legislatures of the Several States, Pursuant to the Fifth Article of the Original Constitution.

AMENDMENT I [1791]

Congress shall make no law respecting an establishment of religion, or prohibiting the free exercise thereof; or abridging the freedom of speech, or of the press; or the right of the people peaceably to assemble, and to petition the Government for a redress of grievances.

AMENDMENT II [1791]

A well regulated Militia, being necessary to the security of a free State, the right of the people to keep and bear Arms shall not be infringed.

AMENDMENT III [1791]

No Soldier shall, in time of peace, be quartered in any house, without the consent of the Owner, nor in time of war, but in a manner to be prescribed by law.

* Also signed the Declaration of Independence

AMENDMENT IV [1791]

The right of the people to be secure in their persons, houses, papers, and effects, against unreasonable searches and seizures, shall not be violated, and no Warrants shall issue, but upon probable cause, supported by Oath or affirmation, and particularly describing the place to be searched, and the persons or things to be seized.

AMENDMENT V [1791]

No person shall be held to answer for a capital or otherwise infamous crime, unless on a presentment or indictment of a Grand Jury, except in cases arising in the land or naval forces, or in the Militia, when in actual service in time of War or public danger; nor shall any person be subject for the same offence to be twice put in jeopardy of life or limb; nor shall be compelled in any criminal case to be a witness against himself, nor be deprived of life, liberty, or property, without due process of law; nor shall private property be taken for public use, without just compensation.

AMENDMENT VI [1791]

In all criminal prosecutions, the accused shall enjoy the right to a speedy and public trial, by an impartial jury of the State and district wherein the crime shall have been committed, which district shall have been previously ascertained by law, and to be informed of the nature and cause of the accusation; to be confronted with the winesses against him; to have compulsory process for obtaining witnesses in his favor, and to have the Assistance of Counsel for his defence.

AMENDMENT VII [1791]

In suits at common law, where the value in controversy shall exceed twenty dollars, the right of trial by jury shall be preserved, and no fact tried by a jury, shall be otherwise reexamined in any Court of the United States, than according to the rules of the common law.

AMENDMENT VIII [1791]

Excessive bail shall not be required, nor excessive fines imposed, nor cruel and unusual punishments inflicted.

AMENDMENT IX [1791]

The enumeration in the Constitution, of certain rights, shall not be construed to deny or disparage others retained by the people.

AMENDMENT X [1791]

The powers not delegated to the United States by the Constitution, nor prohibited by it to the States, are reserved to the States respectively, or to the people.

AMENDMENT XI [1798]

The Judicial power of the United States shall not be construed to extend to any suit in law or equity, commenced or prosecuted against one of the United States by Citizens of another State, or by Citizens or Subjects of any Foreign State.

AMENDMENT XII [1804]

The Electors shall meet in their respective States and vote by ballot for President and Vice-President, one of whom, at least, shall not be an inhabitant of the same State with themselves; they shall name in their ballots the person voted for as President, and in distinct ballots the person voted for as Vice-President, and they shall make distinct lists of all persons voted for as President, and of all persons voted for as Vice-President, and of the number of votes for each, which lists they shall sign and certify, and transmit sealed to the seat of the government of the United States, directed to the President of the Senate;—The President of the Senate shall, in the presence of the Senate and House of Representatives, open all the certificates and the votes shall then be counted;—The person having the greatest number of votes for President, shall be the President, if such number be a majority of the whole number of Electors appointed; and if no person have such majority, then from the persons having the highest numbers not exceeding three on the list of those voted for as President, the House of Representatives shall choose immediately, by ballot, the President. But in choosing the President, the votes shall be taken by states, the representation from each state having one vote; a quorum for this purpose shall consist of a member or members from two-thirds of the states, and a majority of all the states shall be necessary to a choice. And if the House of Representatives shall not choose a President whenever the right of choice shall devolve upon them, before the fourth day of March next following, then the Vice-President shall act as President, as in the case of the death or other constitutional disability of the President.—The person having the greatest number of votes as Vice-President, shall be the Vice-President, if such number be a majority of the whole number of Electors appointed, and if no person have a majority, then from the two highest numbers on the list, the Senate shall choose the Vice-President; a quorum for the purpose shall consist of two-thirds of the whole number of Senators, and a majority of the whole number shall be necessary to a choice. But no person constitutionally ineligible to the office of President shall be eligible to that of Vice-President of the United States.

AMENDMENT XIII [1865]

Section 1. Neither slavery nor involuntary servitude, except as a punishment for crime whereof the party shall have been duly convicted, shall exist within the United States, or any place subject to their jurisdiction.

Section 2. Congress shall have power to enforce this article by appropriate legislation.

AMENDMENT XIV [1868]

Section 1. All persons born or naturalized in the United States, and subject to the jurisdiction thereof, are citizens of the United States and of the State wherein they reside. No State shall make or enforce any law which shall abridge the privileges or immunities of citizens of the United States; nor shall any State deprive any person of life, liberty, or property, without due process of law; nor deny to any person within its jurisdiction the equal protection of the laws.

Section 2. Representatives shall be apportioned among the several States according to their respective numbers, counting the whole number of persons in each State, excluding Indians not taxed. But when the right to vote at any election for the choice of electors for President and Vice-President of the United States, Representatives in Congress, the Executive and Judicial officers of a State, or the members of the Legislature thereof, is denied to any of the male inhabitants of such State, being twenty-one years of age, and citizens of the United States, or in any way abridged, except for participation in rebellion, or other crime, the basis of representation therein shall be reduced in the proportion which the number of such male citizens shall bear to the whole number of male citizens twenty-one years of age in such State.

Section 3. No person shall be a Senator or Representative in Congress, or elector of President and Vice-President, or hold any office, civil or military, under the United States, or under any State, who, having previously taken an oath, as a member of Congress, or as an officer of the United States, or as a member of any State legislature, or as an executive or judicial officer of any State, to support the Constitution of the United States, shall have engaged in insurrection or rebellion against the same, or given aid or comfort to the enemies thereof. But Congress may by a vote of two-thirds of each House, remove such disability.

Section 4. The validity of the public debt of the United States, authorized by law, including debts incurred for payment of pensions and bounties for services in suppressing insurrection or rebellion, shall not be questioned. But neither the United States nor any State shall assume or pay any debt or obligation incurred in aid of insurrection or rebellion against the United States, or any claim for the loss or emancipation of any slave; but all such debts, obligations, and claims shall be held illegal and void.

Section 5. The Congress shall have the power to enforce, by appropriate legislation, the provisions of this article.

AMENDMENT XV [1870]

Section 1. The right of citizens of the United States to vote shall not be denied or abridged by the United States or by any State on account of race, color, or previous condition of servitude—

Section 2. The Congress shall have power to enforce this article by appropriate legislation.

AMENDMENT XVI [1913]

The Congress shall have power to lay and collect taxes on incomes, from whatever source derived, without apportionment among the several States, and without regard to any census or enumeration.

AMENDMENT XVII [1913]

The Senate of the United States shall be composed of two Senators from each State, elected by the people thereof, for six years; and each Senator shall have one vote. The electors in each State shall have the qualifications requisite for electors of the most numerous branch of the State legislatures.

When vacancies happen in the representation of any State in the Senate, the executive authority of such State shall issue writs of election to fill such vacancies: *Provided,* That the legislature of any State may empower the executive thereof to make temporary appointments until the people fill the vacancies by election as the legislature may direct.

This amendment shall not be so construed as to affect the election or term of any Senator chosen before it becomes valid as part of the Constitution.

AMENDMENT XVIII [1919]

Section 1. After one year from the ratification of this article the manufacture, sale, or transportation of intoxicating liquors within, the importation thereof into, or the exportation thereof from the United States and all territory subject to the jurisdiction thereof for beverage purposes is hereby prohibited.

Section 2. The Congress and the several States shall have concurrent power to enforce this article by appropriate legislation.

Section 3. This article shall be inoperative unless it shall have been ratified as an amendment to the Constitution by the legislatures of the several States, as provided in the Constitution, within seven years from the date of the submission hereof to the States by the Congress.

AMENDMENT XIX [1920]

The right of citizens of the United States to vote shall not be denied or abridged by the United States or by any State on account of sex.

Congress shall have power to enforce this article by appropriate legislation.

AMENDMENT XX [1933]

Section 1. The terms of the President and Vice-President shall end at noon on the 20th day of January, and the terms of Senators and Representatives at noon on the 3d day of January, of the years in which such terms would have ended if this article had not been ratified; and the terms of their successors shall then begin.

Section 2. The Congress shall assemble at least once in every year, and such meeting shall begin at noon on the 3d day of January, unless they shall by law appoint a different day.

Section 3. If, at the time fixed for the beginning of the term of the President, the President elect shall have died, the Vice-President elect shall become President. If a President shall not have been chosen before the time fixed for the beginning of his term, or if the President elect shall have failed to qualify, then the Vice-President elect shall act as President until a President shall have qualified; and the Congress may by law provide for the case wherein neither a President elect nor a Vice-President elect shall have qualified, declaring who shall then act as President, or the manner in which one who is to act shall be selected, and such person shall act accordingly until a President or Vice-President shall have qualified.

Section 4. The Congress may by law provide for the case of the death of any of the persons from whom the House of Representatives may choose a President whenever the right of choice shall have devolved upon them, and for the case of the death of any of the persons from whom the Senate may choose a Vice-President whenever the right of choice shall have devolved upon them.

Section 5. Sections 1 and 2 shall take effect on the 15th day of October following the ratification of this article.

Section 6. This article shall be inoperative unless it

shall have been ratified as an amendment to the Constitution by the legislatures of three-fourths of the several States within seven years from the date of its submission.

AMENDMENT XXI [1933]

Section 1. The eighteenth article of amendment to the Constitution of the United States is hereby repealed.

Section 2. The transportation or importation into any State, Territory, or possession of the United States for delivery or use therein of intoxicating liquors, in violation of the laws thereof, is hereby prohibited.

Section 3. This article shall be inoperative unless it shall have been ratified as an amendment to the Constitution by conventions in the several States, as provided in the Constitution, within seven years from the date of the submission hereof to the States by the Congress.

AMENDMENT XXII [1951]

No person shall be elected to the office of the President more than twice, and no person who has held the office of President, or acted as President, for more than two years of a term to which some other person was elected President shall be elected to the office of the President more than once.

But this Article shall not apply to any person holding the office of President when this Article was proposed by the Congress, and shall not prevent any person who may be holding the office of President, or acting as President, during the term within which this Article becomes operative from holding the office of President or acting as President during the remainder of such term.

AMENDMENT XXIII [1961]

Section 1. The District constituting the seat of Government of the United States shall appoint in such manner as the Congress may direct:

A number of electors of President and Vice President equal to the whole number of Senators and Representatives in Congress to which the District would be entitled if it were a State, but in no event more than the least populous State; they shall be in addition to those appointed by the States, but they shall be considered, for the purposes of the election of President and Vice President, to be electors appointed by a State; and they shall meet in the District and perform such duties as provided by the twelfth article of amendment.

Section 2. The Congress shall have power to enforce this article by appropriate legislation.

AMENDMENT XXIV [1964]

Section 1. The right of citizens of the United States to vote in any primary or other election for President or Vice President, for electors for President or Vice President, or for Senator or Representative in Congress, shall not be denied or abridged by the United States or any State by reason of failure to pay any poll tax or other tax.

Section 2. The Congress shall have the power to enforce this article by appropriate legislation.

AMENDMENT XXV [1967]

Section 1. In case of the removal of the President from office or his death or resignation, the Vice President shall become President.

Section 2. Whenever there is a vacancy in the office of the Vice President, the President shall nominate a Vice President who shall take the office upon confirmation by a majority vote of both houses of Congress.

Section 3. Whenever the President transmits to the President pro tempore of the Senate and the Speaker of the House of Representatives his written declaration that he is unable to discharge the powers and duties of his office, and until he transmits to them a written declaration to the contrary, such powers and duties shall be discharged by the Vice President as Acting President.

Section 4. Whenever the Vice President and a majority of either the principal officers of the executive departments, or of such other body as Congress may by law provide, transmit to the President pro tempore of the Senate and the Speaker of the House of Representatives their written declaration that the President is unable to discharge the powers and duties of his office, the Vice President shall immediately assume the powers and duties of the office as Acting President.

Thereafter, when the President transmits to the President pro tempore of the Senate and the Speaker of the House of Representatives his written declaration that no inability exists, he shall resume the powers and duties of his office unless the Vice President and a majority of either the principal officers of the executive departments, or of such other body as Congress may by law provide, transmit within four days to the President pro tempore of the Senate and the Speaker of the House of Representatives their written declaration that the President is unable to discharge the powers and duties of his office. Thereupon Congress shall decide the issue, assembling within 48 hours for that purpose if not in session. If the Congress, within 21 days after receipt of the latter written declaration, or, if Congress is not in session, within 21 days after Congress is required to assemble, determines by two-thirds vote of both houses that the President is unable to discharge the powers and duties of his office, the Vice President shall continue to discharge the same as Acting President; otherwise, the President shall resume the powers and duties of his office.

AMENDMENT XXVI [1971]

Section 1. The right of citizens of the United States, who are 18 years of age or older, to vote shall not be denied or abridged by the United States or any state on account of age.

Section 2. The Congress shall have the power to enforce this article by appropriate legislation.

Presidential Elections, 1789–1988

Year	Candidates	Party	Popular Vote*	Electoral Vote**
1789	**George Washington**			69
	John Adams			34
	Others			35
1792	**George Washington**			132
	John Adams			77
	George Clinton			50
	Others			5
1796	**John Adams**	Federalist		71
	Thomas Jefferson	Democratic Republican		68
	Thomas Pinckney	Federalist		59
	Aaron Burr	Democratic Republican		30
	Others			48
1800	**Thomas Jefferson**	Democratic Republican		73
	Aaron Burr	Democratic Republican		73
	John Adams	Federalist		65
	Charles C. Pinckney	Federalist		64
1804	**Thomas Jefferson**	Democratic Republican		162
	Charles C. Pinckney	Federalist		14
1808	**James Madison**	Democratic Republican		122
	Charles C. Pinckney	Federalist		47
	George Clinton	Independent Republican		6
1812	**James Madison**	Democratic Republican		128
	DeWitt Clinton	Federalist		89
1816	**James Monroe**	Democratic Republican		183
	Rufus King	Federalist		34
1820	**James Monroe**	Democratic Republican		231
	John Quincy Adams	Independent Republican		1
1824	**John Quincy Adams**	Democratic Republican	108,704 (30.5%)	84
	Andrew Jackson	Democratic Republican	153,544 (43.1%)	99
	Henry Clay	Democratic Republican	47,136 (13.2%)	37
	William H. Crawford	Democratic Republican	46,618 (13.1%)	41
1828	**Andrew Jackson**	Democratic	647,231 (56.0%)	178
	John Quincy Adams	National Republican	509,097 (44.0%)	83

* Because only the leading candidates are listed, popular vote percentages do not always total 100.
** The elections of 1800 and 1824, in which no candidate received an electoral vote majority, were decided in the House of Representatives.

Year	Candidates	Party	Popular Vote*	Electoral Vote**
1832	**Andrew Jackson**	Democratic	687,502 (55.0%)	219
	Henry Clay	National Republican	530,189 (42.4%)	49
	William Wirt	Anti-Masonic	33,108 (2.6%)	7
	John Floyd	National Republican		11
1836	**Martin Van Buren**	Democratic	761,549 (50.9%)	170
	William H. Harrison	Whig	549,567 (36.7%)	73
	Hugh L. White	Whig	145,396 (9.7%)	26
	Daniel Webster	Whig	41,287 (2.7%)	14
1840	**William H. Harrison** (**John Tyler,** 1841)	Whig	1,275,017 (53.1%)	234
	Martin Van Buren	Democratic	1,128,702 (46.9%)	60
1844	**James K. Polk**	Democratic	1,337,243 (49.6%)	170
	Henry Clay	Whig	1,299,068 (48.1%)	105
	James G. Birney	Liberty	62,300 (2.3%)	
1848	**Zachary Taylor** (**Millard Fillmore,** 1850)	Whig	1,360,101 (47.4%)	163
	Lewis Cass	Democratic	1,220,544 (42.5%)	127
	Martin Van Buren	Free Soil	291,263 (10.1%)	
1852	**Franklin Pierce**	Democratic	1,601,474 (50.9%)	254
	Winfield Scott	Whig	1,386,578 (44.1%)	42
1856	**James Buchanan**	Democratic	1,838,169 (45.4%)	174
	John C. Frémont	Republican	1,335,264 (33.0%)	114
	Millard Fillmore	American	874,534 (21.6%)	8
1860	**Abraham Lincoln**	Republican	1,865,593 (39.8%)	180
	Stephen A. Douglas	Democratic	1,382,713 (29.5%)	12
	John C. Breckinridge	Democratic	848,356 (18.1%)	72
	John Bell	Constitutional Union	592,906 (12.6%)	39
1864	**Abraham Lincoln** (**Andrew Johnson,** 1865)	Republican	2,206,938 (55.0%)	212
	George B. McClellan	Democratic	1,803,787 (45.0%)	21
1868	**Ulysses S. Grant**	Republican	3,013,421 (52.7%)	214
	Horatio Seymour	Democratic	2,706,829 (47.3%)	80
1872	**Ulysses S. Grant**	Republican	3,596,745 (55.6%)	286
	Horace Greeley	Democratic	2,843,446 (43.9%)	66
1876	**Rutherford B. Hayes**	Republican	4,036,572 (48.0%)	185
	Samuel J. Tilden	Democratic	4,284,020 (51.0%)	184
1880	**James A. Garfield** (**Chester A. Arthur,** 1881)	Republican	4,449,053 (48.3%)	214
	Winfield S. Hancock	Democratic	4,442,035 (48.2%)	155
	James B. Weaver	Greenback Labor	308,578 (3.4%)	
1884	**Grover Cleveland**	Democratic	4,874,986 (48.5%)	219
	James G. Blaine	Republican	4,851,981 (48.2%)	182
	Benjamin F. Butler	Greenback Labor	175,370 (1.8%)	

Year	Candidates	Party	Popular Vote*	Electoral Vote**
1888	**Benjamin Harrison**	Republican	5,444,337 (47.8%)	233
	Grover Cleveland	Democratic	5,540,050 (48.6%)	168
1892	**Grover Cleveland**	Democratic	5,554,414 (46.0%)	277
	Benjamin Harrison	Republican	5,190,802 (43.0%)	145
	James B. Weaver	People's	1,027,329 (8.5%)	22
1896	**William McKinley**	Republican	7,035,638 (50.8%)	271
	William Jennings Bryan	Democratic; Populist	6,467,946 (46.7%)	176
1900	**William McKinley** **(Theodore Roosevelt,** 1901)	Republican	7,219,530 (51.7%)	292
	William Jennings Bryan	Democratic; Populist	6,356,734 (45.5%)	155
1904	**Theodore Roosevelt**	Republican	7,628,834 (56.4%)	336
	Alton B. Parker	Democratic	5,084,401 (37.6%)	140
	Eugene V. Debs	Socialist	402,460 (3.0%)	
1908	**William H. Taft**	Republican	7,679,006 (51.6%)	321
	William Jennings Bryan	Democratic	6,409,106 (43.1%)	162
	Eugene V. Debs	Socialist	420,820 (2.8%)	
1912	**Woodrow Wilson**	Democratic	6,286,820 (41.8%)	435
	Theodore Roosevelt	Progressive	4,126,020 (27.4%)	88
	William H. Taft	Republican	3,483,922 (23.2%)	8
	Eugene V. Debs	Socialist	897,011 (6.0%)	
1916	**Woodrow Wilson**	Democratic	9,129,606 (49.3%)	277
	Charles E. Hughes	Republican	8,538,221 (46.1%)	254
1920	**Warren G. Harding** **(Calvin Coolidge,** 1923)	Republican	16,152,200 (61.0%)	404
	James M. Cox	Democratic	9,147,353 (34.6%)	127
	Eugene V. Debs	Socialist	919,799 (3.5%)	
1924	**Calvin Coolidge**	Republican	15,725,016 (54.1%)	382
	John W. Davis	Democratic	8,385,586 (28.8%)	136
	Robert M. La Follette	Progressive	4,822,856 (16.6%)	13
1928	**Herbert C. Hoover**	Republican	21,392,190 (58.2%)	444
	Alfred E. Smith	Democratic	15,016,443 (40.8%)	87
1932	**Franklin D. Roosevelt**	Democratic	22,809,638 (57.3%)	472
	Herbert C. Hoover	Republican	15,758,901 (39.6%)	59
	Norman Thomas	Socialist	881,951 (2.2%)	
1936	**Franklin D. Roosevelt**	Democratic	27,751,612 (60.7%)	523
	Alfred M. Landon	Republican	16,681,913 (36.4%)	8
	William Lemke	Union	891,858 (1.9%)	
1940	**Franklin D. Roosevelt**	Democratic	27,243,466 (54.7%)	449
	Wendell L. Willkie	Republican	22,304,755 (44.8%)	82
1944	**Franklin D. Roosevelt** **(Harry S Truman,** 1945)	Democratic	25,602,505 (52.8%)	432
	Thomas E. Dewey	Republican	22,006,278 (44.5%)	99

Year	Candidates	Party	Popular Vote*	Electoral Vote**
1948	**Harry S Truman**	Democratic	24,105,812 (49.5%)	303
	Thomas E. Dewey	Republican	21,970,065 (45.1%)	189
	J. Strom Thurmond	States' Rights	1,169,063 (2.4%)	39
	Henry A. Wallace	Progressive	1,157,172 (2.4%)	
1952	**Dwight D. Eisenhower**	Republican	33,936,234 (55.2%)	442
	Adlai E. Stevenson	Democratic	27,314,992 (44.5%)	89
1956	**Dwight D. Eisenhower**	Republican	35,590,472 (57.4%)	457
	Adlai E. Stevenson	Democratic	26,022,752 (42.0%)	73
1960	**John F. Kennedy** **(Lyndon B. Johnson,** 1963)	Democratic	34,227,096 (49.9%)	303
	Richard M. Nixon	Republican	34,108,546 (49.6%)	219
1964	**Lyndon B. Johnson**	Democratic	43,126,233 (61.1%)	486
	Barry M. Goldwater	Republican	27,174,989 (38.5%)	52
1968	**Richard M. Nixon**	Republican	31,783,783 (43.4%)	301
	Hubert H. Humphrey	Democratic	31,271,839 (42.7%)	191
	George C. Wallace	Amer. Independent	9,899,557 (13.5%)	46
1972	**Richard M. Nixon** **(Gerald R. Ford,** 1974)	Republican	45,767,218 (60.6%)	520
	George S. McGovern	Democratic	28,357,668 (37.5%)	17
1976	**Jimmy Carter**	Democratic	40,828,657 (50.6%)	297
	Gerald R. Ford	Republican	39,145,520 (48.4%)	240
1980	**Ronald Reagan**	Republican	43,899,248 (51%)	489
	Jimmy Carter	Democratic	36,481,435 (41%)	49
	John B. Anderson	Independent	5,719,437 (6%)	
1984	**Ronald Reagan**	Republican	54,455,075 (59%)	525
	Walter F. Mondale	Democratic	37,577,185 (41%)	13
1988	**George Bush**	Republican	48,881,221 (54%)	426
	Michael Dukakis	Democratic	41,805,422 (46%)	111

Vice-Presidents and Cabinet Members, by Administration

Washington, 1789–1797

Vice-President	John Adams	1789–1797
Secretary of State	Thomas Jefferson	1789–1793
	Edmund Randolph	1794–1795
	Timothy Pickering	1795–1797
Secretary of War	Henry Knox	1789–1794
	Timothy Pickering	1795–1796
	James McHenry	1796–1797
Secretary of Treasury	Alexander Hamilton	1789–1795
	Oliver Wolcott, Jr.	1795–1797
Postmaster General	Samuel Osgood	1789–1791
	Timothy Pickering	1791–1794
	Joseph Habersham	1795–1797
Attorney General	Edmund Randolph	1789–1793
	William Bradford	1794–1795
	Charles Lee	1795–1797

John Adams, 1797–1801

Vice-President	Thomas Jefferson	1797–1801
Secretary of State	Timothy Pickering	1797–1800
	John Marshall	1800–1801
Secretary of War	James McHenry	1797–1800
	Samuel Dexter	1800–1801
Secretary of Treasury	Oliver Wolcott, Jr.	1797–1800
	Samuel Dexter	1800–1801
Postmaster General	Joseph Habersham	1797–1801
Attorney General	Charles Lee	1797–1801
Secretary of Navy	Benjamin Stoddert	1798–1801

Jefferson, 1801–1809

Vice-President	Aaron Burr	1801–1805
	George Clinton	1805–1809
Secretary of State	James Madison	1801–1809
Secretary of War	Henry Dearborn	1801–1809
Secretary of Treasury	Samuel Dexter	1801
	Albert Gallatin	1801–1809
Postmaster General	Joseph Habersham	1801
	Gideon Granger	1801–1809
Attorney General	Levi Lincoln	1801–1805
	Robert Smith	1805
	John C. Breckinridge	1805–1806
	Caesar A. Rodney	1807–1809
Secretary of Navy	Robert Smith	1801–1809

Madison, 1809–1817

Vice-President	George Clinton	1809–1813
	Elbridge Gerry	1813–1817
Secretary of State	Robert Smith	1809–1811
	James Monroe	1811–1817
Secretary of War	William Eustis	1809–1812
	John Armstrong	1813–1814
	James Monroe	1814–1815
	William H. Crawford	1815–1817
Secretary of Treasury	Albert Gallatin	1809–1813
	George W. Campbell	1814
	Alexander J. Dallas	1814–1816
	William H. Crawford	1816–1817
Postmaster General	Gideon Granger	1809–1814
	Return J. Meigs, Jr.	1814–1817
Attorney General	Caesar A. Rodney	1809–1811
	William Pinkney	1811–1814
	Richard Rush	1814–1817
Secretary of Navy	Paul Hamilton	1809–1813
	William Jones	1813–1814
	Benjamin W. Crowninshield	1814–1817

Monroe, 1817–1825

Vice-President	Daniel D. Tompkins	1817–1825
Secretary of State	John Quincy Adams	1817–1825
Secretary of War	George Graham	1817
	John C. Calhoun	1817–1825
Secretary of Treasury	William H. Crawford	1817–1825

Monroe, 1817–1825 (continued)

Postmaster General	Return J. Meigs, Jr.	1817–1823
	John McLean	1823–1825
Attorney General	Richard Rush	1817
	William Wirt	1817–1825
Secretary of Navy	Benjamin W. Crowninshield	1817–1818
	Smith Thompson	1818–1823
	Samuel L. Southard	1823–1825

John Quincy Adams, 1825–1829

Vice-President	John C. Calhoun	1825–1829
Secretary of State	Henry Clay	1825–1829
Secretary of War	James Barbour	1825–1828
	Peter B. Porter	1828–1829
Secretary of Treasury	Richard Rush	1825–1829
Postmaster General	John McLean	1825–1829
Attorney General	William Wirt	1825–1829
Secretary of Navy	Samuel L. Southard	1825–1829

Jackson, 1829–1837

Vice-President	John C. Calhoun	1829–1832
	Martin Van Buren	1833–1837
Secretary of State	Martin Van Buren	1829–1831
	Edward Livingston	1831–1833
	Louis McLane	1833–1834
	John Forsyth	1834–1837
Secretary of War	John H. Eaton	1829–1831
	Lewis Cass	1831–1837
	Benjamin Butler	1837
Secretary of Treasury	Samuel D. Ingham	1829–1831
	Louis McLane	1831–1833
	William J. Duane	1833
	Roger B. Taney	1833–1834
	Levi Woodbury	1834–1837
Postmaster General	William T. Barry	1829–1835
	Amos Kendall	1835–1837
Attorney General	John M. Berrien	1829–1831
	Roger B. Taney	1831–1833
	Benjamin F. Butler	1833–1837
Secretary of Navy	John Branch	1829–1831
	Levi Woodbury	1831–1834
	Mahlon Dickerson	1834–1837

Van Buren, 1837–1841

Vice-President	Richard M. Johnson	1837–1841
Secretary of State	John Forsyth	1837–1841
Secretary of War	Joel R. Poinsett	1837–1841
Secretary of Treasury	Levi Woodbury	1837–1841
Postmaster General	Amos Kendall	1837–1840
	John M. Niles	1840–1841
Attorney General	Benjamin F. Butler	1837–1838
	Felix Grundy	1838–1840
	Henry D. Gilpin	1840–1841
Secretary of Navy	Mahlon Dickerson	1837–1838
	James K. Paulding	1838–1841

William Harrison, 1841

Vice-President	John Tyler	1841
Secretary of State	Daniel Webster	1841
Secretary of War	John Bell	1841
Secretary of Treasury	Thomas Ewing	1841
Postmaster General	Francis Granger	1841
Attorney General	John J. Crittenden	1841
Secretary of Navy	George E. Badger	1841

Tyler, 1841–1845

Vice-President	None	
Secretary of State	Daniel Webster	1841–1843
	Hugh S. Legaré	1843
	Abel P. Upshur	1843–1844
	John C. Calhoun	1844–1845
Secretary of War	John Bell	1841
	John C. Spencer	1841–1843
	John M. Porter	1843–1844
	William Wilkins	1844–1845
Secretary of Treasury	Thomas Ewing	1841
	Walter Forward	1841–1843
	John C. Spencer	1843–1844
	George M. Bibb	1844–1845
Postmaster General	Francis Granger	1841
	Charles A. Wickliffe	1841
Attorney General	John J. Crittenden	1841
	Hugh S. Legaré	1841–1843
	John Nelson	1843–1845

Secretary of Navy	George Badger	1841
	Abel P. Upshur	1841
	David Henshaw	1843–1844
	Thomas W. Gilmer	1844
	John Y. Mason	1844–1845

Polk, 1845–1849

Vice-President	George M. Dallas	1845–1849
Secretary of State	James Buchanan	1845–1849
Secretary of War	William L. Marcy	1845–1849
Secretary of Treasury	Robert J. Walker	1845–1849
Postmaster General	Cave Johnson	1845–1849
Attorney General	John Y. Mason	1845–1846
	Nathan Clifford	1846–1848
	Isaac Toucey	1848–1849
Secretary of Navy	George Bancroft	1845–1846
	John Y. Mason	1846–1849

Taylor, 1849–1850

Vice-President	Millard Fillmore	1849–1850
Secretary of State	John M. Clayton	1849–1850
Secretary of War	George W. Crawford	1849–1850
Secretary of Treasury	William M. Meredith	1849–1850
Postmaster General	Jacob Collamer	1849–1850
Attorney General	Reverdy Johnson	1849–1850
Secretary of Navy	William Preston	1849–1850
Secretary of Interior	Thomas Ewing	1849–1850

Fillmore, 1850–1853

Vice-President	None	
Secretary of State	Daniel Webster	1850–1852
	Edward Everett	1852–1853
Secretary of War	Charles M. Conrad	1850–1853
Secretary of Treasury	Thomas Corwin	1850–1853
Postmaster General	Nathan K. Hall	1850–1852
	Sam D. Hubbard	1852–1853

Attorney General	John J. Crittenden	1850–1853
Secretary of Navy	William A. Graham	1850–1852
	John P. Kennedy	1852–1853
Secretary of Interior	Thomas M. T. McKennan	1850
	Alexander H. H. Stuart	1850–1853

Pierce, 1853–1857

Vice-President	William R. King	1853
Secretary of State	William L. Marcy	1853–1857
Secretary of War	Jefferson Davis	1853–1857
Secretary of Treasury	James Guthrie	1853–1857
Postmaster General	James Campbell	1853–1857
Attorney General	Caleb Cushing	1853–1857
Secretary of Navy	James C. Dobbins	1853–1857
Secretary of Interior	Robert McClelland	1853–1857

Buchanan, 1857–1861

Vice-President	John C. Breckinridge	1857–1861
Secretary of State	Lewis Cass	1857–1860
	Jeremiah S. Black	1860–1861
Secretary of War	John B. Floyd	1857–1861
	Joseph Holt	1861
Secretary of Treasury	Howell Cobb	1857–1860
	Philip F. Thomas	1860–1861
	John A. Dix	1861
Postmaster General	Aaron V. Brown	1857–1859
	Joseph Holt	1859–1861
	Horatio King	1861
Attorney General	Jeremiah S. Black	1857–1860
	Edwin M. Stanton	1860–1861
Secretary of Navy	Isaac Toucey	1857–1861
Secretary of Interior	Jacob Thompson	1857–1861

Lincoln, 1861–1865

Vice-President	Hannibal Hamlin	1861–1865
	Andrew Johnson	1865
Secretary of State	William H. Seward	1861–1865

Lincoln, 1861–1865 (continued)

Secretary of War	Simon Cameron	1861–1862
	Edwin M. Stanton	1862–1865
Secretary of Treasury	Samuel P. Chase	1861–1864
	William P. Fessenden	1864–1865
	Hugh McCulloch	1865
Postmaster General	Horatio King	1861
	Montgomery Blair	1861–1864
	William Dennison	1864–1865
Attorney General	Edward Bates	1861–1864
	James Speed	1864–1865
Secretary of Navy	Gideon Welles	1861–1865
Secretary of Interior	Caleb B. Smith	1861–1863
	John P. Usher	1863–1865

Andrew Johnson, 1865–1869

Vice-President	None	
Secretary of State	William H. Seward	1865–1869
Secretary of War	Edwin M. Stanton	1865–1867
	Ulysses S. Grant	1867–1868
	John M. Schofield	1868–1869
Secretary of Treasury	Hugh McCulloch	1865–1869
Postmaster General	William Dennison	1865–1866
	Alexander W. Randall	1866–1869
Attorney General	James Speed	1865–1866
	Henry Stanbery	1866–1868
	William M. Evarts	1868–1869
Secretary of Navy	Gideon Welles	1865–1869
Secretary of Interior	John P. Usher	1865
	James Harlan	1865–1866
	Orville H. Browning	1866–1869

Grant, 1869–1877

Vice-President	Schuyler Colfax	1869–1873
	Henry Wilson	1873–1875
Secretary of State	Elihu B. Washburne	1869
	Hamilton Fish	1869–1877
Secretary of War	John A. Rawlins	1869
	William T. Sherman	1869
	William W. Belknap	1869–1876
	Alphonso Taft	1876
	James D. Cameron	1876–1877
Secretary of Treasury	George S. Boutwell	1869–1873
	William A. Richardson	1873–1874
	Benjamin H. Bristow	1874–1876
	Lot M. Morrill	1876–1877

Postmaster General	John A. J. Creswell	1869–1874
	James W. Marshall	1874
	Marshall Jewell	1874–1876
	James N. Tyner	1876–1877
Attorney General	Ebenezer R. Hoar	1869–1870
	Amos T. Ackerman	1870–1871
	G. H. Williams	1871–1875
	Edwards Pierrepont	1875–1876
	Alphonso Taft	1876–1877
Secretary of Navy	Adolph E. Borie	1869
	George Robeson	1869–1877
Secretary of Interior	Jacob D. Cox	1869–1870
	Columbus Delano	1870–1875
	Zachariah Chandler	1875–1877

Hayes, 1877–1881

Vice-President	William A. Wheeler	1877–1881
Secretary of State	William B. Evarts	1877–1881
Secretary of War	George W. McCrary	1877–1879
	Alexander Ramsey	1879–1881
Secretary of Treasury	John Sherman	1877–1881
Postmaster General	David M. Key	1877–1880
	Horace Maynard	1880–1881
Attorney General	Charles Devens	1877–1881
Secretary of Navy	Richard W. Thompson	1877–1880
	Nathan Goff, Jr.	1881
Secretary of Interior	Carl Schurz	1877–1881

Garfield, 1881

Vice-President	Chester A. Arthur	1881
Secretary of State	James G. Blaine	1881
Secretary of War	Robert T. Lincoln	1881
Secretary of Treasury	William Windom	1881
Postmaster General	Thomas L. James	1881
Attorney General	Wayne MacVeagh	1881
Secretary of Navy	William H. Hunt	1881
Secretary of Interior	Samuel J. Kirkwood	1881

VICE-PRESIDENTS AND CABINET MEMBERS, BY ADMINISTRATION

Arthur, 1881–1885

Vice-President	None	
Secretary of State	Frederick T. Frelinghuysen	1881–1885
Secretary of War	Robert T. Lincoln	1881–1885
Secretary of Treasury	Charles J. Folger Walter Q. Gresham Hugh McCulloch	1881–1884 1884 1884–1885
Postmaster General	Timothy O. Howe Walter Q. Gresham Frank Hatton	1881–1883 1883–1884 1884–1885
Attorney General	Benjamin H. Brewster	1881–1885
Secretary of Navy	William H. Hunt William E. Chandler	1881–1882 1882–1885
Secretary of Interior	Samuel J. Kirkwood Henry M. Teller	1881–1882 1882–1885

Cleveland, 1885–1889

Vice-President	Thomas A. Hendricks	1885
Secretary of State	Thomas F. Bayard	1885–1889
Secretary of War	William C. Endicott	1885–1889
Secretary of Treasury	Daniel Manning Charles S. Fairchild	1885–1887 1887–1889
Postmaster General	William F. Vilas Don M. Dickinson	1885–1888 1888–1889
Attorney General	Augustus H. Garland	1885–1889
Secretary of Navy	William C. Whitney	1885–1889
Secretary of Interior	Lucius Q. C. Lamar William F. Vilas	1885–1888 1888–1889
Secretary of Agriculture	Norman J. Colman	1889

Benjamin Harrison, 1889–1893

Vice-President	Levi P. Morton	1889–1893
Secretary of State	James G. Blaine John W. Foster	1889–1892 1892–1893
Secretary of War	Redfield Proctor Stephen B. Elkins	1889–1891 1891–1893
Secretary of Treasury	William Windom Charles Foster	1889–1891 1891–1893
Postmaster General	John Wanamaker	1889–1893
Attorney General	William H. H. Miller	1889–1891
Secretary of Navy	Benjamin F. Tracy	1889–1893
Secretary of Interior	John W. Noble	1889–1893
Secretary of Agriculture	Jeremiah M. Rusk	1889–1893

Cleveland, 1893–1897

Vice-President	Adlai E. Stevenson	1893–1897
Secretary of State	Walter Q. Gresham Richard Olney	1893–1895 1895–1897
Secretary of War	Daniel S. Lamont	1893–1897
Secretary of Treasury	John G. Carlisle	1893–1897
Postmaster General	Wilson S. Bissell William L. Wilson	1893–1895 1895–1897
Attorney General	Richard Olney Judson Harmon	1893–1895 1895–1897
Secretary of Navy	Hilary A. Herbert	1893–1897
Secretary of Interior	Hoke Smith David R. Francis	1893–1896 1896–1897
Secretary of Agriculture	Julius Sterling Morton	1893–1897

McKinley, 1897–1901

Vice-President	Garret Hobart Theodore Roosevelt	1897–1899 1901
Secretary of State	John Sherman William R. Day John M. Hay	1897–1898 1898 1898–1901
Secretary of War	Russell A. Alger Elihu Root	1897–1899 1899–1901
Secretary of Treasury	Lyman J. Gage	1897–1901
Postmaster General	James A. Gary Charles E. Smith	1897–1898 1898–1901
Attorney General	Joseph McKenna John W. Griggs Philander C. Knox	1897–1898 1898–1901 1901
Secretary of Navy	John D. Long	1897–1901
Secretary of Interior	Cornelius N. Bliss Ethan A. Hitchcock	1897–1899 1899–1901
Secretary of Agriculture	James Wilson	1897–1901

Theodore Roosevelt, 1901–1909

Vice-President	Charles Warren Fairbanks	1905–1909
Secretary of State	John M. Hay Elihu Root Robert Bacon	1901–1905 1905–1909 1909
Secretary of War	Elihu Root William Howard Taft Luke E. Wright	1901–1904 1904–1908 1908–1909
Secretary of Treasury	Lyman J. Gage Leslie M. Shaw George B. Cortelyou	1901–1902 1902–1907 1907–1909
Postmaster General	Charles Emory Smith Henry C. Payne Robert J. Wynne George B. Cortelyou George von L. Meyer	1901–1902 1902–1904 1904–1905 1905–1907 1907–1909
Attorney General	Philander C. Knox William H. Moody Charles J. Bonaparte	1901–1904 1904–1906 1906–1909
Secretary of Navy	John D. Long William H. Moody Paul Morton Charles J. Bonaparte Victor H. Metcalf Truman H. Newberry	1901–1902 1902–1904 1904–1905 1905–1906 1906–1908 1908–1909
Secretary of Interior	Ethan A. Hitchcock James R. Garfield	1901–1907 1907–1909
Secretary of Agriculture	James Wilson	1901–1909
Secretary of Labor and Commerce	George B. Cortelyou Victor H. Metcalf Oscar S. Straus	1903–1904 1904–1906 1906–1909

Taft, 1909–1913

Vice-President	James S. Sherman	1909–1912
Secretary of State	Philander C. Knox	1909–1913
Secretary of War	Jacob M. Dickinson Henry L. Stimson	1909–1911 1911–1913
Secretary of Treasury	Franklin MacVeagh	1909–1913
Postmaster General	Frank H. Hitchcock	1909–1913
Attorney General	George W. Wickersham	1909–1913
Secretary of Navy	George von L. Meyer	1909–1913
Secretary of Interior	Richard A. Ballinger Walter Lowrie Fisher	1909–1911 1911–1913
Secretary of Agriculture	James Wilson	1909–1913
Secretary of Labor and Commerce	Oscar S. Straus Charles Nagel	1909 1909–1913

Wilson, 1913–1921

Vice-President	Thomas R. Marshall	1913–1921
Secretary of State	William Jennings Bryan Robert Lansing Bainbridge Colby	1913–1915 1915–1920 1920–1921
Secretary of War	Lindley M. Garrison Newton D. Baker	1913–1916 1916–1921
Secretary of Treasury	William Gilbert McAdoo Carter Glass David F. Houston	1913–1918 1918–1920 1920–1921
Postmaster General	Albert Sidney Burleson	1913–1921
Attorney General	James Clark McReynolds Thomas Watt Gregory A. Mitchell Palmer	1913–1914 1914–1919 1919–1921
Secretary of Navy	Josephus Daniels	1913–1921
Secretary of Interior	Franklin Knight Lane John Barton Payne	1913–1920 1920–1921
Secretary of Agriculture	David F. Houston Edwin T. Meredith	1913–1920 1920–1921
Secretary of Commerce	William C. Redfield	1913–1919
Secretary of Labor	William Bauchop Wilson	1913–1921

Harding, 1921–1923

Vice-President	Calvin Coolidge	1921–1923
Secretary of State	Charles Evans Hughes	1921–1923
Secretary of War	John W. Weeks	1921–1923
Secretary of Treasury	Andrew W. Mellon	1921–1923
Postmaster General	Will H. Hays Hubert Work Harry S. New	1921–1922 1922–1923 1923
Attorney General	Harry M. Daugherty	1921–1923
Secretary of Navy	Edwin Denby	1921–1923
Secretary of Interior	Albert B. Fall Hubert Work	1921–1923 1923
Secretary of Agriculture	Henry C. Wallace	1921–1923
Secretary of Commerce	Herbert C. Hoover	1921–1923
Secretary of Labor	James J. Davis	1921–1923

Coolidge, 1923–1929

Vice-President	Charles G. Dawes	1925–1929
Secretary of State	Charles Evans Hughes	1923–1925
	Frank B. Kellogg	1925–1929
Secretary of War	John W. Weeks	1923–1925
	Dwight F. Davis	1925–1929
Secretary of Treasury	Andrew W. Mellon	1923–1929
Postmaster General	Harry S. New	1923–1929
Attorney General	Harry M. Daugherty	1923–1924
	Harlan Fiske Stone	1924–1925
	John G. Sargent	1925–1929
Secretary of Navy	Edwin Derby	1923–1924
	Curtis D. Wilbur	1924–1929
Secretary of Interior	Hubert Work	1923–1928
	Roy O. West	1928–1929
Secretary of Agriculture	Henry C. Wallace	1923–1924
	Howard M. Gore	1924–1925
	William M. Jardine	1925–1929
Secretary of Commerce	Herbert C. Hoover	1923–1928
	William F. Whiting	1928–1929
Secretary of Labor	James J. Davis	1923–1929

Hoover, 1929–1933

Vice-President	Charles Curtis	1929–1933
Secretary of State	Henry L. Stimson	1929–1933
Secretary of War	James W. Good	1929
	Patrick J. Hurley	1929–1933
Secretary of Treasury	Andrew W. Mellon	1929–1932
	Ogden L. Mills	1932–1933
Postmaster General	Walter F. Brown	1929–1933
Attorney General	William D. Mitchell	1929–1933
Secretary of Navy	Charles F. Adams	1929–1933
Secretary of Interior	Ray L. Wilbur	1929–1933
Secretary of Agriculture	Arthur M. Hyde	1929–1933
Secretary of Commerce	Robert P. Lamont	1929–1932
	Roy D. Chapin	1932–1933
Secretary of Labor	James J. Davis	1929–1930
	William N. Doak	1930–1933

Franklin D. Roosevelt, 1933–1945

Vice-President	John Nance Garner	1933–1941
	Henry A. Wallace	1941–1945
	Harry S Truman	1945
Secretary of State	Cordell Hull	1933–1944
	Edward R. Stettinius, Jr.	1944–1945
Secretary of War	George H. Dern	1933–1936
	Henry A. Woodring	1936–1940
	Henry L. Stimson	1940–1945
Secretary of Treasury	William H. Woodin	1933–1934
	Henry Morgenthau, Jr.	1934–1945
Postmaster General	James A. Farley	1933–1940
	Frank C. Walker	1940–1945
Attorney General	Homer S. Cummings	1933–1939
	Frank Murphy	1939–1940
	Robert H. Jackson	1940–1941
	Francis Biddle	1941–1945
Secretary of Navy	Claude A. Swanson	1933–1940
	Charles Edison	1940
	Frank Knox	1940–1944
	James V. Forrestal	1944–1945
Secretary of Interior	Harold L. Ickes	1933–1945
Secretary of Agriculture	Henry A. Wallace	1933–1940
	Claude R. Wickard	1940–1945
Secretary of Commerce	Daniel C. Roper	1933–1939
	Harry L. Hopkins	1939–1940
	Jesse H. Jones	1940–1945
	Henry A. Wallace	1945
Secretary of Labor	Frances Perkins	1933–1945

Truman, 1945–1953

Vice-President	Alben W. Barkley	1949–1953
Secretary of State	Edward R. Stettinius, Jr.	1945
	James F. Byrnes	1945–1947
	George C. Marshall	1947–1949
	Dean G. Acheson	1949–1953
Secretary of War	Robert P. Patterson	1945–1947
	Kenneth C. Royall	1947
Secretary of Treasury	Fred M. Vinson	1945–1946
	John W. Snyder	1946–1953
Postmaster General	Frank C. Walker	1945
	Robert E. Hannegan	1945–1947
	Jesse M. Donaldson	1947–1953
Attorney General	Tom C. Clark	1945–1949
	J. Howard McGrath	1949–1952
	James P. McGranery	1952–1953
Secretary of Navy	James V. Forrestal	1945–1947
Secretary of Interior	Harold L. Ickes	1945–1946
	Julius A. Krug	1946–1949
	Oscar L. Chapman	1949–1953

Truman, 1945–1953 (continued)

Secretary of Agriculture	Clinton P. Anderson	1945–1948
	Charles F. Brannan	1948–1953
Secretary of Commerce	Henry A. Wallace	1945–1946
	W. Averell Harriman	1946–1948
	Charles W. Sawyer	1948–1953
Secretary of Labor	Lewis B. Schwellenbach	1945–1948
	Maurice J. Tobin	1948–1953
Secretary of Defense	James V. Forrestal	1947–1949
	Louis A. Johnson	1949–1950
	George C. Marshall	1950–1951
	Robert A. Lovett	1951–1953

Eisenhower, 1953–1961

Vice-President	Richard M. Nixon	1953–1961
Secretary of State	John Foster Dulles	1953–1959
	Christian A. Herter	1959–1961
Secretary of Treasury	George M. Humphrey	1953–1957
	Robert B. Anderson	1957–1961
Postmaster General	Arthur E. Summerfield	1953–1961
Attorney General	Herbert Brownell, Jr.	1953–1958
	William P. Rogers	1958–1961
Secretary of Interior	Douglas McKay	1953–1956
	Fred A. Seaton	1956–1961
Secretary of Agriculture	Ezra Taft Benson	1953–1961
Secretary of Commerce	Sinclair Weeks	1953–1958
	Lewis L. Strauss	1958–1959
	Frederick H. Mueller	1959–1961
Secretary of Labor	Martin P. Durkin	1953
	James P. Mitchell	1953–1961
Secretary of Defense	Charles E. Wilson	1953–1957
	Neil H. McElroy	1957–1959
	Thomas S. Gates, Jr.	1959–1961
Secretary of Health, Education, and Welfare	Oveta Culp Hobby	1953–1955
	Marion B. Folsom	1955–1958
	Arthur S. Flemming	1958–1961

Kennedy, 1961–1963

Vice-President	Lyndon B. Johnson	1961–1963
Secretary of State	Dean Rusk	1961–1963
Secretary of Treasury	C. Douglas Dillon	1961–1963
Postmaster General	J. Edward Day	1961–1963
	John A. Gronouski	1963
Attorney General	Robert F. Kennedy	1961–1963

Secretary of Interior	Stewart L. Udall	1961–1963
Secretary of Agriculture	Orville L. Freeman	1961–1963
Secretary of Commerce	Luther H. Hodges	1961–1963
Secretary of Labor	Arthur J. Goldberg	1961–1962
	W. Willard Wirtz	1962–1963
Secretary of Defense	Robert S. McNamara	1961–1963
Secretary of Health, Education, and Welfare	Abraham A. Ribicoff	1961–1962
	Anthony J. Celebrezze	1962–1963

Lyndon Johnson, 1963–1969

Vice-President	Hubert H. Humphrey	1965–1969
Secretary of State	Dean Rusk	1963–1969
Secretary of Treasury	C. Douglas Dillon	1963–1965
	Henry H. Fowler	1965–1969
Postmaster General	John A. Gronouski	1963–1965
	Lawrence F. O'Brien	1965–1968
	Marvin Watson	1968–1969
Attorney General	Robert F. Kennedy	1963–1964
	Nicholas Katzenbach	1965–1966
	Ramsey Clark	1967–1969
Secretary of Interior	Stewart L. Udall	1963–1969
Secretary of Agriculture	Orville L. Freeman	1963–1969
Secretary of Commerce	Luther H. Hodges	1963–1964
	John T. Connor	1964–1967
	Alexander B. Trowbridge	1967–1968
	Cyrus R. Smith	1968–1969
Secretary of Labor	W. Willard Wirtz	1963–1969
Secretary of Defense	Robert F. McNamara	1963–1968
	Clark Clifford	1968–1969
Secretary of Health, Education, and Welfare	Anthony J. Celebrezze	1963–1965
	John W. Gardner	1965–1968
	Wilbur J. Cohen	1968–1969
Secretary of Housing and Urban Development	Robert C. Weaver	1966–1969
	Robert C. Wood	1969
Secretary of Transportation	Alan S. Boyd	1967–1969

Nixon, 1969–1974

Vice-President	Spiro T. Agnew	1969–1973
	Gerald R. Ford	1973–1974
Secretary of State	William P. Rogers	1969–1973
	Henry A. Kissinger	1973–1974
Secretary of Treasury	David M. Kennedy	1969–1970
	John B. Connally	1971–1972
	George P. Shultz	1972–1974
	William E. Simon	1974
Postmaster General	Winton M. Blount	1969–1971
Attorney General	John N. Mitchell	1969–1972
	Richard G. Kleindienst	1972–1973
	Elliot L. Richardson	1973
	William B. Saxbe	1973–1974
Secretary of Interior	Walter J. Hickel	1969–1970
	Rogers Morton	1971–1974
Secretary of Agriculture	Clifford M. Hardin	1969–1971
	Earl L. Butz	1971–1974
Secretary of Commerce	Maurice H. Stans	1969–1972
	Peter G. Peterson	1972–1973
	Frederick B. Dent	1973–1974
Secretary of Labor	George P. Shultz	1969–1970
	James D. Hodgson	1970–1973
	Peter J. Brennan	1973–1974
Secretary of Defense	Melvin R. Laird	1969–1973
	Elliot L. Richardson	1973
	James R. Schlesinger	1973–1974
Secretary of Health, Education, and Welfare	Robert H. Finch	1969–1970
	Elliot L. Richardson	1970–1973
	Caspar W. Weinberger	1973–1974
Secretary of Housing and Urban Development	George W. Romney	1969–1973
	James T. Lynn	1973–1974
Secretary of Transportation	John A. Volpe	1969–1973
	Claude S. Brinegar	1973–1974

Ford, 1974–1977

Vice-President	Nelson A. Rockefeller	1974–1977
Secretary of State	Henry A. Kissinger	1974–1977
Secretary of Treasury	William E. Simon	1974–1977
Attorney General	William B. Saxbe	1974–1975
	Edward H. Levi	1975–1977
Secretary of Interior	Rogers C. B. Morton	1974–1975
	Stanley K. Hathaway	1975
	Thomas S. Kleppe	1975–1977
Secretary of Agriculture	Earl L. Butz	1974–1976
	John A. Knebel	1976–1977
Secretary of Commerce	Frederick B. Dent	1974–1975
	Rogers C. B. Morton	1975–1976
	Elliot L. Richardson	1976–1977
Secretary of Labor	Peter J. Brennan	1974–1975
	John T. Dunlop	1975–1976
	W. J. Usery, Jr.	1976–1977
Secretary of Defense	James R. Schlesinger	1974–1975
	Donald H. Rumsfeld	1975–1977
Secretary of Health, Education, and Welfare	Caspar W. Weinberger	1974–1975
	F. David Mathews	1975–1977
Secretary of Housing and Urban Development	James T. Lynn	1974–1975
	Carla Anderson Hills	1975–1977
Secretary of Transportation	Claude S. Brinegar	1974–1975
	William T. Coleman, Jr.	1974–1977

Carter, 1977–1981

Vice-President	Walter F. Mondale	1977–1981
Secretary of State	Cyrus R. Vance	1977–1980
	Edmund S. Muskie	1980–1981
Secretary of Treasury	W. Michael Blumenthal	1977–1979
	G. William Miller	1979–1981
Attorney General	Griffin B. Bell	1977–1979
	Benjamin R. Civiletti	1979–1981
Secretary of Interior	Cecil D. Andrus	1977–1981
Secretary of Agriculture	Robert Bergland	1977–1981
Secretary of Commerce	Juanita M. Kreps	1977–1979
	Philip M. Klutznick	1979–1981
Secretary of Labor	F. Ray Marshall	1977–1981
Secretary of Defense	Harold Brown	1977–1981
Secretary of Health, Education, and Welfare	Joseph A. Califano, Jr.	1977–1979
	Patricia Roberts Harris	1979
Secretary of Health and Human Services	Patricia Roberts Harris	1979–1981
Secretary of Housing and Urban Development	Patricia Roberts Harris	1977–1979
	Moon Landrieu	1979–1981
Secretary of Transportation	Brock Adams	1977–1979
	Neil E. Goldschmidt	1979–1981
Secretary of Energy	James R. Schlesinger, Jr.	1977–1979
	Charles W. Duncan, Jr.	1979–1981
Secretary of Education	Shirley M. Hufstedler	1979–1981

Reagan, 1981–1989

Vice-President	George Bush	1981–1989
Secretary of State	Alexander M. Haig, Jr.	1981–1982
	George P. Shultz	1982–1989
Secretary of Treasury	Donald T. Regan	1981–1985
	James A. Baker, III	1985–1988
	Nicholas F. Brady	1988–1989
Attorney General	William French Smith	1981–1985
	Edwin A. Meese, III	1985–1988
	Richard Thornburgh	1988–1989
Secretary of Interior	James C. Watt	1981–1983
	William P. Clarke, Jr.	1983–1985
	Donald P. Hodel	1985–1989
Secretary of Agriculture	John R. Block	1981–1986
	Richard Lyng	1986–1989
Secretary of Commerce	Malcolm Baldrige	1981–1987
	C. William Verity, Jr.	1987–1989
Secretary of Labor	Raymond J. Donovan	1981–1985
	William E. Brock	1985–1987
	Ann D. McLaughlin	1987–1989
Secretary of Defense	Caspar W. Weinberger	1981–1987
	Frank C. Carlucci	1987–1989
Secretary of Health and Human Services	Richard S. Schweiker	1981–1983
	Margaret M. Heckler	1983–1985
	Otis R. Bowen	1985–1989
Secretary of Housing and Urban Development	Samuel R. Pierce, Jr.	1981–1989
Secretary of Transportation	Andrew L. Lewis, Jr.	1981–1983
	Elizabeth Hanford Dole	1983–1987
	James H. Burnley	1987–1989
Secretary of Energy	James B. Edwards	1981–1982
	Donald P. Hodel	1982–1985
	John S. Herrington	1985–1989
Secretary of Education	Terrel H. Bell	1981–1985
	William J. Bennett	1985–1988
	Lauro F. Cavazos	1988–1989

Bush, 1989–

Vice-President	Dan Quayle	1989–
Secretary of State	James A. Baker	1989–
Secretary of Treasury	Nicholas F. Brady	1989–
Attorney General	Richard Thornburgh	1989–
Secretary of Interior	Manuel Lujan, Jr.	1989–
Secretary of Agriculture	Clayton K. Yeutter	1989–
Secretary of Commerce	Robert A. Mosbacher	1989–
Secretary of Labor	Elizabeth Hanford Dole	1989–
Secretary of Defense	Richard Cheney	1989–
Secretary of Health and Human Services	Louis Sullivan	1989–
Secretary of Housing and Urban Development	Jack Kemp	1989–
Secretary of Transportation	Samuel K. Skinner	1989–
Secretary of Energy	James D. Watkins	1989
Secretary of Education	Lauro F. Cavazos	1989–
Secretary of Veterans Affairs	Edward J. Derwinski	1989–

Justices of the Supreme Court

Chief Justices in italics.

	Term of Service	Years of Service		Term of Service	Years of Service
John Jay	1789–1795	5	Ward Hunt	1873–1882	9
John Rutledge	1789–1791	1	*Morrison R. Waite*	1874–1888	14
William Cushing	1789–1810	20	John M. Harlan	1877–1911	34
James Wilson	1789–1798	8	William B. Woods	1880–1887	7
John Blair	1789–1796	6	Stanley Matthews	1881–1889	7
Robert H. Harrison	1789–1790	—	Horace Gray	1882–1902	20
James Iredell	1790–1799	9	Samuel Blatchford	1882–1893	11
Thomas Johnson	1791–1793	1	Lucius Q. C. Lamar	1888–1893	5
William Paterson	1793–1806	13	*Melville W. Fuller*	1888–1910	21
*John Rutledge**	1795	—	David J. Brewer	1890–1910	20
Samuel Chase	1796–1811	15	Henry B. Brown	1890–1906	16
Oliver Ellsworth	1796–1800	4	George Shiras, Jr.	1892–1903	10
Bushrod Washington	1798–1829	31	Howell E. Jackson	1893–1895	2
Alfred Moore	1799–1804	4	Edward D. White	1894–1910	16
John Marshall	1801–1835	34	Rufus W. Peckham	1895–1909	14
William Johnson	1804–1834	30	Joseph McKenna	1898–1925	26
H. Brockholst Livingston	1806–1823	16	Oliver W. Holmes, Jr.	1902–1932	30
Thomas Todd	1807–1826	18	William R. Day	1903–1922	19
Joseph Story	1811–1845	33	William H. Moody	1906–1910	3
Gabriel Duval	1811–1835	24	Horace H. Lurton	1910–1914	4
Smith Thompson	1823–1843	20	Charles E. Hughes	1910–1916	5
Robert Trimble	1826–1828	2	Willis Van Devanter	1911–1937	26
John McLean	1829–1861	32	Joseph R. Lamar	1911–1916	5
Henry Baldwin	1830–1844	14	*Edward D. White*	1910–1921	11
James M. Wayne	1835–1867	32	Mahlon Pitney	1912–1922	10
Roger B. Taney	1836–1864	28	James C. McReynolds	1914–1941	26
Philip P. Barbour	1836–1841	4	Louis D. Brandeis	1916–1939	22
John Catron	1837–1865	28	John H. Clarke	1916–1922	6
John McKinley	1837–1852	15	*William H. Taft*	1921–1930	8
Peter V. Daniel	1841–1860	19	George Sutherland	1922–1938	15
Samuel Nelson	1845–1872	27	Pierce Butler	1922–1939	16
Levi Woodbury	1845–1851	5	Edward T. Sanford	1923–1930	7
Robert C. Grier	1846–1870	23	Harlan F. Stone	1925–1941	16
Benjamin R. Curtis	1851–1857	6	*Charles E. Hughes*	1930–1941	11
John A. Campbell	1853–1861	8	Owen J. Roberts	1930–1945	15
Nathan Clifford	1858–1881	23	Benjamin N. Cardozo	1932–1938	6
Noah H. Swayne	1862–1881	18	Hugo L. Black	1937–1971	34
Samuel F. Miller	1862–1890	28	Stanley F. Reed	1938–1957	19
David Davis	1862–1877	14	Felix Frankfurter	1939–1962	23
Stephen J. Field	1863–1897	34	William O. Douglas	1939–1975	36
Salmon P. Chase	1864–1873	8	Frank Murphy	1940–1949	9
William Strong	1870–1880	10	*Harlan F. Stone*	1941–1946	5
Joseph P. Bradley	1870–1892	22	James F. Byrnes	1941–1942	1
			Robert H. Jackson	1941–1954	13
			Wiley B. Rutledge	1943–1949	6

* Never confirmed as Chief Justice.

	Term of Service	Years of Service
Harold H. Burton	1945–1958	13
Fred M. Vinson	1946–1953	7
Tom C. Clark	1949–1967	18
Sherman Minton	1949–1956	7
Earl Warren	1953–1969	16
John Marshall Harlan	1955–1971	16
William J. Brennan, Jr.	1956–	—
Charles E. Whittaker	1957–1962	5
Potter Stewart	1958–1981	23
Byron R. White	1962–	—
Arthur J. Goldberg	1962–1965	3
Abe Fortas	1965–1969	4
Thurgood Marshall	1967–	—
Warren E. Burger	1969–1986	18
Harry A. Blackmun	1970–	—
Lewis F. Powell, Jr.	1971–1987	15
*William H. Rehnquist***	1971–	—
John P. Stevens III	1975–	—
Sandra Day O'Connor	1981–	—
Antonin Scalia	1986–	—
Anthony M. Kennedy	1988–	—

** Chief Justice from 1986 on.

Territorial Expansion

Louisiana Purchase	1803
Florida	1819
Texas	1845
Oregon	1846
Mexican Cession	1848
Gadsden Purchase	1853
Alaska	1867
Hawaii	1898
Philippines	1898–1946
Puerto Rico	1899
Guam	1899
American Samoa	1900
Canal Zone	1904
U.S. Virgin Islands	1917
Pacific Islands Trust Territory	1947

Population, 1790–1980

1790	3,929,214
1800	5,308,483
1810	7,239,881
1820	9,638,453
1830	12,866,020
1840	17,069,453
1850	23,191,876
1860	31,443,321
1870	39,818,449
1880	50,155,783
1890	62,947,714
1900	75,994,575
1910	91,972,266
1920	105,710,620
1930	122,775,046
1940	131,669,275
1950	151,325,798
1960	179,323,175
1970	204,765,770
1980	226,504,825

Picture Credits

Chapter-opening Illustrations

Chapter 17 Edgar Degas, *New Orleans Cotton Merchants:* Art Resource Center, N.Y.
Chapter 18 Arthur F. Tait, *Life of the Hunter:* SuperStock.
Chapter 19 S. B. Shiley, *Teeming Ingots at the Bessamer Shop,* 1895: Bethlehem Steel Corporation, Bethlehem, Pa.
Chapter 20 Theodore Groll, *Washington Street, Indianapolis at Dusk,* 1892–1895: © 1990, Indianapolis Museum of Art, Gift of a Couple of Old Hoosiers.
Chapter 21 Poster, *Harper's/February:* Joseph Martin/Scala/Art Resource.
Chapter 22 H. Schuldt, *The Traffic Halt,* 1878: The Rhode Island School of Design.
Chapter 23 Naval demonstration near Havana, 1898: The Free Library of Philadelphia, Joseph Martin/Scala/Art Resource.
Chapter 24 Maurice Prendergast, *Central Park, 1901,* 1901: Collection of Whitney Museum of Art.
Chapter 25 World War I poster: SuperStock.
Chapter 26 *Rhapsody in Blue,* Advertising poster for Steinway pianos, 1928: Courtesy of Steinway & Sons.
Chapter 27 John Sloan, *Sixth Avenue Elevated At Third Street,* 1928: Collection of Whitney Museum of American Art.
Chapter 28 Isaac Soyer, *Employment Agency,* 1937: Collection of the Whitney Museum of American Art.
Chapter 29 Pearl Harbor: SuperStock.
Chapter 30 President Dwight D. Eisenhower: Wayne Miller/Magnum Photos.
Chapter 31 Martin Luther King, Jr.: Flip Schulke/Black Star.
Chapter 32 Woodstock Weekend, August 1969: Bill Pierce/Sygma.
Chapter 33 President George Bush, Vice-President Dan Quayle, their wives, at inaugural festivities, January 1989: Tom Sobolik/Black Star.

Portfolios *(listed by page number)*

Portfolio Four: **472** "Freedom to Slaves," 1863: Library Company of Philadelphia. **473** Edwin White, *Thoughts of Liberia,* ca. 1830–1840: New-York Historical Society. George Fuller, "Cotton Press and Gin, Feb. 2, 1858": Private Collection. Five generations of a South Carolina slave family, photo by T. H. O'Sullivan, 1862: Library of Congress. **474** "Meeting in the African Church, Cincinnati, Ohio," *Frank Leslie's Illustrated Newspaper,* April 30, 1853: Library of Congress. Thomas Rice playing "Jump Jim Crow" on the Bowery, 1833: Museum of the City of New York. **475** Edwin Taylor, *American Slave Market,* 1852: Chicago Historical Society. Bill of sale for Ned: The Old Slave Mart Museum, Charleston, S.C. **476** Winslow Homer, *A View from the Old Mistress,* 1876: National Museum of American Art, Smithsonian Institution. **477** Sharecropper cabin with slaughtered hogs: Library of Congress. W. L. Sheppard, "Workers Stripping Tobacco in Danville, Va.," *Harper's Weekly,* Jan. 29, 1887: Virginia State Library.

Portfolio Five: **562** Charles W. Witham, "Grand View of Baxter Street": Theatre and Music Collection, Museum of the City of New York. **563** Lewis Hine, Italian mother and child, Ellis Island: New York Public Library. Ellis Island—stethoscope examination: Brown Brothers. **564** Orchard Street looking south from Hester Street, 1898: The Byron Collection, Museum of the City of New York. Lewis Hine, communal faucet in tenement: International Museum of Photography at George Eastman House. Mulbery Bend, ca. 1890. **565** Lewis Hine, labor agency on lower West Side, New York City, 1910: New York Public Library. Immigrant family sewing garments in tenement: Culver Pictures. Italian district of Manhattan's Lower East Side, photo by Langill & Darling: Museum of the City of New York. **566** Lévi Strauss ad, 1870s: Lévi Strauss & Co. **567** Jacob Riis: The Granger Collection. Emma Goldman: Brown Brothers. Nikola Tesla: The Bettmann Archive. Felix Frankfurter: UPI/Bettmann Newsphotos. Sidney Hillman: The Granger Collection. Irving Berlin: The Bettmann Archive.

Portfolio Six: **672** "Look! The Boss Has a Woman to Write His Letters": National Archives and Record Service. **673** Visiting nurse on Henry Street rooftop: Visiting Nurse Service of New York. Lewis Hine, *Carolina Cotton Mill,* 1908: George Eastman House. Black domestic servant: Valentine Museum, Richmond, Virginia. **674** Triangle Shirtwaist Co. fire: Brown Brothers. Women's Trade Union League demonstration: Brown Brothers. **675** YWCA war effort poster: The Granger Collection. Cooking class, Vassar College, ca. 1918: Brown Brothers. **676** Woman streetcar conductors, 1918: Brown Brothers. Women polishing cars, Northern Pacific Railroad: Brown Brothers. Women welding bombs, munitions factory, ca. 1917: The Granger Collection. **677** Reginald Marsh, *Subway, 14th St.,* 1930: Private collection, New York; photo by Ronald L. C. Kienhuis.

Portfolio Seven: **736** Edward Hopper, *Early Sunday Morning,* 1930: Whitney Museum of American Art. John Marin, *Sun Spots,* 1920: The Metropolitan Museum of Art; Alfred Stieglitz Collection. **737** Georgia O'Keeffe, *Cow Skull: Red, White, and Blue,* 1931: The Metropolitan Museum of Art; Alfred Stieglitz Collection. Thomas Hart Benton, *Romance,* 1931–1932: Archer M. Huntington Art Gallery, The University of Texas at Austin; lent by James and Mari Michener. **738** Reginald Marsh, *Twenty Cent Movie,* 1936: Whitney Museum of American Art. Ben Shahn, *Willis Avenue Bridge,* 1940: Collection, The Museum of Modern Art, New York; gift of Lincoln Kirstein. Mark Rothko, *Number 10,* 1950: Collection, The Museum of Modern Art, New York; gift of Philip Johnson. **739** Robert Motherwell, *Elegy to the Spanish Republic 108,* 1965–1967: Collection, The Museum of Modern Art, New York; Charles Mergentine Fund. Willem de Kooning, *Woman and Bicycle,* 1952–1953: Whitney Museum of American Art. **740** Jasper Johns, *Target With Four Faces,* 1955: Collection, The Museum of Modern Art, New York; gift of Mr. and Mrs. Robert C. Scull. Josef Albers, *Homage to the Square: Apparition,* 1959: Solomon R. Guggenheim Museum. **741** Andrew Wyeth, *Albert's Son,* 1959: National Gallery, Oslo, Norway; photo by J. Lathion.

Portfolio Eight: **908** Albert Bierstadt, *Yosemite Landscape:* SuperStock. President Theodore Roosevelt with John Muir and others in Yosemite National Park, May 1903: Magnum Photos. Earth First Protest in Yellowstone National Park, 1989: Gamma-

Liaison/Neal Palumbo.**909** Forest fires in Yellowstone: Gamma-Liaison/B. Willcox. Trees felled by forest fires in Yellowstone: Photo Researchers/William Munoz. Yellowstone in bloom: Gamma-Liaison/B. Willcox. Pike's Peak in the Rocky Mountains, 1891: Culver Pictures. Automobile graveyard near Pike's Peak: Photo Researchers/Maurice and Sally Landre. Ever-mounting solid waste in landfills in Portland, Oregon: Photo Researchers/David Weintraub. **911** Workers clean up after oil spill in Valdez, 1989: Sygma/J. L. Atlan. Valdez, Alaska, on Prince William sound, 1940: Culver Pictures. Sea otter rescued after oil spill recuperates at salmon hatchery, 1989: Sygma/J. L. Atlan. **912** Recycled waste used to produce electricity for Fairfield County, Connecticut: Photo Researchers/Hank Morgan/Science Source. Solar-powered telephone: Photo Researchers/Eunice Harris. Windmills, as alternate sources of energy to electricity, provide power to Altamont, California: Photo Researchers/Lowell Georgia. **913** 19th-century view of Florida Everglades: Culver Pictures. Pollution and other environmental problems threaten the Everglades: Photo Researchers/Max Hunn. Effects of acid rain on North Carolina forest: Stock, Boston/Judy Canty.

American Lives (listed by page number)

Clement Vann Rogers and George William Norris: **506** Clement Vann Rogers: Oklahoma Historical Society. **507** Beaver City, late 19th-century: Nebraska State Historical Society.

The Steltzles and the Smiths: **534** Lower East Side: Culver Pictures. **535** Swimming in the East River: Brown Brothers. Fulton Fish Market in the 1880s: Brown Brothers.

The Johnson Family of Nebraska: **588** Settlers entering Nebraska: The Bettmann Archive. **589** Family farm in northern Nebraska: The Nebraska Historical Society. Country school: The Bettmann Archive.

Emma Goldman: **638** Emma Goldman in the 1890s: Culver Pictures. **639** Emma Goldman and Alexander Berkman: The Bettmann Archive.

Text (listed by page number)

Chapter 17: **450** Matthew Brady, daguerreotype of Andrew Johnson: Library of Congress. **451** Matthew Brady, daguerreotype of Thaddeus Stevens: Library of Congress. **453** Freedman's Bureau: Library Company of Philadelphia. **455** The Bettmann Archive. **457** Cartoon: American Antiquarian Society, Worcester, Mass. **458** The First Colored Senators and Representatives in the 41st and 42nd Congress of the United States, 1842 Lithograph by Currier & Ives: Granger Collection. **460** "Primary School for Freedman, in Charge of Mrs. Green," *Harper's Weekly*, June 23, 1866: New-York Historical Society. **462** Black sharecroppers: Culver Pictures. **465** Carpetbaggers being hanged, *Tuscaloosa Independent Monitor*, September 1, 1868: Alabama Dept. of Archives and History, Montgomery. **467** Nast cartoon: *Harper's Weekly*, August 24, 1872. **Chapter 18:** **481** Joseph Keppler, "None but Millionaires Need Apply," *Puck*, March 12, 1890: New-York Historical Society. **482** Louis Dalrymple, "Getting Troublesome Again," 1896: The Granger Collection. **484** Frances Benjamin Johnston, students working on construction, ca. 1900–1905: Library of Congress: courtesy of National Park Service, Tuskegee Institute National Historical Site; photo by John Scott. **487** Immigrant construction crew laying tracks along west slope of the Cascades in 1885: The Bettman Archive. **488** Kills Two, "An Indian Horse Dance": Yale University Library, Coe Collection. **490** Comanche, the only survivor on the Army's side at the Battle of Little Big Horn: The Bettmann Archive. **492** Ge-

ronimo and Natiche with their sons, preparing to surrender to Gen. Crook: National Archives and Record Service. **493** Nat Love, a cowboy in the Dakotas in the 1880s: The Bettman Archive. **494** Illustration by T. L. Dawes, "Mining in the Comstock," 1872: Bancroft Library, University of California. **496** 30-horse combines, wheat harvest, Stockton, California, 1907: Oregon Historical Society. **497** J. K. Hillers, railroad bridge near Santa Fe, New Mexico: National Archives and Record Service. **499** Old map of Atlantic & Pacific Railroad: National Archives and Record Service. **503** S. D. Butcher, masked Nebraska ranchers cutting fence, 1885: Nebraska State Historical Society, S. D. Butcher Collection.
Chapter 19: **512** Circular inviting settlers to come to Iowa and Nebraska, 1873: The Bettmann Archive. **513** Strip mining, Mesabi Range, 1899: Minnesota Historical Society. **515** Thomas A. Edison with wax-cylinder phonograph, 1888: Edison National Historic Site, National Park Service, U.S. Dept. of the Interior. **517** Edward Steichen, photo of J. P. Morgan, 1906: Museum of Modern Art; gift of A. Conger Goodyear. **518** Theobald Chartran, portrait of Andrew Carnegie, 1895: Museum of Art, Carnegie Institute, Pittsburgh; gift of Mr. Henry Clay Frick. **519** Cartoon of John D. Rockefeller, *Puck*, March 6, 1901: New-York Historical Society. **521** The glove counter in Rike's Department Store, Dayton, Ohio, 1893: The Bettmann Archive. **526** Thomas Nast cartoon ridiculing the willingness of the U.S. Senate to do the bidding of the railroad lobbyists in 1888: New York Public Library.
Chapter 20: **539** Student nurses in New York City in 1899. Library of Congress. **541** Minnesota farming family in front of house, 1895: The Bettmann Archive. **543** An 1890s public school classroom: The Bettmann Archive. **547** Frank Beard cartoon about unrestricted immigration, 1885: The Granger Collection. **550** Jacob Riis, "Bandit's Roost, Lower East Side": New York *Sun*. **551** Herald Square, New York City, 1900: The New-York Historical Society. **553** Design for Chicago's 1893 World Fair by Daniel H. Burham. John Ross Key, *Administration, Mining and Electrical Buildings from Wooded Islands, World's Columbian Exposition*, 1894: Chicago Historical Society. **555** Thomas Eakins's *Baseball Players Practicing*, 1875: Museum of Art, Rhode Island School of Design; Jesse Metcalf and Walter H. Kimball Funds. **557** Henry Ward Beecher, widely admired minister in the second half of the 19th century: The Bettmann Archive. **559** Portrait of Jane Addams by Alice Kellog Tyler, 1896: Chicago Historical Society.
Chapter 21: **570** John Singer Sargent, portrait of Joseph Pulitzer, 1905: Courtesy of Joseph Pulitzer, Jr. **571** William Randolph Hearst in 1906: The Bettmann Archive. **574** Smith College students setting out on geology field trip, ca. 1880–1890: Smith College Archives. **577** John Dewey, progressive educator: Brown Brothers. **578** Oliver Wendell Holmes, Associate Supreme Court Justice, 1902: Brown Brothers. **580** Mark Twain in his easy chair, ca. 1905 in Hartford, Conn.: The Bettmann Archive. Frederick Waddy, caricature of Mark Twain, 1872: The Granger Collection. **583** Thomas Eakins, Marey wheel photo of an unidentified model, 1884: Philadelphia Museum of Art; gift of Charles Bregler. **584** Thomas Eakins, *The Swimming Hole*, 1883: Permanent Collection, The Fort Worth Art Museum; photo by David Wharton. **585** Mary Cassatt, *Mother and Child:* Metropolitan Museum of Art; George A. Hearn, 1909. **586** Henry and William James, ca. 1900: The Bettmann Archive.
Chapter 22: **593** Thomas Nast, "Let Us Pray," *Harper's Weekly,* September 23, 1887: Library of Congress. **595** Currier & Ives, "Farmer Garfield Cutting a Swath to the White House," 1880: The Granger Collection. **597** Anders Zorn, portrait of Grover Cleveland: National Portrait Gallery, Smithsonian Institution. **599** F. M. Howarth, "Put Your Application in The Slot and Get An Office," 1889: The Bettmann Archive. **600** Bernhard Gillan, "Phryne Before the Chicago Tribunal," *Puck*, 1884: Culver Pictures. **601** Guthrie, Oklahoma, May 1889: University of Oklahoma Library, Western History Collection. **603** Mary Elizabeth Lease: Culver Pictures. **604** Jeremiah "Sockless Jerry" Simpson, a Populist and a flamboyant campaigner, speaking at a political debate, 1892: The Kansas State Historical Society, Topeka. **607** William Jennings Bryan: The Granger Collec-

tion. **608** Louis Dalrymple, "Making-Up for a New Role," *Judge:* The Bettmann Archive.

Chapter 23: 618 Admiral Alfred Thayer Mahan, 1904: The Bettmann Archive. **622** Louis Dalrymple, "Some Time in the Future," 1895: The Granger Collection. **624** Highly decorated female recruiting officer during Spanish-American War, 1898: The Bettmann Archive. **626** "His Foresight," *Puck,* 1901: Culver Pictures. **628** Emilio Aguinaldo and his son: The Bettmann Archive. **633** Rendering of a multinational assault upon Chinese militants, the Boxers, 1900: Library of Congress. **634** Panama Canal under construction: The Bettmann Archive.

Chapter 24: 643 Ida Tarbell: UPI/Bettmann Newsphotos. *McClure's* Magazine Cover, 1903: Culver Pictures. **645** George Luks's "The Miner," 1924, from the "ashcan" school of American painting: SuperStock. **646** William Balfour-Ker, *From the Depths,* in John Ames Mitchell, *The Silent War,* 1906, New York Public Library, Astor, Lenox and Tilden Foundations. **648** Robert La Follette, Cumberland, Wisconsin, 1897: State Historical Society of Wisconsin. **651** Suffrage Parade, New York, May 6, 1911: Culver Pictures. **654** President Theodore Roosevelt: Brown Brothers. **655** Theodore Roosevelt in the lions' den: Culver Pictures. **657** Coal miners' strike, Shenandoah, Pa. **659** "Best" tonic advertisement, ca. 1890–1900: The Granger Collection. **660** William Howard Taft playing golf: Culver Pictures. **662** Cartoon caricaturing Presidents Theodore Roosevelt and William H. Taft: The Bettmann Archive. **665** Woodrow Wilson at 1906 Princeton graduation with Andrew Carnegie: Brown Brothers. **668** Winold Reiss, portrait of W. E. B. DuBois, ca. 1925: National Portrait Gallery, Smithsonian Institution.

Chapter 25: 680 Francisco "Pancho" Villa, on his capture by the Mexican Army in 1920: Brown Brothers. **681** Antiwar protesters in 1916: The Bettmann Archive. **684** Warning poster to transatlantic passengers by German embassy, New York *Times,* 1915: Brown Brothers. **686** Wilson 1916 campaign van: UPI/Bettmann Newsphotos. **687** "*U-Boote Heraus!*" poster, ca. 1914, encouraging German submarine crews: The Granger Collection. **690** Rival Horse Meat & Sausages, Inc., 1917: National Archives and Record Service. **691** Removing statue of Germania, April 1, 1918: New-York Historical Society. **693** Young women in their "victory" garden during World War I: UPI/Bettmann Newsphotos. **696** American infantrymen under shell fire in France during World War I: The Bettmann Archive. **700** "Big Four," Hotel Crillon, Paris, December 1918: The Granger Collection. **701** President and Mrs. Woodrow Wilson during the Versailles Peace Conference, 1919: Culver Pictures. **702** "Overweighted," *Punch,* March 26, 1919: Punch Publications, Ltd. **704** William Gropper cartoon: *The Liberator,* February 1920.

Chapter 26: 710 Immigrants entering the United States through New York City's Ellis Island: The Bettmann Archive. **712** Illustration by John Held, Jr., which appeared on the cover of *McClure's* Magazine in the 1920s: Culver Pictures. **714** Young saleswoman at work in ready-to-wear store in the 1920s: Brown Brothers. **716** Charlie Chaplin in *One A.M.:* Museum of Modern Art/Film Stills Archive, New York. **718** Gertrude Ederle, 1926, greased for swim across the English Channel. UPI/Bettmann Newsphotos. **719** John Steuart Curry, *Baptism in Kansas,* 1928: Whitney Museum of American Art, purchase acq. no. 31.159. **722** Ben Shahn, *Prohibition Alley:* Museum of the City of New York. **723** Ku Klux Klan initiation ceremony, ca. 1920–1925: Kansas State Historical Society. **724** Sacco and Vanzetti arriving at court, April 1927: Brown Brothers. **726** F. Scott Fitzgerald: Brown Brothers. Ernest Hemingway: John F. Kennedy Library. **729** Jacob Lawrence, *The Migration of the Negro* (Panel 1), 1940–1941: The Phillips Collection. **731** Henry Ford: Courtesy of Ford Motor Company. **733** Charles A. Lindbergh, two years before his solo flight across the Atlantic: Culver Pictures.

Chapter 27: 744 President Warren G. Harding throwing first ball: Culver Pictures. **746** *Life,* cover, March 6, 1924: Culver Pictures. **747** Cartoon satirizing President Calvin Coolidge: Culver Pictures. **749** Members of the Women's International League for Peace and Freedom, ca. 1918: Library of Congress. **751** "They Shall Pay!" Los Angeles *Times* cartoon re-

printed in *The Outlook,* January 1923: Library of Congress. **753** President Herbert Hoover during 1928 presidential campaign: The Bettmann Archive. **755** James Rosenberg, "Oct. 29 Dies Irae": Philadelphia Museum of Art, Lola Downin Peck Fund. **758** Children begging for money beside signs blaming Hoover for problems of the Depression: Art Resource. **759** Bonus Marchers demonstrating in front of the Capitol Building, July 5, 1932: The Bettmann Archive. **760** Bread line: National Archives and Record Service. **762** Franklin D. Roosevelt and John N. Garner campaigning, 1932: UPI/Bettmann Newsphotos.

Chapter 28: 766 Franklin D. Roosevelt and admirers, Warm Springs, Ga., 1933: UPI/Bettmann Newsphotos. **771** WPA workers widening streets in government work program in 1935: The Bettmann Archive. **773** John Steinbeck: Magnum Photos/ Erich Hartmann. William Faulkner: Black Star/Bern Keating. **774** Huey Long: The Bettmann Archive. **775** Father Charles Coughlin, Detroit: UPI/Bettmann Newsphotos. **780** "No Boost for the Administration Make-Up Department," New York *Tribune,* 1937: Culver Pictures. **781** Sit-down strikers: Wide World Photos. **783** Cartoon, Uncle Sam and federal agencies: © 1935, 1963 Conde-Nast Publications, Inc. *Vanity Fair,* July 1935. New York Public Library, Lenox and Tilden Foundations. **784** Frances Perkins visiting steel plant: Brown Brothers. **786** Arthur Rothstein, photo of evicted sharecroppers, Missouri, 1939: Library of Congress. **788** Eleanor and Franklin D. Roosevelt with their son, Franklin, Jr., at the family home in Hyde Park, New York: UPI/Bettmann Newsphotos. **790** Students and faculty at the University of Chicago demonstrate for peace in 1937: Wide World Photos. **791** American volunteers for the Lincoln Brigade, which fought on the side of the Loyalists in the Spanish Civil War: Magnum Photos/Robert Capa. **792** German poster, 1938: The Granger Collection. **793** Wendell Willkie, Republican candidate for the presidency, 1940: UPI/Bettmann Newsphotos.

Chapter 29: 801 Black graduates of the Advanced Flying School, 1942: Culver Pictures. **802** Zoot suiter, 1943: UPI/Bettmann Newsphotos. **803** Dorothea Lange, Mochida family, Hayward, California, May 8, 1942: National Archives and Record Service. **805** Margeret Bourke-White, "Women in Steel": *Life* Magazine, © 1943 Time Inc. **808** Victorious American troops entering Sicilian town, 1943: Magnum Photos/Robert Capa. **809** Scene from "The True Glory," General Dwight D. Eisenhower's film report as he inspects the horrific conditions in a German concentration camp: Culver Pictures. **812** American soldiers in hand-to-hand combat with the Japanese on the Pacific island of Bougainville, 1944: Black Star. **813** Ruins of Hiroshima's Museum of Science and Industry: UPI/Bettmann Newsphotos. **817** Churchill, Roosevelt, and Stalin at Yalta, February 1945: The Granger Collection.

Chapter 30: 823 Postwar communities of single-family homes developed to house returning veterans and their families: Magnum Photos/Elliott Erwitt. **828** The Berlin Airlift: The Bettmann Archive. **829** Truman with Chicago *Daily Tribune* headline, November 1948: UPI/Bettmann Newsphotos. **832** David Douglas Duncan, 1st Marine Division, November 1950: © David Douglas Duncan, *Life.* **834** Alger Hiss being asked to identify Whittaker Chambers at congressional hearings in 1948: UPI/Bettmann Newsphotos. **837** John Foster Dulles, 1956: UPI/Bettmann Newsphotos. **838** Senator Joseph McCarthy conferring with aide Roy M. Cohn during televised congressional hearings, 1954: UPI/Bettmann Newsphotos. **841** Vice-President Richard M. Nixon debates Nikita Khrushchev over the future of capitalism, 1959: Magnum Photos/Elliott Erwitt. **842** Fidel Castro and his military advisers at secret base in Cuba, 1957: UPI/Bettmann Archive. **845** Little Rock Central High School, September 4, 1957: UPI/Bettmann Archive. **847** Vice-President Richard M. Nixon and Senator John F. Kennedy debating in presidential campaign, 1960: UPI/Bettmann Newsphotos. **849** Aerial photographs of Soviet missiles in Cuba being displayed to the U.N. Security Council, 1962: UPI/Bettmann Newsphotos. **850** Jacqueline and Robert F. Kennedy returning from burial ceremony of President John F. Kennedy, 1963: Magnum Photos/Elliott Erwitt.

Chapter 31: 853 Lyndon B. Johnson, July 6, 1966: UPI/Bett-

Index

Note: Italicized page numbers refer to maps and graphs.